Encyclopedia of Law and Economics
Volume IV

Encyclopedia of Law and Economics
Edited by Boudewijn Bouckaert and Gerrit De Geest

Volume I	The History and Methodology of Law and Economics
Volume II	Civil Law and Economics
Volume III	The Regulation of Contracts
Volume IV	The Economics of Public and Tax Law
Volume V	The Economics of Crime and Litigation

Encyclopedia of Law and Economics Volume IV

The Economics of Public and Tax Law

Edited by

Boudewijn Bouckaert

Professor of Law, University of Ghent, Belgium

Gerrit De Geest

Professor of Law and Economics, University of Ghent and University of Antwerp, Belgium and Researcher, Economic Institute/CIAV Utrecht University, The Netherlands

Edward Elgar

Cheltenham, UK • Northampton, MA, USA

Published by
Edward Elgar Publishing Limited
Glensanda House
Montpellier Parade
Cheltenham
Glos GL50 1UA
UK

Edward Elgar Publishing, Inc.
136 West Street
Suite 202
Northampton
Massachusetts 01060
USA

Reprinted 2001

A catalogue record for this book
is available from the British Library

Library of Congress Cataloguing in Publication Data

Encyclopedia of law and economics / edited by Boudewijn Bouckaert, Gerrit De Geest.
Contents: v. 1. The history and methodology of law and economics — v. 2. Civil law and economics — v. 3. The regulation of contracts — v. 4. The economics of public and tax law — v. 5. The economics of crime and litigation.
Includes bibliographical references.
1. Law and economics Encyclopedias. I. Bouckaert, Boudewijn. II. Geest, Gerrit De.
K487 .E3E53 2000
330—dc 21 99–38062
CIP

ISBN 1 85898 987 6
1 85898 565 X (5 volume set)

Printed and bound in Great Britain by MPG Books Ltd, Bodmin, Cornwall

CONTENTS

EDITORIAL BOARD

Board of Referees

Foreword

Richard A. Posner
Chief Judge, US Court of Appeals for the Seventh Circuit
Senior Lecturer, University of Chicago Law School

The law and economics movement was for a long time regarded as an American movement. This was never completely correct. Its origins, certainly, are international. British economists, Adam Smith and Jeremy Bentham to begin with, and later A.C. Pigou and Ronald Coase (among others), played a founding role, as did Max Weber - himself both a lawyer and an economist. Friedrich Hayek and Bruno Leoni are other examples of scholars from outside the Anglo-American sphere whose thought has had an influence on the movement. And there are others. Today, at any rate, it is plain that the movement is international. There are law and economics associations in Europe and Latin America as well as in North America, law and economics scholarship is being produced in every major country and in many minor ones, and several of the leading journals are published outside the United States. Improvements in transportation and communications, and the rapid diffusion of English as the international language of scholarship, has fostered the internationalisation of law and economics. And there is growing recognition that comparative studies are an indispensable tool for gaining a better understanding of the economic nature and consequences of law. It is, for example, most unlikely that we will ever gain an adequate understanding of the efficiency of the Anglo-American 'adversarial' system of legal procedure without comparing it to the 'inquisitorial' system that prevails in Continental Europe; or understand the role of property rights in economic growth without studying the experience of the Central and European nations that have recently emerged from Communism.

Along with the internationalisation of the field has come an extraordinary growth in breadth of coverage and in specialisation of focus. Few areas of legal scholarship remain untouched by economics. Apart from the obvious examples - areas such as taxation and antitrust and securities regulation and (other) regulated industries and commercial law, all areas where the law is explicitly engaged in regulating economic activity - recent decades have seen a broadening of interest to include tort, contract, family, intellectual property, constitutional, criminal, admiralty, labour, arbitration, and antidiscrimination law, among others. But not only have more and more areas of law been brought under the lens of economics; more and more of the increasingly technical tools of economics - itself a field undergoing rapid growth and increased specialisation - have been brought to bear on the law, along with the latest in game theory. An immense and difficult body of monographic and journal scholarship is the result.

When a field becomes large, diverse and technical, it cries out for encyclopedic coverage. Thirty years ago one person, in one book, could map most of the terrain of law and economics. That is no longer possible. It has become infeasible for any single individual to keep fully abreast of the field of law and economics. He or she cannot be fully expert in every area of the field. And yet from time to time the scholar will find it necessary to cross the boundary that demarcates his own area of primary interest. For such a person, the opportunity of getting a quick overview of another part of the field by reading an encyclopedia article is welcome and even essential. It is even more welcome to those scholars, consultants, and practitioners who do not consider themselves 'law and economics' people, but whose work intersects the law and economics field. Law and economics has had interesting things to say about virtually every area of law, and this makes it of potential relevance to anyone working in one of those areas, who might be a practising lawyer, an economic consultant, a sociologist, psychologist, historian, or philosopher. For these 'outsiders', facing a research or practical task to which law and economics may be relevant, the opportunity to consult an encyclopedia article as the initial port of entry into the law and economics field is of immense potential value - as it is to students, and to scholars who are beginning to work in law and economics and want a broader view of the field before they decide where to specialise within it.

The *Encyclopedia of Law and Economics* endeavours, I think very successfully, to provide the kind of encyclopedic coverage - comprehensive and sophisticated but lucid, international without being esoteric, uniform without being monochrome, collective but individual - that the field of law and economics requires. It will help to make the field accessible to outsiders and to promote mutual intelligibility among insiders. It provides a meeting place for and an overview of a vast activity of scholarship, and will thus help to unify and advance the field. It is a milestone in an advancing field.

INTRODUCTION

Boudewijn Bouckaert and Gerrit De Geest

General editors

General Aims

The *Encyclopedia of Law and Economics* is an ambitious reference work that attempts to survey the whole law and economics literature in nearly 5,000 pages. Most entries contain two elements: a review of the literature, written by an authority in the field, and a quasi complete bibliography (not just a selection).

Economic analysis of law has expanded dramatically in recent years. In many branches, the literature is now at a 'mature' stage, where scholars agree on basic concepts, theories and even on policy recommendations. Yet, this scholarship does not reach many policymakers, lawyers or judges. Outside the USA, it even does not seem to reach law professors. This is not so much due to the fact that policymakers, judges or law professors are not interested in the economic consequences of legal rules, but rather to the fact that the literature is too inaccessible. There is a clear need for reference works that give a reliable overview of the literature in a way that is understandable also for non-specialists. This is the primary purpose of the *Encyclopedia of Law and Economics*.

Reviews of the Literature

The reviews are relatively lengthy articles (on average nearly 10,000 words) in which the basic questions and items of discussion are explained, the literature is summarized, critical reflections on these publications and on the evolution of the discussion in general are developed, and perhaps suggestions for further research are made.

The authors have been asked not to make their surveys too technical in order to make sure that readers without a mathematical training can still understand them. The result is in-depth and up-to-date syntheses of the literature that are still accessible for non-specialists, like judges, politicians or undergraduate students. All review articles have been anonymously refereed.

Bibliographies

The *Encyclopedia of Law and Economics* is to a great extent also a bibliographical work. In most cases, authors have tried to be quasi-complete.

The bibliographical lists at the end of all entries are not a 'list of cited works'. They list many more references than could be discussed in the text. Beside the bibliography of law and economics studies on the topic itself, many entries contain a second list, entitled 'Other References', which are references cited in the text, but either purely legal, philosophical, sociological, or cited law and economics publications that are not directly related to the very topic (for instance, many authors have cited Coase, 1960).

There is no doubt a need for these such specialized bibliographies. The law and economics literature has exploded in recent years (this Encyclopedia lists over 20,000 law and economics publications). However, to date it has not been so easy for readers to find the relevant publications, because they are spread out over law reviews, economics journals, conference volumes and so on. The fact that economic analysis of law is an interdisciplinary approach means that the specialized bibliographies in economics (like Econlit) or the specialized sources on law (like Lexis or Westlaw) give a very incomplete overview. Moreover, titles of articles or books do not always make clear whether the research was purely legal, purely economic, or truly interdisciplinary.

Quotation Style

As anyone can experience every day, there is no uniformity concerning the quotation style in law and economics, nor in economics or legal science. To make the bibliographies useful for as many scholars and students as possible, it is the policy of the *Encyclopedia of Law and Economics* to provide the maximum of information, but within certain limits. More specifically, the references to articles contain in principle the volume number of the journal and the year of publication, as well as the number of the first and the last pages of an article. Journal titles are written out in full. Titles of works in languages other than English are translated into English.

Structure

The *Encyclopedia of Law and Economics* has a pyramidal structure. The question was what structure had to be chosen. The general division of legal rules into branches differs fundamentally among legal systems. Most continental (European) legal classification systems are based, for instance, on the division between public law and private law. They also unify contract law, tort law and the law on restitution into one branch of law, called 'law of obligations'. American lawyers would have a hard time trying to find their way in such a system. The classification system of Econlit (where K is 'law and economics') was in our opinion no perfect alternative either, since it is not detailed enough and not much common-law oriented to satisfy continental lawyers.

Therefore we decided to elaborate a new, detailed classification system, inspired by both legal theory and law and economics insights. After a methodological and historical part (0000-0900), the law is divided into substantial norms (1000-6000) and meta-norms.

Substantial norms are divided into property (private property 1000 ff., common property 2000 ff.) and the transfer of property (involuntary transfer between private parties - tort law and restitution - 3000 ff.), voluntary transfer of property between private parties (general contract law, 4000 ff., and the regulation of contracts, 5000 ff.) and involuntary transfers between citizens and the state (taxation, social security, takings, 6000 ff.).

Meta-norms include litigation and evidence law (7000 ff.), criminal law (putting some additional incentives on legal rules defined in other branches of law) and rules on the production of legal rules (9000 ff.).

A correct classification system can improve analyses by suggesting what kind of models are to be applied. Medical malpractice, for instance, is considered by Anglo-American rules as a branch of tort law. It is more correct from an economic viewpoint to consider it as a regulation of contracts between physicians and patients (therefore it is treated in the volume on the regulation of contracts and not in the general part on tort law). Marriage law is according to many legal systems a part of 'family law'. Again, it is better to see it as the regulation of a specific contract. Modern economic scholarship on marriage law tries to apply the models on optimal contract remedies to the problem of unstable marriages.

Acknowledgments

A massive undertaking requires the help of an enormous amount of people. We would like to thank, first of all, the members of the editorial board and the board of referees. Second, we owe a lot to the publisher, Edward Elgar, and his staff - especially to Dymphna Evans for supporting the project in many ways. Third, we would like to acknowledge the financial support of the Economic Institute/CIAV of Utrecht University and of the Department of General Jurisprudence and History of Law of the University of Ghent. Finally, we can give no more than a sample of the people that have substantially contributed to this project: Luc Bosman, Olivier Delbecque, Ben Depoorter, Anja De Wilde, Niky D'Hulster, Wim Dubois, Regine Goemaes, Ghislain Hoffman, Steven Mels, Geert Premereur, An Saerens, Gianni Trovisi, Frieda Van Caneghem and Nancy Van Nuffel.

6000
OPTIMAL TAXATION: GENERAL

Bibliography Collected by the Editors

Auerbach, Alan J. and Hines, James R., Jr (1988), 'Investment Tax Incentives and Frequent Tax Reforms', **78** *American Economic Review. Papers and Proceedings*, 211-216.

Backhaus, Jürgen G. (1990), 'Die Politische Ökonomie der Schutzzolltheorie (Political Economics of the Protection Tariff Theory)', in Schefold, Bertram (ed.), *Studien zur Entwicklung der oekonomischen Theorie X*, Berlin, Duncker and Humblot, 103-113.

Barnett, Richard, Barrow, Michael and Smith, Peter (1991), 'Representation Without Taxation: An Empirical Assessment of the Validity of the Accountability Argument Underlying the Reform of Local Government Finance in England', **12(3)** *Fiscal Studies*.

Becker, Gary S. (1986), 'The Public Interest Hypothesis Revisited: A New Test of Peltzman's Theory of Regulation', **49** *Public Choice*, 223 ff.

Bell, Edward B., Bodenhorn, Diran and Taub, Allan J. (1983), 'Taxes and Compensation for Lost Earnings', **12** *Journal of Legal Studies*, 181-194.

Bell, Edward B., Bodenhorn, Diran and Taub, Allan J. (1985), 'Taxes and Compensation for Lost Earnings: Reply', **14** *Journal of Legal Studies*, 457-458.

Benson, Bruce L. (1990), 'Interstate Tax Competition, Incentives to Collude, and Federal Influences', **10** *Cato Journal*, 75-90.

Benson, Bruce L. and Engen, Eric M. (1988), 'The Market for Laws: An Economic Analysis of Legislation', **54** *Southern Economic Journal*, 732-745.

Benson, Bruce L. and Faminow, Merle D. (1986), 'The Incentives to Organize and Demand Regulation: Two Ends against the Middle', **24** *Economic Inquiry*, 473-484.

Bizer, David S. and Judd, Kenneth L. (1989), 'Taxation and Uncertainty', **79** *American Economic Review. Papers and Proceedings*, 331-336.

Bohanon, Cecil E. and Van Cott, T. Norman (1991), 'Product Quality andTaxation: A Reconciliation', **19** *Public Finance Quarterly*, 233-237.

Bossons, John (1970), 'The Value of a Comprehensive Tax Base as a Tax Reform Goal', **13** *Journal of Law and Economics*, 327-363.

Browning, Edgar K. and Browning, Jacquelene M. (1985), 'Why not a True Flat Rate Tax?', **5** *Cato Journal*, 629-650.

Buchanan, James M. (1978), 'Tax Reform in Constitutional Perspective', in Skogh, Göran (ed.), *Law and Economics. Report from a Symposium in Lund*, Lund, Juridiska Föreningen, 103-120.

Buchanan, James M., Tollison, Robert D. and Tullock, Gordon (eds) (1980), *Toward a Theory of the Rent Seeking Society*, College Station, Texas, A&M University Press.

Bucovetsky, Sam (1991), 'Choosing Tax Rates and Public Expenditure Levels Using Majority Rule', **46** *Journal of Public Economics*, 113-131.

Caanen, Ch. and Essers, P.H.J. (1990), 'Rechtseconomie en Belastingrecht (Law and Economics and Taxation Law)', **39(10)** *Ars Aequi*, 677-681.

Carbajo, Domingo and Ruesca, Santos M. (1994), 'La Incidencia de la Fiscalidad Sobre Bienes Inmuebles en la Movilidad de los Factores Productivos en el Mercadonico Europeo (Especial Referencia a la Movilidad del Capital) (The Effect of Real State Taxes on the Mobility of the Factors in the E.U. Market Special Regard to Capital Mobility)', **18** *Actualidad Tributaria*, 475-490.

Collard, David (ed) (1989), *Fiscal Policy: Essays in Honour of Cedric Sandford*, Aldershot, Gower, 173 p.

Cooper, Graeme S. (1986), 'Income Tax Law and Contributive Justice: Some Thoughts on Defining and Expressing a Consistent Theory of Tax Justice and Its Limitations', **3** *Australian Tax Forum*, 297-332.

Cooter, Robert D. (1978), 'Optimal Tax Schedules and Rates', **68** *American Economic Review*.

Cooter, Robert D. and Helpman, Elhanan (1974), 'Optimal Income Taxation for Transfer Payments Under Different Social Welfare Functions', **88** *Quarterly Journal of Economics*, 656 ff.

Crain, W. Mark and Oakley, Lisa K. (1995), 'The Politics of Infrastructure', **38** *Journal of Law and Economics*, 1-17.

Crain, W. Mark and Tollison, Robert D. (1979), 'The Executive Branch in the Interest-Group Theory of Government', **8** *Journal of Legal Studies*, 555-567.

Creedy, J. (1988), 'Taxation and Compensation to Dependents of Accident Victims', **8** *International Review of Law and Economics*, 85-95.

Davis, Karen (1989), 'National Health Insurance: A Proposal', **79** *American Economic Review. Papers and Proceedings*, 349-352.

De Clercq, Marc and Naert, Frank (1985), *De Politieke Markt* (The Political Market), Antwerpen, Kluwer, 163 p.

De Geest, Gerrit (1990), 'Public Choice en Rechtseconomie (Public Choice and Law and Economics)', **39(10)** *Ars Aequi* in Bock, Ruth de, et al. (eds), *Themanummer Rechtseconomie*, 666-673.

Degenkamp, J.Th. and Heynen, H.M. (1980), *Tolvrije Gedachten* (Free Thoughts), Deventer, Kluwer, 304 p.

Department of the Treasury (1984), *Tax Reform for Fairness, Simplicity, and Economic Growth - The Treasury Department Report to the President,* 2 vols, Washington, US Treasury, 262 p.

Diamond, Stephen (1983), 'The Death and Transfiguration of Benefit Taxation: Special Assessments in Nineteenth-Century America', **12** *Journal of Legal Studies*, 201-240.

Dilorenzo, T.J. (1984), 'The Domain of Rent-Seeking Behaviour: Private or Public Choice?', **4** *International Review of Law and Economics*, 185-197.

Dilorenzo, T.J. (1988), 'Property Rights, Information Costs, and the Economics of Rent Seeking', **144** *Journal of Institutional and Theoretical Economics*, 318-322.

Dye, Thomas R. (1985), 'Impact of Federal Tax Reform on State-Local Finances', **5** *Cato Journal*, 597 ff.

Eden, Lorraine (1991), 'Free Trade, Tax Reform, and Transfer Pricing', **39(1)** *Canadian Tax Journal*, 90-112.

Ekelund, Robert B., Jr and Tollison, Robert D. (1981), *Mercantilism as a Rent Seeking Society: Economic Regulation in Historical Perspective*, College Station, Texas, A&M University Press, 169 p.

Fane, George (1991), 'Piecemeal Tax Reforms, and the Compensated Radial Elasticities of Tax Bases', **45** *Journal of Public Economics*, 263-270.

Fazzari, Steven, Hubbard, R. Glenn and Petersen, Bruce (1988), 'Investment, Financing Decisions, and Tax Policy', **78** *American Economic Review. Papers and Proceedings*, 200-205.

Fellows, Mary Louise (1990), 'A Comprehensive Attack on Tax Deferral', **88** *Michigan Law Review*, 722-813.

Flowers, Marilyn R. (1987), 'Rent Seeking and Rent Dissipation: A Critical View', **7** *Cato Journal*, 431-440.

Formby, John P., Keeler, James P. and Thistle, Paul D. (1988), 'X-Efficiency, Rent-Seeking, and Social Costs', **57** *Public Choice*, 115-126.

Formby, John P., Keeler, James P. and Thistle, Paul D. (1991), 'X-Efficiency, Rent-Seeking and Social Costs: Reply', **68** *Public Choice*, 267-271.

Frey, Donald E. (1991), 'Optimal-Sized Tuition Tax Credits Reconsidered: Comment', **19(3)** *Public Finance Quarterly*, 347-354.

Garcia Villarejo, Salinas, Avelino and Sánchez, Javier (1993), *Manual de Hacienda Pública General y de España* (Public Treasury Manual), Madrid, Tecnos.

Gephardt, Richard (1985), 'The Economics and Politics of Tax Reform', **5** *Cato Journal*, 455-464.

Gillette, Clayton P. and Hopkins, Thomas D. (1987), 'Federal User Fees: A Legal and Economic Analysis', **67** *Boston University Law Rèview*, 795-874.

Gimeno Ullastres, Juan A. (1980), 'La Incidencia del Gasto Público por Niveles de Renta: España 1990 vs. 1980 (The Effect of Public Expenditure by Levels of Income: Spain 1990 vs. 1980)', in X (ed), *I Simposio Sobre la Igualdad y Distribución de la Renta y la Riqueza*, Fundación Argentaria, 63-121.

Gimeno Ullastres, Juan A. (1981), 'Reforma Fiscal y Sistema Tributario (Reforming the Tax System)', in X (ed), *Las Reformas Urgentes*, Madrid, Taller Ediciones JB, 481-490.

Gimeno Ullastres, Juan A. (1983), *¿A Quién Beneficia el Gasto Público?* (Who Does Public Expenditure Favour?), Número Monografico de la Revista de Economía Pública e Historia Económica.

Gimeno Ullastres, Juan A. (1984), 'Los Recargos Locales sobre Impuestos Estatales (Local Overcharges on Central Taxes)', **1114(21)** *La ley*, 1-4.

Gimeno Ullastres, Juan A. and Ruiz Huerta, Jesús (1979), 'Descentralización Fiscal y Corresponsablidad a Través de las Grandes Figuras Tributarias (Tax Descentralization and Corresponsability)', **3(1);2°ép** *Cuadernos Aragoneses de Economía*, 29-40.

Gimeno Ullastres, Juan A. and Ruiz Huerta, Jesús (1980), 'Financiación Autonómica: Un Modelo Alternativo de Corresponsabilidad Fiscal (Financing the Communities: An Alternative Model for Tax Corresponsability)', **15** *Revista Valenciana de Hacienda Pública*, 149-179.

Gimeno Ullastres, Juan A. and Ruiz Huerta, Jesús (1981), *El Nuevo Estado Fiscal Español* (The New Spanish Fiscal State), Madrid, H. Blume, 315 p.

Gimeno Ullastres, Juan A. and Ruiz Huerta, Jesús (1986), 'Reforma Fiscal y Financiación del las CCAA: El Régimen Especial (Financing The Communities and Tax Reform: The Special Regime)', in X (ed), *Estado Federal/Estado Regional: La Financianción de las Comunidades Autónomas*, Salamanca, Ediciones de la Diputación de Salamanca, 245-263.

Gimeno Ullastres, Juan A., Ruiz Huerta, Jesús and Olleros, Jaime (1987), *Una Reforma Fiscal para España* (Tax Reform in Spain), Moneda y Credito S.A.

Gordon, James P.F. (1991), 'Tax Reform and Uniformity: Explaining the Hatta Result', **45(2)** *Journal of Public Economics*, 161-190.

Graetz, Michael J. and Wilde, Louis L. (1985), 'The Economics of Tax Compliance: Fact and Fantasy', **38** *National Tax Journal*, 355-363.

Graetz, Michael J., Reinganum, Jennifer F. and Wilde, Louis L. (1986), 'The Tax Compliance Game: Toward an Interactive Theory of Law Enforcement', **2** *Journal of Law, Economics, and Organization*, 1-32.

Hansen, Susan B. (1985), 'Tax Reform: Sound Economics or Power Politics? Comment on Dye', **5** *Cato Journal*, 609-612.

Hettich, Walter and Winer, Stanley L. (1988), 'Economic and Political Foundations of Tax Structure', **78** *American Economic Review*, 701-712.

Hofmann, E. and Wehrt, Klaus (1992), 'Die Reform der Kfz-Steuer - Wirtschaftspolitisch Betrachtet (Economic Analysis of the Reform of the Motor Vehicle Tax)', **4** *Zeitschrift für Verkehrswissenschaft*, 263-271.

Inman, Robert P. and Fitts, Michael A. (1990), 'Political Institutions and Fiscal Policy: Evidence from the U.S. Historical Record', **6(S)** *Journal of Law, Economics, and Organization*, 79-132.

Jackman, Richard (1986), 'The Economic Effects of Tax Based Incomes Policy', in Colander, David C. (ed), *Incentive Based Incomes Policies: Advances in TIP and MAP*, Cambridge, MA, Harper and Row, 95-109.

Johnson, Calvin H. (1989), 'Why Have Anti-Tax Legislation? A Response to Professor Zelenak', **67** *Texas Law Review.*, -625.

Kalt, Joseph P. and Zupan, Mark A. (1990), 'The Apparent Ideological Behavior of Legislators: Testing for Principal-Agent Slack in Political Institutions', **33** *Journal of Law and Economics*, 103-131.

Kaplow, Louis (1989), 'Horizontal Equity: Measures in Search of a Principle', **42** *National Tax Journal*, 139-154.

Kaplow, Louis (1992a), 'A Note on Horizontal Equity', **1** *Florida Tax Review*, 191-196.

Kaplow, Louis (1992b), 'Government Relief for Risk Associated with Government Action', **94** *Scandinavian Journal of Economics*, 525-541.

Kaplow, Louis (1993), 'Should the Government's Allocation Branch be Concerned About the Distortionary Cost of Taxation and Distributive Effects?', Program in Law and Economics Discussion Paper, 122 ff.

Kaplow, Louis (1994), 'Taxation and Risk Taking: A General Equilibrium Perspective', **47** *National Tax Journal*, 789-798.

Kaplow, Louis (1995a), 'A Note on Subsidizing Gifts', **58** *Journal of Public Economics*, 469-477.

Kaplow, Louis (1995b), 'A Fundamental Objection to Tax Equity Norms: A Call for Utilitarianism', **48** *National Tax Journal*, 497-514.

Kaplow, Louis (1996a), 'Tax and Non-Tax Distortions', **57** *Journal of Public Economics*.

Kaplow, Louis (1996b), 'Regional Cost-of-Living Adjustments in Tax-Transfer Schemes', **51** *Tax Law Review*.

Kaplow, Louis (1996c), 'Fiscal Federalism and the Deductibility of State and Local Taxes in a Federal Income Tax', **82** *Virginia Law Review*.

Karp, Larry S. and Perloff, Jeffrey M. (1989), 'Estimating Market Structure and Tax Incidence: The Japanese Television Market', **37(3)** *Journal of Industrial Economics*, 225-239.

Katz, Avery and Mankiw, Gregory (1985), 'How Should Fringe Benefits be Taxed?', **38** *National Tax Journal*, 37-45.

Kau, James B. and Rubin, Paul H. (1979), 'Self-Interest, Ideology, and Logrolling in Congressional Voting', **22** *Journal of Law and Economics*, 365-384.

Kay, John A. and King, M.A. (1986), *The British Tax System*, Oxford, Oxford University Press, 261 p.

Kerwin, Cornelis M. (1983), 'Assessing the Effects of Consensual Processes in Regulatory Programs: Methodological and Policy Issues', **32** *American University Law Review*, 401 ff.

Kiesling, Herbert J. (1990), 'Economic and Political Foundations of Tax Structure: Comment', **80** *American Economic Review*.

Krueger, Anne O. (1974), 'The Political Economy of the Rent-seeking Society', **64** *American Economic Review*, 291-303.

Labovitz, John R. (1974), 'The Impact of the Private Foundation Provisions of the Tax Reform Act of 1969: Early Empirical Measurements', **3** *Journal of Legal Studies*, 63-105.

Landry, Raymond A. (1991), 'La Priorité Fiscale sur les Meubles et le Projet de Code Civil du Québec (Fiscal Priority on Movables and the Quebec Civil Code Bill)', **22** *Revue générale de droit*, 649-658.

Lehmann, Michael (1991), 'Umwelthaftungsrecht dient der Internalisierung negativer Extemalitäten, Kommentar (Environmental Liability Law is to Internalize Negative Externalities. A Comment)', in Ott, Claus and Schäfer, Hans-Bernd (eds), *Ökonomische Probleme des Zivilrechts*, Berlin, Springer, 290-294.

Lindsey, Lawrence (1990), *The Growth Experiment: How the New Tax Policy is Transforming the U.S. Economy*, New York, Basic Books, 260 p.

Maddock, Rodney (1982), 'Comment', in Cranston, Ross and Schick, Anne (eds), *Law and Economics*, Canberra, Australian National University, 190-191.

Marlow Michael L. and Orzechowski, William P. (1997), 'The Separation of Spending from Taxation: Implications for Collective Choices', **8** *Constitutional Political Economy*, 151-163.

McCaffery, Edward J. (1990), 'The Holy Grail of Tax Simplification', **66** *Wisconsin Law Review*, 1267-1322.

McChesney, Fred S. (1987), 'Rent Extraction and Rent Creation in the Economic Theory of Regulation', **16** *Journal of Legal Studies*, 101-118.

McCubbins, Mathew D. (1990), 'Note: Budget Policy-making and the Appearance of Power', **6(S)** *Journal of Law, Economics, and Organization*, 133-153.

McGee, Robert W. (1993), 'Principles of Taxation for Emerging Economies: Some Lessons from the U.S. Experience', **12(1)** *Dickinson Journal of International Law*, 29-93.

McGee, Robert W. (1996a), 'Tax Advice for Latvia and Other Similarly Situated Emerging Economies', **13(2)** *International Tax and Business Lawyer*, 223-308.

McGee, Robert W. (1996b), *Essays on Accounting, Taxation and Public Finance*, Dumont Institute for Public Policy Research. <<http:/ww.hili.com~dumontin>>

McGee, Robert W. (1996c), *Taxation, Ethics and Public Policy*, Dumont Institute for Public Policy Research. http:/ww.hili.com~dumontin

McGee, Robert W. (1997), 'Some Principles of Taxation for Latin America: Lessons from the USA and European Experiences', in Gertner, David, Bocater, Paulo F. and Leal, Ricardo R.C. (eds), *Regionalism and Globalization in Latin America: A Contradiction?*, Rio de Janeiro, Business Association of Latin American Studies and Instituto de Administração e Gerência Pontifícia Universidade Católica do Rio de Janeiro, 266-280.

Mintz, Jack M. and Whalley, John (eds) (1989), *The Economic Impacts of Tax Reform*, Toronto, Canadian Tax Foundation, 463 p.

Musgrave, Richard A. and Musgrave, Peggy B. (1985), *Public Finance in Theory and Practice*, Tokyo, McGraw-Hill, 824 p.

Naert, Frank (1984), 'De Politieke Economie van Pressiegroepen (The Political Economy of Pressure Groups)', **69** *Economisch-Statistische Berichten*, 56-61.

Naert, Frank (1987), 'Overheidsuitgaven en Pressiegroepen in België', **32** *Tijdschrift voor Economie en Management*, 165-187.

Page, William H. (1987), 'Interest Groups, Antitrust, and State Regulation: Parker v. Brown in the Economic Theory of Legislation', **37** *Duke Law Journal*, 618-668.

Pauly, Mark V. (1986), 'Taxation, Health Insurance, and Market Failure in the Medical Economy', **24** *Journal of Economic Literature*, 629-675.

Peacock, Alan T. and Forte, Francesco (eds) (1981), *The Political Economy of Taxation*, Oxford, Blackwell, 211 p.

Pechman, Joseph A. (1987), *Federal Tax Policy* (5th edn), Washington, Brookings Institution, 430 p.

Pechman, Joseph A. (1989), *Tax Reform, the Rich and the Poor*, Washington, Brookings Institution, 211 p.

Pechman, Joseph A. (1990), 'The Future of Income Tax', **80** *American Economic Review*, 1-20.

Peltzman, Sam (1980), 'The Growth of Government', **23** *Journal of Law and Economics*.

Peltzman, Sam (1984), 'Constituent Interest and Congressional Voting', **27** *Journal of Law and Economics*, 181-210.

Peterson, Pamela P. (1985), 'Lingering Questions About Tax Reform: Comment on Browning and Browning', **5** *Cato Journal*, 651-656.

Priest, W. Curtiss (1988), *Risks, Concerns, and Social Regulation: Forces that Led to Laws on Health, Safety, and the Environment*, Boulder, CO, Westview Press, 204 p.

Pritchard, A.C. (1991), 'Note: Government Promises and Due Process: An Economic Analysis of the "New Property"', **77** *Virginia Law Review*, 1053-1090.

Provopoulos, George and Zambaras, Athanassios (1991), 'Testing for Causality Between Government Spending and Taxation', **68** *Public Choice*, 277-282.

Puy Fraga, Pedro, Suárez, A. Iglésias and Ron Romero, Ron J. (1985), 'Una Nota Sobre los Problemas que Plantea la Imposición Autonómica y la Municipal (A Note on Autonomic and Local Taxes)', in X (ed), *Actas de la X Reunión de Estudios Regionales, T. II, Asociación Española de Ciencia Regional - Junta de Castilla León*, 901-909.

Ramseyer, J. Mark and Nakazato, Minoru (1989), 'Tax Transitions and the Protection Racket: A Reply To Professors Graetz and Kaplow', **75** *Virginia Law Review*, 1155 ff.

Reinganum, Jennifer F. and Wilde, Louis L. (1991), 'Equilibrium Enforcement and Compliance in the Presence of Tax Practitioners', **7** *Journal of Law, Economics, and Organization*, 163-181.

Rice, Edward M. and Ulen, Thomas S. (1981), 'Rent Seeking and Welfare Loss', **3** *Research in Law and Economics*, 53-65.

Rodios, Nikos D. (1986), 'E Kampyle tou Laffer e Peri tes Phthinousas Apodoseos tes Phorologias (The Laffer Curve or On the Diminishing Return of Taxation)', **53** *Ephemeris ton Hellenon Nomikon*, 216-218.

Rogers, Carol Ann (1991), 'A Simple Model of Endogenous Tax Reform', **46** *Journal of Public Economics*, 91-111.

Rogerson, William P. (1990), 'Comment (on "Political Institutions and Fiscal Policy: Evidence from the U.S. Historical Record")', **6(S)** *Journal of Law, Economics, and Organization*, 155-166.

Rose-Ackerman, Susan (1990), 'Comment (on Ferejohn and Shipan's "Congressional Influence (on Bureaucracy)"', **6(S)** *Journal of Law, Economics, and Organization*, 21-27.

Ross, Thomas W. (1986), 'Store Wars: The Chain Tax Movement', **29** *Journal of Law and Economics*, 125-137.

Rowley, Charles K., Tollison, Robert D. and Tullock, Gordon (eds) (1988), *The Political Economy of Rent-Seeking*, Boston, Kluwer Academic Publishers.

Ru, H.J. De (1988), *Prijst de Wet Zich uit de Markt*? (Does the Law Price Itself Out of the Market?), Zwolle, Tjeenk Willink.

Ruiz-Huerta Carbonell, Jesús (1992), 'Vigencia y Operatividad del Principio de la no Confiscatoriedad de los Tributos en el Ordenamiento Español (The Principle of Non Confiscation of Taxes: Enforcement in Spain)', **64** *Revista Crónica Tributaria*.

Ruiz-Huerta Carbonell, Jesús and Giménez, Antonio (eds) (1993), *Estructura Institucional y Gestión del Gasto Público en algunos Paises de la OCDE* (Institutuional Structure and Managment of Public Expenditure in Some Countries), Estudios de Hacienda Pública, Instituto de Estudios Fiscales.

Russo, Enzo (1992), 'L'Impatto Amministrativo della Riforma del Contenzioso: Spunti di Analisi Economica del Diritto (The Administrative Impact of the Reform of the Contentious Procedure: Hints of Economic Analysis of Law)', *Il Fisco*, 10471-10479.

Salinas, Javier (1990), *Economía Política del Federalismo Fiscal España* (The Political Economy of Spanish Fiscal Federalism), Madrid, Instituto de Estudios Fiscales.

Schmalbeck, Richard L. and Myers, Gary (1986), 'A Policy Analysis of Fee-Shifting Rules under the Internal Revenue Code', **66** *Duke Law Journal*, 970-1002.

Seidl, Christian (1980), 'Historischer Abriß österreichischer Steuerstrukturen und Steuerreformen (A History of Austrian Tax Structures and Tax Reforms)', in Helige, O. (ed), *Dokumentation zur Steuerreformkommission, Wirtschaftsverlag Dr. Anton Orac*, Wien, 219-231.

Shachar, Avishai (1985), 'The Importance of Considering Liabilities in Tax Transitions', **98** *Harvard Law Review*, 1842-1868.

Shaviro, Daniel N. (1988), 'The New Alternative Minimum Tax: Perception, Reality, and Strategy', **66** *Taxes*, 91-113.

Shaviro, Daniel N. (1989a), 'Risk and Accrual: The Tax Treatment of Nonrecourse Debt', **44** *Tax Law Review*, 401-457.

Shaviro, Daniel N. (1989b), 'Selective Limitations on Tax Benefits', **56** *University of Chicago Law Review*, 1189-1260.

Shaviro, Daniel N. (1990), 'Beyond Public Choice and Public Interest: A Study of the Legislative Process As Illustrated by Tax Legislation in the 1980s', **139** *University of Pennsylvania Law Review*, 1-123.

Shaviro, Daniel N. (1992a), 'An Economic and Political Look at Federalism in Taxation,', **90** *Michigan Law Review*, 895-991.

Shaviro, Daniel N. (1992b), 'An Efficiency Analysis of Realization and Recognition Rules Under the Federal Income Tax', **48** *Tax Law Review*, 1-68.

Shaviro, Daniel N. (1993a), *Federalism in Taxation: The Case for Greater Uniformity*, Washington, AEI Press.

Shaviro, Daniel N. (1993b), 'Commentary: Uneasiness and Capital Gains', **48** *Tax Law Review*, 393-417.

Shaviro, Daniel N. (1995), 'Risk-Based Rules and the Taxation of Capital Income', **50** *Tax Law Review*, 643-724.

Shaviro, Daniel N. (1997), 'The Minimum Wage, the Earned Income Tax Credit, and Optimal Subsidy Policy', **64** *University of Chicago Law Review*.

Shughart, William F., II (1987), 'Durable Tax Reform', **7** *Cato Journal*, 273-281.

Shughart, William F., II and Tollison, Robert D. (1986), 'On the Growth of Government and the Political Economy of Legislation', **9** *Research in Law and Economics*, 111-127.

Smith, Tom and Whaley, Robert E. (1994), 'Assessing the Costs of Regulation: The Case of Dual Trading', **37** *Journal of Law and Economics*, 215-246.

Spinnewyn, F. (1987), 'Inkomensvorming en Deregulering van de Arbeidsmarkt: 4. Sociale Zekerheid (Income Formation and Deregulation of the Labour Market: Social Security)', in X (ed.), *18de Vlaams Wetenschappelijk Economisch Congres, Brussel 8 en 9 mei 1987, Sociaal-economische Deregulering*, Brussel, V.E.H.U.B., 305-320.

Stake, Jeffrey E. (1995), 'Loss Aversion and Involuntary Transfers of Title', in Malloy, Robin P. and Braun, Christopher K. (eds), *Law and Economics: New and Critical Perspectives*, New York, Peter Lang, 331-360.

Stein, Herbert (1966), 'Pre-Revolutionary Fiscal Policy: The Regime of Herbert Hoover', **9** *Journal of Law and Economics*, 189-223.

Steuerle, C. Eugene (1986), *Who Should Pay for Collecting Taxes?*, Washington, American Enterprise Institute for Public Policy Research, 75 p.

Stout, Lynn A. (1981), 'Note: The Case for Mandatory Separate Filing by Married Persons', **91** *Yale Law Journal*, 363-382.

Stout, Lynn A. (1995), 'Are Stock Markets Costly Casinos? Disagreement, Market Failure, and Securities Regulation', **81** *Virginia Law Review*, 611 ff.

Tiebout, Charles M. (1956), 'A Pure Theory of Local Government Expenditures', **64** *Journal of Political Economy*, 416-424. Reprinted in Cowen, T. (ed.) (1992), *Public Goods and Market Failures*, Chapter 9, London: Transaction Publishers.

Tillman, Georg (1989), *Equity, Incentives, and Taxation*, Berlin, Springer, 132 p.

Tollison, Robert D. (1982), 'Rent-Seeking: a Survey', **35** *Kyklos*, 575-602.

Trebilcock, Michael J. and Engelhart, Kenneth (1981), 'A Tax Credit for Public Interest Groups', **3** *Canadian Taxation: A Journal of Tax Policy*, 29-33.

Tullock, Gordon (1988), 'The Costs of Rent-Seeking: A Metaphysical Problem', **57** *Public Choice*, 15-24.

Tullock, Gordon (1989), *The Economics of Special Privilege and Rent Seeking*, Boston, Kluwer Academic Publishers, 104 p.

Turnbull, Shann (1982), 'Resource Tax Alternative', **1(2)** *Economic Papers, The Economic Society of Australia, Sydney*, 85-88.

Van den Hauwe, Ludwig (1995), 'Review of: Flair and de Boussieu, Fiscal Policy, Taxation and the Financial System in an Increasingly Integrated Europe', **85** *Public Choice*, 400-405.

Vanberg, Viktor J. and Buchanan, James M. (1986), 'Organization Theory and Fiscal Economics: Society, State and Public Debt', **2** *Journal of Law, Economics, and Organization*, 215-227.

Vedder, Richard (1985), 'Federal Tax Reform: Lessons from the States', **5** *Cato Journal*, 571-590.

Vickrey, William (1947), *Agenda for Progressive Taxation*, New York, Ronald Press, 496 p.

Walz, W. Rainer (1988), 'Rechtssicherheit und Risikozuweisung bei Steuerrechtsänderungen - Verbotene Rückwirkung, gebotene Übergangsregelung, richterliche Vertragsanpassung (Legal Certainty and Risk Allocation for Changes in Tax Law - Illegal Retroaction, Transitional Rules)', *Recht und Risiko*, 252-286.

Waters, Melissa and Moore, William J. (1990), 'The Theory of Economic Regulation and Public Choice and the Determinants of Public Sector Bargaining Legislation', **66** *Public Choice*, 161-175.

Webb, V.C. (1990), 'The Taxation Rulings System - A Helpful Child or a Potential Bully?', **7(2)** *Australian Tax Forum*, 217 252.

Wenders, John T. (1987), 'On Perfect Rent Dissipation', **77** *American Economic Review*, 456-459.

White, P.D. (1990), 'Realization, Recognition, Reconciliation, Rationality and the Structure of the Federal Income Tax System', **88** *Michigan Law Review*, 2034-2096.

Wibaut, Serge (1989), *Tax Reform in Disequilibrium Economies*, Cambridge, Cambridge University Press, 113 p.

Wildasin, David E. (1990), 'R.M. Haig: Pioneer Advocate of Expenditure Taxation?', **28** *Journal of Economic Literature*, 649-654.

Wilson, John Douglas (1991), 'Optimal Public Good Provision With Limited Lump-Sum Taxation', **81** *American Economic Review*, 153-166.

Wood, John C. (1980), 'Alfred Marshall and the Tariff-Reform Campaign of 1903', **23** *Journal of Law and Economics*, 481-495.

Yandle, Bruce (1989), *The Political Limits of Environmental Regulation: Tracking the Unicorn*, Westport, Greenwood, 180 p.

Yorio, Edward (1985), 'The President's Tax Proposals: A Major Step in the Right Direction', **53** *Fordham Law Review*, 1255 ff.

Zelenak, Lawrence (1989), 'When Good Preferences Go Bad: A Critical Analysis of the Anti-Tax Shelter Provisions of the Tax Reform Act of 1986', **67** *Texas Law Review*, 499 ff.

Zelinsky, Edward A. (1986), 'Efficiency and Income Taxes: The Rehabilitation of Tax Incentives', **64** *Texas Law Review*, 973-1037.

Zwemmer, J.W. (1995), 'Belastingrecht op het Grensvlak van Economie en Recht (Tax Law on the Borderline of Economics and Law)', in X (ed), *Ondernemen tussen Macht en Ordening: Opstellen op het Grensvlak van Economie en Recht*, Amsterdam, Thesis Publishers, 37-45.

6010
TAXATION: MACRO ASPECTS

Jef Vuchelen
Vrije Universiteit Brussel

Abstract

This chapter on macro aspects of taxation begins with a discussion of the contribution of taxation to stabilization policies. The budget constraint of the government and the expectations of economic agents about taxation are crucial elements here. The effectiveness of countercyclical policies has, however, been challenged by questions about the relevancy of the timing of taxation. We therefore cover the Barro-Ricardo equivalence theorem. Next we review the literature on taxation and inflation and the positive approaches to taxation. The discussion so far relates primarily to closed economies. The last section surveys some of the publications on the macro aspects of taxation in open economies.
JEL classification: H10, H30, H70
Keywords: Taxation, Government Budget Constraint, Stabilization Policies, Ricardian Equivalence, Inflation

1. Introduction

Over the past decades taxation has increased to levels not experienced before, which has stimulated theoretical and empirical research on the effects of taxation. The search for policy instruments to stimulate economic growth, led most governments to reform taxation (= lower marginal rates), especially income taxation. Notwithstanding, for most economic agents total taxes are still the main single item on the expenditure side of their accounts. Reactions to current and expected taxation are therefore among the more important economic decisions to be made. These decisions cannot be neglected by policymakers. For economists, the sheer size of taxation implies that no macroeconomic shock can be analyzed without considering the effects on the government finances. Frequently in theoretical research the tax rate is assimilated to the income tax rate. The discussion about the effects of this tax could serve as a guide for the theoretical macroeconomic effects.

The interest in taxation or, more generally, in public finances, has not only been stimulated by the rise in 'instant' taxation but also by the tax-postponing policies pursued by many governments since the mid 1970s through the accumulation of government debt. Analyses of the long-run problems related to large stocks of government debt were never as relevant. Data for, for example, the 15 countries of the European Union illustrate the extent of the accumulation of government debt. Total debt amounts now (1998) to about 5,270 billion ECU or 70.5 percent of GDP. This represents 153 percent of current yearly taxation. The per capita debt of every EU citizen equals nearly 14,000 ECU.

Just as it does for any economic entity, a budget constraint unites all operations of the government. This constraint thus links tax policy with expenditures policy, deficits and monetary policy. Any distinction between the different policies is therefore somewhat arbitrary. Evidently some choices had to be made in this survey. We restrict this survey to issues that are directly related to the macroeconomic aspects of taxation. This implies that we will not discuss the relative merits of monetary and fiscal policy, or the link between taxation and government expenditures. We agree here with Kay (1990, p. 18): 'The link between tax and spending is now close and symmetric. But this symmetry is rarely reflected in the theory, or the practice, of tax policy'. Furthermore, we will not consider sectorial, regional or local aspects. As a result, studies concerning, for example, the taxation of international income or commodity flows (tariffs) will not be surveyed. References related to the government debt will only be discussed when they have a direct impact on taxation. This explains, for example, the absence of studies on the world debt problem. Similarly, studies on the political determinants of the deficit or debt policies will not be surveyed; however, the political aspects of taxation will be covered. The literature on the history of taxation and the early discussion about the effects of taxation will not be surveyed. We refer to, for example, Webber and Wildavsky (1986) and Musgrave and Shoup (1959). Taxation is considered in a narrow sense so we will not cover alternatives to taxation such as regulation (see Chapter 5000). Note that because of lack of space, we could not include the literature on taxation and growth and the general equilibrium approach to taxation. We also refer the reader to other related chapters (6000 for optimal taxation, 6020 for tax evasion, 6030 property taxes, 6040 consumption taxes, 6050 income taxation, 6060 corporate taxation, 6070 inheritance taxation and 6080 international taxation).

Our survey can be viewed as integrating the macroeconomic effects of taxation into the intertemporal budget constraint of the government. This constraint determines the sustainability of announced fiscal policies and therefore the perception of fiscal policy by economic agents.

We start our survey with the contribution of taxation to stabilization policies (Section 2). In this discussion, the budget constraint of the government (Section 3) and the expectations of economic agents about taxation (Section 4) are crucial. The effectiveness of countercyclical policies has, however, been challenged by questions about the relevancy of the timing of taxation (Section 5). In the next section (Section 6) we review the literature on taxation and inflation. Section 7 provides an overview of the positive approaches to taxation. The previous discussion relates primarily to closed economies. The last section (Section 8) surveys taxation in open economies.

2. Taxation and Stabilization Policies

The macroeconomic aspects of taxation and fiscal policy have systematically been assimilated with the stabilization function. (The allocative and distribution function being the subject of more specific instruments; they are part of other surveys.) More recent research has, however, been rather critical about the traditional approach because of the formulation of anticipations and medium and longer-run implications of the models under consideration.

In the Keynesian tradition (see any textbook on macroeconomics or public finance; for expositions and extensions Modigliani, 1944; Peacock and Shaw, 1976; Turnovsky, 1977, and Frenkel and Razin, 1987; for an adaptation of traditional Keynesian demand management to the stagflation situation of the 1980s, we refer to Vines, Macriejowski and Meade, 1983; see also Baily, 1978, for a discussion of the changing economic environment and its impact on stabilization policies) fiscal policy, and therefore taxation, is one of the main instruments to stabilize the economy. Stabilization policies are designed to minimize the gap between current and potential production and employment and to limit the inflation rate. This importance of fiscal policy derived from the economic situation in the 1930s and 1950s and the perceived properties of the economy (deficient aggregate demand, rigid prices and wages, an elastic money demand and an inelastic investment function). The asymmetry in its implementation (expenditures and taxes were increased but rarely reduced) resulted in a structural increase in the relative size of the government budget. This was further stimulated by the Haavelmo effect (Haavelmo, 1945) or the balanced-budget multiplier. This effect holds that no deficit penalty for higher public spending financed by an increase in taxes exists since a similar increase in taxes and government expenditures would increase income by the same amount. Later Knoester (1980, 1983) disputed this result by stressing that instead an inverted effect exists as a result of the link between taxes and wages. Furthermore, much faith was placed in the automatic stabilizing properties of expansive policies: any budget deficit would soon disappear thanks to the induced beneficial effects on economic growth (recent work is by Rodseth, 1984; Kyer, Mixon and Uri, 1988; Uri, Mixon and Kyer, 1989a, 1989b). Cameron (1978) argues that the increasing openness of countries 'created' a demand for stabilization policies.

The mainstream approach in the 1960s was to view the economy as similar to a system that, by a clever use of impulses, could be controlled. This led to an intensive search for the value of the multipliers. It explained, partly, the exploding use of large-scale econometric models (see Hickman, 1972, for the state of the debate at the beginning of the 1970s; see Sims, 1982, for an evaluation). However, also reduced form models gained some popularity. This could be explained by the success of the St. Louis model (named after the Federal Reserve Bank of St. Louis). That model (Anderson and Jordan, 1968) intensified the discussion between Keynesians and the monetarists since it was shown that monetary policy and not fiscal policy affected income. In these reduced forms no attention was paid to incentives effects, so we do not survey these studies.

On the empirical level, one should remember the Goldfeld and Blinder (1972) point that reduced forms could give misleading results on the efficacy of fiscal policy if this policy is designed to stabilize the economy. Intuitively, if fiscal policy manages to stabilize income, no correlation between the deficit and income will be found.

In the late 1960s and early 1970s thus a lively discussion about the most appropriate policy course emerged. Buchanan and Wagner (1977) argued that the Keynesian theory destroyed the classical thesis, strengthened by consititutional rules, that budgets should balance and that deficits were immoral.

Until the early 1970s, the main - if not the only - argument to denounce fiscal policy concerned crowding out; that is, that the impact of an increase in government expenditures on total demand would be offset by lower private investment or consumption expenditures. (The traditional result could thus also be defined as 'crowding in'.) Obviously, at full employment a complete crowding out of private by public expenditures occurs so fiscal policy can only determine the division of output between the public and the private sector. When resources are not fully employed, different effects matter such as the increase in the interest rate (financial crowding out), in wealth, the composition of wealth (portfolio crowding out) and inflation (see Spencer and Yohe, 1970; Carlson and Spencer, 1975, 1980; Meyer, 1975; Buiter, 1977; Cavaco-Silva, 1977; Scarth, 1977; Turnovsky, 1977; Cohen and McMenamin, 1978; Floyd and Hynes, 1978; Friedman, 1978; Bruce and Purvis, 1979; Stevens, 1979; Taylor, 1979; Aschauer, 1985, 1988; Aschauer and Greenwood, 1985).

Besides crowding-out, many other questions on the business cycle stabilization potential of fiscal policy have been raised. How is a tax reduction or a deficit financed? Is the policy credible? Is the policy sustainable? What about the foreign effects? What motivates policymakers to modify taxes? The literature on some answers to these questions will be surveyed later.

We will not extend the discussion into different versions of the Keynesian and classical models like the Tobin (Tobin and Buiter, 1976; Buiter and Tobin, 1980) or Brunner-Meltzer (Brunner and Meltzer, 1976) models, since they focus on and refine monetary transmission mechanisms, or extend on the neo-

Keynesian or disequilibrium models.

Finally, note that in recent research shocks in taxes are considered to produce business cycles fluctuations (Christiano and Eichenbaum, 1992; Braun, 1994b; McGrattan, 1994; Johnsson and Klein, 1996). This feeds the criticisms about the possibility to use taxes as a stabilization tool.

3. The Budget Constraint

In the early stages of demand management policies, the 'loose' reasoning was that, by a judicious timing, no public finance instrument would, over the business cycle, create financing problems. This would be the result of the automatic stabilizing properties of taxation. This view was supported by the spectacular decline in the debt ratio after the Second World War. Later, however, the criticism by monetarists was supplemented by the argument that the budget constraint was neglected. By explicitly incorporating the financing aspects of government decisions two important modifications had to be made to the traditional analysis: fiscal and monetary policy became interrelated and the long-run multipliers were no longer uncertain. References to the basic articles and developments are: Ott and Ott (1965), Christ (1967, 1979), Silber (1970), Steindl (1971), Blinder and Solow (1973, 1976), Meyer (1975), Brunner and Meltzer (1976), Currie (1976), Tobin and Buiter (1976), Cavaco-Silva (1977), Smyth (1978), Cohen and De Leeuw (1980) and Mayer (1984) (surveys are to be found in Turnovsky, 1977; Artis, 1979; and Burrows, 1979). In these contributions, it is stressed that any tax reduction has to be financed implying that the budget constraint must be included in the analysis. This endogenized at least the supply of bonds, possibly money creation and therefore monetary policy. The longer-run consequences on the multipliers strengthened the macroeconomic importance of the marginal tax rate: any change in expenditures (or taxes) must be offset by an identical change in taxes (or expenditures) since no deficit and therefore no monetary or bond financing is allowed. The consequence is the irrelevancy of the method of financing the deficit; only the fiscal structure determines the long-run impact of fiscal policy. Note, however, that this attractive result disappears when interest payments are explicitly included into the budget constraint (Blinder and Solow, 1973, 1974). The size of the long-run multiplier associated with a bond-financed fiscal expansion increases, since taxes must now also finance the higher interest charges. The Blinder-Solow model was extended to include explicit stock-flows interaction of capital and bonds by Tobin and Buiter (1976). Calvo (1985) allows for price increases in a model were the money-bond ratio is important.

4. Rational Expectations

The budgetary constraint criticism of the traditional stabilization instruments is based on the accounting argument that expenditures and revenues are linked by the budget constraint. In the 1970s, further blows on the stabilization approach were inflicted on the basis of more behavioral arguments. Indeed, the traditional approach assumes, although implicitly, that all policy changes occur unexpectedly. The rational expectation assumption, based on Muth (1961), argues that economic agents form expectations about future events. These expectations are rational in the sense that they combine all the available information and therefore do not lead to systematic forecasting errors. The implication of the rational expectations hypothesis is that policies will only be effective when they produce surprises (= forecast errors). By definition, this is not possible in the long run since rational economic agents will detect any policy rule and will therefore no longer be surprised. This is also known as the 'irrelevance hypothesis'. This view has been applied to several policy instruments, most of the time of monetary policy; the core arguments are, however, also relevant to fiscal policy and taxation. The main contributions can be found in Fischer (1980b) and Lucas and Sargent (1981); Baily (1978) and McCallum and Whitaker (1979) apply the monetary policy results to fiscal policy. For our problem at hand it implies that any general expected tax change will already have been discounted by the economic agents in their decision process. An unexpected transitory change in taxation will leave permanent income unchanged. Only permanent unexpected changes are of interest. When government expenditures remain constant, the Ricardo equivalence theorem applies (see below) so the new tax policy will be ineffective. If government expenditures are reduced, the traditional expansive effects, depending on the tax rate change, will apply. The final effects on macroeconomic variables depend on the specification of the model. For example, what is the impact of an increased demand on inflationary expectations? One important policy implication is that fiscal consolidations should not necessarily contract demand due to the benign effects on the expectations about future taxation (see Giavazzi and Pagano, 1990, for an application to Denmark and Ireland). Note that the introduction of uncertain shocks modifies the previous picture slightly in the sense that built-in stabilizers will reduce the variability of income since they provide an automatic and immediate adjustment to current disturbances (McCallum and Whitaker, 1979).

The main publications are Lucas (1972, 1973, 1975, 1976), Sargent (1973), Sargent and Wallace (1975), Barro (1976), Infante and Stein (1976), Sargent and Wallace (1976), Fischer (1977, 1979a, 1979b), Kydland and Prescott (1977, 1980), McCallum (1977, 1980), Phelps and Taylor (1977), Shiller (1978), McCallum and Whitaker (1979), Begg (1980, 1982), Buiter (1980b), Taylor (1985), Lovell (1986) and Lucas (1986b).

Notwithstanding the previous conclusion on the ineffectiveness of stabilization policies in a rational expectations framework, microeconomic considerations such as the incentives effects of marginal tax rates, social security payments, subsidies, and so on, on labor supply, saving behavior, investment, and so on, imply that even perfectly anticipated policy changes will have some real effects in the medium run. Furthermore, the previous analysis assumes a systematic clearing of the markets. If this assumption is relaxed and a disequilibrium framework is accepted, the standard Keynesian effects reappear even when expectations are rational (see Taylor, 1979; Begg, 1982; Neary and Stiglitz, 1983, and Buiter, 1980b).

5. The Timing of Taxation

In the traditional stabilization approach, higher deficits are a crucial instrument to increase growth. However, if expenditures remain unchanged this implies, that sometime in the future taxes will have to be raised. Deficits are thus an instrument to transfer taxes intertemporally. Will citizens be aware of this and take future taxes into account in their decision process? In other words, is there a burden associated with government debt? The discussion on the burden of the government debt emerged forcefully around 1960 (most contributions are in Ferguson, 1964, and Kaounides and Wood, vol. 2, 1992; see also Buchanan, 1958; Modigliani, 1961; Bailey, 1962; Pesek and Saving, 1967, and Cavaco-Silva, 1977).

The mainstream Keynesian position (also known as 'the new orthodoxy') was that government debt was different from private debt (repayment of principal and payment of interest is mortgaging future resources) since 'we owe government debt to ourselves': future generations pay interest and principal to themselves so leaving disposable income unaffected. This argument was reinforced by the proposition that the deficit cannot be a burden on future generations because their resources are unaffected; the exception being foreign debt. These views were criticized since higher deficits implied lower taxation. This allows current generations to consume more and so to crowd out investment. Future generations thus inherit less capital. The distinction between domestic and foreign debt is not relevant since, although foreign debt does not crowd out investment, the revenue from the capital will benefit foreign lenders. Posner (1987) extends this view by arguing that foreign borrowing allows higher investment. *Ceteris paribus*, the burden of the internally held debt will be higher than for foreign debt.

In 1974, Barro rephrased the problem of the debt burden in 'Are Government Bonds Net Wealth?'. By doing so, he could focus the attention on the behavior of taxpayers. Barro showed that the real burden on current and future generations occurs when government uses resources for consumption; the financing of government expenditures (taxes or borrowing) is not relevant: they are equivalent (tax neutrality). This proposition is now known as the 'Ricardian equivalence theorem' (some of the papers by Ricardo are reprinted in Kaounides and Wood, vol. 1, 1992; for a discussion on the historical origins see Buchanan, 1976; O'Driscoll, 1977, and Asso and Barucci, 1988; see also Hakes and McCormick, 1996).

The novel feature of Barro's approach is that he showed that intergenerational gifts and bequests turn an overlapping-generations economy with finite-lived households into an infinite-lived households economy whose consumption would not be affected by intertemporal redistributions of lump-sum taxes.

Phrased in a stabilization framework, the Ricardian equivalence theorem holds that when the government issues bonds, at the same time a liability is incurred to pay interest annually and to reimburse the par value at the date of maturity. Formulated from a wealth point of view, the net present value of the future tax liabilities equals the price of the bond. If taxpayers do capitalize future tax liabilities, the positive gross wealth effects of a bond issue will be offset by an equivalent liability leaving net wealth unchanged. Government bonds will then not be part of net private wealth. In other words, a decrease in public saving will be exactly offset by an increase in private saving, leaving total saving unchanged. Formulated from a financing point of view, the financing of government deficits is irrelevant for the real side of the economy so a substitution of debt for taxation does not affect economic development. As a result, in this ultrarational situation fiscal policy is ineffective. This can be viewed as 'ex ante crowding out' (David and Scadding, 1974). If the macroeconomic effects of current taxation are comparable to those of deficits, a choice between current or future taxation will have to be made by considering allocative effects (see Ihori, 1988).

General discussions of the Ricardian equivalence theorem can be found in Buiter and Tobin (1979), Brennan and Buchanan (1980b), Tobin (1980), Bernheim (1987, 1989), Modigliani (1987), Perasso (1987), Leiderman and Blejer (1988), Flemming (1988), Morris (1988), Barro (1989), Thornton (1990), Seater (1993), Van Velthoven, Verbon and Van Winden (1993). Tramontana (1985) and Fields and Hart (1990) place the discussion in a traditional IS-LM framework.

The Barro proposition resulted in an intense discussion and many empirical tests. Several authors, especially Keynesians, questioned his assumptions. Since taxes are in general not lump-sum taxes, tax changes involve modifications in the size and timing of marginal taxation. This affects incentives and induces intertemporal substitution effects (Buiter, 1989, and Trostel, 1993). One can also question whether taxpayers are interested or informed about taxes and the government debt. This refers to the existence of fiscal illusion (Stiglitz, 1988). Similarly, is the public not assuming that government has no intention of paying off the principal (Cox, 1985)?

Barro (1974) showed that the infinite life assumption is sufficient but not necessary for his proposition. A finite life assumption has the same implication if one assumes that the current generation considers the wellbeing of future generations and adjust intergenerational transfers (bequests or transfers inter vivos) to interventions of the government (for example, a tax reduction will be matched by an increase in voluntary tranfers). Expenditures on education are different since a government deficit can increase welfare: parents will be allowed to invest more in their children's education (see Drazen, 1978). Further discussion about this issue is to be found in Blanchard (1985), Hubbard and Judd (1986), Auerbach and Kotlikoff (1987), Frenkel and Razin (1987), Poterba and Summers (1987), Weil (1987), Abel (1988), Bernheim and Bagwell (1988), Musgrave (1988), Kotlikoff, Razin and Rosenthal (1990), Lopez and Angel (1990), Abel and Bernheim (1991), Lord and Rangazas (1993) and Jaeger (1993).

The assumption of perfect capital markets has been critized by several authors. Hubbard and Judd (1986) stress that consumers may face a liquidity constraint, so they prefer future taxes to be substituted for current taxes. Artis (1979) and Leiderman and Blejer (1988) argue that a higher discount rate may be applied to future tax liabilities (for example, as a result of a higher risk of default) compared to future interest payments so there is a gain in present wealth by using debt rather than taxes. In other words, since market imperfections create liquidity constraints, borrowing by the government is cheaper compared to household borrowing. Government surpluses and deficits may thus be used to reallocate consumption through time: a net positive effect of indebtness would thus occur if the government is more efficient than the private sector in carrying out the loan process between generations or if the government acts like a monopolist in the production of the liquidity services associated with debt issue (see Daniel, 1993). Webb (1981) stresses, however, differences in the ability to repay debt between households and the government. A point somewhat related to capital market imperfections is that bequests cannot be negative, which would be required if it is expected that future generations would be richer (Modigliani, 1987). Yotsuzuka (1987) stresses the importance of the exact type of capital market imperfections. The general conclusion that capital market imperfections imply debt non-neutrality is rejected.

Buchanan and Wagner (1977) and Feldstein (1988) discuss the perfect certainty assumption of future tax liabilities. The complexity of the tax system would lead to an underestimation of future tax liabilities. Note that Barro (1974) argues that uncertainty would result in an overcompensation of future tax liabilities if, as could be advocated, households are risk averse (see also Chan, 1983, and Barsky, Mankiw and Zeldes, 1986). Boskin and Kotlikoff (1985),

Leiderman and Razin (1988), Bomberger (1990), Croushore (1990, 1992, 1996), Handa (1993) and Strawczynski (1995) study the impact of uncertainty in income and returns in an intergenerational altruistic model. Cukierman (1986) considers uncertain lifetimes.

The assumption made by Barro that taxes are lump sum has been frequently critized. A modification does, however, not lead to straightforward effects since many alternatives exist (taxation of consumption, income, profit, and so on) (see Abel, 1986, and Basu, 1996). Note also that transaction costs associated with the issue of debt are neglected (Carmichael, 1982). A point that surfaced only infrequently in the recent discussion on the Ricardian equivalence, but was omnipresent in the discussion of the early 1960s is the source of the deficit. Does it matter that a deficit is the result of an increase in government investment instead of in transfer payments? Barro assumed government spending to be constant so the only issue was the financing one. Buchanan and Roback (1987) discuss the importance of the source of the deficit; Kormendi (1983) and Bohn (1992) of spending (see also Katsaitis, 1987, and Cebula and Hung, 1996b).

Liviatan (1982) critizes the neglect of the inflation tax as a source of government revenue. Since additional government debt is frequently financed by money creation, this revenue could partly offset increases in interest charges linked to the issue of government debt. Government bonds will then no longer be neutral.

The list of empirical verifications of the Ricardian equivalence theorem by testing for the effect of the deficit and/or government debt, however defined, on consumption, saving or interest rates is long. Therefore, we are not able to provide any further guidance. Note that any article testing for the effect of the government debt or deficit on an economic or financial variable could be listed. This is especially the case for interest rate equations estimated before the publication of the 1974 article by Barro; we only list those articles that explicitly test for the Ricardo equivalence: (some of the papers are reprinted in Kaounides and Wood, vol. 3, 1992) Kochin (1974), Yawitz and Meyer (1976), Buiter and Tobin (1979), Tanner (1979), Holcombe, Jackson and Zardkoohi (1981), Dwyer (1982), Feldstein (1982), Plosser (1982), Seater (1982), Bennett and Dilorenzo (1983), Kormendi (1983), Koskela and Viren (1983), Makin (1983), Mascaro and Meltzer (1983), Blanchard (1984), Summers (1988), Aschauer (1985), Boskin and Kotlikoff (1985), Evans (1985), King and Plosser (1985), Kormendi (1985), Modigliani, Jappelli and Pagano (1985), Seater and Mariano (1985), Tanzi (1985), Barth, Iden and Russek (1986), Evans (1986), Hoelscher (1986), Kessler, Perelman and Pestieau (1986), Kormendi and Meguire (1986), Merrick and Saunders (1986), Modigliani and Sterling (1986), Barro (1987), Carroll and Summers (1987), Modigliani (1987), Evans (1987a, 1987b), Jones (1987), Modigliani and Japelli (1987), Motley (1987), Poterba and Summers (1987), Boskin (1988), De Haan and Zelhorst (1988), Evans (1988a, 1988b), Gruen (1988), Ihori (1988), Knight and

Masson (1988), Leiderman and Razin (1988), Morris (1988), Nicoletti (1988), Tanzi and Blejer (1988), Viren (1988), Walsh (1988), Boothe and Reid (1989), Buiter (1989), Croushore (1989), Darrat (1989), Evans (1989), Reid (1989), Kormendi and Meguire (1990), McMillin and Koray (1990), Cadsby and Murray (1991), Evans (1991), Gruen (1991), Lee (1991), Standish and Beelders (1991), Whelan (1991), Dalamagas (1992a and 1992b), Graham (1992), Gupta (1992), Kazmi (1992), Nicoletti (1992), Beck (1993), Dalamagas (1993), Evans (1993), Jaeger (1993), Perelman and Pestieau (1993), Akai (1994), Beck (1994), Evans and Hasan (1994), Dalamagas (1994), Mukhopadhyay (1994), Graham (1995), Himarios (1995), Rose and Hakes (1995), Slate (1995), Cebula and Hung (1996a), Chakraborty and Farah (1996), Ghatak and Ghatak (1996), Leachman (1996) and Wagner (1996). Note that no standard approach exists so results are not always comparable. For a discussion of the robustness of the results, see Cardia (1997).

Drawing conclusions from the empirical analysis is difficult. I am inclined to follow Seater (1993, p. 182) when he writes: 'I think it is reasonable to conclude that Ricardian equivalence is strongly supported by the data'. This should not be interpreted absolutely but as a statement that the Ricardian equivalence theorem is an acceptable working hypothesis.

The implication of the Ricardian equivalence theorem for the design of taxation policy (we refer to the chapter on optimal taxation for a more profound discussion) is that taxes should be kept as fixed as possible ('tax smoothing') to minimize the deadweight losses (Barro, 1979). This contradicts the countercyclical approach implied by the standard Keynesian models. In a tax smoothing framework the permanent tax rate should be set so as to finance the permanent primary government expenditures plus interest payments (see also Chari, Christiano and Kehoe, 1991, 1994). Government debt then functions as a cushion for deviations of government spending from its permanent level. We do not extend this analysis since it is part of the optimal taxation literature, covered in another survey.

The Ricardian equivalence theorem does not, by definition, consider any problems related to the financing of the government debt. From a microeconomic point of view an automatic channeling of additional savings into government bonds cannot be assumed. Portfolio holders and tax payers do have alternatives for government bonds but their participation is required to defer taxes to the future. So the constraint should be imposed that bondholders evaluate the policy pursued by the government as credible. If, for example, an increase in inflation is to be feared, no bond issue will be possible (eventually issues of very short run bills are still conceivable). In the more extreme case of a possible repudiation, the demand for government debt will vanish completely. The difference between macro- and microeconomic considerations reflects that taxpayers will not only attempt to minimize their tax share but also to maximize the return on their savings so as to benefit from the postponement of taxes. This is nothing but another application of the saving paradox.

The credibility of fiscal policy depends on expectations by taxpayers about future policies. The determinants of credibility can therefore not be straightforwardly determined. However, some crucial factors are evident such as a combination of taxes and expenditures that respect the intertemporal budget or present value constraint, that is, the solvency condition of the government. This constraint implies that the discounted value of future primary surpluses equals the outstanding stock of government debt. Note that this does not guarantee that the rise in the debt-income ratio will be bounded. All that matters is that the real growth rate of the debt should be lower than the real rate of interest; the growth rate of income or the tax base is not directly involved (see Persson and Tabellini, 1990, and the collection of papers in Persson and Tabellini, 1994).

Although not identical to the Domar approach (Domar, 1944) (in its simple version a stabilization of the debt-income ratio requires that the real after tax interest rate be smaller than the real rate of growth) it is comparable. The Domar requirement was especially very popular in the early 1980s with international organizations such as the OECD and the European Commission, withsgovernment agencies and even governments since, given the high level of the interest rates, its policy implications were relatively straightforward: reduce the primary deficit to stabilize the debt-income ratio.

Articles on this subject are Chouraqui, Jones and Montador (1986), Hamilton and Flavin (1986), Bispham (1987), Spaventa (1987), Kremers (1988, 1989), Trehan and Walsh (1988, 1991), Wilcox (1989), Blanchard et al. (1990), MacDonald and Speight (1990), Corsetti (1991), Hakkio and Rush (1991), Haug (1991), Smith and Zin (1991), Buiter and Patel (1992), MacDonald (1992), Bagliani and Cherubini (1993), De Haan and Siermann (1993), Heinemann (1993), Frisch (1995) and Vanhoorebeek and Van Rompuy (1995).

Violations of the intertemporal budget constraint cannot be excluded, but what are the implications? Feldstein (1982) and Masson (1985) consider uncertainty about the required policy switch in case current policies are unsustainable and Leiderman and Blejer (1988) discuss the uncertainty as to how the spending-tax plan will be adjusted to satisfy the constraint. Bohn (1991) shows that in the United States over the past centuries 50-65 percent of deficits due to tax cuts and 65-70 percent of deficits due to spending cuts have been eliminated later by spending cuts; Kremers (1989) finds that the deficit policy of the 1980s is not consistent with the pattern of the previous decades. The extreme solution to violations of the intertemporal budget constraint is, of course, a default by the government on its debt. Chari and Kehoe (1993) present a general equilibrium model of optimal taxation were this is a policy option.

6. Taxation and Inflation

The literature on inflation is vast. We limit ourselves to two aspects that are especially relevant from a fiscal policy point of view. First, inflation as a tax. Inflation should indeed, as a process of price increases, be at least acknowledged, if not stimulated, by the government. The second question concerns the relationship between deficits and inflation.

Unexpected inflation redistributes wealth between debtors and creditors. Since frequently the government is the major debtor, the budgetary consequences of inflation cannot be neglected. Inflation is thus an alternative for traditional taxation. Furthermore, tax systems are most of the time not indexed so, in general, the direct impact of inflation is a more than proportional rise in tax revenues. This is also the case for the taxation of the inflation premium included in interest rates (Darby,1975), Feldstein,1976, and Feldstein and Summers, 1978; see also Tanzi, 1984). In this approach inflation is viewed as exogenous. In the optimal inflation literature, inflation is explicitly considered as a policy instrument to generate seignorage revenues for the government. Without considering the numerous country applications, we mention Bailey (1956), Friedman (1971), Tower (1971), Barro (1972), Marty (1973), Phelps (1973), Auernheimer (1974), Cathart (1974), Kahn and Knight (1982), Barro (1983), Calvo and Peel (1983), Cox (1983), Remolona (1983), Brock (1984), Mankiw (1987), Weil (1987), Marty and Chaloupka (1988), Brock (1989), Kigel (1989), Vegh (1989), Bohanon, McClure and Van Cott (1990), Bruno and Fischer (1990), Calvo and Leiderman (1992), Calvo and Guidotti (1993), Guidotti and Vegh (1993a, 1993b), Steindl (1993), Banaian, McClure and Willett (1994), Braun (1994a), Chang (1994), Marty (1994), Mourmoras and Tijerina (1994) and Vegh (1995).

The traditional assumption is that no alternative payment instruments to domestic money are available. Hercowitz and Sadka (1987) allow for currency substitution. As this limits the revenues from the inflation tax, governments will broaden financial regulations to minimize the domestic use of foreign currencies.

Taxation and inflation are also, although less directly, linked by the budget constraint of the government. Note that taxation will directly affect the price level but since, in general, changes in tax rates do not occur continuously, they will not explain inflation. It is therefore more the decision not to increase taxation by incurring budget deficits that could be important for the inflation process. In general two main channels can be distinguished that link the budget deficit to inflation. A first link results from a monetization of deficits; a second, less direct link, is the consequence of crowding out. Indeed, when higher government expenditures substitute for investment, potential production declines which, when the stock of money remains constant, implies a price increase. Note that this is not the case when the deficit results from a decline in taxes since, following the previous argument, the price level will decline. Modigliani (1987), however, stresses reverse causation effects running from inflation to higher interest rates and so to deficits; furthermore, restrictive monetary policy to fight inflation lowers income which leads to increased deficits.

Concerning the monetization of the deficit, references mentioned above about the budget constraint are also relevant here. The link between budget deficits, whatever the origin, and inflation was forcefully formulated by Sargent and Wallace (1981) in their 'Some Unpleasant Monetarist Arithmetic': interest payments will, when the government debt exceeds some upper limit, have to be financed by money creation due to a shortage of savings. The 'unpleasant arithmetic' stresses thus that a bond-financed deficit will eventually have to be financed by money creation and therefore lead to a higher inflation rate. Darby (1984) (reply by Miller and Sargent, 1984) argues that the situation described by Sargent and Wallace is unlikely to occur since it requires that the real bond rate exceeds the real rate of growth for a considerable time (see also McCallum, 1984). King and Plosser (1985) discuss, test and reject (for the US as well as for several other developed countries) the link between seignorage revenues and different policy variables. Sargent and Wallace assume that monetary policy accomodates fiscal policy ('fiscal dominance'); Buiter (1987) and Buti (1990) consider different policy regimes (cooperation or leadership between monetary and fiscal authorities). Drazen and Helpman (1990) stress the importance of the policies expected to be used to reduce the deficit (see also Niskanen, 1978; Blinder, 1983; Miller, 1983, and Congdon, 1987).

7. The Positive Approach to Taxation

In democratic societies, tax rates are fixed by politicians and not by technicians who aim for an optimal taxation. The traditional approach holds that taxation or government expenditures are instruments that policymakers modify to realize goals such as a stabilization of the economy, a reallocation of resources or a modification in the distribution of income and wealth. This fine-tuning policy faces several problems and risks. For example, the government can misjudge both the size and timing of interventions, many conflicting objectives need to be pursued, the effects of instruments are not known with certainty, data contain errors, the theoretical structure of the model, the parameters, the value of exogenous variables, the nature of exogenous disturbances are not perfectly known, time lags are involved (recognition, decision, execution and response lag), frequent changes in policy instruments affects policy credibility, and so on. See, for example, Friedman (1960), Okun (1972), Kydland and Prescott (1977), Lucas (1980), Cooley, Leroy and Raymon (1984); and see also the recent literature on taxation as a source of business cycle fluctuations: Christiano and Eichenbaum (1992), Braun (1994b), McGrattan (1994) and Johnsson and Klein

(1996). The previous arguments (partly) explain the preference of several authors for policy rules. See the chapter on optimal taxation for more detail. In the public choice literature a different approach is taken. A typical formulation is Brennan and Buchannan (1980a) where a government is seen as a revenue-maximizing leviathan and taxes result out of a struggle between the government and citizens. Taxation is thus essentially viewed as an instrument to satisfy the wellbeing of the policymakers, not of the community and taxes are required to finance government expenditures. In this way taxes are more directly linked to government expenditures than in the 'traditional' approach. We refer to Downs (1957), Meltzer and Richard (1978), Anderson, Wallace and Warner (1986), Blackley (1986), Manage and Marlow (1986), Von Furstenberg, Green and Jeong (1986), Hibbs (1987), Ram (1988), Ahriakpor and Amirkhalkhali (1989), Mueller (1989), Blackley (1990), Holmes and Hutton (1990), Miller and Russek (1990), Cukierman and Meltzer (1991), Hoover and Sheffrin (1992) and Bella and Quinteri (1995). Consider also the collection of papers in Buchanan, Rowley and Tollison (1986). Several articles and books apply public choice arguments to a discussion of taxation or tax reform. It is impossibble to survey and list them. A pronounced view is Rose and Karran (1987).

Citizens bear, however, also some responsibility: the aggregate demand for budgetary programs will be excessive since any taxpayer bases his demand on the asymmetry between his small share in the cost of the program he supports and the perceived benefits. Furthermore, they suffer from fiscal illusion (see Dollery and Worthington, 1996, for a recent survey of this literature) that is reinforced by debt finance. As a result, the perceived price of public goods is lower than the effective price resulting in a rise in the demand for these goods. On the other hand, there is little incentive to combat tax increases since the individual share is negligible. As a result the upward pressure on the supply of government programs is stronger than the incentive to hold down the budget so government expenditures tend to rise and be financed by tax increases.

The literature on the 'political business cycle' should also be mentioned here. It concerns the creation of favorable economic conditions at election time so as to increase the re-election chances of the incumbent politicians. Obviously taxation is an instrument that could be used to generate these cycles. We refer to Alesina and Roubini (1992), Borooah and Van der Ploeg (1983), Nordhaus (1989) and Schneider and Frey (1988) for a general review of this literature. Unfortunately not much research has been performed on the use of taxes to generate a political business cycle (see, however, Tufte, 1978; Edwards and Tabellini, 1991; Grilli, Masciandaro and Tabellini, 1991, and Alesina and Rosenthal, 1995).

Econometric tax functions, most of the time for separate taxes and, eventually, specified as reaction functions, have been estimated in many econometric models. More relevant here but much less numerous, are general tax equations that contain political determinants. We refer, however, to Frey and Schneider (1978), Alt and Chrystal (1981), Pommerehne and Schneider (1983), Renaud and Van Winden (1987), Van Velthoven (1989) and Ohlsson and Vredin (1996).

8. Open Economies

The literature on fiscal policies is too vast to cover here in a few paragraphs so we limit ourselves to some general points (we refer to Chapter 6080 for international taxation). The point of departure for the analysis of the impact of taxation-fiscal policy in open economies is the Mundell-Fleming model (see Kenen, 1995, and Marston, 1995, for surveys). The magnitude and size of the multipliers depend on different parameters such as the effect on domestic interest rates (the assumption about the country size and capital mobility is relevant here) and the exchange rate regime. For example, a fiscal expansion in a 'large' country will raise world interest rates and appreciate the exchange rate; in a 'small' country a depreciation can be expected since the trade effects will tend to dominate. In the limiting case of perfect capital mobility, fiscal policy will not affect income: any tendency for interest rates to rise will be matched by a currency appreciation leaving total demand unchanged. In other words, exports are completely crowded out. Textbook references are relevant here.

Extensions by McKinnon (1973), Floyd (1980), Dixit (1985), Persson (1985) and Frenkel and Razin (1987) make use of an intertemporal approach covering aspects ranging from the impact of capital mobility and overlapping generations to different specific tax instruments. One general result is that deficits increase world interest rates and lower consumption but the effects depend on whether a country experiences a surplus or deficit. McKibbin and Sachs (1988) and Kole (1988) consider the importance of country size. In the traditional view financial crowding out will not occur in small open economies since, assuming fixed exchange rates, interest rates are given on the world market. Adjustments to imbalances between saving and investment occur through foreign borrowing by way of current account deficits. As a consequence, fiscal policies in all countries determine crowding out, also in countries with balanced budget. In a Ricardo world, this no longer holds.

The previous results must, however, be modified when non-traded goods are introduced. Some models focus more explicitly on the dynamics and on the budget constraint of the government. Work by Frenkel and Razin (1987) and Knight and Masson (1988) demonstrates that, if bonds are net wealth, fiscal expansions will appreciate the exchange rate so as to finance the government deficit. Buiter (1987) takes the impact of interest rates on investment into account so deficits increase interest rates and as a result lower future domestic and foreign income. For a given level of government expenditures this constrains future taxes (see also Blanchard et al., 1990; Frisch, 1995).

An interesting collection of additional work on the international aspects of fiscal policy is Frenkel (1988). The survey by Dixit (1985), although limited to tax policy in open economies, should also be mentioned.

Concerning the Ricardian equivalence theorem in an open economy, (see Morris, 1988, for a discussion of the Barro-Ricardo equivalence in open economies) we recall earlier comments about the burden of external versus internal debt.

Note that a huge literature exists about the international coordination of fiscal policy and about fiscal policy in a monetary union. We also stress the important literature on the Maastricht convergence criteria for the European monetary union.

9. Conclusion

The macroeconomic aspects of taxation have evolved considerably over the past decades.This is linked to the changing ideas about the role of the government. In a nutshell the dominating current views hold that the government should focus on longer-term goals and be very critical about short-term intervention. Due to the difficulty in modifying tax instruments, this is especially true for taxation. This also holds for the process of shifting taxes through time by piling up debt. Such policies do, however, create uncertainty as to the type of taxes and time at which they will be collected. A modern view of the goals of government intervention will therefore be much less ambitious compared to thirty or forty years ago: the actions by the government should be as predictable as possible so as to reduce uncertainty and support the development of the private sector.

Bibliography on Taxation: Macro Aspects (6010)

Abel, Andrew B. (1986), 'The Failure of Ricardian Equivalence under Progressive Wealth Taxation', **30** *Journal of Public Economics*, 117-128.

Abel, Andrew B. (1988), 'An Analysis of Fiscal Policy under Operative and Inoperative Bequest Motives', in Helpman, Elhanan, Razin, Assaf and Sadka, Efraim (eds), *Economic Effects of the Government Budget*, Cambridge, MA, MIT Press, 91-106.

Abel, Andrew B. and Bernheim, B. Douglas (1991), 'Fiscal Policy with Impure Intergenerational Altruism', **59** *Econometrica*, 1687-1711.

Ahmed, Shaghil (1987), 'Government Spending, the Balance of Trade and the Terms of Trade in British History', **20** *Journal of Monetary Economics*, 195-220.

Ahriakpor, James C.W. and Amirkhalkhali, Saleh (1989), 'On the Difficulty of Eliminating

Deficits with Higher Taxes: Some Canadian Evidence', **56** *Southern Economic Journal*, 24-31.

Akai, Nobuo (1994), 'Ricardian Equivalence for Local Government Bonds: Budget Constraint Approach', **44** *Economics Letters*, 191-195.

Alesina, Alberto and Rosenthal, Howard (1995), *Partisan Politics Divided Government, and the Economy*, Cambridge, Cambridge University Press.

Alesina, Alberto and Roubini, Nouriel (1992), 'Political Cycles in OECD Economies', **59** *Review of Economic Studies*, 663-688.

Alexander, J. Davidson (1989), 'The Political Economy of Tax Based Incomes Policy: Wealth Effects of Post Keynesian TIP', **23** *Journal of Economic Issues*, 135-146.

Alt, James and Chrystal, Alec (1981), 'Politico-economic Models of British Fiscal Policy', in Hibbs, Douglas A., Fassbender, Heino and Rivers, Douglas R. (eds), *Contemporary Political Economy*, Amsterdam, North-Holland, 1985-1208.

Anderson, Leonell C. and Jordan, Jerry (1968), 'Monetary and Fiscal Actions: A Test of their Relative Importance in Economic Stabilization', **50** *Federal Reserve Bank of St. Louis Review*, 11-24.

Anderson, William, Wallace, Myles S. and Warner, John T. (1986), 'Government Spending and Taxation: What Causes What?', **52** *Southern Economic Journal*, 630-639.

Andreoni, James (1989), 'Giving with Impure Altruism: Applications to Charity and Ricardian Equivalence', **97** *Journal of Political Economy*, 1447-1458.

Argy, Victor (1994), *International Macroeconomics: Theory and Policy*, London, Routledge.

Artis, Michael (1979), 'Recent Development in the Theory of Fiscal Policy: A Survey', in Cook, S.T. and Jackson, Peter M. (eds), *Current Issues in Fiscal Policy*, London, Martin Robertson, 15-43.

Aschauer, David A. (1985), 'Fiscal Policy and Aggregate Demand', **75** *American Economic Review*, 117-127.

Aschauer, David A. (1988), 'The Equilibrium Approach to Fiscal Policy', **20** *Journal of Money, Credit, and Banking*, 41-62.

Aschauer, David A. and Greenwood, Jeremy (1985), 'Macroeconomic Effects of Fiscal Policy', **23** *Carnegie-Rochester Conference Series on Public Policy*, 91-138.

Asso, Pier F. and Barucci, Emilio (1988), 'Ricardo on the National Debt and its Redemption, Some Notes on an Unpublished Ricardian Manuscript', **17** *Economic Notes*, 5-36.

Atkinson, Anthony B. and Stiglitz, Joseph E. (1980), *Lectures in Public Economics*, London, McGraw Hill.

Auerbach, Alan J. and Kotlikoff, Laurence J. (1987), *Dynamic Fiscal Policy*, Cambridge, Cambridge University Press.

Auerbach, Alan J., Gokhale, Jagadeesh and Kotlikoff, Laurence J. (1993), 'Generational Accounts and Lifetime Tax Rates, 1900-1991', **29** *Federal Reserve Bank of Cleveland Economic Review*, 2-13.

Auernheimer, Leonardo (1974), 'The Honest Government Guide to the Revenue from the Creation of Money', **82** *Journal of Political Economy*, 598-606.

Backhaus, Jürgen G. (1989), 'Taxation and Entrepreneurship: An Austrian Approach to Public Finance', **16(2)** *Journal of Economic Studies*, 5-22.

Backus, David, Devreux, Michael and Purvis, Douglas (1988), 'A Positive Theory of Fiscal Policy in Open Economies', in Frenkel, Jacob E. (ed.), *International Aspects of Fiscal Policies*, Chicago, University of Chicago Press, 173-196.

Bagliani, Angelo and Cherubini, Umberto (1993), 'Intertemporal Budget Constraint and Public Debt Sustainability: The Case of Italy', **25** *Applied Economics*, 275-283.

Bagliani, Fabio C. (1994), 'Do Anticipated Tax Changes Matter? Further Evidence from the United Kingdom', **48** *Ricerche Economiche*, 87-108.

Bailey, Martin J. (1956), 'The Welfare Cost of Inflationary Finance', **64** *Journal of Political Economy*, 93-110.

Bailey, Martin J. (1962), *National Income and the Price Level*, New York, McGraw-Hill.

Bailey, Martin J. (1993), 'Note on Ricardian Equivalence', **51** *Journal of Public Economics*, 437-446.

Baily, Martin N. (1978), 'Stabilization and Private Economic Behavior', *Brookings Papers on Economic Activity*, 11-50.

Banaian, King, McClure, Harold and Willett, Thomas D. (1994), 'The Inflation Tax is Likely to be Inefficient at any Level', **27** *Kredit und Kapital*, 30-42.

Bandin Tomislav (1988), 'Politicko Jedinstvo kao Faktor Ostvarivanja Dogovorene Ekonomske i Razvojne Politike (Political Unity as a Factor of Implementation of Agreed Economic and Development Policy)', **1** *Ekonomist*, 29-31.

Bankman, Joseph and Griffith, Thomas (1987), 'Social Welfare and the Rate Structure: A New Look at Progressive Taxation', **75** *California Law Review*, 1905-1967.

Barro, Robert J. (1972), 'Inflationary Finance and the Welfare Cost of Inflation', **80** *Journal of Political Economy*, 978-1001.

Barro, Robert J. (1974), 'Are Government Bonds Net Wealth?', **82** *Journal of Political Economy*, 1095-1117.

Barro, Robert J. (1976), 'Rational Expectations and the Role of Monetary Policy', **2** *Journal of Monetary Economics*, 1-33.

Barro, Robert J. (1978), *The Impact of Social Security on Private Savings - Evidence from U.S. Time Series*, Washington, American Enterprise Institute.

Barro, Robert J. (1979), 'On the Determination of the Public Debt', **87** *Journal of Political Economy*, 940-971.

Barro, Robert J. (1980), 'A Capital Market in an Equilibrium Business Cycle Model', **48** *Econometrica*, 1393-1417.

Barro, Robert J. (1983), 'Inflationary Finance under Discretion and Rules', **41** *Canadian Journal of Economics*, 1-16.

Barro, Robert J. (1987), 'Government Spending, Interest Rates, Prices, and Budget Deficits in the United Kingdom', **10** *Journal of Monetary Economics*, 221-247.

Barro, Robert J. (1989), 'The Ricardian Approach to Budget Deficits', **3** *Journal of Economic Perspectives*, 37-54.

Barro, Robert J. and Gordon, David B. (1983), 'Rules, Discretion, and Reputation in a Model of Monetary Policy', **12** *Journal of Monetary Economics*, 101-121.

Barry, Frank G. (1985), 'Fiscal Policy in a Small Open Economy with Unemployment and Capital Accumulation', **87** *Scandinavian Journal of Economics*, 474-486.

Barry, Frank G. (1987), 'Fiscal Policy in a Small Open Economy. An Integration of the Short-run, Heckscher-Ohlin and Capital Accumulation Models', **22** *Journal of International Economics*, 103-121.

Barsky, Robert B., Mankiw, Gregory N. and Zeldes, Stephen P. (1986), 'Ricardian Consumers with Keynesian Propensities', **76** *American Economic Review*, 676-691.

Barth, James R., Iden, George and Russek, Frank S. (1986), 'Government Debt, Government Spending and Private Behavior: Comment', **76** *American Economic Review*, 1158-1167.

Basu, Parantap (1996), 'Proportional Income Tax and the Ricardian Equivalence in a Non-expected Utility Maximizing Model', **63** *Southern Economic Journal*, 223-243.

Baum, Donald N. (1991), 'Economic Effects of Including Services in the Sales Tax Base: An Applied General Equilibrium Analysis', **19(2)** *Public Finance Quarterly*, 166-192.

Beck, Stacie E. (1993), 'The Ricardian Equivalence Proposition: Evidence from Foreign Exchange Markets', **12** *Journal of International Money and Finance*, 154-169.

Beck, Stacie E. (1994), 'The Effect of Budget Deficits on Exchange Rates: Evidence from Five Industrialized Countries', **46** *Journal of Economics and Business*, 397-408.

Begg, David K. (1980), 'Rational Expectations, Wage Rigidity, and Involuntary Unemployment', **34** *Oxford Economic Papers*, 23-47.

Begg, David K. (1982), *The Rational Expectations Revolution in Macroeconomics*, Oxford, Philip Allen.

Bella, Mariano and Quinteri, Beniamino (1995), 'Causality between Public Expenditure and Taxation: Evidence from the Italian Case', **24** *Economic Notes*, 45-68.

Bennett, James T. and Dilorenzo, Thomas J. (1983), 'The Ricardian Equivalence Theorem: Evidence from the Off-Budget Public Sector', **38** *Public Finance*, 309-316.

Benson, Bruce L. (1986), 'Do Taxes Matter? The Impact of State and Local Taxes on Economic Development', **10** *Economic Development Commentary*, 13-17.

Benson, Bruce L. (1990), 'Interstate Tax Competition, Incentives to Collude, and Federal Influences', **10** *Cato Journal*, 75-90.

Benson, Bruce L. and Johnson, Ronald N. (1986), 'The Lagged Impact of State and Local Taxes on Economic Activity and Political Behavior', **24** *Economic Inquiry*, 389-402.

Benson, Bruce L. and Johnson, Ronald N. (1986b), 'Capital Formation and Interstate Tax Competition', in Lee, Dwight (ed), *Taxation and the Deficit Economy: Fiscal Policy and Capital Formation in the United States*, Cambridge, MA, Ballinger, 407-436.

Bernheim, B. Douglas (1987), 'An Evaluation of Theory and Evidence', in Fischer, Stanley, (ed), *NBER Macroeconomics Annual*, Cambridge, MA, MIT Press, 263-304.

Bernheim, B. Douglas (1989), 'A Neoclassical Perspective in Budget Deficits', **3** *Journal of Economic Perspectives*, 55-72.

Bernheim, B. Douglas and Bagwell, Kyle (1988), 'Is Everything Neutral?', **96** *Journal of Political Economy*, 308-338.

Bernstein, Jeffrey I. (1986), *Research and Development, Tax Incentives*, Toronto, University of Toronto Press, 107 p.

Biorn, E. (1989), *Taxation, Technology and the User Cost of Capital*, Amsterdam, North-Holland, 325 p.

Bispham, John A. (1987), 'Rising Public-sector Indebtedness: Some more Unpleasant Arithmetic', in Boskin, Michael, Flemming, John and Gorini, Stefano (eds), *Private Saving and Public Debt*, Oxford, Basil Blackwell, 40-71.

Biwas, R., Johns, C. and Savage, D. (1985), 'The Measurement of Fiscal Stance', **113** *National Institute Economic Review*, 50-64.

Blackley, Paul R. (1986), 'Causality between Revenues and Expenditures and the Size of the Federal Budget', **14** *Public Finance Quarterly*, 139-156.

Blackley, Paul R. (1990), 'A Symmetric Causality between Federal Spending and Tax Changes: Avoiding a Fiscal Loss', **66** *Public Choice*, 1-13.

Blanchard, Olivier Jean (1984), 'The Lucas Critique and the Volcker Deflation', **74** *American Economic Review*, 211-215.

Blanchard, Olivier Jean (1985), 'Debt, Deficits, and Finite Horizons', **93** *Journal of Political*

Economy, 223-247.

Blanchard, Olivier Jean (1993), 'Suggestions for a New Set of Fiscal Indicators', in Verbon, Harrie H.A. and Van Winden, Frans A.A.M. (eds), *The Political Economy of Government Debt*, Amsterdam, North-Holland, 307-325.

Blanchard, Olivier Jean, Chouraqui, Jean Claude, Hagemann, R.P. and Satar, N. (1990), 'The Sustainability of Fiscal Policy, New Answers to an Old Question', **15** *OECD Economic Studies*.

Blejer, Mario and Cheasty, A. (1991), 'The Measurement of Fiscal Deficits: Analytical and Methodological Issues', **24** *Journal of Economic Literature*, 1644-1678.

Blinder, Alan S. (1983), 'On the Monetization of Debt', in Meyer, Laurence (ed), *The Economic Consequences of Government Deficits*, Boston, Kluwer-Nijhoff.

Blinder, Alan S. and Goldfeld, Stephen M. (1976), 'New Measures of Fiscal and Monetary Policy, 1958-73', **66** *American Economic Review*, 780-796.

Blinder, Alan S. and Solow, Robert M. (1973), 'Does Fiscal Policy Matter?', **2** *Journal of Public Economics*, 319-337.

Blinder, Alan S. and Solow, Robert M. (1974), 'Analytical Foundations of Fiscal Policy', in Blinder, Alan S., Solow, Robert M., Break, George F., Steiner, Peter O. and Netzer, Dick (eds), *The Economics of Public Finance*, Washington, The Brookings Institution, 3-115.

Blinder, Alan S. and Solow, Robert M. (1976), 'Does Fiscal Policy Still Matter?', **2** *Journal of Monetary Economics*, 501-510.

Bohanon, Cecil E. and McClure, James E. and Van Cott, T. Norman (1990), 'Government Inflation Statistics and the Inflation Tax on Money', **45** *Public Finance*, 164-166.

Bohn, Henning (1991), 'Budget Balance through Revenue or Spending Adjustments', **27** *Journal of Monetary Economics*, 333-359.

Bohn, Henning (1992), 'Endogenous Government Spending and Ricardian Equivalence', **102** *Economic Journal*, 588-597.

Bomberger, William A. (1990), 'The Effects of Fiscal Policies when Incomes are Uncertain: A Contradiction to Ricardian Equivalence: Comment', **80** *American Economic Review*, 309-312.

Boothe, Paul M. and Reid, Bradford G. (1989), 'Asset Returns and Government Budgets in a Small Open Economy: Empirical Evidence for Canada', **23** *Journal of Monetary Economics*, 65-77.

Borooah, Vani and Van der Ploeg, Frederick (1983), *Political Aspects of the Economy*, Cambridge, Cambridge University Press.

Boskin, Michael J. (1982), 'Federal Government Deficits: Some Myths and Realities', **72** *American Economic Review*, 196-203.

Boskin, Michael J. (1988), 'Concepts and Measures of Federal Deficits and Debt and their Impact on Economic Activity', in Arrow, Kenneth J. and Boskin, Michael J. (eds), *The Economics of Public Debt*, London, Macmillan, 77-115.

Boskin, Michael J. and Kotlikoff, Laurence J. (1985), 'Public Debt and United States Saving: A New Test of the Neutrality Hypothesis', **23** *Carnegie-Rochester Conference Series on Public Policy*, 55-86.

Bovenberg, A. Lans (1989), 'The Effects of Capital Income Taxation on International Competitiveness and Trade Flows', **79** *American Economic Review*, 1051-1064.

Braun, Anton R. (1994a), 'How Large is the Optimal Inflation Tax?', **34** *Journal of Monetary Economics*, 201-214.

Braun, Anton R. (1994b), 'Tax Disturbances and Real Economic Activity in Postwar United States', **33** *Journal of Monetary Economics*, 441-462.

Bray, Margaret (1982), 'Learning, Estimation, and the Stability of Rational Expectations', **26** *Journal of Economic Theory*, 318-339.

Brennan, Geoffrey and Buchanan, James M. (1980a), *The Power to Tax*, Cambridge, Cambridge University Press.

Brennan, Geoffrey and Buchanan, James M. (1980b), 'The Logic of the Ricardian Equivalence Theorem', **38** *Finanzarchiv*, 4-16.

Brock, Philip L. (1984), 'Inflationary Finance in an Open Economy', **14** *Journal of Monetary Economics*, 37-53.

Brock, Philip L. (1989), 'Reserve Requirements and the Inflation Tax', **21** *Journal of Money, Credit, and Banking*, 106-121.

Brown, Cary E. (1956), 'Fiscal Policy in the Thirties: A re-appraisal', **46** *American Economic Review*, 857-579.

Browning, Edgar K. (1987), 'On the Marginal Welfare Cost of Taxation', **77** *American Economic Review*, 11-23.

Bruce, Neil and Purvis, Douglas (1979), 'Deficit Finance and First Round Crowding-Out: A Correction and Further Clarification', **14** *Canadian Journal of Economics*, 728-734.

Brunner, Karl and Meltzer, Allan H. (1976), 'An Aggregative Theory for a Closed Economy', in Stein, Jerome (ed), *Monetarism*, Amsterdam, North-Holland, 69-103.

Bruno, Michael and Fischer, Stanley (1990), 'Seigniorage, Operating Rules and the High Inflation Trap', **105** *Quarterly Journal of Economics*, 353-374.

Buchanan, James M. (1958), *Public Principles of Public Debt*, Homewood, IL, Richard D. Irwin.

Buchanan, James M. (1976), 'Barro on the Ricardian Equivalence Theorem', **84** *Journal of Political Economy*, 337-342.

Buchanan, James M. and Roback, Jennifer Morse (1987), 'The Incidence and Effects of Public Debt in the Absence of Fiscal Illusion', **15** *Public Finance Quarterly*, 5-25.

Buchanan, James M. and Wagner, Richard E. (1977), *Democracy in Deficit*, New York, Academic Press.

Buchanan, James M., Rowley, Charles K. and Tollison, Robert D. (eds) (1986), *Deficits*, Oxford, Basil Blackwell.

Buchholz, Wolfgang (1991), 'Tax Effect in General Equilibrium Models with Uncertainty: A Generalization', **45** *Journal of Public Economics*, 397-399.

Buiter, William H. (1977), 'Crowding Out and the Effectiveness of Fiscal Policy', **7** *Journal of Public Economics*, 309-328.

Buiter, William H. (1980a), 'Death, Birth, Productivity Growth and Debt Neutrality', **98** *Economic Journal*, 279-283.

Buiter, William H. (1980b), 'The Macroeconomics of Dr. Planglos', **90** *Economic Journal*, 34-50.

Buiter, William H. (1983), 'Measurement of the Public Sector Deficit and its Implications for Policy Evaluation and Design', **30** *International Monetary Fund Staff Papers*, 306-349.

Buiter, William H. (1985), 'A Guide to Public Sector Debt and Deficits', **1** *Economic Policy*, 13-79.

Buiter, William H. (1987), 'A Fiscal Theory of Hyperdeflations? Some Surprising Monetarist Arithmetic', **39** *Oxford Economic Papers*, 111-118.

Buiter, William H. (1988), 'Macroeconomic Policy Design in an Interdependent World Economy: An Analysis of Three Contingencies', in Frenkel, Jacob E. (ed), *International Aspects of Fiscal Policies*, Chicago, University of Chicago Press, 121-172.

Buiter, William H. (1989), 'Debt Neutrality, Professor Vickrey and Henry George: ASingle Tax', **29** *Economics Letters*, 43-47.

Buiter, William H. (1990), *Principles of Budgetary and Financial Policy*, New York, Harvester Wheatsheaf.

Buiter, William H. and Tobin, James (1979), 'Debt Neutrality: A Brief Review of Doctrine and Evidence', in Von Furstenberg, George M. (ed), *Social Security versus Private Saving*, Cambridge, MA, Ballinger, 39-63.

Buiter, William H. and Tobin, James (1980), 'Fiscal and Monetary Policies, Capital Formations, and Economic Activity', in Von Furstenberg, George M. (ed), *The Government and Capital Formation*, Cambridge, MA, Ballinger, 73-151.

Buiter, William H. and Patel, Urjit R. (1992), 'Debt, Deficits and Inflation: An Application to the Public Finances of India', **47** *Journal of Public Economics*, 171-205.

Burrows, Paul (1979), 'The Government Budget Constraint and the Monetarist-Keynesian Debate', in Cook, S.T. and Jackson, Peter M. (eds), *Current Issues in Fiscal Policy*, London, Martin Robertson, 62-85.

Buti, Marco (1990), 'Monetary and Fiscal Rules for Public Debt Sustainability', **44** *Economic Papers, European Commission.*

Cadsby, Charles Bram and Murray, Frank (1991), 'Experimental Tests of Ricardian Equivalence', **29** *Economic Inquiry*, 645-664.

Calvo, Guillermo A. (1978), 'On the Time Consistency of Optimal Policy in a Monetary Economy', **46** *Econometrica*, 1411-1428.

Calvo, Guillermo A. (1985), 'Macroeconomic Implications of the Government Budget', **15** *Journal of Monetary Economics*, 95-112.

Calvo, Guillermo A. and Guidotti, Pablo E. (1993), 'On the Flexibility of Monetary Policy: The Case of the Optimal Inflation Tax', **60** *Review of Economic Studies*, 667-687.

Calvo, Guillermo A. and Leiderman, Leonardo (1992), 'Optimal Inflation Tax under Precommitment: Theory and Evidence', **82** *American Economic Review*, 179-194.

Calvo, Guillermo A. and Peel, David A. (1983), 'Growth and Inflationary Finance: Variations on a Mundellian Theme', **91** *Journal of Political Economy*, 880-887.

Cameron, David R. (1978), 'The Expansion of the Public Economy: A Comparative Analysis', **72** *American Political Science Review*, 1243-1261.

Cardia, Emanuela (1997), 'Replicating Ricardian Equivalence Tests with Simulated Series', **87** *American Economic Review*, 65-79.

Carlson, Keith M. and Spencer, Roger W. (1975), 'Crowding Out and its Critics', **57** *Federal Reserve Bank of St. Louis Review*, 2-17.

Carmichael, Jeffrey (1982), 'On Barro's Theorem of Debt Neutrality: The Irrelevance of Net Wealth', **72** *American Economic Review*, 351-372.

Carmichael, Jeffrey and Hawtrey, Kim (1981), 'Social Security, Government Finance, and Savings', **57** *Economic Record*, 332-343.

Carroll, Chris and Summers, Lawrence H. (1987), 'Why have Private Savings Rates in the United States and Canada Diverged?', **20** *Journal of Monetary Economics*, 249-279.

Cathart, Charles (1974), 'Monetary Dynamics, Growth and the Efficiency of Inflationary Finance', **6** *Journal of Money, Credit, and Banking*, 169-190.

Cavaco-Silva Anibal A. (1977), *Economic Effects of Public Debt*, London, Martin

Robertson.

Cebula, Richard J. and Hung, Chao Shun (1996a), 'Ricardian Equivalence, Budget Deficits, and Saving in the United States, 1955:1-1991:4', **3a** *Applied Economics Letters*, 525-528.

Cebula, Richard J. and Hung, Chao Shun (1996b), 'Ricardian Equivalence, the Structural Deficit, and the Cyclical Deficit: A Note', **49b** *Economia Internazionale*, 19-27.

Chakraborty, Atreva and Farah, Abdikarim (1996), 'Ricardian Equivalence: Further Evidence', **10** *International Economic Journal*, 19-31.

Chan, Louis K.C. (1983), 'Uncertainty and the Neutrality of Government Financing Policy', **11** *Journal of Monetary Economics*, 351-372.

Chang, Roberto (1994), 'Endogenous Currency Substitution, Inflationary Finance, and Welfare', **26** *Journal of Money, Credit, and Banking*, 906-916.

Chari, Varadarajan V. (1985), 'Macroeconomic Effects of Fiscal Policy: A Comment', **23** *Carnegie-Rochester Conference Series on Public Policy*, 139-141.

Chari, V. and Kehoe, Patrick J. (1990), 'International Coordination of Fiscal Policy in Limiting Economies', **98** *Journal of Political Economy*, 617-636.

Chari, Varadarajan V. and Kehoe, Patrick J. (1993), 'Sustainable Plans and Debt', **61** *Journal of Economic Theory*, 230-261.

Chari, Varadarajan V., Christiano, Lawrence J. and Kehoe, Patrick J. (1991), 'Optimal Fiscal and Monetary Policy: Some Recent Results', **23** *Journal of Money, Credit, and Banking*, 519-539.

Chari, Varadarajan V., Christiano, Lawrence J. and Kehoe, Patrick J. (1994), 'Optimal Fiscal Policy in a Business Cycle Model', **102** *Journal of Political Economy*, 617-652.

Chouraqui, Jean Claude, Jones, Brian and Montador, Robert B. (1986), 'Public Debt in a Medium-term Perspecitve', **7** *OECD Economic Studies*, 103-153.

Christ, Carl A. (1967), 'A Short-Run Aggregate-Demand Model of the Interdependence and Effects of Monetary and Fiscal Policies with Keynesian and Classical Interest Elasticities', **57** *American Economic Review*, 434-443.

Christ, Carl A. (1968), 'A Simple Macroeconomic Model with a Government Budget Restraint', **76** *Journal of Political Economy*, 53-67.

Christ, Carl F. (1979), 'On Fiscal and Monetary Policies and the Government Budget Restraint', **69** *American Economic Review*, 526-538.

Christiano, Lawrence J. and Eichenbaum, Martin (1992), 'Current Real-Business Cycle Theories and Aggregate Labor-market Fluctuations', **82** *American Economic Review*, 430-450.

Cohen, Darrel and De Leeuw, Frank (1980), 'A Note on the Government Budet Restraint', **6** *Journal of Monetary Economics*, 547-560.

Cohen, Darrel and McMenamin, Stuart J. (1978), 'The Role of Financial Policy in a Financially Disaggregated Macroeconomic Model', **10** *Journal of Money, Credit, and Banking*, 322-336.

Congdon, Tim G. (1987), 'The Link between Budget Deficits and Inflation: Some Contrasts between Developed and Developing Countries', in Boskin, Michael, Flemming, John and Gorini, Stefano (eds), *Private Saving and Public Debt*, Oxford, Basil Blackwell, 40-71.

Cooley, Thomas F., Leroy, Stephen F. and Raymon, Neil (1984), 'Econometric Policy Evaluation: Note', **74** *American Economic Review*, 467-470.

Corsetti, Giancarlo (1991), 'Testing for Solvency of the Public Sector: An Application to Italy', **20** *Economic Notes*, 571-599.

Cox, Michael W. (1983), 'Government Revenue from Deficit Finance', **16** *Canadian Journal of Economics*, 264-274.

Cox, Michael W. (1985), 'Inflation and Permanent Government Debt', *Federal Reserve Bank of Dallas Economic Review*, 13-26.

Croushore, Dean D. (1989), 'The Effect of Government Deficits on Consumption and Interest Rates: A Two Equation Approach', **28** *Quarterly Journal of Business and Economics*, 85-129.

Croushore, Dean D. (1990), 'Taxation as Insurance Against Income Uncertainty', **15** *Federal Reserve Bank of Philadelphia*, 29 ff.

Croushore, Dean D. (1992), *Ricardian Equivalence Under Income Uncertainty*, Federal Reserve Bank of Philadelphia Research Working Paper, No. 6/13.

Croushore, Dean D. (1996), 'Ricardian Equivalence with Wage-Rate Uncertainty', **28** *Journal of Money, Credit, and Banking*, 279-293.

Croushore, Dean D., Koot, Ronald S. and Walker, David A. (1990), 'Economic Stability and the Government Deficit', **12** *Journal of Post Keynesian Economics*, 390-403.

Cukierman, Alex (1986), 'Uncertain Lifetimes and the Ricardian Equivalence Proposition', **45** *Tel Aviv Foerder Institute for Economics*, 24 ff.

Cukierman, Alex and Meltzer, Allan H. (1991), 'Theory of Progressive Income Taxation', in Meltzer, Alan H., Cukierman, Alex and Richard, Scott F. (eds), *Political Economy*, New York, Oxford University Press, 76-108.

Currie, David A. (1976), 'Optimal Stabilization Policies and the Government Budget Constraint', **43** *Economica*, 159-167.

Dalamagas, Basil A. (1992a), 'How Rival are the Ricardian Equivalence Proposition and the Fiscal Policy Potency View?', **39(a)** *Scottish Journal of Political Economy*, 457-476.

Dalamagas, Basil A. (1992b), 'Testing Ricardian Equivalence: A Reconsideration', **24b** *Applied Economics*, 59-68.

Dalamagas, Basil A. (1993), 'Fiscal Illusion and the Level of Indebtedness: An International Comparison', **61** *South African Journal of Economics*, 45-58.

Dalamagas, Basil A. (1994), 'Testing the Debt-Illusion Hypothesis', *Revue Economique*, 1079-1094.

Daniel, Betty C. (1993), 'Tax Timing and Liquidity Constraints: A Heterogenous-Agent Model', **25** *Journal of Money, Credit, and Banking*, 176-196.

Darby, Michael R. (1975), 'The Financial and Tax Effects of Monetary Policy on Interest Rates', **13** *Economic Inquiry*, 266-276.

Darby, Michael R. (1984), 'Some Pleasant Monetarist Arithmetic', **8** *Federal Reserve Bank of Minneapolis Quarterly Review*, 15-20.

Darrat, Ali F. (1989), 'Fiscal Deficits and Long-term Interest Rates: Further Evidence from Annual Data', **56** *Southern Economic Journal*, 363-374.

David, Paul A. and Scadding, John L. (1974), 'Private Savings: Ultrarationality, Aggregation and Denison's Law', **82** *Journal of Political Economy*, 225-249.

Davidson, Carl and Martin, Lawrence (1991), 'Tax Incidence in a Simple General Equilibrium Model with Collusion and Entry', **45** *Journal of Public Economics*, 161-190.

De Haan, Jakob and Siermann, Clemens L. (1993), 'The Intertemporal Government Budget Constraint: An Application for the Netherlands', **48** *Public Finance*, 243-249.

De Haan, Jakob and Zelhorst, Dick (1988), 'The Empirical Evidence on the Ricardian Equivalence Hypothesis', **21** *Kredit und Kapital*, 407-421.

Diamond, Peter A. and Mirlees, James A. (1977), 'Optimal Taxation and Public Production, I: Production Efficiency, and II: Tax Rules', **61** *American Economic Review*, 8-278.

Dixit, Avinash K. (1985), 'Tax Policy in Open Economics', in Auerbach, Alan and Feldstein, Martin (eds), *Handbook in Public Economics*, North-Holland, Amsterdam, 313-374.

Djajic, Slobodan (1987), 'Effects of Budgetary Policies in Open Economies: The Role of Intertemporal Consumption Substitution', **6** *Journal of International Money and Finance*, 373-383.

Dollery, Brian E. and Worthington, Andrew C. (1996), 'The Empirical Analysis of Fiscal Illusion', **10** *Journal of Economic Surveys*, 261-298.

Domar, Evsey (1944), 'The Burden of the Debt and the National Income', **34** *American Economic Review*, 798-827.

Downs, Anthony (1957), *An Economic Theory of Democracy*, New York, Harper and Row.

Drazen, Allen (1978), 'Government Debt, Human Capital, and Bequests in a Life Cycle Model', **86** *Journal of Political Economy*, 305-516.

Drazen, Allen and Helpman, Elhanan (1990), 'Inflationary Consequences of Anticipated Macroeconomic Policies', **57** *Review of Economic Studies*, 147-164.

Dwyer, Gerald P., Jr (1982), 'Inflation and Government Deficits', **20** *Economic Inquiry*, 315-329.

Edwards, Sevastian and Tabellini, Guido (1991), 'Explaining Fiscal Policies and Inflation in Developing Countries', **10S** *Journal of International Money and Finance*, 16-48.

Eisner, Robert (1984), 'Which Budget Deficit? Some Issues of Measurement and their Implications', **14** *American Economic Review*, 138-143.

Eisner, Robert and Pieper, Paul (1984), 'A New View of the Federal Debt and Budget Deficits', **74** *American Economic Review*, 11-29.

Eisner, Robert and Pieper, Paul (1988), 'Deficits, Monetary Policy and Real Economic Activity', in Arrow, Kenneth J. and Boskin, Michael J. (eds), *The Economics of Public Debt*, London, Macmillan, 40 ff.

Enders, Walter and Lee, Bong Soo (1990), 'Current Account and Budget Deficits: Twins or Distant Cousins?', **72** *Review of Economics and Statistics*, 373-381.

Evans, Paul (1985), 'Do Large Deficits Produce High Interest Rates?', **75** *American Economic Review*, 68-87.

Evans, Paul (1986), 'Is the Dollar High because of Large Budget Deficits?', **18** *Journal of Monetary Economics*, 227-249.

Evans, Paul (1987a), 'Interest Rates and Expected Future Budget Deficits in the United States', **95a** *Journal of Political Economy*, 34-58.

Evans, Paul (1987b), 'Do Budget Deficits Raise Nominal Interest Rates? Evidence from Six Countries', **20b** *Journal of Monetary Economics*, 281-300.

Evans, Paul (1988a), 'Are Consumers Ricardian? Evidence for the United States', **96** *Journal of Political Economy*, 983-1004.

Evans, Paul (1988b), 'Are Government Bonds Net Weath? Evidence for the United States', **26** *Economic Inquiry*, 551-566.

Evans, Paul (1989), 'A Test of Steady-State Government-Debt Neutrality', **27** *Economic Inquiry*, 39-55.

Evans, Paul (1991), 'Is Ricardian Equivalence a Good Approximation?', **29** *Economic Inquiry*, 626-644.

Evans, Paul (1993), 'Consumers are not Ricardian: Evidence from Nineteen Countries', **31**

Economic Inquiry, 534-548.

Evans, Paul and Hasan, Iftekhar (1994), 'Are Consumers Ricardian? Evidence for Canada', **34** *Quarterly Review of Economics and Finance*, 5-40.

Feldstein, Martin (1976), 'Inflation, Income Taxes and the Rate of Interest: A Theoretical Analysis', **66** *American Economic Review*, 809-820.

Feldstein, Martin (1982), 'Government Deficits and Aggregate Demand', **9** *Journal of Monetary Economics*, 1-20.

Feldstein, Martin (1983), *Behavioral Simulation Methods in Tax Policy Analysis*, Chicago, University of Chicago Press.

Feldstein, Martin (1987a), 'The Welfare Cost of Social Security's Impact on Private Saving', in Boskin, Michael J. (ed), *Modern Developments in Public Finance*, Oxford, Basil Blackwell, 1-13.

Feldstein, Martin (1987b), *The Effects of Taxation on Capital Accumulation*, Chicago, University of Chicago Press.

Feldstein, Martin (1988), 'The Effects of Fiscal Policies when Incomes are Uncertain: A Contradiction to Ricardian Equivalence', **78** *American Economic Review*, 14-23.

Feldstein, Martin and Elmendorf, Douglas W. (1989), 'Budget Deficits, Tax Incentives and Inflation: A Surprising Lesson from the 1983-84 Recovery', in Summers, Lawrence H. (ed), *Tax Policy and the Economy*, Cambridge, National Bureau of Economic Research, 1-23.

Feldstein, Martin and Summers, Lawrence (1978), 'Inflation, Tax Rules, and the Long-Term Interest Rate', *Brookings Papers on Economic Activity*, 61-99.

Ferguson, James M. (1964), *Public Debt and Future Generations*, Chapel Hill, University of North Carolina Press.

Fields, T. Windsor and Hart, William R. (1990), 'On Integrating the Ricardian Equivalence Theorem and the IS-LM Framework', **28** *Economic Inquiry*, 185-193.

Fischer, Stanley (1977), 'Long-Term Contracts, Rational Expectations and the Optimal Money Supply Rule', **85** *Journal of Political Economy*, 191-205.

Fischer, Stanley (1979a), 'Anticipation and the Nonneutrality of Money', **87** *Journal of Political Economy*, 225-252.

Fischer, Stanley (1979b), 'Capital Accumulation on the Transition Path in a Monetary Optimising Economy', **47** *Econometrica*, 1433-1440.

Fischer, Stanley (1980a), 'Dynamic Inconsistency, Cooperation and the Benevolent Dissembling Government', **2** *Journal of Economic Dynamics and Control*, 93-107.

Fischer, Stanley (ed) (1980b), *Rational Expectations and Economic Policy*, Chicago, University of Chicago Press.

Fischer, Stanley (1988), 'Recent Developments in Macroeconomics', **98** *Economic Journal*, 294-339.

Fisher, Douglas (1988), *Monetary and Fiscal Policy*, London, Macmillan.

Flemming, John S. (1988), 'Debt and Taxes in War and Peace: The Closed Economy Case', in Arrow, Kenneth J. and Boskin, Michael J. (eds), *The Economics of Public Debt*, London, Macmillan, 201-229.

Flowers, Marilyn R. (1985), 'Public Choice and the Flat Tax', **5** *Cato Journal*, 625-628.

Floyd, John E. (1980), 'Tax Policy in the Small Open Economy: A Monetary Approach to a Keynesian Problem', **78** *Scandinavian Journal of Economics*, 378-397.

Floyd, John E. and Hynes, Allan J. (1978), 'Deficit Finance and First Round Crowding-Out: A Clarification', **11** *Canadian Journal of Economics*, 97-105.

Frenkel, Jacob A. (1988), *International Aspects of Fiscal Policies*, Chicago, University of Chicago Press.

Frenkel, Jacob A. and Razin, Assaf (1985), 'Government Spending, Debt, and International Economic Interdependence', **95** *Economic Journal*, 619-636.

Frenkel, Jacob A. and Razin, Assaf (1986a), 'Fiscal Policy in the World Economy', **94** *Journal of Political Economy*, 564-594.

Frenkel, Jacob A. and Razin, Assaf (1986b), 'The International Transmission and Effects of Fiscal Policies', **76** *American Economic Review*, 330-335.

Frenkel, Jacob A. and Razin, Assaf (1987), *Fiscal Policies and the World Economy*, Cambridge, MA, MIT Press.

Frey, Bruno S. and Schneider, Friedrich (1978), 'A Politico-Economic Model of the United Kingdom', **88** *Economic Journal*, 243-253.

Frey, Bruno S. and Schneider, Friedrich (1981), 'Central Bank Behavior: A Positive Empirical Analysis', **7** *Journal of Monetary Economics*, 291-315.

Friedman, Benjamin M. (1978), 'Crowding Out or Crowding In? Economic Consequences of Financing Government Deficits', *Brookings Papers on Economic Activity*, 593-642.

Friedman, Milton (1960), *A Program for Monetary Stability*, New York, Fordham University Press.

Friedman, Milton (1966), 'Interest Rates and the Demand for Money', **9** *Journal of Law and Economics*, 71-85.

Friedman, Milton (1971), 'Government Revenue from Inflation', **79** *Journal of Political Economy*, 846-856.

Frisch, Helmut (1995), 'Government Debt and Sustainable Fiscal Policy', **24** *Economic Notes*, 561-580.

Galli, Giampaolo and Mascra, Rainer (1988), 'Government Deficits and Debts. The Necessity and Cost of Adjustment: The Case of Italy', in Eltis, Walter and Sinclair, Peter (eds), *Keynes and Economic Policy, The Relevance of the General Theory after Fifty Years*, London, Macmillan, 175-215.

Ghatak, Anita and Ghatak, Subrata (1996), 'Budgetary Deficits and Ricardian Equivalence: The Case of India, 1950-1986', **60** *Journal of Public Economics*, 267-282.

Giavazzi, Francesca and Pagano, Marco (1990), 'Can Severe Fiscal Contractions be Expenionary? Tales of two Small European Countries', in Blanchard, Olivier J. and Fischer, Stanley (eds), *NBER Macroeconomics Annual: 1990*, Cambridge, MA, MIT Press, 75-111.

Gimeno Ullastres, Juan A. (1987), 'Las Causas del Déficit Público (Trying to Explain Public Deficit)', **88** *Hacienda Pública Espanola*, 85-105.

Gimeno Ullastres, Juan A. (1989), 'Sector Público y Patrocinio (Public Sector and Sponsorship)', in X (ed.), *Cultura y Desarrollo*, Madrid, Ministerio de Cultura, 116-132.

Goldfeld, Stephen M. and Blinder, Alan S. (1972), 'Some Implications of Endogenous Stabilization Policy', *Brookings Papers on Economic Activity*, 585-641.

Graham, Fred C. (1992), 'On the Importance of the Measurement of Consumption in Tests of Ricardian Equivalence', **38** *Economics Letters*, 431-434.

Graham, Fred C. (1995), 'Government Debt, Government Spending and Private Sector Behavior: Comment', **85** *American Economic Review*, 1348-1356.

Graham, Fred C. and Himarios, Daniel (1996), 'Consumption, Wealth and Finite Horizons: Tests of Ricardian Equivalence', **34** *Economic Inquiry*, 527-544.

Grbich, Yuri (1982), 'Towards a More Substantial Jurisprudence to Replace Legalism: a

Welfare Economics Model of Decision- Making in Tax Cases', in Cranston, Ross and Schick, Anne (eds), *Law and Economics*, Canberra, Australian National University, 192-205.

Grilli, Vittorio, Masciandaro, Donato and Tabellini, Guido (1991), 'Political and Monetary Institutions and Public Financial Policies in the Industrial Countries', **11** *Economic Policy*, 342-392.

Gruen, David W.R. (1988), *Ignorance and Ricardian Equivalence (or Keynesians of the World Unite, You have Nothing to Lose but Your Bonds)*, Australian National University, 165.

Gruen, David W.R. (1991), 'What People Know and what Economists Think They Know: Surveys on Ricardian Equivalence', **30** *Australian Economic Papers*, 1-9.

Guidotti, Pablo E. and Vegh, Carlos A. (1993a), 'Currency Substitution and the Optimal Inflation Tax', **42** *Economics Letters*, 65-70.

Guidotti, Pablo E. and Vegh, Carlos A. (1993b), 'The Optimal Inflation Tax when Money Reduces Transactions Costs: A Reconsideration', **31** *Journal of Monetary Economics*, 189-205.

Gullason, Edward T., Kolluri, Bharat R. and Panik, Michael J. (1993), 'Social Security and Household Wealth Accumulation: Refined Microeconometric Evidence', **75** *Review of Economics and Statistics*, 548-551.

Gupta, Kanhaya L. (1992), 'Ricardian Equivalence and Crowding out in Asia', **24** *Applied Economics*, 19-25.

Haavelmo, T. (1945), 'Multiplier Effects of a Balanced Budget', **13** *Econometrica*, 311-318.

Hakes, David R. and McCormick, Ken (1996), 'Did Smith Address Ricardian Equivalence before Ricardo?', **22** *Eastern Economic Journal*, 57-61.

Hakkio, Craig, S. and Rush, Mark S. (1991), 'Is the Budget Deficit too Large?', **29** *Economic Inquiry*, 429-445.

Hamilton, James T. and Flavin, Majorie (1986), 'On the Limitations of Government Borrowing: A Framework for Empirical Testing', **76** *American Economic Review*, 808-819.

Handa, Jagdish (1993), 'Consumption, Uncertainty and Ricardian Equivalence', in Baldassarri, M., Mundell, Robert and McCallum, Bennett J. (eds), *Debt, Deficit and Economic Performance*, London, St. Martin's Press, 291-318.

Hansen, Bent (1969), *Fiscal Policy in Seven Countries, 1955-65*, Paris, OECD.

Haug, Alfred A. (1990), 'Ricardian Equivalence, Rational Expectations, and the Permanent Income Hypothesis', **22** *Journal of Money, Credit, and Banking*, 305-326.

Haug, Alfred A. (1991), 'Cointegration and Government Borrowing Constraints: Evidence for the United States', **9** *Journal of Business and Economic Statistics*, 96-101.

Hayford, Marc (1989), 'Liquidity Constraints and the Ricardian Equivalence Theorem: A Note', **21** *Journal of Money, Credit, and Banking*, 380-387.

Heinemann, Friedrich (1993), 'Sustainability of National Debt in Europe', *Intereconomics*, 61-68.

Hercowitz, Zvi and Sadka, Efraim (1987), 'On Optimal Currency Substitution Policy and Public Finance', in Razin, Assaf and Sadka, Efraim (eds), *Economic Policy in Theory and Practice*, New York, St. Martin's Press, 147-164.

Hibbs, Douglas A. (1987), 'Political Parties and Macroeconomic Policy', **71** *American Political Science Review*, 1467-1487.

Hickman, Bert G. (ed.) (1972), *Econometric Models of Cyclical Behavior*, New York,

Columbia University Press.

Himarios, Daniel (1995), 'Euler Equation Tests of Ricardian Equivalence', **48** *Economic Letters*, 165-171.

Hodrick, Robert J. (1988), 'Expansionary Fiscal Policy and International Interdependence', in Frenkel, Jacob E. (ed.), *International Aspects of Fiscal Policies*, Chicago, University of Chicago Press, 229-272.

Hoelscher, Gregory P. (1986), 'New Evidence on Deficits and Interest Rates', **18** *Journal of Money, Credit, and Banking*, 1-17.

Holcombe, Randall G., Jackson, John D. and Zardkoohi, Asghar (1981), 'The National Debt Controversy', **34** *Kyklos*, 186-202.

Holmes, James M. and Hutton, Patricia (1990), 'On the Causal Relationship between Government Expenditure and National Income', **72** *Review of Economics and Statistics*, 87-95.

Hoover, Kevin D. and Sheffrin, Steven M. (1992), 'Causation, Spending, and Taxes: Sand in the Sandbox or Tax Collector for the Welfare State?', **82** *American Economic Review*, 225-248.

Hotelling, Harold (1938), 'The General Welfare in Relation to Problems of Taxation and Railway and Utility Rates', **6** *Econometrica*, 242-269.

Hubbard, R. Glenn and Judd, Kenneth L. (1986), 'Liquidity Constraints, Fiscal Policy and Consumption', *Brookings Papers on Economic Activity*, 1-50.

Ihori, Toshihiro (1988), 'Debt Burden and Intergeneration Equity', in Arrow, Kenneth J. and Boskin, Michael J. (eds), *The Economics of Public Debt*, London, Macmillan, 149-200.

Infante, Ettore F. and Stein, Jerome L. (1976), 'Does Fiscal Policy Matter?', **2** *Journal of Monetary Economics*, 473-500.

Jaeger, Albert (1993), 'Debt Neutrality, Finite Horizons and Private Savings Behavior', in Verbon, Harrie H.A. and Van Winden, Frans A.A.M. (eds), *The Political Economy of Government Debt*, Amsterdam, North-Holland, 195-205.

Johnsson, Gunnar and Klein, Paul (1996), 'Stochastic Fiscal Policy and the Swedish Businesscycle', **38** *Journal of Monetary Economics*, 245-268.

Jones, Jonathan D. (1987), 'Are Future Taxes Anticipated by Consumers? More Evidence for the U.S., 1946-1985', **16** *Economic Notes*, 141-144.

Kahn, Mohsin S. and Knight, Malcolm D. (1982), 'Unanticipated Monetary Growth and Inflationary Finance', **14** *Journal of Money, Credit, and Banking*, 347-364.

Kaounides, Lakis and Wood, Geoffrey (eds) (1992), *Debt and Deficits, Volume I, II and III, International Library of Macroeconomic and Financial History, vol. 9*, Aldershot, Brookfield.

Katsaitis, Odysseus (1987), 'On the Substitutability between Private Consumer Expenditure and Government Spending in Canada', **20** *Canadian Journal of Economics*, 533-543.

Kay, John A. (1990), 'Tax Policy: A Survey', **100** *Economic Journal*, 18-75.

Kazmi, Aqdas Ali (1992), 'Ricardian Equivalence: Some Macro-econometric Tests for Pakistan', **31** *Pakistan Development Review*, 743-755.

Kenen, Peter (1995), 'Macroeconomic Theory and Policy: How the Closed Economy was Opened', in Jones, Ronald and Kenen, Peter (eds), *Handbook of International Economics, Vol. 2*, Amsterdam, North-Holland.

Kessler, Denis, Perelman, Sergio and Pestieau, Pierre (1986), 'Public Debt, Tax and Consumption: A Test on OECD Countries', **41** *Public Finance*, 43-70.

Kiesling, Herbert J. (1992), *Taxation and Public Goods*, Ann Arbor, University of Michigan Press.

Kigel, Miguel A. (1989), 'Budget Deficits, Stability and the Monetary Dynamics of Hyperinflation', **21** *Journal of Money, Credit, and Banking*, 148-157.

Kimbrough, Kent P. (1988), 'Optimal Tax Policy for Balance of Payments Objectives', in Frenkel, Jacob E. (ed.), *International Aspects of Fiscal Policies*, Chicago, University of Chicago Press, 309-348.

King, Robert G. and Plosser, Charles L. (1985), 'Money, Deficits, and Inflation', **22** *Carnegie-Rochester Conference Series on Public Policy*, 147-196.

Kingston, Geoffrey (1991), 'Should Marginal Tax Rates be Equalized Through Time', *Quarterly Journal of Economics*.

Knight, Malcolm D. and Masson, Paul R. (1988), 'Fiscal Policies, Net Saving, and Real Exchange Rates: The United States, the Federal Republic of Germany, and Japan', in Frenkel, Jacob E. (ed.), *International Aspects of Fiscal Policies*, Chicago, University of Chicago Press, 21-72.

Knoester, Anthonie (1980), 'The Haavelmo Effect Revisited', **1** *Finnish Economic Papers* in Frech, H.E. (ed.), *Regulating Doctors' Fees: Competition, Benefits, and Controls under Medicare*, Washington, DC, American Enterprise Institute, 121-125.

Knoester, Anthonie (1983), 'Stagnation and the Inverted Haavelmoo Effect, some International Evidence', **131** *De Economist*, 548-584.

Koch, Walter A.S. (1984), 'Negative Einkommensteuern und Konjunkturpolitik (Negative Income Taxes and Stabilization Policy)', **30** *Konjunkturpolitik*, 348-373.

Kochin, Levis A. (1974), 'Are Future Taxes Discounted by Consumers', **6** *Journal of Money, Credit, and Banking*, 385-394.

Kole, Linda S. (1988), 'Expansionary Fiscal Policy and International Interdependence', in Frenkel, Jacob E. (ed.), *International Aspects of Fiscal Policies*, Chicago, University of Chicago Press, 229-265.

Kormendi, Roger C. (1983), 'Government Debt, Government Spending and Private Sector Behaviour', **75** *American Economic Review*, 994-1010.

Kormendi, Roger C. (1985), 'Does Deficit-financing affect Economic Growth? Cross Country Evidence', **2** *Journal of Banking and Finance*, 243-255.

Kormendi, Roger C. and Meguire, Philip (1986), 'Government Debt Government Spending and Private Sector Behavior: Reply', **76** *American Economic Review*, 1180-1187.

Kormendi, Roger C. and Meguire, Philip (1990), 'Government Debt, Government Spending and Private Sector Behavior: Reply and Update', **80** *American Economic Review*, 604-617.

Koskela, Erkki and Viren, Matti (1983), 'National Debt Neutrality: Some International Evidence', **36** *Kyklos*, 575-588.

Kotlikoff, Laurence J. and Summers, Laurence T. (1981), 'The Role of Intergenerational Transfers in Aggregate Capital Accumulation', **89** *Journal of Political Economy*, 706-732.

Kotlikoff, Laurence J., Razin, Assaf and Rosenthal, Robert W. (1990), 'A Strategic Altruism Model in Which Ricardian Equivalence Does not Hold', **100** *Economic Journal*, 1261-1268.

Kremers, Jeroen M. (1988), 'Long-Run Limits on the US Federal Debt', **28** *Economic Letters*, 259-262.

Kremers, Jeroen M. (1989), 'Federal Indebtedness and the Conduct of Fiscal Policy', **23**

Journal of Monetary Economics, 219-238.

Kydland, Finn E. and Prescott, Edward C.v (1977), 'Rules rather than discretion. The Inconsistency of Optimal Plans', **85** *Journal of Political Economy* in Frech, H.E. (ed.), *Regulating Doctors' Fees: Competition, Benefits, and Controls under Medicare*, Washington, DC, American Enterprise Institute, 473-491.

Kydland, Finn E. and Prescott, Edward C.v (1980), 'A Competitive Theory of Fluctuations and the Feasibility and Desirability of Stabilization Policies', in Fischer, Stanley (ed.), *Rational Expectations and Economic Policy*, Chicago, University of Chicago Press, 169-187.

Kyer, Ben L., Mixon, J. Wilson, Jr and Uri, Noel D. (1988), 'Taxes, Transfer Payments and Automatic Stabilization in the United States. Impact and Trends', **2** *Economic Notes*, 50-60.

Laney, Leroy O. and Willett, Thomas D. (1983), 'Presidential Politics, Budget Deficits and Monetary Policy in the United States: 1960-1976', **40** *Public Choice*, 53-69.

Leachman, Lori (1996), 'New Evidence on the Ricardian Equivalence Theorem: A Multicointegration Approach', **28** *Applied Economics* in Frech, H.E. (ed.), *Regulating Doctors' Fees: Competition, Benefits, and Controls under Medicare*, Washington, DC, American Enterprise Institute, 695-704.

Lee, Bong Soo (1991), 'Government Deficits and the Term Structure of Interest Rates', **27** *Journal of Monetary Economics*, 425-443.

Leiderman, Leonardo and Blejer, Mario (1988), 'Modeling and Testing Ricardian Equivalence: A Survey', **35** *International Monetary Fund Staff Papers*, 1-35.

Leiderman, Leonardo and Razin, Assaf (1988), 'Testing Ricardian Neutrality with an Intertemporal Stochastic Model', **20** *Journal of Money, Credit, and Banking*, 1-21.

Lipford, Jody and Dougan, William R. (1995), 'A Public Choice Theoretic Test of Ricardian Equivalence', **23** *Public Finance Quarterly*, 467-483.

Liversey, David A. (1980), 'The Uncertain Foundation of Fiscal Policy', in Hughes, G.A. and Heal, Geoffrey M. (eds), *The Public Policy and the Tax System*, London, George Allen & Unwin, 194-224.

Liviatan, Nissan (1982), 'Neutrality of Government Bonds Reconsidered', **19** *Journal of Public Economics*, 261-270.

Lopez, Garcia and Angel, Miguel (1990), 'On Debt Neutrality in Life-Cycle Models', **33** *Economics Letters*, 233-238.

Lord, William and Rangazas, Peter (1993), 'Altruism, Deficit Policies, and the Wealth of Future Generations', **31** *Economic Inquiry*, 609-639.

Lovell, Michael C. (1986), 'Tests of the Rational Expectations Hypothesis', **76** *American Economic Review*, 110-114.

Lucas, Robert E. (1972), 'Expectations and the Neutrality of Money', **4** *Journal of Economic Theory*, 103-124.

Lucas, Robert E. (1973), 'Some International Evidence on Output-Inflation Tradeoffs', **63** *American Economic Review*, 326-334.

Lucas, Robert E. (1975), 'An Equilibrium Model of the Business Cycle', **83** *Journal of Political Economy*, 1113-1144.

Lucas, Robert E. (1976), 'Econometric Policy Evaluation: A Critique', **1** *Carnegie-Rochester Conference Series on Public Policy*, 19-46.

Lucas, Robert E. (1980), 'Rules, Discretion and the Role of the Economic Advisor', in Fischer, Stanley (ed.), *Rational Expectations and Economic Policy*, Chicago, University of Chicago Press, 199-210.

Lucas, Robert E. (1986a), 'Adaptive Behavior and Economic Theory', **59S** *Journal of Business*, 401-426.

Lucas, Robert E. (1986b), 'Principles of Fiscal and Monetary Policy', **17** *Journal of Monetary Economics*, 117-134.

Lucas, Robert E. and Sargent, Thomas J. (eds) (1981), *Rational Expectations and Econometric Practice, Vol 1 and Vol. 2*, Minneapolis, University of Minnesota Press.

Lucas, Robert E. and Stokey, Nancy L. (1983), 'Optimal Fiscal and Monetary Fiscal in an Economy without Capital', **12** *Journal of Monetary Economics*, 55-93.

MacDonald, Ronald (1992), 'Some Tests of the Government's Intertemporal Budget constraint using US Data', **24** *Applied Economics*, 1287-1292.

MacDonald, Ronald and Speight, Alan E.M. (1990), 'The Intertemporal Government Budget Constraint in the UK', **58** *Manchester School of Economic and Social Studies*, 329-347.

Makin, John (1983), 'Real Interest, Money Surprises, Anticipated Inflation and Fiscal Deficits', **32** *Review of Economics and Statistics*, 281-299.

Manage, Neela and Marlow, Michael L. (1986), 'The Causal Relation between Federal Expenditure and Receipts', **52** *Southern Economic Journal*, 617-629.

Mankiw, Gregory (1987), 'The Optimal Collection of Seigniorage: Theory and Evidence', **20** *Journal of Monetary Economics*, 327-341.

Mariger, Randall P. (1986), *Consumption Behavior and the Effects of Government Fiscal Policies*, Cambridge, MA, Harvard University Press.

Marston, Richard (1995), 'Stabilization Policies in Open Economies', in Jones, Ronald and Kenen, Peter (eds), *Handbook of International Economics, Vol. 2*, Amsterdam, North-Holland.

Marty, Alvin L. (1973), 'Growth Satiety and the Tax Revenue from Money Creation', **8** *Journal of Political Economy*, 1136-1152.

Marty, Alvin L. (1994), 'The Inflation Tax and the Marginal Welfare Cost in a World of Currency and Deposits', **76** *Federal Reserve Bank of St. Louis Review*, 67-71.

Marty, Alvin L. and Chaloupka, Frank J. (1988), 'Optimal Inflation Rates: A Generalization', **20** *Journal of Money, Credit, and Banking*, 141-144.

Mascaro, Angelo and Meltzer, Allen (1983), 'Long and Short-term Interest Rates in a Risky World', **12** *Journal of Monetary Economics*, 485-518.

Masson, Paul R. (1985), 'The Sustainability of Fiscal Deficits', **32** *International Monetary Fund Staff Papers*, 577-605.

Mayer, Thomas (1984), 'The Government Budget Constraint and Standard Macro-Theory', **13** *Journal of Monetary Economics*, 371-379.

McCallum, Benneth T. (1977), 'Price Level Stickiness and the Feasibility of Monetary Stabilization Policy with Rational Expectations', **86** *Journal of Political Economy*, 627-634.

McCallum, Benneth T. (1980), 'Rational Expectations and Macroeconomic Stabilisation Policy: An Overview', **12** *Journal of Money, Credit, and Banking*, 716-746.

McCallum, Benneth T. (1984), 'Are Bond-financed Deficits Inflationary? A Ricardian Analaysis', **92** *Journal of Political Economy*, 123-135.

McCallum, Benneth T. and Whitaker, John K. (1979), 'The Effectiveness of Fiscal Feedback Rules and Automatic Stabilizers under Rational Expectations', **5** *Journal of Monetary Economics*, 171-186.

McGrattan, Ellen R. (1994), 'The Macroeconomic Effects of Distortionary Taxation', **33** *Journal of Monetary Economics*, 573-601.

McKibbin, Warwick J. and Sachs, Jeffrey D. (1988), 'Coordination of Monetary and Fiscal Policies in the Industrial Economies', in Frenkel, Jacob E. (ed.), *International Aspects of Fiscal Policies*, Chicago, University of Chicago Press, 73-120.

McKinnon, Ronald I. (1973), 'The Value Added Tax and the Liberalization of Foreign Trade in Developing Economics: A Comment', **11** *Journal of Economic Literature*, 520-524.

McMillin, Douglas W. and Koray, Faik (1990), 'Does Government Debt Affect the Exchange Rate? An Empirical Analysis of the U.S. Canadian Exchange Rate', **42** *Journal of Economics and Business*, 279-288.

Meltzer, Allen and Richard, Scott H. (1978), 'A Rational Theory of the Size of Government', **89** *Journal of Political Economy*, 914-927.

Merrick, John and Saunders, Allen (1986), 'International Expected Real Interest Rates', **18** *Journal of Monetary Economics*, 312-322.

Meyer, Laurence H. (1975), 'The Balance Sheet Identity, the Government Financing Constraint, and the Crowding-Out Effect', **1** *Journal of Monetary Economics*, 65-78.

Meyer, Laurence H. (1980), 'Financing Constraints and the Short-Run Response to Fiscal Policy', **62** *Federal Reserve Bank of St. Louis Review*, 24-31.

Miller, J. Preston (1983), 'Higher Deficit Policies Lead to Higher Inflation', **7** *Federal Reserve Bank of Minneapolis Quarterly Review*, 8-19.

Miller, J. Preston and Sargent, Thomas J. (1984), 'A Reply to Darby', **8** *Federal Reserve Bank of Minneapolis Quarterly Review*, 21-26.

Miller, Marcus H. (1985), 'Measuring the Stance of Fiscal Policy', **4** *Oxford Review of Economic Policy*, 44-57.

Miller, Stephen M. and Russek, Frank S. (1990), 'Cointegration and Error-correction Models: The Temporal Causality between Government Taxes and Spending', **57** *Southern Economic Journal*, 221-229.

Modigliani, Franco (1944), 'Liquidity Preference and the Theory of Interest and Money', **12(1)** *Econometrica*, 45-88. Reprinted in Friedrich A. Lutz and Lloyd W. Mints (eds) (1951), *Readings in Monetory Theory*, Philadelphia, Balkiston, 186-239.

Modigliani, Franco (1961), 'Long-Run Implications of Alternative Fiscal Policies and the Burden of the National Debt', **71** *Economic Journal*, 730-755.

Modigliani, Franco (1987), 'The Economics of Public Deficits', in Razin, Assaf and Sadka, Efraim (eds), *Economic Policy in Theory and Practice*, New York, St. Martin's Press, 3-44.

Modigliani, Franco and Jappelli, Tullio (1987), 'Fiscal Policy and Saving in Italy since 1860', in Boskin, Michael, Flemming, John and Gorini, Stefano (eds), *Private Saving and Public Debt*, Oxford, Basil Blackwell, 126-170.

Modigliani, Franco and Sterling, Arlie G. (1986), 'Government Debt, Government Spending and Private Sector Behavior: Comment', **76** *American Economic Review*, 1168 ff.

Modigliani, Franco, Jappelli, Tullio and Pagano, Marco (1985), 'Policy and Inflation on National Saving: The Italian Case', *Banca Nazionale del Lavoro Review*, 91-126.

Monadjemi, Mehdi and Kearney, Colm (1991), 'The Interest Rate Neutrality of Fiscal Deficits: Testing for Ricardian Equivalence and Capital Inflow', **10** *Journal of International Money and Finance*, 541-551.

Morris, Dirk (1988), *Government Debt in International Financial Markets*, London, Pinter Publishers.

Motley, Brian (1987), 'Ricardo or Keynes: Does the Government Debt Affect Consumption?', *Federal Reserve Bank of San Francisco Economic Review*, 47-62.

Mourmouras, Alex and Tijerina, Jose A. (1994), 'Collection Lags and the Optimal Inflation Tax: A Reconsideration', **41** *International Monetary Fund Staff Papers*, 30-54.

Mueller, Dennis C. (1989), *Public Choice II*, Cambridge, Cambridge University Press.

Mukhopadhyay, Arun K. (1994), 'Are Haligonians Ricardian? A Survey of Households' Saving Response to the Government's Budget Deficits', **23** *Journal of Socio-Economics*, 457-477.

Musgrave, Richard A. (1988), 'Public Debt and Intergeneration Equity', in Arrow, Kenneth J. and Boskin, Michael J. (eds), *The Economics of Public Debt*, New York, St. Martin Press, 133-146.

Musgrave, Richard A. and Shoup, Carl S. (1959), *Readings in the Economics of Taxation*, Homewood, IL, Richard D. Irwin.

Muth, John F. (1961), 'Rational Expectations and the Theory of Price Movements', **29** *Econometrica*, 315-335.

Neary, Peter and Stiglitz, Joseph E. (1983), 'Toward a Reconstruction of Keynesian Economics: Expectations and Constrained Equilibria', **98** *Quarterly Journal of Economics*, 199-228.

Nicoletti, Giuseppe (1988), 'A Cross-Country Analysis of Private Consumption, Inflation and the Debt Neutrality Hypothesis', **11** *OECD Economic Studies*.

Nicoletti, Giuseppe (1992), 'Is Tax Discounting Stable over Time?', **54** *Oxford Bulletin of Economics and Statistics*, 121-144.

Niskanen, William A. (1978), 'Deficits, Government Spending and Inflation: What is the Evidence?', **8** *Journal of Monetary Economics*, 591-602.

Nordhaus, William D. (1989), 'Alternative Approaches to the Political Business Cycle', **19** *Brookings Papers on Economic Activity*, 1-68.

O'Driscoll, Gerald P., Jr (1977), 'The Ricardian Nonequivalence Theorem', **85** *Journal of Political Economy*, 207-210.

Ohlsson, Henry and Vredin, Anders (1996), 'Political Cycles and Cyclical Policies', **98** *Scandinavian Journal of Economics*, 203-218.

Okun, Arthur (1972), 'Fiscal-Monetary Activism: Some Analytical Issues', **1** *Brookings Papers on Economic Activity*, 123-172.

Ott, David J. and Ott, Attiat F. (1965), 'Budget Balance and Equilibrium Income', **20** *Journal of Finance*, 71-77.

Pasula, Kit (1994), 'Sterilization, Ricardian Equivalence and Structural and Reduced-Form Estimates of the Offset Coefficient', **16** *Journal of Macroeconomics*, 683-699.

Peacock, Alan and Shaw, G.K. (1976), *The Economic Theory of Fiscal Policy* (2nd edn), London, George Allen and Unwin.

Pemberton, James (1994), 'Ricardian Equivalence: Are the Required Assumptions Defensible?', **46** *Economics Letters*, 223-227.

Perasso, Giancarlo (1987), 'The Ricardian Equivalence Theorem and the Consumption Function: A Survey of the Literature', **34** *Revista Internazionale di Scienze Economiche e Commerciali*, 649-674.

Perelman, Sergio and Pestieau, Pierre (1993), 'The Determinants of the Ricardian Equivalence in the OECD', in Verbon, Harrie H.A. and Van Winden, Frans A.A.M. (eds), *The Political Economy of Government Debt*, Amsterdam, North-Holland, 181-193.

Persson, Torsten (1985), 'Deficits and Intergenerational Welfare in Open Economies', **19**

Journal of International Economics, 67-84.

Persson, Torsten and Svensson, Lars E.O. (1984), 'Time-consistent Fiscal Policy and Government Cash-flow', **14** *Journal of Monetary Economics*, 365-374.

Persson, Torsten and Svensson, Lars E.O. (1986), 'International Borrowing and Time-consistent Fiscal Policy', **88** *Scandinavian Journal of Economics*, 273-295.

Persson, Torsten and Tabellini, Guido (1990), *Macroeconomic Policy, Credibility and Politics*, New York, Harwood Academic.

Persson, Torsten and Tabellini, Guido (1994), *Monetary and Fiscal Policy, Volume 1: Credibility, Volume 2: Politics*, Cambridge, MA, MIT Press.

Pesek, Boris P. and Saving, Thomas R. (1967), *Money, Wealth and Economic Theory*, New York, Macmillan.

Phelps, Edmund S. (1973), 'Inflation in the Theory of Public Finance', **75** *Swedish Journal of Economics*, 67-82.

Phelps, Edmund S. and Taylor, John B. (1977), 'The Stabilising Powers of Monetary Policy under Rational Expectations', **85** *Journal of Political Economy*, 163-190.

Phelps, Edmund S. and Velupillai, Kumaraswanny (1988), 'Optimum Fiscal Policy when Monetary Policy is Bound by a Rule: Ramsey Redux', in Arrow, Kenneth J. and Boskin, Michael J. (eds), *The Economics of Public Debt*, London, Macmillan, 116-130.

Pissarides, Christopher A. (1986), 'Equilibrium Effects of Tax Based Incomes Policies', in Colander, David C. (ed.), *Incentive Based Incomes Policies: Advances in TIP and MAP*, Cambridge, MA, Harper and Row, 111-127.

Plosser, Charles I. (1982), 'Government Financing Decisions and Asset Returns', **9** *Journal of Monetary Economics*, 325-352.

Plosser, Charles I. (1987), 'Ricardian Equivalence: An Evaluation of Theory and Evidence: Comment', in Fischer, Stanley (ed.), *NBER Macroeconomics Annual*, Cambridge, MA, MIT Press, 309-313.

Pommerehne, Werner W. and Schneider, Friedrich (1983), 'Does Government in a Representative Democracy Follow a Majority of Voters' Preferences? An Empirical Examination', in Hanusch, Horst (ed.), *Anatomy of Government Deficiencies*, Berlin, Springer-Verlag, 61-84.

Posner, Michael V. (1987), 'Private Saving and Public Debt: A Survey of the Debate', in Boskin, Michael, Flemming, John and Gorini, Stefano (eds), *Private Saving and Public Debt*, Oxford, Basil Blackwell, 395-414.

Poterba, James M. and Rotemberg, Julio J. (1990), 'Inflation and Taxation with Optimizing Governments', **12** *Journal of Money, Credit, and Banking*, 1-18.

Poterba, James M. and Summers, Lawrence H. (1987), 'Finite Lifetimes and the Effects of Budget Deficits on National Saving', **20** *Journal of Monetary Economics*, 369-391.

Purvis, Douglas (1985), 'Public Sector Deficits, International Capital Movements, and the Domestic Economy, the Medium-Term is the Message', **18** *Canadian Journal of Economics*, 723-742.

Ram, Rati (1988), 'Additional Evidence on Causality between Revenue and Government Expenditure', **54** *Southern Economic Journal*, 763-769.

Razin, Assaf (1990), 'Fiscal Policies and the Integrated World Stock Market', **29** *Journal of International Economics*, 109-122.

Razin, Assaf and Sadka, Efraim (1987), *Economic Policy in Theory and Practice*, London, Macmillan.

Razin, Assaf and Svensson, Lars E.O. (1983), 'The Current Account and Optimal

Government Debt', **2** *Journal of International Money and Finance*, 215-224.

Reid, Bradford G. (1989), 'Government Budgets and Aggregate Consumption: Cross-sectional Evidence from Canadian Provincial Data', **11** *Journal of Macroeconomics*, 121-132.

Remolona, Eli M. (1983), 'A Pitfall in the Welfare Cost of Inflationary Finance', **20** *Philippine Review of Economics and Business*, 205-213.

Renaud, Paul S.A. and Van Winden, F.A.A.M. (1987), 'Tax Rate and Government Expenditure', **40** *Kyklos*, 349-367.

Reynolds, Alan (1985), 'Some International Comparisons of Supply-Side Tax Policy', **5** *Cato Journal*, 543-569.

Rodseth, Asbjorn (1979), 'Macroeconomic Policy in a Small Open Economy', **81** *Scandinavian Journal of Economics*, 48-59.

Rodseth, Asbjorn (1984), 'Progressive Taxes and Automatic Stabilization in an Open Economy', **6** *Journal of Macroeconomics*, 265-282.

Rose, David C. and Hakes, David R. (1995), 'Deficits and Interest Rates as Evidence of Ricardian Equivalence', **21** *Eastern Economic Journal*, 57-66.

Rose, Richard and Karran, Terence (1987), *Taxation by Political Inertia*, London, Unwin Hyman.

Ruiz-Huerta Carbonell, Jesús (1994), 'The Dimension, Effectiveness and Efficiency of Public Expenditure', in X (ed.), *National Budgeting for Economic and Monetary Union*, European Institute of Public Administration, 195-199.

Ruiz-Huerta Carbonell, Jesús (1995), *Las Rentas de las Personas Mayores (*Eldest Citizens' Income), SECOT.

Ruiz-Huerta Carbonell, Jesús and Gim,nez, Antonio (eds) (1993), *Estructura Institucional y Gestión del Gasto Público en algunos Paises de la OCDE* (Institutional Structure and Managment of Public Expenditure in Some Countries), Estudios de Hacienda Pública, Instituto de Estudios Fiscales.

Sargent, Thomas J. (1973), 'Rational Expectations, the Real Rate of Interest and the Natural Rate of Unemployment', *Brookings Papers on Economic Activity*, 429-472.

Sargent, Thomas J. (1976), 'The Observational Equivalence of Natural and Unnatural Rate Theories of Macroeconomics', **84** *Journal of Political Economy*, 631-640. Reprinted in Lucas and Sargent, 1981, 553-562.

Sargent, Thomas J. and Smith, Bruce D. (1987), 'Irrelevance of Open Market Operations in Some Economies with Government Currency Being Dominated in Rate of Return', **77** *American Economic Review*, 78-92.

Sargent, Thomas J. and Wallace, Neil (1975), '"Rational Expectations": The Optimal Monetary Instrument and the Optimal Money Supply Rule', **83** *Journal of Political Economy*, 241-254. Reprinted in Sargent and Lucas, 1981, 215-228.

Sargent, Thomas J. and Wallace, Neil (1976), 'Rational Expectations and the Theory of Economic Policy', **2** *Journal of Monetary Economics*, 169-183.

Sargent, Thomas J. and Wallace, Neil (1981), 'Some Unpleasant Monetarist Arithmetic', **5** *Federal Reserve Bank of Minneapolis Quarterly Review*, 1-17.

Scarth, William M. (1977), 'The Government Budget Constraint in an Open Economy: A Further Comment', **77** *Oxford Economic Papers*, 145-151.

Schneider, Friedrich and Frey, Bruno (1988), 'Politico-economic Models of Macroeconomic Policy: A Review of the Empirical Evidence', in Willett, Thomas (ed.), *Political Business Cycles*, Durban, Duke University Press, 239-275.

Seater, John J. (1982), 'Are Future Taxes Discounted', **14** *Journal of Money, Credit, and*

Banking, 376-389.

Seater, John J. (1993), 'Ricardian Equivalence', **31** *Journal of Economic Literature*, 142-190.

Seater, John J. and Mariano, Roberto S. (1985), 'New Tests of the Lifecycle and Tax Discounting Hypotheses', **15** *Journal of Monetary Economics*, 195-215.

Shaviro, Daniel N. (1997), *Do Deficits Matter?*, Chicago, University of Chicago Press.

Shaw, G.K. (1979), 'The Measurement of Fiscal Influence', in Cook, S.T. and Jackson, Peter M. (eds), *Current Issues in Fiscal Policy*, London, Martin Robertson, 44-60.

Shiller, Robert J. (1978), 'Rational Expectations and the Dynamic Structure of Macro-economic Models', **4** *Journal of Monetary Economics*, 1-44.

Siegfried, John J. and Smith, Paul A. (1991), 'The Distributional Effects of A Sales Tax on Services', **44(1)** *National Tax Journal*, 41-54.

Silber, William L. (1970), 'Fiscal Policy in IS-LM Analysis: A Correction', **2** *Journal of Money, Credit, and Banking*, 461-472.

Sims, Christopher A. (1982), 'Policy Analysis with Econometric Models', *Brookings Papers on Economic Activity*, 107-152.

Slate, Stephen (1995), 'Testing Ricardian Equivalence under Uncertainty', **85** *Public Choice*, 11-29.

Smith, Gregor and Zin, Stanley E. (1991), 'Persistent Deficits and the Market Value of Government Debt', **6** *Journal of Applied Econometrics*, 31-44.

Smyth, David J. (1978), 'Built-in Flexibility of Taxation, the Government Budget Constraint, the Specification of the Demand for Money Function, and the Stability of an IS-LM System', **33** *Public Finance*, 367-375.

Soderstrom, Hans T. (1985), 'Exchange Rate Strategies and Real Adjustment after 1970. The Experience of the Smaller European Economies', in Peeters, Theo, Praet, Peter and Reding, Paul (eds), *International Trade and Exchange Rates in the Late Eighties*, Amsterdam, North Holland, 227-264.

Soderstrom, Hans T. (1987), 'Sectoral Saving and Investment Patterns in 16 OECD Countries, 1965-82', in Boskin, Michael, Flemming, John and Gorini, Stefano (eds), *Private Saving and Public Debt*, Oxford, Basil Blackwell, 3-39.

Spaventa, Luigi (1987), 'The Growth of Public Debt: Sustainability, Fiscal Rules, and Monetary Rules', **34** *International Monetary Fund Staff Papers*, 577-605.

Spencer, Roger W. and Yohe, William P. (1970), 'The Crowding out of Private Expenditures by Fiscal Actions', **52** *Federal Reserve Bank of St. Louis Review*, 12-24.

Standish, Barry and Beelders, O. (1991), 'Do South African Fiscal Deficits Matter?', **15** *Journal for Studies in Economics and Econometrics*, 1-17.

Steindl, Frank G. (1971), 'A Simple Macroeconomic Model with a Government Budget Restraint: A Comment', **79** *Journal of Political Economy*, 675-679.

Steindl, Frank G. (1993), 'Making a Dishonest Government Credible: The Inflation Tax', **26** *Kredit und Kapital*, 239-245.

Stevens, Neil A. (1979), 'Government Debt Financing - Its Effects in View of Tax Discounting', **61** *Federal Reserve Bank of St. Louis Review*, 11-19.

Stiglitz, Joseph E. (1988), 'On the Relevance or Irrelevance of Public Financial Policy', in Arrow, Kenneth J. and Boskin, Michael J. (eds), *The Economics of Public Debt*, London, Macmillan, 41-76.

Stockman, Alan C. (1988), 'Fiscal Policies and International Financial Markets', in Frenkel, Jacob E. (ed.), *International Aspects of Fiscal Policies*, Chicago, University of Chicago

Press, 196-228.

Strawczynski, Michel (1995), 'Income Uncertainty and Ricardian Equivalence', **85** *American Economic Review*, 964-967.

Summers, Lawrence H. (1988), 'Tax Policy and International Competitiveness', in Frenkel, Jacob E. (ed.), *International Aspects of Fiscal Policies*, Chicago, University of Chicago Press, 349-386.

Sumner, Michael T. (1983), 'The Incentive Effects of Taxation', in Millward, Robert, Parker, David, Rosenthal, Leslie, Summner, Michael and Topham, Neville (eds), *Public Sector Economics*, London, Longman, 6-77.

Svensson, Lars E.O. (1987), 'International Fiscal Policy Transmission', **89** *Scandinavian Journal of Economics*, 89-118.

Svensson, Lars E.O. (1988), 'Fiscal Policy, Sticky Goods Prices, and Resource Utilization', in Kohn, Meir and Tsiang, Sho-Chieh (eds), *Finance Constraints, Expectations, and Macroeconomics*, Oxford, Oxford University Press, 185-205.

Tanner, John E. (1979), 'An Empirical Investigation of Tax Discounting', **11** *Journal of Money, Credit, and Banking*, 214-218.

Tanzi, Vito (ed.) (1984), *Taxation, Inflation and Interest Rates*, Washington, International Monetary Fund.

Tanzi, Vito (1985), 'Fiscal Deficits and Interest Rates in the United States: An Empirical Analysis', **32** *International Monetary Fund Staff Papers*, 551-576.

Tanzi, Vito and Blejer, Mario (1988), 'Public Debt and Fiscal Policy in Developing Countries', in Arrow, Kenneth J. and Boskin, Michael J. (eds), *The Economics of Public Debt*, New York, St. Martin's Press, 230-263.

Taylor, John B. (1979), 'Staggered Wage Setting in a Macro Model', **69** *American Economic Review*, 108-113.

Taylor, John B. (1985), 'Rational Expectations Models in Macroeconomics', in Honkapohja, Seppo and Arrow, Kenneth J. (eds), *Frontiers of Economics*, Helsinki, Y. Jahnsson Foundation, 391-425.

Thornton, Daniel L. (1990), 'Do Government Deficits Matter?', **72** *Federal Reserve Bank of St. Louis Review*, 25-39.

Tobin, James (1980), *Asset Accumulation and Economic Activity*, Chicago, University of Chicago Press.

Tobin, James and Buiter, William H. (1976), 'Long-run Effects of Fiscal and Monetary Policy on Aggregate Demand', in Stein, Jerome (ed.), *Monetarism*, Amsterdam, North-Holland, 273-309.

Tower, Edward (1971), 'More the Welfare Cost of Inflation Finance', **3** *Journal of Money, Credit, and Banking*, 850-860.

Tramontana, Antonino (1985), 'The Wealth Effect of Public Debt: A Macroeconomic Approach', **14** *Economic Notes*, 71-103.

Trehan, Bharat and Walsh, Carl E. (1988), 'Common Trends, the Government Budget Constraint, and Revenue Smoothing', **12** *Journal of Economic Dynamics and Control*, 425-444.

Trehan, Bharat and Walsh, Carl E. (1991), 'Testing Intertemporal Budget Constraints: Theory and Applications to US Federal Budget and Current Account Deficits', **23** *Journal of Money, Credit, and Banking*, 206-223.

Trostel, Philip A. (1993), 'The Nonequivalence between Deficits and Distortionary Taxation', **31** *Journal of Monetary Economics*, 207-227.

Tufte, Edward R. (1978), *Political Control of the Economy*, Princeton, Princeton University Press.

Turnovsky, Stephen J. (1977), *Macroeconomic Analysis and Stabilization Policy*, Cambridge, Cambridge University Press.

Uri, Noel D., Mixon, J. Wilson, Jr and Kyer, Ben L. (1989a), 'An Analysis of the Automatic Stabilizers Associated with Taxes and Transfers Payments', **3** *International Review of Applied Economics*, 46-56.

Uri, Noel D., Mixon, J. Wilson, Jr and Kyer, Ben L. (1989b), 'Automatic Stabilizers Reconsidered', **44** *Public Finance*, 476-496.

Van Der Ploeg, Frederick (1995), 'Political Economy of Monetary and Budgetary Policy', **36** *International Economic Review*, 427-439.

Van Velthoven, B.C.J. (1989), *The Endogenization of Government Behavior in Macroeconomic Models*, Berlin, Springer.

Van Velthoven, B.C.J., Verbon, H.A.A. and Van Winden, F.A.A.M. (1993), 'The Political Economy of Government Debt: A Survey', in Verbon, Harrie H.A. and Van Winden, Frans A.A.M. (eds), *The Political Economy of Government Debt*, Amsterdam, North-Holland, 3-32.

Van Wijnbergen, Sweder (1988), 'Fiscal Policy, Trade Intervention, and World Interest Rates: An Empirical Analysis', in Frenkel, Jacob E. (ed.), *International Aspects of Fiscal Policies*, Chicago, University of Chicago Press, 273-308.

Vanhorebeek, Filip and Van Rompuy, Paul (1995), 'Solvancy and Sustainability of Fiscal Policies in the EU', **143** *De Economist*, 457-473.

Vasic B. Vukasin (1986), 'Makroekonomska Politika kao Javno Dobro (Macroeconomic Policy as a Public Good)', **3** *Ekonomist*, 429-430.

Vaughn, Karen I. and Wagner, Richard E. (1992), 'Public Debt Controversies: An Essay in Reconciliation', **45** *Kyklos*, 37-49.

Vedder, Richard (1991), 'Taxes, and Economic Growth', **10** *Cato Journal*, 91-108.

Vegh, Carlos A. (1989), 'The Optimal Inflation Tax in the Presence of Currency Substitution', **24** *Journal of Monetary Economics*, 139-146.

Vegh, Carlos A. (1995), 'Inflationary Finance and Currency Substitution in a Public Finance Framework', **14** *Journal of International Money and Finance*, 679-693.

Vines, David, Macriejowski, Jan and Meade, James E. (1983), *Demand Management*, London, George Allen and Unwin.

Viren, Matti (1988), 'Interest Rates and Budget Deficits: Cross-Country Evidence from the Period 1924-1938', **28** *Economics Letters*, 235-238.

Von Furstenberg, George M., Green, Jeffrey R. and Jeong, Jin-Ho (1986), 'Tax and Spend or Spend and Tax?', **68** *Review of Economics and Statistics*, 179-188.

Wagner, Richard E. (1996), 'Who Ows What, and to Whom? Public Debt, Ricardian Equivalence and Governmental Form', **9** *Review of Austrian Economics*, 129-142.

Wallace, Neil (1981), 'A Modigliani-Miller Theorem for Open-Market Operations', **71** *American Economic Review*, 267-274.

Walsh, Brendan M. (1988), 'Ricardian Equivalence and the Irish Consumption Function: A Comment', **20** *Economic and Social Review*, 49-52.

Webb, David C. (1981), 'The Net Wealth Effect of Government Bonds when Credit Markets are Imperfect', **91** *Economic Journal*, 405-414.

Webber, Carolyn and Wildavsky, Aaron (1986), *A History of Taxation and Expenditure in the Western World*, New York, Simon and Schuster.

Weil, Philippe (1987a), 'Permanent Budget Deficits and Inflation', **20** *Journal of Monetary Economics*, 393-410.

Weil, Philippe (1987b), 'Love the Children's Reflections on the Barro Debt Neutrality Theorem', **19** *Journal of Monetary Economics*, 377-391.

Whelan, Karl (1991), 'Ricardian Equivalence and the Irish Consumption Function: The Evidence Re-examined', **22** *Economic and Social Review*, 229-238.

Wilcox, David H. (1989), 'The Sustainability of Government Deficits: Implications of the Present-value Borrowing Constraint', **3** *Journal of Money, Credit, and Banking*, 291-306.

Wohar, Mark (1988), 'How Effective is Fiscal Policy? The U.S. Experience', **124** *Weltwirtschaftliches Archiv*, 458-479.

Yawitz, Jess B. and Meyer, Laurence H. (1976), 'An Empirical Investigation of the Extent of Tax Discounting', **8** *Journal of Money, Credit, and Banking*, 247-254.

Yotsuzuka, Toshiki (1987), 'Ricardian Equivalence in the Presence of Capital Market Imperfections', **20** *Journal of Monetary Economics*, 411-436.

6020
TAX EVASION AND TAX COMPLIANCE

Luigi Alberto Franzoni
University of Bologna, Italy

Abstract

This chapter offers an overview of the theoretical and empirical research on tax evasion, delineating the variety of factors affecting noncompliance and examining possible remedies. Particular emphasis is placed on the institutional and procedural rules governing the tax enforcement policy.
JEL classification: K34
Keywords: Tax Enforcement, Compliance, Taxpayer's Behavior, Tax Gap

1. Introduction

Tax evasion is said to occur when individuals deliberately fail to comply with their tax obligations. The resulting tax revenue loss may cause serious damage to the proper functioning of the public sector, threatening its capacity to finance its basic expenses.

Although tax compliance is a major concern for all governments and analytical investigation of tax evasion can be traced as far back as the work, one of the pioneers of 'law and economics', Cesare Beccaria (1764), the problem was long segregated from the main body of economics and left essentially to the attention of tax authorities and jurisprudence. The modern use of economic tools for the analysis of tax compliance can be credited to Allingham and Sandmo ([1972] 1991), who extended the influential work of Becker (1968) on law enforcement to taxation using modern risk theory.

In the decades since, the literature on tax evasion has blossomed (as witnessed by the voluminous bibliography enclosed). Probably no aspect of tax compliance has escaped at least preliminary scrutiny. Detailed introductions to this theme are now available, as in the monographs of Cowell (1990) (theoretically oriented) and Roth, Scholtz and Witt (1989) (an interdisciplinary perspective), and the surveys of Andreoni, Erard and Feinstein (1998) (including a thorough discussion of empirical results) and Slemrod and Yitzhaki (1998) (with large sections devoted to avoidance and administration).

As a complex phenomenon, tax compliance can be addressed from a variety of perspectives. Taxpayers' stance is influenced by many factors, including their disposition towards public institutions, the perceived fairness of the taxes, prevailing social norms, and the chances of noncompliance being detected and punished. Without questioning the relevance of ethical and sociological motivations, the economic analysis of tax compliance has focused mainly on how evasion can be deterred through detection and sanctions. The thesis is that the taxpayer's behavior can be fruitfully seen as the result of a rational calculus, a careful assessment of the costs and benefits of evasion. Since even in the simplest tax and enforcement systems the incentives to comply are far from obvious, this economic perspective offers precious insights that can be used to derive suitable policy measures. Yet, given the complexity of the economic set-up in which the taxpayer usually makes compliance decisions, no simple policy prescription should be expected. In fact, as we will see, to date theoretical and empirical research has managed to establish very few firm points. Nevertheless, the general picture of tax compliance is much clearer now than just a few decades ago. At least the literature has shown that evasion is a serious problem, too complex to be solved by simple policy adjustments, and that the set of instruments for controlling it is vast.

This chapter provides an overview of the findings of the theoretical and the empirical literature on tax evasion. Section 2 defines tax evasion, as opposed to tax avoidance and other unlawful activities. In Section 3, Allingham and Sandmo's basic model of tax evasion is presented and discussed, with a brief review of its numerous extensions. Section 4 surveys the empirical evidence on taxpayer compliance. Section 5 deals with optimal tax enforcement policy, and investigates some possible strategies for combating evasion. Section 6 examines additional policy issues, connected with the institutional and procedural aspects of tax enforcement. Section 7 provides some concluding observations.

2. Definition and Extent of Tax Evasion

By distancing effective payments from statutory taxes, tax evasion defines a specific revenue deficiency, known as the 'tax gap' (in the US, for example, the federal income tax gap has been estimated at 17 percent).

Let us emphasize from the outset that the tax gap is not equal to the amount of additional revenue that would be collected by stricter enforcement, for perfect enforcement would significantly affect the economic scenario (some firms would go bankrupt, taxpayers would modify their labor supply, prices and incomes would change, and so on), so the tax base would surely be altered. As a result, at least in theory, net revenue could even turn out to be smaller. Thus standard measures of tax gaps must be interpreted cautiously. They are only roughly suggestive of the likely immediate effects of marginal improvements in enforcement. Also, one should be wary of the cliché that statutory taxes represent the ideal world and tax gaps an intrinsic evil. This is not only because taxes may not be 'just', but also because statutory taxes themselves are usually determined by a legislature that is perfectly aware that they will only be partially enforced and therefore differ from those that would be optimal under perfect enforcement.

On closer scrutiny, therefore, estimation of the tax gap merely portrays the wedge between economic reality and a purely legal construct called 'statutory taxes'. Reality and its legal representation may differ for any number of reasons, among which, as we shall see, the willful misrepresentation of tax liabilities is just one.

In economic terms, evasion problems originate in the fact that the variables that define the tax base (incomes, sales, revenues, wealth, and so on) are often not 'observable'. That is, an external observer cannot usually see the actual magnitude of an individual's tax base, and hence cannot know his true tax liability. Sometimes this knowledge can be obtained by means of costly audits, in which case we say that the tax base is verifiable (at a cost). In other cases, as when it is related to cash payments, the tax base cannot be verified at all. Taxpayers can take advantage of the imperfect information about their liability and elude taxation.

A related concept is tax avoidance (or reduction), by which individuals reduce their own tax in a way that may be unintended by tax legislators but is permissible by law. Avoidance is typically accomplished by structuring transactions so as to minimize tax liability. In some cases, avoidance is encouraged by legislation granting favorable tax treatment to specific activities in contrast to general taxation principles. From a legal standpoint, evasion differs from avoidance in being unlawful, and hence punishable (at least in theory). As far as economic function is concerned, however, evasion and avoidance obviously have very strong similarities; sometimes, indeed, they can hardly be distinguished (see for instance Feldman and Kay, 1981; Cowell, 1990; McBarnet, 1992). This adds to the difficulty of interpreting the real implications of the tax gap.

Another problem with the measurement of tax evasion relates to its proper delimitation within the broader set of the informal economy. No taxes are generally levied on transactions in the home and criminal sectors, which are usually beyond the reach of authorities and official statistics. Hence, proper determination of the boundaries of evasion is a formidable task, in that evasion is often inextricable from other illegal and unrecorded activities. What, one might ask, is the evaded tax of a hired killer?

Aggregate estimates of evasion must deal with all these problems, in addition to the classic problem of lack of direct data. Various estimation methods have been devised, some based on data collected by fiscal authorities, others - less reliable - on data derived from national accounts and surveys. Their application suggests that in the Western industrialized countries evaded taxes amount to between 5 percent and 25 percent of potential tax revenue, depending on the technique adopted and the country (see monographs by Feige, 1989; Pyle, 1989, and Thomas, 1992), with higher figures (up to 30-40 percent) for less-developed countries (Tanzi and Shome, 1994).

As noted, one should not attach too much importance to such estimates, which essentially tell us that statutory taxes are not the whole story. What matters is *effective taxation*, that is, the net tax burden on individuals. This has major implications bearing on the economic consequences of evasion: the main question is not how evasion alters the shape of statutory allocation of the fiscal burden, but how it constrains the set of policies that can be implemented. When taxes can be evaded, taxation will prove to be an imperfect tool for pursuing government aims (be they redistribution, efficiency, or whatever), which will be only partly achieved. Indeed, effective taxation may turn regressive, as the more affluent usually have better opportunities to evade (or avoid) taxes. Also, evasion may be powerfully deleterious to horizontal equity, owing to unequal distribution of opportunities to evade and of the willingness to seize them. This in turn may induce production inefficiencies, because competition would be distorted by the unequal distribution of the tax burden among firms.

The adverse consequences of tax evasion are sometimes exacerbated by laws, or even constitutions, drafted *as if* the tax base were observable, limiting the set of corrective instruments available to the government (which cannot, for instance, set tax rates according to their presumed degree of enforceability).

In order to evaluate the way in which noncompliance affects the actual tax payment of individuals, one must examine taxpayers' compliance behavior more closely. This can be done by developing a theoretical model to predict how taxpayers' behavior is affected by the relevant variables. The following section reviews some models and assesses their fit with observed practise.

3. The Decision to Evade

Compliance with the tax law typically means: (i) true reporting of the tax base, (ii) correct computation of the liability, (iii) timely filing of the return, and (iv) timely payment of the amounts due. The bulk of tax evasion involves the first point. Most evaders either do not declare their liability at all, or declare it only in part. In the following, we concentrate on the problem faced by an individual who has to decide how much of his tax aggregate to report, or whether to report it at all. The focus is on income taxes (which account for a large part of fiscal revenue in most countries). However, the insights provided can be applied to other taxes as well.

3.1 Allingham and Sandmo

A useful model of taxpayers' evasion decision is that developed by Allingham and Sandmo ([1972] 1991) and Srinivasan (1973), and revised by Yitzhaki (1974). Evasion is viewed as a portfolio allocation problem: the taxpayer must decide what portion of his income y (postulated as exogenous) to invest in the risky activity labeled 'tax evasion'. If the taxpayer does not want to take any risk, he reports his income in full; otherwise, he reports only a fraction of it and bears the risk of being caught and fined. The problem is thus to choose the optimal tax return, when the income reported is taxed at a fixed rate t and evasion is fined at a penalty rate f proportional to the tax evaded. The probability of an audit, that is, the probability that the true income level will be discovered, is a constant denoted by a. The taxpayer decides the amount to conceal so as to maximize his expected utility from net income. If we call y_{NA} the net income when the evader is not audited (gross income less taxes on reported income) and y_A the net income when he is audited (gross income less taxes on true income less the fine), we can write the taxpayer's expected utility as

$$EU(e) = (1-a)\, u(y_{NA}) + a\, u(y_A) = (1-a)\, u[y-t(y-e)] + a\, u(y-ty-fte),$$

where e denotes the amount of income concealed.

This representation yields some interesting results from the standpoint of comparative statics. On the reasonable assumption that the taxpayer is risk averse, it can be shown that the *amount* of tax evaded, te^*, varies inversely with the audit rate a and the penalty rate f, while it depends negatively on the tax rate t and positively on income y if and only if the taxpayer's utility function displays Decreasing Absolute Risk Aversion. Further, the *proportion* of tax evaded, te^*/y, increases with income if and only if taxpayer's utility function displays Decreasing Relative Risk Aversion (see Cowell, 1990). Of these results, the least obvious is surely the inverse correlation between the amount of evasion and the tax rate (with DARA). This stems from the fact that both the direct gain from evasion (taxes saved) and the expected fine depend proportionally on t. Hence, an increase in the tax rate does not induce the 'substitution' of the risky asset for the safe one, but operates solely through the reduction in disposable income (Yitzhaki, 1974).

Once the optimal amount of underreporting, e^*, has been calculated, one can easily derive the 'evasion rent', defined as the monetary benefit accruing to the evader (more precisely, the amount of income that he would be willing to pay to switch from a virtual system of perfect enforcement to the actual, imperfect, one):

$$\textit{Evasion rent} = [1 - a(1+f)]te^* - RP(e^*),$$

where $RP(e^*)$ is the risk premium associated with the audit lottery. The evasion rent is therefore equal to the net return on evasion (evaded taxes less expected sanctions) less the 'loss' due to the riskiness associated with random auditing (note, incidentally, that if taxpayers were risk-lovers, the risk premium would effectively represent a 'gain').

Several observations are in order. First, for evasion rent to be positive, the net return on evasion has to be positive (the evasion gamble needs to be 'better than fair'). That is, for evasion to occur at all, it is necessary that $a(1+f)<1$; that is, the penalty and audit rates must be sufficiently low. Second, when the net return on evasion is positive, the only reason why taxpayers may not evade their whole taxes is the fear of uncertainty (the risk premium loss). Indeed, if taxpayers were infinitely averse to risk, they would report their income in full even if the net return on evasion were positive (taxpayers are hyper-pessimists and behave as if they were to be audited for sure). Finally, the risk premium produces a differential between the rent to the taxpayer and the net revenue loss to the tax authorities. Hence, it provides a monetary measure of the 'deadweight loss' due to the randomness of tax enforcement (Yitzhaki, 1987).

3.2 Extensions

This basic model gives an account of taxpayers' evasion decisions in a very simple set-up: taxes and penalties are proportional, the audit rate is constant, only one form of evasion is available. In addition, the taxpayer is assumed to rely on expected utility theory and to be perfectly amoral, that is, to make compliance decisions with exclusive reference to the consequences for net income. All these assumptions are open to criticism, and models based on alternative assumptions have been developed. The following touches briefly on these contributions.

One standard criticism of the Allingham and Sandmo model is grounded in the belief that compliance decisions depend on moral views. This is clearly a problematic issue, one that cannot be captured by the consequentialistic set-up of standard decision theory. Bordignon (1993) makes an interesting attempt to account for non-self-motivated decisions in tax evasion. He develops a compliance model in which taxpayers are guided by suitably defined 'Kantian principles', which determine the amount that each taxpayer considers fair to pay. Under this assumption, it turns out that tax evasion is generally lower than under selfish behavior, that compliance depends on the level of public expenditure, and that evasion is likely to increase with tax rates.

Other authors have stressed the 'social' factors at the basis of the taxpayers' decision (see Roth, Scholtz and Witt, 1989, for an excellent account of the sociological research). Economists have emphasized the 'stigma' attached to the violation of social norms and shown that tax evasion may have strong spillover effects. Social stigma is likely to give rise to a multiplicity of possible equilibria: when most people evade, the stigma effect is small and evasion is not in fact discouraged; when few evade, the stigma effect is great and evasion is discouraged. The transition from one equilibrium to the other takes the form of a 'noncompliance epidemic': if, for some reason, more people start to evade, the stigma decreases and evasion spreads to an ever larger fraction of the population (see Benjamini and Maital, 1985; Gordon, 1989, and Myles and Naylor, 1996).

Alm and McCallin (1990), Landskroner, Paroush and Swary (1990), Yaniv (1990), and Wrede (1995) have extended Allingham and Sandmo with models in which taxpayers face more complex 'portfolio' set-ups offering other risky activities and alternative forms of evasion. Wadhawan (1992) posits that audits detect only a fraction of taxpayers' evasion, while Das-Gupta (1994) analyses the case in which taxpayers' income derives from a multiplicity of transactions.

Scotchmer and Slemrod (1989) and Scotchmer (1989) consider the effect of randomness in tax liability assessments. Among other things, both papers conclude that uncertainty over the true liability level or outcome of the audit increases net tax revenue, either because increased uncertainty makes evasion more costly (when taxpayers are risk averse) or because it may lead taxpayers to underreport their income and be subject to a fine (whereas overreporting only yields a rebate of the overpaid tax).

Several authors have tried to extend Allingham and Sandmo's model to include the labor supply decision, so as to endogenize taxpayers' gross income (see, among others, Andersen, 1977; Pencavel, 1979; Isachsen and Strom, 1980; Isachsen, Samuelsen and Strom, 1985, and Cowell, 1985). The problem is that as soon as the labor decision is factored in, the simple comparative statics of Allingham and Sandmo are lost. Depending on the taxpayer's marginal disutility from labor and her risk-attitudes, all predictions become possible. This problem is usually overcome by imposing strong restrictions on the utility function. Cowell (1985) takes a different course, assuming that decisions are made in two separate stages: first, the taxpayer decides how many hours to work; then he allocates this total labor supply between legal and illegal activities (alternatively, between reported and unreported income). On this assumption, Cowell is able to show that Allingham and Sandmo's results carry over (with some qualifications) to the extended set-up if taxpayer's labor supply is forward rising. Perhaps more importantly, he shows that the comparative statics results are strictly dependent on the nature of the evasion choice, as it can be tied either to the amount of income to report (for the self-employed) or to the amount of time to spend in 'off the books' activities (for the moonlighter).

The insights drawn from analysis of income tax evasion usually apply to other forms of evasion as well. Different considerations may be relevant, however, when the taxpayer is a firm subject to indirect taxation, as the evasion decision may affect output or pricing policy (tax shifting). However, Marrelli (1984) derives a separability result for the case of a monopolist: the evasion and shifting decisions are independent of one another as long as the audit probability is constant (see also Yaniv, 1995). The same result applies to oligopolistic markets when firms compete à la Cournot (Marrelli and Martina,

1988). Here, the amount of evasion by each firm is shown to depend, apart from the enforcement parameters, on the degree of collusion and on market shares.

Gordon (1990) offers an interesting insight on sales tax evasion. He suggests that under-the-counter cash sales may serve as a means of price discrimination: cash discounts are the best pricing strategy when the demand for cash purchases is highly elastic. The author also shows that, in order to reduce cash sales, a liability on detected cash customers could be imposed, but on the condition that this is an *additional* liability, and not just a transfer of a part of the supplier's existing liability onto the consumer.

As is clear from the foregoing, taxpayer noncompliance decisions may be very complex and are likely to be powerfully affected by the practical framework in which decisions are made. This thesis is strongly supported by the empirical evidence, which we now briefly review.

4. Empirical Evidence on Taxpayers' Behavior

Evidence on taxpayers' behavior is notoriously difficult to come by. Data on the extent of evasion may be confidential (not available for external analysis) or not completely reliable (such as those derived from national accounting sources). All the same, empirical studies on the determinants of taxpayers' compliance decisions have proliferated. The most detailed are based on the American Taxpayer Compliance Measurement Program (TCMP), conducted regularly by the IRS and based on a 'line by line' audit of a sample of 45,000 to 55,000 tax returns. In addition to statistical estimates, major insights on the dynamics of compliance have been obtained from questionnaires and experimentation.

In his pioneering analysis, Clotfelter (1983) uses TCMP data for 1969 to investigate the determinants of underreporting, which is defined as the difference between the income reported and that assessed by IRS examiners. He finds that both the marginal tax rate and after-tax income have significant effects on individual underreporting. In contrast to Allingham and Sandmo's prediction, he finds that elasticities with respect to marginal tax rates are positive and range from 0.5 for non-farm business to 0.8 for non-business returns. In line with Allingham and Sandmo, elasticities with respect to after-tax income are positive and range from 0.3 for non-business returns to 0.65 for farm returns. Also, wages, interest and dividends are associated with better compliance and underreporting is higher for the youngest age-groups. Witte and Woodbury (1985) also analyze data from the TCMP for 1969, but focus on the effect of enforcement parameters. They find that the percentage of underreporting is related inversely to the probability of audit (with a lagged effect), and directly to the 'opportunities' for tax evasion (absence of withholding and information reporting) and to income, though in a decreasing way. Dubin and Wilde (1988) criticize Witte and Woodbury's results and highlight the potential endogeneity of audit rates. The idea is that audit rates are decided by the IRS in view of their potential yield: a decrease in noncompliance rates reduces the net return from auditing and leads the IRS to devote less effort to auditing. Using the IRS budget per return as an instrumental variable for the audit rates, they find the audit rate to be endogenous in 5 out of 7 audit classes. They also find that audits have a deterrent effect on evasion, and that noncompliance is positively related to the unemployment rate and the nonwhite fraction of the population. Feinstein (1991) uses a sophisticated estimation technique, which allows for partial detection by IRS examiners. His results confirm the great unevenness in compliance attitudes between groups of taxpayers, with 'own business' and 'farm' filers scoring the lowest compliance rates. Using TCMP data for 1982 and 1985, Feinstein more easily disentangles the effects of marginal tax rates and gross income (taxpayers with identical incomes filing in different years face different marginal tax rates). He finds that the effect of marginal tax rates on evasion is negative and highly significant, while the effect of income is essentially zero. The former finding is consistent with Allingham and Sandmo's predictions, while the latter is not. Another finding is that greater propensity to evade is accompanied by a higher detection rate (thanks to greater IRS examination effort).

Studies based on IRS data provide a picture of the compliance phenomenon in which many factors come into play: income source, socioeconomic grouping (age, sex, location), detection probability, marginal tax rate and income level. Notably, the severity of the sanction does not seem to play a significant role (partly because in the US sanctions are rarely inflicted). Estimates based on IRS data, however, are subject to several weaknesses. First, by definition, TCMP programs relate to filers only, whereas in 1976, for example, strategic non-filers accounted for an estimated 36 percent of all unreported income. In addition, it is well known that IRS examiners have only limited capacity to detect evasion, especially on income from moonlighting and cash-only businesses. Finally, strong assumptions underlie the choice of instruments and variables as exogenous regressors.

Another important source of information about taxpayers' attitudes is surveys. Much work has been done in this area, and results cannot be easily generalized (see, among others, Vogel, 1974; Spicer and Lundstedt, 1976; Lewis, 1979; Westat, 1980; Scott and Grasmick, 1981; Mason and Calvin, 1984; Yankelovich, Skelly and White, 1984; Kinsey, 1992; Sheffrin and Triest, 1992; and de Juan, Lasheras and Mayo, 1994). On the whole, though, these studies would support the deterrence hypothesis. Specifically, the following factors have been found to be significant determinants of tax compliance: (1) the perceived probability of detection; (2) the severity of informal sanctions; (3) moral beliefs about tax compliance; (4) experience with other noncompliers and past experience with IRS enforcement (both encouraging evasion), and, (5) demographic characteristics (older people seem to be more compliant) (Klepper and Nagin, 1989). These results are largely concordant with those based on TCMP data. The main additional insight they provide lies in the importance of sociological factors, which can hardly be detected by other means.

Survey studies face several problems, however. First, results depend crucially on the representativeness of the sample, which is often difficult to assess. Second, respondents are reluctant to report acts of noncompliance (see, for instance, Elffers, Weigel and Hessing, 1987). Third, causal relationships are difficult to establish. The finding that respondents who perceive the highest probability of detection are most compliant, for instance, is consistent both with the standard 'deterrence hypothesis' and with the 'experiential hypothesis' whereby taxpayers initially overestimate detection probabilities and evaders later lower their estimates if they are not detected (Saltzman et al., 1982). Finally, individuals often seek to provide a consistent image of themselves, offering ad hoc rationalizations for their behavior (Elffers, Weigel and Hessing, 1987).

A third, increasingly widespread empirical approach is based on 'laboratory' experiments (see, for instance, Baldry, 1987); Webley et al., 1991; Alm, Cronshaw and McKee, 1993; Alm, Jackson, and McKee, 1993; and Alm, Sanchez and de Juan, 1995). Individuals (often students) are asked to participate in games simulating tax compliance, where they can underreport and incur the risk of a penalty. At the end, they receive a real reward proportional to their laboratory performance. The results tend to be very sensitive to the particular design of the experiment. In general, this research suggest that audit rates may play an important role in compliance decisions (especially for those who have already been audited), and that compliance is an increasing function of income and a decreasing function of the tax rate, while it is hardly affected by the size of fines (unless the audit rate is very high). These experiments also suggest that social norms and ethical attitudes play an important part in evasion choices, that individuals often take an all-or-nothing stance, that they tend to overweight low probabilities, and that the structure of the taxes is important (Baldry, 1987).

While the empirical research is far from conclusive, it does appear to support the hypothesis that expected punishment (that is, the size of sanctions discounted by the probability of incurring them) is relevant. Sociological and ethical factors surely play an important role too, although their effect is subtler and harder to measure. This suggests that standard enforcement polices based on apprehension and punishment should not be abandoned. They could be supplemented by alternative approaches, seeking to appeal to taxpayers' moral conscience or to reinforce social cohesion.

The following section treats the question of optimal design of tax enforcement policy, focusing on detection and punishment of evaders.

5. Evasion and Enforcement

Let us go back to the model of Allingham and Sandmo. While it provides a fairly sophisticated description of taxpayers' evasion decisions, it leaves very little scope for enforcement policy. The latter is essentially reduced to two parameters: the penalty rate and the audit rate. The main policy prescription implicit in the model and most of its variants is that, in order to curb evasion, audits have to be stepped up and fines increased. And given that raising the audit rate is likely to require public resources while an increase in the penalty rate is not, the end result is likely to be one with Draconian but rare punishment, a rule such as '*hang evaders with probability (close to) zero*'.

This is a difficult prescription to elude. But in fact it is not clear whether curbing or eliminating evasion is always a desirable goal. In general terms, the desirability of perfect enforcement is tied to the 'goodness' of the tax to be enforced. For instance, when perfect enforcement of income tax would result in the collapse of the taxed activity, one may well ask whether such unbearable burden represents the right policy.

Even if perfect enforcement were theoretically beneficial, however, it would not be likely to be cost free, as suggested by the Draconian rule. For instance, when adjudication is not perfect and innocent individuals can be convicted, infinite sanctions may entail very high welfare costs. Also, when individuals may engage in activities to avoid conviction, the social cost of enforcement may increase with the penalty (Malik, 1990)).

From a practical point of view, the major impediment to infinite fines derives from taxpayers' limited wealth. Since convicted evaders cannot be forced to labor, they will be able to foot a penalty at most as great as their own wealth. The Draconian rule thus needs to be rephrased as follows: when strict enforcement is desirable, the optimal penalty is that which expropriates the taxpayer of all his wealth.

Enforcement policies, however, can be much more sophisticated than the combination of two variables, the penalty and the audit rate. The audit probability itself, for instance, need not be the same for all taxpayers. Indeed, a simple way of making audit strategy more effective is to base it on information specific to the taxpayer, which may include any observable characteristic correlated with real tax liability, from compliance records to consumption patterns. Clearly, the relation of an individual's reported tax liability to the average for similar taxpayers may then become the key to singling out candidates for auditing.

In an important article, Reinganum and Wilde (1985) prove that by making audits conditional on the level of reported liability, the enforcer can increase net revenue. They analyze a simple cut-off rule, whereby an audit is triggered if and only if reported income is 'too low'. They show that this rule dominates the random audit rule considered by Allingham and Sandmo, and that it is the most economical way to foster truthful reporting when taxpayers are risk neutral and taxes and fines are lump sum. Scotchmer (1987) and Sanchez and Sobel (1993) extend this result, proving that the cut-off audit rule is the *optimal* policy for a net revenue-maximizing enforcer when taxes and fines are proportional and taxpayers are risk-neutral. These findings prompt the following observations. First, cost-efficient enforcement requires that audits be used primarily as a deterrent rather than as a means to collect fines. Their function is to foster correct self-reporting by individuals. Indeed, under the optimal policy audits will be performed only on people who are found (ex-post) to be honest - hence no fines will ever be collected. Second, the optimal cut-off level is strictly dependent on the distribution of income among the population: effective auditing requires reliable information on taxpayers' expected liability. Finally, optimal enforcement is likely to induce a strong regressive bias, as it provides high-income taxpayers with better chances to evade than low-income taxpayers. The idea is that high-income individuals have greater opportunities to misreport, and since it is more costly to dissuade them from evading, one should let them off the hook (on this, see also Scotchmer, 1992). This problem may be alleviated by shaping audit policy according to indexes correlated with true income (Scotchmer, 1987) and, to a lesser extent, by suitably adjusting the tax rate (Cremer, Marchand and Pestieau, 1990).

These considerations indicate that simple models in the Allingham and Sandmo mold are not adequate to the problematic issues underlying the design of an effective enforcement policy. The matter becomes still more complex when one considers the interrelation between optimal enforcement and optimal taxation.

Border and Sobel (1987), Mookherjee and Png (1989), Marhuenda and Ortuno-Ortin (1994), Hindriks (1994), and Chander and Wilde (1998) address the simultaneous definition of the optimal audit and tax schedules, assuming that taxpayers are subject to limited liability and risk neutral, and that the enforcer seeks to maximize net tax revenue. The main finding of this literature is that, at the optimum, effective taxation is regressive and the audit function is non-increasing in reported income. Hence, the repercussions of noncompliance for effective taxation indicated by Scotchmer (1987) and Sanchez and Sobel (1993) carry over to this more general set-up. An interesting insight (Border and Sobel, 1987) is that when sanctions are upper-bounded and taxpayers are risk neutral, it is optimal to audit taxpayers with a very small probability and to provide infinite rewards for truthful reporting.

The so-called 'principal-agent' approach to enforcement discussed in the foregoing paragraphs constitutes one of the most general frameworks for analyzing tax evasion and its relation to public policy. The main pitfall is its extremely demanding assumptions concerning the enforcer's ability to devise and execute the optimal policy. Indeed, one may argue that actual tax enforcers do not always possess the features that would qualify them as 'rational'. Like other branches of the public administration, they often have conflicting or ill-defined incentives, they may be governed by 'process'- rather than 'outcome'-oriented rules, and they are likely to have short-sighted and perhaps multiple goals. This suggests that the enforcer may tend to act myopically and just 'react' to impulses from the economic system. Thus the enforcer may decide auditing policy taking the amount of evasion in the economy as given and aiming to maximize detection, disregarding deterrence. This view, based on the assumption that the tax enforcer cannot credibly precommit to any specific auditing policy, is forcefully advanced by Graetz, Reinganum and Wilde (1986) and Reinganum and Wilde (1991). Their argument is that since actual audit rates are not observed by taxpayers, the enforcer has an incentive to relax any announced auditing policy once taxpayers have reported their incomes, that is, after the policy has performed its deterrent effect. Since taxpayers will anticipate the enforcer's ex-post deviation, they will not rely on the announced policy and will engage in greater evasion. The bottom line is that, in equilibrium, audits will be performed on likely evaders rather than on compliant (that is, deterred) taxpayers. This would appear to be a most reasonable prediction, and it tallies with actual enforcement practices.

The comparative statics of the no-commitment model differ in nature from those of commitment models. With no-commitment, the evasion rate and the audit rate are determined simultaneously, whereas under commitment the audit rate determines the evasion rate. Consider, for instance, the effect of an increase in the audit cost. In the no-commitment model, evaders will evade more because they know that, *ceteris paribus*, the enforcer will react less harshly (due to the higher enforcement costs). The higher evasion rate, however, rises the net return from auditing and restores the enforcer's incentive to exert effort. In equilibrium, the evasion rate will increase and the audit rate will not decrease. In the models with commitment, an increase in the audit cost means that audits become a more expensive deterrent tool. The enforcer will hence use them more parsimoniously and evasion rate will increase. In contrast to the no-commitment model, the equilibrium audit rate will decrease.

The two types of model provide different insights on tax enforcement. 'Principal-agent' models (with commitment) are probably best used to define the constraints that tax evasion puts on the effective tax system. They neatly define the set of implementable allocations on the assumption that the enforcer performs at maximum capacity. The 'no-commitment' approach, with a lower profile, aims at capturing a version of tax enforcement closer to actual practice. On the whole, however, these models still provide a very 'stylized' view of enforcement practice. They focus on just two enforcement tools, that is, the penalty and the audit probabilities, and ignore most of the institutional features of real enforcement.

6. Procedures and Institutions

It is clear by now that real compliance decisions are much more complex than those depicted by standard economic models, in that taxpayers are subject to a wide variety of sociological and ethical factors. Nor is even the effect of enforcement policy itself fully captured by standard models. Real enforcement is unquestionably more than a mere combination of penalty and audit probabilities (regardless of how sophisticated these can be made). The process that leads from the checking of tax returns to the conviction of evaders is lengthy and complex, perhaps involving various bodies (tax administration, tax courts) and procedures (interviews, cross-examinations, settlements, and so on). The shape of the prosecution process affects taxpayers' attitudes towards compliance in two ways. First, it determines the actual probability that a sanction will be imposed on evaders and, possibly, innocent taxpayers; and second, it may affect the degree of 'hostility' in the taxpayer's perception of the tax system.

In a word, institutional and procedural features matter. They impose costs on taxpayers and affect the outcome of the prosecution process. We will touch briefly on some of these aspects, starting with the costs.

According to a number of studies, the cost to the taxpayer of compliance with the most common taxes (income and VAT) in industrialized countries can be as high as 10-13 percent of the total tax liability (see the pioneering contribution of Sandford, 1973, as well as Sanford et al., 1981; Slemrod, 1989; Pitt and Slemrod ,1989; Sandford, Goodwin, and Hardwick, 1989; Blumenthal and Slemrod, 1992, and Sandford, 1995a). High compliance costs, which may be due to complex tax schedules and rules, not only tilt the 'cost-benefit analysis' towards evasion, but may also generate resentment, weakening taxpayers' moral conscience or even prompting them to evade as a form of 'punishment' for the tax administration. Legislatures should accordingly avoid the vicious circle of countering evasion by increasing the complexity of tax regulations, which raises compliance costs and fosters further evasion.

When the tax legislation is very complex, taxpayers usually have to turn to tax experts (CPAs or tax preparers), who have great power to influence their clients' attitudes towards evasion, thanks to their superior knowledge of enforcement patterns. An interesting empirical study by Klepper and Nagin (1989b) on the United States suggests that tax preparers encourage compliance with regard to unequivocal items, and discourage it with regard to ambiguous ones. (Other investigations of this issue can be found in Scotchmer, 1989; Reinganum and Wilde, 1991; Erard, 1993, and Franzoni, 1998a.)

Costs are also entailed in mandatory record-keeping and reporting, whose role is to increase the visibility of offenses, that is, the 'frequency and ease with which they come to the attention of and can be proved by enforcement officials' (Kagan, 1989). As noted in Section 3, noncompliance varies greatly with economic grouping, as tax violation by different groups has different degrees of 'visibility'. Unsurprisingly, therefore, evasion is apparently most common among independent contractors, professionals, and farmers. Conversely, compliance is highest among payroll employees subject to withholding.

In a technical sense, higher visibility makes it easier both to 'observe' the real situation or behavior of the taxpayer (by signaling potential violations) and to 'verify' it (prove it in court). Some forms of mandatory record-keeping, for example, serve a legal evidentiary function, implying a *de facto* shift in the burden of proof. It is the taxpayer who has to prove his compliance with the law, and bear the costs thereof. The question of the optimal amount of compliance duties to impose on taxpayers is therefore bound up with the optimal allocation of the burden of proof. Generally, the efficient allocation is that which places the onus of the proof on the party for which it is least costly (given its level of informativeness).

Another important factor in the 'visibility' of tax law violations is the standard of proof. Indeed, the difference between the 'observability' and the 'verifiability' of the tax base is precisely defined by the type of evidence that is necessary to asses it legally (and possibly prove that the original payments were not correct). In most countries, tax authorities have the power to estimate taxpayer's liability by discretionary means when the information supplied by the taxpayer is deemed insufficient or clearly incorrect (OECD, 1990). Clearly, under these circumstances the standard of proof can be rather lax, and the use of mere statistical evidence can be used to prove taxpayers' obligations. Presumptive taxation is a case in which statistical estimates and proxies are used *ab origine* to define the tax obligation, resulting in the automatic visibility of the activities covered and imposing virtually no compliance costs on taxpayers (see Tanzi, 1991). Note that simplifications and reductions in compliance costs will ordinarily be achieved only at the expense of reduced ability to discriminate among taxpayers (for purposes of either vertical or horizontal equity). As is pointed out by Kaplow (1996), a trade-off is likely to arise between containing compliance costs and accuracy in liability assessment.

On the procedural side, another important consideration is the possibility of resolving disputes through amicable settlements between taxpayers and the administration. In most countries, taxpayers can make a 'deal' with inspectors and obtain substantial penalty discounts in exchange for collaboration (OECD, 1990). When deals are left to the discretion of the revenue service, enforcement is likely to be adversely affected. Discretionary deals not only reduce the administration's ability to precommit itself to any specific enforcement policy but may also foster opportunism, tempting the administration to increase its inefficiencies (for example, lengthy and invasive prosecution procedures) so as to increase its 'take' at the settlement stage (Franzoni, 1995). Tax amnesties, though sharing some of these problems, may prove desirable, as they offer taxpayers social insurance against unexpected shocks, allowing them to complete their payments after uncertainty (about their income or their true preferences) has been resolved (Andreoni, 1991; Malik and Schwab, 1991).

A fundamental problem in considering the optimal institutional design of tax enforcement relates to incentives for enforcers. More fundamentally, the question is whether enforcement should be the job of public or private agents. First raised in general terms by Becker and Stigler (1974), the issue has been examined in the specific context of tax evasion by several authors. While in most countries taxes are collected by a public agency, in a few cases (as with import duties in Indonesia) collection is delegated to private contractors. Melumad and Mookherjee (1989) show that delegation of tax enforcement to a private party may be viable (that is, it can replicate the full-commitment solution) if it is backed by an incentive scheme based on publicly observable aggregate variables (audit expenditure, taxes filed and fines collected). This scheme rewards the agent for collecting fines, or, when no fine is collected, for meeting the target audit budget. Toma and Toma (1992) observe that different institutional arrangements may entail different agency costs so that depending on their incidence either public or private enforcement may be desirable.

A key agency cost is that associated with the danger of corruption. Since the personal aim of enforcement officers may not correspond to institutional purposes, there is scope for collusion with taxpayers. This seriously complicates the analysis, as a third constraint (no collusion) must now be taken into account. For while it may be contended that combating corruption can help control tax evasion, it may well be that anti-evasion measures as such ultimately just increase the scope and the extent of corruption (see Chu, 1990a; Chander and Wilde, 1992a; Besley and McLaren, 1993; Mookherjee and Png, 1995; Flatters and McLoad, 1995; Hindriks, Keen and Muthoo, 1996). This confirms that the institutional features of the enforcement system represent a point of fundamental importance. These features define the incentive structure governing the conduct of enforcers and crucially affect the actual functioning of all enforcement tools.

7. Conclusions

The foregoing offers an analytical framework for treating some salient aspects of tax noncompliance, suggesting causes and possible remedies. As must be clear by now, tax evasion is a complex phenomenon that cannot be eradicated by marginal changes in enforcement practice. Social and moral attitudes, which play a very important role, are very slow to change and are often beyond the reach of public policy. Standard enforcement therefore remains crucial. The empirical evidence suggests that a stricter enforcement regime is likely to induce greater compliance; the key variable here is the probability of detection.

To date, most studies in this field have focused on two enforcement tools: penalty rates and auditing probabilities. Much work remains to be done to ascertain the impact on compliance of less striking but nonetheless important procedural and institutional factors.

Actually, closer examination of institutional reality suggests that the audit rate may not be the relevant variable. What really matters is the probability that an investigation will eventually result in conviction and sanction for the wrongdoer. Here a host of additional factors come into play: whether evasion leaves detectable traces, the specific ability and expertise of the auditors, the set of investigative tools at their disposal (for example, the degree of banking secrecy), the possibility of inducing taxpayer collaboration, the feasibility of out-of-court settlements, the standard of proof, the definition of 'fault', the clarity of the tax law, the number of levels of appeal, and so on.

Research into the impact that these procedural aspects have on taxpayer compliance is still in its infancy. Better integration of the research on tax evasion with the 'law and economics' analysis of legal rules is definitely desirable. As theoretical analysis proceeds, additional empirical work will be needed together with more extensive study of comparative tax enforcement law and procedure.

Bibliography on Tax Evasion and Tax Compliance (6020)

Aaron, Henry J. and Munnell, Alicia H. (1992), 'Reassessing the Role for Wealth Transfer Taxes', **45(3)** *National Tax Journal*, 119-143.

Agapitos, George and Mavraganis, George (1995), 'Tax Evasion: The Case of Greece: Greece', **49** *Bulletin for International Fiscal Documentation*, 569-576.

Al Zakari, Ibrahim A. (1994), *Corporate Tax Compliance: A Case Study of Saudi Arabia*, University of New Mexico, Ph.D.

Alexeev, Michael V., Gaddy, Clifford and Leitzel, Jim (1995), 'Economic Crime and Russian Reform', **151** *Journal of Institutional and Theoretical Economics*, 677-692.

Alford, Robert R. and Feige, Edgar L. (1989), 'Information Distortions in Social Systems: The Underground Economy and Other Observer-Subject-Policymaker Feedbacks', in Feige, Edgar L. (ed.), *The Underground Economies: Tax Evasion and Information Distortion*, Cambridge, Cambridge University Press, 57-79.

Allingham, Michael G. and Sandmo, Agnar ([1972] 1991), 'Income Tax Evasion: A Theoretical Analysis', in Atkinson, A.B. (ed.), *Modern Public Finance. Volume 1*, Aldershot, Edward Elgar, 50-65.

Alm, James (1988), 'Compliance Costs and the Tax Avoidance-Tax Evasion Decision', **16** *Public Finance Quarterly*, 31-66.

Alm, James (1991), 'A Perspective on the Experimental Analysis of Taxpayer Reporting', **66(3)** *Accounting Review*, 577-593.

Alm, James and Beck, William (1991), 'Wiping the Slate Clean: Individual Response to State Tax Amnesties', **57** *Southern Economic Journal*, 1043-1053.

Alm, James and Beck, William (1993), 'Tax Amnesties and Compliance in the Long Run: A Time Series Analysis', **46** *National Tax Journal*, 53-60.

Alm, James and McCallin, Nancy J. (1990), 'Tax Avoidance and Tax Evasion as a Joint Portfolio Choice', **45** *Public Finance*, 193-200.

Alm, James, Bahl, Roy and Murray, Matthew N. (1990), 'Tax Structure and Tax Compliance', **72** *Review of Economics and Statistics*, 603-613.

Alm, James, Bahl, Roy and Murray, Matthew N. (1991a), 'Income Tax Evasion', in Bahl, Roy (ed.), *The Jamaican Tax Reform*, Cambridge, MA, Lincoln Institute of Land Policy, 181-214.

Alm, James, Bahl, Roy and Murray, Matthew N. (1991b), 'Tax Base Erosion in Developing Countries', **39** *Economic Development and Cultural Change*, 849-872.

Alm, James, Bahl, Roy and Murray, Matthew N. (1993), 'Audit Selection and Income Tax Underreporting in the Tax Compliance Game', **42(1)** *Journal of Development Economics*, 1-33.

Alm, James, Cronshaw, Mark B. and McKee, Michael (1993), 'Tax Compliance with Endogenous Audit Selection Rules', **46** *Kyklos*, 27-45.

Alm, James, Jackson, Betty R. and McKee, Michael (1992a), 'Institutional Uncertainty and Taxpayer Compliance', **82** *American Economic Review*, 1018-1026.

Alm, James, Jackson, Betty R. and McKee, Michael (1992b), 'Deterrence and Beyond: Toward a Kinder, Gentler IRS', in Slemrod, Joel (ed.), *Why People Pay Taxes: Tax Compliance and Enforcement*, Ann Arbor, University of Michigan Press, 311-329.

Alm, James, Jackson, Betty R. and McKee, Michael (1992c), 'Estimating the Determinants of Taxpayer Compliance with Experimental Data', **45** *National Tax Journal*, 107-114.

Alm, James, Jackson, Betty R. and McKee, Michael (1993), 'Fiscal Exchange, Collective Decision Institutions, and Tax Compliance', **22** *Journal of Economic Behavior and Organization*, 285-303.

Alm, James, McClelland, Gary H. and Schulze, William D. (1992), 'Why Do People Pay Taxes?', **48** *Journal of Public Economics*, 21-38.

Alm, James, Sanchez, Isabel and de Juan, Ana (1995), 'Economic and Noneconomic Factors in Tax Compliance', **48** *Kyklos*, 3-18.

Altshuler, Rosanne and Fulghieri, Paolo (1992), *Dynamic Effects of Foreign Tax Credits on Multinational Corporations*, Columbia University Department of Economics Discussion Paper, No. 611.

Altshuler, Rosanne and Newlon, T. Scott (1991), *The Effects of U.S. Tax Policy on the Income Repatriation Patterns of U.S. Multinational Corporations*, National Bureau of Economic Research Working Paper, No. 3925.

Andersen, Per (1977), 'Tax Evasion and Labor Supply', **79** *Scandinavian Journal of Economics*, 375-383.

Andjelkovic Mileva (1995), 'Koncept Zloupotrebe Prava u Poreskoj Materiji (Concept of Abuse of Law in Fiscal Matters)', **5-6** *Finansije*, 269-277.

Andreoni, James (1991), 'The Desirability of a Permanent Tax Amnesty', **45** *Journal of Public Economics*, 143-160.

Andreoni, James (1992), 'IRS as Loan Shark: Tax Compliance with Borrowing Constraints', **49(3)** *Journal of Public Economics*, 35-46.

Andreoni, James, Erard, Brian and Feinstein, Jonathan S. (1996), *Tax Compliance*, University of Wisconsin Working Paper, No. 9610.

Andreoni, James, Erard, Brian and Feinstein, Jonathan S. (1998), 'Tax Compliance', *Journal of Economic Literature*, forthcoming.

Antonides, Gerrit and Robben, Henry S.J. (1995), 'True Positives and False Alarms in the Detection of Tax Evasion', **16** *Journal of Economic Psychology*, 617-640.

Asorey, Ruben O. (1991), 'Transfer Pricing and the New Criminal Tax Law: Argentina', **45** *Bulletin for International Fiscal Documentation*, 74-75.

Baldry, Jonathan C. (1987), 'Income Tax Evasion and the Tax Schedule: Some Experimental Results', **42** *Public Finance*, 357-383.

Baldry, Jonathan C. (1994), 'Economic Analysis and Taxpayer Compliance: Time for a New Agenda', **11** *Australian Tax Forum*, 45-62.

Banerji, Arup (1991), *Tax Evasion Enforcement and Intertemporal Choice*, University of Pennsylvania, Ph.D.

Bardsley, Peter (1994), 'Tax Compliance Research: An Economic Perspective on the Research Agenda', **11** *Australian Tax Forum*, 271-290.

Barthelemy, Philippe (1989), 'The Underground Economy in France', in Feige, Edgar L. (ed.), *The Underground Economies: Tax Evasion and Information Distortion*, Cambridge, Cambridge University Press, 281-294.

Batina, Raymond G. (1992), 'Time-Consistent Income Taxation', **32** *Quarterly Review of Economics and Finance*, 68-81.

Bayar, Ali and Frank, Max (1987), 'The Erosion of the Different Tax Bases', **42** *Public Finance*, 341-356.

Bazzoni, Stefania and Mori, Antonella (1994), 'Politiche Fiscali e Crescita Endogena in un'Economia con un Settore Informale (Fiscal Policy and Endogenous Growth in an Economy with an Informal Sector)', **53** *Giornale degli Economisti e Annali di Economia*, 219-234.

Beams, Mark K. (1992), 'Obtaining Relief through Competent Authority Procedures and Treaty Exchange of Tax Information: The U.S. Approach', **46** *Bulletin for International Fiscal Documentation*, 119-122.

Beaumont, Marion S. (1991), 'Proposition 13 Winners and Losers: Were First-Time Home Buyers Affected Adversely?', in Stocker, Frederick D. (ed.), *Proposition 13: A Ten Year Retrospective*, Cambridge, MA, Lincoln Institute of Land Policy, 135-173.

Becker, G. (1968), 'Crime and Punishment: An Economic Approach', **76** *Journal of Political Economy*, 169-217.

Becker, G. and Stigler, G. (1974), 'Law Enforcement, Malfeasance, and Compensation of Enforcers, **3** *Journal of Legal Studies*, 1 ff.

Becker, Winfried, Buchner, Heinz Jurgen and Sleeking, Simon (1987), 'The Impact of Public Transfer Expenditures on Tax Evasion: An Experimental Approach', **34** *Journal of Public Economics*, 243-252.

Benjamini, Yael and Maital, Shlomo (1985), 'Optimal Tax Evasion and Optimal Tax Evasion Policy: Behavioral Aspects', in Gaertner, Wulf and Wenig, Alois (eds), *The Economics of the Shadow Economy: Proceedings of the International Conference on the Economics of the Shadow Economy Held at the University of Bielefeld, West Germany, October 10-14, 1983*, Berlin, Springer, 245-264.

Beron, Kurt, Tauchen, Helen V. and Witte, Ann Dryden (1988), *A Structural Equation Model for Tax Compliance and Auditing*, National Bureau of Economic Research Working Paper, No. 2556.

Beron, Kurt, Tauchen, Helen V. and Witte, Ann Dryden (1992), 'The Effect of Audits and Socioeconomic Variables on Compliance', in Slemrod, Joel (ed.), *Why People Pay Taxes: Tax Compliance and Enforcement*, Ann Arbor, University of Michigan Press, 67-89.

Besley, Timothy and McLaren, John (1993), 'Taxes and Bribery: The Role of Wage Incentives', **103** *Economic Journal*, 119-141.

Besley, Timothy, Preston, Ian and Ridge, Michael (1993), *Fiscal Anarchy in the U.K. Modelling Poll Tax Noncompliance*, National Bureau of Economic Research Working Paper, No. 4498.

Besley, T., Preston, Ian and Ridge, Michael (1994), *Fiscal Anarchy in the UK*, University College London Discussion Paper, No. 94-01.

Bird, Richard M. (1992), 'Does Deterrence Deter? Measuring the Effect of Deterrence on Tax Compliance in Field Studies and Experimental Studies: Commentary', in Slemrod, Joel (ed.), *Why People Pay Taxes: Tax Compliance and Enforcement*, Ann Arbor, University of Michigan Press, 306-310.

Bird, Richard M. and Miller, Barbara (1991), 'The Incidence of Indirect Taxes on Low-Income Households in Jamaica', in Bahl, Roy (ed.), *The Jamaican Tax Reform*, Cambridge, MA, Lincoln Institute of Land Policy, 793-811.

Blumenthal, Marsha and Slemrod, Joel B. (1992), 'The Compliance Cost of the U.S. Individual Income Tax System: A Second Look After Tax Reform', **45** *National Tax Journal*, 185-202.

Blumenthal, Marsha and Slemrod, Joel B. (1995), 'The Compliance Cost of Taxing Foreign-Source Income: Its Magnitude, Determinants, and Policy Implications', **2** *International Tax and Public Finance*, 37-53.

Boadway, Robin W. and Keen, Michael (1993), 'Evasion and Time Consistency in the Taxation of Capital Income', Queen's Institute for Economic Research Discussion Paper.

Boadway, Robin, Marchand, Maurice and Pestieau, Pierre (1992), 'Towards a Theory of the Direct-Indirect Tax Mix', Queen's Institute for Economic Research Discussion Paper.

Bogetic, Zeljko and Ilman, Arye L. (eds) (1995), *Financing Government in the Transition: Bulgaria: The Political Economy of Tax Policies, Tax Bases, and Tax Hvasion*, Regional and Sectoral Studies. Washington, DC, World Bank, 254 p.

Boidman, Nathan (1983), 'Tax Evasion: The Present State of Non-Compliance', **37(9-10)** *Bulletin for International Fiscal Documentation*, 451-479.

Bolderson, Sarah and Huiskes, Theodoor (1994), 'Central and Eastern Europe: Meeting Tax Obligations in Central and Eastern Europe', **48** *Bulletin for International Fiscal Documentation*, 648-654.

Boone, Catherine (1994), 'Trade, Taxes, and Tribute: Market Liberalizations and the New Importers in West Africa', **22** *World Development*, 453-467.

Border, K. and Sobel, J. (1987), 'Samurai Accountant: A Theory of Auditing and Plunder', **54(4)** *Review of Economic Studies*, 525-540.

Bordignon, Massimo (1993), 'A Fairness Approach to Income Tax Evasion', **52(3)** *Journal of Public Economics*, 345-362.

Bowles, Roger A. and Jones, Philip (1993), 'Nonpayment of Poll Tax: An Exploratory Analysis of Tax Resistance', **13** *International Review of Law and Economics*, 445-455.

Brenner, Reuven and Brenner, Gabrielle A. (1990), *Gambling and Speculation*, Cambridge, Cambridge University Press. Reprinted in French edition by Presses Universitaires de France, 1993.

Broesterhuizen, G.A.A.M. (1989), 'The Unrecorded Economy and the National Income Accounts in the Netherlands: A Sensitivity Analysis', in Feige, Edgar L. (ed.), *The Underground Economies: Tax Evasion and Information Distortion*, Cambridge, Cambridge University Press, 159-174.

Brown, C.V. et al. (1984), 'Tax Evasion and Avoidance on Earned Income: Some Survey Evidence', **5(3)** *Fiscal Studies*, 1-22.

Burgess, Robin and Stern, Nicholas (1992), *Taxation and Development*, London School of Economics Suntory Toyota International Centre for Economics and Related Disciplines Working Paper, No. DEP 42.

Burgess, Robin and Stern, Nicholas (1993), *A VAT in India, Problems and Options*, London School of Economics Suntory Toyota International Centre for Economics and Related Disciplines Working Paper, No. EF/4.

Burgess, Robin, Howes, Stephen and Stern, Nicholas (1993), *The Reform of Indirect Taxes in India*, London School of Economics Suntory Toyota International Centre for Economics and Related Disciplines Working Paper, No. EF/7.

Carroll, John S. (1992), 'How Taxpayers Think about Their Taxes: Frames and Values', in Slemrod, Joel (ed.), *Why People Pay Taxes: Tax Compliance and Enforcement*, Ann Arbor, University of Michigan Press, 43-63.

Cassone, Alberto and Marchese, Carla (1995), 'Tax Amnesties as Special Sales Offers: the Italian Experience', **50** *Public Finance/Finances Publiques*, 51-66.

Chadha, V. and Singh, Gurjeet (1988), 'An Analysis of Tax Evasion in Punjab', in Raikhy, P.S. and Gill, Sucha Singh (eds), *Resource Mobilisation and Economic Development: A Regional Perspective*, Amritsar, India, Guru Nanak Dev University, Punjab School of Economics, 140-151.

Chander, Parkash and Wilde, Louis (1992), 'Corruption in Tax Administration', **49** *Journal of Public Economics*, 333-349.

Chander, P. and Wilde, Louis (1998), 'A General Characterization of Optimal Income Tax Enforcement', **65** *Review of Economic Studies*, 165-183.

Chelvathurai, S.I. (1990), 'Tax Avoidance, Tax Evasion and the Underground Economy - The CATA Experience: International', **44** *Bulletin for International Fiscal Documentation*, 594-599.

Christiansen, Vidar (1980), 'Two Comments on Tax Evasion', **13** *Empirical Economics*, 389-393.

Chu, C.Y. Cyrus (1990a), 'A Model of Income Tax Evasion with Venal Tax Officials: The Case of Taiwan', **45(3)** *Public Finance*, 392-408.

Chu, C.Y. Cyrus (1990b), 'Plea Bargaining with the IRS', **41(3)** *Journal of Public Economics*, 1319-1333.

Chu, C.Y. Cyrus (1992), 'Analyzing Income Tax Evasion Using Amnesty Data with Self-Selection Correction: The Case of the Michigan Tax Amnesty Program: Commentary', in Slemrod, Joel (ed.), *Why People Pay Taxes: Tax Compliance and Enforcement*, Ann Arbor, University of Michigan Press, 190-192.

Clotfelter, Charles T. (1983), 'Tax Evasion and Tax Rates: An Analysis of Individual Returns', **65** *Review of Economics and Statistics*, 363-373.

Cnossen, Sijbren (1991), 'The Future Development of the Sales Tax in Jamaica', in Bahl, Roy (ed.), *The Jamaican Tax Reform*, Cambridge, MA, Lincoln Institute of Land Policy, 519-535.

Coffey, Sergia (1995), *Tax Evasion and the Development of a Financial Sector in LDCs*, New York University, Ph.D.

Coleman, Cynthia and Freeman, Lynne (1994), 'The Development of Strategic Marketing Options Directed at Improving Compliance Levels in Small Business', **11** *Australian Tax Forum*, 347-367.

Collins, Julie H. (1992), 'Deterrence and Beyond: Toward a Kinder, Gentler IRS: Commentary', in Slemrod, Joel (ed.), *Why People Pay Taxes: Tax Compliance and Enforcement*, Ann Arbor, University of Michigan Press, 330-332.

Collins, Julie H. and Plumlee, R. David (1991), 'The Taxpayer's Labor and Reporting Decision: The Effect of Audit Schemes', **66** *Accounting Review*, 559-576.

Collins, Julie H., Murphy, Daniel P. and Plumlee, R. David (1992), 'The Taxpayer's Dilemma: How Hard to Work and What to Report?', in Stern, Jerrold J. (ed.), *Advances in Taxation. Volume 4*, Greenwich, CT, JAI Press, 31-53.

Commerce Clearing House Tax Law (eds) (1989), *Understanding IRS Communications*, Chicago, Commerce Clearing House, 120 p.

Contini, Bruno (1989), 'The Irregular Economy of Italy: A Survey of Contributions', in Feige, Edgar L. (ed.), *The Underground Economies. Tax Evasion and Information Distortion*, Cambridge, Cambridge University Press, 237-250.

Cowell, Frank A. (1985a), 'Public Policy and Tax Evasion: Some Problems', in Gaertner, Wulf and Wenig, Alois (eds), *The Economics of the Shadow Economy: Proceedings of th International Conference on the Economics of the Shadow Economy Held at the University of Bielefeld, West Germany, October 10-14, 1983*, Berlin, Springer, 273-284.

Cowell, Frank A. (1985b), 'The Economic Analysis of Tax Evasion', **37** *Bulletin of Economic Research*, 163-193.

Cowell, Frank A. (1985c), 'Tax Evasion with Labour Income', **26** *Journal of Public Economics*, 19-34.

Cowell, Frank A. (1987), 'The Economic Analysis of Tax Evasion', in Hey, John D. and Lambert, Peter J. (eds), *Surveys in the Economics of Uncertainty*, Oxford, Blackwell, 173-203.

Cowell, Frank A. (1990a), *Cheating the Government: The Economics of Evasion*, Cambridge, MA, MIT Press, 267 p.

Cowell, F.A. (1990b), 'Tax Sheltering and the Cost of Evasion', **42** *Oxford Economic Papers*, 231-243.

Cowell, Frank A. (1991), 'Tax Sheltering and the Cost of Evasion', in Sinclair, Peter J. N. and Slater, Martin D.E. (eds), *Taxation, Private Information and Capital. Oxford Economic Papers, Special Issue 1990*, Oxford, Oxford University Press, 231-243.

Cowell, F.A. (1992), 'Tax Evasion and Inequity', **13** *Journal of Economic Psychology*, 521-543.

Cowell, Frank A. and Gordon, James P.F. (1988), 'Unwillingness to Pay: Tax Evasion and Public Good Provision', **36** *Journal of Public Economics*, 305-321.

Crane, Steven E. and Nourzad, Farrokh (1985), 'Time Value of Money and Income Tax Evasion under Risk-averse Behavior: Theoretical Analysis and Empirical Evidence', **40** *Public Finance*, 481-494.

Crane, Steven E. and Nourzad, Farrokh (1986a), 'Inflation and Tax Evasion: An Empirical Analysis', **68** *Review of Economics and Statistics*, 217-223.

Crane, Steven E. and Nourzad, Farrokh (1986b), 'Federal Income Tax Evasion', in Lindholm, Richard W. (ed.), *Examination of Basic Weaknesses of Income as the Major Federal Tax Base*, New York, Greenwood Press, 140-162.

Crane, Steven E. and Nourzad, Farrokh (1987), 'On the Treatment of Income Tax Rates in Empirical Analysis of Tax Evasion', **40** *Kyklos*, 338-348.

Crane, Steven E. and Nourzad, Farrokh (1990), 'Tax Rates and Tax Evasion: Evidence from California Amnesty Data', **43** *National Tax Journal*, 189-199.

Crane, Steven E. and Nourzad, Farrokh (1992), 'Analyzing Income Tax Evasion Using Amnesty Data with Self-Selection Correction: The Case of the Michigan Tax Amnesty Program', in Slemrod, Joel (ed.), *Why People Pay Taxes: Tax Compliance and Enforcement*, Ann Arbor, University of Michigan Press, 167-189.

Crane, Steven E. and Nourzad, Farrokh (1994), 'An Empirical Analysis of Factors that Distinguish those who Evade on their Tax Return from those who Choose Not to File a Return', **49(Suppl)** *Public Finance*, 106-116.

Creedy, John (1994), *Taxation, Poverty and Income Distribution*, Aldershot, Edward Elgar, 255 p.

Creedy, John and McDonald, Ian M. (1990), 'A Tax Package to Reduce the Marginal Rate of Income Tax and the Wage Demands of Trade Unions', **66** *Economic Record*, 195-202.

Cremer, H., Marchand, M. and Pestieau, P. (1990), 'Evading, Auditing and Taxing: The Equity-Compliance Tradeoff', **43** *Journal of Public Economics*, 67-92.

Cremer, Helmuth and Gahvari, Firouz (1992), 'Tax Evasion and the Structure of Indirect Taxes and Audit Probabilities', **47(Suppl)** *Public Finance*, 351-365.

Cremer, Helmuth and Gahvari, Firouz (1993), 'Tax Evasion and Optimal Commodity Taxation', **50(2)** *Journal of Public Economics*, 261-275.

Cremer, Helmuth and Gahvari, Firouz (1994), 'Tax Evasion, Concealment and the Optimal Linear Income Tax', **96** *Scandinavian Journal of Economics*, 219-239.

Cronshaw, Mark B. and Alm, James (1995), 'Tax Compliance with Two-Sided Uncertainty', **23** *Public Finance Quarterly*, 139-166.

Cunningham, William T. (1989), 'Withholding Taxes: Portugal', **43** *Bulletin for International Fiscal Documentation*, 223-224.

Cunningham, William T. (1994), 'Portugal: Recent Developments', **48** *Bulletin for International Fiscal Documentation*, 185-190.

Danesh, Abol Hassan (1991), *The Informal Economy: Underground Economy, Moonlighting, Subcontracting, Household Economy, Uunorganized Sector, Barter, Ghetto Economy, Second Economy: A Research Guide*, New York, Garland Inc., 420 p.

Das Gupta, Arindam (1994), 'A Theory of Hard-to-Tax Groups', **49(Suppl)** *Public Finance*, 28-39.

Das Gupta, Arindam, Lahiri, Radhika and Mookherjee, Dilip (1995), 'Income Tax Compliance in India: An Empirical Analysis', **23** *World Development*, 2051-2064.

Dassesse, Marc (1994), 'Introduction of the "Economic Reality" Test in Belgian Tax Law: Years of Uncertainty Ahead?', **48** *Bulletin for International Fiscal Documentation*, 127-129.

de Jantscher, Milka Casanegra, Silvani, Carlos and Holland, Graham (1991), 'The Audit of VAT', in Tait, Alan A. (ed.), *Value Added Tax: Administrative and Policy Issues. Occasional Paper, no. 88*, Washington, International Monetary Fund, 67-88.

de Juan, Ana, Lasheras, Miguel A. and Mayo, Rafaela (1994), 'Voluntary Tax Compliant Behavior of Spanish Income Tax Payers', **49(Suppl)** *Public Finance*, 90-105.

Dermine, J. (1994), *EC Banking Regulation, Centralization or National Autonomy*, INSEAD Working Papers, No. 94/13/FIN/EPS.

Drummond, Don et al. (1994), 'The Underground Economy: Moving the Myth Closer to Reality', **2** *Canadian Business Economics*, 3-17.

Dubin, Jeffrey A. (1992), 'Can Brute Deterrence Backfire? Perceptions and Attitudes in Taxpayer Compliance: Commentary', in Slemrod, Joel (ed.), *Why People Pay Taxes: Tax Compliance and Enforcement*, Ann Arbor, University of Michigan Press, 219-222.

Dubin, Jeffrey A. and Wilde, Louis L. (1988), 'An Empirical Analysis of Federal Income Tax Auditing and Compliance', **41** *National Tax Journal*, 61-74.

Dubin, Jeffrey A., Graetz, Michael J. and Wilde, Louis L. (1987), 'Are We a Nation of Tax Cheaters? New Econometric Evidence on Tax Compliance', **77** *American Economic Review. Papers and Proceedings*, 240-245.

Dubin, Jeffrey A., Graetz, Michael J. and Wilde, Louis L. (1989), 'The Effect of Audit Rates on Federal Income Tax Filings and Collections, 1977-1986', Caltech Social Science Working Paper.

Dubin, Jeffrey A., Graetz, Michael J. and Wilde, Louis L. (1992), 'State Income Tax Amnesties: Causes', **107** *Quarterly Journal of Economics*, 1057-1070.

Elffers, Henk and Hessing, Dick J. (1988), 'A Linear Structural Model for Tax Evasion Measurements', in Maital, Shlomo (ed.), *Applied Behavioural Economics Volume 2*, New York, New York University Press, 562-567.

Elffers, H., Robben, H.S.J. and Hessing, D.J. (1991), 'Under-reporting Income: Who is the Best Judge - Tax-payer or Tax Inspector?', **154** *Journal of Royal Statistical Society, Series A*, 125-127.

Elffers, Henk, Robben, Henry S.J. and Hessing, Dick J. (1992), 'On Measuring Tax Evasion', **13** *Journal of Economic Psychology*, 545-567.

Ellfers, H., Weigel, R. and Hessing, D. (1987), 'The Consequences of Different Strategies for Measuring Tax Evasion Behavior', **8** *Journal of Economic Psychology*, 311-337.

Erard, Brian (1990), *Tax Practitioners and Tax Compliance: A Microeconometric Analysis of the Decision to Engage a Tax Preparer and Its Consequences*, University of Michigan, Ph.D.

Erard, Brian (1992), 'The Influence of Tax Audits on Reporting Behavior', in Slemrod, Joel (ed.), *Why People Pay Taxes: Tax Compliance and Enforcement*, Ann Arbor, University of Michigan Press, 95-114.

Erard, Brian (1993), 'Taxation with Representation: An Analysis of the Role of Tax Practitioners in Tax Compliance', **52(2)** *Journal of Public Economics*, 163-197.

Erard, Brian and Feinstein, Jonathan S. (1994a), 'The Role of Moral Sentiments and Audit Perceptions in Tax Compliance', **49(Suppl)** *Public Finance*, 70-89.

Erard, Brian and Feinstein, Jonathan S. (1994b), 'Honesty and Evasion in the Tax Compliance Game', **25** *Rand Journal of Economics*, 1-19.

Erbas, S. Nuri (1993), *Presumptive Taxation: Revenue and Automatic Stabilizer Aspects*, International Monetary Fund Working Paper, No. WP/93/69.

Falkinger, Josef (1988), 'Tax Evasion and Equity: A Theoretical Analysis', **43** *Public Finance*, 388-395.

Falkinger, Josef (1991), 'On Optimal Public Good Provision with Tax Evasion', **45** *Journal of Public Economics*, 127-133.

Falkinger, Josef (1995), 'Tax Evasion, Consumption of Public Goods and Fairness', **16** *Journal of Economic Psychology*, 63-72.

Falkinger, Josef and Walther, Herbert (1991a), 'Separating Small and Big Fish: The Case of Income Tax Evasion', **54** *Journal of Economics (Zeitschrift für Nationalökonomie)*, 55-67.

Falkinger, Josef and Walther, Herbert (1991b), 'Rewards versus Penalties: On a New Policy Against Tax Evasion', **19** *Public Finance Quarterly*, 67-79.

Feige, Edgar L. (1986), 'A Re-examination of the "Underground Economy' in the United States: A Comment', **33** *International Monetary Fund Staff Papers*, 768-781.

Feige, Edgar L. (1989a), 'The Meaning and Measurement of the Underground Economy', in Feige, Edgar L. (ed.), *The Underground Economies: Tax Evasion and Information Distortion*, Cambridge, Cambridge University Press, 13-56.

Feige, Edgar L. (1989b), 'The Underground Economies: Tax Evasion and Information Distortion: Introduction', in Feige, Edgar L. (ed.), *The Underground Economies: Tax Evasion and Information Distortion*, Cambridge, Cambridge University Press, 1-9.

Feige, Edgar L. (1989c), *The Underground Economies: Tax Evasion and Information Distortion*, Cambridge, Cambridge University Press, 378 p.

Feinstein, Jonathan S. (1991), 'An Econometric Analysis of Income Tax Evasion and its Detection', **22** *Rand Journal of Economics*, 14-35.

Feinstein, Jonathan S. (1992), 'The Effect of Audits and Socioeconomic Variables on Compliance: Commentary', in Slemrod, Joel (ed.), *Why People Pay Taxes: Tax Compliance and Enforcement*, Ann Arbor, University of Michigan Press, 90-94.

Feldbrugge, F.J.M. (1989), 'The Soviet Second Economy in a Political and Legal Perspective', in Feige, Edgar L. (ed.), *The Underground Economies: Tax Evasion and Information Distortion*, Cambridge, Cambridge University Press, 297-338.

Feldman, J. and Kay, John A. (1981), 'Tax Avoidance', in Burrows, Paul and Veljanovski, Cento G. (eds), *The Economic Approach to Law*, London, Butterworths, 320-333.

Filosa, Vincenzo (1979), 'Evasione Fiscale: Sanzioni Anche per il governante e il Legislatore (Tax Evasion: Sanctions Also for the Government and the Legislature)', **26** *Rivista Internazionale di Scienze Economiche e Commerciali*, 705-713.

Fishburn, Geoffrey (1981), 'Tax Evasion and Inflation', **20(37)** *Australian Economic Papers*, 325-332.

Fisher, Vickie L. (1985), 'Recent Innovations in State Tax Compliance Programs', **38** *National Tax Journal*, 565-571.

Fishlow, Albert and Friedman, Jorge (1994), 'Tax Evasion, Inflation and Stabilization', **43** *Journal of Development Economics*, 105-123.

Flatters, Frank and MacLeod, W. Bentley (1995), 'Administrative Corruption and Taxation', **2** *International Tax and Public Finance*.

Fluet, Claude (1987), 'Fraude Fiscale et Offre de Travail au Noir (Tax Evasion and the Supply of Unofficial Labour)', **63** *L'Actualité Economique*, 225-242.

Fortin, Bernard and Lacroix, Guy (1994), 'Labour Supply, Tax Evasion and the Marginal Cost of Public Funds: An Empirical Investigation', **55** *Journal of Public Economics*, 407-431.

Fortin, Bernard, Garneau, Gaétan, Lacroix, Guy, Lemieux, Thomas and Montmarquette, Claude (1996), *L'Économie Souterraine au Québec - Mythes et Réalités* (The Underground Economy in Quebec - Myths and Realities), Sainte-Foy, Presses de l'Université Laval.

Fossati, Amedeo, Cavalletti, Barbara and Pench, Alberto (1992), 'From Personal to Indirect Taxation: A General Equilibrium Approach', in Galeotti, G. and Marrelli, M. (eds), *Design and Reform of Taxation Policy. Financial and Monetary Policy Studies, vol. 25*, Dordrecht, Kluwer Academic Publishers, 95-112.

Frank, Max (1976), 'Fraude des Revenus Soumis a l'Impot des Personnes Physiques et Perte d'Impot qui en Resulte pour le Tresor-Etude Methodologique. (Income Tax Evasion and Resulting Revenue Losses for the Treasury-Methodological Study. With English summary)', **31** *Public Finance*, 1-30.

Frank, Max and Dekeyser Meulders, Daniele (1977), 'A Tax Discrepancy Coefficient Resulting from Tax Evasion or Tax Expenditures', **8** *Journal of Public Economics*, 67-78.

Franzoni, Luigi Alberto (1994), 'Costly Prosecution, Tax Evasion and Amnesties', **23** *Economic Notes*, 248-265.

Franzoni, Luigi Alberto (1995), *On the Economics of Tax Amnesties (D.Phil. thesis)*, Nuffield College, Oxford.

Franzoni, Luigi Alberto (1998a), 'Punishment and Grace: on the Economics of Tax Amnesties', *Public Finance*; forthcoming.

Franzoni, Luigi Alberto (1998b), 'Independent auditors as fiscal gatekeepers', *International Review of Law and Economics*, forthcoming

Frey, Bruno (1989), 'How Large (or Small) Should the Underground Economy Be?', in Feige, Edgar L. (ed.), *The Underground Economies: Tax Evasion and Information Distortion*, Cambridge, Cambridge University Press, 111-126.

Friedland, Nehemiah, Maital, Shlomo and Rutenberg, Aryeh (1978), 'A Simulation Study of Income Tax Evasion', **10** *Journal of Public Economics*, 107-116.

Friedman, Jorge Ricardo (1993), *Essays in Tax Evasion*, University of California, Berkeley, Ph.D. 1993.

Fullerton, Don and Karayannis, Marios (1993), *Tax Evasion and the Allocation of Capital*, National Bureau of Economic Research Working Paper, No. 4581.

Fullerton, Don and Karayannis, Marios (1994), 'Tax Evasion and the Allocation of Capital', **55** *Journal of Public Economics*, 257-278.

Gabor, Istvan R. (1989), 'Second Economy and Socialism: The Hungarian Experience', in Feige, Edgar L. (ed.), *The Underground Economies: Tax Evasion and Information Distortion*, Cambridge, Cambridge University Press, 339-360.

Gangemi, Avv. Bruno (1993), 'Tax Avoidance: The Italian Experience', **47** *Bulletin for International Fiscal Documentation*, 522-528.

Geeroms, Hans J.A. and Wilmots, Hendrik (1985), 'An Empirical Model of Tax Evasion and Tax Avoidance', **40** *Public Finance*, 190-209.

Gentry, William M. (1994), 'Review of: Why People Pay Taxes: Tax Compliance and Enforcement', **32** *Journal of Economic Literature*, 1248-1249.

Giovannini, Alberto (1987a), *Capital Controls and Public Finance: The Experience in Italy*, Columbia First Boston Series in Money, Economics and Finance Working Paper, FB-87-19.

Giovannini, Alberto (1987b), *International Capital Mobility and Tax Evasion*, National Bureau of Economic Research Working Paper, No. 2460.

Gordon, James P.F. (1989), 'Individual Morality and Reputation Costs as Deterrents to Tax Evasion', **33** *European Economic Review*, 797-805.

Gordon, James P.F. (1990), 'Evading Taxes by Selling for Cash', **42** *Oxford Economic Papers*, 244-255.

Gordon, James P.F. (1991), 'Evading Taxes by Selling for Cash', in Sinclair, Peter J.N. and Slater, Martin D.E. (eds), *Taxation, Private Information and Capital. Oxford Economic Papers, Special Issue 1990*, Oxford, Oxford University Press, 244-255.

Gordon, Richard K., Jr (1988), 'Income Tax Compliance and Sanctions in Developing Countries: An Outline of Issues', **42(1)** *Bulletin for International Fiscal Documentation*, 3-12.

Gottlieb, Daniel (1985), 'Tax Evasion and the Prisoner's Dilemma', **10(1)** *Mathematical Social Sciences*, 81-89.

Graetz, Michael J. and Wilde, Louis L. (1985), 'The Economics of Tax Compliance: Fact and Fantasy', **38** *National Tax Journal*, 335-363.

Graetz, Michael J. and Wilde, Louis L. (1993), 'The Decision by Strategic Nonfilers to Participate in Income Tax Amnesties', **13** *International Review of Law and Economics*, 271-283.

Graetz, Michael J., Reinganum, Jennifer F. and Wilde, Louis L. (1984), 'A Model of Tax Compliance with Budget-Constrained Auditors', Caltech Social Science Working Paper.

Graetz, Michael J., Reinganum, Jennifer F. and Wilde, Louis L. (1986), 'The Tax Compliance Game: Toward an Interactive Theory of Law Enforcement', **2** *Journal of Law, Economics, and Organization*, 1-32.

Graetz, Michael J., Reinganum, Jennifer F. and Wilde, Louis L. (1989), 'Expert Opinions and Taxpayer Compliance: A Strategic Analysis', Caltech Social Science Working Paper.

Green, Susan (1992), *Schedule D Non-Compliance: Would an Amnesty Help?*, University of Bristol Discussion Paper, No. 92/334.

Greenberg, Joseph (1984), 'Avoiding Tax Avoidance: A (Repeated) Game Theoretic Approach', **32(1)** *Journal of Economic Theory*, 1-13.

Greenfield, Harry I. (1993), *Invisible, Outlawed, and Untaxed: America's Underground Economy*, Westport, Praeger, 137 p.

Greenspan, Edward L. (1988), *Tax Evasion is a Crime!*, Canadian Tax Foundation. Income Tax Enforcement, Compliance, and Administration: Corporate Management Tax Conference, Toronto, Author.

Groenland, Edward A.G. (1992), 'Developing a Dynamic Research Strategy for the Economic Psychological Study of Taxation', **13** *Journal of Economic Psychology*, 589-596.

Gros, Daniel (1990), 'Tax Evasion and Offshore Centres', in Siebert, Horst (ed.), *Reforming Capital Income Taxation. Symposien und Konferenzbande Series*, Tübingen, Mohr, 113-127.

Hagemann, Robert P. (1990), 'Tax Evasion and Offshore Centres: Comment', in Siebert, Horst (ed.), *Reforming capital income taxation. Symposien und Konferenzbande series*, Tübingen, Mohr, 128-131.

Hansson, Ingemar (1985), 'Tax Evasion and Government Policy', in Gaertner, Wulf and Wenig, Alois (eds), *The Economics of the Shadow Economy: Proceedings of th International Conference on the Economics of the Shadow Economy Held at the University of Bielefeld, West Germany, October 10-14, 1983*, Berlin, Springer, 285-300.

Hansson, Ingemar (1989), 'The Underground Economy in Sweden', in Feige, Edgar L. (ed.), *The Underground Economies: Tax Evasion and Information Distortion*, Cambridge, Cambridge University Press, 219-236.

Harris, David et al. (1991), *Income Shifting in U.S. Multinational Corporations*, National Bureau of Economic Research Working Paper, No. 3924.

Harriss, C. Lowell (1994), 'An Address on Land Taxation as an Evasion-Proof Revenue Source', **53** *American Journal of Economics and Sociology*, 97-98.

Hasseldine, D. John and Bebbington, K. Jan (1991), 'Blending Economic Deterrence and Fiscal Psychology Models in the Design of Responses to Tax Evasion: The New Zealand Experience', **12** *Journal of Economic Psychology*, 299-324.

Hasseldine, D. John and Kaplan, Steven E. (1992), 'The Effect of Different Sanction Communications on Hypothetical Taxpayer Compliance: Policy Implications from New Zealand', **47** *Public Finance*, 45-60.

Hepburn, Glen (1992), 'Estimates of Cash-Based Income Tax Evasion in Australia', **0(2)** *Australian Economic Review*, 54-62.

Herschel, Federico J. (1978), 'Tax Evasion and Its Measurement in Developing Countries', **33** *Public Finance*, 232-268.

Hessing, Dick J. et al. (1988), 'Tax Evasion Research: Measurement Strategies and Theoretical Models', in van Raaij, W. Fred, van Veldhoven, Gery M., Warneryd, Karl Erik (eds), *Handbook of Economic Psychology*, Dordrecht, Kluwer Academic Publishers, 517-537.

Hessing, Dick J. et al. (1992), 'Does Deterrence Deter? Measuring the Effect of Deterrence on Tax Compliance in Field Studies and Experimental Studies', in Slemrod, Joel (ed.), *Why People Pay Taxes: Tax Compliance and Enforcement*, Ann Arbor, University of Michigan Press, 291-305.

Hessing, Dick J., Elffers, Henk and Weigel, Russell H. (1988), 'Research in Tax Resistance: An Integrative Theoretical Scheme for Tax Evasion Behavior', in Maital, Shlomo (ed.), *Applied Behavioural Economics Volume 2*, New York, New York University Press, 568-576.

Hey, John D. and Lambert, Peter J. (eds) (1987), *Surveys in the Economics of Uncertainty*, Oxford, Blackwell, 232 p.

Hindriks, J. (1994), *On the Equity-Compliance Tradeoff*, mimeo, University of Namur.

Hindriks, J., Keen, M. and Muthoo, A. (1996), *Corruption, Extortion and Evasion*, mimeo, University of Essex.

Hines, James R., Jr (1990), *The Flight Paths of Migratory Corporations*, John M. Olin Program for the Study of Economic Organization and Public Policy, No. 65.

Hite, Peggy A. (1990), 'An Experimental Investigation of the Effects of Tax Shelters on Taxpayer Noncompliance', **45** *Public Finance*, 90-108.

Holland, Daniel M. (1984), 'Measuring and Combatting Income Tax Evasion', in Hanusch, Horst (ed.), *Public Finance and the Quest for Efficiency: Proceedings of the 38th Congress of the International Institute of Public Finance, Copenhagen*, Detroit, Wayne State University Press, 329-348.

Holland, Daniel M. (1991), 'Property Taxes: Section Postscript', in Bahl, Roy (ed.), *The Jamaican Tax Reform*, Cambridge, MA, Lincoln Institute of Land Policy, 673-676.

Hunter, William C. (1992), 'Cheating the Government: The Economics of Evasion: Review Essay', **77** *Federal Reserve Bank of Atlanta Economic Review*, 35-41.

Hunter, William J. and Nelson, Michael A. (1995), 'Tax Enforcement: A Public Choice Perspective', **82** *Public Choice*, 53-67.

Inhaber, Herbert and Carroll, Sidney (1992), *How Rich is too Rich? Income and Wealth in America*, Westport, Praeger, 252 p.

International Fiscal Association (ed.) (1989), *Administrative and Compliance Costs of Taxation*, Deventer, Kluwer, 650 p.

Isachsen, Arne Jon and Ström, Steinar (1980), 'The Hidden Economy: The Labor Market and Tax Evasion', **82** *Scandinavian Journal of Economics*, 304-311.

Isachsen, Arne Jon and Ström, Steinar (1981), *Skattefritt. Svart Sektor i Vekst* (Taxfree. The Growth of the Black Sector), Oslo, Universitetsforlaget.

Isachsen, Arne Jon and Strom, Steinar (1989), 'The Hidden Economy in Norway with Special Emphasis on the Hidden Labor Market', in Feige, Edgar L. (ed.), *The Underground Economies: Tax Evasion and Information Distortion*, Cambridge, Cambridge University Press, 251-265.

Isachsen, Arne Jon, Samuelson, S.S. and Strom, Steinar (1985), 'The Behavior of Tax Evaders', in Gaertner, Wulf and Wenig, Alois (eds), *The Economics of the Shadow Economy: Proceedings of the International Conference on the Economics of the Shadow Economy Held at the University of Bielefeld, West Germany, October 10-14, 1983*, Berlin, Springer.

Ishi, Hiromitsu (1984), 'International Tax Evasion and Avoidance in Japan', **25(1)** *Hitotsubashi Journal of Economics*, 276-294.

Jain, Anil Kumar (1972), 'The Problem of Income Tax Evasion in India', **26(7)** *Bulletin for International Fiscal Documentation*, 276-294.

Jensen, Richard, Toma, Eugenia Froedge and Toma, Mark (1994), 'Privatization of Tax Collection and the Time-Consistency Problem', **49** *Public Finance*, 57-71.

Jepsen, Gunnar Thorlund (1991a), *Wage Contracts and Design of Tax Enforcement Policy in the Shadow Economy*, Aarhus Institute of Economics Memo, No. 1991-21.

Jepsen, Gunnar Thorlund (1991b), *How to Close 'The Gap'? Wage Contracts and Design of Tax Enforcement Policy in the Shadow Economy*, Aarhus Institute of Economics Memo, No. 1991-14.

Jepsen, Gunner Thorlund (1992), *Measuring the Tax Evaders' Aversion Against Evading: An Introduction to an Empirical Research*, Aarhus Institute of Economics Memo, No. 1991-7.

Jepsen, Gunnar Thorlund (1994), *Is There Aversion Against Moonlighting?*, Aarhus Institute of Economics Memo, No. 1991-19.

Jonathan, R. Kesselman (1988), *Income Tax Evasion in General Equilibrium*, University of British Columbia Department of Economics Discussion Paper, No. 88-03.

Jou, Jyh Bang (1992), *Income Tax Evasion: Theory and Empirical Evidence from the U.S. State-Level Data, Tax Year 1976-1989*, University of Chicago, Ph.D. 1992.

Jung, Young Heon (1992), *Contributions to the Economic Theory of Tax Evasion*, University of Georgia, Ph.D. 1992.

Jung, Young H., Snow, Arthur and Trandel, Gregory A. (1994), 'Tax Evasion and the Size of the Underground Economy', **54(3)** *Journal of Public Economics*, 391-402.

Kagan, Robert A. (1989), 'On the Visibility of Income Tax Violations', in Roth, Jeffrey A. and Scholz, John T. (eds), *Taxpayer Compliance*, Philadelphia, University of Pennsylvania Press.

Kamdar, Nipoli (1993), *Essays on Tax Compliance*, Syracuse University, Ph.D.

Kamdar, Nipoli (1995), 'Information Reporting and Tax Compliance: An Investigation Using Individual TCMP Data', **23** *Atlantic Economic Journal*, 278-292.

Kaplan, Richard L. (1989), 'Perspectives on International Tax Compliance and Enforcement: Transfer Pricing in the United States', **6** *Australian Tax Forum*, 423-454.

Kaplan, Steven E. and Reckers, Philip M.J. (1985), 'A Study of Tax Evasion Judgments', **38** *National Tax Journal*, 97-102.

Kaplow, Louis (1989), *The Optimal Probability and Magnitude of Fines for Acts that are Definitely Undesirable*, National Bureau of Economic Research Working Paper, No. 3008.

Kaplow, Louis (1990), 'Optimal Taxation with Costly Enforcement and Evasion', **43** *Journal of Public Economics*, 221-236.

Kaplow, Louis (1995), 'A Model of the Optimal Complexity of Legal Rules', **11** *Journal of Law, Economics, and Organization*, 150-163.

Kaplow, Louis (1996), 'How Tax Complexity and Enforcement Affect the Equity and Efficiency of the Income Tax', **49** *National Tax Journal*, 135-150.

Karayannis, Marios (1991), *Tax Evasion, Portfolio Choice, and the Allocation of Capital in the U.S. Economy*, University of Virginia, Ph.D.

Karoly, Lynn A. (1994), 'Review of: How Rich is too Rich? Income and Wealth in America', **32** *Journal of Economic Literature*, 130-131.

Kazemier, Brugt and van Eck, Rob (1992), 'Survey Investigations of the Hidden Economy: Some Methodological Results', **13** *Journal of Economic Psychology*, 569-587.

Kelsey, David and Schepanski, Al (1988), *Testing for Regret and Disappointment in Tax Compliance Decisions*, University of Cambridge Economic Theory Discussion Paper, No. 124.

Kemp, Robert, Reckers, Philip M.J. and Arrington, C. Edward (1986), 'U.S. Tax Reform: Tax Evasion Concerns', **21** *Business Economics*, 55-57.

Kesselman, Jonathan R. (1986), *Evasion of Taxes in General Equilibrium*, University of British Columbia Department of Economics Discussion Paper, No. 86-45.

Kesselman, Jonathan R. (1989), 'Income Tax Evasion: An Intersectoral Analysis', **38** *Journal of Public Economics*, 137-182.

Kesselman, Jonathan R. (1993a), *Compliance, Enforcement, and Administrative Factors in Improving Tax Fairness*, University of British Columbia Department of Economics Discussion Paper, No. 93-45.

Kesselman, Jonathan R. (1993b), 'Evasion Effects of Changing the Tax Mix', **69** *Economic Record*, 131-148.

Kim, Chungkweon (1994), *The Effects of Public Transfers and Tax Rate Changes on Reported Income: Experimental Evidence*, University of Pittsburgh, Ph.D.

Kinsey, Karyl A. (1992), 'Deterrence and Alienation Effects of IRS Enforcement: An Analysis of Survey Data', in Slemrod, Joel (ed.), *Why People Pay Taxes: Tax Compliance and Enforcement*, Ann Arbor, University of Michigan Press, 259-285.

Klepper, Stephen and Nagin, Daniel (1989a), 'The Criminal Deterrence Literature: Implications for Research on Taxpayer Compliance', in Roth, Jeffrey A. and Scholz, John T. (eds), *Taxpayer Compliance*, Philadelphia, University of Pennsylvania Press.

Klepper, Steven and Nagin, Daniel (1989b), 'The Role of Tax Preparers in Tax Compliance', **22** *Policy Sciences*, 167-194.

Klepper, Steven, Mazur, Mark and Nagin, Daniel S. (1991), 'Expert Intermediaries and Legal Compliance: The Case of Tax Preparers', **34** *Journal of Law and Economics*, 205-229.

Klepper, Steven, Nagin, Daniel and Spurr, Stephen (1991), 'Tax Rates, Tax Compliance, and the Reporting of Long-Term Capital Gains', **46** *Public Finance*, 236-251.

Klovland, Jan Tore (1984), 'Tax Evasion and the Demand for Currency in Norway and Sweden. Is There a Hidden Relationship?', **86** *Scandinavian Journal of Economics*, 423-439.

Kolm, Serge Christophe (1973), 'A Note on Optimum Tax Evasion', **2** *Journal of Public Economics*, 265-270.

Kong, Randolph (1988), 'Cooperative Approaches among Tax Administrations to Prevent and Counteract International Tax Evasion and Avoidance: Trinidad and Tabago', **42** *Bulletin for International Fiscal Documentation*, 526-530.

Koskela, Erkki (1983), 'On the Shape of Tax Schedule, the Probability of Detection, and the Penalty Schemes as Deterrents to Tax Evasion', **38** *Public Finance*, 70-80.

Koskela, Erkki (1983), 'A Note on Progression, Penalty Schemes and Tax Evasion', **22** *Journal of Public Economics*, 127-133.

Kreutzer, David and Lee, Dwight R. (1988), 'Tax Evasion and Monopoly Output Decisions: A Reply', **41** *National Tax Journal*, 583-584.

Krupsky, Kenneth J. (1992), 'IRS Access to Foreign Transfer Pricing Information: United States', **46** *Bulletin for International Fiscal Documentation*, 113-118.

Kuboniwa, Masaaki (1995), 'From Upward to Downward Bias of the Russian Output Statistics. (In Japanese, with English summary)', **46** *Economic Review (Keizai Kenkyu)*, 289-302.

Laban, Raul and Sturzenegger, Federico (1992), 'La Economia Politica de los Programas de Estabilizacion (The Political Economy of Stabilization Programs. With English summary)', **0(36)** *Coleccion Estudios CIEPLAN*, 41-66.

Lai, Ching Chong (1991), 'The Effect of Tax Evasion on Tax Collections: The Implication of the Cebula Model', **38** *Rivista Internazionale di Scienze Economiche e Commerciali*, 639-647.

Lai, Ching Chong and Chang, Wen Ya (1988), 'Tax Evasion and Tax Collections: An Aggregate Demand-Aggregate Supply Analysis', **43** *Public Finance*, 138-146.

Landsberger, Michael and Meilijson, Isaac (1982), 'Incentive Generating State Dependent Penalty System: The Case of Income Tax Evasion', **19** *Journal of Public Economics*, 333-352.

Landskroner, Yoram, Muller, Eitan and Swary, Itzhak (1991), 'Tax Evasion and Financial Equilibrium', **43** *Journal of Economics and Business*, 25-35.

Landskroner, Yoram, Paroush, J. and Swary, Itzhak (1990), 'Tax Evasion and Portfolio Decisions', **45** *Public Finance*, 409-422.

Langfeldt, Enno (1989), 'The Underground Economy in the Federal Republic of Germany: A Preliminary Assessment', in Feige, Edgar L. (ed.), *The Underground Economies: Tax Evasion and Information Distortion*, Cambridge, Cambridge University Press, 197-217.

Lazos, Vaios (1996), 'E Kambyle Adiaforias enos Eglematos (The Indifference Curve of a Crime)', **6** *Aissymnetes*.

Lemieux, Thomas, Fortin, Bernard and Frechette, Pierre (1994), 'The Effect of Taxes on Labor Supply in the Underground Economy', **84** *American Economic Review*, 231-254.

Lempert, Richard (1992), 'Reciprocity and Fairness: Positive Incentives for Tax Compliance: Commentary', in Slemrod, Joel (ed.), *Why People Pay Taxes: Tax Compliance and Enforcement*, Ann Arbor, University of Michigan Press, 251-257.

Leonard, Herman B. and Zeckhauser, Richard J. (1986), *Amnesty, Enforcement and Tax Policy*, National Bureau of Economic Research Working Paper, No. 2096.

Lewis, A. (1979), 'An Empirical Assessment of Tax Mentality', **43** *Public Finance/Finances Publiques*, 245-257.

Lindholm, Richard W. (1986), *Examination of Basic Weaknesses of Income as the Major Federal Tax Base*, New York, Greenwood Press, 320 p.

Long, Susan B. (1992), 'The Influence of Tax Audits on Reporting Behavior: Commentary', in Slemrod, Joel (ed.), *Why People Pay Taxes: Tax Compliance and Enforcement*, Ann Arbor, University of Michigan Press, 115-123.

Lovely, Mary E. (1994), 'Crossing the Border: Does Commodity Tax Evasion Reduce Welfare and Can Enforcement Improve It?', **27** *Canadian Journal of Economics*, 157-174.

Lugaresi, Sergio and Di Nicola, Fernando (1991), *Tax Policy and Income Redistribution in Italy*, London School of Economics Suntory Toyota International Centre for Economics and Related Disciplines Working Paper, No. TIDI/152.

Lyttkens, Carl Hampus (1992), 'Effects of the Taxation of Wealth in Athens in the Fourth Century B.C.', **40** *Scandinavian Economic History Review*, 3-20.

Macho-Stadler, I. and Pérez-Castrillo, J. David (1994), *Random Audits in Tax Evasion Models*, W.P. UAB-IAE, No. 287.94.

Macho-Stadler, I. and Pérez-Castrillo, J. David (1996), 'Optimal Tax Auditing when Some Individuals Need Not File', *Economic Design*, forthcoming.

Macho-Stadler, I. and Pérez-Castrillo, J. David (1997), 'Optimal Auditing Policy with Heterogeneous Incomes Sources', **38** *International Economic Review*.

Macho-Stadler, I., Olivella-Cunill, P. and Pérez-Castillo, J. David (1993), *Tax Amnesties in a Dynamic Model of Tax Evasion*, W.P. UAB-IAE, No. 247.94.

MacKie Mason, Jeffrey K. (1992), 'The Corporate Tax Gap: Evidence on Tax Compliance by Small Corporations: Commentary', in Slemrod, Joel (ed.), *Why People Pay Taxes: Tax Compliance and Enforcement*, Ann Arbor, University of Michigan Press, 162-166.

Madeo, Silvia A. (1992), 'How Taxpayers Think about Their Taxes: Frames and Values: Commentary', in Slemrod, Joel (ed.), *Why People Pay Taxes: Tax Compliance and Enforcement*, Ann Arbor, University of Michigan Press, 64-66.

Madeo, Silvia A., Schepanski, Albert and Uecker, Wilfred C. (1987), 'Modeling Judgments of Taxpayer Compliance', **62** *Accounting Review*, 323-342.

Maital, Shlomo (1988), *Applied Behavioural Economics. 2 vols*, New York, New York University Press, 831 p.

Malik, Arun S. (1990), 'Avoidance, Screening and Optimum Enforcement', **21** *Rand Journal of Economics*, 341-353.

Malik, Arun S., and Schwab, R. (1991), 'The Economics of Tax Amnesties', **46** *Journal of Public Economics*, 29-49.

Mann, Arthur J. and Smith, Robert (1988), 'Tax Attitudes and Tax Evasion in Puerto Rico: A Survey of Upper Income Professionals', **13** *Journal of Economic Development*, 121-141.

Marhuenda, F. and Ortuno-Ortin, I. (1994), *Honesty versus Progressiveness in Income Tax Enforcement Problems*, University of Alicante WP, No. 94-06.

Marrelli, Massimo (1984), 'On Indirect Tax Evasion', **25** *Journal of Public Economics*, 181-196.

Marrelli, M. (1987), 'The Economic Analysis of Tax Evasion: Empirical Aspects', in Hey, John D. and Lambert, Peter J. (eds), *Surveys in the Economics of Uncertainty*, Oxford, Blackwell, 204-228.

Marrelli, Massimo and Martina, Riccardo (1988), 'Tax Evasion and Strategic Behaviour of the Firms', **37** *Journal of Public Economics*, 55-69.

Martinez Vazquez, Jorge, Harwood, Gordon B. and Larkins, Ernest R. (1992), 'Withholding Position and Income Tax Compliance: Some Experimental Evidence', **20** *Public Finance Quarterly*, 152-174.

Mason, Robert and Calvin, Lyle D. (1984), 'Public Confidence and Admitted Tax Evasion', **37** *National Tax Journal*, 489-496.

McBarnet, Doreen (1992), 'The Construction of Compliance and the Challenge for Control: The Limits of Noncompliance Research', in Slemrod, Joel (ed.), *Why People Pay Taxes: Tax Compliance and Enforcement*, Ann Arbor, University of Michigan Press, 333-345.

McCaleb, Thomas S. (1976), 'Tax Evasion and the Differential Taxation of Labor and Capital Income', **31** *Public Finance*, 287-294.

McCracken, Gerald H. (1988), *Preventing Tax Evasion through Enforcement: The Government Perspective*, Canadian Tax Foundation. Income Tax Enforcement, Compliance, and Administration: Corporate Management Tax Conference.

McGee, Robert W. (1994), 'Is Tax Evasion Unethical?', **42(2)** *University of Kansas Law Review*, 411-435.

McGee, Robert W. (1996a), *Taxation, Ethics and Public Policy*, Dumont Institute for Public Policy Research. <<http:// ww.hili.com~dumontin>>

McGee, Robert W. (1996b), *Essays on Accounting,Taxation and Public Finance*, Dumont Institute for Public Policy Research.

McGee, Robert W. and Feige, Edgar L. (1989), 'Policy Illusion, Macroeconomic Instability, and the Unrecorded Economy', in Feige, Edgar L. (ed.), *The Underground Economies: Tax Evasion and Information Distortion*, Cambridge, Cambridge University Press, 81-109.

Mehta, Shekhar (1990), *Evasion of State Taxes in India*, New Delhi, Criterion.

Melumad, Nahum D. and Mookherjee, D. (1989), 'Delegation as Commitment: The Case of Income Tax Audits', **104(2)** *Rand Journal of Economics*, 399-415.

Mintz, Jack M. and Seade, Jesus (1991), 'Cash Flow or Income? The Choice of Base for Company Taxation', **6** *World Bank Research Observer*, 177-190.

Mirus, Rolf and Smith, Roger S. (1989), 'Canada's Underground Economy', in Feige, Edgar L. (ed.), *The Underground Economies: Tax Evasion and Information Distortion*, Cambridge, Cambridge University Press, 267-280.

Mookherjee, D. and Png, Ivan Paak-Liang (1989), 'Optimal Auditing, Insurance and Redistribution', **20(2)** *Quarterly Journal of Economics*, 139-163.

Mork, Knut Anton (1975), 'Income Tax Evasion: Some Empirical Evidence', **30** *Public Finance*, 70-76.

Moser, Donald V., Evans, John H., III and Kim, Chung K. (1995), 'The Effects of Horizontal and Exchange Inequity on Tax Reporting Decisions', **70** *Accounting Review*, 619-634.

Mtatifikolo, Fidelis P. (1990), 'An Economic Analysis of Tanzania's Tax Performance Experiences since the 1973 Tax Act', **6** *Eastern Africa Economic Review*, 55-67.

Mullin, Ronald David (1993), *Enhancing Taxpayer Compliance: Experimental Evidence on Alternative Policies*, University of Virginia, Ph.D.

Murray, Matthew N. (1986), *A Theoretical and Empirical Analysis of Tax Evasion and Tax Avoidance*, Syracuse University, Ph.D.

Murray, Matthew N. (1995), 'Sales Tax Compliance and Audit Selection', **48** *National Tax Journal*, 515-530.

Myles, G. and Naylor, R. (1996), 'A Model of Tax Evasion with Group Conformity and Social Customs', **12** *European Journal of Political Economy*, 49-66.

Nagin, Daniel (1992), 'The Construction of Compliance and the Challenge for Control: The Limits of Noncompliance Research: Commentary', in Slemrod, Joel (ed.), *Why People Pay Taxes: Tax Compliance and Enforcement*, Ann Arbor, University of Michigan Press, 346-348.

Nayak, P.B. (1978), 'Optimal Income Tax Evasion and Regressive Taxes', **33** *Public Finance*, 358-366.

Nguyen, Trien T. (1989), 'The Parallel Market of Illegal Aliens: A Computational Approach', **17** *World Development*, 1965-1978.

Nitzan, Shmuel and Tzur, Joseph (1987), *Taxpayers, Auditors and the Government - an Extended Tax Evasion Game*, Universitat Bonn Sonderforschungsbereich 303 Discussion Paper, No. A-105.

O'Higgins, Michael (1989), 'Assessing the Underground Economy in the United Kingdom', in Feige, Edgar L. (ed.), *The Underground Economies: Tax Evasion and Information Distortion*, Cambridge, Cambridge University Press, 175-195.

OECD (1990), *Taxpayers' Rights and Obligations*, Paris, OECD.

OKeeffe, Mary (1986), *Audit Strategies with Heterogeneous Agents: Is Efficient Deterrence Compatible with Efficient Detection?*, Harvard Kennedy School of Government Discussion Paper, No. 145D.

Olivella, P. (1992a), 'Un Estudio de la Evasion Fiscal desde la Perspectiva de las Relaciones Principal-Agente (A Principal-Agent Approach of Tax Evasion)', **9(2)** *Revista Española de Economía.*

Olivella, P. (1992b), *Las Amnistias Fiscales: Descripcion y Analisis Economico* (Economic analysis of Tax Amnesties), Universitat Autonoma de Barcelona.

Olivella, P. (1996), *Tax Amnesties and Tax Evasion Inertia*, Universitat Autonoma de Barcelona.

Panagariya, Arvind and Narayana, A.V.L. (1988), 'Excise Tax Evasion: A Welfare cum Crime Theoretic Analysis', **43** *Public Finance*, 248-260.

Panagariya, Arvind and Narayana, A.V.L. (1989), 'Excise Tax Evasion: Reply', **44** *Public Finance*, 510-512.

Pandit, V. and Sundaram, K. (1977), 'Aggregate Demand under Conditions of Tax Evasion', **32** *Public Finance*, 333-342.

Parikh, Parimal M. (1986), 'India: Is Tax Avoidance Merging into Tax Evasion? A Change in the Judiciaries' Approach to Tax Avoidance', **40(1)** *Bulletin for International Fiscal Documentation*, 11-14.

Pasha, Hafiz A. (1993), 'Tax Audit Schemes in Pakistan and the Level of Income Declaration', **38** *Singapore Economic Review*, 167-184.

Pastor, Santos (1995), 'Qué Hacer en los Conflictos Fiscales? Un Análisis Económico de las Propuestas de Actas de Conformidad (The Resolution of Tax Disputes)', *Hacienda Pública Española*, 225-244.

Peacock, Alan and Shaw, G.K. (1982), 'Tax Evasion and Tax Revenue Loss', **37** *Public Finance*, 269-278.

Pencavel, John H. (1979), 'A Note on Income Tax Evasion, Labor Supply, and Nonlinear Tax Schedules', **12** *Journal of Public Economics*, 115-124.

Persson, Mats and Wissen, Pehr (1984), 'Redistributional Aspects of Tax Evasion', **86** *Scandinavian Journal of Economics*, 131-149.

Persson, Mats and Wissen, Pehr (1985), 'Redistributional Aspects of Tax Evasion', in Forsund, Finn R. and Honkapohja, Seppo (eds), *Limits and Problems of Taxation*, New York, St. Martin's Press, 33-51.

Pestieau, Pierre and Possen, Uri M. (1991), 'Tax Evasion and Occupational Choice', **45** *Journal of Public Economics*, 107-125.

Pestieau, Pierre, Possen, Uri M. and Slutsky, Steve (1994a), 'Optimal Differential Taxes and Penalties', **49(Suppl)** *Public Finance*, 15-27.

Pestieau, Pierre, Possen, Uri M. and Slutsky, Steven M. (1994b), *The Penalty for Tax Evasion When Taxes are Set Optimally*, Universite Catholique de Louvain CORE Discussion Paper, No. 9416.

Peters, B. Guy (1991), *The Politics of Taxation: A Comparative Perspective*, Oxford, Blackwell, 338 p.

Pitt, Mark M. and Slemrod, Joel (1989), 'The Compliance Cost of Itemizing Deductions: Evidence from Individual Tax Returns', **79** *American Economic Review*, 1224-1232.

Plumley, Alan H. (1992), 'Deterrence and Alienation Effects of IRS Enforcement: An Analysis of Survey Data: Commentary', in Slemrod, Joel (ed.), *Why People Pay Taxes: Tax Compliance and Enforcement*, Ann Arbor, University of Michigan Press, 286-290.

Png, Ivan Paak-Liang (1987), 'Litigation, Liability, and Incentives for Care', **34** *Journal of Public Economics*, 61-85.

Pommerehne, Werner W. (1983), 'Steuerhinterziehung und Schwarzarbeit als Grenzen der Staatstatigkeit (Tax Evasion and Underground Activities as Limits of Government's Growth)', **119** *Schweizerische Zeitschrift für Volkswirtschaft und Statistik*, 261-284.

Pommerehne, Werner W. and Zweifel, Peter (1991), 'Success of a Tax Amnesty: At the Polls, for the FISC?', **72** *Public Choice*, 131-165.

Pommerehne, Werner W., Hart, Albert and Frey, Bruno S. (1994), 'Tax Morale, Tax Evasion and the Choice of Policy Instruments in Different Political Systems', **49(Suppl)** *Public Finance*, 52-69.

Pope, Jeff (1994), 'Compliance Costs of Taxation: Policy Implications', **11** *Australian Tax Forum*, 85-121.

Pope, Jeff and Fayle, Richard (1991), 'The Compliance Costs of Public Companies' Income Taxation in Australia 1986/87: Empirical Results', **8** *Australian Tax Forum*, 485-538.

Porcano, Thomas M. (1988), 'Correlates of Tax Evasion', **9** *Journal of Economic Psychology*, 47-67.

Porter, Richard D. and Bayer, Amanda S. (1989), 'Monetary Perspective on Underground Economic Activity in the United States', in Feige, Edgar L. (ed.), *The Underground Economies: Tax Evasion and Information Distortion*, Cambridge, Cambridge University Press, 129-157.

Poterba, James M. (1987), 'Tax Evasion and Capital Gains Taxation', **77** *American Economic Review*, 234-239.

Prebble, Mark (1990), 'Tax Compliance and the Use of Tax Information', **7** *Australian Tax Forum*, 207-216.

Pyle, David J. (1989), *Tax Evasion and the Black Economy*, New York, St. Martin's Press, 212 p.

Pyle, D.J. (1991), 'The Economics of Taxpayer Compliance', **5** *Journal of Economic Surveys*, 163-198.

Pyle, D.J. (1992), 'The Economics of Taxpayer Compliance', in Jackson, Peter M. (ed.), *Current Issues in Public Sector Economics*, New York, St. Martin's Press, 58-93.

Raikhy, P.S. and Gill, Sucha Singh (1988), *Resource Mobilisation and Economic Development: A Regional Perspective*, Amritsar, India, Guru Nanak Dev University, Punjab School of Economics, 227 p.

Rao, J. Mohan (1987), 'Class Relations in an "Asiatic" Regime', **11** *Cambridge Journal of Economics*, 229-250.

Reckers, Philip M.J., Sanders, Debra L. and Roark, Stephen J. (1994), 'The Influence of Ethical Attitudes on Taxpayer Compliance', **47** *National Tax Journal*, 825-836.

Reinganum, Jennifer F. (1984), *Sequential Equilibrium Detection and Reporting Policies in a Model of Tax Evasion*, Caltech Social Science Working Paper, No. 525.

Reinganum, Jennifer F. and Wilde, Louis L. (1985), 'Income Tax Compliance in a Principal-Agent Framework', **26** *Journal of Public Economics*, 1-18.

Reinganum, Jennifer F. and Wilde, Louis L. (1986), 'Equilibrium Verification and Reporting Policies in a Model of Tax Compliance', *International Economic Review*, 739-760.

Reinganum, Jennifer F. and Wilde, Louis L. (1991), 'Equilibrium Enforcement and Compliance in the Presence of Tax Practitioners', **7** *Journal of Law, Economics, and Organization*, 163-181.

Rice, Eric M. (1990), *Skirting the Law: Essays on Corporate Tax Evasion and Avoidance*, Harvard University, Ph.D.

Rice, Eric M. (1992), 'The Corporate Tax Gap: Evidence on Tax Compliance by Small Corporations', in Slemrod, Joel (ed.), *Why People Pay Taxes: Tax Compliance and Enforcement*, Ann Arbor, University of Michigan Press, 125-161.

Richupan, Somchai (1984), 'Measuring Tax Evasion', **21(4)** *Finance and Development*, 38-40.

Rickard, J.A., Russell, A.M. and Howroyd, T.D. (1982), 'A Tax Evasion Model with Allowance for Retroactive Penalties', **58** *Economic Record*, 379-385.

Ricketts, Martin (1984), 'On the Simple Macroeconomics of Tax Evasion: An Elaboration of the Peacock-Shaw Approach', **39** *Public Finance*, 420-424.

Robben, Henry S.J. et al. (1989), 'A Cross-National Comparison of Attitudes, Personality, Behaviour, and Social Comparison in Tax Evasion Experiments', in Grunert, Klaus-G. and Olander, Folke (eds), *Understanding Economic Behaviour. Theory and Decision Library Series A: Philosophy and Methodology of the Social Sciences, vol. 11*, Dordrecht, Kluwer Academic Publishers, 121-134.

Robben, Henry S.J. et al. (1990a), 'Decision Frame and Opportunity as Determinants of Tax Cheating: An International Experimental Study', **11** *Journal of Economic Psychology*, 341-364.

Robben, Henry S.J. et. al. (1990b), 'Decision Frames, Opportunity and Tax Evasion: An Experimental Approach', **14** *Journal of Economic Behavior and Organization*, 353-361.

Roberts, Michael L. and Englebrecht, Ted D. (1992), 'Potential Application of Civil Tax Penalties for Undervaluation of Assets: Evidence and Policy Analysis', in Stern, Jerrold J. (ed.), *Advances in Taxation. Volume 4*, Greenwich, CT, JAI Press, 211-223.

Roth, J., Scholtz, J. and Witt A. (1989), *Taxpayer Compliance: An Agenda for Research. Vol. 1*, Philadelphia, University of Pennsylvania Press.

Roubini, Nouriel and Sala i Martin, Xavier (1995), 'A Growth Model of Inflation, Tax Evasion, and Financial Repression', **35** *Journal of Monetary Economics*, 275-301.

Ruesca, Santos M. (1982), 'La Economía Irregular en el Mercado de Trabajo (Irregular Economy in the Labour Market)', **587** *Información Comercial Española*, 91-102.

Ruesca, Santos M. (1986), 'Economía Oculta: de la Definición y los Métodos de Estimación (Underground Economy: Definition and Estimation Methods)', in X (ed.), *Problemas Estadísiticos de la Economía Sumergida*, Madrid, Instituto Nacional de Estadística, 25-48.

Ruesca, Santos M. (1987), 'La Economía Sumergida en España (Underground Economy in Spain)', *Revista del Instituto de Estudios Económicos*.

Russell, A.M. and Rickard, J.A. (1987), 'A Model of Tax Evasion Incorporating Income Variation and Retroactive Penalities', **26** *Australian Economic Papers*, 254-264.

Saltzman, L., Paternoster, R., Waldo, G. and Chiricos, T. (1982), 'Deterrent and Experiental Effects: the Problem of Causal Order in Percepual Deterrence Research', **19** *Journal of Research on Crime and Delinquency*, 172-189.

Samuelson, Paul A. (1954), 'The Pure Theory of Public Expenditure', **36** *Review of Economic Statistics*, 387-389.

Sanchez, Isabel (1990), 'Evasión Fiscal, Regulación y Mecanismos Óptimos de Inspección (Tax Evasion, Regulation, and Optimal Auditing Mechanisms)', **2** *Cuadernos Económicos de ICE*, 45 ff.

Sanchez, Isabel (1993), 'Hierarchical Design and Enforcement of Income Tax Policies', **50** *Journal of Public Economics*, 345-369.

Sanchez, Isabel (1994), *Determinantes Individuales de la Evasión Fiscal: un Enfoque Experimental* (Individual Determinants of Tax Evasion: an Experimental Approach), Monografía, Instituto de Estudios Fiscales.

Sanchez, Isabel (1995a), 'Unraveling the Puzzle of Tax Compliance Using Experimental Methods', **48** *Kyklos*, 3-18.

Sanchez, Isabel (1995b), 'Experimental Analysis of Individuals' Tax Compliance Rate', in de Juan, A. (ed.), *Frontiers in Economic Psychology, Proceedings of the IAREP Conference*, Agosto.

Sanchez, Isabel and Sobel, Joel (1993), 'Hierarchical Design and Enforcement of Income Tax Policies', **50(3)** *Journal of Public Economics*, 345-369.

Sandford, Cedric T. (1973), *Hidden Costs of Taxation*, Institute for Fiscal Studies, London.

Sandford, Cedric T. (1994), 'International Comparisons of Administrative and Compliance Costs of Taxation', **11** *Australian Tax Forum*, 291-309.

Sandford, Cedric T. (ed.) (1995a), *Tax Compliance Costs: Measurement and Policy*, Bath, Fiscal Publications, 413 p.

Sandford, Cedric T. (1995b), *More Key Issues in Tax Reform*, Bath, Fiscal Publications, 214 p.

Sandford, C., Goodwin, M., Hardwick, P. and Butterworth, M. (1981), *Costs and Benefits of VAT*, London, Heinemann Educational Books.

Sandford, C., Goodwin, M. and Hardwick, P. (1989), *Administrative and Compliance Costs of Taxation*, Bath, Fiscal Publications.

Sandmo, Agnar (1981), 'Income Tax Evasion, Labour Supply, and the Equity-Efficiency Tradeoff', **16** *Journal of Public Economics*, 265-288.

Sansing, Richard C. (1993), 'Information Acquisition in a Tax Compliance Game', **68** *Accounting Review*, 874-884.

Sawyer, Adrian J. (1994), 'New Zealand: Raising the Threshold for Taxpayer Compliance: A New Era of Compliance Standards and Penalties', **48** *Bulletin for International Fiscal Documentation*, 655-664.

Sawyer, Adrian J. (1995), 'Taxpayer Compliance Standards and Penalties: Version II Signifies Progress: New Zealand', **49** *Bulletin for International Fiscal Documentation*, 510-521.

Sawyer, Adrian J. (1996), 'Taxpayer Compliance, Penalties and Disputes Resolution Bill: An Update: New Zealand', **50** *Bulletin for International Fiscal Documentation*, 72-78.

Schenk, Karl-Ernst (1983), 'Second Economy und Wirtschaftsordnung - Ein sSstemübergreifender, Transaktionsökonomischer Erklärungsansatz (Second Economy and Economic Constitution. An Explanation Approach Encompassing Different Systems on the Basis of Transaction Economics mit A. Wass von Czege)', in Hedtkamp, G. (ed.), *Beiträge zum Problem der Schattenwirtschaft, Schriften des Vereins für Socialpolitik N.F., Bd. 132*, Berlin, 33-51.

Schjelderup, Guttorm (1993), 'Optimal Taxation, Capital Mobility and Tax Evasion', **95** *Scandinavian Journal of Economics*, 377-386.

Schmidtchen, Dieter (1994), 'Vom nichtmarginalen Charakter der Steuermoral (On the Non-marginal Character of Tax Morals)', in Smekal, Chr. And Theurl, E. (eds), *Stand und Entwicklung der Finanzpsychologie*, Baden-Baden, 185-211.

Schulze, Gunther G. (1994), 'Misinvoicing Imports: The Interdependence of Tax and Tariff Evasion', **22** *Public Finance Quarterly*, 335-365.

Schweizer, Urs (1984), 'Welfare Analysis of Excise Tax Evasion', **140** *Journal of Institutional and Theoretical Economics*, 247-258.

Scotchmer, Suzanne (1987), 'Audit Classes and Tax Enforcment Policy', **77** *American Economic Review*, 229-233.

Scotchmer, Suzanne (1989), 'Who Profits fromTaxpayer Confusion?', **29(1)** *Economic Letters*, 49-55.

Scotchmer, Suzanne (1992), 'The Regressive Bias in Tax Enforcement', **47(Suppl)** *Public Finance*, 366-371.

Scotchmer, Suzanne and Slemrod, Joel (1989), 'Randomness in Tax Enforcement', **38** *Journal of Public Economics*, 17-32.

Scott, W. and Grasmick, H. (1981), 'Deterrence and Income Tax Cheating: Testing Interaction Hypotheses in Utilitarian Theories', **17** *Journal of Applied Behavioral Science*, 395-408.

Sen, Tapas Kumar (1990), 'Sales Tax Evasion in India: Some Issues', **44** *Bulletin for International Fiscal Documentation*, 605-608.

Sengupta, Partha (1991), *Essays on the Theory of Tax Evasion*, Virginia Polytechnic Institute and State University, Ph.D.

Shea, Jia Dong and Wu, Jy Wen (1994), 'Tax Evasion, Anti-monitoring Activities and the Impacts of Government Policies (in Chinese, with English summary)', **22(1)** *Academia Economic Papers*, 81-100.

Sheffrin, Steven M. and Triest, Robert K. (1992), 'Can Brute Deterrence Backfire? Perceptions and Attitudes in Taxpayer Compliance', in Slemrod, Joel (ed.), *Why People Pay Taxes: Tax Compliance and Enforcement*, Ann Arbor, University of Michigan Press, 193-218.

Siebert, Horst (ed.) (1990), *Reforming Capital Income Taxation*, Tübingen, Mohr, 298 p.

Silvani, Carlos and Vehorn, Charles L. (1991), 'Invoices, Books of Account, and Tax Return Forms for VAT', in Tait, Alan A. (ed.), *Value Added Tax: Administrative and Policy Issues. Occasional Paper, no. 88*, Washington, International Monetary Fund, 40-48.

Simon, V.O. and Rao, D.N. (1993), 'Estimation of Leakages in Sales Tax Revenue of Delhi', **25(2)** *Margin*, 178-215.

Skinner, Jonathan and Slemrod, Joel (1985), 'An Economic Perspective on Tax Evasion', **38** *National Tax Journal*, 345-353.

Slemrod, Joel (1985), *The Return to Tax Simplification: An Econometric Analysis*, National Bureau of Economic Research Working Paper, No. 1756.

Slemrod, Joel (1989a), 'Are Estimated Tax Elasticities Really Just Tax Evasion Elasticities? The Case of Charitable Contributions', **71** *Review of Economics and Statistics*, 517-522.

Slemrod, Joel (1989b), *Optimal Taxation and Optimal Tax Systems*, National Bureau of Economic Research Working Paper, No. 3038.

Slemrod, Joel (1992a), 'Why People Pay Taxes: Introduction', in Slemrod, Joel (ed.), *Why People Pay Taxes: Tax Compliance and Enforcement*, Ann Arbor, University of Michigan Press, 1-8.

Slemrod, Joel (1992b), *Why People Pay Taxes: Tax Compliance and Enforcement*, Ann Arbor, University of Michigan Press, 361 p.

Slemrod, Joel and Yitzhaki, Shlomo (1998), 'Tax Avoidance, Evasion and Administration', in Auerbach, Alan and Feldstein, Martin (eds), *Handbook in Public Economics*, North-Holland, Amsterdam.

Slemrod, Joel B. (1985b), 'An Empirical Test for Tax Evasion', **67** *Review of Economics and Statistics*, 232-238.

Slemrod, Joel B. (1989c), 'Complexity, Compliance Costs, and Tax Evasion', in Roth, Jeffrey A. and Scholz, John T. (eds), *Taxpayer Compliance*, Philadelphia, University of Pennsylvania Press.

Smith, Andrew M.C. (1991), 'The Implications of the Commissioner's Statement on Section 99: New Zealand', **45** *Bulletin for International Fiscal Documentation*, 60-66.

Smith, Kent W. (1992), 'Reciprocity and Fairness: Positive Incentives for Tax Compliance', in Slemrod, Joel (ed.), *Why People Pay Taxes: Tax Compliance and Enforcement*, Ann Arbor, University of Michigan Press, 223-250.

Smith, Rodney T. (1976), 'The Legal and Illegal Markets for Taxed Goods: Pure Theory and Application to State Governement Taxation of Distilled Spirits', **19** *Journal of Law and Economics*, 393-429.

Snavely, Keith (1990), 'Governmental Policies to Reduce Tax Evasion: Coerced Behavior versus Services and Values Development', **23** *Policy Sciences*, 57-72.

Soldatos, Gerasimos T. (1994), 'An Analysis of the Conflict between Underground Economy and Tax Evasion', **213** *Jahrbuch für Nationalökonomie und Statistik*, 292-304.

Sommerhalder, Ruud A. and Elffers, Henk (1994), 'Compliance Effects of Some European Tax Reforms', **11** *Australian Tax Forum*, 185-202.

Son, Gwang Lag (1991), *A Model of Tax Compliance with Endogenous Probability of Audit*, University of Washington, Ph.D.

Spicer, Michael W. (1986), 'Civilization at a Discount: The Problem of Tax Evasion', **39** *National Tax Journal*, 13-20.

Spicer, Michael W. (1987), 'The Effect of Tax Evasion on Tax Rates under Leviathan', **40** *National Tax Journal*, 625-628.

Spicer, Michael W. (1990), 'On the Desirability of Tax Evasion: Conventional versus Constitutional Economic Perspectives', **45** *Public Finance*, 119-127.

Spicer, Michael W. and Becker, Lee A. (1980), 'Fiscal Inequity and Tax Evasion: An Experimental Approach', **33(2)** *National Tax Journal*, 171-175.

Spicer, Michael W. and Hero, Rodney E. (1985), 'Tax Evasion and Heuristics: A Research Note', **26** *Journal of Public Economics*, 263-267.

Spicer, M.W. and Lundstedt, S.B. (1976), 'Understanding Tax Evasion', **31** *Public Finance*, 295-305.

Spiro, Peter S. (1994), 'The Underground Economy: Toward a More Balanced View of Alternative Methodologies', **2** *Canadian Business Economics*, 18-21.

Sproule, Robert A. (1985), 'Tax Evasion and Labor Supply under Imperfect Information about Individual Parameters of the Tax System', **40** *Public Finance*, 441-456.

Sproule, Robert, Komus, David and Tsang, Eric (1980), 'Optimal Tax Evasion: Risk-neutral Behaviour under a Negative Income Tax', **35** *Public Finance*, 309-317.

Srinivasan, T.N. (1973), 'Tax Evasion: A Model', **2** *Journal of Public Economics*, 339-346.

Steenbergen, Marco R., McGraw, Kathleen M. and Scholz, John T. (1992), 'Taxpayer Adaptation to the 1986 Tax Reform Act: Do New Tax Laws Affect the Way Taxpayers Think about Taxes?', in Slemrod, Joel (ed.), *Why People Pay Taxes: Tax Compliance and Enforcement*, Ann Arbor, University of Michigan Press, 9-37.

Stella, Peter (1991), 'An Economic Analysis of Tax Amnesties', **46** *Journal of Public Economics*, 383-400.

Stella, Peter (1993), 'Tax Farming: A Radical Solution for Developing Country Tax Problems?', *International Monetary Fund Staff Papers*, 217 ff.

Stern, Jerrold J. (1993), *Advances in Taxation. Volume 5. A Research Annual*, Greenwood, JAI Press, 272 p.

Steuerle, C. Eugene (1992), 'Taxpayer Adaptation to the 1986 Tax Reform Act: Do New Tax Laws Affect the Way Taxpayers Think about Taxes? Commentary', in Slemrod, Joel (ed.), *Why People Pay Taxes: Tax Compliance and Enforcement*, Ann Arbor, University of Michigan Press, 38-41.

Stroope, John C. (1988), *An Empirical Analysis of the Impact of ERTA and TEFRA on Tax Compliance*, Pennsylvania Economic Association. Proceedings of the Third Annual Meeting, May 27 and 28, 1988. University Park: Pennsylvania State University.

Stroope, John C. (1991), 'Changing Perceptions of Taxation and the Impact of Recent Tax Legislation on Tax Compliance and Budget Deficits', in Long, Stanley G. (ed.), *Pennsylvania Economic Association: Proceedings of the Sixth Annual Meeting, May 23-25, 1991*, Johnstown, University of Pittsburgh, 178-186.

Tanzi, V. (1991), *Public Finance in Developing Countries*, Aldershot, Edward Elgar.

Tanzi, Vito and Shome, Parthasarathi (1994), 'International: A Primer on Tax Evasion', **48** *Bulletin for International Fiscal Documentation*, 328-337.

Tauchen, Helen V., Witte, Ann Dryden and Beron, Kurt J. (1989), *Tax Compliance: An Investigation Using Individual TCMP Data*, National Bureau of Economic Research Working Paper, No. 3078.

Thalmann, Philippe (1992), 'Factor Taxes and Evasion in General Equilibrium', **22** *Regional Science and Urban Economics*, 259-283.

Thomas, J. (1992), *Informal Economic Activity*, Ann Arbor, University of Michigan Press.

Thurman, Quint C. (1991), 'Taxpayer Noncompliance and General Prevention: An Expansion of the Deterrence Model', **46** *Public Finance*, 289-298.

Tillmann, Georg (1992), *Tax Evasion in an Open Economy*, Universitat Bonn Sonderforschungsbereich 303 Discussion Paper, No. A-377.

Toma, Eugenia Froedge and Toma, Mark (1992), 'Tax Collection with Agency Costs: Private Contracting or Government Bureaucrats?', **59** *Economica*, 107-120.

Tomasic, Roman and Pentony, Brendan (1991), 'Tax Compliance and the Rule of Law: From Legalism to Administrative Procedure?', **8** *Australian Tax Forum*, 85-116.

Tower, Edward (1989), 'Excise Tax Evasion: Comment', **44** *Public Finance*, 506-509.

Trandel, Gregory (1992), *Essays on Commodity Taxation: Evasion, Tax Competition, and the Form of the Tax*, Princeton University, Ph.D.

Trandel, Gregory A. (1992), 'Evading the Use Tax on Cross-Border Sales: Pricing and Welfare Effects', **49** *Journal of Public Economics*, 313-331.

Troup, Edward (1992), 'Unacceptable Discretion: Countering Tax Avoidance and Preserving the Rights of the Individual', **13(4)** *Fiscal Studies*, 128-138.

Udell, Michael A. (1995), *Essays in Applied Economics: New Techniques in Aggregate Data Analysis*, California Institute of Technology, Ph.D.

Urbiztondo, Santiago (1993), 'Un Sistema de Incentivos para Mejorar la Recaudacion Impositiva (An Incentive System to Improve the Impositive Collecting. With English Summary)', **39** *Economica (National University of La Plata)*, 141-162.

Usher, Dan (1986), 'Tax Evasion and the Marginal Cost of Public Funds', **24** *Economic Inquiry*, 563-586.

Van Raaij, W. Fred, van Veldhoven, Gery M. and Warneryd, Karl Erik (1988), *Handbook of Economic Psychology*, Dordrecht, Kluwer Academic Publishers, 683 p.

Viren, Matti (1992), 'Financial Innovations and Currency Demand: Some New Evidence', **17** *Empirical Economics*, 451-461.

Virmani, Arvind (1989), 'Indirect Tax Evasion and Production Efficiency', **39** *Journal of Public Economics*, 223-237.

Vogel, Kenneth R. (1974), 'Taxation and Public Opinion in Sweden: An Interpretation of Recent Survey Data', **27(4)** *National Tax Journal*, 499-513.

von Zameck, Walburga (1989), 'Tax Evasion and Tax Revenue Loss: Another Elaboration of the Peacock-Shaw Approach', **44** *Public Finance*, 308-315.

Wadhawan, Satish C. (1992), 'Evasion, Partial Detection and Optimal Tax Policy', **47(Suppl)** *Public Finance*, 372-383.

Wahlund, Richard (1992), 'Tax Changes and Economic Behavior: The Case of Tax Evasion', **13** *Journal of Economic Psychology*, 657-677.

Wallschutzky, Ian (1991), 'Reforming a Tax System to Reduce Opportunities for Tax Evasion: Australia', **45** *Bulletin for International Fiscal Documentation*, 165-175.

Wallschutzky, Ian G. and Gibson, Brian (1993), 'Small Business Cost of Tax Compliance', **10** *Australian Tax Forum*, 511-543.

Wang, Leonard F.S. (1990), 'Tax Evasion and Monopoly Output Decisions with Endogenous Probability of Detection', **18** *Public Finance Quarterly*, 480-487.

Wang, Leonard F.S. and Conant, John L. (1988), 'Corporate Tax Evasion and Output Decisions of the Uncertain Monopolist', **41** *National Tax Journal*, 579-581.

Wang, Xuejun (1995), 'Equilibrium Models of Asset Pricing with Progressive Taxation and Tax Evasion', **2** *Applied Economics Letters*, 440-443.

Watson, Harry (1985), 'Tax Evasion and Labor Markets', **27** *Journal of Public Economics*, 231-246.

Waud, Roger N. (1985), 'Tax Aversion, Deficits and the Tax Rate - Tax Revenue Relationship', National Bureau of Economic Research Working Paper.

Waud, Roger N. (1988), 'Tax Aversion, Optimal Tax Rates, and Indexation', **43** *Public Finance*, 310-325.

Webley, Paul, Cowell, Frank A., Long, Susan B. and Swingen, Judyth A. (1991), *Tax Evasion: An Experimental Approach. European Monographs in Social Psychology*, Cambridge, Cambridge University Press.

Webley, Paul, Robben, Henry and Morris, Ira (1988), 'Social Comparison and Tax Evasion in a Shop Simulation', in Maital, Shlomo (ed.), *Applied Behavioural Economics Volume 2*, New York, New York University Press, 553-561.

Weck-Hannemann, Hannelore and Pommerehne, Werner W. (1989), 'Einkommenssteuerhinterziehung in der Schweiz. Eine empirische Analyse (An Empirical Analysis of Income Tax Evasion in Switzerland)', **125(4)** *Schweizerische Zeitschrift für Volkswirtschaft und Statistik*, 515-556.

Westat, Inc. (1980), *Individual Income Tax Compliance Factors Study: Qualitative Research Results*, Prepared for the Internal Revenue Service, Rockville, MD.

White, Michelle J. (1990), *Why are Taxes So Complex and Who Benefits?*, University of Michigan Center for Research on Economic and Social Theory Working Paper, No. 90-7.

Wickerson, John (1994), 'Measuring Taxpayer Compliance: Issues and Challenges Facing Tax Administrations', **11** *Australian Tax Forum*, 1-44.

Wiegand, Bruce (1993), 'Petty Smuggling as "Social Justice": Research Findings from the Belize-Mexico Border', **42** *Social and Economic Studies*, 171-193.

Wirth, Andrew (1994), 'Changing Taxpayer Compliance: The Impact of Business Auditors as Service Providers', **11** *Australian Tax Forum*, 63-84.

Witte, Ann Dryden and Woodbury, Diane F. (1985), 'The Effect of Tax Laws and Tax Administration on Tax Compliance: The Case of the U.S. Individual Income Tax', **38** *National Tax Journal*, 1-13.

Wolf, Holger, C. (1993), *Anti-Tax Revolutions and Symbolic Prosecutions*, National Bureau of Economic Research Working Paper, No. 4337.

Wrede, Matthias (1995), 'Tax Evasion and Risk Taking: Is Tax Evasion Desirable?', **50(2)** *Public Finance*, 303-316.

Wrede, Matthias (1995), 'Tax Evasion and Growth', **8(2)** *Finnish Economic Papers*, 82-90.

Yamada, Masatoshi (1990), 'An Analysis of Optimal Taxation with Tax Evasion', **45** *Public Finance*, 470-490.

Yaniv, Gideon (1986), 'Fraudulent Collection of Unemployment Benefits: A Theoretical Analysis with Reference to Income Tax Evasion', **30** *Journal of Public Economics*, 369-383.

Yaniv, Gideon (1988), 'Withholding and Non-withheld Tax Evasion', **35** *Journal of Public Economics*, 183-204.

Yaniv, Gideon (1990a), 'On the Interpretation of the Income Effect in Tax Evasion Models', **45** *Public Finance*, 235-239.

Yaniv, Gideon (1990b), 'Tax Evasion under Differential Taxation: The Economics of Income Source Misreporting', **43** *Journal of Public Economics*, 327-337.

Yaniv, Gideon (1994), 'Tax Evasion and the Income Tax Rate: A Theoretical Reexamination', **49** *Public Finance*, 107-112.

Yaniv, Gideon (1995), 'A Note on the Tax-Evading Firm', **48** *National Tax Journal*, 113-120.

Yankelovich, Skelly and White, Inc. (1984), 'Taxpayer Attitudes Study: Final Report. Public opinion survey prepared for the Public Affairs Division', *Internal Revenue Service, New York.*

Yitzhaki, Shlomo (1974), 'A Note on Income Tax Evasion: A Theoretical Analysis', **3** *Journal of Public Economics*, 201-202.

Yitzhaki, Shlomo (1987), 'On the Excess Burden of Tax Evasion', **15** *Public Finance Quarterly*, 123-137.

Yitzhaki, Shlomo and Vakneen, Yitzhak (1989), 'On the Shadow Price of a Tax Inspector', **44** *Public Finance*, 492-505.

Zheng, Kangbin (1992), *Four Essays on Linear Tax Evasion Games*, Georgetown University, Ph.D.

Other References

Beccaria, Cesare (1764), 'An Attempt at an Analysis of Smuggling (Tentativo Analitico sui Contrabbandi)', *Il Caffè*, Brescia, Italy, 118-199, in Baumol, William J. and Goldfeld, S. (eds), *Precursors in Mathematical Economics: An Anthology*, London, London School of Economics and Political Science.

Border, K. and Sobel, J. (1987), 'Samurai Accountant: A Theory of Auditing and Plunder', **54(4)** *Review of Economic Studies*, 525-540.

Elfers, H., Weigel, R. and Hessing, D. (1987), 'The Consequences of Different Strategies Measuring Tax Evasion Behavior', **8** *Journal of Economic Psychology*, 311-337.

Mookherjee, D. and Png, I. (1995), 'Corruptible Law Enforcers: How Should they be Compensated?', **105(428)** *Economic Journal*, 145-159.

Roth, J. and Scholtz, J. (eds) (1989), *Taxpayer Compliance, Vol. 2: Social Science Perspectives*, University of Pennsylvania Press, Philadelphia.

Saltzman, L., Paternoster, R., Waldo, G. and Chiricos, T. (1982), 'Deterrent and Experiental Effects: The Problem of Causal Order in Perceptual Deterrence Research', **19** *Journal of Research on Crime and Delinquency*, 172-189.

Scotchmer, Suzanne (1987), 'Audit Classes and Tax Enforcement Policy', **77(2)** *American Economic Review*, 229-233.

Scotchmer, Suzanne (1989), 'The Effect of Tax Advisors on Tax Compliance' in Roth, J. and Scholtz, J. (eds), *Taxpayer Compliance*, Vol. 2, University of Pennsylvania Press, Philadelphia.

Slemrod, Joel and Yitzhaki, Shlomo (1987), 'The Optimal Size of a Tax Collection Agency', **89(2)** *Scandinavian Journal of Economics*, 183-192.

Thomas, J. (1992), *Informal Economic Activity*, Ann Arbor, University of Michigan Press.

6030
PROPERTY TAXES

David L. Cameron
Professor of Law, Willamette University, College of Law

Abstract

The consideration of property taxation has long been a part of the development of economic analysis beginning with the French Physciocrats, through Ricardo, and then George. As a result, the economic literature concerning property taxation is vast. This chapter surveys an important slice of that literature which considers the incidence of property taxes. Over the past thirty years, three theories have been proposed to describe the economic effect of property taxes. The 'Traditional View' suggests that, because of the fixed supply of land, taxes on land will be borne by the owners or renters of land. The 'New View,' however, concludes that a tax on land is largely equivalent to a general tax on all capital. Finally, the 'Benefit View' suggests that property taxes are appropriately viewed, not as a tax, but as an efficient user charge for local public services. Empirical study to date has not determined whether the new view or the benefit view is the more appropriate model of property taxation.
JEL classification: H2, H22, K3, K34
Keywords: Property Taxation, Economic Rent, User Fee, Fiscal Zoning

1. Introduction

Property taxes are typically defined to encompass those taxes levied on both real and personal property that are dependent on the value of the property itself. Generally, a property tax is administered through the use of a uniform tax rate imposed on the assessed value of the property subject to tax. Within a given jurisdiction, the tax rates frequently vary depending on the type or class of property being taxed. More importantly perhaps for comparative purposes, property tax systems vary significantly across jurisdictions with respect to the types of property that comprise the tax base as well as the exclusions for specific types of property, the assessment techniques used to determine the value of the property subject to the tax, and the tax rates applicable to the various classes of property. Within the United States, the property tax is the principal source of revenue for county and municipal governments.

The economic literature that considers the law of property taxation is extremely broad in scope. Economists have developed various theories concerning the incidence of property taxes and have conducted empirical studies to test those theories. The study of property taxation is closely tied to the study of the provision of public goods as any general equilibrium analysis of property taxation must consider the public benefits provided through a system of property taxation. The following discussion will consider the three principal models of the incidence of property taxes, and in particular the taxation of land, that form the basis for the examination of property taxes from an economic perspective. These economic models of property taxation have also served as the basis for public policy proposals under which differential property tax rates or assessment procedures could be used to protect agricultural lands or encourage development in urban areas. Economists have also examined the administration of property tax systems, including the proper assessment procedures for the valuation of property for tax purposes.

A. Conceptual History of the Property Tax

2. Survey

As described by Winfrey (1973), as well as Buchanan and Flowers (1975), property taxes were one of the earliest forms of taxation to be considered from an economic perspective. Beginning with the French Physiocrats of the mid-eighteenth century, including Francois Quesnay their leader, early economists concluded that property, and more specifically land, was the only logical base for taxation. The Physiocrats viewed agricultural land as the only 'productive' sector of the economy, producing a surplus over the real costs of production. All other sectors of the economy simply provided services or transformed goods from one form to another.

The English classical economist David Ricardo also maintained that land was the appropriate factor of production to be taxed. According to Ricardo, increases in population increased the demand for agricultural goods, thus causing more marginal lands to be brought into use. Because greater labor was necessary to make these more marginal lands productive, Ricardo reasoned that these greater costs would be reflected in higher prices for agricultural goods. These higher prices, in turn, increased the return to the owners of the more productive land who did not confront the greater costs of production applicable to the more marginal lands. According to Ricardo, this increased return or 'rent' represented 'the original and indestructible powers of the soil'. Ricardo maintained that this 'surplus' should be taxed as it did not represent a real cost of production.

The views of the Physciocrats and Ricardo served as the basis for the single tax movement which gained strong support in the United States at the end of the nineteenth century under Henry George. George (1879) maintained that the return on land represented an economic rent that could be taxed away without distorting the allocation of resources that would otherwise result in the absence of the tax. In today's terminology, an economic rent is defined as the return to any factor of production in excess of that which the factor could receive in its next best employment. Thus, the taxing of only the economic rent attributable to any particular factor will not result in the transfer of that factor from its current use to an alternative use. In addition, the Georgists maintained that any increase in the value of land resulting from growth in the economy was viewed as a surplus created by society that could rightfully be taxed. As stated by George:

> Taxes levied upon the value of land cannot check production in the slightest degree, until they exceed rent, or the value of land taken annually, for unlike taxes upon commodities, or exchange, or capital, or any of the tools or processes of production, they do not bear upon production. The value of land does not express the reward of production, as does the value of crops, of cattle, of buildings, or of any of the things which are styled personal property or improvements. It expresses the exchange value of a monopoly. It is not in any case the creation of the individual who owns the land; it is created by the growth of the community. Hence the community can take it all without in any way lessening the incentive to improvement or in the slightest degree lessening the production of wealth. Taxes may be imposed upon the value of land until all rent is taken by the State, without reducing the wages of labor or the reward of capital one iota; without increasing the price of a single commodity, or making production in any way more difficult. (George, 1879, p. 413)

George's claim that a tax on the value of land is nondistortionary has been supported by modern commentators such as Wildasin (1982), Vickrey (1970), and Tideman (1982) provided the tax is imposed on pure land rentals, defined as the value of the land independent of anything that might be done with the land, and not, as Bentick (1982) and Mills (1981) point out, on the current market value of land which reflects present and future uses of the land.

Unfortunately, the Physciocrats, Ricardo, and George all failed to recognize that rents may be attributable to all factors of production. Under a marginal analysis, each factor of production - labor and capital, as well as land - will receive the value of its marginal product in a competitive economy. Land alone cannot be viewed as receiving the residual value of all production. As noted by Fischel (1985, pp. 16-17), 'the only economic difference between land and the other factors of production is that [land] is fixed in supply by virtue of its immobility'. As discussed below, this characteristic - the fixed supply of land as a result of its immobility - remains important in understanding the economic effects of property taxation.

In the United States, the use of property taxation is largely limited to state and local jurisdictions. In addition, revenues collected through the imposition of property taxes on personal property has declined in relation to the imposition of property taxes on real property (Netzer, 1966). Although George's single tax movement was never fully implemented, principally because of administrative difficulties (Holland, 1970), it remains visible in those property tax regimes under which land is more heavily taxed than other forms of property (Oates and Schwab, 1997).

B. The Modern Theoretical Framework

3. Overview

Economists have developed three principal theories under which the incidence of property taxation has been considered. Importantly, each theory distinguishes between taxes on land and taxes on capital. The observation that a property tax may have a differential effect on land as opposed to other forms of capital results from the difference in elasticity of the supply of each item. Based on the assumption that the supply of land subject to taxation in a given jurisdiction is fixed, the 'Traditional View' suggests that taxes on land will be borne by the users of land, that is, the owners or renters of the land (Netzer, 1966). The 'New View,' however, concludes that a local tax on land can be broken into two components, a 'profits tax' and an 'excise tax' (Mieszkowski, 1972b; Aaron 1975). Because the profits tax component is equivalent to a general tax on all capital, that portion of any property tax will fall on the owners of all capital. Finally, the 'Benefit View' suggests that property taxes are appropriately viewed as a user charge for local public services (Hamilton, 1975b, 1976b; Fischel, 1985, 1992). Because consumers of public services are mobile, the benefits view suggests that a property tax is in many situations is an efficient financing mechanism for public services.

4. The Traditional View

The traditional view of property taxes was originally articulated by Simon (1943) and Netzer (1966). The traditional view adopts a partial-equilibrium approach under which property taxes are considered as separate payments for capital and land. The supply of capital is considered to be perfectly elastic, and the supply of land is considered to be perfectly inelastic. As shown in Figure 1, the return to owners of capital is at a nationally determined rental rate for capital (R_n). If a jurisdiction enacts an ad valorem property tax (t) on capital, the price of capital will rise to R_n (1 + *t*) in order to maintain an after-tax return on capital of R_n and the amount of capital in the jurisdiction will fall from C_0 to C_1. This effect can be modeled as a decline in the demand for capital from *D* to *D'*. This effect will also occur if the jurisdiction enacts an increase in the rate of an existing property tax.

Figure 1

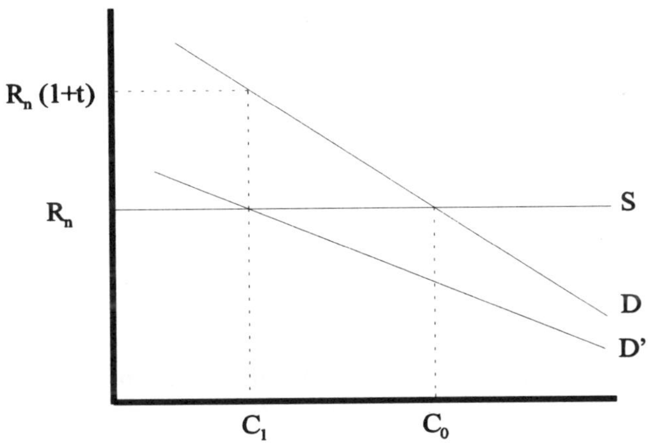

If the ad valorem property tax is also imposed on the jurisdiction's perfectly inelastic supply of land, the result is the perfect capitalization of the tax in the return of the land. As shown in Figure 2, the return on the land will fall from R_n to R_n (1- *t*). Nevertheless, because the supply of land in the jurisdiction is fixed, the tax has no effect on the quantity of land but results only in a reduction in the price of land.

Figure 2

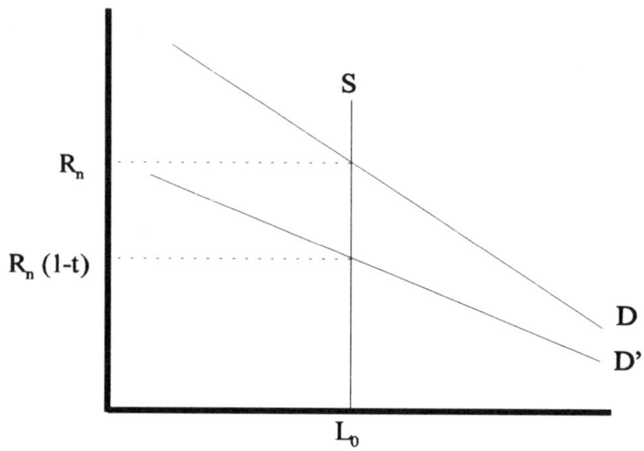

The traditional view has been employed to conclude that the imposition of a property tax on residential land is regressive in nature. This conclusion is based on the assumption that the proportion of income spent on housing falls as income rises. Based on the traditional view, Netzer (1966), however, concluded that, in the aggregate, the property tax was more nearly proportional than regressive. Nevertheless, with respect to housing, Netzer recognized that the property tax was regressive based on empirical studies available at that time. Netzer (1973) later cautioned that studies concluding that the property tax was regressive in nature were biased because they typically adopted current income rather than normal or permanent income. He hypothesized that the regressive aspects of the property tax would be diminished if the studies, like consumers themselves when making housing decisions, considered income prospects over periods longer than a single year.

5. The New View

The new view of property taxation was originally developed by Thomson (1965), Mieszkowski (1972b) and Aaron (1975) and reformulated byMieszkowski and Zodrow (1986). The new view adopts a general equilibrium analysis for all jurisdictions in a country, and assumes that both the capital in the country and the land in any one jurisdiction are fixed.

As described by Wassmer (1993), the analysis underlying the new view is often simplified by assuming that only three types of jurisdictions exist which differ in the demand for local services - low, medium, and high. In the short run, property, which is made up of capital as well as land, is considered fixed in each jurisdiction at P_0. Prior to the introduction of the tax, the return on capital is at a nationally determined rate, R_n. Following the introduction of the tax, the return on capital declines by the amount of the tax in the same manner as that described under the traditional view for land alone. The decline will be greatest in the jurisdiction for which the demand for services is highest as greater revenues are necessary to provide the services demanded. As shown in Figure 3, the return declines to R_{h1} in the high demand jurisdiction, R_{m1} in the medium demand jurisdiction, and R_{l1} in the low demand jurisdiction.

The decline in the return on property in the medium-demand type jurisdiction from R_n to R_{m1} has been referred to as the 'profits tax' effect, a decline in the market value of property across all jurisdictions by the average rate of taxation. (Zodrow and Mieszkowski, 1989). The profits tax effect is exacerbated in the high-demand type jurisdiction by a negative 'excise tax' effect equal to the difference between R_{h1} and R_{m1} resulting from a higher tax rate in the high-demand type jurisdiction as compared to the medium-demand type. The profits tax effect is partially offset, however, in the low-demand type jurisdiction by a positive excise tax effect equal to the difference between R_{l1} and R_{m1} resulting from a lower tax rate in the low-demand type jurisdiction as compared to the medium-demand type jurisdiction.

Because the relative return on property among the three types of jurisdictions differ and because capital is assumed to be perfectly mobile in the long run, capital will exit the high-demand type jurisdiction where the return on property is the lowest, decreasing the supply of property in that jurisdiction from P_0 to P_1. This capital will enter the low-demand type jurisdiction where the return on property is the highest, increasing the supply of property in that jurisdiction from P_0 to P_1. The decrease in the supply of property in the high-demand type jurisdiction will increase the return on property from R_{h1} to R_{h2}. The increase in the supply of property in the low-demand type jurisdiction will decrease the return on property from R_{l1} to R_{l2}. Equilibrium will be achieved when the after-tax return on property is equalized across all three types of jurisdictions at R_{h2}, R_{m1}, and R_{l2}. Importantly, however, the excise tax effects of the property tax, as described above, will result in distortionary effects in the high- and low-demand type jurisdictions.

Figure 3

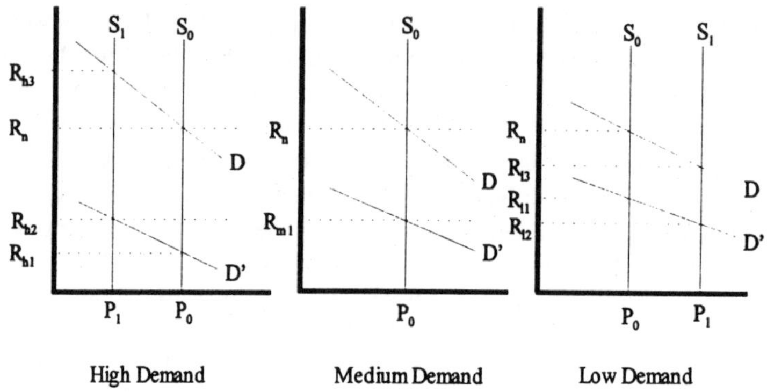

As shown in Figure 3, the rental rates paid for property in the three types of jurisdictions differ. The rental rate in the high-demand type jurisdiction, R_{h3}, exceeds the rental rate in the medium-demand type jurisdiction, R_n, which, in turn, exceeds the rental rate in the low-demand type jurisdiction, R_{l3}. To the extent that the higher rental rates in high-demand type jurisdictions are not offset by increased utility from higher service levels, individuals may move from high-demand type jurisdictions to medium- or low-demand type jurisdictions. Conversely, to the extent that higher rental rates are offset by increased utility from higher service levels, individuals may move from low-demand type jurisdictions to medium- or high-demand type jurisdictions. Such a movement would cause rental rates across all three types of jurisdictions to converge but, unless individuals are assumed to be perfectly mobile, rent differentials will persist.

Unlike the traditional view, the incidence of the property tax under the new view is generally seen as progressive. This is because the property tax results principally in a decline in the return on capital by the 'average' rate of taxation in the nation. Because capital is disproportionately held by those with higher incomes, Mieszkowski and Zodrow (1989) conclude that the profits tax portion of any property tax under the new view is 'highly progressive'.

6. The Benefit View

The benefit view, which extends the analysis of the new view, includes within its analysis the benefits conferred on property owners through property taxes. As developed by Hamilton (1975b, 1976b), the benefit view adopts the assumptions underlying the new view but also assumes the perfect mobility of individual consumers and the ability of jurisdictions to engage in fiscal zoning. If the provision of public services is viewed as a public good, the new view suggests that incentives exist to utilize land in a high-demand type jurisdiction in such a manner that the benefit of public services exceeds the burden of the property tax. The benefit view assumes that jurisdictions will engage in fiscal zoning under which the value of the housing units permitted within the jurisdiction will be restricted to some minimum value, typically through the use of the jurisdiction's zoning authority or through some other power to control land uses and intensities. At this minimum value, the revenues generated through the property tax will exactly offset the value of the public services obtained.

The benefit view, thus, follows a Tiebout (1956) model under which the property tax becomes a head tax or nondistortionary user charge for public services. Assuming a sufficiently large number of jurisdictions within a larger metropolitan region offering a diversity of public services and assuming further the mobility of consumers for those services, the property tax represents an efficient means of financing the provision of public services. Importantly, the benefit view does not require that any particular jurisdiction be homogenous with respect to residential values. Hamilton (1976b) demonstrated that, in heterogenous communities, differentials between benefits received through public services and taxes paid will be capitalized into the price of the property. Fischel (1975) and White (1975a) have extended the benefit view to the taxation of commercial and industrial property.

Viewing the property tax as a head tax or a user charge for the provision of public services under the benefit view, the concerns involving the progressivity or regressivity of the property tax under the traditional and new views do not arise based on the relationship between the property tax and the provision of public goods and services and the assumption of consumer mobility.

7. Evidence Concerning the Validity of the Alternative Theories

Commentary and empirical studies concerning the validity of the traditional, new, and benefit views have reached no definitive results. For example, Netzer (1973), a proponent of the traditional view, suggests that the lack of uniformity of the property tax, at least on a national level in the United States, means that it is not even 'sensible' to speak of a partial tax on capital (such as a property tax in only one jurisdiction) in terms of a tax that lowers the average rate of return on all capital as proposed under the new view. This observation is disputed by Mieszkowski and Zodrow (1989) who suggest that the work of Lin (1986) concludes otherwise.

The proponents of the new view have suggested, in turn, that little evidence exists to support the view that jurisdictions engage in perfect fiscal zoning or that any benefit or burden differentials are perfectly capitalized into the value of property as required by the benefit view. Nevertheless, Fischel (1985, 1992) suggests that the multi-dimensional land use restrictions available to communities under typical zoning enabling acts can be effective mechanisms to engage in fiscal zoning. In addition, Fischel (1992) maintains that the widespread use of exactions or impact fees may directly substitute for expenditures otherwise financed by property taxes. The existence and relative importance of exactions and impact fees are typically overlooked in studies of the property tax itself. Fischel (1989) also maintains that the benefit view is supported by voter hostility towards property taxation when the level of benefits typically paid for through the imposition of property taxes, such as expenditures for education, are no longer related to the property taxes paid. Fischel suggests that the overwhelming voter support for property tax reduction in California in 1978 under Proposition 13 was the result of the California Supreme Court's 1976 decision in *Serrano v. Priest* (135 Cal. Rptr. 345) requiring stringent equality in spending per pupil across California school districts.

Empirical studies of various types have not succeeded in fully determining whether the new view or the benefit view provides the more valid description of the property tax. As summarized by Mieszkowski and Zodrow (1989), the majority of empirical studies have focused on the extent to which property taxes and local government expenditures are capitalized into property values. These studies by Oates (1969), Edel and Sclar (1974), and Hamilton (1976b, 1983) as well as others indicate that property taxes and government expenditures are capitalized into property values. This observation does not confirm the benefit view, however, because the new view also implies some capitalization. The existence of capitalization of benefits, such as school quality, further supports the benefits view (Gurwitz, 1980; Hoxby, 1997). Responding to the suggestion of Mieszkowski and Zodrow (1989, p. 1131), Wassmer (1993), Carroll and Yinger (1994) and Man (1995) conducted studies considering changes in the aggregate value of the property tax base and intermetropolitan rent differentials. The results of these studies support the new view's conception of the property tax as, at least in part, a distortionary tax on capital. Wildasin (1986a) has suggested that neither the new view nor the benefit view may be entirely correct, however, and that, because of imperfect fiscal zoning and imperfect capitalization, the property tax may best be considered as a combination of a capital tax and user charge.

Despite the fact that the benefit view has not been entirely validated based on empirical study, it has focused inquiry on the question whether property taxation can be properly analyzed in isolation from the public goods and services that it finances. This aspect of the benefits view, in turn, has spurred more recent research into the political behavior of local governments, particularly in the area of tax competition as governments compete for capital through adjustments in property tax rates (Coates, 1993; Edwards and Keen, 1996; Nechyba, 1997).

Bibliography on Property Taxes (6030)

Aaron, Henry J. (1969), 'Some Observations on Property Tax Valuation and the Significance of Full Value Assessment', in Lynn, A.D., Jr (ed.), *The Property Tax and Its Administration*, Madison, University of Wisconsin.

Aaron, Henry J. (1973), 'What Do Circuit-Breaker Laws Accomplish?', in Peterson, George E. (ed.), *Property Tax Reform*, Washington, DC, Urban Institute Press.

Aaron, Henry J. (1974), 'A New View of Property Tax Incidence', **64** *American Economic Review*, 212-221.

Aaron, Henry J. (1975), *Who Pays the Property Tax? A New View*, Washington, Brookings Institution.

Agapos, A.M. and Dunlap, Paul R. (1973), 'Elimination of Urban Blight Through Inverse Proportional Ad Valorem Property Taxation', **32** *American Journal of Economics and Sociology*, 143-152.

Almy, Richard R. (1977), 'The Impact of Assessment Practices Upon Assessment Performance', in *Analyzing Assessment Equity: Techniques for Measuring and Improving the Quality of Property Tax Administration*, Chicago, Illinois, International Association of Assessment Officers.

Anderson, John E. (1986), 'Property Taxes and the Timing of Land Development', **16** *Regional Science and Urban Economics*, 483-492.

Anderson, John E. and Bunch, Howard C. (1989), 'Agricultural Property Tax Relief: Tax Credits, Tax Rates, and Land Values', **65** *Land Economics*, 13-22.

Andrews, R.B. and Dasso, Jerome J. (1961), 'The Influence of Annexation on Property Tax Burdens', **14** *National Tax Journal*, 88-97.

Arnott, Richard J. and MacKinnon, James G. (1977), 'The Effects of the Property Tax: A General Equilibrium Simulation', **4** *Journal of Urban Economics*, 389-407.

Arnott, Richard J. and Stiglitz, Joseph E. (1979), 'Aggregate Land Rents, Expenditure on Public Goods, and Optimal City Size', **93** *Quarterly Journal of Economics*, 471-500.

Aronson, J. Richard (1966), 'Intangible Taxes - A Wisely Neglected Revenue Source for States', **19** *National Tax Journal*, 184-186.

Ashworth, John and Gemmell, Norman (1996), 'Local Governments' Monopoly Power and Local Tax Reform: Theory and Evidence from the U.K.', **89** *Public Choice*, 393-417.

Auerbach, Alan J. (1981), 'Taxation of Wealth', in Eatwell, John, Milgate, Murray and Newman, Peter (eds), *The New Palgrave: A Dictionary of Economics*, New York, Stockton Press.

Aull, G.H. (1959), 'The Situation and Outlook for Property Taxation in the South', **12** *National Tax Journal*, 86-92.

Back, Kenneth (1970), 'Land Value Taxation in Light of Current Assessment Theory and Practice', in Beck, Athur P. (ed.), *The Assessment of Land Value - A Symposium, Committee on Taxation, Resources and Economic Development*, Madison, University of Wisconsin.

Bahl, Roy (ed.) (1979), *The Taxation of Urban Property in Less Developed Countries*, Madison, University of Wisconsin.

Bahl, Roy (ed.) (1991), *The Jamaican Tax Reform*, Cambridge, MA, Lincoln Institute of Land Policy.

Bahl, Roy and Linn, Johannes F. (1992), *Urban Public Finance in Developing Countries*, Oxford, Oxford University Press.

Bahl, Roy, Sjoquist, David Lawrence and Williams, W. Loren (1990), *School Finance Reform and Impact on Property Taxes*, Proceedings of the Eighty-Third Annual Conference on Taxation, National Tax Association-Tax Institute of America.

Barkume, Anthony (1976), 'Criteria for Voting Judgments on a Property Tax Initiative: An Analysis of the Watson Amendment', **29** *National Tax Journal*, 448-460.

Barnes, Ralph and Raymond, George (1955), 'The Fiscal Approach to Land Use Planning', **21** *Journal of the American Institute of Planners*, 2-3.

Barr, James L. and Davis, Otto A. (1966), 'An Elementary Political and Economic Theory of the Expenditures of Local Governments', **33** *Southern Economic Journal*, 149-165.

Bartik, Timothy J. (1991), 'The Effects of Property Taxes and Other Local Public Policies on the Intrametropolitan Pattern of Business Location', in Herzog, Henry W., Jr and Schlottmann, Alan M. (eds), *Industry Location and Public Policy*, Knoxville, Tennessee, University of Tennessee Press.

Bates, Laurie J. and Santerre, Rexford E. (1993), 'Property Tax Collector Performance and Pay', **46** *National Tax Journal*, 23-31.

Beck, John H. (1983), 'Tax Competition, Uniform Assessment, and the Benefit Principle', **13** *Journal of Urban Economics*, 127-146.

Beck, John H. (1993), 'Tax Abatements and Tax Rates in a System of Overlapping Revenue-Maximizing Governments', **23** *Regional Science and Urban Economics*, 645-665.

Beck, Morris (1963), *Property Taxation and Urban Land Use in Northeastern New Jersey*, Washington, DC, Urban Land Institute.

Beck, Morris (1965), 'Determinants of the Property Tax Level: A Case Study of Northeastern New Jersey', **18** *National Tax Journal*, 74-77.

Becker, Arthur P. (ed.) (1969), *Land and Building Taxes: Their Effect on Economic Development - A Symposium, Committee on Taxation, Resources, and Economic Development*, Madison, University of Wisconsin.

Becker, Arthur P. (ed.) (1970), *The Assessment of Land Value - A Symposium, Committee on Taxation, Resources, and Economic Development*, Madison, University of Wisconsin.

Behrens, John O. (1980), 'Property Taxes and Property Values: What's New About Base, Burden, and Other Mysteries', in Tron, Esther O. (ed.), *Public School Finance Programs*, Washington, DC, U.S. Government Printing Office.

Bell, Earl J. (1984), 'Administrative Inequity and Property Assessment: The Case for the Traditional Approach', **3** *Property Tax Journal*, 123-131.

Bendick, Marc, Jr (1974), 'Designing Circuit-Breaker Property Tax Relief', **27** *National Tax Journal*, 19-28.

Bennion, Fred W. (1958), 'Veteran Tax Exemption in Wyoming', **11** *National Tax Journal*, 377-378.

Benson, G.C.S., Benson, Sumner, McClelland, Harold and Thomson, Procter (1965), *The American Property Tax: Its History, Administration and Economic Impact*, Claremont, California, Claremont College Print Service.

Bentick, Brian L. (1972), 'Improving the Allocation of Land Between Speculators and Users: Taxation and Paper Land', **48** *Economic Record*, 18-41.

Bentick, Brian L. (1974), 'The Allocation of Land Between Speculators and Users under a Land Ownership Tax: Reply', **50** *Economic Record*, 451-452.

Bentick, Brian L. (1979a), 'The Impact of Taxation and Valuation Practices on the Timing and Efficiency of Land Use', **87** *Journal of Political Economy*, 859-868.

Bentick, Brian L. (1979b), 'The Capitalization of the Property Tax and Idle Land', **55** *Land Economics*, 545-548.

Bentick, Brian L. (1980a), 'Property and Income Taxation in Rural Industries with Different Rotation Periods', **33** *National Tax Journal*, 219-225.

Bentick, Brian L. (1980b), 'Capitalized Property Taxes and the Viability of Rural Enterprise Subject to Urban Pressure', **56** *Land Economics*, 451-456.

Bentick, Brian L. (1982), 'A Tax on Land Value May Not be Neutral', **35** *National Tax Journal*, 113 ff.

Bentick, Brian L. (1996), 'The Differential Incidence of an Urban Land Tax Depends on the Travel Intensities of Substitutes for Land', **33** *Urban Studies*, 1729-1732.

Bentick, Brian L. and Pogue, Thomas F. (1988), 'The Impact on Development Timing of Property and Profit Taxation', **64** *Land Economics*, 317-324.

Berglas, Eitan (1982), 'User Charges, Local Public Services, and Taxation of Land Rents', **32** *Public Finance*, 178-188.

Bevins, Robert J. (1975), 'Real Property Taxes and Farm Real Estate Values: Incidence and Implications: Comment', **57** *American Journal of Agricultural Economics*, 725 ff.

Billings, R. Bruce and Folsom, Roger Nils (1980), 'Voter Perception of Property Tax Incidence as Revealed by School Expenditure Decisions', **33** *National Tax Journal*, 459-471.

Birch, John W., Sunderman, Mark A. and Hamilton, Thomas W. (1990), 'Adjusting for Vertical Inequity in Property Assessment', **3** *Property Tax Journal*, 197-211.

Bird, Frederick L. (1960), *The General Property Tax: Findings of the 1957 Census of Governments*, Chicago, Illinois, Public Administration Service.

Bird, Richard M. (1960), 'A National Tax on the Unimproved Value of Land: The Australian Experience 1910-52', **13** *National Tax Journal*, 386-392.

Bird, Richard M. (1976), 'The Incidence of the Property Tax: Old Wine in New Bottles', **4** *Canadian Public Policy*, 323-334.

Bird, Richard M. (1993), 'Threading the Fiscal Labyrinth: Some Issues in Fiscal Decentralization', **46** *National Tax Journal*, 207-227.

Black, David E. (1972), 'The Nature and Extent of Effective Property Tax Rate Variation Within the City of Boston', **25** *National Tax Journal*, 203-210.

Black, David E. (1974), 'The Incidence of Differential Property Taxes on Urban Housing: Some Further Evidence', **27** *National Tax Journal*, 367-369.

Black, David E. (1977), 'Property Tax Incidence: The Excise-Tax Effect and Assessment Practices', **30** *National Tax Journal*, 429-434.

Blackburn, John O. (1965), 'Intangibles Taxes: A Neglected Revenue Source for States', **18** *National Tax Journal*, 214-218.

Blank, David M. (1954), 'The Role of the Real Property Tax in Municipal Finance', **7** *National Tax Journal*, 319-326.

Bloom, Howard S. (1979), 'Public Choice and Private Interest: Explaining the Vote for Property Tax Classification in Massachusetts', **32** *National Tax Journal*, 527-534.

Bloom, Howard S. and Ladd, Helen F. (1982), 'Property Tax Revaluation and Tax Levy Growth', **11** *Journal of Urban Economics*, 73-84.

Boadway, Robin W. (1982), 'On the Method of Taxation and the Provision of Local Public Goods: Comment', **72** *American Economic Review*, 846-851.

Bogart, William T. and Bradford, David F. (1989), 'Incidence and Allocation Effects of the Property Tax and a Proposal for Reform', **45** *Tax Notes*, 223-234.

Borgia, Daniel (1994), 'How a Land Value Tax System Promotes Economic Development', **9** *Real Estate Finance Journal*, 89 ff.

Borland, Melvin and Lile, Stephen (1980), 'The Property Tax Rate and Assessment Uniformity', **33** *National Tax Journal*, 99-102.

Boskin, Michael J. (1973), 'Local Government Tax and Product Competition and the Optimal Provision of Public Goods', **81** *Journal of Political Economy*, 203-210.

Botha, D. (1971), 'Towards a New Variant of Property Taxation', **39** *South African Journal of Economics*, 1-12.

Bourassa, Steven C. (1987), 'Land Value Taxation and New Housing Development in Pittsburgh', **18** *Growth and Change*, 44-55.

Bourassa, Steven C. (1990), 'Land Value Taxation and Housing Development: Effects on the Property Tax Reform in Three Types of Cities', **49** *American Journal of Economics and Sociology*, 101-111.

Bourassa, Steven C. (1992), 'Economic Effects of Taxes on Land: A Review', **51** *American Journal of Economics and Sociology*, 109-113.

Bowman, John H. (ed.) (1995), *Taxation of Business Property: Is Uniformity Still a Valid Norm?*, Westport, Connecticut, Greenwood, Praeger Publishing Company.

Bowman, John H. and Mikesell, John (1978), 'Uniform Assessment of Property: Returns From Institutional Remedies', **31** *National Tax Journal*, 137-152.

Bowman, John H., Hoffer, George E. and Pratt, Michael D. (1990), 'Current Patterns and Trends in State and Local Intangible Taxation', **43** *National Tax Journal*, 439-450.

Bradbury, Katherine, Ladd, Helen F., Perrault, Michael, Reschovsky, Andrew and Yinger, John (1984), 'State Aid to Offset Fiscal Disparities Across Communities', **37** *National Tax Journal*, 151-170.

Bradbury, Katherine and Ladd, Helen F. (1987), 'City Property Taxes: The Effects of Economic Change and Competitive Pressures', **1989** *New England Economic Review*, 22-36.

Bradford, David F., Malt, R.A. and Oates, Wallace E. (1969), 'The Rising Cost of Local Public Services: Some Evidence and Reflections', **22** *National Tax Journal*, 185-202.

Bradley, James F. (1988), 'Property Tax Proposals for the Republic of Ireland', *British Tax Review*, 446-461.

Brainin, David and Germanis, John J. (1967), 'Comments on "Distribution of Property, Retail Sales and Personal Income Tax Burdens in California: An Empirical Analysis of Inequity in Taxation" by Gerhard N. Rostvold', **20** *National Tax Journal*, 106-111.

Brazer, Harvey E. (1961),'The Value of Industrial Property as a Subject of Taxation', **55** *Canadian Public Administration*, 137-147.

Brazer, Harvey E. (ed.) (1967), *Essays in State and Local Finance*, Ann Arbor, Michigan, University of Michigan, Institute of Public Administration.

Break, George F. (1974), 'The Incidence and Economic Effects of Taxation', in *The Economics of Public Finance*, Washington, DC, Brookings Institution.

Bridges, Benjamin (1964a), 'The Elasticity of the Property Tax Base: Some Cross Section Estimates', **40** *Land Economics*, 449-451.

Bridges, Benjamin (1964b), 'Income Elasticity of the Property Tax Base', **17** *National Tax Journal*, 253-264.

Brown, Harry Gunnison (1924), *The Economics of Taxation*, New York, NY, Henry Holt and Company.

Brown, Harry Gunnison (1955), *Land Taxation Around the World*, New York, NY, Robert Schalkenbach Foundation.

Brown, J. Bruce (1968), 'The Incidence of Property Taxes Under Three Alternative Systems in Urban Areas in New Zealand', **21** *National Tax Journal*, 237-252.

Brueckner, Jan K. (1979), 'Property Values, Local Public Expenditure, and Economic Efficiency', **11** *Journal of Public Economics*, 223-245.

Brueckner, Jan K. (1981a), 'Zoning and Property Taxation in a System of Local Governments: Further Analysis', **18** *Urban Studies*, 113-120.

Brueckner, Jan K. (1981b), 'Labor Mobility and the Incidence of the Residential Property Tax', **10** *Journal of Urban Economics*, 173-182.

Brueckner, Jan K. (1982), 'A Test for Allocative Efficiency in the Local Public Sector', **19** *Journal of Public Economics*, 311-331.

Brueckner, Jan K. (1986), 'A Modern Analysis of the Effects of Site Value Taxation', **39** *National Tax Journal*, 49-58.

Buchanan, James M. and Flowers, Marilyn R. (1975), *The Public Finances: An Introductory Textbook*, 4th edn, Homewood , IL, Richard D. Irwin.

Buchanan, James M. and Weber, Bruce A. (1982), 'Growth in Residential Property Taxes: A Model for Estimating Direct and Indirect Population Impacts', **58** *Land Economics*, 324-337.

Buehler, Alfred G. (1939), *Property Taxes*, Tax Policy League, Inc.

Buehler, Alfred G. (1950), 'The Capitalization of Taxes', **3** *National Tax Journal*, 283-297.

Buehler, Alfred G., St. George, John F., Long, Henry F., Bird, Frederick L., Pond, Chester B. and Soule, Raymond L. (1948), 'Improving the Property Tax: New England Tax Conference', **1** *National Tax Journal*, 369-372.

Calvo, Guillermo A., Kotlikoff, Laurence J. and Rodriquez, Carlos Alfredo (1979), 'The Incidence of a Tax on Pure Rent: A New (?) Reason for an Old Answer', **87** *Journal of Political Economy*, 869-874.

Carlton, Dennis W. (1981), 'The Spacial Effects of a Tax on Housing and Land', **11** *Regional Science and Urban Economics*, 509-527.

Carman, Hoy F. and Polson, Jim G. (1971), 'Tax Shifts as a Result of Differential Assessment of Farmland: California, 1968-69', **24** *National Tax Journal*, 449-457.

Carroll, Robert J. and Yinger, John (1994), 'Is the Property Tax a Benefit Tax? The Case of Rental Housing', **47** *National Tax Journal*, 295-316.

Case, Karl E. (1978), *Property Taxation: The Need for Reform*, Cambridge, MA, Ballinger.

Case, Karl E. and Grant, James H. (1991), 'Property Tax Incidence in a Multijurisdictional Neoclassical Model', **19** *Public Finance Quarterly*, 379-392.

Cebula, Richard J. (1982), 'Property Taxation and Prices: An Exploratory Note', **17** *Review of Business and Economic Research*, 85-87.

Chang, Cyril F. and Tuckman, Howard P. (1990), 'Do Higher Property Tax Rates Increase the Market Share of Nonprofit Hospitals?', **43** *National Tax Journal*, 175-187.

Cheng, Pao Lun (1970), 'The Common Level of Assessment in Property Taxation', **23** *National Tax Journal*, 50-65.

Cheng, Pao Lun (1974), 'Property Taxation, Assessment Performance and Its Measurement', **29** *Public Finance Quarterly*, 268-284.

Cheng, Pao Lun and Edwards, Alfred L. (1959), 'Compensatory Property Taxation: An Alternative', **12** *National Tax Journal*, 270-275.

Cheng, Yung-Ping (1965), 'Present Status and Fiscal Significance of Property Tax Exemptions for the Aged', **18** *National Tax Journal*, 162-174.

Ching, C.T.K. and Frick, G.E. (1970), 'Effect of Use Value Assessment on Property Tax Rates', **52** *American Journal of Agricultural Research*, 603-606.

Chinloy, Peter T. (1978), 'Effective Property Taxes and Tax Capitalization', **11** *Canadian Journal of Economics*, 740-750.

Church, Albert M. (1974), 'Capitalization of the Effective Property Tax Rate on Single Family Residences', **27** *National Tax Journal*, 113-122.

Church, Albert M. (1981), 'The Effects of Local Government Expenditures and Property Taxes on Investment', **9** *American Real Estate and Urban Economics Association Journal*, 165-180.

Clapp, John M. (1990), 'A New Test for Equitable Real Estate Tax Assessment', **3** *Journal of Real Estate Finance and Economics*, 233-249.

Clatanoff, Robert M. (1986), *Patterns of Property Tax Administration in the U.S.*, Research and Information Series, No. 5, Chicago, Illinois, International Association of Assessment Officers.

Coates, Dennis (1993), 'Property Tax Competition in a Repeated Game', **23** *Regional Science and Urban Economics*, 111-119.

Coen, Robert M. and Powell, Brian J. (1972), 'Theory and Measurement of the Incidence of Differential Property Taxes on Rental Housing', **25** *National Tax Journal*, 211-216.

Colberg, Marshall R. (1955), 'Utility Profits: A Substitute for Property Taxes', **8** *National Tax Journal*, 382-387.

Coughlin, Robert E. and Isard, Walter (1957), *Municipal Costs and Revenues Resulting from Community Growth*, Wellesley, Massachusetts, Chandler-Davis Publishing Company.

Coughlin, Robert E., Berry, David and Plaut, Thomas (1979), 'Differential Assessment of Real Property as an Incentive to Open Space Preservation and Farmland Retention', **31** *National Tax Journal*, 165-179.

Courant, Paul N. (1977), 'A General Equilibrium Model of Heterogenous Local Property Taxes', **8** *Journal of Public Economics*, 313-327.

Courant, Paul N., Gramlich, Edward M. and Rubinfeld, Daniel L. (1979), 'Tax Limitation and the Demand for Public Services in Michigan', **32** *National Tax Journal*, 147-157.

Cowing, T.G. (1974), 'Real Property Taxes, Local Government Services and Residential Property Values: Comment', **41** *Southern Economic Journal*, 325-329.

Daicoff, Darwin W. (1967), 'Capitalization of the Property Tax', in Brazer, Harvey E. (ed.), *Essays in State and Local Finance*, Ann Arbor, Michigan, University of Michigan, Institute of Public Administration.

Davenport, Herbert Joseph (1917), 'Theoretical Issues in the Single Tax', **7** *American Economic Review*, 1-30.

David, E.L. and Skurski, Roger B. (1966), 'Property Tax Assessment and Absentee Owners', **19** *National Tax Journal*, 421-426.

Davies, Edgar J. (1948), 'The Louisana Property Tax Relief Fund: A Source of Financial Assistance for Local Governments', **1** *National Tax Journal*, 270-272.

Davis, Otto and Wertz, Kenneth (1969), 'The Consistency of the Assessment of Property: Some Empirical Results and Managerial Suggestions', **1** *Applied Economics*, 151-157.

Davisson, Malcolm M. and Schmelzle, William K. (1950), 'Equalization of Property Tax Assessments in California', **3** *National Tax Journal*, 221-232.

De Tray, Dennis and Fernandez, Judith (1986), 'Distributional Impacts of the Property Tax Revolt', **39** *National Tax Journal*, 435-450.

Deaton, Brady J. and Mundy, S. Darrell (1975), 'Real Property Taxation and Farm Real Estate Values: Incidence and Implications: Comment', **57** *American Journal of Agricultural Economics*, 125-126.

Delipalla, Sophia and Keen, Michael (1992), 'The Comparison Between ad Valorem and Specific Taxation Under Imperfect Competition', **49** *Journal of Public Economics*, 351-367.

DeSalvo, Joseph S. (1971), 'Effects of the Property Tax on Operating and Investment Decisions of Rental Property Owners', **24** *National Tax Journal*, 45-50.

DeSalvo, Joseph S. (1973), 'Effects of the Property Tax on Operating and Investment Decisions of Rental Property Owners: Reply', **26** *National Tax Journal*, 129-131.

Diamond, Stephen (1983), 'The Death and Transfiguration of Benefit Taxation: Special Assessments in Nineteenth-Century America', **12** *Journal of Legal Studies*, 201-240.

Dimasi, Joseph A. (1986), 'Property Tax Classification and Welfare in Urban Areas: A General Equilibrium Computational Approach', **23** *Journal of Urban Economics*, 131-149.

Dimasi, Joseph A. (1987), 'The Effects of Site Value Taxation in an Urban Area: A General

Equilibrium Computational Approach', **40** *National Tax Journal*, 577-590.

DiPasquale, Denise and Wheaton, William C. (1996), *Urban Economics and Real Estate Markets*, Englewood Cliffs, NJ, Simon and Schuster, Prentice Hall.

Do, A. Quang and Sirmans, C.F. (1994), 'Residential Property Tax Capitalization: Discount Rate Evidence from California', **47** *National Tax Journal*, 341-348.

Dornfest, Alan S. (1993), 'Assessment Ratio Study Issues: 1992 Survey Results', **12** *Property Tax Journal*, 3 ff.

Douglas, Richard W., Jr (1980), 'Site Value Taxation and the Timing of Land Development', **39** *American Journal of Economics and Sociology*, 289-294.

Dowding, Keith, John, Peter and Biggs, Stephen (1994), 'Tiebout: A Survey of the Empirical Literature', **31** *Urban Studies Abstracts*, 767-797.

Due, John F. (1961), 'Studies of State-Local Tax Differences on Location of Industry', **14** *National Tax Journal*, 163-173.

Due, John F. (1963), *Government Finance, An Economic Analysis*, Homewood, IL, Richard D. Irwin.

Dushansky, Richard, Ingber, Melvin and Karatjas, Nicholas (1981), 'The Impact of Property Taxation on Housing Values and Rents', **10** *Journal of Urban Economics*, 240-255.

Eaton, Jonathan (1988), 'Foreign-Owned Land', **78** *American Economic Review*, 76-88.

Ebel, Robert D. and Ortbal, James (1989), 'Direct Residential Property Tax Relief', **15** *Intergovernmental Perspective*, 9-14.

Eckart, Wolfgang (1983), 'The Neutrality of Land Taxation in an Uncertain World', **36** *National Tax Journal*, 237-241.

Eckert, Joseph K. (ed.) (1990), *Property Tax Appraisal and Assessment Administration*, Chicago, Illinois, International Association of Assessing Officers.

Edel, Matthew and Sclar, Elliot (1974), 'Taxes, Spending, and Property Values: Supply Adjustment in a Tiebout-Oates Model', **82** *Journal of Political Economy*, 941-954.

Edwards, J. and Keen, Michael (1996), 'Tax Competition and Leviathan', **40** *European Economic Review*, 113-134.

Ellis, Larry V., Combs, J. Paul and Weber, William (1983), 'Administrative Inequity in the Property Tax: Further Evidence', **11** *Public Finance Quarterly*, 491-506.

Engle, Robert F. (1975), 'De Facto Discrimination in Residential Assessments: Boston', **28** *National Tax Journal*, 445-451.

Epple, Dennis, Filimon, Radu and Romer, Thomas (1993), 'Existence of Voting and Housing Equilibrium in a System of Communities With Property Taxes', **23** *Regional Science and Urban Economics*, 585-610.

Erickson, Robert A. and Wollover, David R. (1987), 'Local Tax Burdens and the Supply of Business Sites in Suburban Municipalities', **27** *Journal of Regional Science*, 25-37.

Feldman, Edward S. (1949), 'Exemption of House Furnishings from Property Taxation', **2** *National Tax Journal*, 334-342.

Feldstein, Martin S. (1977), 'The Surprising Incidence of a Tax on a Pure Rent: A New Answer to an Old Question', **85** *Journal of Political Economy*, 349-360.

Fischel, William A. (1975), 'Fiscal and Environmental Considerations in the Location of Firms in Suburban Communities', in Mills, Edwin S. and Oates, Wallace E. (eds), *Fiscal Zoning and Land Use Controls*, Lexington, MA, Lexington Books.

Fischel, William A. (1976), 'An Evaluation of Proposals for Metropolitan Sharing of Commercial and Industrial Property Tax Base', **3** *Journal of Urban Economics*, 253-263.

Fischel, William A. (1980), 'Zoning and Land Use Reform: A Property Rights Perspective', **1** *Virginia Journal of Natural Resources Law*, 69-93.

Fischel, William A. (1981), 'Is Local Government Structure in Large Urbanized Areas

Monopolistic or Competitive?', **34** *National Tax Journal*, 95-104.

Fischel, William A. (1985), *The Economics of Zoning Laws: A Property Rights Approach to American Land Use Controls*, Baltimore, MD, John Hopkins University Press.

Fischel, William A. (1989), 'Did Serrano Cause Proposition 13?', **42** *National Tax Journal*, 465-474.

Fischel, William A. (1992), 'Property Taxation and the Tiebout Model: Evidence for the Benefit View from Zoning and Voting', **30** *Journal of Economic Literature*, 163-169.

Fischel, William A. (1995), 'Review of: "Property Taxes and Tax Revolts: The Legacy of Proposition 13"', **33** *Journal of Economic Literature*, 239-240.

Fischel, William A. (1996), 'How Serrano Caused Proposition 13', **12** *Journal of Law and Politics*, 407-434.

Fischel, William A. and Campbell, Colin D. (1996), 'Preferences for School Finance Systems: Voters versus Judges', **49** *National Tax Journal*, 1-15.

Fisher, Glen W. (1987), 'The Evolution of the General Property Tax in the Nineteenth Century: The Search for Equality', **6** *Property Tax Journal*, 99-117.

Fisher, Peter S. (1980), 'Adjustments for Household Size in Property Tax Circuit-Breaker Programs', **33** *National Tax Journal*, 161-170.

Flaherty, Shelia M. (1992), 'Property Tax Limitations: Do We Need a New Approach for the 1990s?', **45** *Tax Lawyer*, 827-843.

Follain, James R. and Miyake, Tamar Emi (1986), 'Land Versus Capital Taxation: A General Equilibrium Analysis', **39** *National Tax Journal*, 451-470.

Frech, H. Edward III, Deacon, Rovert, Decanio, Stephen J. and Johnson, Bruce M. (1990), *Taxing Energy: Oil Severence Taxation and the Economy*, New York, Holmes and Meyer.

Fuerst, J.S. and Ditton, Andrew (1975), 'Reducing Property Taxes: An Evaluation of a Collective Action', **51** *Land Economics*, 94-97.

Fullerton, Don and Gordon, Roger H. (1983), 'A Reexamination of Tax Distortions in General Equilibrium Models', in Feldstein, Martin S. (ed.), *Behavioral Simulation Methods in Tax Policy Analysis*, Chicago, University of Chicago Press.

Fullerton, Don and Henderson, Yolanda K. (1984), 'Incentive Effects of Taxes on Income from Capital: Alternative Policies in the 1980s', in Hulten, Charles R. and Sawhill, Isabel V. (eds), *The Legacy of Reaganomics: Prospects for Long-Term Growth*, Washington, Urban Institute Press.

Funk, Gerald M. and Kryscio, Richard J. (1978), 'Equity and the Property Tax: Comments on Two Seemingly Unrelated Conceptual Frameworks', **31** *National Tax Journal*, 411-413.

Gaffney, Mason (1972), *The Property Tax is a Progressive Tax*, Proceedings of the Sixty-Fourth Annual Conference on Taxation, Columbus, Ohio, National Tax Association, 1972.

Gaffney, Mason (1972), 'What is Property Tax Reform?', **31** *American Journal of Economics and Sociology*, 139-152.

Gaffney, Mason (1973), 'An Agenda for Strengthening the Property Tax', in Peterson, George E. (ed.), *Property Tax Reform*, Washington, Urban Institute Press.

Garwood, John D. (1952), 'Taxes and Industrial Location', **5** *National Tax Journal*, 365-369.

Garwood, John D. (1956), 'Kansas Citizens Examine Their Property Taxes', **9** *National Tax Journal*, 258-267.

George, Henry (1879), *Progress and Poverty*, New York, NY, Robert Schalkenbach Foundation.

George, Henry (1883), *Social Problems*, New York, NY, Robert Schalkenbach Foundation.

George, Henry (1885), *Land and Taxation*, Our Land and Land Policy, Speeches, Lectures, and Miscellaneous Writings, New York, NY, National Single Tax League.

Geraci, Vincent J. (1977), 'Measuring the Benefits from Property Tax Assessment Reform', **30** *National Tax Journal*, 195-205.

Geraci, Vincent J. and Plourde, James L. (1976), 'The Determinants of Uniform Property Tax Assessment', **11** *Assessors Journal*, 235-251.

Ghaus, Aisha, F.A. and Pasha, Hafiz A. (1996), 'Excess Burden of the Property Tax: The Open Jurisdiction Case', **24** *Public Finance Quarterly*, 120-128.

Gibb, Kenneth (1992), 'The Council Tax: The Distributional Implications of Returning to a Tax on Property', **39** *Scottish Journal of Political Economy*, 302-317.

Glaeser, E.L. (1996), 'The Incentive Effects of Property Taxes on Local Government', **89** *Public Choice*, 93-111.

Gold, Steven D. (1976), 'A Note on Designing Property Tax Circuit-Breakers', **29** *National Tax Journal*, 477-481.

Gold, Steven D. (1979), *Property Tax Relief*, Lexington, MA, Heath.

Gold, Steven D. (1981), 'Homeowner Property Taxes, Inflation and Property Tax Relief', **34** *National Tax Journal*, 167-184.

Goodman, Allen C. (1978), 'Hedonic Prices, Price Indices, and Housing Markets', **5** *Journal of Urban Economics*, 471-484.

Goodman, Allen C. (1983), 'Capitalization of Property Tax Differentials Within and Among Municipalities', **59** *Land Economics*, 211-219.

Goodman, Allen C. (1988), 'An Econometric Model of Housing Price, Permanent Income, Tenure Choice, and Housing Demand', **23** *Journal of Urban Economics*, 327-353.

Gouldemans, Robert (1974), *Use-Value Farmland Assessments: Theory, Practice, Impacts*, Chicago, Illinois, International Association of Assessing Officers.

Grieson, Ronald E. (1973), 'Effects of the Property Tax on Operating and Investment Decisions of Rental Property Owners: A Note', **26** *National Tax Journal*, 127-128.

Grieson, Ronald E. (1974), 'The Economics of Property Taxes and Land Values: The Elasticity of Supply of Structures', **1** *Journal of Urban Economics*, 367-381.

Grieson, Ronald E. (1975), 'The Incidence of Profits Taxes in a Neoclassical Growth Model', **4** *Journal of Public Economics*, 75-85.

Gronouski, John A. (1957), 'State Supervision of Property Tax Administration', **10** *National Tax Journal*, 158-170.

Groves, Harold M. (1967), 'Property Taxation of Intangibles', in Lindholm, Richard W. (ed.), *Property Taxation USA*, Madison, Wisconsin, University of Wisconsin Press.

Groves, Harold M. and Kahn, C. Harry (1952), 'The Stability of State and Local Tax Yields', **42** *American Economic Review*, 87-102.

Groves, Harold M. and Riew, John (1963), 'The Impact of Industry on Local Taxes - A Simple Model', **16** *National Tax Journal*, 137-146.

Gurwitz, Aaron S. (1980), 'The Capitalization of School Finance Reform', **5** *Journal of Education Finance*, 297-319.

Gustely, Richard D. (1976), 'Local Taxes, Expenditures and Urban Housing: A Reassessment of the Evidence', **42** *Southern Economic Journal*, 659-665.

Gyourko, Joseph and Tracy, Joseph (1989), 'On the Political Economics of Land Value Capitalization and Local Public Sector Rent Seeking in a Tiebout Model', **26** *Journal of Urban Economics*, 152-173.

Hady, Thomas F. (1962), 'The Incidence of the Personal Property Tax', **15** *National Tax Journal*, 368-384.

Hady, Thomas F. (1970), 'Differential Assessment of Farmland on the Rural-Urban Fringe', **52** *American Journal of Agricultural Economics*, 25-32.

Haig, Robert Murray (1914), *A History of the General Property Tax in Illinois*, Illinois, Urbana, Illinois, University of Illinois Studies in the Social Sciences.

Hall, James K. (1956a), 'Sales-Assessment Ratio Survey in Washington', **9** *National Tax Journal*, 177-192.

Hall, James K. (1956b), 'Assessment Equalization in Washington', **9** *National Tax Journal*, 302-325.

Hamilton, Bob and Whalley, John (1985), 'Tax Treatment of Housing in a Dynamic Sequenced General Equilibrium Model', **27** *Journal of Public Economics*, 157-175.

Hamilton, Bruce W. (1975a), 'Property Taxes and the Tiebout Hypothesis: Some Empirical Evidence', in Mills, Edwin S. and Oates, Wallace E. (eds), *Fiscal Zoning and Land Use Controls*, Lexington, MA, Lexington Books, 13-29.

Hamilton, Bruce W. (1975b), 'Zoning and Property Taxation in a System of Local Governments', **12** *Urban Studies*, 205-211.

Hamilton, Bruce W. (1976a), 'The Effects of Property Taxes and Local Public Spending on Property Values: A Theoretical Comment', **84** *Journal of Political Economy*, 647-650.

Hamilton, Bruce W. (1976b), 'Capitalization of Intrajurisdictional Differences in Local Tax Prices', **66** *American Economic Review*, 743-753.

Hamilton, Bruce W. (1977), 'Local Government, the Property Tax, and the Quality of Life: Some Findings on Progressivity', in Wingo, Lowdon and Evans, Alan (eds), *Public Economics and the Quality of Life*, Baltimore, MD, John Hopkins Press for Resources for the Future.

Hamilton, Bruce W. (1979), 'Capitalization and the Regressivity of the Property Tax: Empirical Evidence', **32** *National Tax Journal*, 169-180.

Hamilton, Bruce W. (1983), 'A Review: Is the Property Tax a Benefit Tax?', in Zodrow, George R. (ed.), *Local Provision of Public Services: The Tiebout Model After Twenty-Five Years*, New York, Academic Press.

Hansen, David E. and Schwartz, Seymour I. (1975), 'Landowner Behavior at the Rural-Urban Fringe in Response to Preferential Taxation', **51** *Land Economics*, 341-354.

Hansmann, Henry B. (1991), 'Condominium and Co-operative Housing: Transactional Efficiency, Tax Subsidies, and Tenure Choice', **20** *Journal of Legal Studies*, 25-71.

Harmon, O.R. (1989), 'A New View of the Incidence of the Property Tax: The Case of New Jersey', **17** *Public Finance Quarterly*, 323-348.

Harriss, C. Lowell (1952), 'The British Revaluation of Real Estate for Local Taxation', **5** *National Tax Journal*, 239-244.

Harriss, C. Lowell (1968), 'Economic Evaluation of Real Property Taxation', in Connery, Robert H. (ed.), *Municipal Income Taxes, Academy of Political Science Proceedings*, New York, Columbia University Press.

Harriss, C. Lowell (1974), 'Property Taxation: What's Good and What's Bad About It', **33** *American Journal of Economics and Sociology*, 89-102.

Harriss, C. Lowell (ed.) (1983), *The Property Tax and Local Finance*, New York, NY, Academy of Political Science.

Haurin, Donald (1980), 'The Effect of Property Taxes on Urban Areas', **7** *Journal of Urban Economics*, 384-396.

Haurin, Donald (1981), 'Property Taxation and the Structure of Urban Areas', in Henderson, J. Vernon (ed.), *Research in Urban Economics, Vol. 1*, Greenwood, JAI Press.

Heilbrun, James (1966), *Real Estate Taxes and Urban Housing*, New York, Columbia University Press.

Heinburg, John D. and Oates, Wallace E. (1970), 'The Incidence of Differential Property Taxes on Urban Housing: A Comment and Some Further Evidence', **23** *National Tax*

Journal, 92-98.

Heinburg, John D. and Oates, Wallace E. (1972), 'The Incidence of Differential Property Taxes on Rental Housing: An Addendum', **25** *National Tax Journal*, 221-222.

Hellerstein, Jerome R. (1959), 'Judicial Review of Property Tax Assessments', **14** *Tax Law Review*, 327-352.

Hellman, Daryl A. and Sifniotis, Costas (1977), 'Distributional Considerations of Property Tax Exemption: An Analytical Framework', **5** *Public Finance Quarterly*, 127-136.

Henderson, J. Vernon (1985), 'Property Tax Incidence Within a Public Sector', **93** *Journal of Political Economy*, 649-665.

Henderson, J. Vernon (1994), 'Community Choice of Revenue Instruments', **24** *Regional Science and Urban Economics*, 159-183.

Henderson, J. Vernon (1995), 'Will Homeowners Impose Property Taxes?', **25** *Regional Science and Urban Economics*, 153-181.

Henry, Edward L. (1951), 'The Farmer's Tax Burden', **4** *National Tax Journal*, 341-350.

Hickelman, Jac C. and Wallis, J. (1997), 'Railroads and Property Taxes', **34** *Explorations in Economic History*, 77-99.

Hobson, Paul A. R. (1986), 'The Incidence of Heterogeneous Residential Property Taxes', **29** *Journal of Public Economics*, 363-373.

Hochman, Oded (1981), 'Land Rents, Optimal Taxation and Local Fiscal Independence in an Economy with Local Public Goods', **15** *Journal of Public Economics*, 59-85.

Hoff, Karla (1991), 'Land Taxes, Output Taxes, and Sharecropping: Was Henry George Right?', **5** *World Bank Economic Review*, 93-111.

Holland, Daniel M. (ed.) (1970), *The Assessment of Land Value*, Madison, University of Wisconsin.

Holtz-Eakin, Douglas (1986), 'Unobserved Tastes and the Determination of Municipal Services', **39** *National Tax Journal*, 527-532.

Holtz-Eakin, Douglas and Rosen, Harvey S. (1989), 'The 'Rationality of Municipality Capital Spending: Evidence from New Jersey', **19** *Regional Science and Urban Economics*, 517-536.

Howards, Irving (1963), 'Property Tax Rate Limits in Illinois and Their Effect Upon Local Government', **16** *National Tax Journal*, 285-293.

Hoxby, Coroline Minter (1997), 'Are Efficiency and Equity in School Finance Substitutes or Complements?', **10** *Journal of Economic Perspectives*, 51-72.

Hoyt, William H. (1990), 'Local Government Inefficiency and the Tiebout Hypothesis: Does Competition Among Municipalities Limit Local Government Inefficiencies?', **57** *Southern Economic Journal*, 481-496.

Hoyt, William H. (1991), 'Competitive Jurisdictions, Congestion, and the Henry George Theorem: When Should Property be Taxed Instead of Land?', **21** *Regional Science and Urban Economics*, 351-370.

Hoyt, William H. (1991), 'Property Taxation, Nash Equilibrium, and Market Power', **30** *Journal of Urban Economics*, 123-131.

Hyman, David N. and Pasour, Ernest C., Jr (1973a), 'Real Property Taxes, Local Public Services and Residential Property Values', **39** *Southern Economic Journal*, 601-611.

Hyman, David N. and Pasour, Ernest C., Jr (1973b), 'Property Tax Differentials and Residential Rents in North Carolina', **26** *National Tax Journal*, 303-307.

Hyman, David N. and Pasour, Ernest C., Jr (1974), 'Real Property Taxes, Local Public Services and Residential Property Values: A Reply', **41** *Southern Economic Journal*, 329-331.

Ihlanfeldt, Keith (1979), 'The Incidence of the Property Tax on Homeowners: Evidence from the Panel Study of Income Dynamics', **32** *National Tax Journal*, 535-541.

Ihlanfeldt, Keith (1982), 'Property Tax Incidence on Owner-Occupied Housing: Evidence from the Annual Housing Survey', **35** *National Tax Journal*, 89-97.

Ihlanfeldt, Keith (1984), 'Property Taxation and the Demand for Housing: An Econometric Analysis', **16** *Journal of Urban Economics*, 208-224.

Ihlanfeldt, Keith and Boehm, Thomas P. (1983), 'Property Taxation and the Demand for Home Ownership', **11** *Public Finance Quarterly*, 47-66.

Ihlanfeldt, Keith and Jackson, John D. (1982), 'Systematic Assessment Error and Intrajurisdictional Property Tax Capitalization', **49** *Southern Economic Journal*, 417-427.

Ihori, Toshihiro (1990), 'Economic Effects of Land Taxes in an Inflationary Economy', **42** *Journal of Public Economics*, 195-211.

Inman, Robert P. (1979), 'The Fiscal Performance of Local Governments: An Interpretative Review', in Mieszkowski, Peter and Straszheim, Mahlon (eds), *Current Issues in Urban Economics*, Baltimore, MD, John Hopkins University Press.

International Association of Assessing Officers (1992), *Assessment Administrative Practices in the U.S. and Canada*, Chicago, Illinois.

Islam, Mohammed N. (1989), 'Tiebout Hypothesis and Migration Impact of Local Fiscal Policies', **44** *Public Finance*, 406-418.

Islam, Mohammed N. and Sahni, Balbir S. (1987), 'Property Taxation and Regional Public Services in Canada: A Causality Analysis', **58** *Annals of Public and Cooperative Economy*, 275-286.

Jaffee, Bruce L. (1978), 'State Taxation of Intangibles: The Problem of Evasion', **6** *Public Finance Quarterly*, 485-502.

James, F.J. (1975), *Assessment Procedures, Community Characteristics and the Accuracy of Property Tax Assessments*, Washington, Urban Institute Press.

Jensen, Jens P. (1931), *Property Taxation in the United States*, Chicago, Illinois, University of Chicago Press.

Johnson, David B. (1993), 'A Review of Taxation of Property: Local Government Rates in Victoria', **61** *Review of Marketing and Agricultural Economics*, 455-477.

Johnson, Dudley W. (1958), 'A Note on Local Administration of the Property Tax : A Case Study of Bethlehem, Pennsylvania', **11** *National Tax Journal*, 265-271.

Kanemoto, Yoshitsugu (1985), 'Housing as an Asset and the Effects of Property Taxation on the Residential Development Process', **17** *Journal of Urban Economics*, 145-166.

King, A. Thomas (1973), *Property Taxes, Amenities, and Residential Land Values*, Cambridge, MA, Ballinger.

King, A. Thomas (1977), 'Estimating Property Tax Capitalization: A Critical Comment', **85** *Journal of Political Economy*, 425-431.

Kish-Goodling, Donna M. (1995), *Property Taxes and Local Economic Development*, New York, Garland Inc.

Kitchen, Harry M. (1987), 'Property Taxation as a Tax on Wealth: Some New Evidence', **35** *Canadian Tax Journal*, 953-963.

Kitchen, Harry M. (1992), *Property Taxation in Canada*, Canadian Tax Paper No. 92, Toronto, Canada, Canadian Tax Foundation.

Klemperer, W. David (1974), 'Forests and the Property Tax - A Re-Examination', **27** *National Tax Journal*, 645-651.

Klemperer, W. David (1977), 'An Economic Analysis of the Case Against ad Valorem Property Taxation in Forestry - A Comment', **30** *National Tax Journal*, 469 ff.

Knapp, John L. (1974), *Virginia Issues: The Real Property Tax*, Charlottesville, VA, University Press of Virginia.

Kochin, Lewis A. and Parks, Richard W. (1982), 'Vertical Equity in Real Estate Assessment:

A Fair Appraisal', **20** *Economic Inquiry*, 511-531.

Kochin, Lewis A. and Parks, Richard W. (1984), 'Testing for Assessment Uniformity: A Reappraisal', **3** *Property Tax Journal*, 27-53.

Kotlikoff, Laurence J. and Summers, Lawrence H. (1987), 'Tax Incidence', in Auerbach, Alan and Feldstein, Martin (eds), *Handbook in Public Economics*, North-Holland, Amsterdam.

Krelove, R. (1992), 'Do Local Governments Use Their Tax Bases Efficiently', **31** *Journal of Urban Economics*, 285-300.

Krelove, R. (1993), 'The Persistence and Inefficiency of Property Tax Finance of Local Public Expenditures', **51** *Journal of Public Economics*, 415-435.

Kurnow, Ernest (1963), 'On the Elasticity of the Real Property Tax', **18** *Journal of Finance*, 36-38.

Ladd, Helen F. (1973), 'The Role of the Property Tax: A Reassessment', in Musgrave, Richard A. (ed.), *Broad Based Taxes, New and Old*, Baltimore, MD, John Hopkins University Press.

Ladd, Helen F. (1975), 'Local Education Expenditures, Fiscal Capacity, and the Composition of the Property Tax Base', **28** *National Tax Journal*, 145-158.

Ladd, Helen F. (1976a), 'State Wide Taxation of Commercial and Industrial Property for Education', **29** *National Tax Journal*, 143-153.

Ladd, Helen F. (1976b), 'Municipal Expenditures and the Composition of the Property Tax Base', in Lynn, Arthur D., Jr (ed.), *Property Taxation, Land Use, and Public Policy*, Washington, Brookings Institution.

Ladd, Helen F. (1992), 'Population Growth, Density and the Cost of Providing Public Services', **29** *Urban Studies*, 273-295.

Ladd, Helen F. and Bradbury, Katherine (1988), 'City Taxes and Property Tax Bases', **41** *National Tax Journal*, 503-524.

Lea, Michael J. (1982), 'Local Tax and Expenditure Capitalization: Integrating Evidence from the Market and Political Process', **10** *Public Finance Quarterly*, 95-117.

Lee, Eugene C. (1953), 'State Equalization of Local Assessments', **6** *National Tax Journal*, 177-187.

Lent, George E. (1966), *Taxation of Unimproved Land Value*, Washington, International Monetary Fund.

Lent, George E. (1982), 'Property Taxes in the Carribean Community', **36** *Bulletin for International Fiscal Documentation*, 439-444.

Leonard, Lawrence A. (1958), 'Property Taxation in Kansas, An Historical Analysis', **11** *National Tax Journal*, 230-240.

Leong, Y.S. and Kamins, Robert M. (1961), 'Property Taxation in the 50th State', **14** *National Tax Journal*, 59-69.

Leroy, Stephen F. (1976), 'Urban Land Rent and the Incidence of Property Taxes', **3** *Journal of Urban Economics*, 167-179.

Lewis, Chris W. and McNutt, Paul J. (1979), 'The Incidence of Property Taxes on Single Family Housing', **7** *American Real Estate and Urban Economics Association Journal*, 344-361.

Lin, Chuan (1986), 'A General Equilibrium Analysis of Property Tax Incidence', **29** *Journal of Public Economics*, 113-132.

Lin, Chuan (1994), 'Property Taxation as a National Policy Tool in Taiwan', in Musgrave, Richard A., Chang, Ching-huei and Riew, John (eds), *Taxation and Economic Development Among Pacific Asian Countries*, Boulder, CO, Westview Press.

Lindauer, John H. and Singh, Sarjit (1966), 'Effects of the Punjab Land Tax', **19** *National Tax Journal*, 427-433.

Lindholm, Richard W. (ed.) (1967), *Property Taxation USA - A Symposium*, Committee on Taxation, Resources, and Economic Development, Madison, Wisconsin, University of Wisconsin Press.

Linn, Johannes F. (1980), 'Property Taxation in Bogota, Columbia: An Analysis of Poor Revenue Performance', **8** *Public Finance Quarterly*, 457-476.

Lockner, Allyn O. and Kim, Han J. (1973), 'Circuit-Breakers on Farm-Property-Tax Overload: A Case Study', **26** *National Tax Journal*, 233-240.

Lowenstein, Louis K. (1963), 'The Impact of New Industry on the Fiscal Revenues and Expenditures of Suburban Communities', **16** *National Tax Journal*, 113-136.

Lynn, Arthur D. (1967), 'Trends in Taxation of Personal Property', in Buehler, Alfred G. (ed.), *The Property Tax: Problems and Potentials*, Princeton, NJ, Tax Institute of America.

Lynn, Arthur D. (ed.) (1976), *Property Taxation, Land Use and Public Policy*, Madison, Wisconsin, University of Wisconsin Press.

Mair, Douglas (1991), 'The Incidence of the Property Tax: A Survey', **13** *British Review of Economic Issues*, 1-27.

Mair, Douglas and Damania, Richard (1988), 'The Richardian Tradition and Local Property Taxation', **12** *Cambridge Journal of Economics*, 435-449.

Mair, Douglas and Laramie, Anthony J. (1992), 'The Incidence of Business Rates on Manufacturing Industry in Scotland and the Rest of the UK', **39** *Scottish Journal of Political Economy*, 76-94.

Man, Joyce Y. (1995), 'The Incidence of Differential Commercial Property Taxes: Empirical Evidence', **48** *National Tax Journal*, 479-496.

Manning, Glenn H. and Thompson, Emmett F. (1969), 'Forest Property Taxation: Another Look', **47** *Journal of Forestry*, 556-559.

Manning, Raymond E. (1949), 'Burden of State and Local Taxes in 18 Large Cities', **2** *National Tax Journal*, 173-178.

Margolis, Julius (1956a), 'The Variation of Property Tax Rates Within a Metropolitan Region', **9** *National Tax Journal*, 326-330.

Margolis, Julius (1956b), 'On Municipal Land Policy For Fiscal Gains', **9** *National Tax Journal*, 247-257.

Marshall, Alfred (1890), *Principles of Economics*, London, Macmillan.

Martinez Vazquez, Jorge and Ihlanfeldt, Keith (1987), 'Why Property Tax Capitalization Rates Differ: A Critical Analysis', in Quigley, J.M. and Smolensky, E. (eds), *Modern Public Finance*, Cambridge: Harvard University Press.

May, Peter J. (1982), 'Local Tax Burdens, Benefit Levels and Fiscal Illusion', **35** *National Tax Journal*, 465-475.

McCluskey, William J. (ed.) (1991), *Comparative Property Tax Systems*, Aldershot, Ashgate, Avebury.

McDonald, John F. (1993), 'Incidence of the Property Tax on Commercial Real Estate: The Case of Downtown Chicago', **46** *National Tax Journal*, 109-120.

McDougall, Gerald S. (1976), 'Local Public Goods and Residential Property Values: Some Insights and Extensions', **29** *National Tax Journal*, 436-447.

McEachern, William A. (1981), 'Tax Exempt Property, Tax Capitalization, and the Cumulative-Urban-Decay Hypothesis', **34** *National Tax Journal*, 185-192.

McGuire, Therese J. (1985), 'Are Local Property Taxes Important in the Intrametropolitan Location Decisions of Firms? An Empirical Analysis of the Minneapolis-St. Paul Metropolitan Area', **18** *Journal of Urban Economics*, 226-234.

McGuire, Therese J. (1987), 'The Effect of New Firm Locations on Local Property Taxes', **22** *Journal of Urban Economics*, 223-229.

McLure, Charles E., Jr (1967), 'The Interstate Exporting of State and Local Taxes: Estimates for 1962', **20** *National Tax Journal*, 49-77.

McLure, Charles E., Jr (1977), 'The "New View" of the Property Tax - A Caveat', **30** *National Tax Journal*, 69-75.

McLure, Charles E., Jr (1979), 'The Relevance of the "New View" of the Incidence of the Property Tax in Developing Countries', in Bahl, Roy (ed.), *The Taxation of Urban Property in Less Developed Countries*, Madison, University of Wisconsin.

McLure, Charles E., Jr (1981), 'Market Dominance and the Exporting of State Taxes', **34** *National Tax Journal*, 483-485.

McLure, Charles E., Jr and Thirsk, Wayne R. (1975), 'A Simplified Exposition of the Harberger Model, I: Tax Incidence', **28** *National Tax Journal*, 24-25.

McMillan, Melville and Carlson, Richard (1977), 'The Effect of Property Taxes and Local Public Services Upon Residential Property Values in Small Wisconsin Cities', **59** *American Journal of Agricultural Economics*, 81-87.

Meng, Ronald (1986), 'Horizontal Equity and Property Taxation in Canada', **39** *National Tax Journal*, 221-228.

Meng, Ronald and Gillespie, W. Irwin (1986), 'The Regressivity of Property Tax in Canada: Another Look', **34** *Canadian Tax Journal*, 1417-1430.

Metha, Shekhar and Giertz, J. Fred (1996), 'Measuring the Performance of the Property Tax Assessment Process', **49** *National Tax Journal*, 73-85.

Meyer, Charles W. (1965), 'Geographic Inequalities in Property Taxes in Iowa, 1962', **18** *National Tax Journal*, 388-397.

Mieszkowski, Peter (1969), 'Tax Incidence Theory: The Effects of Taxes on the Distribution of Income', **7** *Journal of Economic Literature*, 1103-1124.

Mieszkowski, Peter (1972a), 'On the Theory of Tax Incidence', **75** *Journal of Political Economy*, 250-262.

Mieszkowski, Peter (1972b), 'The Property Tax: An Excise or Profits Tax', **1** *Journal of Public Economics*, 73-96.

Mieszkowski, Peter and Straszheim, Mahlon (eds) (1979), *Current Issues in Urban Economics*, Baltimore, MD, John Hopkins University Press.

Mieszkowski, Peter and Zodrow, George R. (1983), 'The Incidence of the Property Tax: The Benefit View Versus the New View', in Zodrow, George R. (ed.), *Local Provision of Public Services: The Tiebout Model After Twenty-Five Years*, New York, Academic Press.

Mieszkowski, Peter and Zodrow, George R. (1989), 'Taxation and the Tiebout Model: The Differential Effects of Head Taxes, Taxes in Land Rents, and Property Taxes', **27** *Journal of Economic Literature*, 1098-1146.

Mikesell, John (1992), 'Patterns of Exclusion of Personal Property from the American Property Tax Systems', **20** *Public Finance Quarterly*, 528-542.

Mills, David E. (1981), 'The Non-Neutrality of Land Value Taxation', **34** *National Tax Journal*, 125-130.

Mills, David E. (1982), 'Reply to Tideman', **35** *National Tax Journal*, 115 ff.

Mills, Edwin S. and Oates, Wallace E. (eds) (1975), *Fiscal Zoning and Land Use Controls: The Economic Issues*, Lexington, MA, Lexington Books.

Miner, Ralph E. (1974), 'Property Taxes, Services, and Calculating Voters', **2** *Public Finance Quarterly*, 139-154.

Mitchell, George (1948), 'Using Sales Data to Measure the Quality of Property Tax Administration', **1** *National Tax Journal*, 330-340.

Moomau, Pamela H. and Morton, Rebecca B. (1992), 'Revealed Preferences for Property Taxes: An Empirical Study of Tax Incidence', **74** *Review of Economics and Statistics*, 176-179.

Moss, William G. (1977), 'Large Lot Zoning, Property Taxes, and Metropolitan Area', **4** *Journal of Urban Economics*, 408-427.

Mullen, John K. (1990), 'Property Tax Exemptions and Local Fiscal Stress', **43** *National Tax Journal*, 467-479.

Murphy, Louis S. (1915), 'The Single Tax in Relation to Forestry', **18** *The Public*, 217-223.

Murphy, Louis S. (1925), 'The General Property Tax and Forest Property', **23** *Journal of Forestry*, 762-780.

Murray, William G. (1952), 'Improvement in Real Estate Taxation Through Assessment-Sales Studies', **5** *National Tax Journal*, 86-92.

Murray, William G. and Bivens, Gordon E. (1952), 'Clinics, Bench Marks, and Improved Assessments', **5** *National Tax Journal*, 370-375.

Musgrave, Richard A. (1974), 'Is a Property Tax On Housing Regressive?', **64** *American Economic Review, Papers and Proceedings*, 222-229.

Musgrave, Richard A. (ed.) (1973), *Broad Based Taxes, New and Old*, Baltimore, MD, John Hopkins University Press.

Musgrave, Richard A. and Musgrave, Peggy B. (1989), *Public Finance in Theory and Practice*, 5th edn, New York, McGraw-Hill.

Musgrave, Richard A., Chang, Ching-huei and Riew, John (eds) (1994), *Taxation and Economic Development Among Pacific Asian Countries*, Boulder, CO, Westview Press.

Myers, Eugene A. and Stout, Randall S. (1950), 'Recent Trends in Property Tax Equalization', **3** *National Tax Journal*, 179-186.

Nechyba, Thomas J. (1997), 'Local Property and State Income Taxes: The Role of Interjurisdictional Competition and Collusion', **105** *Journal of Political Economy*, 351-384.

Netzer, Dick (1964), 'Income Elasticity of the Property Tax: A Post-Mortem Note', **17** *National Tax Journal*, 205-207.

Netzer, Dick (1966), *Economics of the Property Tax*, Washington, DC, Brookings Institution.

Netzer, Dick (1973), 'The Incidence of the Property Tax Revisited', **26** *National Tax Journal*, 515-535.

Netzer, Dick (1984), 'On Modernizing Local Public Finance: Why Aren't Property Taxes in Urban Areas Being Reformed into Land Value Taxes?', **43** *American Journal of Economics and Sociology*, 497-501.

Netzer, Dick (1993), 'Property Taxes: Their Past, Present, and Future in Government Finance', in Swartz, Thomas R. and Bonello, Frank J. (eds), *Urban Finance Under Siege*, Armonk, NY, Sharpe.

Neufeld, Ernest (1965), 'Is Tax Exempt Property a Municipal Asset?', **18** *National Tax Journal*, 414-419.

Newcomer, Mabel (1953a), 'The Decline in the General Property Tax', **6** *National Tax Journal*, 38-51.

Newcomer, Mabel (1953b), 'The Growth of Property Tax Exemptions', **6** *National Tax Journal*, 116-128.

Noguchi, Yukio (1982), 'On the Neutrality of the Property Tax', **58** *Land Economics*, 383-385.

Noiset, Luc (1995), 'Pigou, Property Taxation, and the Underprovision of Local Public Goods: Comment', **38** *Journal of Urban Economics*, 312-316.

Noonan, Albert W. (1947), 'Improvements in Personal Property Taxation', in Groves, Harold M. (ed.), *Viewpoints on Public Finance: A Book of Readings*, New York, NY, Henry Holt and Company.

Note (1962), 'Inequality in Property Tax Assessment: New Cures for an Old Ill', **75**

Harvard Law Review, 1374-1395.

O'Sullivan, Arthur M., Sexton, Terri A. and Sheffrin, Steven M. (1994), 'Differential Burdens from the Assessment of Proposition 13', **47** *National Tax Journal*, 721-729.

O'Sullivan, Arthur M., Sexton, Terri A. and Sheffrin, Steven M. (1995), *Property Taxes and Tax Revolts: The Legacy of Proposition 13*, Cambridge, Cambridge University Press.

Oakland, W.H. (1978), 'Local Taxes and Intra-Urban Industrial Location: A Survey', in Break, George (ed.), *Metropolitan Financing and Growth Management Policies*, Madison, University of Wisconsin.

Oates, Wallace E. (1969), 'The Effects of Property Taxes and Local Public Spending on Property Values: An Empirical Study of Tax Capitalization and the Tiebout Hypothesis', **77** *Journal of Political Economy*, 957-971.

Oates, Wallace E. (1973), 'The Effects of Property Taxes and Local Public Spending on Property Values: A Reply and Yet Further Results', **81** *Journal of Political Economy*, 994-1003.

Oates, Wallace E. (1987), 'Property Taxation', in Eatwell, John, Milgate, Murray and Newman, Peter (eds), *The New Palgrave, a Dictionary of Economics*, New York, The Stockton Press.

Oates, Wallace E. and Schwab, Robert M. (1988), 'Economic Competition Among Jurisdictions: Efficiency Enhancing or Distortion Inducing?', **35** *Journal of Public Economics*, 333-354.

Oates, Wallace E. and Schwab, Robert M. (1997), 'The Impact of Urban Land Taxation: The Pittsburgh Experience', **50** *National Tax Journal*, 1-21.

Oberhauser, Alois (1975), 'Death Duties and Property Taxation as a Means of More Even Distribution of the Stock of Wealth', **13** *German Economic Review*, 1-15.

Oldman, Oliver and Aaron, Henry J. (1965), 'Assessment Sales Ratios Under the Boston Property Tax', **18** *National Tax Journal*, 36-49.

Ordeshook, Peter C. (1979), 'Property Tax Consciousness', **34** *Public Choice*, 285-295.

Orr, Larry L. (1968), 'The Incidence of Differential Property Taxes on Urban Housing', **21** *National Tax Journal*, 253-262.

Orr, Larry L. (1970), 'The Incidence of Differential Property Taxes on Urban Housing: A Response', **23** *National Tax Journal*, 99-101.

Orr, Larry L. (1972), 'The Incidence of Differential Property Taxes on Urban Housing: Reply', **25** *National Tax Journal*, 217-220.

Owen, Michael S. and Thirsk, Wayne R. (1974), 'Land Taxes and Idle Land: A Case Study of Houston', **50** *Land Economics*, 251-260.

Paglin, Morton and Fogarty, Michael (1972), 'Equity and the Property Tax: A New Conceptual Focus', **25** *National Tax Journal*, 557-565.

Paglin, Morton and Fogarty, Michael (1973), 'Equity and the Property Tax: A Reply', **26** *National Tax Journal*, 651-652.

Parai, Amar K. and Beck, John H. (1989), 'The Incidence of Classified Property Taxes in a Three-Sector Model with an Imperfectly Mobile Population', **25** *Journal of Urban Economics*, 77-92.

Parks, Peter J. and Quimio, Wilma-Rose H. (1996), 'Preserving Agricultural Land with Farmland Assessments: New Jersey as a Case Study', **25** *Agricultural and Resource Economics Review*, 22-27.

Pasour, Ernest C., Jr (1973), 'Real Property Taxes and Farm Real Estate Values: Incidence and Implications', **55** *American Journal of Agricultural Economics*, 549-556.

Pasour, Ernest C., Jr (1975), 'The Capitalization of Real Property Taxes Levied on Farm Real Estate', **57** *American Journal of Agricultural Economics*, 539-548.

Pasour, Ernest C., Jr (1980), 'An Economic Analysis of the Case Against ad Valorem

Property Taxation in Forestry: Reply', **33** *National Tax Journal*, 119 ff.

Pasour, Ernest C., Jr and Holley, D.L. (1976), 'An Economic Analysis of the Case Against ad Valorem Property Taxation in Forestry', **29** *National Tax Journal*, 155-164.

Paul, Diane B. (1975), *The Politics of the Property Tax*, Lexington, MA, Lexington Books.

Pauly, Mark V. (1976), 'A Model of Local Government Expenditure and Tax Capitalization', **6** *Journal of Public Economics*, 231-242.

Pechman, Joseph A. (1985), *Who Paid the Taxes? 1966-85*, Washington, Brookings Institution.

Pechman, Joseph A. and Okner, Benjamin A. (1974), *Who Bears the Tax Burden?*, Washington, Brookings Institution.

Penniman, Clara (1956), 'The Role of Property Tax in Wisconsin Since 1929', **9** *National Tax Journal*, 331-338.

Penniman, Clara (1961), 'Property Tax Equalization in Wisconsin', **14** *National Tax Journal*, 182-189.

Perry, David B. (1996), 'Property Taxes in Canada', **44** *Canadian Tax Journal*, 1243-1250.

Peterson, George E. (1972), *The Regressivity of the Residential Property Tax*, Urban Institute Working Paper, 1972.

Peterson, George E. (1973), 'The Issues of Property Tax Reform', in Peterson, George E. (ed.), *Property Tax Reform*, Washington, Urban Institute Press.

Peterson, George E., Solomon, Arthur, Madjid; Hadid and Apgar, William C. (1973), *Property Taxes, Housing and the Cities*, Lexington, MA, Heath.

Pfister, Richard L. (1976), 'A Re-evaluation of the Justification for Property Tax Exemption', **4** *Public Finance Quarterly*, 431-452.

Phares, Donald (1980), *Who Pays State and Local Taxes?*, Cambridge, Massachusetts, Oelgeschlager, Gunn and Hain.

Pillai, Vel (1987), 'Property Taxation in Thailand: An Uncommon Combination of a Land Tax and a Rental Tax', **32** *Singapore Economic Review*, 43-55.

Pines, David (1991), 'Tiebout Without Politics', **21** *Regional Science and Urban Economics*, 469-489.

Polinsky, A. Mitchell and Rubinfeld, Daniel L. (1978), 'The Long-Run Effects of a Residential Property Tax and Local Public Services', **5** *Journal of Urban Economics*, 241-262.

Pollakowski, Henry O. (1973), 'The Effects of Property Taxes and Local Public Spending on Property Values: A Comment and Further Results', **81** *Journal of Political Economy*, 994-1003.

Preston, Anne and Ichniowski, Casey (1991), 'A National Perspective on the Nature and Effects of the Local Property Tax Revolt, 1976-1986', **44** *National Tax Journal*, 123-145.

Property Tax Committee of The National Tax Association (1973), 'The Erosion of the Ad Valorem Real Estate Tax Base', **60** *Tax Policy*, 1-94.

Prud'Homme, Remy and Navarre, Francoise (1992), 'Property Taxation in France', in King, David (ed.), *Local Government Economics in Theory and Practice*, London, Routledge.

Quigley, John M. and Schmenner, Roger W. (1975), 'Property Tax Exemption and Public Policy', **23** *Public Policy*, 259-278.

Raimondo, Henry J. (1980), 'Compensation for Tax Exempt Property in Theory and Practice', **70** *Land Economics*, 410-414.

Reeves, H. Clyde (1973), 'System Value Determinations in the Assessment of Railroads for Property Taxation', **26** *National Tax Journal*, 133-135.

Reeves, H. Clyde and Pardue, Lea (1948), 'Some Reasons why Property is Poorly Assessed for Taxation', **1** *National Tax Journal*, 366-368.

Reeves, H. Clyde and Spaulding, Henry A. (1950), 'Assessment of Coal Producing Properties in Kentucky', **3** *National Tax Journal*, 173-178.

Reinhard, Raymond M. (1981), 'Estimating Property Tax Capitalization: A Further Comment', **89** *Journal of Political Economy*, 1251-1260.

Reinmuth, James E. (1975), 'Innovative Techniques for Measuring Assessment Performance', **8** *International Property Assessment Administration*, 175-185.

Renshaw, Edward F. (1958), 'Scientific Appraisal', **11** *National Tax Journal*, 314-322.

Richardson, David H. and Thalheimer, Richard (1981), 'Measuring the Extent of Property Tax Capitalization for Single Family Residences', **48** *Southern Economic Journal*, 671-689.

Richman, Raymond L. (1967), 'The Incidence of Urban Real Estate Taxes Under Conditions of Static and Dynamic Equilibrium', **43** *Land Economics*, 172-180.

Ricks, R. Bruce (1967), 'Possessory Interests in Publicly Owned Property: Improperly Assessed', **20** *National Tax Journal*, 347-351.

Riew, John (1983), 'Property Taxation and Economic Development: With Focus on Korea', **8** *Journal of Economic Development*, 7-24.

Robertson, Jack E. (1962), 'Comparative Tax Burdens for a Midwestern City', **15** *National Tax Journal*, 308-313.

Romans, J.T. (1970), 'On the Measurement of Assessment Error', **23** *National Tax Journal*, 89-91.

Rosen, Harvey S. and Fullerton, David J. (1977), 'A Note on Local Tax Rates, Public Benefit Levels, and Property Values', **85** *Journal of Political Economy*, 433-440.

Rosett, Richard N. (1970), 'Inequity in the Real Property Tax of New York State and the Aggravating Effects of Litigation', **23** *National Tax Journal*, 66-73.

Ross, Myron H. (1971), 'The Property Tax Assessment Review Process: A Cause for Regressive Property Taxation?', **24** *National Tax Journal*, 37-43.

Rostvold, Gerhard N. (1963), 'Property Tax Payments in Relation to Household Income: A Case Study of Los Angeles County', **16** *National Tax Journal*, 197-199.

Rostvold, Gerhard N. (1966), 'Distribution of Property, Retail Sales, and Personal Income Tax Burdens in California: An Empirical Analysis of Inequity in Taxation', **19** *National Tax Journal*, 38-47.

Rostvold, Gerhard N. (1967), 'Reply', **20** *National Tax Journal*, 112-113.

Rubinfeld, Daniel L. (1979), 'Judicial Approaches to Local Public Sector Equity: An Economic Analysis', in Mieszkowski, Peter and Straszheim, Mahlon (eds), *Current Issues in Urban Economics*, Baltimore, MD, John Hopkins University Press.

Rubinfeld, Daniel L. (1987), 'The Economics of the Local Public Sector', in Auerbach, Alan and Feldstein, Martin (eds), *Handbook in Public Economics*, North-Holland, Amsterdam, 571-645.

Sabella, Edward M. (1973), 'Equity and the Property Tax: A Comment and an Alternative Conceptual Framework', **26** *National Tax Journal*, 645-650.

Sanders, Joe C. (1967), 'A Defense of Personal Property Taxation', in Buehler, Alfred G. (ed.), *The Property Tax: Problems and Potentials*, Princeton, NJ, Tax Institute of America.

Sazama, Gerald W. (1965), 'Equalization of Property Taxes for the Nation's Largest Central Cities', **18** *National Tax Journal*, 151-161.

Sazama, Gerald W. (1970), 'Land Taxes - Prerequisites and Obstacles: Boliva', **23** *National Tax Journal*, 315-323.

Schaaf, A.H. (1969), 'Effects of Property Taxation on Slums and Renewal: A Study of Land-Improvement Assessment Ratios', **45** *Land Economics*, 111-117.

Schmidt, E.B. (1952), 'Categorical Inequalities in Assessment in Nebraska, 1930-1950', **5** *National Tax Journal*, 130-144.

Schmitt, Robert C. (1951), 'Fringe Growth and Tax Rates', **4** *National Tax Journal*, 370-371.

Schmitt, Robert C. (1952), 'Annexation and Tax Rates', **5** *National Tax Journal*, 176-178.

Schoettle, Ferdinand P. (1972), 'Judicial Requirements for School Finance and Property Tax Redesign: The Rapidly Evolving Case Law', **25** *National Tax Journal*, 455-472.

Schoettle, Ferdinand P. (1985), 'A Three-Sector Model for Real Property Taxation', **27** *Journal of Public Economics*, 355-370.

Schroeder, Larry D. (1975), *The Property Tax and Alternative Local Taxes: An Economic Analysis*, New York, Praeger.

Sears, G. Alden (1964), 'Incidence of Profiles of a Real Estate Tax and Earned Income Tax: A Study in the Formal, Differential Incidence of Selected Local Taxes', **17** *National Tax Journal*, 340-356.

Seligman, Edwin R. (1925), *Essays in Taxation*, New York, Macmillan.

Seligman, Edwin R. (1927), *The Shifting and Incidence of Taxes,* 5th edn, New York, Columbia University Press.

Sexton, Terri A. (1987), 'Forecasting Property Taxes: A Comparison and Evaluation of Methods', **40** *National Tax Journal*, 47-59.

Sexton, Terri A. and Sexton, Richard J. (1986), 'Re-Evaluating the Income Elasticity of the Property Tax Base', **62** *Land Economics*, 182-191.

Shah, A. (1992), 'Empirical Test for Allocative Efficiency in the Local Public Sector', **20** *Public Finance Quarterly*, 359-377.

Shannon, Francis John (1950), 'Assessment Improvement Program in Kentucky', **3** *National Tax Journal*, 233-241.

Shannon, John (1971), 'Federal Assistance in Modernizing State Sales and Local Property Taxes', **24** *National Tax Journal*, 379-388.

Shannon, John (1973), 'The Property Tax: Reform or Relief?', in Peterson, George E. (ed.), *Property Tax Reform*, Washington, Urban Institute Press.

Shapiro, Harvey (1965), 'Assessment and Taxation of Tangible Personal Property on Farms', **18** *National Tax Journal*, 25-35.

Shoup, Carl S. (1940), 'Capitalization and Shifting of the Property Tax', in Woodworth, L.D. (ed.), *Property Taxes*, New York, Tax Policy League Symposium, Inc.

Shoup, Carl S. (1969), *Public Finance*, Chicago, Aldine-Atherton.

Simon, Herbert A. (1943), 'The Incidence of a Tax on Urban Real Property', **57** *Quarterly Journal of Economics*, 398-421.

Sinha, K.K. (1978), 'Theory of Property Taxation: Some Issues', **26** *Indian Economic Journal*, 8-17.

Sirmans, G. Stacy and Sirmans, C.F. (1991), 'Rents, Selling Prices and Financing Premiums', **28** *Urban Studies*, 267-276.

Sirmans, G. Stacy, Diskin, Barry A. and Friday, H. Swint (1995), 'Vertical Inequity in the Taxation of Real Property', **48** *National Tax Journal*, 71-84.

Sjoquist, David Lawrence (1981), 'A Median Voter Analysis of Variations in the Use of Property Taxes Among Local Governments', **36** *Public Choice*, 273-285.

Skinner, Jonathan (1991), 'If Agricultural Land Taxation is so Efficient, Why is it so Rarely Used?', **5** *World Bank Economic Review*, 113-133.

Skouras, Athanassios (1973), 'On the Analysis of Property Tax Effects on Operating and Investment Decisions of Rental Property Owners', **26** *National Tax Journal*, 123-125.

Skouras, Athanassios (1974), 'The Allocation of Land Between Speculators and Users under a Land Ownership Tax: A Comment', **50** *Economic Record*, 449-450.

Slinn, R.J. (1968), 'Taxes on Private Forests in Australia', **32** *Australian Forestry*, 163-170.

Smith, Lawrence B. (1976), 'The Ontario Land Speculation Tax: An Analysis of an Unearned Increment Land Tax', **52** *Land Economics*, 1-12.

Smith, R. Stafford (1970), 'Property Tax Capitalization in San Francisco', **23** *National Tax Journal*, 177-193.

Smith, Roger S. (1990), 'Why the Canadian Property Tax(payer) is not Revolting', **38** *Canadian Tax Journal*, 298-327.

Smith, Theodore R. (1970), 'Land Value vs. Real Property Taxation: A Case Study Comparison', **46** *Land Economics*, 305-313.

Sonstelie, Jon C. (1979), 'The Incidence of a Classified Property Tax', **12** *Journal of Public Economics*, 75-85.

Spears, McGehee H. (1958), 'Veterans' Property Tax Exemptions', **11** *National Tax Journal*, 129-137.

Starrett, David A. (1980), 'On the Method of Taxation and the Provision of Local Public Goods', **70** *American Economic Review*, 380-392.

Starrett, David A. (1981), 'Land Value Capitalization in Local Public Finance', **89** *Journal of Political Economy*, 306-327.

Starrett, David A. (1982), 'On the Method of Taxation and the Provision of Local Public Goods: A Reply', **72** *American Economic Review*, 852-853.

Steen, Robert C. (1987), 'Effect of the Property Tax in Urban Areas', **21** *Journal of Urban Economics*, 146-165.

Stiglitz, Joseph E. (1983), 'The Theory of Local Public Goods Twenty-Five Years after Tiebout: A Perspective', in Zodrow, George R. (ed.), *Local Provision of Public Services: The Tiebout Model After Twenty-Five Years*, New York, Academic Press.

Stober, William J. and Falk, Laurence H. (1967), 'Property Tax Exemption: An Efficient Subsidy to Industry', **20** *National Tax Journal*, 386-394.

Sullivan, Arthur M. (1984), 'The General Equilibrium Effects of the Industrial Property Tax: Incidence and Excess Burden', **14** *Regional Science and Urban Economics*, 547-563.

Sullivan, Arthur M. (1985), 'The General Equilibrium Effects of the Residential Property Tax: Incidence and Excess Burden', **18** *Journal of Urban Economics*, 235-250.

Sullivan, Arthur M. (1987), 'The Spatial Effects of a General Capital Tax', **17** *Regional Science and Urban Economics*, 209-222.

Sunderman, Mark A., Birch, John W., Cannaday, Roger A. and Hamilton, Thomas W. (1990), 'Testing for Vertical Inequity in Property Tax Systems', **5** *Journal of Real Estate Research*, 319-334.

Thather, George W. (1951), 'Taxation of Intangible Personal Property in Ohio', **4** *National Tax Journal*, 351-360.

Thirsk, Wayne R. (1979), 'The Capitalization of the Property Tax and Idle Land: Reply', **55** *Land Economics*, 549-552.

Thomassen, Henry (1978), 'Circuit Breaking and Life-Cycle Lock-In', **31** *National Tax Journal*, 59-65.

Thompson, James H. (1951), 'Effects of Property Tax Limitations in West Virginia', **4** *National Tax Journal*, 129-138.

Thomson, Procter (1965), 'The Property Tax and the Rate of Interest', in Benson, George C.S., Benson, Sumner, McClelland, Harold and Thomson, Procter (eds), *The American Property Tax*, Claremont, California, Lincoln School of Public Finance.

Tideman, T. Nicolaus (1982), 'A Tax on Land Value is Neutral', **35** *National Tax Journal*, 109-111.

Tiebout, Charles M. (1956), 'A Pure Theory of Local Expenditures', **64** *Journal of Political Economy*, 416-424.

Topham, Neville (1982), 'A Note on Zoning and Property Taxation in a System of Local Governments', **19** *Urban Studies*, 197-199.

Topham, Neville and Ward, Robert (1992), 'Property Prices, Tax and Expenditure Levels and Local Fiscal Performance', **24** *Applied Economics*, 1225-1232.

Townsend, Roswell G. (1951), 'Inequalities of Residential Property Taxation in Metropolitan Boston', **4** *National Tax Journal*, 361-369.

Trestrail, Richard W. (1969), 'Forests and the Property Tax - Unsound Accepted Theory', **22** *National Tax Journal*, 347-356.

Trestrail, Richard W. (1980), 'An Economic Analysis of the Case Against Ad Valorem Property Taxation in Forestry: Comment', **33** *National Tax Journal*, 117-118.

Turnbull, Geoffrey K. (1987), 'Land Taxes, Income Taxes, and Land Use', **40** *National Tax Journal*, 265-269.

Vedder, Richard (1990), 'Tiebout, Taxes, and Economic Growth', **10** *Cato Journal*, 91-108.

Vickery, William (1970), 'Defining Land Value for Tax Purposes', in Holland, Daniel M. (ed.), *The Assessment of Land Value - A Symposium*, Madison, Wisconsin, University of Wisconsin Press.

Vickery, William (1977), 'The City as a Firm', in Feldstein and Inman (eds), *The Economics of Public Services*, London, Macmillan.

Vitaliano, Donald F. and Hill, Constance (1994), 'Agricultural Districts and Farmland Prices', **8** *Journal of Real Estate Finance and Economics*, 213-223.

Vuuren, Willem (1970), 'An Evaluation of Ontario's Farm Assessment Proposals for Property Taxation', **18** *Canadian Journal of Agricultural Economics*, 87-94.

Vuuren, Willem and Cumming, John R. (1978), 'The Impact of Housing Development in Rural Areas on Farm Property Taxes', **26** *Canadian Journal of Agricultural Economics*, 31-37.

Wald, Haskell P. (1959), *The Taxation of Agricultural Land in Underdeveloped Economies*, Cambridge, MA, Harvard University Press.

Wales, T.J. and Wiens, E.G. (1974), 'Capitalization of Residential Property Taxes: An Empirical Study', **56** *Review of Economics and Statistics*, 329-333.

Wassmer, Robert W. (1990), 'Local Fiscal Variables and Intrametropolitan Firm Location: Regression Evidence from U.S. and Research Suggestions', **8** *Environment and Planning*, 283-296.

Wassmer, Robert W. (1993), 'Property Taxation, Property Base, and Property Value: An Empirical Test of the "New View"', **46** *National Tax Journal*, 135-159.

Waters, Edward C., Holland, David W. and Weber, Bruce A. (1977), 'Economic Impacts of Property Tax Limitation: A Computable General Equilibrium Analysis of Oregon's Measure 5', **73** *Land Economics*, 72-89.

Weil, Rolf A. (1953), 'Property Tax Equalization in Illinois', **6** *National Tax Journal*, 157-167.

Weinberg, Daniel H., Friedman, Joseph and Mayo, Stephen K. (1981), 'Intra-Urban Residential Mobility: The Role of Transactions Costs, Market Imperfections, and Household Disequilibrium', **9** *Journal of Urban Economics*, 332-348.

Weir, Michael and Peters, Lillian E. (1986), 'Development, Equity, and the Graded Tax in the City of Pittsburgh', **5** *Property Tax Journal*, 71-84.

Welch, Ronald B. (1957), 'Intercounty Equalization in California, Part 1: The Mechanics', **10** *National Tax Journal*, 57-66.

Welch, Ronald B. (1957), 'Intercounty Equalization in California, Part 2: Action and Reaction', **10** *National Tax Journal*, 148-157.

Welch, Ronald B. (1964), 'Some Observations on Assessment Ratio Measurement', **17** *National Tax Journal*, 13-21.

Welch, Ronald B. (1974), 'Disclosure of Property Tax Information', **27** *National Tax Journal*, 409-411.

Welch, Ronald B. (1976), 'Property Tax Developments: Modernization, Classification, Site Value Taxation', **29** *National Tax Journal*, 323-327.

Wheaton, William C. (1975), 'Consumer Mobility and Commodity Tax Bases: The Financing of Local Public Goods', **4** *Journal of Public Economics*, 377-384.

Wheaton, William C. (1984), 'The Incidence of Inter-Jurisdictional Differences in Commercial Property Taxes', **37** *National Tax Journal*, 515-527.

White, Michelle J. (1975a), 'Firm Location in a Zoned Metropolitan Area', in Mills, Edwin S. and Oates, Wallace E. (eds), *Fiscal Zoning and Land Use Controls*, Lexington, MA, Lexington Books, 175-201.

White, Michelle J. (1975b), 'Fiscal Zoning in Fragmented Metropolitan Arreas', in Mills, Edwin S. and Oates, Wallace E. (eds), *Fiscal Zoning and Land Use Controls*, Lexington, MA, Lexington Books, 31-100.

White, Michelle J. (1979), 'Suburban Growth Controls: Liability Rules and Pigouvian Taxes', **8** *Journal of Legal Studies*, 207-230.

White, Michelle J. (1986a), 'Property Taxes and Urban Housing Abandonment', **20** *Journal of Urban Economics*, 312-330.

White, Michelle J. (1986b), 'Property Taxes and Firm Location: Evidence from Proposition 13', in Rosen, Harvey S. (ed.), *Studies in State and Local Public Finance*, Chicago, Illinois, University of Chicago Press.

Wicks, John H., Little, Robert A. and Beck, Ralph A. (1968), 'A Note on Capitalization of Property Tax Changes', **21** *National Tax Journal*, 263-265.

Wildasin, David E. (1982), 'More on the Neutrality of Land Taxation', **35** *National Tax Journal*, 105-108.

Wildasin, David E. (1986a), 'Theoretical Analyzes of Local Public Economics', in Mills, Edwin S. (ed.), *Handbook of Urban Economics*, Amsterdam, Elsevier/North Holland, 1131-1178.

Wildasin, David E. (1986b), *Urban Public Economics*, New York, Harwood.

Wildasin, David E. (1989), 'Interjurisdictional Capital Mobility: Fiscal Externalities and a Corrective Subsidy', **25** *Journal of Urban Economics*, 193-212.

Williams, Alan (1966), 'The Optimal Provision of Public Goods in a System of Local Governments', **74** *Journal of Political Economy*, 18-33.

Williams, Ellis T. (1961), 'Trends in Forest Taxation', **14** *National Tax Journal*, 113-144.

Williams, Ellis T. (1974), 'Site Value Taxation - How Does it Relate to Forest Land?', **27** *National Tax Journal*, 29-44.

Wilson, John D. (1984), 'The Excise Tax Effects of the Property Tax', **24** *Journal of Public Economics*, 309-329.

Wilson, John D. (1985), 'Optimal Property Taxation in the Presence of Interregional Capital Mobility', **18** *Journal of Urban Economics*, 73-89.

Wilson, John D. (1986), 'A Theory of Interregional Tax Competition', **19** *Journal of Urban Economics*, 296-315.

Wilson, John D. (1987), 'Trade, Capital Mobility, and Tax Competition', **95** *Journal of Political Economy*, 835-856.

Wilson, John D. (1997), 'Property Taxation, Congestion, and Local Public Goods', **64** *Journal of Public Economics*, 207-217.

Windsor, Duane (1979), *Fiscal Zoning in Suburban Communities*, Lexington , MA, Lexington Books.

Winfrey, John C. (1973), *Public Finance: Public Choices and the Public Economy*, New York, NY, Harper & Row Publishers.

Woodard, F.O. and Brady, Ronald W. (1965), 'Inductive Evidence on Tax Capitalization', **18** *National Tax Journal*, 193-201.

Woodruff, A.M. (1967), 'Land Value Taxation - A 1966 Evaluation', in Buehler, Alfred G. (ed.), *The Property Tax Problems and Potentials*, Princeton, NJ, Tax Institute of America.

Wunderlich, Gene (1997), 'Land Taxes in Agriculture: Preferential Rate and Assessment Effects', **56** *American Journal of Economics and Sociology*, 215-228.

Wunderlich, Gene (ed.) (1993), *Land Ownership and Taxation in American Agriculture*, Boulder, CO, Westview Press.

Yang, Chin Wei, Means, Dwight B., Jr and Moody, George E. (1993), 'Tax Rates and Total Tax Revenues from Local Property Taxes', **21** *Public Finance Quarterly*, 355-377.

Yinger, John (1982), 'Capitalization and the Theory of Local Public Finance', **90** *Journal of Political Economy*, 917-943.

Yinger, John (1985), 'Inefficiency and the Median Voter: Property Taxes, Capitalization, Heterogeneity, and the Theory of Second Best', in Quigley, John M. (ed.), *Perspectives on Local Public Finance and Public Policy*, Greenwood, JAI Press.

Yinger, John, Bloom, Howard S., Borsch-Supan, Axel and Ladd, Helen F. (1988), *Property Taxes and Housing Values: The Theory and Estimation of Intrajurisdictional Property Tax Capitalization, Studies in Urban Economics Series*, San Diego, Harcourt, Brace, Jovanovich, Academic Press.

Zimmer, Basil G. (1958), 'Differential Property Taxation in a Metropolitan Area', **11** *National Tax Journal*, 280-286.

Zodrow, George R. (1983a), 'The Tiebout Model After Twenty-Five Years: An Overview', in Zodrow, George R. (ed.), *Local Provision of Public Services: The Tiebout Model After Twenty-Five Years*, New York, Academic Press.

Zodrow, George R. (ed.) (1983b), *Local Provision of Public Services: The Tiebout Model After Twenty-Five Years*, New York, Academic Press.

Zodrow, George R. (1984), 'The Incidence of Metropolitan Property Tax Base Sharing and Rate Equalization', **15** *Journal of Urban Economics*, 210-229.

Zodrow, George R. (1986), 'Pigou, Tiebout, Property Taxation and the Underprovision of Local Public Goods', **19** *Journal of Urban Economics*, 356-370.

Zodrow, George R. and Mieszkowski, Peter (1983), 'The Incidence of the Property Tax: The Benefit View versus the New View', in Zodrow, George R. (ed.), *Local Provision of Public Services: The Tiebout Model After Twenty-Five Years*, New York, Academic Press.

Zodrow, George R. and Mieszkowski, Peter (1986), 'The New View of Property Taxation: A Reformulation', **16** *Regional Science and Urban Economics*, 309-327.

6040
CONSUMPTION TAX, VALUE ADDED TAX, EXCISE TAX AND SALES TAX

Bibliography Collected by the Editors

Aguirre, Carlos A. and Shome, Parthasarathi (1988), 'The Mexican Value Added Tax (VAT): Methodology for Calculating the Base', **41(4)** *National Tax Journal*, 543-554.

Ashenfelter, Orley and Sullivan, Daniel (1987), 'Nonparametric Tests of Market Structure: An Application to the Cigarette Industry', **35(4)** *Journal of Industrial Economics*, 483-498.

Barham, Vicky, Poddar, S.N. and Whalley, John (1987), 'The Tax Treatment of Insurance under a Consumption Type, Destination Basis VAT', **40(2)** *National Tax Journal*, 171-182.

Barker, Phyllis A. (1972), 'Projected Compliance Costs Associated with the Value Added Tax as Proposed', **47** *Indiana Business Review*, 22-27.

Barlow, Robin and Snyder, Wayne (1994), 'The Tax That Failed: The VAT in Niger', **14(3)** *Public Budgeting and Finance*, 77-89.

Barman, Kiran and Bisonoi, Usha (1983), 'Value Added Tax as an Alternative to Corporation Tax', **28(4)** *Economic Affairs*, 860-865.

Barnett, Paul G., Keeler, Theodore E. and Hu, Teh Wei (1995), 'Oligopoly Structure and the Incidence of Cigarette Excise Taxes', **57(3)** *Journal of Public Economics*, 457-470.

Barthold, Thomas A. (1994), 'Issues in the Design of Environmental Excise Taxes', **8(1)** *Journal of Economic Perspectives*, 133-151.

Bates, Christopher (1993), 'Value Added Tax and Holding Companies: A Major Change of Policy or a Small Problem of Translation?', **14(2)** *Fiscal Studies*, 117-127.

Becker, Gary S., Grossman, Michael and Murphy, Kevin M. (1994), 'An Empirical Analysis of Cigarette Addiction', **84(3)** *American Economic Review*, 396-418.

Bell, Michael E., Dearborn, Philip M. and Hunter, Roland (1993), 'Financing the Post Apartheid City in South Africa', **30(3)** *Urban Studies*, 581-591.

Berglas, Eitan (1971), 'The Effect of the Public Sector on the Base of the Value Added Tax', **24(4)** *National Tax Journal*, 459-464.

Bergstrom, Theodore C. (1982), 'On Capturing Oil Rents with a National Excise Tax', **72(1)** *American Economic Review*, 194-201.

Besley, Timothy and Suzumura, Kotaro (1992), 'Taxation and Welfare in an Oligopoly with Strategic Commitment', **33(2)** *International Economic Review*, 413-431.

Bhatia, Kul B. (1982), 'Value Added Tax and the Theory of Tax Incidence', **19(2)** *Journal of Public Economics*, 203-223.

Black, David E. (1977), 'Property Tax Incidence: The Excise Tax Effect and Assessment Practices', **30(4)** *National Tax Journal*, 429-434.

Blazic, Helena (1993), 'Adaptacija Oporezivanja Potrosnje u Hrvatskoj (With English summary) (Adaptation of Consumption Taxation in Croatia)', **11(0)** *Zbornik Radova Ekonomskog Fakulteta Rijeka*, 3-22.

Brannon, Gerald M. (1973), 'Death Taxes in a Structure of Progessive Taxes', **26** *National Tax Journal*, 451-457.

Brannon, Gerald M. (1984), 'The Value Added Tax is a Good Utility Infielder', **37(3)** *National Tax Journal*, 303-312.

Brashares, Edith, Speyrer, Janet Furman and Carlson, George N. (1988), 'Distributional Aspects of a Federal Value Added Tax', **41(2)** *National Tax Journal*, 155-174.

Burgess, Robin, Howes, Stephen and Stern, Nicholas (1995), 'Value Added Tax Options for India', **2(1)** *International Tax and Public Finance*, 109-141.

Carlson, George N. and Patrick, Melanie K. (1989), 'Addressing the Regressivity of a Value Added Tax', **42(3)** *National Tax Journal*, 339-351.

Caspersen, Erik and Metcalf, Gilbert E. (1994), 'Is a Value Added Tax Regressive? Annual versus Lifetime Incidence Measures', **47(4)** *National Tax Journal*, 731-746.

Chiles, Ted W., Jr and Sollars, David L. (1993), 'Estimating Cigarette Tax Revenue', **17(3)** *Journal of Economics and Finance*, 1-15.

Chowdhury, Osman H. (1989), 'Equity and Efficiency Tradeoff in Bangladesh Tax Policy Reform: A Computable General Equilibrium Model', **26(2)** *Philippine Review of Economics and Business*, 262-286.

Chowdhury, Osman Haider (1991), 'Revenue Neutral Value Added Tax (VAT) in Bangladesh: Some General Equilibrium Illustrations', **19(4)** *Bangladesh Development Studies*, 49-63.

Clotfelter, Charles T. and Cook, Philip J. (1987), 'Implicit Taxation in Lottery Finance', **40(4)** *National Tax Journal*, 533-546.

Cnossen, Sijbren (1981), 'Dutch Experience with the Value Added Tax', **39(2)** *Finanzarchiv*, 223-254.

Cnossen, Sijbren (1982), 'What Rate Structure for a Value Added Tax?', **35(2)** *National Tax Journal*, 205-214.

Cnossen, Sijbren (1989), 'The Value Added Tax: Key to a Better Tax Mix', **6(3)** *Australian Tax Forum*, 265-281.

Cnossen, Sijbren (1992), 'Key Questions in Considering a Value Added Tax for Central and Eastern European Countries', **39(2)** *International Monetary Fund Staff Papers*, 211-255.

Cosciani, Cesare (1970), 'Sulle Probabili Conseguenze dell'Introduzione dell'I. V. A. in Italia. (With English summary) (On the Probable Consequences of the Introduction of the Added Value Tax in Italy)', **26(8)** *Bancaria*, 909-916.

Dahl, Henrik and Mitra, Pradeep (1991), 'Applying Tax Policy Models in Country Eocnomic Work: Bangladesh, China, and India', **5(3)** *World Bank Economic Review*, 553-572.

Davie, Bruce F. (1994), 'Tax Expenditures in the Federal Excise Tax System', **47(1)** *National Tax Journal*, 39-62.

Devers, M. (1969), 'De B.T.W. Aangifte en de Factuur (The Value Added Tax Declaration and the Invoice with English summary)', **23(3)** *Economisch en Sociaal Tijdschrift*, 287-303.

Dewatripont, C. et al. (1991), 'The Effects on Unemployment of Reducing Social Security Contributions: A General Equilibrium Analysis for Belgium', **139(2)** *De Economist*, 272-290.

Dosser, Douglas and Hitiris, Theodore (1972), 'Trade Effects of Tax Harmonisation: Harmonisation of Value Added Tax in E.E.C. A Reply', **40(2)** *Manchester School of Economic and Social Studies*, 189-191.

Dosser, Douglas, Han, S.S. and Hitiris, Theodore (1969), 'Trade Effects of Tax Harmonisation: Harmonisation of the Value added Tax in E.E.C.', **37(4)** *Manchester School of Economic and Social Studies*, 337-346.

Due, John F. (1974), 'The Value Added Tax Sense and Nonsense', **13(4)** *Nebraska Journal of Economics and Business*, 54-65.

Due, John F. (1990), 'Some Unresolved Issues in Design and Implementation of Value Added Taxes', **43(4)** *National Tax Journal*, 383-394.

Due, John F. and Greaney, Francis (1991), 'The Development of a Value Added Tax: Trinidad and Tobago', **45(6)** *Bulletin for International Fiscal Documentation*, 260-268.

Dye, Richard F. and McGuire, Therese J. (1991), 'Growth and Variability of State Individual Income and General Sales Taxes', **44(1)** *National Tax Journal*, 55-66.

Edwards, Franklin R. (1993), 'Taxing Transactions in Futures Markets: Objectives and Effects', **7(1)** *Journal of Financial Services Research*, 75-91.

Engineer, Merwan (1989), 'Taxes, Public Goods, and the Ruling Class: An Exploration of the Territory between Brennan and Buchanan's Leviathan and Conventional Public Finance', **44(1)** *Public Finance*, 19-30.

Epley, Donald R. (1978), 'A Note on the Substitution of a Value Added Tax for the Corporate Income Tax, and Its Impact upon Stabilization', **17(1)** *Nebraska Journal of Economics and Business*, 47-56.

Fourie, F.C.V.N. and Owen, A. (1993), 'Value Added Tax and Regressivity in South Africa', **61(4)** *South African Journal of Economics*, 281-300.

Frech, H. Edward III, Deacon, Rovert, Decanio, Stephen J. and Johnson, Bruce M. (1990), *Taxing Energy: Oil Severence Taxation and the Economy*, New York, Holmes and Meyer.

Frenkel, Jacob A. (1988), 'Budget Deficits under Alternative Tax Systems: International Effects', **35(2)** *International Monetary Fund Staff Papers*, 297-315.

Frenkel, Jacob A., Razin, Assaf and Symansky, Steven (1991), 'International VAT Haromonization: Macroeconomic Effects', **38(4)** *International Monetary Fund Staff Papers*, 789-827.

Gantner, Manfred (1993), 'Anmerkungen zur Universitätsreform aus Finanzwissenschafltlicher Sicht (Notes on Reforming Universities from a Public Finance Perspective)', in Strasser, R. (ed.), *Beiträge zum Universitätsrecht*, Vienna, 119-139.

Gantner, Manfred (1995), 'Energieabgaben als Ländersteuern? Wirkungsanalyse und Fnanzverfassungsrechtliche Überlegungen am Beispiel des Feldversuch Vorarlbergs (Duties on Energy as Provincial Taxes?)', **21** *Wirtschaft und Gesellschaft*, 47-76.

Garton, Steven D. (1974), 'The Value Added Tax', **55(8)** *Management Accounting*, 16-18.

Gelauff, G.M.M. et al. (1991), 'Towards an Analysis of Tax Effects on Labour Market and Allocation: A Micro/Macro Approach', **139(2)** *De Economist*, 243-271.

Georgakopoulos, Theodore A. (1972), 'Trade Effects of Tax Harmonisation: Harmonisation of the Value Added Tax in E.E.C. A Comment and a Suggested Methodology', **40(2)** *Manchester School of Economic and Social Studies*, 177-188.

Georgakopoulos, Theodore A. (1975), 'Stabilisation Aspects of Tax Substitution: The Value Added Tax in the UK', **30(3)** *Public Finance*, 333-346.

Georgakopoulos, Theodore A. (1991), 'Some Economic Effects of Value Added Tax Substitution in Greece: A First Ex post Assessment', **13(1)** *Greek Economic Review*, 117-134.

Gimeno Ullastres, Juan A., 'Los Beneficios de los Gastos Indivisibles (Benefits of Indivisible Expenses)', **133** *Hacienda Pública Española*, 115-130.

Gimeno Ullastres, Juan A. (1980), *Imposición Sobre el Consumo y Distribución Personal de Rentas* (Consumption Taxes and Personal Distribution of Income), Madrid, Instituto de Estudios Fiscales, 341 p.

Gimeno Ullastres, Juan A. (1985), 'La Incidencia del I.V.A. sobre los Consumidores (How V.A.T. Affects Consumers)', **4** *Estudio Sobre le Consumo*, 37-55.

Gimeno Ullastres, Juan A. (1994), *La Fiscalidad del Tabaco en la CEE* (Taxing Tobacco in the E.C.), Madrid, Editorial Cívitas, 127 p.

Goffin, R. (1970), 'An Account of T.V.A. in Belgium (Value Added Tax V.A.T.)', **24(789)** *Bulletin for International Fiscal Documentation*, 299-347.

Goode, Richard (1993), 'Tax Advice to Developing Countries: An Historical Survey', **21(1)** *World Development*, 37-53.

Gottfried, Peter and Wiegard, Wolfgang (1991), 'Exemption versus Zero Rating: A Hidden Problem of VAT', **46(3)** *Journal of Public Economics*, 307-328.

Guerard, Michele (1973), 'The Brazilian State Value Added Tax', **20(1)** *International Monetary Fund Staff Papers*, 118-169.

Hafer, R.W. and Trebing, Michael E. (1980), 'The Value Added Tax A Review of the Issues', **62(1)** *Federal Reserve Bank of St. Louis Review*, 3-10.

Hamilton, Bob and Kuo, Chun-Yan (1991), 'Reforming the Canadian Sales Tax System: A Regional General Equilibrium Analysis', **39(1)** *Canadian Tax Journal*, 113 ff.

Hilzenbecher, Manfred (1990), 'Horizontale und vertikale Verteilungswirkungen einer Mehrwertsteuererhohung (With English summary) (Horizontal and Vertical Distribution Effects of an Increase of the Value Added Tax)', **36(23)** *Konjunkturpolitik*, 63-79.

Holcombe, Randall G. (1990), 'The Value Added Tax and the Sales Tax', **37(9)** *Rivista Internazionale di Scienze Economiche e Commerciali*, 799-815.

Homma, Masaaki, Atoda, Naosumi and Hashimoto, Kyoji (1989), 'Welfare Analysis of the 1988 Tax Reform in Japan', **40(4)** *Economic Studies Quarterly*, 336-348.

Hong, Lee Fook (1995), 'People's Republic of China: Value Added Tax, Consumption Tax and Business Tax', **49(1)** *Bulletin for International Fiscal Documentation*, 23-26.

Hossain, Shahabuddin M. (1995), 'The Equity Impact of the Value Added Tax in Bangladesh', **42(2)** *International Monetary Fund Staff Papers*, 411-430.

Hu, Sheng Cheng (1983), 'Value Added Tax as a Source of Social Security Financing', **11(2)** *Public Finance Quarterly*, 154-180.

Hunter, William J. and Nelson, Michael A. (1990), 'Excise Taxation and the Theory of Tax Exploitation', **45(2)** *Public Finance*, 268-282.

Ichioka, Osamu (1988), 'The Value Added Tax in Japan: A Numerical General Equilibrium Evaluation', **2(1)** *Journal of the Japanese and International Economy*, 11-41.

Ingberg, Mikael (1990), 'Steg mot Mervardesomsattningsskatt (With English summary) (Steps toward a Value Added Tax)', **43(4)** *Ekonomiska Samfundets Tidskrift*, 251-252.

Jap, Kim Siong (1986), 'Taiwan: An Outline of the Proposed Value Added Tax System', **40(1)** *Bulletin for International Fiscal Documentation*, 18-19.

Jhun, U. Jin (1976), 'Value Added Tax and Balance of Trade', **1(1)** *Journal of Economic Development*, 139-147.

Johnson, Darwin G. (1980), 'The Inflation Elasticity of a Specific Excise Tax', **33(1)** *National Tax Journal*, 107-110.

Johnson, Peter and Parker, Simon (1994), 'The Interrelationships between Births and Deaths', **6(4)** *Small Business Economics*, 283-290.

Kaiser, Helmut and Spahn, P. Bernd (1989), 'On the Efficiency and Distributive Justice of Consumption Taxes: A Study on VAT in West Germany', **49(2)** *Journal of Economics (Zeitschrift für Nationalökonomie)*, 199-218.

Kaplow, Louis (1988), 'Savings Incentives in a Hybrid Income Tax: Comment', in Aaron, Henry J., Galper, Harveu and Pechman, Joseph A. (eds), *Uneasy Compromise: Problems of a Hybrid Income-Consumption Tax*, Washington, Brookings Institution.

Kaplow, Louis (1994), 'Human Capital under An Ideal Income Tax', **80** *Virginia Law Review*, 1477-1514.

Kaplow, Louis (1995), 'Recovery of Pre-Enactment Basis Under a Consumption Tax: The USA Tax System', **68** *Tax Notes*, 1109-1118.

Kaplow, Louis (1996), 'On the Divergence Between 'Ideal' and Conventional Income Tax Treatment of Human Capital', *American Economic Review. Papers and Proceedings*.

Kaplow, Louis and Warren, Alvin (1986), 'An Income Tax by Any Other Name - A Reply to Professor Strnad', **38** *Stanford Law Review*, 339-421.

Kaplow, Louis and Warren, Alvin (1987), 'Professor Strnad's Rejoinder: Simply Semantics', **39** *Stanford Law Review*, 419-425.

Kay, John A. and Keen, Michael (1991), 'Product Quality Under Specific and Ad Valorem Taxation', **19** *Public Finance Quarterly*, 238-247.

Kehoe, Timothy J. et al. (1989), 'Un Analisis de Equilibrio General de la Reforma Fiscal de 1986 en Espana (A General Equilibrium Analysis of the Spanish Fiscal Reform of 1986) (with English Summary)', **13(3)** *Investigaciones Económicas*, 337-385.

Krauss, Melvyn B. and Bird, Richard M. (1971), 'The Value Added Tax: Critique of a Review', **9** *Journal of Economic Literature*, 1167-1173.

Kudrle, Robert Thomas (1984), 'Excise Tax Incidence in Limit Price Oligopoly', **39(3)** *Public Finance*, 321-346.

Lakdawala, D.T. (1976), 'Value Added Tax', **24(2)** *Indian Economic Journal*, 183-207.

Lent, George E. (1974), 'Value Added Tax in Developing Countries', **11(4)** *Finance and Development*, 35-37.

Lent, George E., Casanegra, Milka and Guerard, Michele (1973), 'The Value Added Tax in Developing Countries', **20(2)** *International Monetary Fund Staff Papers*, 318-378.

Li, Jinyan (1988), 'Value Added Tax: People's Republic of China', **42(1)** *Bulletin for International Fiscal Documentation*, 17-22.

Lindholm, Richard W. (1970), 'The Value Added Tax: A Short Review of the Literature', **8** *Journal of Economic Literature*, 1178-1189.

Lindholm, Richard W. (1971), 'The Value Added Tax: Rejoinder to a Critique', **9** *Journal of Economic Literature*, 1173-1179.

Lott, William F. and Miller, Stephen M. (1974), 'Excise Tax Revenue Maximization', **40(4)** *Southern Economic Journal*, 657-664.

Lyons, Susan M. (1992), 'The Taxation of Companies and Individuals in Mexico', **46(9)** *Bulletin for International Fiscal Documentation*, 436-443.

Maital, Shlomo and Krevinsky, Shlomo (1970), 'Shifting Parameters and the Value Added Tax: A Note', **23(2)** *National Tax Journal*, 221-222.

Mann, Arthur J. (1990), 'Bolivia: Tax Reform 1986-1989', **44(1)** *Bulletin for International Fiscal Documentation*, 32-36.

Massone, Pedro F. (1979), 'Recent Developments in Latin America: The Mexican Value Added Tax', **33(12)** *Bulletin for International Fiscal Documentation*, 539-549.

Matthiasson, Bjorn (1970), 'The Value Added Tax', **7(1)** *Finance and Development*, 40-46.

McClure, Charles E., Jr (1980), 'Tax Restructuring Act of 1979: Time for an American Value Added Tax?', **28(3)** *Public Policy*, 301-322.

McGee, Robert W. (1984a), *Software Taxation*, National Association of Accountants, 305 p.

McGee, Robert W. (1984b), 'Loophole of the Month', *CPA Digest*, 4 ff.

McGee, Robert W. (1984c), 'Software Taxation: A New NAA Research Study', **66** *Management Accounting*, 7071-7077.

McGee, Robert W. (1985a), *Accounting for Software*, Homewood, IL, Dow Jones-Irwin, 168 p.

McGee, Robert W. (1985b), 'Sales, Use and Property Taxation of Computer Software', **8** *Hamline Law Review*, 307-342. Reprinted in *Accounting and Tax Aspects of Computer Software Manufacturing*, New York, Praeger Publishing Company, 1987.

McGee, Robert W. (1985c), 'Financial and Tax Accounting for Computer Software', **7** *Western New England Law Review*, 651-704. Reprinted in *Accounting for Data Processing Department Costs*, New York, Greenwood Press, 1988.

McGee, Robert W. (1987), *Accounting and Tax Aspects of Computer Software Manufacturing*, New York, Praeger Publishing Company, 162 p.

McGee, Robert W. (1996a), *Taxation, Ethics and Public Policy*, Dumont Institute for Public Policy Research. http:/ww.hili.com~dumontin

McGee, Robert W. (1996b), *Essays on Accounting. Taxation and Public Finance*, Dumont Institute for Public Policy Research. http:/ww.hili.com~dumontin

McGibany, James M. (1991), 'The Effect of Property Tax Rate Differentials on Single Family Housing Starts in Wisconsin, 1978-1989', **31(3)** *Journal of Regional Science*, 347-359.

McKinnon, Ronald I. (1973), 'The Value Added Tax and the Liberalization of Foreign Trade in Developing Economies: A Comment', **11** *Journal of Economic Literature*, 520-524.

McLure, Charles E., Jr (1991), 'Tax Policy for Bulgaria', **45(5)** *Bulletin for International Fiscal Documentation*, 235-247.

Merriman, David (1994), 'Do Cigarette Excise Tax Rates Maximize Revenue?', **32(3)** *Economic Inquiry*, 419-428.

Meyer, Carrie and Due, John F. (1988), 'Value Added Tax: Dominican Republic', **42(1)** *Bulletin for International Fiscal Documentation*, 13-16.

Militzer, Ken and Ontscherenki, Ilona (1990), 'The Value Added Tax: Its Impact on Saving', **25(2)** *Business Economics*, 32-37.

Modesto, Leonor, Vasco, Alexandra and Bernardes, Luis (1992), 'Macroeconomic Effects of an Energy Tax in Portugal: Simulation Results for 1991-2000', **16(1)** *Economia (Portuguese Catholic University)*, 33-45.

Morrison, Clarence C. (1995), 'Comparing the Welfare Effects of Income and Excise Taxes in the Presence of the Other Taxation Paradox', **23(3)** *Atlantic Economic Journal*, 189-202.

Musgrave, Richard A. (1972), 'Problems of the Value Added Tax', **25(3)** *National Tax Journal*, 425-430.

Nakamura, Kazuo (1979), 'On the Actual State of Value Added Tax in England (In Japanese)', **139(5)** *Kokumin Keizai Zasshi*, 42-57.

Nakamura, Kazuo (1980), 'Value Added Tax in Retail Stage (In Japanese)', **141(5)** *Kokumin Keizai Zasshi*, 17-31.

Nakamura, Kazuo (1982), 'Pros and Cons of Value Added Tax in the United Kingdom (In Japanese)', **145(4)** *Kokumin Keizai Zasshi*, 47-60.

O'Higgins, T.J. (1971), 'Proposals for a Value Added Tax in Ireland', **25(7)** *Bulletin for International Fiscal Documentation*, 243-247.

Panagariya, Arvind and Narayana, A.V.L. (1988), 'Excise Tax Evasion: A Welfare cum Crime Theoretic Analysis', **43** *Public Finance*, 248-260.

Panagariya, Arvind and Narayana, A.V.L. (1989), 'Excise Tax Evasion: Reply', **44** *Public Finance*, 510-512.

Parr, Michael and Day, John (1977), 'Value Added Tax in the United Kingdom', *National Westminster Bank Quarterly Review*, 7-18.

Patel, Himat (1978), 'Scope for Value Added Tax in India', **14(2)** *Artha Vikas*, 70-84.

Peeters, Frans (1969), 'De B.T.W. in de Onderneming (The Value Added Tax and the Enterprise. With English summary)', **23(4)** *Economisch en Sociaal Tijdschrift*, 391-403.

Perraudin, W.R.M. and Pujol, T. (1991), 'European Fiscal Harmonization and the French Economy', **38(2)** *International Monetary Fund Staff Papers*, 399-440.

Perry, John (1990), 'Business Registers the Search for Quality', **7(1)** *Statistical Journal*, 55-61.

Peters, Douglas D. (1991), 'International Perspective: Canada: Recession and Recovery', **26(2)** *Business Economics*, 51-55.

Petersen, Mitchell A. (1992), 'Pension Reversions and Worker Stockholder Wealth Transfers', **107(3)** *Quarterly Journal of Economics*, 1033-1056.

Poterba, James (1989), 'Lifetime Incidence and the Distributional Burden of Excise Taxes', **79** *American Economic Review. Papers and Proceedings*, 325-330.

Ribich, Thomas I. (1973), 'Soft Sell for Soft Drinks: An Excise Tax Problem', **26(1)** *National Tax Journal*, 115-117.

Rienstra, J.G. (1992), 'United States: German Treaty Exemption for Foreign Insurance Premiums', **46(11)** *Bulletin for International Fiscal Documentation*, 545-550.

Ruebling, Charlotte E. (1973), 'A Value Added Tax and Factors Affecting Its Economic Impact', **55(9)** *Federal Reserve Bank of St. Louis Review*, 15-19.

Ruggeri, G.C. and Bluck, K. (1990), 'On the Incidence of the Manufacturers' Sales Tax and the Goods and Services Tax', **16(4)** *Canadian Public Policy*, 359-373.

Saba, Richard P. et al. (1995), 'The Demand for Cigarette Smuggling', **33(2)** *Economic Inquiry*, 189-202.

Saffer, Henry and Grossman, Michael (1987), 'Beer Taxes, the Legal Drinking Age, and Youth Motor Vehicle Fatalities', **16** *Journal of Legal Studies*, 351-374.

Salter, Sarah W. (1982), 'Value Added: Economic Concepts in Tax Policy Analysis', in Cranston, Ross and Schick, Anne (eds), *Law and Economics*, Canberra, Australian National University, 175-189.

Sapona, Ingrid (1990), 'Goods and Services Tax: Canada', **44(10)** *Bulletin for International Fiscal Documentation*, 489-498.

Schlecht, Otto (1987), 'Die Vollendung des Europaischen Binnenmarktes Ziele, Voraussetzungen und Chancen (With English summary) (The Completion of the European Internal Market Goals, Prerequisites, and Opportunities)', **33(6)** *Konjunkturpolitik*, 303-310.

Schweizer, Urs (1984), 'Welfare Analysis of Excise Tax Evasion', **140** *Journal of Institutional and Theoretical Economics*, 247-258.

Sgontz, Larry G. (1992), 'An Excise Tax that Reduces Price', **45(1)** *National Tax Journal*, 115-117.

Shapiro, Perry and Petchey, Jeffrey D. (1994), '"Shall Become Exclusive": An Economic Analysis of Section 90', **70(209)** *Economic Record*, 171-182.

Shoup, Carl S. (1969), 'Experience with the Value Added Tax in Denmark, and Prospects in Sweden', **28(2)** *Finanzarchiv*, 236-252.

Shoup, Carl S. (1988), 'The Value Added Tax and Developing Countries', **3(2)** *World Bank Research Observer*, 139-156.

Shughart, William F., II, Tollison, Robert D. and Higgins, Richard S. (1987), 'Rational Self Taxation: Complementary Inputs and Excise Taxation', **20(3)** *Canadian Journal of Economics*, 527-532.

Siong, Jap Kim (1986), 'Taiwan: The Value Added Tax Law in Force', **40(7)** *Bulletin for International Fiscal Documentation*, 315-318.

Slovin, Myron B., Sushka, Marie E. and Bendeck, Yvette M. (1990), 'The Market Valuation Effects of Reserve Regulation', **25(1)** *Journal of Monetary Economics*, 3-19.

Smith, Dan Throop (1970), 'Value Added Tax: The Case For', **48(6)** *Harvard Business Review*, 77-85.

Spindler, Z.A. (1972), 'A Predicition of the Effects of an Excise Tax Change on the Automobile Market: A Note', **24(2)** *Economic and Business Bulletin*, 66-68.

Steedman, Ian (1986), 'Produced Inputs and Tax Incidence Theory', **41(3)** *Public Finance*, 331-349.

Stephenson, Peter (1970), 'Problems and Political Implications for the United Kingdom of Introducing the EEC Value Added Tax', **8(4)** *Journal of Common Market Studies*, 305-324.

Stout, Lynn A. (1995), 'Are Stock Markets Costly Casinos? Disagreement, Market Failure, and Securities Regulation', **81** *Virginia Law Review*, 611 ff.

Sumner, Daniel A. and Wohlgenant, Michael K. (1985), 'Effects of an Increase in the Federal Excise Tax on Cigarettes', **67(2)** *American Journal of Agricultural Economics*, 235-242.

Surrey, Stanley S. (1970), 'Value Added Tax: The Case Against', **48(6)** *Harvard Business Review*, 86-94.

Tait, Alan A. (1981), 'Is the Introduction of a Value Added Tax Inflationary?', **18(2)** *Finance and Development*, 38-42.

Tait, Alan A. (1989), 'Misconceptions about the Value Added Tax', **26(1)** *Finance and Development*, 25-27.

Tamaoka, Masayuki (1994), 'The Regressivity of a Value Added Tax: Tax Credit Method and Subtraction Method. A Japanese Case', **15(2)** *Fiscal Studies*, 57-73.

Théret, Bruno (1981), 'Un Point de Vue Macroeconomique sur le Traitement de la Taxe sur la Valeur ajoutee dans le Systeme Elargi de Comptabilite Nationale Francaise (A Macroeconomic View on the Treatment of the Value Added Tax in the Extended French National Accounting System)', **36(1)** *Public Finance*, 108-124.

Thirsk, Wayne R. (1987), 'The Value Added Tax in Canada: Saviour or Siren Song?', **13(3)** *Canadian Public Policy*, 259-283.

Thiry, Beranrd (1988), 'Distributive Effects of the Reform of Value Added Tax: The Case of Belgium', **59(3)** *Annals of Public and Cooperative Economy*, 341-368.

Thomson, Trevor (1974), 'The Value Added Tax and the Cost of Change', **42(1)** *South African Journal of Economics*, 56-64.

Tower, Edward (1989), 'Excise Tax Evasion: Comment', **44** *Public Finance*, 506-509.

Van Rensburg, B.P.J. (1990), 'Belasting op Toegevoegde Waarde: Pas dit Suid Afrika? (With English summary) (Value Added Tax: Can it be Applied to South Africa?)', **58(1)** *South African Journal of Economics*, 21-42.

Vandenhouten, F. (1969), 'De Invoering van de B.T.W. in de Ondernemingen (The Value Added Tax in the Administration of the Firms with English summary)', **23(2)** *Economisch en Sociaal Tijdschrift*, 159-171.

Vartholomeos, John (1974), 'Price and Trade Effects of the Substitution of a Value Added Tax for the Corporate Income Tax: The British Case', **32(3)** *Finanzarchiv*, 469-480.

Wajsman, Nathan (1992), 'Indirect Tax Harmonization in Denmark', **128(4)** *Weltwirtschaftliches Archiv - Review of World Economics*, 727-741.

Waldauer, Charles (1981), 'Comment (on 'The Variable Rate Value Added Tax as an Anti Inflation Fiscal Stabilizer')', **34(1)** *National Tax Journal*, 131-132.

Walker, John F. (1974), 'Do Economists Ever Agree? The Case of the Teaching of Excise Tax: Shifting and Incidence', **27(2)** *National Tax Journal*, 351-355.

Wetzler, James W. (1979), 'The Role of a Value Added Tax in Financing Social Security', **32(3)** *National Tax Journal*, 334-345.

White, Daniel L. (1980), 'The Variable Rate Value Added Tax as an Anti Inflation Fiscal Stabilizer', **33(2)** *National Tax Journal*, 227-232.

White, Daniel L. (1981), 'The Variable Rate Value Added Tax as an Anti Inflation Fiscal Stabilizer: A Response', **34(1)** *National Tax Journal*, 133 ff.

Wilson, John Douglas (1984), 'The Excise Tax Effects of the Property Tax', **24(3)** *Journal of Public Economics*, 309-329.

Wilson, John Douglas (1989), 'On the Optimal Tax Base for Commodity Taxation', **79** *American Economic Review*, 1196-1206.

Wright, L. Hart (1983), 'Personal, Living or Family Matters and the Value Added Tax', **82(3)** *Michigan Law Review*, 419-430.

Yeh, Chiou Nan (1979), 'The Incidence of the Value added Tax in a Neoclassical Growth Model', **34(2)** *Public Finance*, 277-292.

Young, Claire F.L. (1991), 'Introduction of a Goods and Services Tax: The Canadian Experience', **8(3)** *Australian Tax Forum*, 259-280.

Zuckerman, Ben Ami (1972), 'Proposals for a Value Added Tax in Israel', **26(6)** *Bulletin for International Fiscal Documentation*, 241-243.

6050
PERSONAL INCOME TAXATION

Yoshihiro Masui
Associate Professor
Graduate School of Law and Politics, The University of Tokyo

Minoru Nakazato
Professor
Graduate School of Law and Politics, The University of Tokyo

Abstract

This survey traces the literature on the three fundamental components of personal income taxation: base, unit and rates. It first discusses the debates between income tax base and consumption tax base in a chronological order, starting from Simons, and continuing up until the law and economics literature in the 1990s. The chapter then reviews recent law review articles on tax units. Finally, it examines discussions on progressive rate structures. This article finds a distinct shift in appproach, due to the emergence of optimal tax theory.
JEL classification: K34
Keywords: Taxation, Income, Consumption, Tax Base, Tax Unit, Tax Rates

1. Introduction

Taxation is an 'old' area of law and economics studies. It has been studied by economists as an important area of public finance as well as by lawyers as an integral branch of law governing private property. Thus, personal income taxation, especially after its emergence as a major revenue raiser in industrially developed countries, could be called one of the oldest research subjects in law and economics.

Indeed, the modern concept of comprehensive income can be traced back to Schantz (1896) who, based on the ability-to-pay (Leistungsfaehigkeit) tradition of tax theory, argued against his predecessors by defining income broadly as the increase of net assets during a given period. It is well known that his conception was well received on the other side of the Atlantic. It was refined by Haig (1921) and Simons (1938). Particularly the latter laid down a conceptual foundation of personal income taxation in the US, refuting the Fisherian concept of income as consumption.

On the other hand, lawyers' inquiries into issues of personal income taxation have differed from country to country. It is by no means the US that has produced the richest volume of academic work on the law and economics concerning taxation. In Germany, legal scholars traditionally have been remote from law and economics studies. Although Germany is the mother country of Adolf Wagner and Georg Schantz, capital gains from personal property have been excluded from the taxable income of individuals, which is a significant deviation from the comprehensive income principle. The UK has traditionally adhered to a schedular system of personal income taxation, rather than comprehensive conception of income; tax lawyers are trained in an environment where they tend to view income tax as a set of various levies on transactions, rather than a personal tax on a single base. In Japan, lawyers began a systematic research on income taxation after the 1949 Shoup Recommendation (for a synthesis, see Kaneko, 1995), and their interest has been recently bolstered by developments in law and economics studies in general.

2. The Scope and Structure of this Survey

Given the long history of tax research and the variety of studies taking place in different regions, it is impossible to introduce all the major works on the subject; by its very nature, the quest for creating an academic inventory has to be partial. Instead of being exhaustive, this chapter shall trace those articles, mainly written in English, which aroused salient debates on the three fundamental components of personal income taxation: base, unit and rates.

Accordingly, the chapter proceeds as follows. Part A will trace the major debates between income tax base and consumption tax base in chronological order, starting from Simons (1938), and continuing up until the law and economics literature in the 1990s. Part B will review recent law review articles on tax units. Part C will examine the literature on progressive tax rate structures. Part D will conclude briefly.

The line taken here is basically within the ET (equitable taxation) paradigm (Musgrave, 1976) in the sense that personal income tax versus consumption tax is contrasted as measures of equitable taxation. However, it is necessary also to introduce the OT (optimal taxation) perspective, since recent articles increasingly employ the OT analysis.

For a convenient anthology of these articles, see White (1995), Baker and Elliot (1990), and McIntyre, Sander and Westfall (1983). The impact of OT perspective is discussed in Cooper (1994).

A. Base

3. Origins

In the late nineteenth century, researchers started to discuss the concept of income as a basis for personal taxation. The various concepts of income of the time were reviewed by Wueller (1938a, 1938b, 1939) as belonging either to an 'accrual type', which focuses upon inflow, or to a 'disposition type', which focuses upon expenditure or disposition.

The latter type of definition was put forward by Irving Fisher, and represents an alternative stream within following discussion. It was advocated most notably by Kaldor (1958), who elaborated an expenditure tax design. However, expenditure tax was considered unpractical until recently. The 'accrual type' income concept has many varieties. Without going into preceding constructions, let us start directly from Henry Simons whose formulation dominates the following debates. For readers interested in a historical review of the scholarly works of this period, McCombs (1990) gives a good summary of discussions by Haig, Hewett, Simons and Vickrey. For analyses of Simons' value judgement, see Hettich (1979), Kiesling (1981) and Long (1990).

4. The Impact of Henry Simons

Simons (1938) measured personal income as 'the algebraic sum of (1) the market value of rights exercised in consumption, and (2) the change in the value of the store of property rights between the beginning and end of the period in question'. The essential feature of this formulation is that it defines income as gain to someone during a specified time period. The definition is comprehensive in the sense it does not make any distinction according to source or recurrence; it includes income in kind, gratuitous receipts such as gifts or bequests, and capital gains. Simons saw the comprehensive income as an appropriate tax base for persons, since, by this construction, taxes may be distributed to persons in an equitable manner, especially using a graduated rate structure. Simons' book covered most of the basic issues in personal income taxation, and his initial definition is modified in order to account for the implementation needs in the real world.

Although never fully implemented in any country, Simons' concept of income became an analytical framework commonly used by researchers especially in the Anglo-Saxon tradition. This was especially true in the US after the Second World War, where numerous casebooks of Federal Income Taxation were compiled with an emphasis on the concept of income as it appeared in legal rules and court cases. Surrey (1973) was one of the most prominent proponents of comprehensive income taxation, arguing that the concessions to deviate from the normal income tax structure constitutes another form of subsidy - the so-called 'tax expenditure'. Based on this idea, the tax expenditure budget was introduced in 1974. Surrey and McDaniel (1985) traced the development since 1973 of the tax expenditure concept, considering its impact on budget policy, on tax policy and administration, and on government decisions between using tax expenditure or direct spending to implement subsidy programs.

It is noteworthy that the idea of comprehensive income taxation as developed elsewhere, too. In Japan, Kaneko (1966-75) carefully traced the various concepts of income by public finance economists and, based on his detailed comparative survey on the legal systems in various countries, applied the comprehensive concept to the Japanese positive tax law on the issues of realization, imputed income, and illegal income.

5. Comprehensive Tax Base Debate

During the same period when proponents of comprehensive income taxation were making efforts to streamline the tax system, growing dissent was emerging, and culminated in the so-called comprehensive tax debate of the late 1960s. The debate was started by Bittker (1967), who argued that a neutral, scientific measure of taxable income is a mirage (for his earlier examination of personal expenditures, see Bittker, 1973). Bittker argues that the concept of Haig-Simons economic income yields no help in many of the contentious areas of income definition. Based on this observation, he concludes that there is no touchstone for tax reform: proposals must be considered provision by provision and policy by policy, on their own particular merits.

Bittker's penetrating criticism invited rejoinders from the proponents of comprehensive income tax such as Musgrave (1967), Pechman (1967) and Galvin (1968). The debate made clear that in many senses the existing income tax base inevitably departed from a pure concept of comprehensive income and that the concept itself has vague outer boundaries. However, Bittker was not formulating a systematic alternative, which may be a reflection of his agnosticism towards the foundations of tax policy. This explains why Surrey, despite Bittker's criticism, was able to institutionalize a tax expenditure budget after the debate.

6. Andrews' Breakthrough

It did not take long for an alternative construction to come to emerge in discussion. Two works by William Andrews changed the landscape of the debate. While agreeing that it is useful to evaluate departures from an ideal income tax as tax expenditures, Andrews (1972) maintained that the ideal for this purpose must be carefully stated and worked out to embody the intrinsic objectives of the tax. Starting from the Simons' formulation, Andrews argued that an ideal income tax is one in which tax burdens are apportioned to a taxpayer's aggregate personal consumption and accumulation. Focusing on the consumption component of the tax base, he contended that there are persuasive reasons why the concept of personal consumption for tax purposes should be elaborated in a way that excludes medical services and whatever satisfactions one obtains from making charitable contributions. One is struck by Andrews' careful reading of the Simons' formulation, distinguishing the consumption and the accumulation components of the personal income tax base. By showing that an exclusion of the accumulation component from the income tax base delivers a graduated personal consumption tax, Andrews paved the way for a renewed discussion of tax on personal consumption.

Andrews (1974) extended this analysis further. He asserted that the worst inequities, distortions and complexities in the present tax, and the most intractable difficulties in approaching the accretion ideal, have essentially to do with the accumulation component of accretion. He therefore urged that consideration be given to an alternative ideal in which personal taxable income would be computed on a simple cash flow basis to reflect only personal consumption, with accumulation in the form of business and investment assets being comprehensively eliminated. He showed how pursuit of this would produce a substantial net simplification of the tax as well as a fairer and more efficient distribution of tax burdens. Unlike Bittker, who tended to take a piecemeal approach, Andrews was able to build on a conceptual framework based on the economics of time value of money, an essential analytical tool for the accumulation component of the income tax base.

Andrews' work was a breakthrough: while the earlier version of the consumption tax scheme required computation of borrowing, dissaving and imputed income from assets, his prepayment system simply exempts the yield from capital, arriving at the consumption component by deducting the accumulation portion from the tax base. Moreover, Andrews successfully showed that the existing personal income tax is a hybrid of the consumption and accretion models in relation to accumulation, and his diagnosis became accepted by tax theorists and policymakers alike, regardless of their positions for or against his specific proposals for reform.

7. Income or Consumption?

Recognizing that the existing personal income tax is a hybrid, opinions diverged whether to pursue a comprehensive income tax ideal or a consumption tax ideal. In the debates that followed, several factors were posited and examined, such as fairness, efficiency and administrative feasibility.

On the fairness issue, Warren (1975) suggested that the neutrality of the consumption-type tax is obtained at the cost of allowing income from wealth to escape taxation. Finding the consumption-based tax to be analogous to a tax on wages alone, Warren rejects it as an insufficient compromise in regard to the various legitimate objectives of a basic tax system. To this, Andrews (1975) replied that Warren's observations do not refute the conclusion that a consumption-type tax would be fairer, pointing out important differences between a wage tax and a consumption-type personal income tax. To Andrews, an income tax, even a true accretion-type tax, was a deficient device for attacking disparities in wealth. Five years later, Warren (1980) further evaluated the arguments that have been advanced in favor of the consumption criterion being superior to the income criterion. He concluded that while either tax can be justified as a means of implementing a plausible principle of distributional equity, the case for superior fairness of the consumption tax is not persuasive on its own terms. Fried (1992), provisionally setting aside the Hobbesian foundational argument that asserts wealth ought not to be regarded as appropriated for private purposes until withdrawn for personal use from the common pool, focused on the unfairness argument of taxing returns to capital per se. She distinguished three theories implicit in the arguments for exempting the return to capital: (1) returns to capital should be exempted as a means of perfecting the income tax; (2) they should be exempted as a means of implementing an endowments tax; and (3) they should be exempted to preserve the relative pre-tax welfare of savers and spenders. Her conclusion was that none presents a persuasive case for the greater fairness of a consumption tax.

On efficiency, economists are almost unanimous in holding that an income tax base discriminates against savings and favors current consumption, whereas a consumption tax base is more neutral as regards the saving decision of individuals. On administrative feasibility, Graetz (1979) applied his general analysis of legal transitions to the issue of substituting a progressive consumption tax for income tax, and suggests that the obstacles to implementing a progressive personal tax on consumption would be substantial, but not prohibitive. Given practical difficulties, however, he warned that proponents of an expenditure tax should be required to demonstrate that its claimed advantages in terms of equity and economic efficiency are real and cannot be achieved in a simpler fashion. He asserted that unless and until this burden of proof is met, replacing the income tax with a progressive personal tax on consumption should remain low on the list of political priorities, and that the principal utility of expenditure tax analysis should continue to lie in illuminating issues of income taxation and increasing the understanding of tax policy. Shachar (1984) examined the issue of transition, proposing that changes in the tax treatment of both assets and liabilities must be considered on a case-by-case basis in order to determine which type of transition rule would place the tax burden on the superior risk bearer. He pointed out that transition rules are necessary to avoid windfalls and double taxation. Serious debates in academic and policy circles followed between income tax proponents and consumption tax proponents (Pechman, 1977; Gulper and Pechman, 1980; Aaron, 1988; and Marshall and Wells, 1993). Some tried to pave the way to an income tax model (Gunn, 1979; Shakow, 1986; Fellows, 1990), while others urged the move to a consumption tax model (Institute for Fiscal Studies, 1978; Bradford et al. 1984; and Bradford, 1986). Nakazato (1991a) supported the consumption tax base from a lifetime perspective, arguing that Simons' income artificially limits the time range of base measurement, that the traditional equity justification of Simons' income lacks grounds, and that the consumption tax base is neutral in the time preferences of individuals.

8. Extension

In the meantime, the relevance of a comparison between income and consumption tax bases was questioned by Strnad (1985). Strnad argued that in a non-general-equilibrium setting where the effect of taxes on pre-tax prices is not included in the analysis, the cash-flow income tax and not the traditional income tax implements the Haig-Simons ideal; thus, the generally accepted income tax analyses of activities as disparate as corporations investing in machines, individuals contributing to pension funds, and businesses financing their operations by debt have no theoretical basis. Strnad's sensational reappraisal was rejected by Kaplow and Warren (1986), who demonstrated that Strnad's conclusion that a cash flow tax properly implements a tax on 'income' is a correct, but tautological, derivation from the starting point of Strnad income, which is not the same as Haig-Simons income. Popkin (1986) agreed with Kaplow and Warren in that Strnad's conclusion rests on a definition of the Haig-Simons ideal that already contains a bias in favor of the consumption tax. Further he added that the Strnad version of the Haig-Simons definition is defective on basic fairness grounds because it adopts a mistaken view of when a taxpayer has fairly discharged a tax obligation to the government. Strnad (1986) and Strnad (1987) are replies to Popkin and to Kaplow and Warren respectively. Strnad (1990) dealt with the question of 'periodicity' - how often changes in value should be assessed and taxed - in the context of implementing accrual taxation. Despite heated debates and strong criticism, the robustness of income tax idea proved itself in the real world. The US Department of the Treasury (1984) opted for an expansion of the income tax base with a less graduated rate structure, which became a basis for the 1986 Reagan Tax Reform. In the late 1980s, similar tax reforms with base-broadening and rate-flattening followed in other countries, although no country ever switched completely to a consumption tax structure. The income tax system remains a hybrid. It has not been perfected as a pure accretion model, nor has it undergone a complete change to a consumption tax model. From his perspective as a political scientist, Witte (1985) attacks Simons' position as ultimately resting on an unclear set of value premises, but still defends a comprehensive income tax on pragmatic grounds such as revenue capacity, administrative efficiency, certainty, simplicity and legitimacy, rather than by traditional value criteria such as fairness and efficiency. While casting a doubt on the future of income taxation, Isenberg (1990) rejects the adoption of a personal tax on consumption, and opts for a value added tax which is essentially a tax on firms. Noting the near consensus among economists that long-term growth would be less hampered by additional taxes if they fell on consumption rather than on income, Graetz (1992), nonetheless, cautions against a broad-based tax on consumption, instead advocates a tax on energy consumption.

9. Enter Optimal Taxation

For traditional income tax idealists the hybrid system may seem like a stalemate, but for newer generations the hybrid tax is already a given. Discussions in 1990s tend to focus on the policy evaluation of specific rules and provisions within the hybrid tax framework, but made little direct normative assessment over the appropriateness of either tax base. Underlying this newer work is the emergence of the optimal tax framework and the elaboration of finance theory. McCaffery (1992) argues that one should accept the fact of a hybrid income-consumption tax and begin to examine how best to structure it. Dividing savings into three categories (life cycle, precautionary, and bequest savings), McCaffery contends that because of the different values one places on the different types of savings, some form of a hybrid may in fact be ideal and not merely a practical necessity. Although more empirical work and normative exploration is necessary, his work exemplifies a new trend of discussion on an old issue. Knoll (1994) seeks to direct scholarly attention towards large-scale redesign of the hybrid, away from both marginal improvements in the existing hybrid and the debate over whether there should be an income tax or a consumption tax. He describes and evaluates three hybrid taxes. A blended hybrid, which would reduce the tax rate on investment income, is rejected because of the impossibility of allocating returns between capital and effort and among various investments. A simple hybrid, which would supplement economic depreciation with an immediate write-off of a given fraction of the investment, and a COCA (Cost of Capital Allowance) system, which would supplement economic depreciation by providing a deduction based on the undepreciated portion of a taxpayer's assets, are held to serve as models for comprehensive reform.

Significance of risk rather than deferral is articulated by Bankman and Griffith (1992). By reviewing historical data, they reveal that substantially all of the real return realized on investments during the past 60 years has been attributable to investment risk, and contend that thus it is appropriate to center the income versus consumption tax debate on the way in which the two tax bases treat risky investments, rather than the way the two tax bases treat interest (interest being defined as the inflation-adjusted return on riskless assets). According to their analysis, taxation of risk premia is much less troublesome than taxation of interest, because many taxpayers will be able to offset the effects of taxation of risk premia by increasing the proportion of risky assets in their portfolios, and because such taxpayers will not be disadvantaged by an income tax. On the other hand, Bankman and Griffith conclude that taxation of risk premia without full loss offsets will disfavor investors in risky assets and raise efficiency concerns. While previous analyses have focused on the time value of money aspect, Bankman and Griffith have highlighted the way in which risk matters.

The conceptual weakness, even as an analytical tool, of the Haig-Simons definition of income as a first-best tax principle is revealed by Shaviro (1989b). Shaviro defines as selective limitation of tax benefits those provisions in the Revenue Code that, in response to preferences and resultant income undermeasurement, make certain tax benefits conditional on the character or amount of other items on the taxpayer's return. He argues that such selective limitations cannot be analyzed solely through the consideration of first-best tax principles, notably the Haig-Simons definition of income, and that the question gives rise to second-best issues that have a discernible theoretical structure with identifiable tradeoffs but are indeterminate in the absence of empirical information. Shaviro (1990) shows the similar indeterminacy of the Haig-Simons definition of income in the measurement of taxable consumption. Shaviro (1992) makes an efficiency analysis of the hybrid tax system and argues that the main advantage of realization and recognition rules, as compared with no tax at all even upon realization, is that they may tend to equalize the ex ante expected taxes from alternative activities or investments. Appeal to definitions, which has been the basic communication code of the income versus consumption tax debate, is set aside by Kaplow (1991), who views that debates about definitions cannot give meaningful guidance to policy unless informed by the objectives underlying the definitions. Kaplow prefers evaluating directly the effects of possible tax rules on individuals' well-being. He reconsiders the justification for casualty loss and medical expense deductions, taking into account the availability of private insurance. He argues that when individuals can insure, the second level of insurance implicit in the casualty loss and medical expense deductions has undesirable effects on consumption choices and insurance decisions: individuals may be more exposed to losses because of tax deductions commonly believed to mitigate them. He concludes that, given the option, individuals would prefer a regime that eliminated the deductions and offered correspondingly lower tax rates. His later work (Kaplow, 1994) is another example of his contribution by the use of direct explorations. Here he shows the arithmetic interchangeability between standard deduction and floors.

Zolt (1996) examines the case for uniform taxation on efficiency and equity grounds. He concludes that neither economic theory or equity considerations require uniform treatment. He contends that even if we could devise rules that taxed 'appropriately' such items as unrealized gains, imputed income, or government services, we may still be able to achieve efficiency and equity gains using tax treatment that varies by type of income or type of taxpayer. He carefully adds, however, that the desirability of the use of nonuniform taxes likely varies among countries and over time.

10. Paradigm Shift

Recent law and economics contributions to the debate thus reflect the mainstream intellectual trends in public sector economics which have leaned away from the traditional ET paradigm and towards the OT framework. It is an interesting question if and how this academic work will have an impact on real-world policymaking.

B. Unit

11. The Choice: Individual, Marital, or Family

In order to measure income during a specified period, it is necessary to identify whose income is in question. Simons (1938) seems to have advanced his theory on the assumption that natural persons should be taxed as isolated individuals. His approach is a logical consequence of methodological individualism. Others may view persons as social beings whose family ties affect their taxpaying capacity. Underlying this view is the rejection of naked individualism in favor of a conception of 'self' which is encumbered with communal conditions.

Personal tax units may be designed as based on either of the following: individual, marital, or family. Which system to adopt has been long discussed in many countries, producing numerous legislative movements. For a comparative survey, see Pechman and Engelhardt (1990), and Kaneko (1996b).

Among OECD countries, the design of tax units differs from country to country: some adopt an individual unit system (Australia, Canada, Denmark, Italy, Japan, the UK, and Sweden), some employ a marital unit system (Belgium, Germany and Spain), and others have a family unit system (France and Luxembourg). The US provides multiple tax rates for (1) single individuals, (2) married individuals filing joint tax returns and surviving spouses, (3) married persons electing separate tax returns and (4) heads of households. In addition to the diversity of treatments among different countries, systems in each country often have undergone numerous changes.

The discussion of tax unit has multiple facets because it is a reflection of how one views a family, a very controversial institution in our swiftly changing societies. The difficulty of finding common ground is aggravated by the fact that the treatment of a family under personal income taxation is related to all three of the fundamental elements of taxation: base, unit and rates. For example, within an individual unit system, personal deductions could be introduced to make adjustments according to the family status of an individual. Moreover, many legal issues concerning family taxation are inherent to progressive rate structure.

12. Early Discussion

Although recognizing the aforementioned difficulty, Oldman and Temple (1960) tried to illuminate the guiding policies for the design of tax units. With a detailed description of the systems then in operation in the Philippines, UK, Sweden, Canada, US and the Netherlands, Oldman and Temple supported the marital unit system as a more reasonable choice than the individual unit system in light of economic realities and administrative feasibility. In so doing they suggested the following: (1) a married couple with only one spouse having an income should pay a greater total tax than a married couple with both spouses working, assuming both couples have the same total income (imputed income from household services); (2) the dual-income couple should pay a greater total tax on its two incomes than would be paid by two single persons with corresponding incomes (economic advantages of joint living); (3) one single person should pay the same or a greater tax than the married couple with one income (the advantages of joint living are never so great that two can live more cheaply than one).

Bittker (1975) questioned the validity of these guiding policies. He demonstrated that it is impossible to have (a) progression, (b) equal taxes on equal-income married couples, and (c) a marriage-neutral tax burden. In discussing the relative tax burdens of married couples and other taxpayers, he examined whether the assumptions of commentators, such as marital burden of supporting a spouse, economies of scale, and unpaid household services, would hold in reality. He concluded that theoreticians, regardless of their backgrounds, be it economics, anthropology or sociology, cannot 'solve' the problem of taxing family income; they can only identify the issues, point out conflicts among objectives, propose alternative approaches, and predict the outcome of picking one route rather than another. Having performed these functions, the expert must give way to the citizen, whose judgments can rest on nothing more precise or permanent than collective social preferences. Bittker thus exposed the fundamental dilemma between neutrality among couples and neutrality on marital decisions under a progressive income tax. No commentators since have been able to escape this dilemma.

In the face of controversy surrounding the treatment of the family in federal income tax, McIntyre and Oldman (1977) developed a normative model for the taxation of the family based on the ideal of a comprehensive tax base. From this ideal, they suggested a program for reform in which tax burdens would be distributed in accordance with practical estimates of the monetary income enjoyed by individual taxpayers.

13. Divergent Family Models, and a Look at Behavioral Response

Although the debate in the 1970s seemed to have led to a fairly widespread consensus that the married couple is an appropriate tax unit, in the 1980s more emphasis was given to the aspect of marriage penalty, rather than the aspect of non-neutrality among couples.

Gann (1980) argues that a marriage-neutral income tax system under which all individuals file separate returns under a single rate structure is the most defensible position in the long run. Gann (1983) criticizes the earned income deduction provisions introduced in the US by the 1981 Act, urging that the earned income deduction cannot be supported on an equity criterion of marriage neutrality, although noting that it produces some efficiency gains.

Kornhauser (1993) examines the premise that married couples share or pool their incomes. She surveys the changing concept and reality of the 'family' and examines several empirical studies that address the issue of the allocation of financial resources between members of a couple living together. Her findings are: not all couples pool assets; that pooling is not confined to married couples, and separation of assets is not confined to non-married couples; that financial arrangements sometimes change during the course of the relationship; and that even among those couples who claim they pool, the non-earner spouse often does not have equal access to assets. Based on this evidence, she argues that the joint filing system is unfair, because it is both under-inclusive (barring some unmarried poolers from its benefits) and over-inclusive (bestowing its benefits on non-pooling married couples).

McCaffery (1993) explores how the tax laws provide behavioral incentives that affect three types of decisions: whether to marry, whether to form a one- or a two-earner household, and whether to work full or part time. He finds that tax laws contribute to the marginalization of women in the workplace, and that they impede a more creative formulation of alternative models of work and family. Pointing out strong class dimensions in the actual patterns of effects, he urges to take steps to put one- and two-earner families on an equal footing. He thus argues a case for altering the basic rate structure to provide significantly lower, even negative, rates for secondary earners, financed by higher rates on primary earners. McCaffery's approach was to focus on behavioral incentives, where traditional tax policy analysis looked at distributive burdens. McCaffery (1997) is a synthesis of his research based on this approach.

Struggling with the dilemma posed by Bittker, Zelenak (1994b) argues that American society at the end of the twentieth century would be better served by separate returns, predicting that the joint return system will eventually disappear, the only question being when.

Nakazato (1995) applies Gary Becker's theory of productive consumption to the treatment of households under the comprehensive income tax model, examining income transfer, imputed income and leisure within a family. He concludes that tax units and income deductions do not provide a satisfactory solution, and that full implementation of a comprehensive income base under an individual unit system would approximately achieve tax neutrality towards the organization of a household. The design of tax units and of various deductions and credits within a household has another dimension: its role as an instrument of welfare and family policies. Alstott (1995) examines the role of tax system in welfare programs, arguing that the case for the EITC (earned income tax credit) has been oversimplified in two significant ways. First, the conventional policy debate over the EITC's behavioral incentives has been framed too narrowly. Second, the EITC, as a tax-based income-transfer program, faces inherent institutional constraints not present in traditional welfare programs. These include problems of inaccuracy, unresponsiveness and noncompliance that are inherent in tax-based administration.

14. Expansion of Arena

In sum, recent studies embody analyses of people's behavioral responses to the structure of tax units, as well as wider examinations of family taxation in interaction with social and welfare policies.

C. Rates

15. The Conundrum Concerning Progression

The most significant issue on the tax rates of personal income tax is progression. The progressive tax rate structure is one component of the progressive tax mechanism, and the overall progression of the tax is dependent on all three elements of personal income taxation: base, unit and rates. Simons (1938) recognized this, arguing against the theory of declining utility and examining the case for redistribution of income and wealth in its own terms.

The support for redistribution and for progressive taxation as a means to more economic equality was strong among New Dealers. One example is Vickrey (1947), who proposed an agenda for progressive taxation: he devoted a chapter on the graduation of taxes, examining the methods of graduation, the choice of graduation curves, the use of mathematical formulas, and the size of tax brackets. Throughout the decades after the Second World War, the patterns of Federal Income Tax legislation in the US were consistently progressive.

16. The Uneasy Case

It is ironic that Blum and Kalven (1953), the most widely acknowledged academic work on the issue of progression, claimed that the case for progressive taxation is uneasy. They traced various affirmative arguments for progressive tax on all incomes over a minimum subsistence exemption, looking at: (1) maintaining economic stability and a high level of business activity; (2) taxes levied in accordance with the benefits received; (3) the declining utility of money (sacrifice theory); and (4) mitigating economic inequality. They also examined the implications of exemptions on the case for progression, and considered whether any of the preceding analysis of the merits of progression would be affected by considerations regarding how the government spends the tax money that it collects. They concluded that the case for progression turns out to be stubborn but uneasy. Galvin and Bittker (1969) made several points in support of a progressive federal income tax rate structure. They note that (1) if the case for progression is 'uneasy', so too is the case for a proportional rate schedule; (2) progression in federal income tax serves to counterbalance the regressive tendencies in other federal, state and local taxes; (3) progression is an inevitable consequence of allowing personal exemption in computing income tax liability; (4) economic security increases more than proportionately as one moves up the income scale; (5) benefits of government expenditures increase progressively with income and wealth; and (6) progressive tax rates serve as a measure to reduce economic inequality, fitting comfortably within the forms of democratic capitalism.

17. Flat Tax and the Optimal Taxation Framework

It was not until the 1980s that the progressive rate structure was overhauled. Various proposals were made to make the personal income tax rates flat in the US Congress. The 1986 Tax Reform reduced the number of brackets and the top marginal income tax rate significantly. Subsequently, rate cutting, coupled with base broadening measures, became a worldwide trend in tax reform in other countries. Graetz (1983) addresses the problem of the transition to a flat-rate tax, arguing that the minimum tax amendments of the 1982 Act in the Internal Revenue Code constitute a transitional mechanism that can be regarded as a first step to phasing in a broad-based tax. Hall and Rabushka (1995) propose a flat-tax plan under which all income would be taxed once at a uniform rate of 19 percent, based on the consumption tax principle. O'Kelley (1985) describes how adopting a flat rate comprehensive income tax that uses personal exemption could result in tax burdens substantially more progressive than under the then current system, arguing for a personal exemption equal in amount to the minimum wage, and for integrating the income tax and the social security systems.

Bankman and Griffith (1987) re-examine the traditional economic arguments against progressive taxation from the perspective of distributive justice. They critically analyze both the labor-related efficiency costs of progressive taxation, and the traditional arguments that progressivity imposes significant administrative costs, promotes misallocation of capital, and increases tax evasion. They go on to describe an optimal tax model for calculating the most desirable tax rate, balancing the costs of progressivity against possible gains from redistribution. Their model suggests that under most welfare theories, the optimal tax rate should be progressive, but not confiscatory, and that a progressive tax is best implemented not in the form of graduated or rising marginal rates, but rather through a combination of cash grants and constant or even declining marginal rates.

D. Conclusion

18. From Definition to Numbers

This chapter briefly reviewed the existing literature on personal income taxation. Overall, the survey shows a shift in approach, which broadly involved a change 'from definition to numbers'. Traditionally, the main interests of researchers were how to define the concept of income, how to structure an appropriate tax unit based on taxpaying capacity, and how to design the rate according to some intuitive notion of vertical equity. More recently, with the emergence of optimal taxation theory, discussions are beginning to focus on the implications of social welfare functions, and on the market responses to particular tax rules. Looking at the names of authors cited, one may note that this intellectual shift is due to the advent of new generation of law and economics scholars armed with analytical devices which connect policy discussions directly to normative criteria such as equity and efficiency.

Personal income taxation has strong connections with other elements of human behavior, including the formation of human capital, the choice between labor and leisure, the investment decision, the compliance and evasion of legal rules, and the geographical location of resources. Hereby, personal income taxation is but one aspect of a larger inquiry into the connection between law and human behavior. As such, interested readers should consult other chapters in this volume relating to the family, finance, labor, social security and administration.

Bibliography on Personal Income Taxation (6050)

Aaron, Henry J., Galper, Harveu and Pechman, Joseph A. (eds) (1988), *Uneasy Compromise: Problems of a Hybrid Income-Consumption Tax*, Washington, Brookings Institution, 441 p.

Alchin, Terry (1985), 'Prota: A New Measure of the Progressivity of Personal Income Taxation', **24(44)** *Australian Economic Papers*, 185-200.

Allen, Tuovi (1985), 'Vahennykset Tuloverotuksessa Tulonsiirtopolitiikan Jatke? (With English summary) (Deductions in Personal Income Taxation Substitutes for Government Transfer Programmes?)', **81(1)** *Kansantaloudellinen Aikakauskirja*, 65-72.

Alstott, Anne L. (1995), 'The Earned Income Tax Credit and the Limitation of Tax-Based Welfare Reform', **108** *Harvard Law Review*, 533-592.

Anderson, Gary M. and Tollison, Robert D. (1993), 'Political Influence and the Ratification of the Income Tax Amendment', **13** *International Review of Law and Economics*, 259-270.

Andrews, William D. (1972), 'Personal Deductions in an Ideal Income Tax', **86** *Harvard Law Review*, 309-385.

Andrews, William D. (1974), 'A Consumption-Type or Cash-Flow Personal Income Tax', **87** *Harvard Law Review*, 1113-1188.

Andrews, William D. (1975), 'Fairness and the Choice Between a Consumption-Type and an Accretion-Type Income Tax: A Reply to Professor Warren', **88** *Harvard Law Review*, 947-958.

Arnold, Brian J. (1983), *Timing and Income Taxation: The Principles of Income Measurement for Tax Purposes*, Canadian Tax Paper, 71.

Baker, Samuel H. and Elliott, Catherine S. (1990), *Readings in Public Sector Economics*, Lexington, D.C. Heath, 603 p.

Bankman, Joseph and Griffith, Thomas (1987), 'Social Welfare and the Rate Structure: A New Look at Progressive Taxation', **75** *California Law Review*, 1905-1967.

Bankman, Joseph and Griffith, Thomas (1992), 'Is the Debate Between an Income Tax and a Consumption Tax a Debate About Risk? Does it Matter?', **47** *Tax Law Review*, 377-406.

Batina, Raymond G. (1991), 'Equity, and the Time Consistent Taxation of Income', **93(3)** *Scandinavian Journal of Economics*, 407-419.

Bhargava, P.K. and Jain, A.K. (1982), 'Personal Income Taxation and Equity in India', **36(12)** *Bulletin for International Fiscal Documentation*, 535-538.

Bittker, Boris I. (1967), 'A Comprehensive Tax Base as a Goal of Income Tax Reform', **80** *Harvard Law Review*, 925-985.

Bittker, Boris I. (1968), 'Comprehensive Income Taxation: A Response', **81** *Harvard Law Review*, 1032-1043.

Bittker, Boris I. (1973), 'Income Tax Deductions, Credits, and Subsidies for Personal Expenditures', **16** *Journal of Law and Economics*, 193-213.

Bittker, Boris I. (1975), 'Federal Income Taxtion and the Family', **27** *Stanford Law Review*, 1389-1463.

Blum, Walter J. and Kalven, Harry, Jr (1953), *The Uneasy Case for Progressive Taxation*, Chicago: University of Chicago Press.

Blum, Walter J. and Kalven, Harry, Jr (1982), 'Revisiting the Uneasy Case for Progressive Taxation', **60** *Taxes*, 16 ff.

Bradford, David F. (1986), *Untangling the Income Tax, A Committee for Economic Development Publication*, Harvard University Press, 386 p.

Bradford, David F. and the U.S. Treasury Tax Policy Staff (1984), *Blueprints for Basic Tax Reform (second edition)*, Arlington, Tax Analysts, 194 p.

Chen, Charng Yi (1990), 'Risk-Preferences and Tax-Induced Dividend Clienteles: Evidence from the Insurance Industry', **57** *Journal of Risk and Insurance*, 199-219.

Chirinko, Robert S. (1981), 'A Further Comment on 'Would Tax Shifting Undermine the Tax Based Incomes Policy?'', **15** *Journal of Economic Issues*, 177-181.

Cooper, Graeme S. (1994), 'An Optimal or Comprehensive Income Tax?', **22** *Federal Law Review*, 414-447.

Coven, G.E. (1981), 'Decline and Fall of Taxable Income', **79** *Michigan Law Review*, 1525-1572.

Davies, John H. (1984), 'Income-Plus-Wealth: In Search of a Better Tax Base', **15** *Rutgers Law Journal*, 849-896.

Fellows, Mary Louise (1990), 'A Comprehensive Attack on Tax Deferral', **88** *Michigan Law Review*, 722-813.

Fortin, Bernard (1988), 'Should the Current Tax-Transfer System be Replaced by a Flat-Rate Income Tax?', **26** *Osgoode Hall Law Journal*, 423-431.

Fried, Barbara H. (1992), 'Fairness and the Consumption Tax', **44** *Stanford Law Review*, 961-1017.

Galvin, Charles (1968), 'More on Boris Bittker and the Comprehensive Tax Base: The Practicalities of Tax Reform and ABA's CSTR', **81** *Harvard Law Review*, 1016-1031.

Galvin, Charles and Bittker, Boris I. (1969), *The Income Tax: How Progressive Should It Be?: Rational Debate Seminars*, Washington, American Enterprise Institute for Public Policy Research, 183 p.

Gann, P.B. (1980), 'Abandoning Marital Status as a Factor in Allocating Income Tax Burdens', **59** *Texas Law Review*.

Gann, P.B. (1983), 'The Earned Income Deduction: Congress's 1981 Response to the "Marriage Penalty" Tax', **68** *Cornell Law Review*, 468-487.

Gavrielidou, Alexandra A. (1990), 'Enallaktikes Protaseis sto Phoro Eisodematos (Alternative Proposals to the Income Tax)', **38** *Nomiko Vema*, 382-400.

Gergen, Mark P. (1988), 'The Case for a Charitable Contributions Deduction', **74** *Virginia Law Review*, 1393-1450.

Gimeno Ullastres, Juan A. (1980), *Imposición Sobre el Consumo y Ddistribución Personal de Rentas (Consumption Taxes and Personal Distribution of Income)*, Madrid, Instituto de Estudios Fiscales, 341 p.

Gimeno Ullastres, Juan A. (1984), 'Los Presupuestos Familiares (Family Budgets)', **1** *Estudios Sobre el Consumo*, 39-45.

Graetz, Michael J. (1975), 'Assessing the Distributional Effects of Income Tax Revision: Some Lessons from Incidence Analysis', **4** *Journal of Legal Studies*, 351-368.

Graetz, Michael J. (1979), 'Implementing a Progressive Consumption Tax', **92** *Harvard Law Review*, 1575-1661.

Graetz, Michael J. (1983), 'The 1982 Minimum Tax Amendments as a First Step in the Transition to a "Flat-Tax"', **56** *Southern California Law Review*, 527-571.

Graetz, Michael J. (1992), 'Revisiting the Income Tax versus Consumption Tax Debate', **7** *Tax Notes*, 1437-1442.

Graetz, Michael J. and McDowell, Barbara (1984), 'Tax Reform 1985: The Quest for a Fairer, More Efficient and Simpler Income Tax', **3** *Yale Law and Policy Review*, 5-40.

Griffith, Thomas (1989), 'Theories of Personal Deductions in the Income Tax', **40** *Hastings Law Journal*, 343-395.

Griffith, Thomas (1994), 'Efficient Taxation of Mixed Personal and Business Expenses', **41** *UCLA Law Review*, 1769-1789.

Gunn, Alan (1979), 'The Case for an Income Tax', **46** *University of Chicago Law Review*, 370-400.

Haig, Robert Murray (1921), *The Federal Income Tax*.

Hall, Robert E. and Rabushka, Alvin (1995), *The Flat Tax*, 2nd edn, Stanford, Stanford University Press, 152 p.

Halperin, Daniel I. (1986), 'Interest in Disguise: Taxing the 'Time Value of Money'', **95** *Yale Law Journal*, 508-552.

Hansmann, Henry B. (1989), 'Unfair Competition and the Unrelated Business Income Tax', **75** *Virginia Law Review*, 605-635.

Hatakeyama, Takemichi (1990), 'Flat Zeiritsu Ronso (Flat Tax Rates Debate)', **964** *Juristen*, 115-119.

Head, John G. and Krever, Richard (1990), *Flattening the Tax Rate Scale: Alternative Scenarios and Methodologies*, Longman Professional, 410 p.

Head, John G. and Krever, Richard (1996), *Tax Units and the Tax Rate Scale*, Australian Tax Research Foundation, 213 p.

Heimler, Alberto and Milana, Carlo (1992), 'Riforma del Salario, Finanziamento del Servizio Sanitario Nazionale e Crescita Economica (With English summary) (Wage Reform, Functioning of the National Health Service and Economic Growth)', **26(1)** *Economia e Lavoro*, 67-78.

Hellmuth, William F. and Oldman, Oliver (1973), *Tax Policy and Tax Reform: 1961-1969, Selected Speeches and Testimony of Stanley S. Surrey*, CCH, 780 p.

Hettich, Walter (1979), 'Henry Simons on Taxation and the Economic System', **32** *National Tax Journal*, 1-9.

Holland, D.M. (1971), 'An Evaluation of Tax Incentives for on- the-Job Training of the Disadvantaged', **2** *Bell Journal of Economics*, 293-327.

Hulten, Charles R. and Schwab, Robert M. (1991), 'A Haig-Simons-Tiebout Comprehensive Income Tax', **44(1)** *National Tax Journal*, 67-78.

Institute for Fiscal Studies (1978), *The Structure and Reform of Direct Taxes: Report of a Committee Chaired by Professor J.E. Meade*, London, George Allen and Unwin Ltd., 533 p.

Isenberg, Joseph (1990), 'The End of Income Taxation', **45** *Tax Law Review*, 283-361.

Jepsen, Gunnar Thorlund (1980), 'Horisontal Lighed og den Personlige Indkomstskat (Horizontal Equity in Personal Income Taxation. With English summary)', **118(1)** *Nationalokonomisk Tidsskrift*, 37-50.

Johnson, Calvin H. (1989), 'Soft Money Investing Under the Income Tax', **1989** *University of Illinois Law Review*, 1019-1093.

Johnson, Manuel H. (1985), 'President Reagan's Modified Flat Tax: Analysis and Comparison', **5** *Cato Journal*, 499-520.

Jones, A.M. and Posnett, J.W. (1991), 'The Impact of Tax Deductibility on Charitable Giving by Covenant in the U.K.', **101** *Economic Journal*, 1117-1129.

Joseph, Richard, J. (1996), 'Why Progressive Taxation?', **15** *Tax Notes*, 313-318.

Kaldor, N. (1958), *An Expenditure Tax*, London, George Allen and Unwin Ltd., 249 p.

Kale, Jayant R. and Noe, Thomas H. (1990), 'Corporate Hedging under Personal and Corporate Taxation', **11(3)** *Managerial and Decision Economics*, 199-205.

Kaneko, Hiroshi (1966-75), 'Sozeiho Ni Okeru Shotoku Gainen No Kosei (1) (3) (Construction of the Concept of Income in Tax Law)', **92** *Hogaku Kyokai Zasshi*, 1081-1143.

Kaneko, Hiroshi (1995), *Shotoku Gainen No Kenkyu* (Studies on the Concept of Income), Tokyo, Yuhikaku, 444 p.

Kaneko, Hiroshi (1996a), *Shotoku Kazei No Ho to Seisaku* (Law and Policy in Income Taxation), Tokyo, Yuhikaku, 481 p.

Kaneko, Hiroshi (1996b), *Kazei Tanni Oyobi Joto Shotoku No Kenkyu* (Studies on the Tax Unit and Capital Gains), Tokyo,Yuhikaku, 364 p.

Kaplow, Louis (1986), 'An Economic Analysis of Legal Transitions', **99** *Harvard Law Review*, 509-617.

Kaplow, Louis (1987), *Optimal Transition Policy: Replacing Horizontal Equity with an Ex Ante Incentives Perspective*, Dissertation accepted by Harvard University Department of Economics.

Kaplow, Louis (1988), 'Savings Incentives in a Hybrid Income Tax: Comment', in Aaron, Henry J., Galper, Harveu and Pechman, Joseph A. (eds), *Uneasy Compromise: Problems of a Hybrid Income-Consumption Tax*, Washington, Brookings Institution.

Kaplow, Louis (1989), 'Horizontal Equity: Measures in Search of a Principle', **42** *National Tax Journal*, 139-154.

Kaplow, Louis (1991), 'The Income Tax as Insurance: The Casualty Loss and Medical Expense Deductions and the Exclusion of Medical Insurance Premiums', **79** *California Law Review*, 1485-1510.

Kaplow, Louis (1992a), 'Government Relief for Risk Associated with Government Action', **94** *Scandinavian Journal of Economics*, 525-541.

Kaplow, Louis (1992b), 'Income Tax Deductions for Losses as Insurance', **82** *American Economic Review*, 1013-1017.

Kaplow, Louis (1993), 'Should the Government's Allocation Branch be Concerned About the Distortionary Cost of Taxation and Distributive Effects?', Program in Law and Economics Discussion Paper, 122 ff.

Kaplow, Louis (1994a), 'Human Capital under An Ideal Income Tax', **80** *Virginia Law Review*, 1477-1514.

Kaplow, Louis (1994b), *Accuracy, Complexity, and the Income Tax*, National Bureau of Economic Research Working Paper, No. 4631. Also Harvard Program in Law and Economics Discussion Paper.

Kaplow, Louis (1994c), 'The Standard Deduction and Floors in the Income Tax', **50** *Tax Law Review*, 1-31.

Kaplow, Louis (1994d), 'A Note on Taxation as Social Insurance for Uncertain Labor Income', **49** *Public Finance*, 244-256.

Kaplow, Louis (1994e), 'Taxation and Risk Taking: A General Equilibrium Perspective', **47** *National Tax Journal*, 789-798.

Kaplow, Louis (1995a), 'A Fundamental Objection to Tax Equity Norms: A Call for Utilitarianism', **48** *National Tax Journal*, 497-514.

Kaplow, Louis (1995b), 'A Note on Subsidizing Gifts', **58** *Journal of Public Economics*, 469-477.

Kaplow, Louis (1996a), 'Tax Treatment of Families', *Encyclopedia of Taxation and Tax Policy*, Maryland, University Press of America.

Kaplow, Louis (1996b), 'Fiscal Federalism and the Deductibility of State and Local Taxes in a Federal Income Tax', *Virginia Law Review*.

Kaplow, Louis (1996c), 'Regional Cost-of-Living Adjustments in Tax-Transfer Schemes', *Tax Law Review*.

Kaplow, Louis (1996d), 'How Tax Complexity and Enforcement Affect the Equity and Efficiency of the Income Tax', **49** *National Tax Journal*, 135-150.

Kaplow, Louis (1996e), 'Tax and Non-Tax Distortions', **24** *Journal of Public Economics*.

Kaplow, Louis (1996f), 'On the Divergence Between 'Ideal' and Conventional Income Tax Treatment of Human Capital', **86** *American Economic Review. Papers and Proceedings*.

Kaplow, Louis (1996g), 'Optimal Distribution and the Family', *Scandinavian Journal of Economics*.

Kaplow, Louis and Shavell, Steven (1994), 'Why the Legal System is Less Efficient than the Income Tax in Redistributing Income', **23** *Journal of Legal Studies*, 667-681.

Kaplow, Louis and Warren, Alvin (1986), 'An Income Tax by Any Other Name - A Reply to Professor Strnad', **38** *Stanford Law Review*, 339-421.

Kaplow, Louis and Warren, Alvin (1987), 'Professor Strnad's Rejoinder: Simply Semantics', **39** *Stanford Law Review*, 419-425.

Katz, Avery and Mankiw N. Gregory (1985), 'How Should Fringe Benefits be Taxed?', **38** *National Tax Journal*, 37-45.

Kelman (1983), 'Time Preference and Tax Equity', **35** *Stanford Law Review*, 649-680.

Kiesling, Herbert J. (1981), 'Henry Simons, Equality, and the Personal Income Tax', **34** *National Tax Journal*, 257-259.

Klein, William A. (1977), 'Timing in Personal Taxation', **6** *Journal of Legal Studies*, 461-481.

Knoll, Michael S. (1994), 'Designing a Hybrid Income-Consumption Tax', **41** *UCLA Law Review*, 1791-1860.

Koren, Stephan (1989), 'Ausgewahlte Steuerreformen im Vergleich. (On the Recent Tax Reforms in Five Industrial Countries) (With English summary)', **35(5)** *Konjunkturpolitik*, 251-275.

Kornhauser, Marjorie E. (1987), 'The Rhetoric of the Anti- Progressive Income Tax Movement: A Typical Male Reaction', **86** *Michigan Law Review*, 465-523.

Kornhauser, Marjorie E. (1993), 'Love, Money and the IRS: Family, Income-Sharing, and the Joint Income Tax Return', **45** *Hastings Law Journal*, 63-111.

Krever, Richard (1984), 'Structural Issues in the Taxation of Capital Gains', **1** *Australian Tax Forum*, 164-184.

Lindholm, Richard W. (ed.) (1986), *Examination of Basic Weaknesses of Income as the Major Federal Tax Base*, New York, Greenwood Press, 320 p.

London, Jack R. (1988), 'The Impact of Changing Perspectives of Social Equity on Tax Policy: The Marital Tax Unit', **26** *Osgood Hall Law Journal*, 287-312.

Long, J.B., Jr (1990), 'In Defense of Henry Simons' Standing as a Classical Liberal', **9** *Cato Journal*, 601-618.

Marshall, Marion B. and Wells, Robert J. (1993), 'Prior Coverage of Consumption Tax Issues', **15** *Tax Notes*, 951-955.

Martinello, F. and West, E.G. (1991), 'Education Budget Reductions Via Tax Credits: Some Further Considerations', **19** *Public Finance Quarterly*, 355-368.

Matthiessen, Lars (1975), 'Recent Trends in Personal Income Taxation in Sweden', **33(2)** *Finanzarchiv*, 272-304.

McCaffery, Edward J. (1992), 'Tax Policy Under a Hybrid Income-Consumption Tax', **70** *Texas Law Review*, 1145-1218.

McCaffery, Edward J. (1993), 'Taxation and the Family: A Fresh Look at Behavioral Gender Biases in the Code', **40** *UCLA Law Review*, 983-1060.

McCaffery, Edward J. (1997), *Taxing Women*, Chicago, University of Chicago Press, 310 p.

McCaleb, Thomas S. (1985), 'Public Choice Perspectives on the Flat Tax Follies', **5** *Cato Journal*, 613-624.

McClelland, Alison and Krever, Rick (1993), 'Social Security, Taxation Law, and Redistribution: Directions for Reform', **31** *Osgood Hall Law Journal*, 63-135.

McCombs, J.B. (1990), 'An Historical Review and Analysis of Early United States Tax Policy Scholarship: Definition of Income and Progressive Rates', **64** *St. John's Law Review*, 471-525.

McGee, Robert W. (1975a), 'Investment Credit for Progress Expenditures Using Phase-In Rule', *Taxation for Accountants*, 250-251.

McGee, Robert W. (1975b), 'T.D. 7352: New Rules on Application of Sick Pay Exclusion to Disability Pension Payments', *Taxes*, 436-441.

McGee, Robert W. (1976), 'The New Imputed Interest Rules: How They Work', *The Practical Accountant*, 63-67.

McGee, Robert W. (1984a), *The History of the Income Tax in the United States*, Occasional Paper, Deakin University, Australia, No. 69.

McGee, Robert W. (1984b), *Software Taxation*, National Association of Accountants, 305 p.

McGee, Robert W. (1985a), 'Computer Software and the Investment Tax Credit', **5** *Computer Law Journal*, 347-362. Reprinted in *Accounting and Tax Aspects of Computer Software Manufacturing*, Praeger Publishing Company, 1987. Reprinted in *The Monthly Digest of Tax Articles*, 1985, 6-21.

McGee, Robert W. (1985b), *Tax Planning in Divorce Settlements*, Prentice Hall, 64 p.

McGee, Robert W. (1985c), 'The 1985 Tax Simplification Act', **1** *Business Planning*, 14-17.

McGee, Robert W. (1985d), 'Keeping Track of Fringe Benefits ... When To Tax and When Not To Tax', **1** *Controllers Quarterly*, 24-27.

McGee, Robert W. (1986a), *Capital Gains and Losses, Alternative Minimum Tax, Accounting Provisions, Prentice-Hall's Explanation of the Tax Reform Act of 1986*, New Jersey, Prentice Hall, 500 p.

McGee, Robert W. (1986b), *How Tax Reform Would Affect Profit-Sharing*, New Jersey, Prentice Hall, 23 p.

McGee, Robert W. (1986c), *Tax-Wise Executive Comensation Strategies*, New Jersey, Prentice Hall, 44 p.

McGee, Robert W. (1986d), *International Revenue Service Special Enrollment Examination Questions and Answers*, New Jersey, Prentice Hall, 59 p.

McGee, Robert W. (1996a), *Taxation, Ethics and Public Policy*, Dumont Institute for Public Policy Research. <<http://ww.hili.com~dumontin>>

McGee, Robert W. (1996b), *Essays on Accounting,Taxation and Public Finance*, Dumont Institute for Public Policy Research. <<http://ww.hili.com~dumontin>>

McIntyre, M.J. and Oldman, Oliver (1977), 'Taxation of the Family in a Comprehensive and Simplified Income Tax', **90** *Harvard Law Review*, 1573-1630.

McIntyre, M.J., Sander, Frank E.A. and Westfall, David (1983), *Readings in Federal Taxation*, 2nd edn, New York, Foundation, 625 p.

Meyer, Peter B. (1976), 'The Acceptance over Time of Personal Income Taxation: Voluntary Compliance in the Philippines', 1965, **15(4)** *Philippine Economic Journal*, 604-613.

Mookherjee, Dilip and Png, Yvan P.L. (1990), 'Enforcement Costs and the Optimal Progressivity of Income Taxes', **6** *Journal of Law, Economics, and Organization*, 411-431.

Musgrave, Richard A. (1967), 'In Defense of an Income Concept', **81** *Harvard Law Review*, 44-62.

Musgrave, Richard A. (1976), 'ET, OT, and SBT', **6** *Journal of Public Economics*, 3-16.

Nadeau, Serge (1988), 'A Model to Measure the Effects of Taxes on the Real and Financial Decisions of the Firm', **41(4)** *National Tax Journal*, 467-481.

Nakazato, Minoru (1991a), 'Shotoku Gainen To Jikan (Income Concept and Timing)', in Kaneko, Hiroshi (ed.), *Shotoku Kazei No Kenkyu* (Studies on Income Taxation), Tokyo, Yuhikaku, 129-163.

Nakazato, Minoru (1991b), 'Shotoku No Kosei Yoso Toshiteno Shohi (Consumption as a component of income)', in Kaneko, Hiroshi (ed.), *Shotoku Kazei No Kenkyu* (Studies on Income Taxation), Tokyo, Yuhikaku, 35-71.

Nakazato, Minoru (1995), 'Katei To Sozei Seido (Family and Tax System)', **1059** *Jurist*, 31-36.

O'Kelley, C.R. (1981), 'Rawls, Justice, and The Income Tax', **16** *Georgia Law Review*, 1-32.

O'Kelley, C.R. (1985), 'Tax Policy for Post-Liberal Society: A Flat-Tax-Inspired Redefinition of the Purpose and Ideal Structure of a Progresive Income Tax', **58** *Southern California Law Review*, 727-776.

Oldman, Oliver and Temple, Ralph (1960), 'Comparative Analysis of the Taxation of Married Persons', **12** *Stanford Law Review*, 585-605.

Paci, Pierella (1988), 'Tax Based Incomes Policies: Will They Work? Have They Worked?', **9(2)** *Fiscal Studies*, 81-94.

Parsons, Ross W. (1986), 'Income Taxation An Institution in Decay?', **3** *Australian Tax Forum*, 233-266.

Pechman, Joseph A. (1967), 'Comprehensive Income Taxation: A Comment', **81** *Harvard Law Review*, 63-67.

Pechman, Joseph A. (1977), *Comprehensive Income Taxation*, Washington, Brookings Institution, 311 p.

Pechman, Joseph A. (1980), *What Should Be Taxed: Income or Expenditure?*, Washington, Brookings Institution, 311 p.

Pechman, Joseph A. and Engelhardt, Gray V. (1990), 'The Income Tax Treatment of the Family', **43** *National Tax Journal*, 1-22.

Peterson, Wallace C. (1991), *Transfer Spending, Taxes, and the American Welfare*, Dordrecht, Kluwer, 192 p.

Pope, Jeff (1989), 'The Compliance Costs of Personal Income Taxation: A Review of the Issues', **6(2)** *Australian Tax Forum*, 125-142.

Pope, Jeff and Fayle, Richard (1990), 'The Compliance Costs of Personal Income Taxation in Australia 1986/87: Empirical Results', **7(1)** *Australian Tax Forum*, 85-126.

Popkin, William D. (1986), 'Tax Ideals in the Real World: A Comment on Professor Strnad's Approach to Tax Fairness', **62** *Indiana Law Journal*, 63-72.

Rea, Samuel A., Jr (1984), 'Taxes, Transfers and the Family', **34** *University of Toronto Law Journal*, 314-340.

Roin, Julie, A. (1988), 'United they Stand, Divided They Fall: Public Choice Theory and the Tax Code', **74** *Cornell Law Review*, 62-134.

Ruiz-Huerta Carbonell, Jesús (1995), *Las Rentas de las Personas Mayores* (Eldest Citizens' Income), SECOT.

Ruiz-Huerta Carbonell, Jesús, Alvarez, Jesús, Ayala, Luis, Iriondo, Iñaki, Martinez, Rosa and Palacios, Juan Ignacio (1995), *La Distribución Funcional y Personal de la Renta en España* (Functional and Personal Distribution of Income in Spain), Premio de Investagión 1995 del Consejo Económico y Social.

Rupley, Lawrence A. (1978), 'Personal Income-based Taxation in the Northern States of Nigeria and the Effect of Uniform Income Taxation', **32(89)** *Bulletin for International Fiscal Documentation*, 401-410.

Russell, R. Robert (1986), 'Tax Based Incomes Policies: Some Skeptical Remarks', in Colander, David C. (ed.), *IncentiveBased Incomes Policies: Advances in TIP and MAP*, Cambridge, MA, Harper and Row, 159-175.

Salzyn, Vladimir (1988), 'Desigining an Optimal Personal Income Tax Rate Structure: Goals and Criteria', **26** *Osgoode Hall Law Journal*, 577-602.

Sanchez, Isabel (1990), 'Evasión Fiscal, Regulación y Mecanismos Óptimos de Inspección (Tax Evasion, Regulation, and Optimal Auditing Mechanisms)', **2** *Cuadernos Económicos de ICE*, 45 ff.

Sanchez, Isabel (1993), 'Hierarchical Design and Enforcement of Income Tax Policies', **50** *Journal of Public Economics*, 345-369.

Schantz, Georg (1896), 'Der Einkommensbefriff und die Einkommensteuergesetze', **13** *Finanzarchiv*, 1-87.

Schmalbeck, Richard L. (1984), 'Income Averaging After Twenty Years: A Failed Experiment in Horizontal Equity', **64** *Duke Law Journal*, 509-580.

Schwartz, Eli and Aronson, J. Richard (1972), 'How to Integrate Corporate and Personal Income Taxation', **27(5)** *Journal of Finance*, 1073-1080.

Seidl, Christian (1979a), 'Reform der Steuern auf Einkommen und Ertrag, Novellierung des herrschenden Steuersystems oder Systemänderung durch eine modifizierte analytische Einkommensteuer? (Reforming the Income Tax, Improving the Traditional Tax or Tax Reform by a Schedule Income Tax?)', **6(4)** *Freie Argumente, Freiheitliche Zeitschrift für Politik*, 1-56.

Seidl, Christian (1979b), 'Das Konzept einer Modifizierten Analytischen Einkommensteuer als Alternative zum Herrschenden System Direkter Steuern (A Schedule Income Tax as an Alternative to the Traditional System of Direct Taxation)', **26(5)** *Wirtschaftspolitische Blätter*, 49-62.

Seidl, Christian (1980), 'Ein Analytisches Einkommensteuerkonzept mit Flankierenden Steuern (A Schedule Income Tax with Matching Other Taxes)', in Helige, O. (ed.), *Dokumentation zur Steuerreformkommission, Wirtschaftsverlag Dr. Anton Orac*, Wien, 128-155.

Sewell, David (1988), 'Towards Longer Time Horizons in Personal Taxation', **26** *Osgoode Hall Law Journal*, 235-258.

Shachar, Avishai (1984), 'From Income to Consumption Tax: Criteria for Rules of Transition', **97** *Harvard Law Review*, 1581-1609.

Shakow, David J. (1986), 'Taxation Without Realization: A Proposal for Accrual Taxation', **134** *University of Pennsylvania Law Review*, 1111-1205.

Shaviro, Daniel N. (1988), 'The New Alternative Minimum Tax: Perception, Reality, and Strategy', **66** *Taxes*, 91-113.

Shaviro, Daniel N. (1989a), 'Risk and Accrual: The Tax Treatment of Nonrecourse Debt', **44** *Tax Law Review*, 401-457.

Shaviro, Daniel N. (1989b), 'Selective Limitations on Tax Benefits', **56** *University of Chicago Law Review*, 1189-1260.

Shaviro, Daniel N. (1990), 'The Man Who Lost Too Much: Zarin v. Commissioner and the Measurement of Taxable Consumption', **45** *Tax Law Review*, 215-258.

Shaviro, Daniel N. (1992), 'An Efficiency Analysis of Realization and Recognition Rules Under the Federal Income Tax', **48** *Tax Law Review*, 1-68.

Shaviro, Daniel N. (1993), 'Commentary: Uneasiness and Capital Gains', **48** *Tax Law Review*, 393-417.

Shaviro, Daniel N. (1995), 'Risk-Based Rules and the Taxation of Capital Income', **50** *Tax Law Review*, 643-724.

Simons, Henry C. (1938), *Personal Income Taxation: The Definition of Income as a Problem of Fiscal Policy*, Chicago, University of Chicago Press, 283 p.

Sommerhalder, Ruud A. (1996), *Comparing Individual Income Tax Reforms: a Dutch Perspective*, IBFD, 471 p.

Steven, Paul B. (1984), 'Federal Income Taxation and Human Capital', **70** *Virginia Law Review*, 1357-1427.

Stout, Lynn A. (1981), 'Note: The Case for Mandatory Separate Filing by Married Persons', **91** *Yale Law Journal*, 363-382.

Strnad, Jeff (1985), 'Taxation of Income from Capital: A Theoretical Reappraisal', **37** *Stanford Law Review*, 1023-1107.

Strnad, Jeff (1986), 'Tax Timing and the Haig-Simons Ideal: A Rejoinder to Professor Popkin', **62** *Indiana Law Journal*, 73-94.

Strnad, Jeff (1987), 'The Bankruptcy of Conventional Tax Timing Wisdom is Deeper Than Semantics: A Rejoinder to Professors Kaplow and Warren', **39** *Stanford Law Review*, 389-417.

Strnad, Jeff (1990), 'Periodicity and Accretion Taxation: Norms and Implementation', **99** *Yale Law Journal*, 1877-1911.

Surrey, Stanley S. (1973), *Pathways to Tax Reform: The Concept of Tax Expenditures*, Harvard University Press, 418 p.

Surrey, Stanley S. and McDaniel, P.R. (1985), *Tax Expenditures*, Harvard University Press, 303 p.

US Department of the Treasury (1984), *Tax Reform for Fairness, Simplicity, and Economic Growth, The Treasury Department Report to the President*, US Department of the Treasury, 262 p.

Veall, Michael R. (1987), 'A Note on the Expenditure Tax and Progressivity', **40** *National Tax Journal*, 261-263.

Vickrey, William (1947), *Agenda for Progressive Taxation*, New York, Ronald Press, 496 p.

Warren, Alvin (1975), 'Fairness and a Consumption-Type or Cash Flow Personal Income Tax', **88** *Harvard Law Review*, 931-946.

Warren, Alvin (1980), 'Would a Consumption Tax be Fairer than an Income Tax?', **89** *Yale Law Journal*, 1081-1124.

Weck-Hannemann, Hannelore (1996), 'Frauenerwerbstätigkeit und Familienbesteuerung (Female Employment and Family Taxation)', in Thöni, Erich and Winner, Hannes (eds), *Die Familie im Sozialstaat. Familienbesteuerung aus ökonomischer und juristischer Sicht Veröffentlichungen der Universität Innsbruck 216*, Innsbruck, 191-207.

Weiss, Deborah (1993), 'Can Capital Tax Be Fair? Stimulating Savings Through Differentiated Tax Rates', **78** *Cornell Law Review*, 206-251.

White, P.D. (1995), *Tax Law I., II.*, Dartmouth, Aldershot, 1008 p.

Witte, John F. (1985), *The Politics and Development of the Federal Income Tax*, Madison, University of Wisconsin, 438 p.

Wittmann, Rolf (1992), *Das Markteinkommen: einfachgesetzlicher Struckturbegriff und verfassungsdirigierter Anknuepfungsgegenstand der Einkommensteuer?*, Augsburg, Verlag Rudolf Wittmann, 132 p.

Wueller, Paul H. (1938a), 'Concepts of Taxable Income I: The German Contribution', **53** *Political Science Quarterly*, 83-110.

Wueller, Paul H. (1938b), 'Concepts of Taxable Income II: The American Contribution', **53** *Political Science Quarterly*, 557-583.

Wueller, Paul H. (1939), 'Concepts of Taxable Income III: The Italian Contribution', **54** *Political Science Quarterly*, 555-576.

Yohe, Gary W. (1985), 'Improving Tax-based Incomes Policies: The Lessons of the Environmental Literature', **13** *Public Finance Quarterly*, 183-205.

Yorio, Edward (1982), 'Federal Income Tax Rulemaking: An Economic Approach', **51** *Fordham Law Review*, 1 ff.

Zelenak, Lawrence (1994a), 'Children and the Income Tax', **49** *Tax Law Review*, 349-418.

Zelenak, Lawrence (1994b), 'Marriage and the Income Tax', **67** *Southern California Law Review*, 339-405.

Zelenak, Lawrence (1995), 'Flat Tax vs. VAT: Progressivity and Family Alloances', **27** *Tax Notes*, 1129-1134.

Zelinsky, Edward P. (1986), 'Efficiency and Income Taxes: The Rehabilitation of Tax Incentives', **64** *Texas Law Review*, 973-1037.

Zolt, Eric M. (1996), 'The Uneasy Case for Uniform Taxation', **16** *Virginia Tax Review*, 39-109.

6060
CORPORATE TAXATION

Charlotte Crane
Northwestern University School of Law

Abstract

Much of the traditional economic literature has until relatively recently ignored almost all of the details of the coverage of the tax and the legal institutions within which the tax has developed. As a result, most of the rules used in establishing corporate tax liabilities are the outgrowth of legal formalisms. Although many discussions of reforms of tax rules use as their starting point some rudimentary assumptions about incentives and effects, few of these discussions consider less obvious incentives and interactions or attempt to verify their analysis empirically.

This chapter will therefore focus primarily on those treatments that go beyond these typical rudimentary assumptions. The bibliography deals only with those works that go well beyond descriptive treatments and practical expositions of the legal rules in question.
JEL classification: K22, K34
Keywords: Corporate Income Tax, Tax Burden and Incidence, Corporate Financial Structure

1. Introduction and Note on Scope

Corporations, measures of corporate profits, and taxes imposed thereon are uniquely legal institutions. They have no physical reality; they are entirely the product of legal and accounting rules. But because of the importance of corporate activity in modern economies, scholars in economics and finance who have no other interest in law or legal institutions have long had an interest in analyzing the effects of corporate taxes. To the extent that this work uses economic analysis to understand and predict the behavior of firms as well as the development of legal rules, this body of literature must be considered in any review of the treatment of the corporate tax as 'law and economics'. References to works in a wide variety of methodologies are therefore included in this bibliographic review.

Much of this traditional economic literature has until relatively recently ignored almost all of the details of the coverage of the tax and the legal institutions within which the tax has developed. At least in the United States, these details have evolved through a continuing dialog between the legislature (which until relatively recently formally prescribed only the most skeletal of rules) and the courts (which have felt free to allow the approaches of the common law to contribute to the development of the legal rules), as prompted by the Internal Revenue Service. As a result, most of the rules used in establishing corporate tax liabilities (for instance, those according to which entities are classified as subject to the tax, those according to which debt is distinguished from equity, those according to which share redemptions are distinguished from dividends, and those according to which corporate reorganizations are classified as taxable or nontaxability) are the outgrowth of legal formalisms, particularly the idea that a corporation can be an entity entirely separate from its participants. These formalisms developed without any conscious attention to their economic effect. There are therefore only a few justifications and analyses of the substantive rules of corporate taxation of the sort those well-read in other areas of law and economics might find familiar. Indeed, a leading monograph analyzing the corporate law through the lens of law and economics makes only scant reference to the possibility that taxes have an influence on the legal relationships between corporations and their shareholders (Easterbrook and Fischel, 1991). Furthermore, the evolution of most of these details has historically been, and continues to be, dominated by manipulation of these formal constructs by institutions for which there is only rudimentary understanding of their nature as 'economic' actors. Although many discussions of reforms of tax rules use as their starting point some rudimentary assumptions about incentives and effects (most commonly, that taxpayers will attempt to minimize tax burdens at least to the extent that the avoided burden exceeds the cost of avoidance and that differential treatment of economically similar transactions will produce inefficient distortions), few of these discussions consider less obvious incentives and interactions or attempt to verify their analysis empirically. (Roin, 1988; Kanda and Levmore, 1991, and Arlen and Weiss, 1995, are notable exceptions). This review will therefore focus primarily on those treatments that go beyond these typical rudimentary assumptions. Thus only a small portion of the literature considered here can be solidly classified as 'law and economics', rather than traditional economic analysis of the effect of tax laws on legal institutions.

This chapter focuses on the effects of taxes that are encountered only by incorporated entities, and does not consider the effects of taxes that are imposed regardless of the legal form in which capital is held. Thus it does not generally consider the effect of taxes on overall capital formation beyond basic questions of corporate financial structure. However, many of the works cited herein, particularly earlier works, may have (in many cases knowingly, but in other cases unwittingly) assumed a substantial congruence between the 'business' and 'corporate' sectors, and there is, therefore, a substantial overlap with that literature. For survey treatments of capital and business taxes generally, see Gravelle (1994) and Halpern and Mintz (1992, with emphasis on Canada).

This bibliography deals only with those works that go well beyond descriptive treatments and practical expositions of the legal rules in question. The reader is cautioned, however, that, perhaps more than other areas of the law, the rules outlining the base of the corporate income tax are complex, and that assumptions about the impact of potential tax liabilities can rarely be made without a relatively sophisticated understanding of them. Comprehensive introductions to the overall income tax systems of various jurisdictions and an introductory bibliography can be found in Ault (1997); additional descriptions of the corporate tax systems in specific jurisdictions can be found in Brooks (1997) (Canada); Pender (1997) (Australia); Muten (1997) (Scandinavia); Teixeira (1997) (Portugal, Great Britain, Holland).

More detailed surveys of tax-base defining rules and rates can be found in the looseleaf services of the International Bureau of Fiscal Documentation, as well as in various pamphlet series of the larger accounting firms, including Coopers and Lybrand, Klynveld Peat Marwick Goerdeler, Price Waterhouse, and Deloitte Touche Tohmatsu International. Useful short summaries of various topics include Auerbach (1990) (the predominant features of the classical double tax), Shoven and Waldfogel (1990) (the treatment of debt and equity), Scholes and Wolfson (1991) (the general pattern of rules for mergers and acquisitions) and the international scheme generally.

Wiseman (1974), Harberger (1983) and Goode (1951) should give the reader good perspective on the early contributions of traditional economists. A useful survey of the issues raised by the presence of taxes in the traditional corporate finance literature is provided by Gordon and Malkiel (1981). Other more recent surveys of slightly different scope include that by Head (1997), Mintz (1995) (including tables showing the prominent features of the tax schemes used in various jurisdictions and providing more general background on taxes, costs of capital and risky investments), and Cnossen (1997), focusing on the OECD jurisdictions.

2. Overview of the Tax

Under the 'classical' scheme for taxation of corporate income, corporations are recognized as separate taxable entities, legitimately subject to tax upon their income. Distributions of earnings to shareholders are also taxed as income to shareholders, as if they represented entirely new values available to be taxed. Such schemes essentially tax the earnings on corporate equity investments twice, once at the corporate level as earned and later upon the distribution of the earnings to the shareholders. Bittker and Eustice (1994) provide a comprehensive summary of the complex US tax rules controlling corporate/shareholder relations. Clark (1977) provides useful insights into legal concepts behind the classification of various corporate/shareholder transactions in the classical scheme. Stephan (1990) provides a slightly more intricate update of US taxation of corporate/shareholder relations, taking into account both the many legislative changes occurring in the 1980s and more recent theoretical analysis of corporate/shareholder relations.

Not all business activity is subject, even nominally, to the corporate tax. Much business activity is undertaken by entities, including charities (Hansmann, 1981; Rose-Ackerman, 1982) and local governments, that may be entirely exempt from income taxation.

Even in the for-profit sector, there is much business activity that is not subject to corporate tax. In the classical system, the corporate tax only attaches to those entities that are in fact incorporated, or are deemed to be operating as if they were in fact incorporated. It does not attach to joint ventures and partnerships. In the US, the legal nature of business entities is a matter of state, not federal law, while the reach of the federal income tax on corporations has been a matter of federal law. As a consequence, in the US, an entity could be subject to the corporate income tax regardless of its formal legal classification as a partnership or trust.

As an historical matter, entities that enjoy limited liability, free transferability of interests, centralized management, and continuity of life traditionally were subject to corporate tax even if unincorporated. In the US, this line proved very difficult to police. See Klein (1972), Lee (1988) and Hobbes (1995) for a review of this history. Recent regulatory changes in the US have made avoidance of the classical double tax scheme elective for all but publicly traded entities. Even a publicly traded entity can also avoid the classic double tax if its activities and capital requirements can fit certain rigid structures, generally designed for entities serving as financial intermediaries, see, for example, Gergen (1997) and Clark (1975). For an overview of current thinking about the scope of the corporate tax base in the US, see Yin (1997) and Klein and Zolt (1995). In other jurisdictions, the formal legal status of the business entity is likely to determine whether the entity is subject to the income tax (Thomas, 1997).

Under the traditional income tax, an increase in the value of corporate stock is not taxed to shareholders until it is 'realized', generally, reduced to cash in the hands of the shareholders. There are recurring proposals to alter this rule, especially with respect to publicly held debt and equity (Slawson, 1967; Davies, 1975; Dodge, 1995). Under the classical scheme, dividends distributed to shareholders are taxed without offset for shareholder investment or credit for corporate taxes paid. Increased share value, however, can be realized by shareholders by selling shares to third parties. This value can be both realized by the shareholder and removed from the corporate solution if it is the corporation, not a third party, who purchases the shares. In the US scheme, the rules applicable to such tactics sometimes leave the consequences of such transactions uncertain. Kingson (1976) and Jassy (1974) explore these rules in detail; Chirelstein (1969) explores the effects of such transactions on the remaining shareholders.

Shareholders can ordinarily enjoy the benefits of increased share value without such values leaving corporation solution merely by selling shares. When such a sale is for cash or other relatively liquid consideration, the shareholder will ordinarily be taxed. However, increased share value can often be enjoyed without any taxation at the shareholder level as a result of tax-free mergers with corporations the stock of which represents more diversified holdings or is more easily pledged, through sophisticated futures and other hedging transactions. Such tactics can result in permanent escape from income tax on increases in share value when stock need not be liquidated until after the shareholder's death because, upon death, the shareholder's basis (that is, deemed after tax investment) is increased to fair market value. Some investors, especially offshore investors, will effectively be subject to income tax upon dividend payments but not on stock sales. Finally, tax exempt shareholders, including pension plans, will be taxed neither on dividend receipt or sale, although their beneficiaries will be subject to tax upon the ultimate payout.

Most classical schemes are designed to avoid full taxation of earnings at more than one corporate level, limiting the tax burden to a 'double tax'. In the United States' income tax this is achieved by allowing a deduction for dividends received, which may vary with the extent of payee ownership in the payor corporation, and through the elimination of the ordinary consequences of asset transfers among very closely related corporations. This feature of the classical scheme, considered together with the number of shareholders that are explicitly exempt from taxation (including pension plans) and effectively exempt (including foreign shareholders), reduces the extent to which the classical scheme in fact results in double taxation of corporate enterprise.

3. Other Taxes Attaching to the Corporate Form

Corporate income taxes can be combined with various other adjunct taxes designed to offset various undesirable effects of the classical income tax or some particular implementation feature of it. Such devices include the undistributed earnings (or accumulated earnings) tax (designed to offset the incentive to retain earnings in corporations rather than distribute them and subject them to the shareholder level tax), excess profits taxes (designed to capture the excessive return thought to be available during war time) and minimum taxes (designed to counteract perceived flaws in the ordinary rules defining the tax base). Lyon (1997) examines the inefficiencies introduced by one such tax in the US, the alternative minimum tax, the aim of which was to reduce the claimed overuse of certain incentive provisions in the US corporate income tax.

Other taxes may be specifically imposed only on corporations, including franchise and capital taxes, property taxes at special rates, net worth and gross asset taxes can be imposed with or without regard for their relation to the corporate income tax. Taxes generally imposed on property, value-added, imports, sales and sales are almost never coordinated with corporate income taxes, although such payments are ordinarily allowed as business expenses in the computation of corporate income.

The problems inherent in defining corporate income have led to recent proposals alternative measures. Knoll (1996), following Bankman (1995) sets out the conditions under which a corporate tax, imposed directly on the corporation, for increases in its total market value would replicate the current, accounting based tax. The possibility that even a perfectly defined income tax creates disincentives for investment has fueled additional proposals for substantial changes in the definition of the tax base that includes corporate income. Zodrow (1997), King (1987) and Auerbach (1990) build on earlier work to propose a corporate cash flow tax that would sever a corporate tax from its routes in profit accounting and eliminate any tax-driven biases regarding corporate structure and investment; the base of such a tax could be approximated to all current distributions to shareholders (both of dividends and share repurchases) by reducing corporate receipts for all new investment.

4. The Origins of the Corporate Income Tax

The earliest attempts to impose taxes upon corporations, rather than upon any particular corporate activity or holding, appear to have origins in efforts to include individual wealth represented by corporate interests in property tax bases. Taxation of the corporation itself could serve as a surrogate for taxation of the wealth of the shareholder, and would be preferred by those jurisdictions which could claim that the corporation was entirely within its taxing jurisdiction, even if its shareholders were not. Initial efforts focused on the par value of the stock, or its paid in capital, but as it became clear that these legal and accounting concepts had no economic meaning, jurisdictions either switched to, or added, corporate income as the measure of the tax.

Further support for the tax derived from the notion that doing business as a corporation was a privilege for which charging a fee or franchise tax was appropriate. (These franchise taxes are thought to have played an important part in the competition among states for the most attractive law governing corporate shareholder relations, see Cary, 1974, pp. 668-669.) With the possible exception of the privilege of limited liability (which is now frequently available without subjection to the classical tax regime), this justification now has limited appeal. A good survey of the historical attitudes in the US can be found in Goode (1951, pp. 24-43).

The introduction of the modern corporate income tax at the federal level in the US has alternatively been explained as an early effort to respond to the popular pressure to regulate corporate activity without infringing upon the state's prerogatives in corporate law (Kornhauser, 1990). The details of its later development has been described (by a political scientist reaching conclusions that except in their general optimism, resemble a public choice approach) as a reflection of a coalition between elected government and the business community to promote economic growth (Martin, 1991).

5. Modern Justifications for the Corporate Income Tax

Some early writers simply assumed that the corporation, as a separate legal entity, was appropriately subject to tax. Corporate income taxes remain politically popular, especially among those who view corporations as sources of wealth entirely independent of shareholders, employees or customers. But most modern justifications for the tax are even less unsatisfying than those relied upon historically. Some justify the tax as necessary to secure the goals of other tax regimes. When corporate income tax is part of a larger scheme of income taxation, particularly a scheme with substantial redistributive goals implemented through progressive rates, the corporate tax can be viewed as an expedient buttress to the income tax. Without a corporate tax, the personal income tax would be substantially undermined by entrepreneurs who could shift the return on their efforts into untaxed corporate profits. (Gordon and Mackie Mason, 1995, explore this rationale as an explanation for the presence of corporate income taxes even in small capital importing jurisidictions.) Even if taxation of return to effort were not at issue, corporate earnings would be retained, providing economic benefit to shareholders, outside of the reach of the income tax. Under this justification, the corporate tax serves as a withholding tax to insure at least minimum correspondence with the nominal personal income tax scheme. This rationale, however, can only justify the imposition of the tax upon the income when realized by the corporation, not the failure to avoid taxing the remaining value again upon its distribution to shareholders (Gabinet and Coffey, 1977). Alternatively, the corporate income tax would be fully justified, however, as a means of buttressing the personal income tax in cases in which jurisdiction is lacking to tax shareholders (Musgrave, 1987). Under this justification, however, some credit for corporate taxes paid should be allowed at least to domestic taxpayers.

Some claims have been made that the corporate tax under the classical scheme can be justified because of certain other economic characteristics of corporations. (Caution must be used in relying upon such justifications, since there is unlikely to be an identity between the entities attracting the tax and these characteristics. Only relatively recently have the rules for determining which entities will attract the tax actually reflected any of these justifications.) Early writers relied upon the benefits of limited liability to justify the imposition of tax. Goode (1951), Break (1969) and Rudnick (1989) all suggest that liquidity, resulting both from marketability and from the limited liability ordinarily afforded to shareholders, justifies attracting an entity level tax. Kose, Senbet and Sundaram (1994) outline the contours of a tax that would more precisely internalize the costs of limited liability.

Stiglitz (1973, 1976) posits that the corporate tax should be viewed as only a tax on pure profits and entrepreneurship, a tax which allows the government a partial return on an implicit partnership with the owners of equity. This view relies heavily on the notion that all ordinary returns to capital can be paid out as returns to debt finance which returns are not subject to tax because they are deducted from corporate income, but does not attempt to reconcile the actual contours of the tax with this description given the fact that corporations frequently do not appear to be so fully leveraged. Head (1997) provides an in-depth examination of these various explanations of the corporate tax in light of the current finance literature.

Even if the corporate tax can only be explained as an historical accident, its persistence in the face of its apparent inefficiencies remains an enigma. One possible explanation is that corporate managers have little incentive to lobby to eliminate the corporate tax, or to otherwise integrate the personal and corporate taxes, when they can enjoy a higher payoff from lobbying to alter the corporate tax base in ways that benefit them as managers even if integration or elimination would benefit shareholders more (Arlen and Weiss 1995).

Still others have suggested that the corporate tax can serve to avoid the agency costs that would be incurred if other means were used to resolve the conflicts over timing of income among stakeholders facing different tax consequences upon corporate asset sales and distributions (Kanda and Levmore, 1991; Snoe, 1993).

Cooper (1994) considers the possibility that corporate managers consider tax compliance as a financing and investment decision, and the implications of this view for tax administrators.

6. The Definition of the Corporate Tax Base

Perhaps because there can be no economically sound justification for the corporate income tax under the classical scheme, there has been little serious effort to develop an economically sound measure of the corporate income tax base (Levmore, 1988). (This is in stark contrast with the individual income tax base, for which the combined articulations of Georg Schanz, Robert M. Haig and Henry C. Simons (Simons, 1938) provides the most common measure.) There is a general consensus, for instance, that the current standards for base-defining are far from that which would justify the corporate tax as merely a tax on economic rents under the Stiglitz view (Bond and Devereux, 1995).

The few preliminary attempts have merely deduced from the existing accounting rules defining the corporate base that their overall purpose seems to be the taxation of all income, above and beyond the contributions made by the shareholders, that the corporation can be expected to make available to shareholders in the future (Bryan, 1984; Crane, 1988). Levmore (1987) suggests that at least some of the rules used to define the corporate tax base and which govern corporate shareholder relations serve to constrain managers in an efficient way. Repetti (1997) explores some more closely tailored efforts in the US to manipulate the incentives of corporate managers through particular base-defining provisions.

The corporate tax base is frequently defined so as to identify a base only roughly equivalent to profit for other purposes. Accounting for tax purposes may deviate substantially from accounting for financial, rate-making or internal purposes. Some such disparities are introduced to overcome the bias of financial accounting against overstating earnings. Cummins, Harris and Hassett (1995) offer some preliminary analysis of the relative effects of such 'one-book' and 'two-book' regimes, as well as survey information on various tax schemes in place. Other disparities between book and tax income are deliberate preferences, introduced to provide incentives for investment, sometimes available only for investment by entities subject to the corporate tax. Auerbach (1982) and Hulten and Robertson (1982) examine the accelerated depreciation scheme in place for a brief time in the US in the early 1980s, which under many plausible conditions, and in connection with mechanisms for transferring tax losses that temporarily moved the US system closer to full loss offsets (see Gravelle, 1982), effectively eliminated the corporate tax. Interest generally is deductible, producing a potential bias against equity and in favor of debt financing (see Warren, 1974, and below). Although preferential treatment may be available for capital gains, the corporate tax base frequently includes extraordinary gains as well as income from operations.

Corporate income is ordinarily computed on an annual basis, with only clumsy mechanisms for carrying back and forward losses to smooth out income. Among the shortcomings in such mechanisms are nonrefundability and an unwillingness to allow the loss incurred with respect to one corporate investment to be available to shelter the gain from a previously unrelated investment, or to allow adjustments for the timing of payment and refund. Many systems provide for carrybacks and carryforwards of losses, but few provide for full loss offsets. Failure to provide such offsets may affect the type of risks undertaken and may provide an advantage for diversified over undiversified firms (Romano and Campisano, 1981). Those firms with loss carryforwards ordinarily face a lower than statutory rate on earnings from new investments (since carryforwards effectively postpone tax payments), while those with carrybacks face the statutory rate (since carrybacks produce current refunds). Auerbach and Poterba (1987b) find that the presence of such carryforwards can have significant effects on investment incentives.

Although corporate income is taxed both to the corporation and when realized by shareholders, most classical tax schemes include some mechanism whereby additional levels of corporate tax are avoided. Dividends from wholly-owned subsidiaries are frequently eliminated entirely in the measure of corporate income; dividends on portfolio stock maybe partially eliminated; certain other transactions among related, and sometimes even among unrelated, corporations may be given special tax accounting treatments (see generally Mundstock, 1988).

As noted above, interest paid on debt is generally deductible, while returns paid on equity are not. Despite the apparently enormous consequences, distinction between debt and equity is not easily maintained, Plumb (1971) contains a thorough examination of the case law attempting to establish the distinction; Bulow, Summers and Summers (1990) examine more recent devices used to obtain debt tax treatment for equity investment. Scholes and Wolfson (1990) explore the extent to which this distinction can be exploited to avoid the double tax completely; and ultimately conclude that, as long as competitive investment is available, full self-help integration is not possible.

7. Measures of Corporate Tax Burden and Incidence. Establishing Effective Corporate Tax Rates

Despite the obvious significance of the question, very little conclusive analysis or reliable data is available regarding the actual burden of the corporate tax. Frequently, information about the tax liabilities of particular firms is simply not available. It is generally accepted that effective corporate tax rates are likely to differ from statutory rates in at least three important ways, even if tax payments can be matched with reliable information about income for tax purposes. First, if the permanent preferences that are available for certain types of corporate income (as are commonly offered for corporate dividends paid on stock held by corporations) have been capitalized, an implicit tax will reduce corporate tax payments without increasing corporate after-tax income. Second, some express preferences reduce current corporate tax liabilities but increase future tax liabilities, resulting in deferred taxes. Third, tax accounting rules (such as the limitation on corporate capital losses) will frequently result in additional timing disparities that make comparisons of tax payments with corporate income in any one year difficult.

Perhaps the most controversial efforts to estimate the effective corporate tax rate in the US have been prepared with the popular press in mind. McIntyre and Folen (1984), McIntyre and Wilhelm (1986), Marovelli and Moser (1990) provide calculations of effective corporate tax rates in the United States based on publicly available data; such analysis frequently is limited by the fact that it can compare only current taxes with current financial income, with no accounting for implicit taxes or even for deferred taxes. Dworin (1985) demonstrates how difficult reliance on such data can be. A somewhat more sophisticated analysis is offered by Shevlin (1990). Collins and Shackelford (1990) attempt to use data available from financial statements to establish average effective tax rates in various jurisdictions. Auerbach and Poterba (1987a) provide some more meaningful measures of corporate tax payments in the United States from the mid-1950s to the mid-1980s. Mintz (Canada, 1985) and Mayer (United Kingdom, 1986) analyze the effect of loss carryovers on tax rates.

It must be noted that effective tax rates on capital are difficult to determine without taking into account personal taxes as well as corporate taxes and the interplay between personal taxes, corporate taxes, the form of business organization and the form of financing, for example, King and Fullerton (1984). But in the presence of an open international market these relationships may not hold.

8. Incidence of Corporate Tax

Although the primary legal incidence of the corporate income tax is on the corporation itself, the economic incidence is uncertain. If corporate investment must take the form of equity, and if current earnings must be distributed, the classical system will create a bias against investments in corporations, but the prevalence of those conditions is uncertain. Furthermore, the use of the corporate form to allow maximum use of preferences for capital gains and basis step-up at death for share appreciation when earnings can be retained, the availability of preferences only for investment in corporate form, and the use of debt as a means of distribution for those returns that cannot be retained all mitigate the bias against investment in corporate form.

Nevertheless, it is generally assumed that the classical corporate tax system raises the corporate cost of capital and therefore increases the share of capital allocated to the noncorporate sector. Under such a view, the burden of the corporate tax might well be ultimately borne equally by corporate and noncorporate capital owners, but the distorting effects on the allocation of capital between corporate and noncorporate are great (Harberger, 1962, 1966; Shoven and Whalley, 1972; Shoven, 1976; Ballard et al., 1985; Gravelle and Kotlikoff, 1989; but Harberger, 1983). McLure (1981) provides a perspective on this literature and applies its insights to questions regarding the determination of sub-national tax incidence. Rogers (1996) provides a useful summary of the research and issues.

Empirical work regarding the incidence of the corporate income tax has been, and is likely to remain, inconclusive. In one early and interesting effort, Krzyzaniak and Musgrave (1963) contended that corporations are in fact able to more than fully recoup additional taxes, but were quickly criticized by many, including Cragg, Harberger and Miezkowski (1967) and Slitor (1966). Fullerton and Lim Rogers (1993) report that because very little corporate tax is actually paid, its effect in the United States is primarily through relative price changes, and that because those who are relatively poorer spend more of their incomes on goods produced in the corporate sector, and thus bear a relatively higher burden.

9. Corporate Tax and the Choice of Business Form

Very few of the jurisdictions committed to a classical corporate tax attempt to impose taxes on aggregations of business capital or business activity that would remove the tax disincentive to use the corporate form. (However, one such proposal was included in US Treasury, 1992.) Hence there is likely to be a bias against incorporation where non-tax considerations allow the activity to be conducted and the required aggregation of capital without incorporation. The bias against suggested by the classical double tax scheme will not be present, however, if the corporate tax rate is substantially lower than the individual tax rate, whether because of difference in statutory rates, or because of special provisions (including deductions for deferred compensation and cost recovery) available only to corporate taxpayers. Such conditions were likely to be present in the US prior to the mid-1980s. Auerbach (1997) summarizes the changes in US law introduced in 1986.

The bias against moving capital into corporate form seems likely to have increased given the increasing availability of limited liability, in the US at least, without submission to a corporate level tax. For summaries of the changes in US legal rules that have led to complete avoidance of corporate level tax for new business investment in the absence of public trading, see Burke (1995).

The overall impact of the incentives against moving capital into corporate form remains undecided. Mackie-Mason and Gordon (1997) and Gordon and Mackie-Mason (1994) report that changes in organizational form are sensitive to changes in tax rates. Gordon and Slemrod (1998) concur, demonstrating that much of the apparent rise in personal incomes in the US after 1986 resulting from shifts in business activity away from the corporate form, implying a strong response.

Finally, even if the double tax aspects of the corporate tax do not entirely discourage incorporation, they are likely to affect the ways in which capital is provided to corporations, since returns provided as wages, interest, rents, and royalties will be deducted from the corporate tax base while returns on equity contributions will not.

10. The Corporate Tax and Corporate Financial Structure

Under the classic corporate tax, dividends are not deducted from corporate income as paid, but in general interest is deducted as it accrues. It is generally accepted that the resulting removal from the corporate tax base of returns to debt is likely to create a strong incentive toward financing with debt. Indeed, if all corporate earnings are paid out as return on debt financing rather than return on equity, the disincentive resulting from presence of the corporate tax to use the corporate form can be eliminated. There is a general consensus, however, that there is not as much corporate debt as would be expected if taxes were the only consideration. Good general summaries of the issues and current research in the US can be found in Scholes and Wolfson (1992) and Auerbach (1990).

The fact that the classical corporate tax provides an incentive to finance through debt does not, however, suggest that only debt be issued, despite Modigliani and Miller's early suggestion (1963) that the optimal source of all capital should be debt in the presence of such a preference. Miller (1977) observed that at some point, the price that must be offered to attract debt financing will offset the tax advantage of debt, at least if there is any preference for returns on equity. Furthermore, other aspects of tax accounting and tax preferences will make some firms less able to take advantage of the tax incentive afforded by debt, and may result in lower levels of debt (DeAngelo and Masulis, 1980).

Although it is hard to explain changes in the amount of corporate leverage without understand more about the phenomenon generally, several empirical studies suggest that corporate debt levels do indeed respond to relative tax rates on corporate income. Auerbach (1985) (finding relation between debt levels and low effective rates resulting from carryforwards, but not composition of asset cost recovery), Bartholdy, Fisher and Mintz (1985) (a one-point increase in Canadian corporate tax results in 3/4 point increase in corporate debt/equity ratio), Mackie-Mason (1990), Graham (1996) and others have attempted to estimate the sensitivity of this relationship (Rangazas and Abdullah, 1987). Gentry (1994) shows an increase in debt by firms who can pass-through tax losses to investors. Schulman et al. (1996) report that imputation integration in New Zealand and Canada reduced debt/equity ratios. Others, however, have failed to find tax effects on levels of corporate borrowing (Ang and Peterson, 1986; Bradley, Jarrel and Kim, 1984). Taggert (1985) concludes that although tax factors have played a role in the increased debt levels of corporations in the United States, they do not provide a complete explanation; Gordon and Mackie-Mason (1990) similarly find less response to taxes than predicted.

Even less certain is whether this possible distortion in favor of debt financing should be considered inefficient. The discipline that debt brings to managers is likely to reduce agency costs, but the losses occurring as a result of the incentive to choose less risky and shorter termed investments which are not wealth-maximizing may outweigh them. Full consideration of equity/debt and corporate financial structure beyond the scope of this article; more general surveys of optimal capital structure can be found in Barclay, Smith and Watts (1995), Myers (1993), Harris and Raviv (1991), Taggert (1985), Auerbach (1985) and Jensen and Meckling (1976).

11. The Corporate Tax and the Incentive to Distribute Corporate Earnings

Under the classic corporate tax, individual shareholders that receive dividends are taxed on the full amount of those dividends, usually without preference and without offset for their investment in their shares. Shareholders who realize their returns through the sale of shares, on the other hand, frequently enjoy a capital gains preference, and can offset proceeds with investment basis on all sales of shares. They may be able to avoid tax entirely through the rules avoiding income tax on gains remaining unrealized at death. (Although this fact is almost entirely overlooked in the analytical literature mentioned below, there are significant exceptions to this general pattern of tax burden on dividend payments in the US. First, payments denominated 'dividends' will be subject to only capital gains taxation if there are no corporate earnings for tax purposes ('earnings and profits'), even though ordinarily there must be earnings for corporate law purposes in order for dividends to be paid. Such 'return of capital' dividends are highly likely when cost recovery allowances for tax purposes exceed similar allowances for corporate law purposes, and when corporations are successful in engaging in restructuring transactions which reduce earnings for tax purposes. Second, only individual shareholders are in fact subject to the double tax: corporate shareholders are allowed to eliminate a substantial portion of dividends paid by domestic corporations, and tax-exempt entities, including pension plans, pay no tax at on dividend receipts at all.)

This disparity between the tax treatment of shareholders who receive dividends and shareholders who participate in sale transactions led to an early debate about whether the regular payment of dividends lowered share prices and required higher dividend rates, for example, Litzenberger and Ramaswamy (1979, 1982), Bradford and Gordon (1980), Miller and Scholes (1982), Morgan (1982), Poterba and Summers (1984), Wu and Hsu (1996). This disincentive would not, however, affect dividend behavior if the share price of corporate stock is set by investors for whom the tax impact of dividends and capital gains are the same (Miller and Scholes, 1978). Miller (1986) reviews this literature. Similarly, it is frequently supposed that the classic corporate tax provides a imposes a cost on the distribution of earnings, and that an increase in the tax cost of dividend distributions should result in a lower level of dividend payouts. Some empirical studies support this view: Brittain (1966) (analyzing US dividend behavior from 1920 to 1960); Feldstein (1970) (British firms from 1953 through 1964); King (1971, 1972) (British firms from 1949 through 1967), but Feldstein (1972); Poterba and Summers (1985); Poterba (1987) (US firms through 1986).

On the other hand, there should be no incentive to avoid distribution of corporate earnings simply to avoid the shareholder level tax on the distribution, if those earnings must eventually be distributed and must be subject to the same tax in the future. (Under this view, the tax cost of a distribution must decrease the overall return to the shareholder, whether it does so on an immediate distribution that reduces the net-after-tax amount received by the shareholder now, or whether, if the earnings are retained, reinvested, and distributed in the future, it reduces the net-after-tax amount received by the shareholder on that future distribution (Auerbach, 1990). Thus, there should be no effect on the *marginal* investment decisions of firms as a result of the double tax resulting from the taxation of dividends. Although the tax treatment of dividends should create a disincentive to new contributions to firms through new share issues and should generally reduce the amount by which such new share issues increase the value of the firm, this tax treatment would not change the firm's dividend behavior, which would be governed by nontax considerations. In the absence of any significant nontax benefits to distributions, the firm would pay dividends only when no profitable investment could be made. A permanent change in the tax on dividends would not affect distributions, but would operate only as a charge on retained earnings and on new equity contributions. Under this view (sometimes still referred to as the 'new' view), equity is 'trapped' in corporate form, and the inevitable tax on payout is capitalized into share price. Early contributions supporting this view include King (1974, 1977), Auerbach (1979, 1983b), Bradford (1981).

In fact, however, the future tax on distributions can be avoided in several ways: (1) if no current distribution of corporate funds is ever made and the shareholder's return is received through the sale of stock (especially when this return is, as is frequently the case, entitled to a special capital gains rate or to the benefit of forgiveness at death through stepped up basis) and (2) distributions are made from the corporation in the form of share redemptions (not permitted in all jurisdictions) and distributions made in connection with acquisitions, both of which may also be subject to more favorable tax treatment. If corporate earnings can be transformed without significant cost to borrowings (for instance through redemptions of stock held by exempt shareholders) there may in fact be little or no disincentive for current distribution of corporate earnings through such non-dividend techniques. Shoven (1987) reviews the tax consequences and provides estimates of such behaviors by firms in the 1970s and 1980s. Bagwell and Shoven (1989) provide a useful summary of the various incentives faced by corporate managers and conclude that the increased use of non-dividend techniques for distributions to shareholders may be attributable to the simple phenomena of an increased awareness and understanding of the 'technology' of implementing such devices under relatively complicated tax rules.

The debate about the limitations inherent in the assumptions necessary to the 'new view' and the implications of the new view remains unresolved. Most agree that for the traditional view to hold, there must be some countervailing benefit to the corporation or its managers upon the distribution of dividends, but there is little agreement as to whether those benefits include signaling or merely provide a mechanism for disciplining corporate management. If there is such a benefit, it may be exceeded by an increased tax cost of dividend distributions and, therefore, increased tax burdens on dividends would decrease dividend payouts. Most also agree that one strong implication of the new view is that the net value of the firm's shares must be less than the total value of the firm's assets. Such a discount to share value would be present unless there were some inherent advantage to investments conducted through the corporate form, but the identification of this advantage has been elusive (and will likely remain elusive as the tax law, at least in the US, continues to shift). This appears to have led some to conclude that the new view can hold only if share repurchases are prohibited, since if they were not, firms would simply repurchase shares until the discount was eliminated. Sinn (1991c) argues that the traditional view implies that corporations do not minimize their cost of capital, and further that the new view is plausible even when share repurchases can be made, so long as limits on such devices are present. Zodrow (1997, 1991), Poterba and Summers (1985) and Sorensen (1995) also elaborate upon the implications of the 'traditional' and 'new' views. Zodrow (1997) and Gerardi, Graetz and Rosen (1990) both conclude, after reviewing the empirical literature, that it primarily supports the traditional view.

Perhaps the most significant practical implication of the new view is that to the extent that the new view is correct, the burden of the double tax on corporate dividends is capitalized in the market value of its shares. Any lessening of the burden of double taxation through any form of integration would therefore create a windfall for shareholders of firms with retained earnings. The likelihood that the new view is correct at least to this extent explains at least part of the reluctance in the US to move toward full integration (Hubbard, 1993; Halperin, 1992, considering the conclusions reached in American Law Institute, 1979, 1989).

12. Jurisdiction over the Corporate Tax Base and Sufficiency of Nexus to Tax

Corporate economic activity frequently ignores the political boundaries by which jurisdiction to tax is ordinarily assigned. Rarely are there constitutional barriers to the assertion by each polity with which the activity has some minimal nexus asserting the power to tax such economic activity and to define the base according to which that tax will be assessed. Nevertheless, most polities acknowledge a need to avoid overtly duplicative taxes, especially when the chosen base is income. A good survey of the issues and patterns of solutions can be found in Easson (1997).

There are two principal approaches that can be used to assign taxing power among competing taxing polities. Under an assignment or sourcing method, each polity adopts rules according to which a corporation's income is categorized as most closely related to one taxing jurisdiction. If more than one jurisdiction asserts the power to tax this income, a credit can be given (generally by the home polity) for the taxes paid elsewhere (generally the foreign site of the economic activity). McIntyre (1994) provides an overview of this approach as applied by the United States; Green (1993) Ault and Bradford (1990) and Hufbauer (1992) highlight the issues inherent in its use. Under the apportionment method, a corporation's income can be apportioned to each taxing jurisdiction according to a formula that takes into account the location of the business activity (frequently sales, payroll and property). Even if two jurisdictions adopt the same approach to avoiding duplicative taxes, there is rarely any device for ensuring that the implementation of the approaches are consistent. Avi-Yonah (1995) explores agency-theory-based rationales for the approaches taken for operational and passive income. Each state in the United States, for instance, is free to define its own apportionment formula so long as that apportionment formula, if adopted by every state, would avoid duplicative taxes (McLure, 1986; Gordon and Wilson, 1986; Hreha and Silhan, 1986).

Each of these approaches must include variants to take into account the fact that frequently corporate activity that encompasses more than one jurisdiction will be undertaken by more than one formal corporate entity. Generally, jurisdictions (including the United States) that rely on an assignment approach will require that transfer prices among entities be at 'arm's length' prices so as to avoid jurisdictional distortions (see generally Avi-Yonah, 1995). Jurisdictions that use an apportionment method are likely to require that all related corporations 'combine' their income, so that apportionment will take into account all related entities.

Each approach must also consider how to treat transfers of dividends to related corporations that are not wholly or exclusively subject to their taxing power. Under the assignment method as implemented by the United States, income of foreign subsidiaries will ordinarily not be subject to United States' tax as earned, but will be subject to United States' tax as it is repatriated as dividends, and a credit for foreign taxes paid will be available upon repatriation. Under a fully combined apportionment method, dividends paid to related corporations should be ignored.

Finally, it is highly likely that any one taxing scheme will, at least in some of its details, include features from both approaches. For instance, despite the fact that the United States in general uses sourcing with arm's length pricing to establish the taxable income of multinational groups, since 1986 interest expense must be apportioned according to asset holdings. (For an analysis of this change, see Froot and Hines, 1995; Altshuler and Mintz, 1995.)

There is at least some evidence that sourcing systems impose significantly greater compliance costs than apportionment systems (Blumenthal and Slemrod, 1996).

13. Effect of Corporate Taxes on Investment in Multinational Economies

Although it might not be obvious to the modern observer, the pattern of taxation for multinational businesses was the product of more systematic thinking than many other areas of US federal taxation. Graetz and O'Hear (1997) recount the role of early economists in this history. Picciotto (1992) provides an exhaustive review and analysis of the current patterns. A good summary of the relevant rules and a straightforward review of the most prominent empirical research can be found in Hines (1997). (In this review, Hines concludes that real responses to taxes are as one would expect: there tends to be more direct investment where corporate tax burdens are anticipated to be lower.) Gordon and Mackie-Mason (1995) offers interesting speculation about the incentives leading to the prevailing patterns of international tax, and conclude that significant parts of the current pattern reflect the need to preserve the personal income tax on the return to entrepreneurial labor.

Some jurisdictions, including the US, claim the right to tax all income, domestic and foreign, of their resident taxpayers, including corporations. However, in keeping with the classical corporate income tax, the income of separately incorporated foreign entities conducting active businesses is ordinarily not subject to US tax until it is repatriated through dividends. Hartman (1985) theorized that if such repatriation taxes are unavoidable, their existence should not affect the decision whether to repatriate or reinvest in the source jurisdiction, essentially applying a 'trapped equity' analysis to the repatriation decision. Hines (1994) and Leechor and Mintz (1993) point out that variations in income-defining rules can be sufficient to alter this result. Empirical studies (Goodspeed and Frisch, 1989; Hines and Hubbard, 1990; Altshuler, Newlon and Randolph, 1995) suggest that repatriation taxes do in fact vary sufficiently to provide other incentives. Hines (1997) suggests that the tax costs of repatriation may encourage undercapitalization of foreign subsidiaries so that profitable opportunities remain for the reinvestment of retained earnings, and notes that this incentive may make attempts to measure the influence of foreign tax rates on foreign direct investment. Roin (1988) develops a public choice analysis of the exceptions to the limitations on deferral for relatively passive foreign acitivities.

In the US, a credit against domestic taxes is allowed for foreign taxes paid. It has sometimes been assumed that the foreign tax crediting device used by the US results in a lower national return on foreign direct investment by US corporations than the national return on displaced domestic investment (for example, Dutton, 1982). Recent analysis suggests that the loss due to taxes yielded to the foreign jurisdiction may be offset by the overall greater return resulting from lower costs of foreign capital (Feldstein, 1995).

At the multinational level, all of the possibility of tax effects on choice of form and financial structure found domestically are present, with additional possibilities resulting from the variety of rates, the special treatments afforded by treaty, and the arbitrary and inconsistent nature of the rules used by the various jurisdictions for allocating items affecting measures of income. Predictably, multinationals structure their transactions in ways that, for instance, yield accounting profits in low tax jurisdictions and place the tax shields afforded by debt finance. Hines (1997) reviews the empirical studies evidencing this behavior.

Among the most difficult, and yet most fundamental, problems in analyzing the effect of national corporate income taxes on corporate behavior and general business investment is a determination of the effective tax rates in the various jurisdictions to be studied. The problem is complicated by the fact that stated nominal tax rates and published legal rules are unlikely to provide complete information about the tax burdens actually felt by corporations. The most ambitious empirical study, and an enormous amount of data regarding rates and bases can be found in OECD (1991). Attempts to further analyze and update such data include Jun (1995).

14. The Corporate Tax and Corporate Mergers and Acquisitions

Any corporate income tax scheme, whether classic or integrated, must set out criteria for determining when transactions relating to corporate assets and to corporate stock interests will be treated as events that will trigger corporate income tax. (Such events frequently will trigger all unrealized gain on assets and will trigger reconciliation of various suspended accounting preferences.) The US scheme has evolved largely through judicial interpretation with only limited statutory modification. Very little attention has been given to the distortions created by the resulting framework, perhaps because the framework, although arcane, provides sufficient flexibility.

Under the US scheme for taxing restructuring transactions, shareholder realization is frequently tied to corporate realization, and flexibility in accommodating all shareholder interests may be difficult. Ginsburg and Levin (1996 and updated regularly) provide an intricate account of the current US rules. Some changes in control will be treated as merely continuing the tax existence of a corporation, and thus will not result in the triggering of gains on assets, the loss of grandfathered accounting methods, or the discontinuance of carryover tax losses. Other changes in control may be treated as discontinuous, and will trigger gains, force new accounting methods and cut off unused losses. Under certain circumstances prior to 1986, however, such a change in control that is treated as discontinuous could have produced a highly desirable result for US corporations, since it allowed a step-up in tax-basis of assets held at the corporate level without the payment of corporate level tax.

These rules must establish highly arbitrary distinctions upon which rest frequently enormous stakes. For instance, sales of stock among shareholders will not ordinarily trigger gain on corporate assets, since the formal identity of the owner of the assets has not changed, but transfers of assets to different corporate entities will trigger gain on those assets unless there is substantial overlap between the owners of the new entity and the owners of the old. Therefore when an existing corporation is acquired, there can be enormous tax differences depending upon whether the transaction is viewed as a transfer of assets or of stock. To complicate things further, corporate tax regimes frequently will include special rules designed to mitigate the arbitrariness of such distinctions, but that make it still harder for observers to ascertain the effect of any particular set of rules. (For instance, until 1986, the United States allowed certain purchases of corporate stock to be treated as purchases of stock for the purpose of taxing shareholders, but as purchases assets for the purpose of the corporate level tax. This special rule was available only if the purchaser was a domestic corporation that acquired at least 80 percent of the stock of the target.)

These arbitrary distinctions clearly have an enormous influence on the form that changes in corporate control take. It is less clear, however, whether they have any effect upon the frequency or price at which changes in corporate control occur. In the older literature it was generally assumed that at least some some changes in corporate control occurred in which the only motivation was tax-related (see Feld, 1982; Hellerstein, 1959; Butters, Lintner and Cary, 1951).

More recent literature suggests that at least in the aggregate, the presence of tax gains are not as certain to have increased acquisition activity.

Auerbach and Reishus (1988a) provides a useful summary of the various incentives in US law. Gilson, Scholes and Wolfson (1988) review the overall interaction of the pre-1986 United States tax rules most frequently thought to produce tax gains from acquisitions, and conclude that many such gains could be accomplished in other ways. Their conclusions seem too dependent on the availability of other means of accomplishing the tax gains, which although plausible for some tax gains when viewed separately, seem less likely to be available in conjunction with other tax gains and with other goals. Another study by Auerbach and Reishus (1988b) however, concluded that in a least a fifth of the mergers studied, occurring between 1968 and 1983, the merger allowed a corporation to free itself from constraints on the use of tax benefits but did not find useful measures either of increased cost recovery or increase debt shields. One survey of transactions concluded that the primary gains from management buyouts were tax gains (Lowenstein, 1985). Jensen, Kaplan and Stiglin (1989) argue that certain acquisition activities actually increase tax revenues, although Bulow, Summers and Summers (1990) demonstrate that an increase in revenue is not necessarily inconsistent with a tax incentive derived subsidy.

Some of the earlier writing regarding tax-motivations for corporate acquisition activity assumed that such activity would be socially undesirable. Several recent writers have challenged this assumption in passing, and offered several possible scenarios in which tax-motivated acquisition activity could produce social gains. Tax gains from various acquisition activities could, for instance, increase the premium for successful searches for operating efficiencies through acquisition activity (Gilson, Scholes and Wolfson, 1988); or restore incentives for investment by restoring tax incentives for investment that are weak in the absence of positive corporate tax liabilities (Auerbach and Reishus, 1988). Changes in the US law in 1984 (eliminating the possibility of stepping up depreciation deductions without a corporate level tax), and in 1986 (generally eliminating the exemption from capital gains taxation for distributed assets imposing additional limits on the use of carryover losses after a merger transaction), have substantially decreased the likely to be obtained through merger activity. The changes appear to have lessened interest in the study of tax motivations for merger activity, despite the possibility that data reflecting the change in tax regimes may be more useful than that studied previously. An analysis of these changes, and some discussion of their impact appear in Scholes and Wolfson (1991). Hayn (1989) provides an interesting study of the effect of the value of tax attributes on merger activity for which a IRS ruling was requested.

15. Integration of Corporate and Individual Level Income Taxes

Under 'integrated' schemes, various devices are used to attempt to eliminate or minimize this double tax effect. Among the simplest of such devices is a 'passthrough' of corporate income to the shareholders even in the absence of a distribution of earnings, producing a liability at the shareholder level even if the corporation retains the funds generating the liability. Later distributions of corporate earnings are not subject to tax. (Although the classic scheme prevails for capital transferred to corporations before 1986, an increasing number of US enterprises can enjoy both passthrough integration and the limited liability associated with incorporation by using either the special rules available under subchapter S of the Internal Revenue Code (at the cost of a being restricted to a very limited number of shareholders and corporate structure), or by using the newly emerging limited liability company (at a cost of uncertainty regarding both the tax consequences and the default rules governing stakeholder relations).) Yin (1992) and Warren (1981) provide an exhaustive summaries of the available choices for implementing integration from the starting point of the classical system in the US.

Integration can also be accomplished by allowing dividends to be paid without tax consequence to shareholders. Other more complicated integration devices include a corporate level tax, with a credit for such tax to be claimed by the shareholder upon the ultimate distribution of the earnings and after the amount of tax actually paid is imputed as part of the distribution (Australia, New Zealand, Canada, France, the United Kingdom and Germany all have used some form of imputation credit to accomplish varying degrees of integration), a split rate tax (under which distributed earnings are taxes at a lower rate than undistributed earnings, used by Japan and Germany), or a credit to the paying corporation upon the distribution of dividends. To the extent that the anticipated burdens of the classical double tax have been capitalized in existing capital, the considerations involved in moving from a classical scheme to an integrated scheme differ from those that would be considered prior to the imposition of any tax because a transition device would be necessary to avoid a windfall to existing corporate holdings. It is not clear, however, that such windfalls would be present, as suggested by the lack of price response to the announcement of integration in the United Kingdom in 1970 revealed by Poterba and Summers (1985). Auerbach (1990), McLure (1979), Sunley (1992), Cnossen (1993) and US Department of the Treasury (1992) provide in-depth discussions of the circumstances under which various approaches to integration might be desirable.

International considerations make integration issues even more difficult, especially since there is no consensus about whether the jursidiction to tax should lie primarily with the jurisdiction in which business activity is conducted or the jurisdiction whose resident is supplying capital through share or debt ownership. Uncertainty about tax effects in open and closed economies makes evaluations of integration proposals especially difficult (Boadway and Bruce, 1992; Devereux and Freeman, 1995). Under the more common approaches to the integration, relief form double taxation is appropriate only for resident shareholders (Ault, 1992; Doernberg, 1992).

Bibliography on Corporate Taxation (6060)

Abbott, Ashok Bjardway (ed.) (1987), *The Valuation Effects of Tax Legislation in Corporate Sell Offs*, Ph.D. Thesis, Virginia Polytechnic Institute and State University.

Aivazian, Varouz A. and Turnbull, Stuart M. (1988), 'Taxation and Capital Structure: A Selected Review', in Coffee, John, Lowenstein, Louis and Rose-Ackerman, Susan (eds), *Knights, Raiders and Targets: The Impact of the Hostile Takeover*, Oxford, Oxford University Press, 230-277.

Allen, Franklin (1989), 'The Changing Nature of Debt and Equity: a Financial Perspective' (Discussion), in Hart Oliver D. and Merton Robert C., *Are the Distinctions Between Debt and Equity Disappearing?*

Allerdings, Jeffrey Paul (ed.) (1992), *The Effects of the Corporate Alternative Minimum Tax on Corporate Tax Liability, MS Thesis*, San Francisco, State University.

Allsop, Peter (1991), 'Taxation Aspects of Corporate Finance', in Coffee, John, Lowenstein, Louis and Rose-Ackerman, Susan (eds), *Knights, Raiders and Targets: The Impact of the Hostile Takeover*, Oxford, Oxford University Press, 443-466.

Alstott, Anne L. and Mackie, James B. (1992), 'Approaches to Corporate Integration: The Treasury Department Report' Ph.D. Dissertation, **45** *National Tax Journal*, 209-223.

Altshuler, Rosanne T. and Auerbach, Alan J. (1990), 'The Importance of Tax Law Asymmetries: An Empirical Investigation', **105** *Quarterly Journal of Economics*, 61-86.

Altshuler, Rosanne T. and Mintz, Jack M. (1995), 'United States Interest-Allocation Rules: Effects and Policy', in Giovannini, A., Hubbard, R.G. and Slemrod, J. (eds), *Studies in International Taxation*, Chicago, University of Chicago Press.

Altshuler, Rosanne T. and Newlon, T. Scott (1993), 'The Effects of U.S. Tax Policy on the Income Repatriation Patterns of U.S. Multinational Corporations', in Giovannini, A., Hubbard, R.G. and Slemrod, J. (eds), *Studies in International Taxation*, Chicago: University of Chicago Press, 77-115.

Altshuler, Rosanne T., Newlon, T. Scott and Randolph, William C. (1995), 'Do Repatriation Taxes Matter? Evidence from the Tax Returns of U.S. Multinationals', in Feldstein, M. (ed.), *The Effects of Taxation on Capital Accumulation*, Chicago: University of Chicago Press, 253-276.

Alworth, J.S. (ed.) (1988), 'Investment and Taxation Decisions of Multinationals', in Coffee, John, Lowenstein, Louis and Rose-Ackerman, Susan (eds), *Knights, Raiders and Targets: The Impact of the Hostile Takeover*, Oxford, Oxford University Press.

Alworth, J.S. (ed.) (1988), *The Finance, Investment and Taxation Decisions of Multinationals*.

American Bar Association (ed.) (1988), *A Report of the Invitational Conference on Subchapter C*.

American Institute of Certified Public Accountants (ed.) (1993), *Integration of the Corporate and Shareholder Tax Systems*, New York.

American Law Institute (1991), 'Federal Income Tax Project, Integration of the Individual and Corporate Income Taxes', **2** *Reporter's Memorandum*.

American Law Institute (ed.) (1979), *Federal Tax Project, Tentative Draft No. 2, Subchapter C - Corporate Distributions,* Philadelphia, The American Law Institute.

American Law Institute (ed.) (1982), *Federal Income Tax Project, Subchapter C: Proposals on Corporate Acquisitions and Dispositions and Reporter's Study on Corporate Distributions*, Philadelphia, The American Law Institute.

American Law Institute (ed.) (1989), *Federal Income Tax Project, Subchapter C, Reporter's Study Draft (Supplemental Study)*, Philadelphia, The American Law Institute.

American Law Institute (ed.) (1990), *Federal Income Tax Project, Integration of the Individual and Corporate Income Taxes, Reporter's Memorandum No. 1*, Philadelphia, The American Law Institute.

American Law Institute (ed.) (1991), *Federal Income Tax Project Integration of the Individual and Corporate Income Taxes, Reporter's Memorandum No. 3*, Philadelphia, The American Law Institute.

American Law Institute (ed.) (1992), *Federal Income Tax Project, Integration of the Individual and Corporate Income Taxes, Reporter's Study of Corporate Tax Integration*, Philadelphia, The American Law Institute.

Amihud, Yakov and Murgia, Maurizio (1997), 'Dividends, Taxes, and Signaling: Evidence from Germany', **52** *Journal of Finance*, 397-408.

Anderson, F.J., Beaudreau, B.C. and Bonsor, N.C. (1983), 'Effective Corporate Tax Rates, Inflation, and Contestability', **16(4)** *Canadian Journal of Economics*, 686-703.

Andersson, Edward (1983), 'Corporate Tax Laws as Instruments of Economic Policy: Some Finnish Experiences', **37(1)** *Bulletin for International Fiscal Documentation*, 35-39.

Andersson, Krister (1991), 'Taxation and the Cost of Capital in Hungary and Poland: A Comparison with Selected European Countries', **38(2)** *International Monetary Fund Staff Papers*, 327-355.

Andrews, William D. (1956), 'Out of Earnings and Profits: Some Reflections on the Taxation of Dividends', **69** *Harvard Law Review*, 1403 ff.

Andrews, William D. (1984), 'Tax Neutrality between Equity and Debt Capital', **30** *Wayne Law Review*, 1057-1071.

Andrews, William D. (1995), *The Unintegrated Economics of Corporate Tax Integration*.

Ang, James S. and Peterson, David, 'Optimal Debt Versus Debt Capacity: A Disequilibrium Model of Corporate Behavior', in Coffee, John, Lowenstein, Louis and Rose-Ackerman, Susan (eds), *Knights,Raiders and Targets: The Impact of the Hostile Takeover*, Oxford, Oxford University Press.

Appelbaum, Elie and Katz, Eliakim (1996), 'Corporate Taxation, Incumbency Advantage and Entry', **40** *European Economic Review*, 1817-1828.

Arbor, Ann (1992), 'Tax Compliance and Enforcement', in Slemrod, Joel (ed.), *Why People Pay Taxes: Tax Compliance and Enforcement*, University of Michigan Press, 125-661.

Aretz, Adward (1991), 'Taxation and Incorporation: An Economic Analysis of Post-1992 Business Incorporations', in Weigel, Wolfgang (ed.), *Economic Analysis of Law - A Collection of Applications*, Vienna, Österreichischer Wirtschaftsverlag, 122-132.

Arlen, Jennifer H. and Weiss, Deborah M. (1995), 'A Political Theory of Corporate Taxation', **105** *Yale Law Journal*, 325 ff.

Arnold, Brian J. (1994), 'Canadian Finance Minister Announces Release of Tax Expenditures Account: Corporate Tax Expenditures Detailed', **8** *Tax Notes International*, 841 ff.

Auerbach, Alan J. (1979a), 'Wealth Maximization and the Cost of Capital', **93** *Quarterly Journal of Economics*, 443-446.

Auerbach, Alan J. (1979b), 'Share Valuation and Corporate Equity Policy', **11** *Journal of Public Economics*, 291-305.

Auerbach, Alan J. (1981a), 'Inflation and the Tax Treatment of Firm Behavior', *American Economic Review*, 419-423.

Auerbach, Alan J. (1981b), *Tax Integration and the New View of the Corporate Tax: a 1980 Perspective*.

Auerbach, Alan J. (1982a), 'The New Economics of Accelerated Depreciation', **23** *Boston College Law Review*, 1327-1355.

Auerbach, Alan J. (1982b), 'Whither the Corporate Tax? Reform after ACRS', **35(3)** *National Tax Journal*, 275-286.

Auerbach, Alan J. (1983a), 'Stockholder Tax Rates and Firm Attributes', **21** *Journal of Public Economics*, 107 ff.

Auerbach, Alan J. (1983b), 'Taxation, Corporate Financial Policy, and the Cost of Capital', **21** *Journal of Economic Literature*, 905-940.

Auerbach, Alan J. (1983c), 'Corporate Taxation in the United States', **2** *Brookings Papers on Economic Activity*, 451-505.

Auerbach, Alan J. (1984), 'Taxes, Firm Financial Policy and the Cost of Capital: An Empirical Analysis', **23** *Journal of Public Economics*, 27-57.

Auerbach, Alan J. (1985), *Real Determinants of Corporate Leverage*, Chicago, University of Chicago Press.

Auerbach, Alan J. (1986), 'The Dynamic Effects of Tax Law Asymmetries', **53** *Review of Economic Studies*, 205-226.

Auerbach, Alan J. (1987), 'The Tax Reform Act of 1986 and the Cost of Capital', **1** *Economic Perspectives*, 73-86.

Auerbach, Alan J. (1989), 'Implications for Public Policy: Tax Policy and Corporate Borrowing', *Proceedings of a conference held at Melvin Village, New Hampshire* in Kopcke, Richard and Rosengren, Eric (eds), *Are the Distinctions between Debt and Equity disappearing ?*, Federal Reserve Bank of Boston.

Auerbach, Alan J. (1998), 'Should Interest Deductions be Limited?', in Aaron, Henry J., Galper, Harveu and Pechman, Joseph A. (eds), *Uneasy Compromise: Problems of a Hybrid Income-Consumption Tax*, Washington, Brookings Institution.

Auerbach, Alan J. and King, Mervyn (1983), 'Taxation, Portfolio Choice and Debt Equity Rations: a General Equilibrium Model', *Quarterly Journal of Economics*, 587-609.

Auerbach, Alan J. and Poterba, James M. (1987a), 'Why Have Corporate Revenues Declined?', in Coffee, John, Lowenstein, Louis and Rose-Ackerman, Susan (eds), *Knights, Raiders and Targets: The Impact of the Hostile Takeover*, Oxford, Oxford University Press, 3-29.

Auerbach, Alan J. and Poterba, James M. (1987b), 'Tax Loss Carryforwards and Corporate Tax Incentives', in Feldstein, M. (ed.), *The Effects of Taxation on Capital Accumulation*, Chicago: University of Chicago Press.

Auerbach, Alan J. and Reishus, David (1988), 'The Impact of Taxation on Mergers and Acquisitions', **69** in Coffee, John, Lowenstein, Louis and Rose-Ackerman, Susan (eds), *Knights,Raiders and Targets: The Impact of the Hostile Takeover*, Oxford, Oxford University Press, 81 ff.

Auerbach, Alan J. and Reishus, David (1988), 'The Effects of Taxation on the Merger Decision', in Coffee, John, Lowenstein, Louis and Rose-Ackerman, Susan (eds), *Knights,Raiders and Targets: The Impact of the Hostile Takeover*, Oxford, Oxford University Press.

Auerbach, Alan J. and Reishus, David (1988), 'Taxes and the Merger Decision', in Coffee, John, Lowenstein, Louis and Rose-Ackerman, Susan (eds), *Knights,Raiders and Targets: The Impact of the Hostile Takeover*, Oxford, Oxford University Press.

Auerbach, Alan J. and Hassett, Kevin A. (1992), 'Tax Policy and Business Fixed Investment in the United States', **47** *Journal of Public Economics*, 141-170.

Auerbach, Alan J., Hassett, Kevin A. and Sodersten, Jan (1995), 'Taxation and Corporate Investment: The Impact of the 1991 Swedish Tax Reform', **2** *Swedish Economic Policy Review*, 361-383.

Auerbach, Alan J. and Slemrod, Joel (1997), 'The Economic Effects of the Tax Reform Act of 1986', **35** *Journal of Economic Literature*, 589-632.

Ault, Hugh J. (1978), 'International Issues in Corporate Tax Integration', **10** *Law and Policy in International Business*, 461 ff.

Ault, Hugh J. (1980), 'Exploration of Income Tax Treaty Policy Issues in the United States: Interaction of the U.S. Tax System and U.S. Tax Treaty Rules with Foreign Integrated Corporate Shareholder Tax Systems', **34(23)** *Bulletin for International Fiscal Documentation*, 62-64.

Ault, Hugh J. (1992), 'Corporate Integration, Tax Treaties and the Division of the International Tax Base: Principles and Practices, with commentary by Kees Van Raad', **47** *Tax Law Review*, 565 ff.

Ault, Hugh J. (ed.) (1997), *Comparative Income Taxation: A Structural Analysis*, Kluwer Law International.

Ault, Hugh J. and Bradford, David F. (1990), 'Taxing International Income: An Analysis of the U.S. System and its Economic Premises', in Razin and Slemrod (eds), *Taxation in the Global Economy*, Chicago: University of Chicago Press, 11 ff.

Avi-Yonah, R.S. and Reuven, S. (1990), 'The Treatment of Corporate Preference Items under an Integrated Tax System: a Comparative Analysis', **44** *Tax Lawyer*, 195 ff.

Avi-Yonah, R.S. and Reuven, S. (1995), 'The Rise and Fall of Arms' Length: A Study in the Evolution of U.S. International Taxation', **15** *Va. Tax Review*, 89 ff.

Ayers, Benjamin, Robinson, John R. and Cloyd, Bryan C. (1996), 'Organizational Form and Taxes: An Empirical Analysis of Small Businesses', *Journal of the American Taxation Association*, 49-67.

Bacon, Frank W., Shin, Tai S. and Murphy, Neil B. (1994), 'Factors Motivating Mergers: The Case of Rural Electric Cooperatives', **46(2)** *Journal of Economics and Business*, 129-134.

Bagwell, Laurie Simon and Shoven, John B. (1989), 'Cash Distributions to Shareholders', **3** *Journal of Economic Perspectives*, 129-140.

Ballard, Billy L. (ed.), *Corporate Tax Rates and the Purchasing Power Parity Doctrine: Thesis (M.S.)*, University of North Texas.

Ballard, Charles L., Fullerton, Don, Shoven, John B. and Walley, A. (eds) (1985), *A General Equilibrium Model for Tax Policy Evaluation*, Chicago.

Ballentine, J. Gregory (1980), 'Sales Maximization and Corporate Tax Shifting', **47(2)** *Southern Economic Journal*, 498-501.

Ballentine, J. Gregory (1986), *Effective Corporate Tax Rates: Their Level and Dispersion Across Industries*.

Bamberg, Gunter and Roder, Klaus (1994), 'Arbitrage institutioneller Anleger am DAX Futures Markt unter Berucksichtigung von Korperschaftsteuern und Dividenden. (With English summary)', **64(12)** *Zeitschrift für Betriebswirtschaft*, 1533-1566.

Bankman, Joseph (1995), 'A Market-Value Based Corporate Income Tax', **68** *Tax Notes*, 1347 ff.

Barclay, Michael J., Smith, C.W. and Watts, Ross L. (1995), 'The Determinants of Corporate Leverage and Dividends Policies', **7** *Journal of Applied Corporate Finance*, 4-19.

Barnes, Tom and Burnie, David A. (1987), 'The Estimation of Corporate Bond Yield Curves as a Function of Term to Maturity and Coupon', **26(4)** *Quarterly Journal of Business and Economics*, 50-64.

Bartholdy, J., Fisher, G. and Mintz, Jack M. (1985), *Some Theory of Taxation and Financial Policy with Application to Canadian Corporate Data*, Econometric Society Fifth World Congress, Cambridge.

Battacharya, Sugato (1980), 'Imperfect Information, Dividend Policy and the "Bird in the Hand Fallacy"', **10** *Bell Journal of Economics*, 259-270.

Batten, Dallas S. and Ott, Mack (1985), 'The President's Proposed Corporate Tax Reforms: A Move toward Tax Neutrality', **67(7)** *Federal Reserve Bank of St. Louis Review*, 5-17.

Benge, Matt (1997a), *The Australian Full Imputation Reform in Company Tax Systems*,.

Benge, Matt (1997b), 'Taxes, Corporate Financial Policy and Investment Decisions in Australia', **73** *Economic Record*, 1-15.

Benge, Matt and Robinson, Tim (eds) (1986), *How to Integrate Company and Shareholder Taxation: Why Full Imputation is the Best Answer*, Wellington University Press for the Institute of Policy Studies.

Bernard, Jean Thomas and Weiner, Robert J. (eds) (1990), 'Multinational Corporations, Transfer Prices, and Taxes: Evidence from the U.S. Petroleum Industry', in Razin and Slemrod (eds), *Taxation in the Global Economy*, Chicago, University of Chicago Press.

Bernard, Victor L. and Hayn, Carla (1986), 'Inflation and the Distribution of the Corporate Income Tax Burden', **39** *National Tax Journal*, 171-187.

Bernheim, B. Douglas (1991), 'Tax Policy and The Dividend Puzzle', **22** *Rand Journal of Economics*, 455-476.

Bernheim, B. Douglas and Shoven, John B. (1987), 'Taxation and the Cost of Capital: An International Comparison', **61**, 74-75.

Bernheim, B. Douglas and Wantz, Adam (1995), 'A Tax-Based Test of the Dividend Signalling Hypothesis', **85** *American Economic Review*, 532-551.

Bernstein, Jeffrey I. and Nadiri, M., *Corporate Taxes and Incentives and the Structure of Production: a Selected Survey*, Kingston, Ontario.

Bernstein, Jeffrey I. and Shah, Anwar (1993), *Corporate Tax Structure and Production*, World Bank Policy Research Dept., 1196.

Berry, Richard J. (ed.) (1978), *Short-run Shifting and Incidence of the Corporate Income Tax for U.S. Manufacturing*.

Bird, Richard M. (ed.) (1980), *Taxing Corporations*, Montreal, Institute for Research on Public Policy.

Bird, Richard M. (1987), 'Corporate-Personal Tax Integration', in Cnossen, S. (ed.), *Tax Coordination In The European Community*, London: Kluwer Law And Taxation, 227 ff.

Bird, Richard M. (1996), *Why Tax Corporations?*, Ottawa, Technical Committee on Business Taxation., 96-2.

Bittker, Boris I. and Rahdert (1976), 'The Exemption of Nonprofit Organizations from Federal Income Taxation', **85** *Yale Law Journal*, 299 ff.

Bittker, Boris I., Eustice, James S. and Cummings, Jasper L., Jr (1994), *Federal Income Taxation of Corporations and Shareholders*.

Blair, Margaret, M. and Litan, Robert (1990), 'Corporate Leverage and Leveraged Buyouts in the Eighties: Taxes, Debt, and Corporate Restructuring', in Coffee, John, Lowenstein, Louis and Rose-Ackerman, Susan (eds), *Knights, Raiders and Targets: The Impact of the Hostile Takeover*, Oxford, Oxford University Press.

Blais, Andre and Vaillancourt, Francois (1986), *The Political Economy of Taxation: the Corporate Income Tax and the Canadian Manufacturing Industry*, Dept. De Science Economique, Universite de Montreal, 8610.

Blum, Walter J. (1975), 'The Earnings and Profits Limitation on Dividend Income: A Reappraisal', **53** *Taxes*, 68 ff.

Blumenthal, Marsha and Slemrod, Joel (1994), *The Compliance Costs of the US Corporate Income Tax for Large Corporations*.

Blumenthal, Marsha and Slemrod, Joel (1995), 'The Compliance Cost of Taxing Foreign-Source Income: Its Magnitude, Determinants and Policy Implications', *International Tax and Public Finance* in Coffee, John, Lowenstein, Louis and Rose-Ackerman, Susan (eds), *Knights,Raiders and Targets: The Impact of the Hostile Takeover*, Oxford, Oxford University Press. Slemrod J. (ed.), The taxation of multinational corporations (1996).

Boadway, Robin W. (1988), 'The Theory and Measurement of Effective Tax Rates', in Coffee, John, Lowenstein, Louis and Rose-Ackerman, Susan (eds), *Knights,Raiders and Targets: The Impact of the Hostile Takeover*, Oxford, Oxford University Press, 60-98.

Boadway, Robin W. (1989), 'Corporate Tax Harmonisation: Lessons from Canada in Gammie, Malcolm, Robinson, Bill, and Fitchew, Geoffrey, Beyond 1992: a European Tax System', in Coffee, John, Lowenstein, Louis and Rose-Ackerman, Susan (eds),

Knights,Raiders and Targets: The Impact of the Hostile Takeover, Oxford, Oxford University Press.

Boadway, Robin W. and Bruce, Neil (1984), 'A General Proposition on the Design of a Neutral Business Tax', **24** *Journal of Public Economics*, 231-239.

Boadway, Robin W. and Bruce, Neil (1992a), 'Problems with Integrating Corporate and Personal Income Taxes in an Open Economy', **24** *Journal of Public Economics*, 231-239.

Boadway, Robin W. and Bruce, Neil (1992b), 'Problems with Integrating Corporate and Personal Income Taxes in an Open Economy', **48(1)** *Journal of Public Economics*, 39-66.

Boadway, Robin W. and Treddenick, John M. (1975a), *The Effects of the U.S. Corporate Tax on Resource Allocation and Welfare Institute for Economic Research*, Queen's University Institute for Economic Research Discussino Paper, 165.

Boadway, Robin W. and Treddenick, John M. (1975b), 'The Effect of Corporate Tax Changes by Industry on Employment in Canada: A Short Run Analysis', **30(1)** *Public Finance*, 46-60.

Boadway, Robin, Bruce, Neil and Mintz, Jack M. (1982), 'Corporate Taxation in Canada: Toward an Efficient System', in Coffee, John, Lowenstein, Louis and Rose-Ackerman, Susan (eds), *Knights, Raiders and Targets: The Impact of the Hostile Takeover*, Oxford, Oxford University Press.

Boadway, Robin, Bruce, Neil and Mintz, Jack M. (1984), 'Taxation, Inflation, and the Effective Marginal Tax Rate in Canada', **17** *Canadian Journal of Economics*, 62-79.

Boadway, Robin, Bruce, Neil and Mintz, Jack M. (1992), 'Corporate Taxation and the Holding of Inventories', **25** *Canadian Journal of Economics*, 278-293.

Bodie, Zvi (1989), 'The Lender's View of Debt and Equity: the Case of Pension Funds', Proceedings of a conference held at Melvin Village, New Hampshire.

Bolderson, Sarah and Huiskes, Theodoor (1994), 'Central and Eastern Europe: Meeting Tax Obligations in Central and Eastern Europe', **48** *Bulletin for International Fiscal Documentation*, 648-654.

Bond, S. and Devereux, Michael P. (1995), 'On the Design of a Neutral Business Tax under Uncertainty', **58** *Journal of Public Economics*, 57-71.

Bonner, Sarah E., Davis, Jon S. and Jackson, Betty R. (1992), 'Expertise in Corporate Tax Planning: The Issue Identification Stage', **30(0)** *Journal of Accounting Research*, 1-28.

Boshoff, Vanessa (1993), 'Corporate Tax Rates and Inter-country Comparisons', **61(4)** *South African Journal of Economics*, 301-316.

Bovenberg, A. Lans (1993), 'Investment Promoting Policies in Open Economies: The Importance of Intergenerational and International Distributional Effects', **51(1)** *Journal of Public Economics*, 3-54.

Bovenberg, A. Lans and Goulder, Lawrence H. (1993), 'Promoting Investment under International Capital Mobility: An Intertemporal General Equilibrium Analysis', **95(2)** *Scandinavian Journal of Economics*, 133-156.

Boyle, Glenn W. (1996), 'Corporate Investment and Dividend Tax Imputation', **31** *Financial Review*, 209-226.

Boynton, Charles E., Dobbins, Paul S. and Plesko, George A. (1992), 'Earnings Management and the Corporate Alternative Minimum Tax in Conference on Accounting Research', *Studies on Accounting and Taxation*.

Bracewell-Milnes, J. Barry (1995), 'Summary of Proceedings in International Fiscal Association. International Taxation of Dividends Reconsidered in Light of Corporate Tax Integration', Proceedings of a seminar organised jointly with the EOCD in Toronto in 1994 during the 48th Congress of the International Fiscal Association.

Bradford, David F. (1981), 'The Incidence and Allocation Effects of a Tax on Corporate Distributions', **15** *Journal of Public Economics*, 1-22.

Bradford, David F. and Fullerton, David J. (1982), 'Pitfalls in the Construction and Use of Effective Tax Rates', in Hulten, Charles R (ed.), *Depreciation, Inflation, and the Taxation of Income from Capital.*, Washington, Urban Insitute, 251-279.

Bradford, David F. and Gordon, Roger H. (1980), 'Taxation and the Stock Market Valuation of Capital Gains and Dividends', **14** *Journal of Public Economics*, 109-136.

Bradley, Cassie Francis (ed.) (1994), *An Empirical Investigation of Factors Affecting Corporate Tax Compliance Behavior: Ph.D. Thesis*, University of Alabama, Culverhouse School of Accountancy.

Bradley, Michael, Jarrell, Gregg A. and Kim, E. Han (1984), 'On the Existence of an Optimal Capital Structure: Theory and Evidence', **39** *The Journal of Finance*, 857 ff.

Bravenec, Lorence L. (1989), 'A Nontraditional Approach to Corporate Integration', *Tax Notes*, 1381 ff.

Break, George F. (1969), 'Integrating Corporate and Personal Income Taxes: The Carter Commission Proposals', **34** *Law and Contemporary Problems*, 726-735.

Break, George F. (1969), 'Integration of the Corporate and Personal Income Taxes', **22** *National Tax Journal*, 39-56.

Break, George F. (1978), 'Corporate Tax Integration: Radical Revisions or Common Sense?', in Boskin, Michael J. (ed.), *Federal Tax Reform Myths and Realities*, San Francisco, Institute for Contemporary Studies Press.

Break, George F. (1991), 'Corporate Income Taxation in Jamaica. A Framework for Policy Formation', in Bahl, Roy (ed.), *The Jamaican Tax Reform*, Cambridge, MA, Lincoln Institute of Land Policy, 251-263.

Break, George F. and Pechman, Joseph A. (1975), 'Relationship Between the Corporation and Individual Income Taxes', **28** *National Tax Journal*, 341 ff.

Brennan, Michael J. (1970), 'Taxes, Market Valuation and Corporate Financial Policy', **23** *National Tax Journal*, 417-427.

Brittain, John A. (1964), 'The Tax Structure and Corporate Dividend Policy', **54** *American Economic Review*, 272 ff. Reprinted by Brookings Institution, Washington, DC Studies of Government Finance reprint no. 78.

Brittain, John A. (ed.) (1966), *Corporate Dividend Policy*, Washington, Brookings Institution.

Brody, Evelyn (1995), 'Agents Without Principals: the Economic Convergence of the Nonprofit and For-Profit Organizational Forms', **40** *New York Law School Law Review*, 457 ff.

Brooke, Peter (1989), 'The Government's Approach to the Community: Some Myths Dispelled', in Gammie, Malcolm, Robinson, Bill and Fitchew Geoffrey, *Beyond 1992: A European Tax System: Proceedings of the Fourth Institute for Fiscal Studies Residential Conference*, Oxford.

Brooks, Janet (1990), 'Tax Reform: A Response to Economic and Social Changes: Korea', **44(6)** *Bulletin for International Fiscal Documentation*, 271-272.

Brooks, Neil (1997), 'Canadian Corporate Tax: Logic, Policies and Politics', in Head, G. And Krever, Richard (eds), *Company Tax Systems*, Australian Research Foundation, 115-158.

Brown, E. (1973), *Cary Recent Studies of the Incidence of the Corporate Income Tax*, Massachusetts Institute of Technology Dept. of Economics Working paper No. 116.

Brown, Fred B. (1993), 'Federal Income Taxation of U.S. Branches of Foreign Corporations: Separate Entity or Separate Rules?', **49** *Tax Law Review*, 195-196.

Brumbaugh, David L. and Gravelle, Jane G. (ed.) (1984), *The Corporate Income Tax and the U.S. Economy*, Washington DC, Congressional Research Service, Library of Congress.

Bryan (1984), 'Cancellation of Indebtedness by Issuing Stock in Exchange, Challenging the Congressional Solution to Debt-Equity Swaps', **63** *Texas Law Review*, 89-130.

Bryan (1987), 'Leveraged Buyouts and Tax Policy', **65** *North Carolina Law Review*, 1039 ff.

Buck, Ingerlise (1990), 'Budgetdepartementets Behandling af Erhvervsbeskatningen (with English summary) (A Critical Evaluation of the Assumptions on Corporate Tax in the Macroeconomic Model Used by the Danish Ministry of Finance)', **128(1)** *Nationalokonomisk Tidsskrift*, 30-39.

Bulow, Jeremy I. and Summers, Lawrence H. (1984), 'The Taxation of Risky Assets', **92** *Journal of Political Economy*, 20-39.

Bulow, Jeremy I., Summers, Lawrence H. and Summers, Victoria P. (1990), 'Distinguishing Debt from Equity in the Junk Bond Era', in Shoven, John B. and Waldfogel, Joel (eds), *In Debt, Taxes, and Corporate Restructuring*, Washington, Brookings Institution.

Burke, Karen C. (1995), 'The Uncertain Future of Limited Liability Companies', **12** *American Jounal of Tax Policy*, 14 ff.

Burns, Arthur Edward (1970), 'The Tax Court and Profit Renegotiation', **13** *Journal of Law and Economics*, 307-326.

Butters, J. Keith, Lintner, John V. and Cary, William L. (1951), *Effects of Taxation on Corporate Mergers*.

Canellos, Peter C. (1985), 'The Over-Leveraged Acquisition', **39** *Tax Lawyer*, 91 ff.

Canellos, Peter C. (1987), 'Corporate Tax Integration: by Design or by Default', *Tax Notes*, 999 ff.

Canellos, Peter C. (1988), 'Corporate Tax Integration: by Design or by Default?', in Yin, George K. and Mundstock, George (eds), *Corporate Tax Reform: A Report of the Invitational Conference on Subchapter C 129*.

Canellos, Peter C. and Yin, George K. (eds) (1987), *Corporate Tax Reform: A Report of the American Bar and New York State Bar Associations Invitational Conference on Subchapter C*.

Caplin, Mortimer M. (1961), 'Income Tax Pressures on the Form of Business Organization: Is it Time for a "Doing Business" Tax?', **47** *Va. Law Review*, 249 ff.

Carrera, Carmen (1991), 'On the Consequences of Legal Constraints and Taxation for Corporate Choice', **24** *Canadian Journal of Economics*, 471-485.

Carter, Mary Ellen and Manzon, Gil B., Jr (1995), 'Evidence on the Role of Taxes on Financing Choice: Consideration of Mandatorily Redeemable Preferred Stock', **18** *Journal of Financial Research*, 103-114.

Cary, William L. (1974), 'Federalism and Corporate Law: Reflections Upon Delaware', **83** *Yale Law Journal*, 663 ff.

Centre for European Policy Studies (ed.) (1992), *Corporate Tax Harmonisation in the European Community*.

Chen, Charng Yi and Ponarul, Richard (1991), 'Tax Sheltering Behavior of Property Liability Insurers: Some Additional Evidence', **58(4)** *Journal of Risk and Insurance*, 722-728.

Cheung, Joseph K. (1987), 'Depreciation, Debt, and Equilibrium Tax Rates: A Reconsideration', **27(1)** *Quarterly Review of Economics and Business*, 6-15.

Chiang, Raymond C. and Narayanan, M.P. (1991), 'Bond Refunding in Efficient Markets: A Dynamic Analysis with Tax Effects', **14(4)** *Journal of Financial Research*, 287-302.

Chirelstein, Marvin A. (1969), 'Optional Redemptions and Optional Dividends: Taxing the Repurchase of Common Shares', **78** *Yale Law Journal*, 739 ff.

Chirinko, Robert S. (1986), 'Business Investment and Tax Policy: a Perspective on Existing Models and Empirical Results', **39** *National Tax Journal*, 137 ff.

Chirinko, Robert S. (1987), 'The Ineffectiveness of Effective Tax Rates on Business Investment: a Critique of Feldstein's Fisher-Schultz Lecture', **32** *Journal of Public Economics*, 369 ff.

Chirinko, Robert S. (ed.), *Business Fixed Investment Spending: A Critical Survey of Modeling Strategies, Empirical Results, and Policy Implications*, University of Munich, Centre for Economic Studies, 27.

Chorvat, Terrence R. (1998), 'Taxing International Corporate Income Efficiently', *Tax Law Review*.

Chown, John (1989), 'Tax Harmonisation in Europe', in Gammie, Malcolm, Robinson, Bill and Fitchew Geoffrey, *Beyond 1992: A European Tax System: Proceedings of the Fourth Institute for Fiscal Studies Residential Conference*, Oxford.

Christie, William G. and Nanda, Vikram (1994), 'Free Cash Flow, Shareholder Value, and the Undistributed Profits Tax of 1936 and 1937', **49** *Journal of Finance*, 1727-1754.

Citizens for Tax Justice (1985), 'Corporate Taxpayers and Corporate Freeloaders: Four Years of Continuing, Legalized Tax Avoidance by America's Largest Corporation, 1981-84', *Tax Notes*, 947-971.

Clark (1975), 'The Federal Income Taxation of Financial Intermediaries', **84** *Yale Law Journal*, 1603 ff.

Clark, Robert C. (1977), 'The Morphogenesis of Subchapter C: An Essay in Statutory Evolution and Reform', **87** *Yale Law Journal*, 90 ff.

Clotfelter, Charles T. (1989), 'Tax-Induced Distortions in the Voluntary Sector: in What is Charity? Implications for Law and Policy', **39** *Case Western Reserve Law Review*, 663 ff.

Clowery, Grant M., Outslay, Edmund and Wheeler, James, E. (1986), 'The Debate on Computing Corporate Effective Tax Rates - an Accounting View', *Tax Notes*.

Cloyd, Bryan C., Limberg, Stephen T. and Robinson, John R. (1997), 'The Impact of Federal Taxes on the Use of Debt by Closely-Held Corporations', *National Tax Journal*, 261-277.

Cnossen, Sijbren (1989), 'How Much Tax Harmonisation in the European Community?', in Gammie, Malcolm, Robinson, Bill and Fitchew, Geoffrey, *Beyond 1992: A*

European Tax System: Proceedings of the Fourth Institute for Fiscal Studies Residential Conference, Oxford.

Cnossen, Sijbren (1993), 'What Kind of Corporation Tax?', **47** *International Bureau of Fiscal Documentation*, 3-16.

Cnossen, Sijbren (1993), 'Must the Corporation Tax be Harmonised?', in Knoester, Anthonie (ed.), *Taxation in the United States and Europe: Theory and Practice: Proceedings of a Conference Held by the Confederation of European Economic Associations at Amsterdam, the Netherlands, 1991*, 165-201. Confederation of European Economic Associations Conference Volumes 1993.

Cnossen, Sijbren (1996), 'Company Taxes in the European Union: Criteria and Options for Reform', **17** *Fiscal Studies*, 67-97.

Cnossen, Sijbren (1997a), 'Reform and Harmonization of Company Tax Systems in the European Union', in *Tax Conversations: A Guide to the Key Issues in the Tax Reform Debate: Essays in Honour of John G. Head, Kluwer*, 365-413.

Cnossen, Sijbren (1997b), 'The Role of the Corporation Tax in OECD Member Countries', in Head, G. and Krever, Richard (eds), *Company Tax Systems*, Australian Research Foundation, 49-84.

Coates, Dennis (1991), 'Endogenous Capital Utilization and Taxation of Corporate Capital', **44** *National Tax Journal*, 79-91.

Cohen, Edwin S. (1975), 'Possible Solutions to Practical Problems in Integration of the Corporate and Shareholder Income Tax', **28** *National Tax Journal*, 359-367.

Cohen, Edwin S., Warren, Alvin C. and Andrews, William D. (1985), 'The Meaning of Changes Within the Framework of Subchapter C and the Impact on Proposals for Integration of the Corporate and Individual Income Tax', **22** *San Diego Law Review*, 317 ff.

Collins, Julie H. and Shackelford, Douglas A. (1990), 'Corporate Domicile and Average Effective Tax Rates: The Cases of Canada, Japan, the United Kingdom, and the United States', in Slemrod, Joel (ed.), *The Taxation of Multinational Corporations*.

Collins, Julie H. and Shackelford, Douglas A. (1992a), 'Foreign Tax Credit Limitations and Preferred Stock Issuances', **30** *Journal of Accounting Research*, 103-124.

Collins, Julie H. and Shackelford, Douglas A. (eds) (1992b), *Foreign Tax Credit Limitations and Preferred Stock Issuances in Conference on Accounting Research, Studies on Accounting and Taxation*, Chicago, University of Chicago.

Collins, Julie H., Kelmsley, D. and Shackelford, Douglas A. (1995), 'Tax Reform and Foreign Acquisitions: A Microanalysis', **48** *National Tax Journal*, 1-21.

Colm, Gerhard (1940), 'Conflicting Theories of Corporate Income Taxation', **7** *Law and Contemporary Problems*, 282 ff.

Commission on Corporations (1977), 'Report on the Integration of Corporate and Individual Income Taxes', **31** *Tax Lawyer*, 37 ff.

Commission of European Communities (ed.) (1992), *Report of the Committee of Independent Experts on Company Taxation*, Brussels.

Cooley, Thomas F. and Salyer, Kevin D. (1987), 'The Effects of Inflation Induced Tax Increases on Stock and Housing Prices', **89(4)** *Scandinavian Journal of Economics*, 421-434.

Cooper, Graeme S. (1994), 'Analyzing Corporate Tax Evasion', **50** *Tax Law Review*, 33 ff.

Cooper, Graeme S. (1996), 'The Return to Corporate Tax Evasion in the Presence of an Income Tax on Shareholders: The Return to Corporate Tax Evasion in the Presence of an Income Tax on Shareholders', **12** *Akron Tax Journal*, 1 ff.

Cooper, Graeme S. (1997), 'The Effect of an Income Tax on Corporate Tax Compliance', in Head, G. and Krever, Richard (eds), *Company Tax Systems*, Australian Research Foundation, 341-378.

Cooper, Graeme S. and Gordon, Richard K., Jr (1988), 'Taxation of Legal Persons and Their Owners', in Coffee, John, Lowenstein, Louis and Rose-Ackerman, Susan (eds), *Knights, Raiders and Targets: The Impact of the Hostile Takeover*, Oxford, Oxford University Press.

Cordes, Joseph J. and Sheffrin, Steven M. (1983), 'Estimating the Tax Advantage of Corporate Debt', **38** *Journal of Finance*, 95-105.

Cosciani, Cesare (1959), *The Effects of Differential Tax Treatment of Corporate and Non-corporate Enterprises*, European Productivity Agency of the Organisation for European Economic Cooperation Project, 314.

Couzin, Robert (1992), 'Taxation and Its Impact on Market Structure: Comment', in Bird, R.M. and Mintz, J.M. (eds), *Taxation to 2000 and Beyond. Canadian Tax Paper*, Toronto: Canadian Tax Foundation, 257-262.

Coyne, Christopher, Fabozzi, Frank J. and Yaari, M.E. (1992), 'How Taxes Transform Corporate Acquisitions into Asset Arbitrage', in Coffee, John, Lowenstein, Louis and Rose-Ackerman, Susan (eds), *Knights, Raiders and Targets: The Impact of the Hostile Takeover*, Oxford, Oxford University Press, 173-203.

Cragg, John C., Harberger, Arnold, C. and Mieszkowski, Peter M. (1967), 'Empirical Evidence on the Incidence of the Corporation Income Tax', *Journal of Political Economy*, 811-822. Reprinted in Harberger, Arnold C. (ed.) *Taxation and Welfare*, 1974, 135-162

Craig, Caroline Kern (ed.) (1987), *The Shifting of Corporate Capital Acquisition Tax Subsidies an Empirical Analysis, Ph.D. Thesis*, University of Illinois at Urbana-Champaign.

Craig, Caroline Kern and Todd, Heidi I. (1993), 'An Overview of Corporate Tax Issues Involving the European Communit', **175** *Journal of Accountancy*, 29 ff.

Crane, Charlotte (1988), 'Toward a Theory of the Corporate Tax Base: The Effect of a Corporate Distribution of Encumbered Property to Shareholders', **44** *Tax Law Review*, 13 ff.

Crockett, Ulysses S. (ed.) (1973), *Tax Exemption for Corporate Mergers and Consolidations: a Legislative History of Congressional Policy, LL.M. Thesis*, Columbia University Press.

Cross, Mark L., Davidson, Wallace N. II and Thornton, John H. (1988), 'Taxes, Stock Returns and Captive Insurance Subsidiaries', **55** *Journal of Risk and Insurance*, 331-338.

Cummings, Jasper L., Jr (1992), 'The Silent Policies of Conservation and Cloning of Tax Basis and Their Corporate Applications', **48** *Tax Law Review*, 126-131.

Cummins, Jason G., Harris, Trevor S. and Hassett, Kevin A. (1995), 'Accounting Standards, Information Flow, and Firm Investment Behavior', in Feldstein, M., Hines, J.R., Jr, Hubbard, R.G. (eds), *The Effects of Taxation on Multinational Corporations*, Chicago, University of Chicago Press, 181-224.

Cutler, David M. (1988), 'Tax Reform and the Stock Market: An Asset Price Approach', **78** *American Economic Review*, 1107-1117.

Daly, Kevin and Hart, Neil (1994), 'Mark-up Pricing and the Forward Shifting of the Corporate Income Tax', **0** *Australian Economic Review*, 45-54.

Daly, Michael and Jung, Jack (1987), 'The Taxation of Corporate Investment Income in Canada: An Analysis of Marginal Effective Tax Rates', **20** *Canadian Journal of Economics*, 555-587.

Daly, Michael and Weiner, Joann (1993), 'Corporate Tax Harmonization and Competition in Federal Countries: Some Lessons for the European Community?', **46(4)** *National Tax Journal*, 441-461.

Dammon, Robert M. and Senbet, Lemma W. (1988), 'The Effect of Taxes and Depreciation on Corporate Investment and Financial Leverage', **43(2)** *Journal of Finance*, 357-373.

Damus, Sylvester, Hobson, Paul A.R. and Thirsk, Wayne R. (1991), 'Foreign Tax Credits, the Supply of Foreign Capital, and Tax Exporting: A Numerical General Equilibrium Model of Corporate Tax Reform in Canada', **45(1)** *Journal of Public Economics*, 29-46.

Darrow, Jill E. (1994), 'Limited Liability Companies and S Corporations: Deciding Which is Optimal and Whether to Convert to LLC Status', **48** *Tax Lawyer*, 1 ff.

Davies, John H. (1975), 'Public Stock, Private Stock: A Model for the Corporate Income Tax', **124** *University of Pennsylvania Law Review*, 299 ff.

de la Fuente, Angel and Gardner, Edward (eds) (1990), *Corporate Income Tax Harmonization and Capital Allocation in the European Community*, International Monetary Fund.

Deangelo, Harry (1991), 'Payout Policy and Tax Deferral', **46(1)** *Journal of Finance*, 357-368.

Deangelo, Harry and Masulis, Ronald W. (1980), 'Optimal Capital Structures under Corporate and Personal Taxation', **8** *Journal of Financial Economics*, 3-30.

Desai, Mihir A. and Hines, James R., Jr (eds) (1996), *"Basket" Cases : International Joint Ventures after the Tax Reform Act of 1986*, National Bureau of Economic Research, 5755.

Devereux, Michael P. (1989), 'Tax Asymmetries: The Cost of Captial and Investment', **99** *Economic Journal*, 103-112.

Devereux, Michael P. and Freeman, Harold (1991), 'A General Neutral Profits Tax', **12(3)** *Fiscal Studies*, 2 ff.

Devereux, Michael P. and Freeman, Harold (1995), 'The Impact of Tax on Foreign Dirrect Investment: Empirical Evidence and the Implications for Tax Integration Schemes', **2** *International Tax and Public Finance*, 85-106.

Devereux, Michael P. and Freeman, Harold (1996), 'The Impact of Tax on Foreign Direct Investment: Empirical Evidence and the Implications for Tax Integration Schemes', in Slemrod, Joel (ed.), *The Taxation of Multinational Corporations*. International Tax and Public Finance, 1995

Devereux, Michael P. and Pearson, Mark (1990), 'Harmonising CorporateYaxes in Europe', **11** *Fiscal Studies*, 21-35.

Devereux, Michael P. and Pearson, Mark (1992), 'The Interactions of Corporate Tax between the EC, Japan and the United States: International', **46(8)** *Bulletin for International Fiscal Documentation*, 367-383.

Devereux, Michael P. and Pearson, Mark (1994), 'Production Efficiency and Corporate Tax Harmonization', *European Economic Review*.

Devereux, Michael P. and Pearson, Mark (eds), *Corporate Tax Harmonisation and Economic Efficiency*,.

Devereux, Michael P., Keen, Michael and Schiantarelli, F. (1994), 'Corporation Tax Asymmetries and Investment: Evidence from UK Panel Data', **53** *Journal of Public Economics*, 3950-3418.

Diamond, Peter and Mirrlees, J.A. (1971), 'Optimal Taxation and Public Production, I: Production Efficiency, and II: Tax Rules', **61** *American Economic Review*, 261-278.

Dodge, Joseph A. (1995), 'A Combined Mark-to-Market and Pass-Through Corporate-Shareholder Integration Proposal', **50** *Tax Law Review*, 265 ff.

Doernberg, Richard L. (1992), 'International Aspects of Individual and Corporate Tax Integration', **4** *Tax Notes International*, 506 ff.

Doernberg, Richard L. (1995), *Amending the OECD Model Treaty and Commentary in Response to Corporate Tax Integration*, Proceedings of a Seminar Organised Jointly with the OECD in Toronto in 1994 During the 48th Congress of the International Fiscal Association.

Doernberg, Richard L. and McChesney Fred S. (1987), 'On the Accelerating Rate and Decreasing Durability of Tax Reform', **71** *Minnesota Law Review*, 913 ff.

Douglas, Richard W., Jr (ed.) (1987), *Consultative Document on Full Imputation*, Wellington, New Zealand Ministry of Finance.

Douvier, Pierre Jean (1993), 'Major Measures Concerning International Taxation: The Finance Act 1993 and Transfer of Assets Abroad', **47(4)** *Bulletin for International Fiscal Documentation*, 214-219.

Downs, Thomas, W. (1992), 'Q and the Tax Bias Theory: The Role of Depreciation Tax Shields', **47** *Journal of Public Economics*, 59-84.

Downs, Thomas, W. (1993), 'Corporate Leverage and Nondebt Tax Shields: Evidence on Crowding-Out', **28** *Financial Review*, 549-583.

Downs, Thomas, W. and Demirgures, Cuneyt (1992), 'The Asset Price Theory of Shareholder Revaluations: Tests with the Tax Reforms of the 1980s', **27** *Financial Review*, 151-184.

Downs, Thomas and Hendershott, Patric H. (1987), 'Tax Policy and Stock Prices', **40(2)** *National Tax Journal*, 183-190.

Downs, Thomas, W. and Shriver, Keith A. (1992), 'The Analytical Derivation and Empirical Test of a Tax-Adjusted Fundamental Value Model', **30** *Journal of Accounting Research*, 77-98.

Downs, Thomas, W. and Tehranian, Hassan (1988), 'Predicting Stock Price Responses to Tax Policy Changes', **78** *American Economic Review*, 1118-1130

Driessen, Patrick A. (1991), 'Net Imports and the U.S. Corporate Tax Base', **44(3)** *National Tax Journal*, 315-324.

Duggal, V.G. and Adams, F.G. (1987), 'Corporate Tax Reform and Business Investment: Empirical Estimates for Structures and Equipment', **12(3)** *Empirical Economics*, 187-195.

Dusansky, Richard (ed.), *Corporate Income Tax Shifting in the U.S.: A Simultaneous Equations Approach Stony Brook*, Economic Research Bureau, State University of New York, 31.

Dutton, John (1982), 'The Optimal Taxation of International Investment Income: A Comment', **97** *Quarterly Journal of Economics*, 373-380.

Dworin, Lowell (1985), 'On Estimating Corporate Tax Liabilities from Financial Statements', **9** *Tax Notes*, 947-971.

Dworin, Lowell (1987), *Impact of the Corporate Alternative Minimum Tax: A Monte Carlo Simulation.*

Easson, Alex J. (1997), *Company Tax Reform and the Inter-nation Allocation of Tax Jurisdiction*, Australian Research Foundation.

Easterbrook, Frank H. (1984), 'Two Agency-cost Explanations of Dividends', **74** *American Economic Review*, 650 ff.

Easterbrook, Frank H. and Fischel, Daniel R. (1991), *The Economic Structure of Corporate Law*, Cambridge, MA, Harvard University Press.

Ebrill, Liam, P. and Hartman, David, G. (1982), 'On the Incidence and Excess Burden of the Corporation Income Tax', **37** *Public Finance*, 48 ff.

Ebrill, Liam, P. and Hartman, David, G. (1983), 'The Corporate Income Tax, Entrepreneurship, and the Noncorporate Sector', **11** *Public Finance Quarterly*, 419-436.

Eckhard, Janeba (1995), 'Corporate Income Tax Competition, Double Taxation Treaties, and Foreign Direct Investment', **56** *Journal of Public Economics*, 311-325.

Eden, Lorraine (ed.) (1998), *Taxing Multinationals: Transfer Pricing and Corporate Income Taxation in North America*, Toronto; University of Toronto Press.

Egger, John, B. (1985), 'Citizens for Tax Justice's Latest Misrepresentation of Corporate Tax Burdens', *Tax Notes*, 947-971.

Eisner, Robert (1969), 'Tax Policy and Investment Behavior: Comment', **59** *American Economic Review*, 379 ff.

Eisner, Robert and Nadiri, M. (1968), 'Investment Behavior and Neoclassical Theory', **50** *Review of Economics and Statistics*, 369 ff.

Elitzur, R. Ramy and Mintz, Jack M. (1994), 'Transfer Pricing Rules and Corporate Tax Competition. Dept. of Economics and Institute for Policy Analysis', in Coffee, John, Lowenstein, Louis and Rose-Ackerman, Susan (eds), *Knights, Raiders and Targets: The Impact of the Hostile Takeover*, Oxford, Oxford University Press, 829-4909.

Elitzur, R. Ramy and Mintz, Jack M. (1996), 'Transfer Pricing Rules and Corporate Tax Competition', **60** *Journal of Public Economics*, 401-422.

Elitzur, R. Ramy and Mintz, Jack M. (1997), 'Corrigendum to Transfer Pricing Rules and Corporate Tax Competition', **64** *Journal of Public Economics*, 287 ff.

Elston, Julie Ann (1992), 'Tax Reform and Corporate Investment: Theory and Evidence of a Q Theoretic Approach', in Coffee, John, Lowenstein, Louis and Rose-Ackerman, Susan (eds), *Knights, Raiders and Targets: The Impact of the Hostile Takeover*, Oxford, Oxford University Press.

Elton, Edwin, J. and Gruber, Martin (1970), 'Marginal Stockholder Tax Rates and the Clientele Effect', **52** *Review of Economics and Statistics*, 68-74.

Esam, Richard, T. (1979), 'International and Comparative Aspects of Corporate/Shareholder Integration: A View from the United Kingdom', **33** *Bulletin for International Fiscal Documentation*, 312-316.

Esenwein, Gregg, A. and Gravelle, Jane G. (1982), *A Comparative Analysis of the Accelerated Cost Recovery System and a Repeal of the Corporate Income Tax*, Washington, DC, Fund for Public Policy Research.

Evans, Thomas L. (1991), 'The Taxation of Multi-Period Projects: An Analysis of Competing Models', **69(5)** *Texas Law Review*, 1109 ff.

Faber, Peter (1985), 'Taxation of Corporations and Shareholders: Premises of the present System', **22** *San Diego Law Review*, 5 ff.

Fabozzi, Frank J. and Fonfeder, Robert (1981), 'Corporate Tax Rates in an Inflationary Environment: 1976 and 1977', **16(1)** *Business Economics*, 55-58.

Fama, Eugene F. and French, Kenneth R. (1998), 'Taxes, Financing Decisions, and Firm Value', *Journal of Finance*.

Fantozzi, Augusto (1993), 'Italy Welcomes Further EC Harmonization', **47(9)** *Bulletin for International Fiscal Documentation*, 474-479.

Fazzari, Steven, Hubbard, R. Glenn and Petersen, Bruce (1988), 'Financing Constraints and Corporate Investment', **1** *Brookings Papers on Economic Activity*, 141 ff.

Feld, Alan (ed.) (1982), *Tax Policy and Corporate Concentration*, Lexington Books.

Feldstein, Martin S. (1970a), *Testimony on Tax Policy Aspects of Mergers and Acquisitions*, House of Representatives, Committee on Ways and Means, No.101-10.

Feldstein, Martin, S. (1970b), 'Corporate Taxation and Dividend Behavior', **37** *Review of Economic Studies*, 57-72.

Feldstein, Martin S. (1972), 'Corporate Taxation and Dividend Behavior: a Reply and Extension', **39** *Review of Economic Studies*, 235 ff.

Feldstein, Martin S. (1987), *Imputing Corporate Tax Liabilities to Individual Taxpayer*, Cambridge: National Bureau of Eocnomic Research, 2349.

Feldstein, Martin S. (1988), 'Imputing Corporate Tax Liabilities to Individual Taxpayers', **41(1)** *National Tax Journal*, 37-59.

Feldstein, Martin S. (1989), 'Tax Policy for the 1990s: Personal Saving, Business Investment, and Corporate Debt', **79** *American Economic Review. Papers and Proceedings*, 108-112.

Feldstein, Martin S. (1995), 'The Effects of Tax Based Saving Incentives on Government Revenue and National Saving', **110(2)** *Quarterly Journal of Economics*, 475-494.

Feldstein, Martin S. and Frisch, Daniel, J. (1977a), 'Corporate Tax Integration: the Estimated Effects on Capital Accumulation and Tax Distribution of Two Integration Proposals', **30** *National Tax Journal*, 37 ff.

Feldstein, Martin S. and Frisch, Daniel, J. (1977b), 'Corporate Tax Integration: The Estimated Effects on Capital Accumulation and Tax Distribution of Two Integration Proposals', **30(1)** *National Tax Journal*, 37-52.

Feldstein, Martin, S. and Frisch, Daniel, J. (1977c), 'Corporate Tax Integration: A Quantitative Comparison of Alternatives Tax Foundation', **28** *Government Finance Brief*.

Feldstein, Martin, S. and Slemrod, Joel (1980), 'Personal Taxation, Portfolio Choice, and the Effect of the Corporate Income Tax', **21** *Journal of Political Economy*, 854-866.

Feltenstein, Andrew and Shah, Anwar (1995), 'General Equilibrium Effects of Investment Incentives in Mexico', **46(2)** *Journal of Development Economics*, 253-269.

Feldstein, Martin S, Hines, James R., Jr and Hubbard, R. Glenn (eds) (1995), *Taxing Multinational Corporations*.

Feltham, Glenn, D. and Paquette, Suzanne, M. (1996), *To Pay or to Delay: an Economic Analysis of the Decision to Delay, and the Incidence of Delaying, the Payment of Corporate Income Tax*.

Fisher (1985), 'Corporate Tax Incentives: The American Version of Industrial Policy', **19** *Journal of Economic Issues*, 9-12.

Fisher, Peter S. (1985), 'Corporate Tax Incentives: The American Version of Industrial Policy', **19** *Journal of Economic Issues*, 1-19.

Fitchew, Geoffrey (1989), *The Single European Market and Tax Harmonisation*.

Flak, Henry (1965), *A Study of the Methods of Shifting the Corporate Income Tax*, Houston University.

Flemming (1976), 'A Reappraisal of the Corporation Income Tax', **6** *Journal of Public Economics*, 163 ff.

Fletcher, Douglas, R. (1994), 'The International Argument for Corporate Tax Integration', **11** *American Jounal of Tax Policy*, 156 ff.

Frech, H. Edward III, Deacon, Rovert, Decanio, Stephen J. and Johnson, Bruce M. (1990), *Taxing Energy: Oil Severence Taxation and the Economy*, New York, Holmes and Meyer.

Freeman, Louis, S. (1996), *Tax Strategies for Corporate Acquisitions, Dispositions, Spin-offs, Joint Ventures, Financings, Reorganizations and Restructurings*.

Frisch, Daniel, J. (1990), 'The Economics of International Tax Policy: Some Old and New Approaches', **47** *Tax Notes* in Coffee, John, Lowenstein, Louis and Rose-Ackerman, Susan (eds), *Knights, Raiders and Targets: The Impact of the Hostile Takeover*, Oxford, Oxford University Press, 581 ff.

From, Gary (ed.) (1971), *Tax Incentives and Capital Spending*.

Froot, Kenneth A. and Hines, James R., Jr (1995), 'Interest Allocation Rules, Financing Patterns, and the Operations of U.S. Multinationals', in Feldstein, M., Hines, J.R., Jr and Hubbard, R.G. (eds), *The Effects of Taxation on Multinational Corporations*, Chicago, University of Chicago Press.

Frost, James Lyon (ed.) (1980), *Corporate Tax and Wealth Redistribution Effects in Mergers and Acquisitions, MS Thesis, MIT*, Alfred P. Sloan School of Management.

Fujisaki, Tetsuya (ed.) (1987), *Effect of 1986 Tax Reform on Corporate Mergers: MS Thesis,* Massachusetts, Institute of Technology, Sloan School of Management.

Fullerton, Don (1981), 'Corporate Tax Integration in the United States: A General Equilibrium Approach', **71** *American Economic Review*, 677-691.

Fullerton, Don (1984), 'Which Effective Tax Rate?', **37** *National Tax Journal*, 23-41.

Fullerton, Don (1987), 'The Indexation of Interest, Depreciation, and Capital Gains and Tax Reform in the United States', **32(1)** *Journal of Public Economics*, 25-51.

Fullerton, Don and Hamdan, Lawrence A. (1983), 'The Aborted Phase in of Marginal Effective Corporate Tax Rates', **11(4)** *Public Finance Quarterly*, 437-464.

Fullerton, Don and Rogers, Diane, Lim (eds) (1993), *Rogers, Diane, Lim*, Washington, DC, Brookings Institution.

Fullerton, Don et al. (1981), 'Corporate Tax Integration in the United States: A General Equilibrium Approach', **71(4)** *American Economic Review*, 677-691.

Fullerton, Don, Gillete, Robert and Mackie, James B. (eds) (1987), *Investment Incentives Under the Tax Reform Act of 1986*.

Funke, Michael and Hubbard, R. Glenn (1992), 'Corporate Financial Policy, Taxation, and Macroeconomic Risk', *US Treasury*.

Funke, Michael and Willenbockel, Dirk (1996), 'Das Jahressteuergesetz 1996 und die private Investitionstatigkeit', **42** *Ifo-Studien*, 221-233.

Gabinet, Leon and Coffey, Ronald, J. (1977), 'The Implications of the Economic Concept of Income for Corporation-Shareholder Income Tax Systems', **27** *Case Western Reserve Law Review*, 895 ff.

Gaffrey, Dennis, J. and Wheeler, James, E. (1977), 'The Double Taxation of Corporate Source Income: Reality or Illusion?', **8** *Tax Advisor*, 523 ff.

Gammie, Malcolm (1991), 'Corporate Tax Harmonization: an "ACE" Proposal', **545** *12 IBFD European Taxation*.

Gammie, Malcolm (1992), 'The Harmonisation of Corporate Income Taxes in Europe: The Ruding Committee Report', **13** *Fiscal Studies*, 108-121.

Gammie, Malcolm (1997), 'The Future of UK Corporation Tax', in Head, G. and Krever, Richard (eds), *Company Tax Systems*, Australian Research Foundation, 207-270.

Gammie, Malcolm and Robinson, Bill (1989), 'Introduction: The Impact of the Single Market on EC Tax Systems', in Coffee, John, Lowenstein, Louis and Rose-Ackerman, Susan (eds), *Knights, Raiders and Targets: The Impact of the Hostile Takeover*, Oxford, Oxford University Press.

Gann, Pamela, B. (1985), 'Neutral Taxation of Capital Income: An Achievable Goal?', **48** *Law and Contemporary Problems*, 77 ff.

Gendron, Pierre-Pascal (1996), 'Corporate Tax Analysis in a Dominant Firm Model with Sunk Capital Investment', **29** *Canadian Journal of Economics*, 298-302.

Gentry, William M. (1994), 'Taxes, Financial Decisions and Organization Form: Evidence from Publicly Traded Partnerships', **53** *Journal of Public Economics*, 223-244.

Gentry, William M. and Hubbard, R. Glenn (1997), 'Fundamental Tax Reform and Corporate Financial Policy', *National Tax Association Proceedings*.

Gerardi, Geraldine, Greatz, Michael, J. and Rosen, Harvey S., 'Corporate Integration Puzzles, US Dept of the Treasury', **3** *National Tax Journal*, 307-314.

Gergen, Mark P. (1997), 'Subchapter K and Passive Financial Intermediation', **51** *Law Review*, 37 ff.

Gertler, Mark and Hubbard, R. Glenn (1990), 'Taxation, Corporate Capital Structure, and Financial Distress', *Tax Policy and the Economy 4* in Coffee, John, Lowenstein, Louis and Rose-Ackerman, Susan (eds), *Knights, Raiders and Targets: The Impact of the Hostile Takeover*, Oxford, Oxford University Press.

Gilson, Ronald J. (1991), 'Unlimited Liability and Law Firm Organization: Tax Factors and the Direction of Causation', **99** *Journal of Political Economy*, 420-425.

Gilson, Ronald J. and Black, Bernard, S. (1995), *The Law and Finance of Corporate Acquisitions*.

Gilson, Ronald J., Scholes, Myron S. and Wolfson, Mark, Alan, 'Taxation and the Dynamics of Corporate Control: the Uncertain Case for Tax Motivated Acquisitions', in Coffee, John, Lowenstein, Louis and Rose-Ackerman, Susan (eds), *Knights, Raiders and Targets: The Impact of the Hostile Takeover*, Oxford, Oxford University Press.

Gilson, Stuart C., 'Transactions Costs and Capital Structure Choice: Evidence from Financially Dostressed Firms', *Journal of Finance*.

Ginsburg, Martin, D. (1992), 'Maintaining Subchapter S in an Integrated Tax World', **47** *Tax Law Review*, 665-680.

Ginsburg, Martin, D. and Mergers, Jack, Levin (eds) (1996), *Acquisitions and Buyouts*, Little, Brown and Company.

Givoly, Dan, Hayn, Carla, Ofer, Aharon, D. and Sarig, Oded (1992), 'Taxes and Capital Structure: Evidence From Firms' Response to The Tax Reform Act of 1986', **5** *Review of Financial Studies*, 331-355.

Goldberg, Daniel, S. (1995), 'The Tax Treatment of Limited Liability Companies: Law in Search of Policy', **50** *Business Lawyer*.

Goode, Richard (1946), 'Postwar Corporate Tax Structure', U.S. Treasury.

Goode, Richard (1951), *The Corporation Income Tax*.

Goode, Richard (1966), 'Rates of Return, Income Shares, and Corporate Tax Incidence', in Krzyzaniak, M. (ed.), *Effects of Corporation Income Tax*, Papers Presented at the Symposium on Business Taxation.

Goode, Richard (1989), 'Forward Shifting of the Corporate Tax in the Presence of Competing Imports: A Reply', **44(2)** *Public Finance*, 327-328.

Goodman, Leonard and Miranti, Paul, J., Jr, *A Bridge between Knowledge and Action: E. R. A.*.

Goodspeed, Timothy J. and Frisch, Daniel, J. (eds), 'US Tax Policy and the Overseas Activities of US Multinational Corporations: A Quantitative Assessment'.

Goolsbee, Austan, 'Taxes, Organizational Form and the Deadweight Loss of the Corporate Income Tax', *Journal of Public Economics*.

Gordon, R.J. (1967), 'The Incidence of the Corporation Tax in U.S. Manufacturing', **57** *American Economic Review*, 731-758.

Gordon, Robert J. (1970), 'Specification Bias and Corporate Tax Incidence', **23(4)** *National Tax Journal*, 373-378.

Gordon, Roger H., 'Taxation of Corporate Capital Income: Tax Revenues Versus Tax Distortions', **53** *Quarterly Journal of Economics*, 223-244.

Gordon, Roger H., 'Taxation of Investment and Savings in a World Economy', **76** *American Economic Review*, 1086-1102.

Gordon, Roger H. (ed.) (1981), 'Uncertainty and the Analysis of Corporate Tax Distortions', Proceedings of the 74th Annual Conference.

Gordon, Roger H. (1984), 'Inflation, Taxation and Corporate Behavior', **99** *Quarterly Journal of Economics*, 313 ff.

Gordon, Roger H. and Bradford, David F. (1980), 'Taxes and Capital Structure: Evidence From Firms' Response to The Tax Reform Act of 1986', **14** *Journal of Public Economics*, 109-136.

Gordon, Roger H. and Jun, Joosung (1993), 'Taxes and the Form of Ownership of Foreign Corporate Equity', in Giovannini, A., Hubbard, R.G. and Slemrod, J. (eds), *Studies in International Taxation*, Chicago, University of Chicago Press, 13-44.

Gordon, Roger H. and Levinsohn, James (1990), 'The Linkage Between Domestic Taxes and Border Taxes', in Razin and Slemrod (eds), *Taxation in the Global Economy*, Chicago, University of Chicago Press.

Gordon, Roger H. and MacKie Mason, Jeffrey K. (1990), 'Effects of the Tax Reform Act of 1986 on Corporate Financial Policy and Organizational Form', in Slemrod, J. (ed.), *Do Taxes Matter?*, Cambridge, MA, MIT Press, 91-131.

Gordon, Roger H. and MacKie Mason, Jeffrey K. (1994), 'Tax Distortions to the Choice of Organization Form', **55** *Journal of Public Economics*, 279-306.

Gordon, Roger H. and MacKie Mason, Jeffrey K. (1995), 'Why is There Corporate Taxation in a Small Open Economy? The Role of Transfer Pricing and Income Shifting', in Feldstein, M., Hines, J.R., Jr and Hubbard, R.G. (eds), *The Effects of*

Taxation on Multinational Corporations, Chicago: University of Chicago Press, 67-94.

Gordon, Roger H. and Malkiel, Burton, G., 'Corporation Finance', in Aaron, Henry and Pechman, Joseph (eds), *How Taxes Affect Economic Behavior*, Washington, DC, Brookings Institution..

Gordon, Roger H. and Slemrod, Joel (1998), *Are 'Real' Responses to Taxes Simply Income Shifting between Corporate and Personal Tax Bases?*, Office of Tax Research, University of Michigan Business School, 98-9.

Gordon, Roger H. and Wilson, John D. (1986), 'An Examination of Multijurisdictional Corporate Income Taxation Under Formula Apportionment', *Econometrica*, 1357-1373.

Gordon, Roger H. and Wilson, John Douglas (1989), 'Measuring the Efficiency Cost of Taxing Risky Capital Income', **79** *American Economic Review*, 427-439.

Goudie, A.W. (1984), 'Tax Exhaustion: Estimates from a Disaggregate Model of Corporate Tax Liabilities', **16(2)** *Applied Economics*, 205-224.

Goulder, Lawrence H. and Summers, Lawrence H. (1989), 'Tax Policy, Asset Prices, and Growth: A General Equilibrium Analysis', **38(3)** *Journal of Public Economics*, 265-296.

Gourevitch, Harry, G. (1977), 'Corporate Tax Integration: The European Experience', **31** *Tax Lawyer*, 65 ff.

Gourevitch, Harry, G. (1978), 'Corporate Tax Integration: The European Experience', **31** *Tax Lawyer*, 65 ff.

Gradus, Raymond and de Zeeuw, Aart (1989), *Corporate Tax Rate Policy and Public and Private Employment*, Discussion paper, Center for Economic Research, Tilburg University.

Graetz, Michael J. (1989), 'The Tax Aspects of Leveraged Buyouts and Other Corporate Financial Restructuring Transactions', **42** *Tax Notes*, 721 ff.

Graetz, Michael J. and O'Hear, Michael, M. (1997), 'The"Original Intent" of U.S. International Taxation', **46** *Duke Law Journal*, 1021 ff.

Graham, John, R. (1996a), 'Debt and the Marginal Tax Rate', *Journal of Financial Economics*.

Graham, John, R. (1996b), 'Proxies for the Corporate Marginal Tax Rate', **42** *Journal of Financial Economics*, 187-221.

Gravelle, Jane G. (1979), 'Differential Taxation of Capital Income: Another Look at the 1986 Tax Reform Act', **42** *National Tax Journal*, 441-463.

Gravelle, Jane G. (1981), 'The Social Cost of Non-Neutral Taxation: Estimates from Nonresidential Capital', in Hulten, Charles R (ed.), *Depreciation, Inflation, and the Taxation of Income from Capital*, Washington, Urban Institute.

Gravelle, Jane G. (1982), *Safe Harbor Leasing under the Economic Recovery Tax Act of 1981 and Investment Efficiency*.

Gravelle, Jane G. (1995), 'The Corporate Income Tax: Economic Issues and Policy Options', **48** *National Tax Journal*, 267-277.

Gravelle, Jane G. (ed.) (1991), *Corporate Tax Integration: Issues and Options*, Washington, DC, Congressional Research Service, Library of Congress.

Gravelle, Jane G. (ed.) (1994), *The Economic Effects of Taxing Capital Income*, Cambridge, MA, MIT Press.

Gravelle, Jane G. and Esenwein, Gregg, A. (1983), 'The Measurement and Interpretation of Effective Corporate Tax Rates: A Comment', *Tax Notes*, 867-872.

Gravelle, Jane G. and Kotlikoff, Laurence J. (1988), 'Does the Harberger Model Greatly Understate the Excess Burden of the Corporate Tax?: Another Model Says Yes'.

Gravelle, Jane G. and Kotlikoff, Laurence J. (1989), 'The Incidence and Efficiency Costs of Corporate Taxation when Corporate and Noncorporate Firms Produce the Same Good', **97** *Journal of Political Economy*, 749-780.

Gravelle, Jane G. and Kotlikoff, Laurence J. (1993), 'Corporate Tax Incidence and Inefficiency when Corporate and Noncorporate Goods Are Close Substitutes', **31(4)** *Economic Inquiry*, 501-516.

Gravelle, Jane G. and Kotlikoff, Laurence J. (1995), 'Corporate Taxation and the Efficiency Gains of the 1986 Tax Reform Act', **6** *Economic Theory*, 51-81.

Green, Richard C. and Talmor, Eli (1985), 'The Structure and Incentive Effects of Corporate Tax Liabilities', **40(4)** *Journal of Finance*, 1095-1114.

Green, Robert, A. (1993), 'The Future of Source-Based Taxation of the Income of Multinational Enterprises', **79** *Cornell Law Review*, 67-70.

Grier, Paul and Strebel, Paul (1980), 'The Empirical Relationship between Taxation and Capital Structure', **15** *Financial Review*, 45-57.

Griffith, Thomas, D. (1983), 'Integration of the Corporate and Personal Income Taxes and the ALI Proposal', **23** *Santa Clara Law Review*, 715 ff.

Gropp, Reint, E. (ed.) (1994), *Corporate Taxation and Capital Structure Choice in the U.S. and Germany*, Wisconsin University.

Gropp, Reint, E. (1995), 'Corporate Taxation and Capital Structure Choice in Germany: A General Equilibrium Model', **52** *Finanzarchiv*, 196-121.

Grubert, Harry and Mutti, John H. (eds) (1987), 'The Impact of the Tax Reform Act of 1986 on Trade and Capital Flows'.

Grubert, Harry and Mutti, John H. (1991), 'Taxes, Tariffs and Transfer Pricing in Multinational Corporate Decision Making', **73** *Review of Economics and Statistics*, 285-293.

Grubert, Harry and Mutti, John H. (1994), 'International Aspects of Corporate Tax Integration: The Contrasting Role of Debt and Equity Flows', **47(1)** *National Tax Journal*, 111-133.

Grubert, Harry, Goodspeed, Timothy J. and Swenson, Deborah (1991), *Explaining the Low Taxable Income of Foreign-controlled Companies in the United States*.

Guenther, David, A. (1992), 'Taxes and Organizational Form: A Comparison of Corporations and Master Limited Partnerships, UCT', **67** *Accounting Review*, 17-45.

Gulley, O. David and Santerre, Rexford E. (1993), 'The Effect of Tax Exemption on the Market Share of Nonprofit Hospitals', **46(4)** *National Tax Journal*, 477-486.

Hadjina, Branko and Sever, Ivo (1995), 'Ucinci Upravljanja Porezom Poduzeca s Posebnim Osvrtom na Mala i Srednja Poduzeca. (Effects of Company Taxation — With Special Regard to SMEs. With English summary.)', **13** *Zbornik Radova Ekonomskog Fakulteta Rijeka*, 479-496.

Hall, Mark A. and Columbo, John D. (1991), 'The Charitable Status of Nonprofit Hospitals: Toward a Donative Theory of Tax Exemption', **66** *Washington Law Review*, 307-411.

Hall, Robert E. (1991), 'Dividends, Capital Gains, and the Corporate Veil: Evidence from Britain, Canada, and the United States: Comment', in Bernheim, B. Douglas and

Shoven, John B. (eds), *National Saving and Economic Performance*, Chicago, University of Chicago Press, 71-73.

Halpem, Paul and Mintz, Jack M. (1992), 'Taxation and Its Impact on Market Structure', in Bird, R.M. and Mintz, J.M. (eds), *Taxation to 2000 and Beyond. Canadian Tax Paper*, Toronto, Canadian Tax Foundation, 214-256.

Halperin, Daniel I. (1992), 'Commentary, Will Integration Increase Efficiency? The Old and New View of Dividend Policy', **47** *Tax Law Review*, 645 ff.

Hamill, Susan, Pace (1995), 'The Taxation of Domestic Limited Liability Companies And Limited Partnerships: a Case For Eliminating The Partnership Classification Regulations', **73** *Washington United Law Quaterly*, 565 ff.

Hamill, Susan, Pace (1996), 'The Limited Liability Company: A Catalyst Exposing the Corporate Integration Question', **95** *Michigan Law Review*, 393 ff.

Hamilton, Bob, Shah, Anwar and Whalley, John (eds) (1986), *A Dynamic General Equilibrium Model for Corporate Tax Policy Evaluation in Canada*, Canada, Dept. of Finance.

Hammer, Richard, M. (1975), 'The Taxation of Income from Corporate Shareholders: Review of Present Systems in Canada, France, Germany, Japan and the UK', **28** *National Tax Journal*, 315 ff.

Hammer, Richard, M. (1979), 'Corporate/Shareholder Tax Integration', **33** *Bulletin for International Fiscal Documentation*, 290-292.

Han, Kim E., 'Optimal Capital Structure in Miller's Equilibrium', in Bhattacharya, S. and Constandtinides, G.M. (eds), *Financial Markets and Incomplete Information.*

Han, Kim E. (1978), 'A Mean-variance Theory of Optimal Captial Structure and Corporate Debt Capacity', **33** *Journal of Finance*, 45-63.

Haney, James, R. (1977), 'Integration of the Corporate and Individual Income Taxes', **3** *National Tax Journal*, 345-358.

Haney, James, R. (1979), 'Integration of Corporate and Individual Income Taxes', **33** *Bulletin for International Fiscal Documentation*, 298-305.

Hanka, Gordon, *The External Effects of Debt: A Back to Basics Evaluation of the Tax Incentive for Leverage.*

Hansmann, Henry (1981), 'The Rationale for Exempting Nonprofit Organizations from Corporate Income Taxation', **91** *Yale Law Journal*, 54 ff.

Harberger, Arnold, C. (1962), 'The Incidence of the Corporation Income Tax', **70** *Journal of Political Economy*, 215-240. Reprinted in Harberger, Arnold C. (1974), *Taxation and Welfare,* 135-62.

Harberger, Arnold, C. (1966), 'Efficiency Effects of Taxes on Income from Capital', in Krzyzaniak, Marian (ed.), *Effects of the Corporation Tax*, Detroit, Wayne State University Press. Reprinted in Harberg, Arnold C; (ed.) (1974), *Taxation and Welfare* 162-184.

Harberger, Arnold, C. (1980), 'Vignettes on the World Capital Market', **70** *American Economic Review*, 331 ff.

Harberger, Arnold, C. (1983), 'The State of the Corporate Income Tax: Who Pays? Should it be Repealed?', in Walker, Charles E. and Bloomfield, Mark A. (eds), *New Directions in Federal Tax Policy for the 1980's*, Cambridge, Ballinger Publishing Company.

Harberger, Arnold, C. (ed.) (1959), *The Corporation Income Tax: An Empirical Appraisal,* U.S. Congress House, Committee on Ways and Means, Tax Revision Compendium.

Hardman, Ann Louise (1992), 'Corporate Tax Reform: The Key to International Competitiveness', **25** *Vanderbilt Journal of Transnational Law*, 509 ff.

Harris, David, G., 'The Impact of US Law Revision on Multinational Corporation Decision Making', **31** *Journal of Accounting Research*, 111-140.

Harris, David, Morck, Randall, Slemrod, Joel and Yeung, Bernard (1993), 'Incoming Shifting in U.S. Multinational Corporations', 277-302.

Harris, M. and Raviv, Artur (1991), 'The Theory of Optinal Capital Structure', **48** *Journal of Finance*, 297-356.

Harris, Peter, A. (1994), 'Passing Corporate Foreign Tax Credits to Shareholders: Lessons from the UK's FID Scheme, Supreme Court of Queensland and of England & Wales', **11** *Australian Tax Forum*, 229-246.

Harris, Peter, A. (ed.) (1996), *Corporate/Shareholder Income Taxation and Allocating Taxinng Rights Between Countries: A Comparison of Imputation Systems*, Amsterdam, IBFD.

Harris, Richard A., Franks, Julian and Mayer, Colin (1987), *Means of Payment in Takeovers: The Results for the U.K. and U.S.*, National Bureau of Economic Research, Inc., 2456.

Hart, Kenneth, D. (ed.) (1987), 'Research and Development Impacts of Corporate Income Tax Reform: A Manuscript Report'.

Hartman, David, G. (1985), 'Tax Policy and Foreign Direct Investment', **26** *Journal of Public Economics*, 107-121.

Haskins, Matthew, P. (1995), 'The Theory and Politics of Tax Integration', **67** *Tax Notes*, 401 ff.

Hayn, Carla (1989), 'Tax Attributes as Determinants of Shareholder Gains in Corporate Acquisitions', **23** *Journal of Financial Economics*, 121 ff.

Head, John G. (1997), 'Company Tax Structure and Company Tax Incidence', **4** *International Tax and Public Finance*, 61-100. 'Company Tax Systems: From Theory to Policy' in Head, John G. and Krever, Richard (eds), *Company Tax Systems*, Australian Research Foundation, Conference Series No. 18 (1997)

Head, John G. and Krever, Richard (eds) (1997), *Company Tax Systems*, Australian Research Foundation, 18.

Heaton, Hal (1986), 'The Relative Yields on Taxable and Tax Exempt Debt', **18(4)** *Journal of Money, Credit, and Banking*, 482-494.

Heaton, Hal (1987), 'On the Bias of the Corporate Tax against High Risk Projects', **22(3)** *Journal of Financial and Quantitative Analysis*, 365-371.

Hein, Scott E., Koch, Timothy W. and MacDonald, S. Scott (1995), 'The Changing Role of Commercial Banks in the Municipal Securities Market', **27(3)** *Journal of Money, Credit, and Banking*, 894-906.

Hellerstein, Jerome R. (1957), 'Mergers, Taxes and Realism', **71** *Harvard Law Review*.

Hellerstein, Jerome R. (1959), 'Judicial Review of Property Tax Assessments', **14** *Tax Law Review*, 327-352.

Hellerstein, Walter (1980), 'State Income Taxation of Multijurisdictional Corporations: Reflections on Mobil, Exxon, and H.R.', **113** *Michigan Law Review*, 160 ff.

Hendershott, Patric H. (1991), 'The Long-Run Impact on Federal Tax Revenues and Capital Allocation of a Cut in the Capital Gains Tax Rate', **19(1)** *Public Finance Quarterly*, 3-21.

Hendershott, Patric H., Toder, H. and Won Yunhi (1991), 'Effects of Capital Gains Taxes on Revenue and Economic Efficiency', **44(1)** *National Tax Journal*, 21-40.

Hershberg, Susan (1979), 'Consolidated Returns: A Tax Policy Perspective', **27** *Canadian Tax Journal*, 552 ff.

Hicks, Samuel, Alton, *The Effect of Corporate Tax Incentives on the Horizontal Equity*.

Higgins, Mark, Marthew (ed.) (1989), *An Empirical Analysis of the Relationship Between Corporate Effective Tax Rates and Book Effective Tax Rates with an Analysis of the Financial Characteristics That Influence Corporate Effective Tax Rates*.

Higson, C. and Eliot, J. (1994), 'The Incentive to Locate a Multinational Firm: The Effect of Tax Reforms in the United Kingdom', **1** *International Tax and Public Finance*, 81-97.

Hines, James R., Jr (1994), 'Credit and Deferral as International Investment Incentives', **2** *Journal of Public Economics*, 323-347.

Hines, James R., Jr (1996), 'Altered States: Taxes and the Location of Foreign Direct Investment in America', **86** *American Economic Review*, 1076-1094.

Hines, James R., Jr (1997), 'Tax Policy and the Activities of Multinational Corporations', in Auerbach, Alan (ed.), *Fiscal Policy*, MIT Press.

Hines, James R., Jr and Hubbard, R. Glenn (1990), 'Coming Home to America: Dividend Repatriations by U.S. Multinationals', in Razin and Slemrod (eds), *Taxation in the Global Economy*, Chicago, University of Chicago Press, 161-207.

Hobbes, Patrick, E. (1995), 'Entity Classification: The One Hundred-year Debate', **44** *Catholic University Law Review*, 437 ff.

Hodder, James E. and Senbet, Lemma W. (1990), 'International Capital Structure Equilibrium', **45(5)** *Journal of Finance*, 1495-1516.

Holland, Daniel, M. (1975), 'Some Observations on Full Integration', **28** *National Tax Journal*, 353 ff.

Hong, Lee Fook (1989), '1989 Budget: Pro business or Pro family? Singapore', **43(6)** *Bulletin for International Fiscal Documentation*, 283-285.

Hong, Lee Fook (1990), '1900: Celebration Budget for a Maturing Nation: Singapore', **44(6)** *Bulletin for International Fiscal Documentation*, 273-276.

Hong, Lee Fook (1991), 'Singapore's 1991 Budget: A Successful Nation's Budget', **45(5)** *Bulletin for International Fiscal Documentation*, 211-213.

Hong, Lee Fook (1992), '1992 Budget: A Carry on Budget with a Few Surprises: Singapore', **46(5)** *Bulletin for International Fiscal Documentation*, 254-256.

Horst, Thomas, 'A Note on Optimal Raxation of International Investment Income Quarterly', **94** *Journal of Economics*, 793-799.

Horst, Thomas (1982), 'Some Issues in the Calculation and Uses of Effective Corporate Income Tax Rates', *Tax Notes*, 347-351.

Howitt, Peter and Sinn, Hans-Werner (1989), 'Gradual Reforms of Capital Income Taxation', **79** *American Economic Review*, 106-124.

Hreha, Karen, S. and Silhan, Peter, A. (1986), 'An Empirical Analysis of Unitary Apportionment', *Journal of the American Taxation Association*, 7-18.

Hubbard, Jeff and Michaely, Roni (1997), 'Do Investors Ignore Dividend Taxation? A Reexamination of the Citizens Utilities Case', **32** *Journal of Financial and Quantitative Analysis*, 117-135.

Hubbard, R. Glenn (1990), *Asymmetric Information, Corporate Finance and Investment*, Chicago.

Hubbard, R. Glenn (1993), 'Corporate Tax Integration: A View from the Treasury Department', **7(1)** *Journal of Economic Perspectives*, 115-132.

Hubbard, R. Glenn and Reiss, Peter C. (1989), 'Corporate Payouts and the Tax Price of Corporate Retentions: Evidence from the Undistributed Profits Tax of 1936-1938'.

Huber, Bernd (1994), 'Dividend Taxes and Investment', **51** *Finanzarchiv*, 457-471.

Hufbauer, Gary, C. (ed.) (1992), *U.S. Taxation of International Income*.

Huizinga, Harry (1992), 'The Tax Treatment of R&D; Expenditures of Multinational Enterprises', **47(3)** *Journal of Public Economics*, 343-359.

Hulten, Charles R. and Robertson, James, W. (1982), *Corporate Tax Policy and Economic Growth: An Analysis of the 1981 and 1982 Tax Acts*, Washington, DC, Urban Institute.

Institute For Fiscal Studies (1991), *Equity for Companies: A Corporation Tax for the 1990s*, Fourth Report of the IFS Capital Taxes Group, 26.

International Fiscal Association (1987), 'The Fiscal Residence of Companies: La Residence Fiscale Des Societes: Die Steuerliche Ansassigkeit von Kapitalgesellschaften: La Residencia Fiscal De Las Sociedades', in Cahiers de Droit Fiscal International.

International Fiscal Association (1987), *Tax Problems of the Liquidation of Corporations: Regime de liquidation des societes: Steuerliche Probleme der Liquidation von Korperschaften: Problemas fiscales de la liquidacion de sociedades*.

International Fiscal Association (1992), 'Tax Consequences of International Acquisitions and Business Combinations - Consequences fiscales des acquisitions et regroupements internationaux d'entreprises', in Cahiers de Droit Fiscal International.

International Fiscal Association (1992), 'Transfer Pricing in the Absence of Comparable Market Prices - Determination des prix de transfert en l'absence de prix de marche camparables', in Cahiers de Droit Fiscal International.

International Fiscal Association (1993), 'Corporate Tax on Distributions (Equalization Tax)', *Proceedings of the 47th Congress of the International Fiscal Association*.

International Fiscal Association (ed.) (1993), 'Interpretation of Double Taxation Conventions', **78a** in Cahiers de Droit Fiscal International.

Iqbal, Mahmood (1994), 'A Corporate Tax Comparison for Canada, the United States and Mexico', **3(1)** *Canadian Business Economics*, 54-64.

Isaac, John (1989), 'Corporate Tax Harmonisation', in Gammie, Malcolm, Robinson, Bill and Fitchew Geoffrey, *Beyond 1992: A European Tax System: Proceedings of the Fourth Institute for Fiscal Studies Residential Conference*, Oxford.

Isaac, John (1997), 'A Comment on the Viability of the Allowance for Corporate Equity', **18** *Fiscal Studies*, 303-318.

Isard, Peter (1990), 'Corporate Tax Harmonization and European Monetary Integration', **43(1)** *Kyklos*, 3-24.

Isenbergh, Joseph (1988), 'Perspectives on the Deferral of United States Taxation of the Earnings of Foreign Corporations', *Taxes*, 1062 ff.

Iwamoto, Yasushi (1992), 'Effective Tax Rates and Tobin's q', **48** *Journal of Public Economics*, 225-237.

Jaffe, Jeffrey F. (1978a), 'Corporate Taxes, Inflation, the Rate of Interest, and the Return to Equity', **13** *Journal of Financial and Quantitative Analysis*, 55-64.

Jaffe, Jeffrey F. (1978b), 'A Note on Taxation and Investment', **33** *Journal of Finance*, 1439-1445.

Jaffe, Jeffrey F. (1991), 'Taxes and the Capital Structure of Partnerships, REIT's, and Related Entities', **46** *Journal of Finance*, 401-407.

Jaffe, Jeffrey F. and Westerfield, Randolph (1984), 'Leverage and the Value of a Firm under a Progressive Income Tax: A Correction and Extension', **8** *Journal of Banking and Finance*, 491-494.

Janeba, Eckhard (1995), 'Corporate Income Tax Competition, Double Taxation Treaties, and Foreign Direct Investment', **56(2)** *Journal of Public Economics*, 311-325.

Janeba, Eckhard (ed.), *Corporate Income Tax Competition, Double Taxation Treaties, and Foreign Direct Investment*, Department of Economics, University of Bonn, A-36.1.

Jassy, B. (1974), 'Treatment of Bootstrap Stock Acquisitions: The Redemption Route vs. Dividend Route', **87** *Harvard Law Review*, 1459 ff.

Jeffcote, Bernard (ed.) (1993), *The Developing European Corporate Tax System*.

Jensen, Michael C. (1986), 'Agency Costs of Free Cash Flow, Corporate Finance, and Takeovers', **32** *American Economic Review*, 323 ff.

Jensen, Michael C. (1988), 'The Takeover Controversy: Analysis and Evidence', in Coffee, John, Lowenstein, Louis and Rose-Ackerman, Susan (eds), *Knights, Raiders and Targets: The Impact of the Hostile Takeover*, Oxford, Oxford University Press.

Jensen, Michael C. and Meckling, W. (1976), 'Theory of the Firm: Managerial Behavior, Agency Costs and Ownership Structures', **3** *Journal of Financial Economics*, 305-360.

Jensen, Michael C., Kaplan, Steven N. and Stiglin, Laura (1989), 'The Effects of LBOs on Tax Revenues of the U.S. Treasury', **42** *Tax Notes*, 727 ff.

Jensen, Ronald, H. (1991), 'Of Form and Substance: Tax Free Incorporations and Other Transactions Under Section 351', **11** *Virginia Tax Review*, 349 ff.

Jones, David D. (1979), 'Corporations, Double Taxation and the Theory of Integration', **27** *Canadian Tax Journal*, 405 ff.

Jones, Robert (1991), 'The Effective Taxation of Australian Corporate Source Income', in Hamilton, Clive (ed.), *The Economic Dynamics of Australian Industry*, Sydney, Allen and Unwin, distributed by Paull, Concord, Mass., 196-215.

Jones, Shirley, A. (1994), 'The Evolution of the Corporate Minimum Tax', **20** *Journal of Corporate Taxation*, 351 ff.

Jun, Joosung (1995), *The Impact of International Tax Rules on the Cost of Capital*.

Kalambokidis, Laura (ed.) (1992), *What Is Being Taxed?: A Test for the Existence of Excess Profit in the Corporate Income Tax Base*, University of Michigan.

Kale, Jayant R. and Noe, Thomas H. (1990), 'Corporate Hedging under Personal and Corporate Taxation', **11(3)** *Managerial and Decision Economics*, 199-205.

Kale, Jayant R. and Noe, Thomas H. (1992), 'Taxes, Financial Distress, and Corporate Capital Structure', **32(1)** *Quarterly Review of Economics and Finance*, 71-83.

Kale, Jayant R., Noe, Thomas H. and Ramirez, Gabriel G. (1991), 'The Effect of Business Risk on Corporate Capital Structure: Theory and Evidence', **46(5)** *Journal of Finance*, 1693-1715.

Kanda, Hideki and Levmore, Saul (1991), 'Taxes, Agency Costs, and the Price of Incorporation', **77** *Virginia Law Review*, 211-256.

Kanniainen, Vesa and Sodersten, Jan (1994), 'Costs of Monitoring and Corporate Taxation', **55** *Journal of Public Economics*, 307-321.

Kanniainen, Vesa and Sodersten, Jan (1995), 'The Importance of Reporting Conventions for the Theory of Corporate Taxation', **57** *Journal of Public Economics*, 417-430.

Kaplan, Steven E. (1989), 'Management Buyouts: Evidence on Taxes as a Source of Value', **44** *Journal of Finance*, 611-632.

Karier, Thomas (1991), 'A Proposal to Restore the Corporate Profit Tax', **49(2)** *Review of Social Economy*, 141-167.

Kassanen, Eero (1992), *Sensitivity of Dividend Decisions to Corporate Tax Reform: Empirical Test with Aggregate Data of Finnish Firms*, Felsingin Kauppakorkoulu, 1235-5674.

Keen, Michael (1993), 'Corporation Tax, Foreign Direct Investment and the Single Market in European Integration', in Winters, L., Venables, Alan and Anthony J (eds), *Trade and Industry*, Cambridge, Cambridge University Press, 165-198.

Keen, Michael and Shiantarelli, Fabio (eds) (1991), 'Corporation Tax Asymmetries and Optimal Financial Policy', **43** *Oxford Economic Papers*, 280-291.

Keller, Robert R. (1985), 'The Tax Effects of a Shareholder's Post-Incorporation Sale of Stock: A Reappraisal', **2** *Tax Law Journal*, 107-111.

Kiefer, Donald W. (1973), 'The 1973 Tax Package: Corporate Tax Restructuring', **48** *Indiana Business Review*, 1-2.

Kiefer, Donald W. (1990), 'Lock-In Effect Within a Simple Model of Corporate Stock Trading', **53** *National Tax Journal.*

Kimbrough, Kent P. (1984), 'The Corporation Income Tax in the Open Economy', **25** *International Economic Review*, 391-407.

King, Mervyn A. (1971), 'Corporate Taxation and Dividend Behavior: A Comment', *Review of Economic Studies*, 377 ff.

King, Mervyn A. (1972), 'Corporate Taxation and Dividend Behavior: a Further Comment', **39** *Review of Economic Studies*, 231 ff.

King, Mervyn A. (1974a), 'Dividend Behavior and the Theory of the Firm', **41** *Economica*, 25-34.

King, Mervyn A. (1974b), 'Taxation and the Cost of Capital', **41** *Review of Economic Studies*, 21-35.

King, Mervyn A. (1975), 'Taxation, Corporate Financial Policy, and the Cost of Capital: A Comment', **4** *Journal of Public Economics*, 271 ff.

King, Mervyn A. (ed.) (1977), *Public Policy and the Corporation*, London, Chapman and Hall.

King, Mervyn A. (1987), 'The Cash Flow Corporate Income Tax', in Feldstein, M. (ed.), *The Effects of Taxation on Capital Accumulation*, Chicago, University of Chicago Press.

King, Mervyn A. and Fullerton, David J. (eds) (1984), *The Taxation of Income from Capital: A Comparative Study of the US, UK, Sweden, and West Germany*, Chicago.

Kingson, Charles I. (1976), 'The Deep Structure of Taxation: Dividend Distributions', **85** *Yale Law Journal*, 861 ff.

Kingson, Charles I. (1991), 'The Foreign Tax Credit and its Critics', **9** *American Jounal of Tax Policy*, 1 ff.

Klassen, Kenneth, Lang, Mark and Wolfson, Alan (1993), 'Geographic Income Shifting by Multinational Corporations in Response to Tax Rate Changes', *Journal of Accounting Research*, 141-173.

Klein (1972), 'Income Taxation and Legal Entities', **20** *UCLA Law Review*, 13 ff.

Klein, William A. (1965), 'The Incidence of the Corporation Income Tax: A Lawyer's View of a Problem in Economics', *Wisconsin Law Review*, 576 ff.

Klein, William A. and Zolt, Eric M. (1995), 'Business Form, Limited Liability, and Tax Regimes: Lurching Toward a Coherent Outcome', **66** *UCLA Law Review*, 1001-1041.

Knauer, Nancy J. (1994), 'The Paradox of Corporate Giving: Tax Expenditures, the Nature of the Corporation, and the Social Construction of Charity', **44** *DePaul Law Review*, 1 ff.

Knoll, Michael S. (1993), 'Taxing Prometheus: How the Corporate Interest Deduction Discourages Innovation and Risk-taking', **38** *Villanova Law Review*, 1461 ff.

Knoll, Michael S. (1996), 'An Accretion Corporate Income Tax', **49** *Stanford Law Review*, 1 ff.

Konrad, Kai A. (1991), 'The Decision to Go Public, Accrued Capital Gains and Taxation', **37** *Economics Letters*, 439-445.

Kopcke, Richard W. and Rosengren, Eric S. (1989), 'Are the Distinctions Between Debt and Equity Disappearing?: An Overview'.

Kopcke, Richard W. and Rosengren, Eric S. (eds) (1989), 'Regulation of debt and equity', Proceedings of a conference held at Melvin Village, New Hampshire.

Kornhauser, Marjorie E. (1990), 'Corporate Regulation and the Origins of the Corporate Income Tax', **66** *Industrial Law Journal*, 53 ff.

Kose John and Senbet, Lemma W. (1989), *Limited Liability, Tax Deductibility of Corporate Debt, and Public Policy*, Salomon Brothers Center for the Study of Financial Institutions, 544.

Kose, John (1987), 'Risk-Shifting Incentives and Signaling Through Corporate Capital Structure', **42** *Journal of Finance*, 623 ff.

Kose, John and Williams, Joseph (1985), 'Dividends, Dilution and Taxes: A Signalling Equilibrium', **40** *Journal of Finance*, 1053-1070.

Kose, John, Teresa, A. and Ronen, Joshua (1996), 'Corporate Taxes, Choice among Accounting Alternatives, and Information Content of Earnings', **11** *Journal of Accounting, Auditing and Finance*, 163-183.

Kose, John, Senbet, Lemma W. and Sundaram, Anant (1994), 'Corporate Limited Liability and the Design of Corporate Taxation'.

Krause-Junk, Gerold (1988), 'Uberlegungen zu einem Kunftigen Europaischen Korperschaftsteuersystem', **34** *Konjunkturpolitik*, 268-290.

Krueger, LaVern Eldon (ed.) (1974), *The Value Added Tax Compared to the Corporate Income Tax: Effects on Capital Formation*, Colorado, Coen Lecture, University Of Colorado Law School.

Krzyzaniak, Marian (ed.) (1966), *Effects of the Corporation Income Tax*, Wayne State University.

Krzyzaniak, Marian and Musgrave, Richard A. (eds) (1963), *The Shifting of the Corporation Income Tax*, Baltimore, MD, John Hopkins University Press.

Kurtz, Jerome (1992), 'The Limited Liability Company and the Future of Business Taxation: A Comment on Professor Berger's Plan', **47** *Tax Law Review*, 815 ff.

Kwall, Jeffrey L. (1990), 'The Uncertain Case Against the Double Taxation of Corporate Income', **68** *Law Review*, 613 ff.

Kwall, Jeffrey L. (1997), 'Taxing Private Enterprise in the New Millenium', **51** *Tax Lawyer*, 229 ff.

Kweit, Catherine and Rubin, Marilyn M. (1982), 'Impact of the Economic Recovery Tax Act on State and Local Revenues: A Case Study of New York City Corporate Tax Revenues', **35(3)** *National Tax Journal*, 295-306.

Lakonishok, Josef and Baruch, Lev (1987), 'Stock Splits and Stock Dividends: Why, Who, and When', **42** *Journal of Finance*, 913 ff.

Lall, Vinay D. (1983), *Fiscal Incentives and Corporate Tax Saving*, New Dehli, National Institute of Public Finance and Policy.

Lall, Vinay D. (ed.) (1984), *Economic Effects of the Corporate Profits Tax*, New Dehli, National Institute of Public Finance and Policy.

Lamoureux, Christopher G. and Poon, Percy (1987), 'The Market Reaction to Stock Splits', **42** *Journal of Finance*, 1347 ff.

Lander, Joel Martin (1989), *Optimal Taxation Policies Which Affect Capital Structure*, Law and Economics Workshop, UCLA Economics Dept..

Lander, Joel Martin (ed.) (1990), *Essays on the Corporate Tax Policy Effects on Investments and Financing Choices*, UCLA.

Langbein, Stanley I. (1986), 'The Unitary Method and the Myth of Arm's Length', **30** *Tax Notes*, 625 ff.

Lapidoth, Arye (1990), 'The 1990 Israeli Tax Reform: Israel', **44(12)** *Bulletin for International Fiscal Documentation*, 609-610.

Laramie, Anthony J., *The Incidence of the Corporate Profits Tax Revisited: A Post Keynesian Approach, Bard College*, Jerome Levy Economics Institute, 109.

Laumas, G.S. (1971), 'The Effectiveness of Corporate Tax Increases as an Anti inflationary Policy', **30(4)** *American Journal of Economics and Sociology*, 397-402.

Leauby, Bruce Alan (ed.) (1990), *Determinants of Corporate Tax Avoidance Strategy: an Empirical Analysis*, Drexel University.

LeClere, Marc J. (1993), 'Commonality among Alternative Measures of Corporate Effective Tax Rates', in Stern, Jerrold J. (ed.), *Advances in Taxation. Volume 4*, Greenwich, CT, JAI Press, 175-195.

Lee, Dwight R. (ed.) (1986), *Taxation and the Deficit Economy: Fiscal Policy and Capital Formation in the United States*, - San Francisco, Pacific Research Institute for Public Policy, 554 p.

Lee, John W. (1988), 'Entity Classification and Integration: Publicly Traded Partnerships, Personal Service Corporations, and the Tax Legislative Process', **8** *Virginia. Tax Review*, 57 ff.

Leechor, Chad and Mintz, Jack M. (1993), 'On the Taxation of Multinational Corporate Investment When the Deferral Method is Used by the Capital Exporting Country', **51(1)** *Journal of Public Economics*, 75-96.

Lehn, Kenneth and Poulsen, Annette B. (1987), *Sources of Value in Leveraged Buyouts*.

Lenhardt, Ingrid Lynn (1996), 'Limited Liability Companies: The Corporate and Tax Advantages of a Limited Liability Company: A German Perspective', **64** *University of Cincinatti Law Review*, 551 ff.

Lent, George E. (1948), *The Impact of the Undistributed Porfits Tax*, Columbia University Press, 1936-1937.

Levinsohn, James and Slemrod, Joel (1993), 'Taxes, Tariffs, and the Global Corporation', **97** *Journal of Public Economics*, 116 ff.

Levis, Mario (1986), 'The 1984 Budget: The Impact on Corporate Tax Payments', **0(0)** *National Westminster Bank Quarterly Review*, 28-42.

Levmore, Saul (1982), 'Identifying Section 306 Stock: The Sleeping Beauty of Revenue Ruling 66-332', **2** *Virginia Tax Review*, 59-78.

Levmore, Saul (1987), 'The Positive Role of Tax Law in Corporate and Capital Markets', **12** *Journal of Corporation Law*, 483-502.

Levmore, Saul (1988), 'Recharacterizations and the Nature of Theory in Corporate Tax Law', **136** *University of Pennsylvania Journal Law Review*, 1019-1065.

Levmore, Saul (1992), 'Partnerships, Limited Liability Companies, and Taxes: A Comment on the Survival of Organizational Forms', **70** *Washington University Law Quarterly (Symposium Comment)*, 489-495.

Lewellen, Wilbur G. and Mauer, David C. (1988), *Tax Options and Corporate Capital Structures*, Graduate School of Business, University of Wisconsin-Madison Wisconsin, 1-88-4.

Lintner, John V. (1956), 'The Distribution of Incomes of Corporations among Dividends, Retained Earnings, and Taxes', **46** *American Economic Review*, 97-113.

Litzenberger, Robert H. and Ramaswamy, K. (1979), 'The Effect of Personal Taxes and Dividends on Capital Asset Prices: Theory and Empirical Evidence', **7** *Journal of Financial Economics*, 163-195.

Litzenberger, Robert H. and Ramaswamy, K. (1982), 'The Effects of Dividends on Common Stock Prices: Tax Effects or Information Effects', **37** *Journal of Finance*, 429-443.

Litzenberger, Robert H. and Van Horne, James C. (1978), 'Elimination of the Double Taxation of Dividends and Corporate Financial Policy', **33** *Journal of Finance*, 737 ff.

Livingston, John (1993), 'Corporate Tax Integration in the United States: A Review of the Treasury's Integration Study', **58** *Modern Law Review*, 717 ff.

Long, Michael S. and Malitz, Ileen B. (1985), 'Investment Patterns and Financial Leverage', in Friedman, Benjamin (ed.), *Financing Corporate Capital Formation*, Chicago, University of Chicago Press.

Lowenstein, Louis K. (1985), 'Management Buyouts', **85** *Columbia Law Review*, 730 ff.

Ludwig, Matthias (ed.) (1993), *A Proposal for a Reform of the U.S. Corporate Income Tax System on the Basis of the Experiences with the Tax System of the Federal Republic of Germany*, American Graduate School of International Management.

Luscombe, Mark A. (1995), 'The Transformation of Entity Classification', **73** *Taxes*, 562 ff.

Lustig, Eric A. (1988), 'The Emerging Role of the Federal Tax Law in Regulating Hostile Corporate Takeover Defenses: The New Section 5881 Excise Tax on Greenmail', **40** *University of Florida Law Review*, 825-827.

Lynch, Howell Jackson, Jr (ed.) (1991), *Effective Corporate Income Tax Rates and Their Relationship to Corporate Attributes: A Multidefinitional, Multiperiod View*, Texas, A&M University.

Lyon, Andrew B.R. (ed.) (1986), *How Do Stock Prices Change When Corporate Tax Laws Change?: An Empirical Analysis of the Effect of Tax Laws on the Value of the Firm*, Princeton University.

Lyon, Andrew B.R. (1990), 'Investment Incentives under the Alternative Minimum Tax', **43** *National Tax Journal*, 451-465.

Lyon, Andrew B.R. (1992), 'Tax Neutrality under Parallel Tax Systems', **20** *Public Finance Quarterly*, 338-358.

Lyon, Andrew B.R. (ed.) (1997), *Cracking the Code: Making Sense of the Corporate Alternative Minimum Tax*, Washington, DC, Brookings Institution.

Lyon, Andrew B.R. and Silverstein, Gerald (1995), 'The Alternative Minimum Tax and the Behavior of Multinational Corporations', in Feldstein, M., Hines, J.R. Jr and Hubbard, R.G. (eds), *The Effects of Taxation on Multinational Corporations*, Chicago: University of Chicago Press, 153-177.

MacKie Mason, Jeffrey K. (1990), 'Do Taxes Affect Corporate Financing Decisions?', **45** *Journal of Finance*, 1471 ff.

MacKie Mason, Jeffrey K. and Gordon, Roger H. (1997), 'How Much Do Taxes Discourage Incorporation?', **52** *Journal of Finance*, 2 ff.

Majd, Saman and Myers, Stewart C. (1987), 'Tax Asymmetries and Corporate Tax Reform', in Feldstein, M. (ed.), *The Effects of Taxation on Capital Accumulation*, Chicago, University of Chicago Press.

Maksimovic, Vojislav and Zechner, Josef (1991), 'Debt, Agency Costs, and Industry Equilibrium', **46(5)** *Journal of Finance*, 1619-1643.

Malcomson, James M. (1981), 'Corporate Tax Policy and the Service Life of Capital Equipment', **48(2)** *Review of Economic Studies*, 311-316.

Mansfield, Edwin (1986), 'The R&D; Tax Credit and Other Technology Policy Issues', **76** *American Economic Review. Papers and Proceedings*, 191-197.

Mansoorian, Arman (1995), 'Budget Deficits, Corporate Income Taxes, and the Current Account', **27** *Journal of Money, Credit, and Banking*, 378-388.

Marovelli, Forrest D. and Moser, Beth (eds) (1990), *Effective Corporate Tax Rates: 1980-84*, Tax Analysts.

Marsh, Paul (1982), 'The Choice Between Equity and Debt: An Empirical Study', **37** *Journal of Finance*, 121 ff.

Martin, Cathie Jo (1989), 'Business Influence and State Power: The Case of U.S. Corporate Tax Policy', **17** *Politics and Society*.

Martin, Cathie Jo (1993), 'Growth Strategies and Corporate Taxation: Politics as Cause and Effect', in Post, James E. (ed.), *Research in Corporate Social Performance and Policy. A Research Annual*, Greenwich, Conn. and London, JAI Press, 57-76.

Martin, Cathie Jo (ed.) (1991), *Shifting the Burden: the Struggle over Growth and Corporate Taxation. American Politics and Political Economy Series Chicago and London*, Chicago, University of Chicago Press.

Masulis, Ronald W. and Trueman, B. (1988), 'Corporate Investment and Dividend Decsions under Differential Personal Taxation', **23** *Journal of Financial and Quantitative Analysis*, 369-385.

Maule, James Edward (1982), 'The Effect of Federal Income Tax Integration on State Tax Systems', *Tax Notes*, 99 ff.

Mavraganis, George (1993), 'Corporate Income Tax Harmonization in the Nineties: European Community', **47(4)** *Bulletin for International Fiscal Documentation*, 220-225.

Mayer, Colin (1986), 'Corporation Tax, Finance and the Cost of Capital', **153** *Review of Economic Studies*, 93 ff.

McClure, Charles E., Jr (1975), 'The Case for Integrating the Income Taxes', **28** *National Tax Journal*, 257-258.

McCutcheon, Maeve (1995), 'The Tax Incentives Applying to US Corporate Investment in Ireland', **26(2)** *Economic and Social Review*, 149-171.

McFetridge, Donald G. (1992), 'Taxation and Its Impact on Market Structure: Comment', in Bird, R.M. and Mintz, J.M. (eds), *Taxation to 2000 and Beyond. Canadian Tax Paper*, Toronto, Canadian Tax Foundation, 263-268.

McGee, Robert W. (1975), 'Investment Credit for Progress Expenditures Using Phase-In Rule', *Taxation for Accountants*, 250-251.

McGee, Robert W. (1976a), 'Tax Impact of Debt v. Equity Financing', *Taxes*, 110-116.

McGee, Robert W. (1976b), 'How to Handle Corporate Obligations that Are Issued at a Discount or Premium', *Monthly Digest of Tax Articles*, 64-69.

McGee, Robert W. (1976c), 'The New Imputed Interest Rules: How They Work', *The Practical Accountant*, 63-67.

McGee, Robert W. (1976d), 'How to Handle Corporate Obligations That Are Issued at a Discount or Premium', *Taxation for Accountants*, 48-50. Reprinted inThe Monthly Digest of Tax Articles, 1976, 64-69.

McGee, Robert W. (1977), 'Planning a Tax-Free Corporate Reorganization: Selecting the One Best Suite to a Client's Needs', *Taxation for Lawyers*, 36-41.

McGee, Robert W. (1983), 'Deferred Taxation', *Bibliography, National Association of Accountants*.

McGee, Robert W. (1984a), *The History of the Income Tax in the United States*, Occasional Paper, Deakin University, Australia, No. 69.

McGee, Robert W. (1984b), 'Loophole of the Month', *CPA Digest*, 4 ff.

McGee, Robert W. (1984c), 'Software Taxation: A New NAA Research Study', *Management Accounting*, 7071-7077.

McGee, Robert W. (1984d), 'The Growth of the Deferred Tax Account', *Management Accounting*, 18 ff.

McGee, Robert W. (1985a), *A Summary of Deferred Income Tax Studies Conducted in the United States and Canada*, Occasional Paper, Deakin University, Australia, No. 74.

McGee, Robert W. (1985b), *Accounting for Software*, Dow Jones Irwin, 168 p.

McGee, Robert W. (1985c), 'Developing Computer Technology With the Research Credit', *The Practical Lawyer*, 13-24.

McGee, Robert W. (1985d), 'The 1985 Tax Simplification Act', **1** *Business Planning*, 14-17.

McGee, Robert W. (1985e), 'Keeping Track of Fringe Benefits ... When To Tax and When Not To Tax', **1** *Controllers Quarterly*, 24-27.

McGee, Robert W. (1985f), 'New IRS Regs on Company Cars Raise Taxes ... And Tempers', **1** *Controllers Quarterly*, 25-27.

McGee, Robert W. (1985g), 'Computer Software and the Investment Tax Credit', **5** *Computer Law Journal*, 347-362. Reprinted in *Accounting and Tax Aspects of Computer Software Manufacturing*, Praeger Publishing Company, 1987. Reprinted in *The Monthly Digest of Tax Articles*, 1985, 6-21.

McGee, Robert W. (1985h), 'Computer Software and the Research Credit', **5** *Computer Law Journal*, 363-378. Reprinted in *The Monthly Digest of Tax Articles*, 1985, 6-21; *Accounting and Tax Aspects of Computer Software Manufacturing*, Praeger Publishing Company, 1987.

McGee, Robert W. (1985i), 'Financial and Tax Accounting for Computer Software', **7** *Western New England Law Review*, 651-704. Reprinted in *Accounting for Data Processing Department Costs*, Greenwood Press, 1988.

McGee, Robert W. (1985j), *A Guide To VEBAs and Funded Welfare Benefite Plans*, New Jersey, Prentice Hall, 32 p.

McGee, Robert W. (1985k), *Employee Stock Ownership Plans: A guide te ESOPs Under The Latest Rules*, New Jersey, Prentice Hall, 44 p.

McGee, Robert W. (1986a), *Capital Gains and Losses, Alternative Minimum Tax, Accounting Provisions, Prentice-Hall's Explanation of the Tax Reform Act of 1986*, New Jersey, Prentice Hall, 500 p.

McGee, Robert W. (1986b), *How Tax Reform Would Affect Profit-Sharing*, New Jersey, Prentice Hall, 23 p.

McGee, Robert W. (1986c), *The Corporate Alternative Minimum Tax*, National Association of Accountants.

McGee, Robert W. (1986d), *Tax-Wise Executive Comensation Strategies*, New Jersey, Prentice Hall, 44 p.

McGee, Robert W. (1986e), *International Revenue Service Special Enrollment Examination Questions and Answers*, New Jersey, Prentice Hall, 59 p.

McGee, Robert W. (1986f), *How the New Tax Law Affects Business*, - National Association of Accountants.

McGee, Robert W. (1987), *Accounting and Tax Aspects of Computer Software Manufacturing*, Praeger Publishing Company, 162 p.

McGee, Robert W. (1996a), *Essays on Accounting, Taxation and Public Finance*, Dumont Institute for Public Policy Research. http:/ww.hili.com~dumontin

McGee, Robert W. (1996b), *Taxation, Ethics and Public Policy*, Dumont Institute for Public Policy Research. http:/ww.hili.com~dumontin

McIntyre, Michael J. (1986), 'Toward a Fairer and Less Complicated Foreign Tax Credit System', *Tax Notes*, 1269 ff.

McIntyre, Michael J. (1989), *The International Income Tax Rules of the United States*. 1995

McIntyre, Michael J. (1996), 'Separate Basket Limitations in Theory and in Practice', *Tax Notes*.

McIntyre, Robert S. and Folen, Robert (1984), *Corporate Income Taxes in the Reagan Years*, Washington DC, Ciitizens for Tax Justice.

McIntyre, Robert S. and Wilhelm, David (eds) (1986), 'Money for Nothing: The Failure of Corporate Tax Incentives 1981-84'.

McKenzie, Kenneth J. (1994), 'The Implications of Risk and Irreversibility for the Measurement of Marginal Effective Tax Rates on Capital', **27(3)** *Canadian Journal of Economics*, 604-619.

McKenzie, Kenneth J. and Mintz, Jack M. (1992), 'Tax Effects on the Cost of Capital', in Shoven, John B. and Whalley, John (eds), *Canada-U.S. Tax Comparisons. A National Bureau of Economic Research Project Report*, Chicago, University of Chicago Press, 189-216.

McLure, Charles E., Jr (1975a), 'The Case for Integrating the Income Taxes', **28** *National Tax Journal*, 255 ff.

McLure, Charles E., Jr (1975b), 'Integration of the Personal and Corporate Income Taxes: The Missing Element in Recent Tax Reform Proposals', **88** *Harvard Law Review*, 532 ff.

McLure, Charles E., Jr (1976), 'Integration of the Income Taxes: Why and How', **2** *Journal of Corporate Taxation*, 458 ff.

McLure, Charles E., Jr (1977), 'Integrating the Income Taxes: How to Do it Right', *Tax Notes*, 3 ff.

McLure, Charles E., Jr (1978), 'A Status Report on Tax Integration in the United States', **31** *National Tax Journal*, 313 ff.

McLure, Charles E., Jr (1980), 'International Aspects of Dividend Relief', **7** *Journal of Corporate Taxation*, 137 ff.

McLure, Charles E., Jr (1980), 'The State Corporate Income Tax: Lambs in Wolves' Clothing', in Aaron, Henry, J. And Boskins, Michael J. (eds), *The Economics of Taxation*, Washington, Brookings Institution, 345 ff.

McLure, Charles E., Jr (1981), 'The Elusive Incidence of the Corporate Income Tax: The State Case', **9** *Public Finance Quarterly*, 4 ff.

McLure, Charles E., Jr (1984), 'Corporate Income Tax: Restoration, Integration, or Elimination?', in Moore, J. (ed.), *To Promote Prosperity: U.S. Domestic Policy in the Mid-1980s*, 303-318.

McLure, Charles E., Jr (1989), 'European Integration and Taxation of Corporate Income at Source: Lessons from the U.S.', in Gammie, Malcolm, Robinson, Bill and Fitchew Geoffrey., *Beyond 1992: A European Tax System: Proceedings of the Fourth Institute for Fiscal Studies Residential Conference*, Oxford.

McLure, Charles E., Jr (ed.) (1979), *Must Corporate Income be Taxed Twice?*, Washington, Brookings Institution.

McLure, Charles E., Jr (ed.) (1984), *The State Corporation Income Tax : Issues in Worldwide Unitary Combination*, Stanford, Hoover Institute Press, Stanford University.

McLure, Charles E., Jr (ed.) (1986), 'Economic Perspectives on State Taxation of Multijurisdictional Corporations'.

McLure, Charles E., Jr and Mieszkowski, Peter (1983), 'Tax Exporting and the Commerce Clause', in McLure, Charles, E., Jr and Mieszkowski, Peter (eds), *Fiscal Federalism and the Taxation of Natural Resources*, 169 ff.

McLure, Charles E., Jr and Surrey, Stanley S. (1977), 'Integration of Income Taxes - Issues for Debate', **55** *Harvard Business Review*, 169 ff.

McLure, Charles E., Jr, Mutti, Jack, Thuronyi, Victor and Zodrow, George R. (eds) (1990), *The Taxation of Income From Business and Capital in Colombia*, Chapel Hill, Duke University.

McNulty, John K. (1983), 'Integrating the Corporate Income Tax?', **31** *American Journal of Comparative Law*, 661-666.

McNulty, John K. (1990), 'Reform of the Individual Income Tax by Integration of the Corporate Income Tax', **46** *Tax Notes*, 1445 ff.

McNulty, John K. (1992), 'Commentary, Preserving the Virtues of Subchapter S in an Integrated World', **47** *Tax Law Review*, 681 ff.

McNulty, John K. (1994), 'Corporate Income Tax Reform in the United States: Proposals for Integration of the Corporate and Individual Income Taxes, and International Aspects', **12** *International Tax & Business Lawyer*, 161 ff.

Meade, James E. (ed.) (1978), *The Taxation of Corporate Reorganizations: How Are We Doing So Far?*, London, Allen and Unwin.

Meier, Donald L. (1991), 'Europe in 1992: A U.S. Tax Perspective, Sara Lee Corporation', **45** *Bulletin for International Fiscal Documentation*, 328-331.

Merski, Paul G. (ed.) (1990), *The Corporate Tax Burden*, Washington, DC, Brookings Institution.

Michaely, Roni (1991), 'Ex-dividend Day Stock Price Behavior: The Case of the 1986 Tax Reform Act', **46** *Journal of Finance*, 845-859.

Michaely, Roni and Murgia, Maurizio (1995), 'The Effect of Tax Heterogeneity on Prices and Volume around the Ex-dividend Day: Evidence from the Milan Stock Exchange', **8** *Review of Financial Studies*, 369-399.

Michaely, Roni and Murgia, Maurizio (1997), 'Fiscalita e Mercato Azionario: Come Interpretare lo Stacco dei Dividendi dei Titoli Italiani? (Dividends and Taxes in the Italian Stock Market. Evidence from the Ex-Dividend Day Behavior)', **13** *Politica Economica*, 117-152.

Mieszkowski, Peter M., 'Integration of the Corporate and Personal Income Taxes: The Bogus Issue of Shifting', **31** *Finanzarchiv*, 286-297.

Mieszkowski, Peter M. (1969), 'Tax Incidence Theory: the Effects of Taxes on the Distribution of Income', **7** *Journal of Economic Literature*, 1103 ff.

Mieszkowski, Peter M. and Zodrow, George R. (1985), 'The Incidence of a Partial State Corporate Income Tax', **38** *National Tax Journal*, 4 ff.

Miller, Merton H. (1977), 'Debt and Taxes', **32** *Journal of Finance*, 261-275.

Miller, Merton H. (1982), *The Corporation Income Tax and Corporate Financial Policies*, New Jersey, Prentice Hall.

Miller, Merton H. (1986), 'Behavioral Rationality in Finance: The Case of Dividends', **59** *Journal of Business*, 451-468.

Miller, Merton H. (1988), 'The Modigliani-Miller Propositions After Thirty Years', **2** *Journal of Economic Perspectives*, 99-120.

Miller, Merton H. and Modigliani, Franco (1961), 'Dividend Policy, Growth and the Valuation of Shares', **34** *Journal of Business*, 41 ff.

Miller, Merton H. and Rock, Kevin (1985), 'Dividend Policy Under Asymmetric Information', **40** *Journal of Finance*, 103 ff.

Miller, Merton H. and Scholes, Myron S. (1979), 'Dividends and Taxes', **6** *Journal of Financial Economics*, 1118-1141.

Miller, Merton H. and Scholes, Myron S. (1982), 'Dividends and Taxes: Some Empirical Evidence', **90** *Journal of Political Economy*, 1118-1141.

Minarik, Joseph J. (1984), 'The Effects of Taxation on the Selling of Corporate Stock and the Realization of Capital Gains: Comment', **99** *Quarterly Journal of Economics*, 93 ff.

Mintz, Jack M. (1976), 'Is there a Future for Capital Income Taxation?', **24** *Canadian Tax Journal*, 1469-1503.

Mintz, Jack M. (1987a), *Alternative Views of the Corporate Tax: A Reassessment of the Carter Report Twenty Years Later*, Department of Economics, Queen's University, Queen's Institute for Economic Research, 56.

Mintz, Jack M. (1987b), *An Empirical Estimate of Corporate Tax Refundability and Effective Tax Rates*, Department of Economics, Carleton University, Carleton Industrial Organization Research Unit, 87-02.

Mintz, Jack M. (1988), 'An Empirical Estimate of Corporate Tax Refundability and Effective Tax Rates', **103(1)** *Quarterly Journal of Economics*, 225-231.

Mintz, Jack M. (1990), 'Corporate Tax Holidays and Investment', **4(1)** *World Bank Economic Review*, 81-102.

Mintz, Jack M. (1991), 'Economic Implications of Non-Refundability of Tax Losses', in X (ed.), *4 Policy Options for the Treatment of Tax Losses*, Toronto, Clarkson Gordon Foundation, 1-43.

Mintz, Jack M. (1995), 'The Corporation Tax: A Survey', **16** *Fiscal Studies*, 23-68.

Mintz, Jack M. and Tsiopoulos, Thomas (1992), 'Contrasting Corporate Tax Policies: Canada and Taiwan', **40** *Canadian Tax Journal*, 902 ff.

Mintz, Jack M. and Tsiopoulos, Thomas (1994), 'The Effectiveness of Corporate Tax Incentives for Foreign Investment in the Presence of Tax Crediting', **55(2)** *Journal of Public Economics*, 233-255.

Moden, Karl, Markus (ed.) (1993), 'Tax Incentives of Corporate Mergers and Foreign Direct Investments', Ph.D. Thesis.

Moden, Karl, Markus (ed.) (1993), *Tax Incentives of Corporate Mergers and Foreign Direct Investments, Ph.D. Dissertation*, University of Pennsylvania.

Modigliani, Franco (1982), 'Debt, Dividend Policy, Taxes, Inflation, and Market Valuation', **37** *Journal of Finance*, 255-273.

Modigliani, Franco and Miller, Merton H. (1961), 'Dividend Policy, Growth, and the Valuation of Shares', **34** *Journal of Business*, 411 ff.

Modigliani, Franco and Miller, Merton H. (1963), 'Corporate Income Taxes and the Cost of Capital: A Correction', **53** *American Economic Review*, 433 ff.

Morgan, Eleanor J. (1987), 'The UK Corporate Tax Reform and Business Investment Decisions', **8(2)** *Managerial and Decision Economics*, 149-159.

Morgan, I.G. (1982), 'Dividends and Capital Asset Prices', **37** *Journal of Finance*, 1071 ff.

Mundstock, G. (1988), 'Taxation of Intercorporate Dividends Under an Unintegrated Regime', **44** *Tax Law Review*, 1 ff.

Musgrave, Peggy B. (1974), 'International Tax Base Division and the Multinational Corporation', **27** *Journal of Public Finance*, 394 ff.

Musgrave, Peggy B. (1987), 'Interjurisdictional Coordination of Capital Income', in Cnossen, S. (ed.), *Tax Coordination In The European Community*, London, Kluwer Law and Taxation.

Mutén, Leif (1997), 'Dual Income Tax: The Scandinavian Experience', in Head, G. and Krever, Richard (eds), *Company Tax Systems*, Australian Research Foundation, 271-285.

Mutti, John H. (1981), 'Tax Incentives and Repatriation Decisions of US Multimational Coporations', **34** *National Tax Journal*, 241-248.

Mutti, John H. and Grubert, Harry (eds) (1984), *Corporate and Personal Taxation of Capital Income in an Open Economy*, Washington, DC, Office of Tax Analysis, U.S. Treasury Dept..

Mutti, John H. and Grubert, Harry (1985), 'The Taxation of Capital Income in an Open Economy: The Importance of Resident-Nonresident Tax Treatment', **27** *Journal of Public Economics*, 291-309.

Myers, Stewart C. (1984), 'The Capital Structure Puzzle', **39** *Journal of Finance*, 575-592.

Myers, Stewart C. (1993), 'Still Searching for Optimal Capital Structure', **6** *Journal of Applied Corporate Finance*, 4-14.

Nadean, Serge and Strauss, Robert P. (1991), 'Tax Policies and the Real and Financial Decisions of the Firm: The Effects of the Tax Reform Act of 1986', **19** *Public Finance Quarterly*, 251-292.

Nadeau, Serge J. (1988), 'A Model to Measure the Effects of Taxes on the Real and Financial Decisions of the Firm', **41** *National Tax Journal*, 467-481.

Nadeau, Serge J. and Strauss, Robert P. (1993), 'Taxation, Equity, and Growth: Exploring the Trade-off Between Shareholder Dividend Tax Relief and Higher Corporate Income Taxes', **6** *National Tax Journal*, 161-172.

Nadeau, Serge J. and Strauss, Robert P. (1993), 'Taxation, Equity, and Growth: Exploring the Trade-Off Between Shareholder Dividend Tax Relief and Higher Corporate Income Taxes, U Victoria; Carnegie Mellon U', **46** *National Tax Journal*, 161-175.

Nadeau, Serge J. and Strauss, Robert P. (1997), 'Observations on US Corporate Tax Policy and the 1992 US Treasury Report on Integration', in Head, G. and Krever, Richard (eds), *Company Tax Systems*, Australian Research Foundation, 85-114.

Narayanan, Suresh (1989), 'Forward Shifting of the Corporate Tax in the Presence of Competing Imports: A Note', **44(2)** *Public Finance*, 320-326.

Neville, Norman (1985), 'The Economics of Tax Ploision and Corporate Tax Integration', **2** *Australian Tax Forum*, 71-77.

Newberry, Kaye J. (ed.) (1994), *Foreign Tax Credit Limitations and Public Issuances by U.S. Multinationals: New Evidence of Tax Clienteles,* Thesis, Arizona State University.

Normadin, Charles P. (1989), 'A Legal Perspective (Discussion)', in Peters, Richard T. and Scott, Robert E. (eds), *Are the Distinctions Between Debt and Equity Disappearing? Proceedings of a conference held at Melvin Village*, New Hampshire Federal Reserve Bank of Boston.

Norr, M. (1982), *The Taxation of Corporations and Shareholders.*

Norregaard, John and Owens, Jeffrey (1992), 'Taxing Profits in a Global Economy: International', **46(5)** *Bulletin for International Fiscal Documentation*, 223-228.

Note (1995), 'Losing Control: Toward a New Understanding of the Taxation of Post-Incorporation Stock Sales', **108** *Harvard Law Review*, 1661 ff.

Ofer, Aharon, R. and Siegel, Daniel R. (1987), 'Corporate Financial Policy, Information, and Market Expectations: an Empirical Investigation of Dividends', **42** *Journal of Finance*, 889 ff.

Officer, Robert R. (1990), *The Australian Imputation System for Company Tax and Its Likely Effect on Shareholders, Financing and Investment Australian Tax Forum.*

Officer, Robert R. (1994), 'The Cost of Capital of a Company under an Imputation Tax System', 1-17.

Olin, John M. (ed.) (1990), '*Taxation and the Cost of Capital: The 'Old' View, the 'New' View, and Another View*.

Omer, Thomas C. and Ziebart, David A. (1993), 'The Effect of the Alternative Minimum Tax on Corporate Tax Burdens', **33(2)** *Quarterly Review of Economics and Finance*, 123-139.

Omer, Thomas C., Molloy, Karen H. and Ziebart, David A. (1991), 'Measurement of Corporate Tax Rates Using Financial Statement Information', *Journal of the American Taxation Association*, 57-72.

Ono, Yoshiyasu and Shibata, Akihisa (1992), 'Spill Over Effects of Supply Side Changes in a Two Country Economy with Capital Accumulation', **33(12)** *Journal of International Economics*, 127-146.

Osterberg, William P. (1989), 'Tobin's q, Investment, and the Endogenous Adjustment of Financial Structure', **40(3)** *Journal of Public Economics*, 293-318.

Parai, Amar K. (1988), 'The Incidence of Corporate Income Tax under Variable Returns to Scale', **43(3)** *Public Finance*, 414-424.

Parai, Amar K. (1991), 'The Incidence of Corporate Income Tax under Variable Returns to Scale: Reply', **46** *Public Finance*, 337-338.

Parai, Amar K. and Choudhary, Munir A.S. (1992), 'Imperfect Labor Mobility and Corporate Tax Incidence', **6(3)** *International Economic Journal*, 75-82.

Pastor, Santos (1991), 'Comment (on Aretz, Taxation and Incorporation)', in Weigel, Wolfgang (ed.), *Economic Analysis of Law - A Collection of Applications*, Vienna, Österreichischer Wirtschaftsverlag, 133-134.

Pearson, Mark (1989), 'Corporate Tax Harmonisation in the European Community', in Gammie, Malcolm, Robinson, Bill and Fitchew Geoffrey, *Beyond 1992: A European Tax System: Proceedings of the Fourth Institute for Fiscal Studies Residential Conference*, Oxford.

Pedersen, Bente Moll (1994), 'Denmark: Joint Taxation: A Unique Way of Reducing Corporate Tax', **48(11)** *Bulletin for International Fiscal Documentation*, 574-578.

Peel, Fred W. (1985), 'A Proposal for Eliminating Double Taxation of Corporate Dividends', **39** *Tax Law Journal*, 29 ff.

Pender, Howard (1997), 'Company Tax in Australia', in Head, G. and Krever, Richard (eds), *Company Tax Systems*, Australian Research Foundation, 195-206.

Pereira, Alfredo M. (ed.) (1989), *Corporate Tax Integration in the United States: A Dynamic General Equilibium Analysis*, San Diego, University of California.

Pereira, Alfredo M. (1993), 'A Dynamic General Equilibrium Analysis of Corporate Tax Integration', **15(1)** *Journal of Policy Modeling*, 63-89.

Peroni, Robert J. (1997), 'Back to the Future: A Path to Progressive Reform of the U.S. International Income Tax Rules', **51** *University of Miami Law Review*, 975 ff.

Petersen, Dorothy Ann (ed.) (1993), *Do Average Tax Rates Matter for Corporate Investment?*, Northwestern University Press.

Peterson, George E. (1985), 'Direct Evidence on the Marginal Rate of Taxation on Dividend Income', **14** *Journal of Financial Economics*, 272-280.

Petit, R.R. (1977), 'Taxes, Transaction Costs and the Clientele Effects of Dividends', *Journal of Financial Economics*, 419-436.

Piccioti, Sol (ed.) (1992), *International Business Taxation: A Study in the Internationalization of Business Regulation* .

Plasmans, J. and Vanneste, J. (1991), 'The Incidence of Corporate Taxation in Belgium on Employment and Investment', **0** *Cahiers Economiques de Bruxelles*, 3-25.

Platt, Joseph S. (1947), 'Integration and Correlation - The Treasury Proposal', **3** *Tax Law Review*, 59 ff.

Plesko, George A. (1994), 'Corporate Taxation and the Financial Characteristics of Firms', **22** *Public Finance Quarterly*, 311 ff.

Plumb, W.T. (1971), 'The Federal Income Tax Significance of Corporate Debt: A Critical Analysis and A Proposal', **26** *Tax Law Review*, 359 ff.

Polito, Anthony P. (1989), 'Note, A Proposal for an Integrated Income Tax', **12** *Harvard Journal of Law and Public Policy*, 1009 ff.

Pomp, Richard D. (1993), 'The Disclosure of State Corporate Income Tax Data: Turning the Clock Back to the Future', **22** *Capital University Law Review*, 373 ff.

Porteba, James M. (1987), 'How Burdensome ae Capital Gains Taxes?: Evidence from the United States', **33** *Journal of Public Economics*, 157 ff.

Porteba, James M. (1987), 'Tax Policy and Corporate Saving', **2** *Brookings Papers on Economic Activity*, 455-515.

Porteba, James M. (1991), 'Dividends, Capital Gains, and the Corporate Veil: Evidence from Britain, Canada, and the United States', in Bernheim, B. Douglas and Shoven, John B. (eds) *National Saving and Economic Performance*, Chicago, University of Chicago Press, 49-71.

Porteba, James M. (1992), 'Why Didn't the Tax Reform Act of 1986 Raise Corporate Taxes?', in X (ed.), *Tax Policy and the Economy*, Cambridge and London, MIT Press, Cambridge, Mass. National Bureau of Economic Research, 43-58.

Porteba, James M. and Summers, Lauwrence H. (1983), 'Dividends, Taxes, Corporate Investment, and "Q"', **22** *Journal of Public Economics*, 135-167.

Porteba, James M. and Summers, Lauwrence H. (1984), 'New Evidence that Taxes Affect the Valuation of Dividends', **39** *Journal of Finance*, 1397-1415.

Porteba, James M. and Summers, Lauwrence H. (1985), 'The Economic Effects of Dividend Taxes', in Altman Edward and Subrahmanyam Marti (eds), *Recent Advances in Corporate Finance*, Homewood: Richard D. Irwin, 227-284.

Posin, Daniel Q. (1985), 'Taxing Corporate Reorganizations: Purging Penelope's Web', **133** *University of Pennsylvania Law Review*, 1381-1382.

Pozdena, Randall Johnston (1987), 'Tax Policy and Corporate Capital Structure', **4** *Economic Review*.

Quirmbach, Herman C., Swenson, Charles W. and Vines, Cynthia Carol (1996), 'An Experimental Examination of General Equilibrium Tax Incidence', **61** *Journal of Public Economics*, 337-358.

Rajagopal, Dagmar (ed.) (1987), *The Corporate Income Tax and the User Cost of Capital a New Method to Test for Short-run Forward Shifting of the Tax, Ph.D. Thesis*, Toronto, University of Toronto Faculty of Law.

Rands, William J. (1995), 'Passthrough Entities and Their Unprincipled Differences Under Federal Tax Law', **49** *SMU Law Review*, 15 ff.

Rangazas, Peter and Dewan, Abdullah (1987), 'Taxes and the Corporate Sector Debt Ratio: Some Time Series Evidence', **69** *Review of Economics and Statistics*, 357 ff.

Rapanos Vassilis T. (1991), 'The Incidence of Corporate Income Tax under Variable Returns to Scale: Comment', **46** *Public Finance*, 335-336.

Razin, Assaf and Sadka, Efraim (1990), 'Integration of International Capital Markets: The Size of Government and Tax Coordination', in Razin and Slemrod, Joel (eds), *Taxation in the Global Economy*, Chicago: University of Chicago Press.

Reamonn, Sean (ed.) (1970), *The Philosophy of the Corporate Tax*, Dublin.

Reaume, David M. (1976), 'Short Run Corporate Tax Shifting by Profit Maximizing Oligopolists', **4(1)** *Public Finance Quarterly*, 33-44.

Repetti, James R. (1990), 'Long-Term Capital Gains, the Long-Term Investment Perspective, and Corporate Productivity', **49** *Tax Notes*, 85 ff.

Repetti, James R. (1992), 'Corporate Governance and Stockholder Abdication: Missing Factors in Tax Policy Analysis', **67** *Notre Dame Law Review*, 983-984.

Repetti, James R. (1997), 'Accounting and Taxation: the Misuse of Tax Incentives to Align Management-Shareholder Interests', **19** *Cardozo Law Review*, 697 ff.

Ribstein, Larry E. (1988), 'An Applied Theory of Limited Partnership', **37** *Emory Law Journal*, 852-854.

Ribstein, Larry E. (1992), 'The Deregulation of Limited Liability and the Death of Partnership', **70** *Washington United Law Quarterly*, 471 ff.

Rice, Eric M. (ed.) (1990), *Eric M. Skirting the Law: Essays on Corporate Tax Evasion and Avoidance, Ph.D. Thesis*, Harvard University Press.

Ritter, Wolfgang (1989), 'Harmonisation of Taxes as a Prerequisite for a Single European Market', in Gammie, Malcolm, Robinson, Bill and Fitchew, Geoffrey, *Beyond 1992: A European Tax System: Proceedings of the Fourth Institute for Fiscal Studies Residential Conference*, Oxford.

Robichek, Alexander and Myers, Eugene A. (1966), 'Stewart Problems in the Theory of Optimal Capital Structure', **1** *Journal of Financial and Quantitative Analysis*, 1-35.

Rocap and Waimon (1989), 'Passthrough Rules for Financial Intermediairies: Different Routes to a Single Tax', **67** *Taxes*, 1025 ff.

Rodios, Nikos D. (1986), 'E Kampyle tou Laffer e Peri tes Phthinousas Apodoseos tes Phorologias (The Laffer Curve or On the Diminishing Return of Taxation)', **53** *Ephemeris ton Hellenon Nomikon*, 216-218.

Rogers, Diane, Lim (ed.) (1996), 'The Incidence of the Corporate Income Tax', *Congressional Office Paper*.

Roin, Julie, A. (1988), 'United They Stand, Divided They Fall: Public Choice Theory and the Tax Code', **74** *Cornell Law Review*, 62 ff.

Roin, Julie, A. (1995), 'Rethinking Tax Treaties in a Strategic World with Disparate Tax Systems', **81** *Virginia. Law Review*, 1753 ff.

Ronen, Joshua and Aharoni, A. (1989), 'The Choice among Accounting Alternatives and Management Compensation: Effects of Corporate Tax', **64(1)** *Accounting Review*, 69-86.

Rooijen, Martin J. (1977), 'Interrelationship of Corporate Tax and Income Tax of Shareholders', **31** *Bulletin for International Fiscal Documentation*, 64-68.

Rose-Ackerman, Susan (1982), 'Unfair Competition and Corporate Income Taxation', **34** *Stanford Law Review*, 1017-1039. Reprinted In Rose Ackerman (ed.), *The Economics of Nonprofit Institutions*, pp. 394 414.

Rousslang, Donald J. (1987), 'The Effects of Recent Corporate Tax Changes on U.S. International Trade', **40(4)** *National Tax Journal*, 603-615.

Rozycki, John J. (1997), 'A Tax Motivation for Smoothing Dividends', **37** *Quarterly Review of Economics and Finance*, 563-578.

Rudnick, Rebecca S. (1988), 'Who Should Pay the Corporate Tax in a Flat Tax World?', **39** *Case Western Reserve Law Review*, 965 ff.

Rudnick, Rebecca S. (1989), 'Corporate Tax Integration: Liquidity of Investment', **42** *Tax Notes*, 1107 ff.

Sadowitz, March (ed.) (1992), *Corporate Tax Policy: a Factor in Environmental Decision Making*, Thesis, Albany, State University of New York Press.

Sahni, Balbir Singh and Mathew, T. (eds) (1976), *The Shifting and Incidence of the Corporation Income Tax*, Rotterdam University Press.

Salinger, Michael A. and Summers, Lawrence H. (eds) (1981), *Tax Reform and Corporate Investment: a Micro-econometric Simulation*, National Bureau of Economic Research, 757.

Sandberg, Milton (1938), 'The Income Tax Subsidy to "Reorganizations"', **38** *Columbia Law Review*, 98 ff.

Sanden, B. Kenneth (1975), 'The Taxation of Income from Corporate Shareholding: Introductory Remarks', **28** *National Tax Journal*, 255 ff.

Sansing, Richard C. (1993), 'Information Acquisition in a Tax Compliance Game', *Accounting Review*, 874-884.

Sarma, J.V.M. (1990), '1990-91 Budget and the New Corporate Tax Proposals: An Evaluation: India', **44(7)** *Bulletin for International Fiscal Documentation*, 347-349.

Sasseville, Jacques (ed.) (1995), 'Article 10 of the OECD Model Tax Convention and the Different Approaches to Integration in International Fiscal Association. International taxation of dividends reconsidered in light of corporate tax integration', Proceedings of a seminar organised jointly with the EOCD in Toronto in 1994 during the 48th Congress of the International Fiscal Association.

Sato, Mitsuo and Bird, Richard M. (1975), 'International Aspects of the Taxation of Corporations and Shareholders', **22** *International Monetary Fund Staff Papers*, 384-455.

Scarborough, Robert H. (1993), 'Risk, Diversification and the Design of Loss Limitations Under a Realization-Based Income Tax', **48** *Tax Law Review*, 677 ff.

Schadewald, Michael S. (1992), 'Discussion of Expertise in Corporate Tax Planning: The Issue Identification Phase', **30(0)** *Journal of Accounting Research*, 29-36.

Schaffer, Daniel C. (1979), 'The Income Tax on Intercorporate Dividends', **33** *Tax Lawyer*, 161 ff.

Schenk, Deborah H. (1992), 'Complete Integration in a Partial Integration World', **47** *Tax Law Review*, 697 ff.

Schipper, Katherine and Smith, Abbie (1988), *Corporate Income Tax Effects of Management Buyouts*.

Schler, Michael L. (1992), 'Taxing Corporate Income Once (or Hopefully Not at All): A Practitioner's Comparison of the Treasury and ALI Integration Models', **47** *Tax Law Review*, 509 ff.

Scholes, Myron S. and Wolfson, Mark, Alan (1980), 'Employee Stock Ownership Plans and Corporate Restructuring: Myths and Realities', in Samets, Arnold W. and Bicksler, James L. (eds), *The Battle for Corporate Control: Shareholder Rights, Stakeholder Interest, and Managerial Responsibilities*.

Scholes, Myron S. and Wolfson, Mark, Alan (1990), 'The Effects of Change in Tax Laws on Corporate Reorganization Activity', **63** *Journal of Business*, 141-164.

Scholes, Myron S. and Wolfson, Mark Alan (1990), 'The Effects of Changes in Tax Laws on Corporate Reorganization Activity', **63(S)** *Journal of Business*, 141-164.

Scholes, Myron S. and Wolfson, Mark, Alan (1991), 'The Role of Tax Rules in the Recent Restructuring of U.S. Corporations, in D. Bradford', **5** *Tax Policy and the Economy*, 1-25.

Scholes, Myron S. and Wolfson, Mark, Alan (eds) (1992), *Taxes and Business Strategy: A Planning Approach*, Englewood Cliffs, NJ, Prentice-Hall.

Scholes, Myron S., Wilson, Peter G. and Wolfson, Mark Alan (1992), 'Firms' Responses to Anticipated Reductions in Tax Rates', **30** *Journal of Accounting Research*, 161-185.

Scholz, John Karl (1988), *The Effect of the Relative Tax Treatment of Dividends and Capital Gains on Corporate Valuation and Behavior, Ph.D. Dissertation*, Stanford University.

Schulman, Graig T., Thomas, Deborah W., Sellers, Keith F. and Kennedy, Duane (1996), 'Effects of Tax Integration and Capital Gains Tax on Corporate Leverage', **49** *National Tax Journal*, 31-54.

Schultz, Michael L. (1990), 'Section 382 and the Pursuit of Neutrality in the Treatment of Net Operating Loss Carryovers', **39** *University of Kansas Law Review*, 84 ff.

Schwidetzky, Walter D. (1995), 'A Comparison of Partnership Income Taxation in the United States and Germany: A Study in Differences', **10** *American University Journal of International Law and Policy*, 1331 ff.

Seidl, Christian (1989), 'Betriebssteuer und Neutralität (On the Neutrality of a Business Tax)', **66/4** *Steuer und Wirtschaft*, 350-357.

Sellers, Keith F., Thomas, Deborah W. and Schulman, Craig T. (eds) (1994), *Effects of Tax Policy on Corporate Financing Decisions: Integration of the Corporate and Personal Income Tax*, Washington, DC, Tax Foundation and Ernst & Young.

Senate Finance Committee Staff (ed.) (1983), *The Reform and Simplification of the Income Taxation of Corporations*, Washington, DC, United States G.P.O.. Preliminary Report of the Staff of the Senate Finance Committee, 'Corporate Tax Study', issued September 27, 1983, by Commerce Clearing House, Chicago no. 45 (Oct. 6, 1983)

Shaikh, Abdul Quader J. (1971), *The Corporate Income Tax and the Growth of the Corporate Sector: a Case Study of India, Ph.D. Thesis*, University of Massachusetts.

Shakow, David J. (1990), 'Wither, C!', **45** *Tax Law Review*, 177 ff.

Shapiro, Robert J. (1997), 'Building a Conceptual Baseline for Corporate Tax Reform', **50** *National Tax Journal*, 507-517.

Sharpe, Donald (1996), 'Unfair Business Competition and the Tax on Income Destined for Charity: Forty Six Years Later', **3** *Florida Tax and Law Review*, 367 ff.

Shaviro, Daniel N. (1992), 'An Efficiency Analysis of Realization and Recognition Rules Under the Federal Income Tax', **48** *Tax Law Review*, 53 ff.

Shaviro, Daniel N. (1995), 'Risk-Based Rules and the Taxation of Capital Income', **50** *Tax Law Review*, 643-724.

Shay, Steven E. (1996), 'Revisiting U.S. Anti-Deferral Rules', **74** *Taxes*, 1042 ff.

Sheffrin, Steven M. (1982), 'What Have We Done to the Corporate Tax System?', **25(2)** *Challenge*, 46-52.

Shefrin, Hersch M. and Statman, Meir (1984), 'Explaining Investor Preference for Cash Dividends', **13** *Journal of Financial Economics*, 253 ff.

Sheppard, Lee A. (1985), 'Corporate Tax Integration, the Proper Way to Eliminate the Corporate Tax', **27** *Tax Notes*, 637 ff.

Shevlin, Terry (1990), 'Estimating Corporate Marginal Tax Rates', *Journal of the American Taxation Association.*

Shim, Ki-Ryon (1976), *The Shifting of the Corporation Income Tax in Japanese Manufacturing, Ph.D. Thesis*, University of Cincinnati.

Shnaider, Eliahu (1987), ' The Use of Fuzzy Set Theory for Forecasting Corporate Tax Revenu', M.S. Thesis.

Shome, Parthasarathi (1982), 'Corporate Tax Shifting: Empirical Evidence from ASEAN', **4** *Papers in Asian Studies.*

Shome, Parthasarathi (1985), 'Is the Corporate Tax Shifted? Empirical Evidence from ASEAN', **13(1)** *Public Finance Quarterly*, 21-46.

Shoven, John B. (1976), 'The Incidence and Efficiency Effects of Taxes on Income from Capital', **84** *Journal of Political Economy*, 1261 ff.

Shoven, John B. (1986), *New Developments in Corporate Finance and Tax Avoidance: Some Evidence*, National Bureau of Economic Research, 2091.

Shoven, John B. (1987), 'The Tax Consequences of Share Repurchases and Other Non-Dividend Cash Payments to Equity Owners', in Summers, Lawrence H. (ed.), *Tax Policy and the Economy*, Cambridge, MIT Press, 29-54.

Shoven, John B. (ed.), 'Using the Corporate Cash Flow Tax to Integrate Corporate and Personal Taxes', Proceedings of the 83rd Annual Conference of the National Tax Association, 19-26.

Shoven, John B. (ed.) (1990), *The Japanese Tax Reform and the Effective Rate of Tax on Japanese Corporate Investments*, Stanford University, Center for Economic Policy Research, 147.

Shoven, John B. and Waldfogel, Joel (eds) (1990), 'Introduction and Summary', in Shoven, John B. and Waldfogel, Joel (eds), *In Debt, Taxes, and Corporate Restructuring*, Washington, Brookings Institution, 1-19.

Shoven, John B. and Whalley, John (1972), 'A General Equilibrium Calculation of the Effects of Differential Taxation of Income from Capital in the U.S.', **1** *Journal of Public Economics*, 281 ff.

Shoven, John B. and Whalley, John (eds) (1992), *Canada-U.S. Tax Comparisons, A National Bureau of Economic Research Project Report*, Chicago, University of Chicago Press.

Shuldiner, Reed H. (1992), 'Corporate Integration: Do the Uncertainties Outweigh the Benefits?', **47** *Tax Law Review*, 653 ff.

Shum, Pauline M. (1996), 'Taxes and Corporate Debt Policy in Canada: An Empirical Investigation', **29** *Canadian Journal of Economics*, 556-572.

Siegel, Stanley (1995), 'The Effects of Tax Laws on the Choice of Organizational Form and Structure: A Comparison of Integrated and Nonintegrated Tax Systems', **29** *International Lawyer*, 1-6.

Siegfried, John J. (1972), *The Relationship Between Economic Structure and the Effect of Political Influence: Empirical Evidence from The Federal Corporation Income Tax Program, Ph.D. Dissertation*, Madison, Wisconsin University.

Siegfried, John J. (1974), 'Effective Average U.S. Corporation Income Tax Rates', **27** *National Tax Journal*, 245-259.

Siegfried, John J. and Weiss, Leonard W. (1974), 'Advertising, Profits, and Corporate Taxes Revisited Review of Economics and Statistics', **56** *National Tax Journal*, 195-200.

Simeone, Gary John (1994), *U.S. Corporate Tax Integration - Analysis of the Alternatives, M.S. Thesis*, San Francisco, State University.

Simmons, Daniel L. (1983), 'Net Operating Losses and Section 382: Searching for a Limitation on Loss Carryovers', **63** *Tulane Law Review*, 1045 ff.

Simon, Herbert A. (1972), 'Antitrust and the "Size" Problem: The "Graduated" Corporate Income Tax as an Anti-Bigness Device', **6** *Antitrust Law and Economics Review*, 53 ff.

Simons, Henry C. (1938), *Personal Income Taxation*.

Sinn, Hans-Werner (1990), *Taxation and the Birth of Foreign Subsidiaries*, National Bureau of Economics, 3519.

Sinn, Hans-Werner (1991a), 'The Vanishing Harberger Triangle', **45** *Journal of Public Economics*, 271-300.

Sinn, Hans-Werner (1991b), 'Taxation and the Cost of Capital: The Old View, the "New" View and Another View', **5** *Tax Policy and the Economy*, 25-54.

Sinn, Hans-Werner (1991c), 'Share Repurchases, the "New" View, and the Cost of Capital', **36** *Economic Letters*, 187-190.

Sinn, Hans-Werner (1993), 'Taxation and the Birth of Foreign Subsidiaries', in Herberg, H. and Long, N.V. (eds), *Trade Welfare, and Economic Policies: Essays in Honor of Murray C Kemp*, Ann Arbor: University of Michigan Press, 325-352.

Slawson (1967), 'Taxing as Ordinary Income the Appreciation of Publicly Held Stock', **76** *Yale Law Journal*, 623 ff.

Slemrod, Joel (1990), 'The Impact of the Tax Reform Act of 1986 on Foreign Direct Investment To and From the United States', in Slemrod, J. (ed.), *Do Taxes Matter?*, Cambridge, MA, MIT Press.

Slemrod, Joel (1990), 'Tax Effects on Foreign Direct Investment in the United States: Evidence from a Cross-Country Comparison', in Razin and Slemrod (eds), *Taxation in the Global Economy*, Chicago, University of Chicago Press.

Slitor, Richard E. (1963), 'The Enigma of Corporate Tax Incidence', **18** *Public Finance*.

Slitor, Richard E. (1966), 'Corporate Tax Incidence: Economic Adjustments to Differentials Under a Two-Tied Tax Structure', in Krzyzaniak, M. (ed.), *Effects of Corporation Income Tax*, Papers Presented at the Symposium on Business Taxation, 136-206.

Sloan, Frank A. et al. (1988), 'Cost of Capital to the Hospital Secto', **7(1)** *Journal of Health Economics*, 25-45.

Smirlock, Michael Randolph and Beatty, Saman Majd (eds) (1986), *Taxes and Mergers: A Survey, Salomon Brothers Center for the Study of Financial Institutions*, New York, University Graduate School of Business Administration.

Smith, Abbie (1990), 'The Effects of Leveraged Buyouts', **25(2)** *Business Economics*, 19-25.

Smith, Andrew M.C. (1991), 'Corporate and International Tax Reforms in 1991 Budget: New Zealand', **45(11)** *Bulletin for International Fiscal Documentation*, 530-537.

Smith, Andrew M.C. (1993), 'Comprehensive Dividend Imputation, Neutrality and Double Taxation of Corporate Profits: New Zealand', **47** *Bulletin for International Fiscal Documentation*, 568-580.

Smith, Andrew M.C. (1994), 'Dividend Imputation and International Equity Investment: Unilateral Extension of Imputation to Non-Resident Investors', **11** *Australian Tax Forum*, 247-269.

Smith, Dan Throop (1977), 'Relief From Double Taxation of Dividend Income', **55** *Harvard Business Review*, 87 ff.

Smith, David Duane (ed.) (1979), *The Relationship Between Market Structure and the Effective Corporate Income Tax Rate, Ph.D. Thesis*, University of Michigan.

Smith, Peter Jefferson (1989), 'Proposals to Date, and Aims for 1992', in Gammie, Malcolm, Robinson, Bill and Fitchew Geoffrey, *Beyond 1992: A European Tax System: Proceedings of the Fourth Institute for Fiscal Studies Residential Conference*, Oxford.

Snoe, Joseph A. (1993), 'The Entity Tax and Corporate Integration: An Agency Cost Analysis and A Call for a Deferred Distributions Tax', *University of Miami Law Review*.

Snow, Sandra L. (ed.) (1976), *A Comparative Model of Corporate Income Tax Shifting Utilizing Cross Sectional Data, Ph.D. Thesis*, University of Missouri, Columbia.

Sommerfeld, Ray M. and Jones, Sally M. (ed.) (1991), *Federal Taxes and Management Decisions*, Homewood, IL, Richard D. Irwin.

Sommerfeld, Ray M. and Jones, Sally M. (1995), *Federal Taxes and Management Decisions*, Chicago, Ill., Richard D. Irwin, Inc..

Sorensen, Peter Birch (1994), 'Some Old and New Issues in the Theory of Corporate Income Taxation', **51** *Finanzarchiv*, 425-456.

Sorensen, Peter Birch (1995a), 'Changing Views of the Corporate Income Tax', **48** *National Tax Journal*, 279-294.

Sorensen, Peter Birch (1995b), 'Comment on Alan J. Auerbach, Kevin Hassett and Jan Sodersten: Taxation and Corporate Investment: The Impact of the 1991 Swedish Tax Reform', **2** *Swedish Economic Policy Review*, 385-390.

Spooner, Gillian M. (1986), 'Effective Tax Rates from Financial Statements', **39** *National Tax Journal*, 293-306.

Spooner, Gillian M. and Sunley, Emil M. (eds) (1988), 'The Corporate Tax Burden in the United States'.

Stapleton, R.C. (1972), 'Taxes, the Cost of Capital and the Theory of Investment', **82** *The Economic Journal*, 1273-1292.

Steenekamp, T.J. (1996), 'Some Aspects of Corporate Taxation in South Africa: The Katz Commission', **64** *South African Journal of Economics*, 1-19.

Stephan, Paul B. III (1990), 'Disaggregation and Subchapter C: Rethinking Corporate Tax Reform', **76** *Virginia Law Review*, 655-711.

Steuerle, C. Eugene (1989), 'A Simplified Integrated Tax', **44** *Tax Notes*, 335 ff.

Stewart, J.C. (1989), 'Transfer Pricing: Some Empirical Evidence from Ireland', **16(3)** *Journal of Economic Studies*, 40-56.

Stiglitz, Joseph E. (1973), 'Taxation, Corporate Financial Policy, and the Cost of Capital', **2** *Journal of Public Economics*, 1-33.

Stiglitz, Joseph E. (1976), 'The Corporation Tax', **5** *Journal of Public Economics*, 303 ff.

Strecker, (1965), 'When Will the Corporate Form Save Taxes', **18** *Vanderbilt Law Review*, 1695 ff.

Sugin, Linda (1997), 'Theories of the Corporation and the Tax Treatment of Corporate Philanthropy', **41** *New York Law School Law Review*, 835 ff.

Summers, Lawrence H. (1980), *Tax Policy and Corporate Investment*, National Bureau of Economic Research, 605.

Summers, Lawrence H. (1981), 'Taxation and Corporate Investment: A Q-Theory Approach', **1** *Brookings Papers on Economic Activity*, 105 ff.

Sunley, Emil M. (1992), 'Corporate Integration: An Economic Perspective', **47** *Tax Law Review*, 621 ff.

Surrey, Stanley S. (1975), 'Reflections on "Integration" of Corporation and Individual Income Taxes', **28** *National Tax Journal*, 335-340.

Suwanmala, Charas (1989), 'Crisis and Response: Treasury Cash Balance Crisis in Thailand 1980-1982', **9(3)** *Public Budgeting and Finance*, 27-36.

Swaine, David (1989), 'The Longer-term Implications for European Tax Systems', in Gammie, Malcolm, Robinson, Bill and Fitchew Geoffrey, *Beyond 1992: A European Tax System: Proceedings of the Fourth Institute for Fiscal Studies Residential Conference*, Oxford.

Swan, Peter L. (1984), 'Capital Gains, Cash Flow Taxes, and Corporate Tax Reform', **1(3)** *Australian Tax Forum*, 292-311.

Swayze, James P. (ed.) (1992), *The Effect of Corporate Income Tax Integration on the Demand for Risky Stock, Ph.D. Thesis*, University of Houston, College of Business Administration.

Swenson, Deborah (1993), 'Explaining the Low Taxable Income of Foreign-Controlled Companies in the United States', in Giovannini, A., Hubbard, R.G. and Slemrod, J. (eds), *Studies in International Taxation*, Chicago, University of Chicago Press.

Taggert, Robert A. (1980), 'Taxes and Corporate Capital Structure in an Incomplete Market', **35** *Journal of Finance*, 645-659.

Taggert, Robert A. (1985), 'Secular Patterns in the Financing of U.S. Corporations', in Friedman, Benjamin (ed.), *Corporate Capital Structures in the United States: An Introduction and Overview*, Chicago, University of Chicago Press.

Tajika, Eiji and Yui, Yuji (1988), 'Cost of Capital and Effective Corporate Tax Rate the Case of Post War Japan (In Japanese)', **39(2)** *Economic Review (Keizai Kenkyu)*, 118-128.

Takirambudde, Peter Nanyenya (1994), 'Botswana: Double Corporate Tax: Untangling the Undergrowth of Company and Shareholder Tax Rules', **48(2)** *Bulletin for International Fiscal Documentation*, 82-88.

Tax Executives Institute (ed.) (1993), *The Structure and Size of the Corporate Tax Department: An Empirical Analysis*, Washington.

Taylor, Scott A. (1990), 'Corporate Integration in the Federal Income Tax: Lessons From the Past and A Proposal for the Future', **10** *Virginia Tax Review*, 237 ff.

Taylor, Willard B. (1977), 'Report on the Integration of Corporate and Individual Income Taxes', **31** *Tax Lawyer*, 37 ff.

Teixeira, Gloria (ed.) (1997), *Taxing Corporate Profits in the EU: A Comparison of the Portuguese, British and Dutch Systems*, London, Kluwer Law International.

Terborgh, George Willard (ed.) (1959), 'Effect of the Corporate Income Tax on Investment. Machinery and Allied Products Institute', **37**.

Tetreault, David T. and Lindsay, Robert F. (1995), 'The Taxation of Corporate Reorganizations: How are we Doing so Far?', **43** *Canadian Tax Journal*, 1441-1464.

The Valabh Committee (ed.) (1988), *International Tax Reform: Full Imputation, an Independent Report to the New Zealand Government*, Wellington.

The Valabh Committee (ed.) (1991), *The Taxation of Distributions from Companies, an Independent Report to the New Zealand Government*, Wellington.

Thomas, Ann F. (1997), 'Square Wheels: U.S. Passthrough Taxation of Privately Held Enterprises in a Comparative Law Context', **17** *New York Law School Journal of International and Comp. Law*, 429-471.

Thompson, Samuel C., Jr (1975), 'Tax Policy Implications of Contributions of Appreciated and Depreciated Property to Partnerships, Subchapter C Corporations and Subchapter S Corporations in Exchange for Ownership Interests', **31** *Tax Law Review*, 51 ff.

Thompson, Samuel C. Jr (ed.) (1993), *Reform of the Taxation of Mergers, Acquisitions, and LBOs*, Durham, NC, Carolina Academic Press.

Thuronyi, Victor (1983), 'The Taxation of Corporate Income - A Proposal for Reform', **2** *American Journal of Tax Policy*, 109 ff.

Tillinghast, David R. (1990), 'International Tax Simplification', **8** *American Jounal of Tax Policy*, 204-205.

Treubert, Patrice and Pavelko, Amy (1991), *Internal Revenue Service, 'The Alternative Minimum Tax: An Analysis of Its Effect on Corporations in 1987'*.

Trezevant, Robert (1981), 'How did Firms Adjust their Tax-Deductible Activities in Response to the Economic Recovery Tax Act of 1981?', **67** *National Tax Journal*, 253-271.

Trezevant, Robert (1992), 'Debt Financing and Tax Status: Test of the Substitution Effect and the Tax Exhaustion Hypothesis Using Firm's Responses to the Economic Recovery Act of 1981', **47** *The Journal of Finance*, 1557-1568.

U.S. Department of the Treasury (1992), 'A Recommendation for Integration of the Individual and Corporate Tax Systems', **14** *Daily Tax Rep. (BNA)*, 7 ff.

U.S. Department of the Treasury (1992), *Report on Integration of the Individual and Corporate Tax Systems: Taxing Business Income Once*.

United States General Accounting Office (ed.), *Tax Policy Implications of Replacing the Corporate Income Tax with a Consumption Tax*.

Unni, Sanjay (1994), 'An Intertemporal Analysis of Optimal Capital Structure under Corporate and Personal Taxation', Ph.D. Dissertation.

Van Den Dempel, A. (1970), *Corporation Tax and Individual Income Tax in the European Communities*.

Van Raad, Kees (1995), 'In a World where Classical and Integration Systems Co-exist, Article 10 OECD Model should not Disregard the Underlying Corporation Income Tax in International Fiscal Association', *Proceedings of a seminar organised jointly with the EOCD in Toronto in 1994 during the 48th Congress of the International Fiscal Association*.

Van Rooijen, Martin J. (1977), 'Interrelationship of Corporate Tax and Income Tax of Shareholders', **31(2)** *Bulletin for International Fiscal Documentation*, 64-68.

Vanistendael, Frans and Gammie, Malcolm (ed.) (1992), *The Ruding Committee Report on European Corporate Tax Harmonisation*, Conference held by the Institute for Fiscal Studies.

Vanthienen, Lambert and Vermaelen, Theo (1987), 'The Effect of Personal Taxes on Common Stock Prices: The Case of a Belgian Tax Reform', **11** *Journal of Banking and Finance*, 243 ff.

Vasquez, Nilda D. (ed.) (1981), *The Corporate Income Tax: its Distributive Implications on Individual Shareholders*, University of the Philippines, School of Economics, 8102.

Vazquez Vega, Pablo (1996), '¿Discriminación positiva? La reforma del impuesto de sociedades en el Pais Vasco (Positive Discrimination? Corporate Tax Reform in Euskadi)', *Revista de la Camara de Comercio, Industria y Navegación*.

Vickrey, William, 'The Corporate Income Tax and How to Get Rid of It', in Eden, Lorraine (ed.).

Village, George Paul (ed.) (1989), *The Effect of Safe Harbor Leasing on Investment and Capital Allocation, Ph.D. Thesis*, Notre Dame Press.

Vines, Cynthia Carol (ed.) (1991), *The Effects of Regulation on Corporate Tax Shifting : an Analysis of the Property and Casualty Insurance Industry, Ph.D. Thesis*, University of Southern Carolina.

Virolainen, Kimmo (1991), 'Corporate Tax Exhaustion and Financial Policy: Evidence on Finnish Data', **4(2)** *Finnish Economic Papers*, 130-141.

Vogel, Klaus (1990), *World-wide vs. Source Taxation of Income - A Review and Reevaluation of Arguments*.

Vogel, Klaus (1995), 'Introductory Notes in International Fiscal Association. International Taxation of Dividends Reconsidered in Light of Corporate Tax Integration', *Proceedings of a seminar organised jointly with the EOCD in Toronto in 1994 during the 48th Congress of the International Fiscal Association*.

Von Martens, Christel (1992), 'Beskattning av Kapitalinkomster och av Foretagsinkomst ur Kommunal Synvinkel (with English summary) (The Effect of the New Capital and Corporate Tax Reform on Local Government Finances)', **45(3)** *Ekonomiska Samfundets Tidskrift*, 131-137.

von Zur Muehlen, Peter (ed.), *Some Partial Equilibrium Effects of Tax Reform on Corporate Policy*, Federal Reserve Board, Washington, Division of Research and Statistics Special Studies, 97.

Waggoner, Michael J. (1977), 'Eliminating the Capital Gains Preference. Part II: The Problem of Corporate Taxation', **19** *University of Colorado Law Review*, 18 ff.

Wang, Leonard F.S. (1993), 'Sector Specific Unemployment and Corporate Income Tax Incidence: A Geometric Exposition', **37(1)** *American Economist*, 64-67.

Wang, Leonard F.S. and Conant, John L. (1988), 'Corporate Tax Evasion and Output Decisions of the Uncertain Monopolist', **41** *National Tax Journal*, 579-581.

Wang, Shiing-wu (1991), 'The Relation between Firm Size and Effective Tax Rates: A Test of Firms' Political Success', **66** *Accounting Review*, 158-169.

Wang, Shiing-wu (1994), 'The Relationship between Financial Reporting Practices and the 1986 Alternative Minimum Tax', **69** *Accounting Review*, 495-506.

Warda, Jacek P. and Zollo, Trancredi (eds) (1987), *The Competitiveness of Canada's Corporate Tax Structure*, Ottawa, Canada Conference Board.

Warren (1981), 'The Relationship Between the Corporate and Individual Federal Income Taxes After the Economic Recovery Tax Act of 1981', **27** *Proc. National Tax Ass'n*.

Warren (1989), 'Recent Corporate Restructuring and the Corporate Tax System', **42** *Tax Notes*, 715 ff.

Warren, Alvin C. (1975), 'Fairness and A Consumption-Type or Cash Flow Personal Income Tax', **88** *Harvard Law Review*, 931 ff.

Warren, Alvin C. (1994), 'Alternatives for International Corporate Tax Reform', **49** *Tax Law Review*, 601 ff.

Warren, Alvin C. Jr (1974), 'The Corporate Interest Deduction: A Policy Evaluation', **83** *Yale Law Journal*, 1585 ff.

Warren, Alvin C. Jr (1981), 'The Relation and Integration of Individual and Corporate Income Taxes', **94** *Harvard Law Review*, 719 ff.

Warren, Alvin C. Jr (1985), 'Corporate Integration Proposals and ACRS', **22** *San Diego Law Review*, 325 ff.

Warren, Alvin C. Jr (1987), 'Taxing Corporate Income in the U.S. Twenty Years After The Carter Commission: Integration or Disintegration?', **4** *Australian Tax Forum*, 465-489.

Weisfelder, Christine J. (ed.) (1991), *Linkages Between Tax Systems: An Analysis of the Corporate Tax Consequences of Transferring Royalties, Interest, and Dividends between Germany, Japan and the United States, Ph.D. Thesis*, University of Michigan.

Weiss, Randall D. (1979), 'Effective Corporation Income Tax Rates', **32** *National Tax Journal*.

Werner, Ingrid M. (1994), 'Capital Income Taxation and International Portfolio Choice', **53** *Journal of Public Economics*, 205-222.

Wetzler, James W. (1993), 'Federal Tax Policy and the States: Corporate Integration', **46** *National Tax Journal*, 393-397.

Whalley, John (1984), 'Regression or Progression: the Taxing Question of Incidence', **17** *Canadian Journal of Economics*, 654-682.

Wheeler, J. (1988), 'An Academic Look at Transfer Pricing in a Global Economy', *Tax Notes*, 87-96.

Wickham, Dale W. and Kerester, Charles J. (1992), 'New Directions Needed for Solution of the International Transfer Pricing Puzzle: Internationally Agreed Rules or Tax Warfare?', **56** *Tax Notes*, 339 ff.

Wilkie, Patrick J. and Limberg, Stephen T. (1993), 'Measuring Explicit Tax (Dis)Advantage for Corporate Taxpayers: An Alternative to Average Effective Tax Rates', *Journal of the American Taxation Association*, 46-71.

Wilkie, Patrick J., Young, James C. and Nutter, Sarah E., *Corporate Business Activity Before and After the Tax Reform Act of 1986*.

Willard, Kristen L. (1994), 'Do Taxes Level the Playing Field? How U.S. Tax Policy Affects the Investment Decisions of Foreign Affiliates in the United States', **29(4)** *Columbia Journal of World Business*, 20-28.

Williams, David (1995), 'An Optimum Form of Article 10 of the OECD Model in International Fiscal Association. International Taxation of Dividends Reconsidered in Light of Corporate Tax Integration', *Proceedings of a seminar organised jointly with the EOCD in Toronto in 1994 during the 48th Congress of the International Fiscal Association.*

Wilson, G. Peter (1993), 'The Role of Taxes in Location and Sourcing Decisions', in Giovannini, A., Hubbard, R.G. and Slemrod, J. (eds), *Studies in International Taxation*, Chicago, University of Chicago Press.

Winsen, Joseph K. (1992), 'The Interaction Between Fringe Benefits Tax, Salary and Franked Dividends', **Sept** *Australian Tax Review*, 149-154.

Wiseman, Jack (1974), *Theoretical and Empirical Aspects of Corporate Taxation*.

Wolfman, Bernard (1979), 'Integration of the Corporate and Individual Income Taxes in the United States', **33** *Bulletin for International Fiscal Documentation*, 305-309.

Wolfson, Mark, Alan, 'The Effects of Ownership and Control on Taxes and Financial Reporting Policy', **22** *Economic Notes*, 318-322.

Woodside, Kenneth (1982), 'The Symbolic Politics of the Corporate Income Taxation: Canada and Britain, 1945-1980', in Stone, Alan and Harpham Edward (eds), *The Political Economy of Public Policy*, Sage, Beverly Hills.

Woodworth, Jay N. (1990), 'Different Economic Systems: Vast New Opportunities for Business Economists: NABE Presidential Address', **25(1)** *Business Economics*, 10-17.

Wozny, James (1991), 'The Taxation of Corporate Source Income in Jamaica', in Bahl, Roy (ed.), *The Jamaican Tax Reform*, Cambridge, MA, Lincoln Institute of Land Policy, 265-323.

Wu, Chunchi (1996), 'Taxes and Dividend Policy', **5** *International Review of Economics and Finance*, 291-305.

Wu, Chunchi and Hsu, Junming (1996), 'The Impact of the 1986 Tax Reform on Ex-Dividend Day Volume and Price Behavior', **49** *National Tax Journal*, 177 ff.

Yin, George K. (1990), 'A Different Approach to the Taxation of Corporate Distributions: Theory and Implementation of a Uniform Corporate-Level Distributions Tax', **78** *Georgetown Law Journal*, 1837 ff.

Yin, George K. (1992a), 'Achieving Corporate Integration Through Double Taxation', **56** *Tax Notes*, 1365-1368.

Yin, George K. (1992b), 'Corporate Tax Integration and the Search for the Pragmatic Ideal', **47** *Tax Law Review*, 449-468.

Yin, George K. (1997), 'The Taxation of Private Business Enterprises: Some Policy Questions Stimulated by the "Check-the-Box" Regulations', **51** *SMU Law Review*, 125 ff.

York, Harold L. (1993), 'An Applied General Equilibrium Model of International Tax Competition among the Group of Seven Countries', **15(56)** *Journal of Policy Modeling*, 653-672.

Young, K. H., 'The Effects of Taxes and Rates of Return on Foreign Direct Investment in the U.S', **41** *National Tax Journal*, 109-121.

Zarin Nejadan, Milad (1992), 'Fiscalite, q de Tobin et Investissement Prive en Suisse', **58(2)** *Recherches Economiques de Louvain*, 213-235.

Zelenak, Lawrence (1984), 'Serving Two Masters: Commercial Hues and Tax Exempt Organizations', **8** *U.P.S. Law Review*, 1 ff.

Zelinsky, Edward A. (1990), 'Greenmail, Golden Parachutes and the Internal Revenue Code: A Tax Policy Critique of Sections 280G, 4999 and 5881', **35** *Villanova Law Review*, 131 ff.

Zelinsky, Edward A. (1993), 'The Tax Policy Case for Denying Deductibility To Excessive Executive Compensation: Disguised Dividends, Reasonable Compensation, and the Protection of the Corporate Income Tax Base', **58** *Tax Notes*, 1123 ff.

Zodrow, George R. (1991), 'On the "Traditional" and "New" Views of Dividend Taxation', **44** *National Tax Journal*, 497-509.

Zodrow, George R. (1997), 'A Corporate Cash Flow Tax as an Income Tax Integration Mechanism', in Head, G. and Krever, Richard (eds), *Company Tax Systems*, Australian Research Foundation, 321-340.

Zolt, Eric M. (1988), 'Corporate Taxation After The Tax Reform Act of 1986: A State of Disequilibrium', **66** *North Carolina Law Review*, 839 ff.

6070
INHERITANCE AND GIFT TAXATION

Paul B. Stephan
Percy Brown, Jr. Professor and Barron F. Blak Research Professor, University of Virginia School of Law

Abstract

This chapter reviews the economic literature on inheritance and gift taxation. It discusses, among other things, the arguments for subsidizing transfers, the advantages of and problems with accessions taxation, the relationship of transfer taxes to income tax, proposals for unification of tax rates, proposals for base integration, special rules for transfers within family units, problems with interspousal transfers, and the implementation of generation-skipping-transfer taxes.
JEL categories: K34
Keywords: Life-Cycle Assets, Transferor Tax, Accessions Tax, Interspousal Transfers, Generational Issues

1. Introduction

Although death duties and comparable excises have existed since ancient times, long outstripping income taxation in length of history, no modern industrial or postindustrial state relies on estate, inheritance, or gifts taxes ('transfer taxes') for a significant portion of its revenues. As a result, transfer taxation plays almost no role in fiscal policy. Moreover, in most countries transfer taxes affect a small proportion of the population. In the United States, for example, less than 1 percent of all decedents who have died since the 1981 rate cuts went into effect have had to file estate tax returns, much less pay any tax. But for the few persons affected by transfer taxation, either as a potential transferor or transferee, the levy can be huge. For the wealthiest persons in the United States, a bequest to grandchild might be taxed at a 78.25 percent marginal rate.

2. Historical Pattern

Perhaps for these reasons, the law and economics literature has not focused on transfer taxation to the extent it has on other tax issues. Rather, one may detect a pattern where, every generation or so, there takes place broad normative discussions of transfer tax design. The discussion plays itself out, usually without much consequence for the actual tax rules. The topic disappears from view, to return some years later. When less radical changes do transpire, the ensuing commentary reflects the broad-based literature but does not necessarily build upon it. Thus in the 1960s Meade (1964), Shoup (1966), Tait (1967), Jantscher (1969), and Andrews (1973), among others, either initiated or responded to proposals for systemic and expansionary transformation of transfer taxation. These proposals in turn drew on ideas propounded in Simons (1938) and Vickrey (1947). Two decades after this flurry of interest in increasing the effectiveness of transfer taxation, Bracewell-Milnes (1989) presented diametrically opposed, but at least as radical, proposals to abolish taxes on gifts and bequests. These works and the scholarly traditions to which they have contributed have framed a number of policy issues, some fundamental and others more technical, but have not provided definitive answers to any of the questions raised.

3. Role in Redistribution of Wealth

Most transfer tax systems, and particular that of the United States, target the rich, either largely or exclusively. Much of the debate about these taxes therefore turn on assumptions about the existing distribution of wealth and the feasibility of effecting a redistribution. Both sides of this debate accept for purposes of argument the legitimacy of wealth redistribution as a social goal. Proponents of transfer taxation argue that ownership of assets is concentrated among a small portion of the population, that this concentration of wealth does not represent only differences in lifetime consumption, and that transfer taxation represents an effective way of redressing the misdistribution of economic power. These points are forcefully put in Vickrey (1947), Meade (1964), Shoup (1966), Tait (1967), Jantscher (1969), Kurtz and Surrey (1970), Brannon (1973), Graetz (1983) and Pechman (1987). Critics argue that measures of the concentration of wealth are underinclusive and therefore exaggerate the exent of concentration, that a large portion of wealth represents provisions against future consumption, and that the causes of inequality in society either are not related to family property holdings or cannot be remedied by a tax on gratuitous transfers of property. Variations of these points can be found in Collie (1973), Covey (1973), McCaffery (1994), Wagner (1977) and Bracewell-Milnes (1989).

4. Life-Cycle Assets versus Capital Assets

One important emprical question that underlies the debate over the efficacy of transfer taxation as a means of redistributing wealth is the proportion of wealth that is transferred gratuitously. The literature has developed a distinction between life-cycle assets, which represent household savings intended to finance future consumption, and capital assets, which households accumulate with the purpose of transferring to future generations. If most wealth is acquired for future consumption, a tax that applies only to transfers will not reach it. People would die holding assets only because of unanticipated mortality, and transfer taxes would serve only to punish the unlucky. If, on the other hand, a large portion of wealth constitutes capital assets, a tax on gratuitous transfers would have a significant impact on its ownership and could contribute to its redistribution.

5. Relative Mix of Life-Cycle and Capital Assets

A sharp disagreement exists among researchers who have tried to estimate the relative mix of life-cycle and capital assets. Modigliani (1988) estimates that 80 percent of US wealth constitutes life-cycle assets, while Summers (1981) and Kotlikoff (1988) argue that more than half of all wealth represents capital assets. The gap reflects a dispute over how to characterize particular types of transfers, in particular income from inherited property and support of children over the age of majority but still in school. Underlying these disagreements are deep problems. In a post-industrial society, one might argue, the education purchased by affluent parents may prove to have greater income-generating capacity than financial property such as stock and bonds. This claim would support the characterization of tuition payments and similar support to students as the creation of a capital asset. But, at least in the United States, a substantial portion of the cost of education is financed by alumni, who make deferred payments in the form of nominally charitable contributions once their investment reaches its peak income-producing potential. If parental funding is incidental to education's wealth-creating potential, then one instead might characterize education-related payments as a form of intrahousehold consumption.

6. Research on Distribution of Wealth

Aaron and Munnell (1992) provide a relatively recent review of the research on the distribution of wealth and the relative distribution of assets used for consumption and other purposes. W_1 consists of tangible assets, equities and bonds, and the cash surrender value of trust funds and pension plans. W_2 adjusts W_1 to take into account the full value of trust funds and pension plans. W_3 adds the discounted present value of future social insurance receipts. The authors further attempt to estimate the distribution of life-cycle wealth and capital wealth by splitting the difference between the Modigliani and Summers-Kotlikoff approaches. If one looks only at W_1, the data suggest that in the United States the proportion of capital wealth to life-cycle wealth has grown significantly between 1930 and 1990, which in turn implies an increase in the power of assets holders to wield dynastic power. If one instead includes W_3, the data indicate that the proportion of capital wealth to total wealth has remained fairly steady. In other words, the rich are getting richer, but only at the same rate as everyone else. Other survey data suggest that the amount of W_1 held by the wealthiest 1 percent of the population increased substantially during the 1980s, after the 1981 transfer tax rate cut went into effect, but these surveys do not measure W_3 after 1983. Studies of Great Britain and Sweden show a marked decline in the concentration of ownership of W_1 between 1940 and 1980.

7. Unconventional Forms of Property

Part of the debate over the efficacy of transfer taxation as a means of redressing wealth inequality turns on the capacity of such taxes to reach not just traditional forms of property, but other kinds of rights, powers, and expectations that might seem analogous to property *simpliciter*. One much-discussed problem is the so-called 'estate freeze', which allows an owner to retain some degree of control over an asset while transferring the formal right to enjoy all further appreciation in the asset's value. A simple example would be a restructuring of a family business in which the sole owner of a company transfers a new class of common stock to children while retaining preferred stock equal in value to the firm's current worth. US lawmakers have taken several stabs at limiting the freedom of owners to achieve these results, notably in the Revenue Act of 1987 and the Budget Act of 1990 (which substituted a new scheme for the one created only three years previously). Most observers, however, believe that the capacity of families to accommodate their business transactions to the forms required by the tax law outstrips the ability of the legislature to attack the problem. As a result, the transfer tax seems largely an excise extracted from the inattentive or improvident wealthy. Shoup (1966) asks the question of why wealthy persons ever find themselves in the position of paying the federal estate tax, given the many means available for avoiding it. At the same time he recounts substantial anectdotal evidence indicating that some extremely rich people do fall prey to this levy.

8. Contribution of US Tax to Progressivity

Reforms proposed in 1969 and to some extent adopted in 1976 broadened the scope of US transfer taxation but did not significantly change the rate schedule as such. In 1981 the United States both lowered the maximum tax rates applicable to gifts and estates and increased the amounts that could be transferred exempt from tax. In real dollar terms, the enlarged exemptions were still smaller than those in effect in 1932, when the federal taxes were made permanent. Nonetheless, a number of commentators contend that the 1981 changes represented a significant departure from the previous policy of promoting the redistribution of wealth. Graetz (1983) argues that the pre-1981 federal transfer taxes, although insignificant in terms of absolute amount of government revenues, were responsible for about a third of the total amount of progressivity in federal taxation. He defines progressivity as the increment in taxes collected from persons with greater than average wealth over the amount they would pay if average tax rates applied at all levels of income. He deplores the move away from redistribution implied by the 1981 changes. However, he does not consider the claim that such progressivity as the pre-1981 taxes achieved represented levies against unusually improvident or poorly advised persons, rather than a systematic effort to redistribute wealth.

9. Welfare Analysis of Voluntary Wealth Transmission

The intuition that a gratuitous transfer represents a form of valuable consumption for the transferor while benefiting the transferee by increasing either capital or the capacity to consume appears in Simons (1938). The transferor has revealed a preference for the transferee's welfare, which the transferor values at least as much as possession of the property transferred. The transferee is enriched by the value of the property, defined as the amount for which the property could be exchanged. A formal statement of the claim can be found in Becker (1974). The implications of this insight for tax policy took longer to work out. For Simons, it was enough to show that gratuitous transfers were economically indistinguishable from other transactions normally subjected to income taxation. Following a principle of strict nondiscrimination among categories of income, he therefore would have included the transfers in the transferee's income tax base while continuing the existing rule of not allowing transferors a deduction. A Canadian government study proposed exactly this step in 1966 (Jantscher, 1969), and a study commissioned by the US Treasury explored the implications of such a system in 1976. Other scholars, notably Dodge (1978), also have advocated including gratuitous transfers in the income tax base.

10. Arguments for Subsidizing Transfers

More recently, scholars have seized on the welfare implications of Simons' insight to argue against transfer taxation. Bracewell-Milnes (1989) puts the argument in nontechnical terms by coining the term 'owner's surplus' to connote the value owners attach to their assets in excess of the discounted present value of the asset's anticipated income stream. He claims that gratuitous transfers, whether charitable or intrafamilial, increase welfare by bestowing owner's surplus on transferees while providing transferors with value equal to the discounted present value of the anticipated income from the asset. Kaplow (1995) states the argument in formal terms and with great rigor. They both conclude that, to the extent welfare maximization is a legitimate social end, society ought to subsidize gratuitous transfers rather than tax them. Kaplow notes that a number of rules found in US law - income tax deductibility of charitable transfers, the treatment of gratuitous transfers as a nonrealization event to the transferor and as excluded from the transferee's income tax base, and the basis increase for assets received from a decedent - might be characterized as a kind of subsidy for giving.

11. Arguments for Subsidizing Earlier Transfers

A variation on this argument looks at evidence suggesting that younger owners may tend to prefer riskier investments than do older persons. To the extent this claim is true, it would imply that, *ceteris paribus*, younger owners might underwrite a greater amount of technological innovation and therefore increase social welfare. The data presented by Menchick and David (1983) is suggestive but not conclusive. Stephan (1986) uses this hypothesis to support an argument for tax rules that subsidize lifetime gifts relative to deathtime bequests. He notes that US law generally encourages gifts: the effective gift tax rates are substantially less because the tax is not included in the base, as it is with respect to estates. US income tax rules do disfavor gifts to the extent that gifts are not eligible for the basis step up to fair market value that applies to bequests, but in many cases this distinction is inconsequential because of the upward basis adjustment available to gifts subject to the gift tax.

12. Rate Differential Depending on Whether First- or Later-Generation Wealth

Economists have made a somewhat different distinction between wealth in the possession of the person who accummulated it and inherited wealth. Rignano (1924) was the first to argue that either an estate or inheritance tax should base the rate of taxation on the age of the wealth. He would have imposed low rates on wealth being transferred by the person who created it and progressively higher rates on those who acquire wealth by inheritance and then seek to pass it on to later generations. He argued that such a system could achieve significant socialization of wealth without destroying the incentive to save and take risks. Kiesling (1992) returned to this proposal and defended it against criticisms based on its difficulty of administration. He proposed operating with a presumption that all wealth passing at death had been 'aged' and then placing the burden on the decedent or his beneficiaries to present evidence justifying lower rates. The US generation-skipping-transfer tax, discussed below in Sections 34-35, offers an alternative approach to an analogous problem.

13. Transferor Tax versus Accessions Tax

Were all transfers taxed at a uniform rate, it would make no difference whether the levy fell on transferors or transferees. For most purposes the administration of these taxes is indistinguishable, especially if one party has secondary liability for the other's tax obligation. But as soon as one introduces exempt amounts and a progressive rate structure, the identification of the taxpayer becomes significant. Estate and gift taxes calculate the amount owed by reference to the size of the decedent's holdings. Inheritance and other accessions taxes look instead at what the transferee receives. The United States and the United Kingdom tax transferors, although their systems differ substantially. Most Continental European countries have accessions taxes instead.

14. Advantages of Accessions Taxation

Advocates of accessions taxes contend that this system has two main advantages over the estate tax (see Andrews, 1973, and Aaron and Munnell, 1992). First, to the extent gratuitious transfers involve life-cycle assets and therefore increase the transferee's consumption, the tax should fall on the person engaged in the higher level of consumption. Second, to the extent that the tax is intended to encourage the redistribution of capital assets through dispersion of ownership, it should impose a lower burden on bequests to multiple beneficiaries. An estate tax, which does not take into account how a decedent spreads the estate among noncharitable beneficiaries, cannot do this.

15. Income Taxation of Transfers as an Alternative Accessions Tax

A variation on the imposition of accessions taxes would be the inclusion of bequests and gifts in the income tax base, as advocated by Simons (1938) and Dodge (1978). The 1966 Canadian proposal contains the most detailed analysis of what this approach would entail. One important collateral consequence of including accessions in income would be the greater likelihood of high taxes during years in which a taxpayer received an extraordinary accession, such as a once-in-a-lifetime bequest. The Canadian proposal would have introduced a form of income-averaging to alleviate this problem.

16. Problems with Accessions Taxes

A complication associated with accessions taxes is the opportunity trusts present for separating the transferor's relinquishment of ownership from the transferee's accession to wealth. The creation of the trust may give beneficiaries an expectation sufficient to alter their behavior but not create property interests substantial enough to sustain immediate taxation (compare Dickens, 1861). The problem does not exist in the case of trusts where all interests are fixed (for example, to A for life, remainder to B), because an inheritance tax can be levied on the discounted present value of a vested future interest. But it is easy enough to design trusts where vesting is delayed (for example, to W for life, then income divided equally among those of my children alive at the time of W's death, then the corpus distributed equally to my issue *per stirpes*; only W's interest would be vested). Nor is there a problem even in such cases, if the trust corpus grows at the rate that the designated discount rate assumes. The increased tax paid on distribution attributable to appreciation of the trust property would offset the benefit of deferral. But discount rates are only guesses as to future value, and become less useful to the extent that trust corpus does not comprise assets for which reliable and thick markets exist. Income taxation of the trust may substitute in part, but is not equivalent to an immediate levy at the inheritance tax rate on the discounted present value of the future distribution.

17. Withholding on Trusts under Accessions Taxation

An alternative approach would be to impose a withholding tax on complex trusts that could be credited against accessions taxes due on distribution of trust property (see Andrews, 1973). To be a complete substitute for the ultimate inheritance tax payable, however, the credits attributable to withholding would have to be refundable and interest would have to be paid, by the taxpayer or the government as the case may be, on any difference between the amount withheld and the amount of tax payable at the time of distribution. Such refinements would add to the administrative burden of the tax and to that extent make it somewhat less attractive.

18. Relationship of Transfer Taxes to Income Tax

Transfer taxes, and in particular taxes levied on transferors, are sometimes defended on the grounds that the property subject to these levies benefits from unavoidable but undesirable gaps in the income tax. Gutman (1981) argues that the US estate and gift taxes compensate for the income tax deferral implicit in the rule treating gifts as nonrealization events, and for the foregone income tax produced by the basis increase enjoyed by holders of propertry received from a decedent. More generally, capital assets tend to benefit from the realization principle, which defers taxation of capital gain until the holder sells or exchanges the asset. Imposition of a substitute tax on persons who benefit from these gaps brings the income tax closer to the ideal of nondiscrimination among types of income.

19. Difficulties with Nondiscrimination Principle

Appeals to the nondiscrimination principle have a certain intuitive attraction but often obscure difficult issues. Recalling the concept of W_3, for example, one might note that most income taxes do not include social insurance in their base. Yet transfer taxes for the most part reach very few people who benefit from this exclusion. The point is illustrative: all income taxes in practice contain many violations of a strict nondiscrimination principle, and the nondiscrimination norm standing alone does not suggest a weighting strategy that can indicate which violations should be seen as more serious than others.

20. Choice of Nondiscrimination Principles

Moreover, as Andrews (1974) was among the first to note, to the extent existing law indicates adherence to any nondiscrimination principle, it suggests a commitment to neutrality among types of consumption, with a surtax on the kinds of capital held by the most wealthy. The US (so-called) income tax, like those of many countries, excludes from the base imputed rents from owner-occupied housing and most employer contributions to retirement savings. The exclusion of imputed rents in turn can be seen as equivalent to allowing an immediate deduction for the cost of acquiring an asset, as a consumption tax would require. And for the nonwealthy, housing and pension plans are the most significant forms of savings. In other words, when considered from the perspective of neutrality among types of consumption, these systems discriminate against financial assets such as stock and bonds, the ownership of which (disregarding tax-favored retirement savings) is heavily concentrated among the wealthiest persons. Taking this point to its logical conclusion, one might argue that the structure of the income tax implies an argument against any further taxation of wealth transfers.

21. Unification of Transfer Taxes

Some countries tax gifts separately from deathtime transfers, others treat gifts as deathtime transfers if the donation precedes death by less than a specified period, and a few attempt to treat gifts and deathtime transfers as functionally equivalent. Aaron and Munnell (1992) and Andrews (1973) advocate development of an accessions tax that would include gifts and bequests in an integrated base, with the tax rate increasing with the amount of the transferee's lifetime receipts. Shoup (1966), Kurtz and Surrey (1970), Brannon (1973) and Sims (1984) instead call for an integrated progressive transfer tax that would determine its rate by reference to the sum of the transferor's lifetime and deathtime transfers.

22. Unification and US Practice

Before 1976 US law subjected lifetime and deathtime transfers to completely different levies. Gifts made in 'contemplation of death', a gloriously open-ended standard, were subjected to both taxes, but the gift tax paid on these transfers was both credited against the estate tax and excluded from the estate tax base. Since 1976, the US has had a partially integrated system. The rate of tax on estates depends on the decedent's lifetime taxable transfers, and all transfers have a single 'unified credit' to offset gift and estate taxes. But gifts occurring more than three years before death (whether made in contemplation of death or not) enjoy a distinct benefit. First, a per-person exemption of $10,000 a year exists for gifts. The gift tax base does not include the amount of tax. By contrast, the estate tax base is tax inclusive. To illustrate, a US transferor in the highest rate bracket would part with $ 1,550,000 to effect a gift of $1,000,000 (disregarding the $10,000 exemption). A decedent in the highest bracket (because of lifetime gifts) would have to have a taxable estate of $2,222,222 to make an after-tax bequest of $1,000,000. Stated differently, the top gift tax rate, translated into tax-inclusive terms, is slightly in excess of 36 percent, while the equivalent estate tax rate is 55 percent.

23. Proposals for Unification of Tax Rates

In 1984 the US Treasury proposed a more complete integration of the gift and estate taxes (Department of the Treasury, 1984). This would have been accomplished by increasing the tax rate on gifts. This proposal was not incorporated into the major tax changes enacted in 1986. Stephan (1986) subsequently criticized it for its failure to take account of differences in both the income tax treatment and welfare implications of gifts and bequests.

24. Issue of Base Integration

A different kind of integration occurs when the same transaction comes under both taxes. A simple example would involve a trust in which the transferor retains income for life, remainder to the beneficiary. The creation of the vested remainder constitutes a completed gift and is subject to tax. This transaction, however, seems functionally indistinguishable from retention of full ownership until death, at least for those persons with no need to invade capital. As a result, US law for many years also has included the full value of the trust corpus in the decedent's taxable estate. The decedent is given a credit against the estate tax for the gift tax payable on the remainder.

25. Historical Dimensions of Problem

The actual rules for determining which lifetime transfers are includible in the estate tax base are complex and inconsistent. During the early years of the US estate tax, the Supreme Court expressed its hostility to this levy by imposing narrow constructions on the statutory language. These decisions in turn provoked the Congress to overrule the Court through new legislation. In the period after World War II, a more liberal Court both repudiated some of its earlier decisions and imposed expansive constructions on the new legislation, provoking a by-then more conservative Congress to enact further legislation. The resulting hodge podge produces rents for professors and specialists but otherwise serves no apparent good.

26. Proposals for Base Integration

Various suggestions have been made for cutting this Gordian knot. The Department of the Treasury (1984) would subject all transfers to either a gift or an estate tax but not both. It would have included transactions where the transferor retained some form of present enjoyment in the estate tax base. In all other cases, it would have imposed a gift tax on the value of the transferred property. Isenbergh (1984) and Sims (1984) offer schemes that differed in detail but in general followed the Treasury's 'easy to complete' preference for earlier gift taxation. Stephan (1986) instead favors 'hard to complete' rules that would classify more transactions as deathtime. His rule would regard any transfer where the determination of the interest depends on the transfer's life as testamentary. Thus in the case of a trust with income to accumulate, then the corpus to B at the transferor's death, only the estate tax would apply.

27. Special Rules for Transfers within Family Units

Most transfer tax systems, whether levied on transferors or transferees, contain special exemptions or reduced rates where the transfers involve specific family relationships. Transfers between spouses present particular problems, because the underlying law of ownership may depend on marital status. In the United States, for example, an asset acquired by a married couple living in a community property state often will become the common property of the couple, regardless of who furnished the consideration for the acquisition. In 1948 the United States sought to create a uniform national tax rule by allowing a 50 percent deduction for gifts to a spouse and a deduction up to half the size of the taxable estate for deathtime transfers. The 1981 amendments exclude most interspousal transfers from both taxes.

28. Implications of Complete Exclusion for Interspousal Transfers

A rule of complete exclusion creates a hypothetical possibility for indefinite avoidance of the transfer taxes in cases where remarriage occurs successively. As a practical matter, however, the progressive nature of the transfer taxes still creates an incentive for most spouses to split their estates between the survivor and other noncharitable beneficiaries. All other things being equal, under a progressive rate structure a tax equal to twice the tax on half of a large sum is less than the tax on that sum. In other words, spouses still will benefit if their property is distributed in such a way that at least one is treated for estate tax purposes as having an estate that does not fall into the top taxable bracket.

29. Problems with Interspousal Transfers

Transfers to spouses in trust continue to present problems. In the simplest case, namely a transfer to a spouse for life, remainder to the children, permitting a deduction for the spouse's interest may present tax avoidance opportunities. If standard actuarial tables overestimated the spouse's actual life expectancy or if the applicable discount rate underestimates the appreciation of the corpus, a present tax on the remainder interest will not be economically equivalent to a deferred tax on the full value of the property. US law instead denies a deduction for the spouse's interest in most cases where that interest terminates and, upon that event, others acquire an interest in the property. The rules implementing this policy, which contain many exceptions, are exceedingly complex and have occasioned much litigation.

30. Nonspousal Intrafamilial Transfers

Interspousal transfers aside, US gift and estate taxation generally attaches little significance to consanguinity. Most inheritance taxes, however, do increase the rate of tax with the degree of separation between transferor and transferee. As Tait (1967) observes, to the extent these taxes are designed to break up economic dynasties, this characteristic seems perverse. Bequests to children suffer lower taxes than bequests to strangers. Nor, in Tait's view, do there exist other reasons for treating transfers among close family members more favorably than others. He dismisses one common claim - that inheritances from distant relatives come as windfalls and therefore are more easily surrendered to the tax authorities - as dependent on what he considers the dubious assumption that expectancy is correlated with closeness of relationship.

31. Defenses of Consanguinity Preferences

In response to Tait, Richter (1987) argues that consanguinity rate reductions make sense if one regards inheritance taxation not as a mechanism to redistribute wealth, but rather as a form of social insurance. Drawing on Friedman (1957), Richter distinguishes between 'permanent' and 'transitory' inheritances. The former are reliable, in the sense that the potential beneficiary reasonably may make plans based on the expectation of receiving them. The latter become reliable only if the beneficiary can insure against nonreceipt. The market does not supply inheritance insurance as such, but a tax on transitory inheritances, to the extent that the tax receipts are converted by the state into commonly shared benefits, serves the same function. To conclude the argument, Richter maintains that consanguinity is a good proxy for the relative mix of permanent and transitory components in any given inheritance.

32. Consanguinity Preferences and Redistribution

Cremer and Pestieau (1988) extend Richter's argument to defend the consanguinity perference on grounds of promoting redistribution. Their model assumes variablity in the number of children, including the existence of childless transferors. They show that under certain plausible assumptions about inheritance patterns, wealth transferred to lineal descendents result in dispersion of property among children and grandchildren. Transfers to collateral relatives, however, may result in concentration of multiple couples' assets in the hands of a single niece or nephew. A rate preference for lineal over collateral transfers thus may reflect a desire to disperse the ownership of property.

33. Generational Issues

Although US estate taxation does not take consanguinity into account, the system does adjust the tax rates to take into account wealth transfers that skip over one or more generations. The argument for this surtax on generation-skipping transfers is that the transfer taxes should function as a once-a-generation levy on financial capital. Moderately wealthy people transfer capital to children, with the assumption that the children will consume the income thrown off by the assets and then transfer them to grandchildren. Persons so wealthy that they can provide for their children and still have capital left over to transfer to grandchildren should be taxed as if their capital first passed through their childrens' hands, whether or not the children directly benefited from the property. An exception to this policy exists for orphaned grandchildren, who are treated as if they were the transferor's children.

34. Implementation of the Generation-Skipping Transfer Tax

The United States first enacted a generation-skipping transfer (GST) tax in 1976 but deferred its implementation for several years. In 1986 Congress created a significantly different tax in place of the earlier one. The current levy imposes a flat rate of 55 percent on generation-skipping transfers in excess of $1,000,000 per transferor. The statute assigns persons to generations based on lineal relationship to the transferor; nonrelative transferees are assigned to a generation on the basis of difference in age with the transferor. The tax is calculated by reference to the amount received by the transferee, which means that any estate or gift tax generated by the transfer will not be included in the tax base. The amount of GST tax is, however, treated as a taxable gift. The GST tax on direct transfers is not included in the GST tax base, but the tax on generation-skipping transfers from trusts, either of income or corpus, is.

35. Technical Issues in Generation-Skipping Transfer Taxation

The GST tax treats direct transfers to grandchildren more favorably than it does trust transactions that encumber financial capital and delay ultimate power to dispose of the property. Stephan (1986) observes that this difference parallels the lower rates imposed on gifts as opposed to deathtime transfers, and may reflect a similar policy of encouraging wealthy people to transfer control over financial capital to younger persons sooner rather than later.

Bibliography on Inheritance and Gift Taxation (6070)

Aaron, Henry J. and Munnell, Alicia H. (1992), 'Reassessing the Role for Wealth Transfer Taxes', **45** *National Tax Journal*, 119-143.

Andrews, William D. (1973), 'What's Fair About Death Taxes?', **26** *National Tax Journal*, 465-469.

Blum, Robert (1973), 'Estate and Gift Taxation Moderator's Remarks', **26** *National Tax Journal*, 439-440.

Bracewell-Milnes, Barry (1989), *The Wealth of Giving: Every One in his Inheritance*, London, Institute of Economic Affairs, 112 p.

Brannon, Gerald M. (1973), 'Death Taxes in a Structure of Progessive Taxes', **26** *National Tax Journal*, 451-457.

Collie, Martin K. (1973), 'Estate and Gift Tax Revision', **26** *National Tax Journal*, 441-449.

Covey, Richard B. (1973), 'Estate and Gift Taxation', **26** *National Tax Journal*, 459-463.

Cremer, Helmuth and Pestieau, Pierre (1988), 'A Case for Differential Inheritance Taxation', **0(9)** *Annales d'Economie et de Statistique*, 167-182.

Dodge, Joseph M. (1978), 'Beyond Estate and Gift Tax Reform: Including Gifts and Bequests in Income', **91** *Harvard Law Review*, 1177-1211.

Graetz, Michael J. (1983), 'To Praise the Estate Tax, Not to Bury It', **93** *Yale Law Journal*, 259-286.

Gutman, Harry L. (1981), 'Reforming Federal Wealth Transfer Taxes after ERTA', **69** *Virginia Law Review*, 1183-1272.

Isenbergh, Joseph (1984), 'Simplifying Retained Life Interests, Revocable Transfers, and the Marital Deduction', **51** *University of Chicago Law Review*, 1-33.

Jantscher, Gerald R. (1969), 'Death and Gift Taxation in the United States after the Report of the Royal Commission', **22(1)** *National Tax Journal*, 121-138.

Kaplow, Louis (1995), 'A Note on Subsidizing Gifts', **58** *Journal of Public Economics*, 469-477.

Kiesling, Herbert J. (1992), *Taxation and Public Goods - A Welfare-Economic Critique of Tax Policy Analysis*, Ann Arbor, MI, University of Michigan Press, 362 p.

Kotlikoff, Laurence J. (1988), 'Intergenerational Transfers and Savings', **2** *Journal of Economic Perspectives*, 41-58.

Kurtz, Jerome and Surrey, Stanley S. (1970), 'Reform of Death and Gift Taxes: The 1969 Treasury Proposals, the Criticisms, and a Rebuttal', **70** *Columbia Law Review*, 1365-1401.

McCaffery, Edward J. (1994), 'The Uneasy Case for Wealth Transfer Taxation', **104** *Yale Law Journal*, 283-365.

Menchik, Paul and David, Martin (1983), 'Income Distribution, Lifetime Savings, and Bequests', **73** *American Economic Review*, 672-690.

Modigliani, Franco (1988), 'The Role of Intergenerational Transfers and Life Cycle Saving in the Accumulation of Wealth', **2** *Journal of Economic Perspectives*, 15-40.

Richter, Wolfram F. (1987), 'Taxation as Insurance and the Case of Rate Differentiation According to Consanguinity under Inheritance Taxation', **33** *Journal of Public Economics*, 363-376.

Rignano, Eugenio (1924), *The Social Significance of the Inheritance Tax*, New York, Knopf, 128 p.

Shoup, Carl S. (1966), *Federal Estate and Gift Taxes*, Washington, Brookings Institution, 253 p.

Sims, Theodore S. (1984), 'Timing Under a Unified Wealth Transfer Tax', **51** *University of Chicago Law Review*, 34-90.

Stephan, Paul B. (1986), 'A Comment on Transfer Tax Reform', **72** *Virginia Law Review*, 1471-1496.

Summers, Lawrence H. (1981), 'Capital Taxation and Capital Accumulation in a Life Cycle Growth Model', **71(4)** *American Economic Review*, 533-544.

Tait, Alan A. (1967), *The Taxation of Personal Wealth*, Urbana, University of Illinois Press, 283 p.

Wagner, Richard E. (1977), *Inheritance and the State-Tax Principles for a Free and Prosperous Commonwealth*, Washington, American Enterprise Institute for Public Policy Research, 95 p.

Other References

Andrews, William D. (1974), 'A Consumption-Type or Cash-Flow Personal Income Tax', **87** *Harvard Law Review*, 1113-1188.

Becker, Gary S. (1974), 'A Theory of Social Interactions', **82** *Journal of Political Economy*, 1063-1091.

Department of the Treasury (1984), *Tax Reform for Fairness, Simplicity, and Economic Growth - The Treasury Department Report to the President,* 2 vols, Washington, US Treasury, 262 and 408 p.

Dickens, Charles (1861), *Great Expectations*, London, Chapman and Hall, 225 p.

Friedman, Milton (1957), *A Theory of the Consumption Function*, Chicago, University of Chicago Press, 243 p.

Meade, James E. (1964), *Efficiency, Equality, and the Ownership of Property*, London, Allen and Unwin, 92 p.

Pechman, Joseph A. (1987), *Federal Tax Policy* (5th edn), Washington, Brookings Institution, 430 p.

Simons, Henry C. (1938), *Personal Income Taxation: The Definition of Income as a Problem of Fiscal Policy*, Chicago, University of Chicago Press, 238 p.

Vickrey, William (1947), *Agenda for Progressive Taxation*, New York, Ronald Press, 496 p.

6080
INTERNATIONAL TAXATION

Timothy J. Goodspeed
Hunter College and CUNY Graduate Center

Ann Dryden Witte
Florida International University, Wellesley College and NBER

Abstract

We consider various systems for taxing international income (source vs. residency systems) and international transactions (origin vs. destination systems) and the empirical literature that has addressed issues related to such systems. The optimal taxation literature finds a conflict between static and dynamic efficiency considerations but fails to consider such important aspects of taxation as the benefits arising from public goods and services, compliance costs and administrative costs. Empirical work finds that the level of taxation significantly affects the location of investment and the way in which investment is financed. However, estimates of the magnitude of these effects of taxation are varied. Non-tax considerations (for example, political and economic stability) often dominate tax considerations in firm decision making. Firms use intra-company prices (for example, transfer prices) to reduce the total amount of taxes paid, but the magnitude of this type of evasion does not appear to be large. Countries often use their tax systems to encourage exports and to attract investment. Many tax treaties between developed and developing countries have tax sparing provisions that allow firms to credit unpaid taxes due to 'tax holidays'. We suggest that future research on international taxation consider second-best worlds, incorporate administrative considerations and consider the effect of regulatory as well as tax regimes. This research could also usefully incorporate equity considerations and such non-tax aspects of international decision making as the availability of skilled labor, infrastructure and legal and regulatory environments.
JEL classification: F2, F3, H2, K3, M4, O0
Keywords: International Taxation, Transfer Pricing, Foreign Investment, Tax Treaties, Capital Taxation

1. Systems of International Taxation

International taxation generally refers to the tax treatment of cross-national transactions. Since each nation has its own tax rules and the rules of one nation are rarely perfectly meshed with those of another, it is possible that income will be taxed more than once (sometimes referred to as double taxation) or that it will go untaxed by any jurisdiction. To prevent this, countries employ different methods. In principal, two methods of taxation have been distinguished for direct taxes such as personal and corporate income taxes: the territorial (or source) system of taxation and the worldwide (or residence) system. Under a pure source system, all income earned in a country is taxed by that country regardless of whether the earner is deemed to be foreign. A pure residence system taxes income regardless of where it was earned as long as the earner is deemed to be a resident of the country. An analogy to the familiar distinction between gross domestic product (GDP) and gross national product (GNP) may be helpful. GDP includes all income produced domestically, whether by domestic or foreign nationals, and is analogous to income taxed under the source method. GNP includes all income produced by nationals, whether at home or abroad, and is analogous to income taxed under the residence method.

As long as those receiving income are classified by all countries in the same mutually exclusive way as residents or nonresidents, and all countries use the same method of taxation, there is no problem of double taxation. (However, there are efficiency issues, which we address in the next section.) Double taxation problems arise because countries have different residency rules and tax systems. For example, some countries use a territorial system when defining income while others use a residence basis for determining what income is taxable. Further, no country uses the pure form of either of these systems. All countries claim the right to tax all income generated within that country's border; that is, all countries begin with a source basis for taxation. This is reasonable in terms of both tax administration and tax compliance. It is always easier to assess and collect taxes on income earned in the taxing jurisdiction. Source taxation also accords with the widely accepted principle of taxing individuals who receive benefits from public expenditures (the benefit principle of taxation). For the most part, the government of the country in which that taxpayer is physically present provides the public goods and services consumed by a taxpayer. Both efficiency and common concepts of fairness dictate that those who benefit from government should help to pay for it.

However, most nations try to tax at least some of the foreign income of their residents. These attempts to tax the foreign income of residents result in a mixed source and residence basis for taxation. For instance, the US Government claims the right to tax all income earned in the US, a source system of taxation. However, it also claims the right to tax some of the income that its permanent residents and citizens earn abroad, a residence basis of taxation. Countries that tax such foreign-source income normally provide a credit for foreign taxes paid (up to a limit discussed below). Other countries such as France come closer to a true source/territorial basis for taxation. These countries generally exclude the foreign income of their residents from domestic taxation.

Regardless of which method of direct taxation is used, the tax code must provide a set of rules determining residency. For individuals, residency is usually determined by a test based on the number of days an individual is present in a country. Unlike other countries, US citizenship also triggers the definition of a resident for US tax purposes. For corporations, this may be triggered by incorporation (as in the US) or by the place of management and control. The UK relied exclusively on the place of management and control until 1988. Since 1988, UK residency for a corporation may be triggered either by incorporation, or by the place of management and control.

A second question in countries that tax foreign source income is the timing of such taxation. For a business, the way in which foreign operations are set up can influence when taxes are paid. For instance, a US corporation can set up an overseas operation as a branch, which is not separately incorporated. The income (or loss) of a foreign branch is combined with domestic income and taxed currently. The companies that tend to set up foreign operations as branches are concentrated in the banking and petroleum industries (Goodspeed and Frisch, 1989). Alternatively, the foreign operation can be set up as a controlled foreign corporation (CFC). CFCs are incorporated in the foreign country, but a controlling share of their stock (over 50 percent for the US) is owned by domestic shareholders. Except for certain types of income (described below), the income of a CFC is only subject to domestic taxation when it is repatriated. Since a CFC can delay subjecting its income to tax by not repatriating income, this feature of international tax law is commonly referred to as 'deferral'. Many countries (for example, the US, Germany and Japan) allow deferral on undistributed income. These countries also generally have 'anti-deferral' regimes that restrict the types of income on which taxation may be deferred until repatriation. The US anti-deferral regime began with the addition of Subpart F to the US Internal Revenue Code by the US Revenue Act of 1962. Subpart F provides for current taxation of certain types of unrepatriated income of US CFCs. Unrepatriated income subject to Subpart F is treated as if it had been repatriated as a dividend. The income subject to Subpart F provisions has been broadened over the years and the US has enacted other anti-deferral rules. However, deferral remains important. The US Treasury estimates that deferral cost $2 billion in lost tax revenue in 1997 (OMB, 1996). See Ault (1997) or Gramwell, Merrill and Dubert (1996) for a detailed discussion of anti-deferral regimes in a number of countries.

Residents of countries that tax on a worldwide basis will have their foreign source income taxed twice, first in the foreign country where the income is earned and next in the home country. Most countries that attempt to tax the worldwide income of their residents allow a credit or deduction for taxes paid to foreign countries. To avoid giving refunds for high foreign taxes, the credit is limited to the tax that would have been paid had the income been earned in the home country (usually given both the home country tax rate and the home country definition of the tax base). This creates two types of resident taxpayers; those that receive full credit for foreign taxes paid and those that do not. Taxpayers who are not able to credit all taxes paid abroad against taxes in their home country are said to be in an 'excess credit' position. Taxpayers who do receive full credit are said to be in a 'deficit of credit' or 'excess limitation' position.

Two methods are used to determine the foreign tax credit. One method treats income in each foreign country separately in determining the credit. The second method determines the credit on a worldwide basis. Income and taxes from all countries are added to determine whether the limitation applies; thus, the taxpayer will be in excess credit if its (weighted) average foreign tax rate is greater than the home country tax rate. Consequently, a taxpayer may be able to reduce its home country tax liability because of the averaging of high and low taxed income. Consider, for instance, a multinational with a large proportion of income coming from investments in high-tax countries and a small proportion of income coming from investments in low-tax foreign countries. The multinational will not obtain full credit for foreign taxes paid; that is, it will be in an excess credit position. This firm would then have an incentive (absent under a per-country limitation) to try to shift income from high-tax to low-tax foreign countries so that the average foreign tax rate falls below the home country rate. The multinational will thereby obtain credit for all foreign taxes paid. (The shifting of income may not require actually shifting production facilities; it could be accomplished through paper transactions - see the later section on transfer pricing.)

To combat this tendency of the worldwide credit system, some countries force multinational companies to make separate credit calculations for particularly high- or low-tax categories called 'baskets' of income. The US basket classification system is particularly complex. Prior to the US Tax Reform Act of 1986 (TRA86), there were five baskets. TRA86 substantially increased the number of baskets by expanding the Internal Revenue Code Section 904(b) interest income basket to include all passive income and adding four new baskets: (1) high withholding tax on interest (defined as 5 percent or more), (2) financial services income, (3) shipping income, and (4) dividends from each uncontrolled foreign corporation. This last basket potentially created a large number of new baskets since the credit on dividends from *each* uncontrolled foreign corporation had to be computed separately. The basket system is designed to prevent US taxpayers from combining high-taxed and low-taxed foreign income in order to receive a credit for taxes paid in excess of the US rate on one portion of income.

To some extent, countries can be classified on the basis of whether their foreign tax credit systems are per-country or worldwide. The US, Japan and Iceland provide credits on a worldwide basis; Canada, Germany, Greece, Ireland, Italy, the Netherlands, New Zealand, Norway, Portugal, Spain, Turkey, and the United Kingdom use a per country limit in determining the foreign tax credit. However, as Ault (1997) notes, this division is somewhat misleading. In the UK, for instance, the per-country credit limitation can be avoided by routing income through a nonresident holding company. The income going through this 'mixer' company is considered all from one source, and hence averaged and the per-country limitation avoided. (There are no 'pass-thru' rules in the UK as there are in the US.) Ault suggests that the use of such companies is common.

In principal, the resident system taxes individuals on their worldwide income. However, since most countries determine resident status by a test based on the number of days one is in a country, most expatriates are not residents of their home country for tax purposes. The US is an exception. Since US citizens are considered US residents, US expatriates are required to file US tax returns as well as tax returns for the country in which they reside. However, if a US citizen is not in the United States for 11 out of 12 consecutive months, the individual can exempt $70,000 of income earned abroad from US personal income taxation. Self-employed US citizens working abroad will still owe the 15 percent US payroll tax for Social Security, but this is often overridden by treaty if the US citizen pays the foreign social security tax, and the foreign social security tax otherwise qualifies for the foreign tax credit.

Lower-level governments that form a federation sometimes use a somewhat different arrangement for apportioning the tax base of firms with operations in a number of different taxing jurisdictions. The approach used is called formula apportionment. The US states that belong to the Multi-State Tax Compact, Canadian provinces, and Swiss cantons use formula apportionment to tax corporations (Daly and Weiner, 1993). Formula apportionment can be considered a source-based approach to taxation. The formula used under a formula apportionment system divides the entire tax base of the corporation (for example, the worldwide base) among a participating set of taxing authorities. Each authority taxes only that portion of the tax base attributed to it. If all regions use the same formula and the same definition of profits, the portions are mutually exclusive and exhaustive, and the 'worldwide' base is taxed only once. Formula apportionment begins by selecting a set of indicators (for example, sales, property value, and wage payments of a corporation in the case of US states) to reflect the level of economic activity of a taxable economic entity in a tax jurisdiction. It then weights these indicators to form an index of economic activity in a jurisdiction. The jurisdictions split the taxable base on the basis of this index. In practice, one problem that this method encounters in the US is that states use different weights in determining the index so that the base ends up being taxed more than once. The economic effects of formula apportionment have been explored by McLure (1980, 1981), and have even been discussed in the context of the European Union (Daly and Weiner, 1993). On a broader international basis, formula apportionment is rarely used because of difficulty agreeing to the 'formula' and enforcing its use.

A second set of taxes on foreign income, both for wage and capital income, are termed 'withholding taxes'. These taxes are applied at source, usually on gross income. For instance, interest income received by a British citizen holding money in an Italian bank would have taxes withheld prior to remittance to the British citizen. The same holds for wage income: a US citizen working in Spain for a few months is subject to a 15 percent withholding tax. The income is also subject to US tax, although the individual can get credit for the 15 percent Spanish withholding tax. The reason for withholding tax on the income of nonresidents is principally for compliance purposes.Without withholding, individuals may fail to report such income in both home and source country. Bilateral treaties generally reduce withholding taxes on dividends and interest. In addition, the US has unilaterally eliminated its withholding tax on interest income (both for individuals and corporations). For a summary of reductions see Gramwell, Merrill and Dubert, 1996. Countries may also enter into information exchange agreements and other cooperative arrangements.

Since tax treaties are bilateral and only cover selective countries, withholding tax rates can vary widely. This creates incentives to funnel income through third countries that have a low withholding tax rate. (See Giovannini, 1989, for an example.) As described in Hufbauer, Elliott, and Maldonado (1988), tax treaties grew out of recommendations by the League of Nations in 1927 as a way to reduce double and zero taxation, and to reduce withholding taxes. They also serve the purpose of stimulating international investment and structuring cooperation among different national taxing authorities. 'Model' tax treaties were developed by the OECD in 1963 and the UN in 1979. The OECD issued its most recent model treaty in 1994. These model treaties are meant to serve as general guidelines. The US has from time to time issued its own model treaty. The most recent US model was issued in 1996. Countries do not have tax treaties with all other countries. For example, France has treaties with approximately 90 countries while the US has treaties with approximately 50 countries (see Gramwell, Merill and Dubert, 1996 for a summary).

Indirect taxes, such as sales and value-added taxes, also suffer from problems of double taxation. As with direct tax systems, international indirect tax systems can in principal be of two types: a destination system or an origin system. The destination system taxes goods where they are consumed and is analogous to resident taxation; the origin system taxes goods where they are produced and is analogous to source taxation. International trade agreements have set rules for indirect taxation so that taxes cannot be used to favor domestically produced goods. Under the General Agreement on Tariffs and Trade (GATT) indirect taxes can be imposed on import and rebated on export. This is consistent with the destination system of indirect taxation.

2. Theory: Equilibrium, Efficiency and Tax Competition

Having outlined various systems of taxation, we turn to the nature of the equilibrium under various forms of taxation and the relative efficiency of different systems. While the residence and source principles of taxation apply to labor as well as capital taxation, most of the literature discussing these concepts relates to capital taxation, and our discussion will therefore proceed in terms of capital taxation. The standard view is that pure residence taxation promotes efficiency in investment decisions while pure source taxation promotes efficiency in savings decisions. To understand why, we must first consider the nature of the equilibrium under source and residence taxation.

Recent discussions of equilibrium in international taxation can be found in Keen (1992); we follow the notation of Keen. Consider two countries, A and B. Each country can be characterized by a representative investor who can earn a pre-tax return r_k in country k. Each investor faces two possibly different tax rates, one on domestic income and one on foreign income. Denoting the foreign income tax rate with an asterisk, this means that there are potentially four different tax rates: T_A, T_B, T_A^*, T_B^*. T_k is the tax rate of an investor from k investing in k, while T_k^* is the tax rate of an investor from k investing abroad. An equilibrium is characterized by a lack of arbitrage possibilities for each investor. Hence, for the investor from A, equilibrium requires equality of after tax returns in each country: $r_A(1 - T_A) = r_B(1 - T_A^*)$. Similarly for the investor from B, $r_A(1 - T_B^*) = r_B(1 - T_B)$. Dividing the arbitrage condition for the investor from A by that for the investor from B yields $(1 - T_A)/(1 - T_B^*) = (1 - T_A^*)/(1 - T_B)$. Since we have four possible variables for only one equilibrium condition, existence of a unique equilibrium is far from guaranteed. Despite these possible problems in the existence of an equilibrium, both pure source taxation by both countries ($T_A = T_B^*$ and $T_B = T_A^*$) or pure residence taxation by both countries ($T_A = T_A^*$ and $T_B = T_B^*$) present no existence problems.

We now consider the implications of an equilibrium under pure source and pure residence taxation. Consider first the case of pure source taxation with differential tax rates so that $T_A \neq T_A^*$ (and similarly for B). Given the equilibrium condition for the investor from A, differential tax rates imply that $r_A \neq r_B$. That is, the before-tax return in A is not equal to that in B. Since factors are paid their marginal product, this implies that the marginal product of capital in A is not equal to that in B. If $T_A > T^*_A$, then $r_A < r_B$, and we could therefore reallocate capital from A to B and increase total production. Another way to think of this is that differential tax rates have set up a fiscal incentive to locate capital in the low-tax country so that too much capital will flow to the low-tax country. Source taxation therefore is said to distort the location of capital and investment decisions.

In its pure form, the residence approach leads to production efficiency. To see this, note that the definition of residence taxation ($T_A = T^*_A$) implies from the equilibrium condition that $r_A = r_B$. There is no tax-induced incentive for capital to locate in one country over another with residence-based taxation. While residence based taxation therefore eliminates the incentive for capital to move from high-to low-tax jurisdictions, it may induce the owners of factors to change their residence. (The effect of such migration incentives are apparent in the decision of high income individuals to locate across the border in Greenwich, Connecticut rather than New York (avoiding taxes on capital income) or the migration of high income individuals from high tax countries such as Sweden.) Moreover, since $T_A \neq T^*_B$, the after-tax return of an investor from A will differ from the after-tax return of an investor from B. Since saving depends on the after-tax return, a given level of world savings will be misallocated between investors from A and B. If $T_A > T^*_B$, investors from A realize a lower after-tax return and will save too little, while investors from B will save too much. Since the value of an extra dollar of savings is greater for investors from A than for investors from B, we could increase welfare by transferring some of the future consumption generated from the savings of investors from B to investors from A. In contrast, source taxation leads to an efficient allocation of savings since investors from A and B face the same after-tax return.

To summarize, source taxation leads capital to locate inefficiently (production inefficiency) but leads to intertemporal exchange efficiency. Resident taxation leads to efficiency in capital location but violates intertemporal exchange efficiency. In a first-best world (that is, when we can raise revenue without distortions), both efficiency conditions are required. These two efficiency concepts have often been captured in the literature by the terms 'capital export neutrality' and 'capital import neutrality'. Capital export neutrality is associated with pure residence taxation: facing the same tax consequences at home or abroad, capital is neutral as to its location. (As mentioned above, it is not neutral as to its choice of residence.) Capital import neutrality is associated with pure source taxation: capital from abroad is taxed the same as domestic capital, so there is no tax discrimination for or against foreign capital.

Horst (1980) and Dutton (1982) suggest that the optimal tax on foreign income will balance these two efficiency concerns; the proper balance, they suggest, depends on the elasticities of capital demand and supply. For instance, Horst shows that if the elasticity of supply of capital is zero and the combined tax on international income is equal to the tax on domestic income in the capital exporting country, the optimal tax on foreign source income results in capital export neutrality. Intuitively, there is no saving distortion for this case. To ensure an efficient allocation of capital, the capital exporting country should tax the worldwide income of its residents and provide an *unlimited* credit for taxes paid abroad. Horst also shows that when the elasticity of demand for capital is zero and the combined tax on international income is equal to the tax on domestic income in the capital-importing country, the optimal tax on foreign source income results in capital import neutrality. To ensure an efficient allocation of capital, the capital-exporting country should exempt foreign source income from tax. It is sometimes argued that capital export neutrality is more important, possibly because savings elasticities are often thought to be low and the elasticity of the demand for capital relatively high.

Gordon (1986) points out an interesting parallel to the 'production efficiency lemma' of Diamond and Mirrlees (1971) that also supports capital export neutrality. Diamond and Mirrlees showed (under some rather stringent assumptions) that the optimal commodity tax system will lead to productive efficiency; that is, no input taxes should be used if commodity tax rates are set optimally. Gordon shows that it will be optimal for a small open economy to set its tax rate on capital equal to zero. As Gordon explains, since capital supply is perfectly elastic for the small open economy, a tax on capital will be borne by labor and hence will create the same labor market distortion as a direct tax on labor; in addition, however, the tax on capital will reduce capital investment in the small open economy, and will therefore be dominated by a direct tax on labor. The implication is that capital export neutrality will be part of the optimal tax system for small open economies.

We suggest below some possible new directions for the literature on the optimal tax on foreign source income. First, given the reality that for administrative reasons all countries start from source taxation, it may be worthwhile for the theoretical literature to incorporate this important institutional detail that turns the problem into one of second-best. An interesting question to analyze is whether it is better to augment the initial source taxation by further source taxation (excluding foreign-source income from tax), by residence-based taxation (using a credit system to avoid double taxation), or perhaps by some combination of the two. Perhaps the difficulties in establishing an equilibrium has precluded this sort of discussion in the past, and this is a formidable problem to overcome; still, one might be able to use the approach of Slemrod (1988), for instance, to model an equilibrium and gain some insight into the efficiency consequences of current practices. Second, the optimal tax should incorporate administrative issues (for example, administrative costs, enforceability) as well as more traditional efficiency issues. (See Slemrod, 1990a, for an excellent and very readable discussion of optimal taxation that also incorporates administrative concerns.) Third, since no country has an unlimited foreign tax credit, the limitation is another institutional constraint that should be incorporated in the theoretical problem. Fourth, the literature tends to ignore benefits provided by the government that tax payments support; presumably owners of capital would willingly pay for government expenditures that enhance capital investments (for example, infrastructure investment). Fifth, externalities generated by capital location decisions have not been dealt with, and would presumably alter optimal taxation rules.

As a normative concept, economic efficiency naturally refers to the maximization of world welfare. Positive issues of why tax systems develop in certain ways presents another set of issues. One of the first issues of a positive nature to be raised concerns the sort of tax system that maximizes national welfare. Musgrave (1969) (also clearly discussed in Caves, 1982) raises the point that a capital exporting country (that is large enough to alter the return on capital) will maximize national income by using a deduction system rather than a tax-credit system. This conclusion has a number of qualifications discussed in Hartman (1980), but still raises the question of why a large capital exporting country like the US relies on a tax-credit system.

While international taxation naturally involves more than one country, analysis until recently has considered the situation of a single country under the assumption that other countries' tax systems do not matter. Several recent papers, however, use game theoretic frameworks to analyze strategic decisions between countries that use a corporate income tax. One of the first is Feldstein and Hartman (1979), who find that if one takes into account the reaction of the (small) capital importer, the optimal tax from the large capital exporter's perspective is even higher than otherwise, which seems to add to the puzzle of why the US has a tax-credit system. A more recent paper Bond and Samuelson (1989), finds that the only Nash equilibrium for two countries under a tax credit system is zero tax rates on capital. This is also found by Razin and Sadka (1991c). Bond and Samuelson find that a deduction system yields positive tax rates on capital, again adding to the puzzle of why we do not typically observe the deduction system in practice. In an interesting variation on strategic behavior, Gordon (1992) finds that if one country (for example, the US) acts as a Stackelberg leader, and countries use tax crediting systems, positive tax rates on capital income emerges as the equilibrium solution.

Strategic considerations have also been a recent focus of international commodity taxation. In an early study, Mintz and Tulkens (1986) analyze the inefficiencies liable to arise from duopolistic competition in commodity taxes. One problem with these early studies is that no equilibrium in pure strategies exists because of discontinuities in reaction functions. More recently, Kanbur and Keen (1993) use a simpler model, in which an equilibrium exists, to examine the merits of cooperative tax agreements versus tax competition. They find that two countries with different tax rates may be worse off if both countries are forced to set an average tax rate, while both may be better off if a minimum tax rate is imposed.

The literature on tax competition and international taxation is closely related to the fiscal federalism and local public finance literatures, a point made by Gordon (1990) and Goodspeed (forthcoming). A seminal treatise on fiscal federalism and local public finance is Oates (1972). Since there are several surveys for the reader (Wildasin, 1986; Zodrow and Mieszkowski, 1986; Rubinfeld, 1987; Oates, 1994) and since the focus of this entry is international taxation, we do not undertake an exhaustive survey. Rather, we briefly point out some similarities and differences, and suggest some ways that research on international taxation can benefit from the local public finance/fiscal federalism perspective.

The key similarity of the literatures on international taxation and local public finance/fiscal federalism is that both study the taxation of mobile factors of production. The heart of the fiscal federalism/local public finance literature begins with the Tiebout (1956) model, which postulates many communities offering different tax-expenditure packages. The basic message from the Tiebout literature is that, given the proper type of financing (that is, given that consumers of publicly provided goods face 'prices' that reflect marginal social cost), individuals and firms will sort themselves among communities in an efficient manner. Tax bills (or effective tax rates) may differ across communities, but this will simply reflect differing demands for public services.

An efficient locational equilibrium in the Tiebout model is therefore characterized by tax rates that differ across regions. This may at first seem in stark contrast to the international tax literature, but the similarity is evident upon further reflection. Two differences are particularly noteworthy. First, the Tiebout model considers both the expenditure and tax sides of a government's budget. In contrast, the international taxation literature ignores the expenditure side, or, equivalently, assumes that the taxed factor gains no benefit from public goods and services that are provided by tax revenues. Secondly, a crucial aspect of locational efficiency in the Tiebout model is the method of taxation. Efficiency requires taxes that reflect the marginal social cost of a resident. However, as suggested by Oates (1972) and others, taxes such as income or property taxes may create externalities so that tax-prices diverge from social marginal cost. If externalities are present, incentives for inefficient location decisions are created. In addition to these problems, taxation in an open economy can result in several other sorts of externalities (for example, benefit spillovers); Gordon (1983) provides an elegant and concise derivation of the many types of externalities that may arise from local (as opposed to national) taxation.

The local public finance literature has focused on cases in which efficiency is achieved in small open economies. Some, such as Hamilton (1976), argue that zoning laws in the US effectively convert the property tax (the major source of locally raised revenue in the US) into a benefit tax. If this is the case, and there are enough jurisdictions to satisfy different preferences both for housing and public goods, the taxation of mobile individuals will lead them to choose their place of residence efficiently. Moreover, a modification of Hamilton's argument made by Fischel (1975) suggests that local property taxes on businesses may represent payment for disamenities suffered by residents from business location. Incidentally, the zoning argument is quite general. If one could zone on the basis of income, income taxes could also be converted to benefit taxes, at least for jurisdictions within a country. Such zoning is generally rejected on the grounds of equity and social stability. However, many immigration laws suggest that countries are well aware of the benefits of wealthy immigrants and the costs of poor ones.

As international taxes may not represent benefit taxes, they may lead to location distortions. However, one of the first studies to measure the efficiency loss that results from income taxes in a general equilibrium model of an open economy (Goodspeed, 1989), finds relatively small differences in the way individuals allocate themselves under a head tax and under an income tax. Consequently, he finds a small welfare loss resulting from income taxation of mobile individuals. This suggests that the magnitude of the welfare loss from income taxes in an open economy may not be very large.

The international tax literature tends to ignore the link between taxes and benefits that is the focus of the Tiebout model. Moreover, Wilson (1993) suggests that such benefits may be as important as taxes in multinational planning decisions. As Hubbard (1993) notes in his comment on Wilson's paper, 'part of the apparent insensitivity to tax considerations could reflect the link between taxes paid and the provision of important infrastructure (for example, in education and transportation support)'. This would be an important area to develop in further studies of international taxation.

The fiscal federalism literature on tax competition has revolved around the type of financing that is used for public services. One of the first modern formulations of tax competition in local public finance is Zodrow and Miezskowski (1986), who show that if communities rely exclusively on taxes on mobile capital, an externality is created by the tax system, and competition leads to an underprovision of public goods. Closer to results obtained in the international tax literature is the finding of Oates and Schwab (1988) that if both benefit taxes and non-benefit taxes on capital are available, efficiency will result if governments choose a zero non-benefit tax on capital and finance entirely from benefit taxes. Goodspeed (1995) shows that political considerations are important for this result to hold. He shows that an asymmetric income distribution may lead to a median voter who chooses to finance via non-benefit taxes despite the inefficiency that results from the mobility of the taxed entity. This work suggests that political considerations could also be used to explain equilibrium outcomes of international tax systems.

3. International Taxation and Corporate Behavior

A key question in the study of any tax is the extent to which the tax distorts behavior and thereby creates economic inefficiencies and alters the revenue potential of the tax. Broadly speaking, one can think of the effects of taxation on the multinational firm as affecting (i) the location of investment, (ii) the method of financing an investment, and (iii) intra-multinational transfer pricing decisions. We begin by discussing two opposing theoretical hypotheses about the effects of the tax system on multinational decisions concerning the location of investment and the method of finance. We then discuss the empirical literature on the effect of taxation on the location of investment, followed by a discussion of the empirical literature on financing decisions. Hines (1996b) provides a thorough review of the empirical literature on the effect of taxation on foreign investment and financial decisions, which we have relied upon. Finally, we discuss tax-related issues concerning transfer pricing and review the empirical literature on the prevalence of tax avoidance by judicious use of transfer prices. We have relied on Goodspeed's (1997) review of the empirical transfer pricing literature. For a comprehensive treatment of transfer pricing issues see Lowell, Burge and Briger (1994).

A starting point for understanding the empirical literature on investment and financial decisions are the theoretical works of Horst (1977) and Hartman (1985). Somewhat surprisingly, these two works come to different conclusions about the incentive effects of a foreign tax credit system.

The traditional view, laid out by Horst (1977), is that incentives are different for excess credit and deficit of credit firms. The excess credit firm faces the tax rate of the country in which it invests on the margin; the deficit of credit firm faces the tax rate of the home country no matter where it invests. One way to interpret this in terms of our previous discussion of source versus resident taxation is that once a firm has hit the limit of creditable taxes (as is the case for an excess credit firm), the marginal return on an investment faces a source tax system, and the firm should compare the home and foreign after-tax returns when deciding where to invest. If a firm has not yet hit the limit of creditable taxes (the case of a deficit of credit firm), the marginal return on an investment faces a resident tax system and hence faces the tax rate of the home country no matter where the investment takes place.

In contrast, Hartman argues that deferral combined with the fact that mature firms finance investment from retained earnings that are already abroad implies that the foreign tax credit position of the multinational is irrelevant for investment decisions. Both deferral and an investment financed from retained earnings that are already abroad are necessary for Hartman's result. These two conditions essentially convert the tax-credit system of the home country into a source-based system; hence, the firm should compare the home and foreign after-tax returns when deciding where to invest, and the tax-credit position of the multinational is irrelevant.

The Hartman result is often explained by reference to an analogy relating to the debate on the effect of dividend taxes in a closed economy setting. The 'old view' of dividend taxes assumes that dividends have some intrinsic value as either a signal (Bhattacharya, 1979) or as a control on managers (Jensen and Meckling, 1976). Hence, there will be an optimal dividend payout rate that balances the intrinsic benefit of dividends and their tax cost. But this implies that dividend taxes matter: a higher tax on dividends leads to a lower optimal dividend payout rate. The 'new view' of dividend taxes (King, 1974; Bradford, 1981; Auerbach, 1983) disputes this and suggests that dividend taxes are irrelevant. In the new view, dividends are ultimately the only way that the returns to equity-financed investment can be distributed to shareholders. Hence, according to the new view, dividend taxes are lump-sum taxes that cannot be avoided; consequently, they have no effect on the dividend payout rate. (See, for instance, Zodrow, 1991, for a nice summary and further discussion of these views.) The Hartman scenario is similar to the new view of dividend taxation. In Hartman's case, deferral does not help firms that invest funds that are already abroad and must eventually be repatriated; the return on those funds must eventually absorb the home country tax. Hence, the investment rule for excess-credit and deficit of credit firms is the same: invest abroad if the after-foreign-tax return is higher than the after-domestic-tax return.

While the Hartman result depends on an unchanging home tax rate (Altshuler and Fulghieri, 1994; Keen, 1990) among other things, it has become a focal point in many studies. Nevertheless, the difference between the traditional and Hartman views may not be of much consequence in terms of economic efficiency. As detailed in Goodspeed and Frisch (1989), there is little difference between the traditional and Hartman views in terms of the amount of US earnings abroad that face the foreign tax rate on the margin. While the Hartman view is that 100 percent of earnings abroad (of mature firms that finance from retained earnings) face the foreign tax rate, data from 1984 indicate that in that year the traditional view implied that 82 percent of foreign earnings faced the foreign tax rate on the margin. Under either view, therefore, most foreign earnings faced the foreign tax rate on the margin, as would be the case for a source-based tax system.

Most studies of the effect of international taxation on investment location have concentrated on the United States, examining both US investment abroad and foreign investment in the US These studies have used time-series data, cross-sectional data, and a pooled approach that combines cross-sectional and time-series data. We first examine the time-series studies, then the cross-sectional studies, and finally the studies that pool cross sectional and time series data.

Time series studies typically use aggregate annual data on direct investment collected by the Bureau of Economic Analysis (BEA), US Department of Commerce Department. Early time-series studies are based on the seminal work of Hartman (1981, 1984), and include Boskin and Gale (1987), Newlon (1987), and Young (1988). These early studies ignore the tax credit position of the parent, and so implicitly assume that the Hartman (1985) model is correct.

More recent time-series studies have used somewhat more disaggregated BEA data. Swenson (1994) disaggregates the BEA data by using 18 industries, and tries to gain insight into the reactions to the Tax Reform Act of 1986. Slemrod (1990b), in the first study to actually attempt to test some implications of Hartman's (1985) model for investment decisions, is able to use information on the tax systems (exemption versus foreign tax-credit) of seven countries that invest in the US. He does not, however, find much evidence that allows him to differentiate between the Hartman and traditional views for foreign firms investing in the US.

Cross-sectional studies have also been able to tap into the BEA data by using country information; for instance, Hines and Rice (1994) use data from 1982 for 73 countries while Grubert and Mutti (1991) use the 1982 data for 33 countries. Hines (1996c) is able to generate enough data points for a meaningful regression using a cross-section of 1987 BEA data for 7 countries by exploiting differences in US state taxes. In contrast to Slemrod's (1990b) study, Hines (1996c), does find evidence of differences in the choice of high- or low-tax US states by foreign firms depending on whether the firm comes from an exemption or a foreign tax credit country, which contradicts the Hartman view (if the investment coming from foreign tax credit countries is financed by retained earnings already in the US). Data from tax returns have also been used in cross-sectional studies, either aggregated from the Statistics of Income (SOI) such as in Frisch and Hartman (1983), or at the firm level as in Grubert and Slemrod (1994).

Several studies that use pooled time-series and cross-sectional data have used Compustat as a data source. Studies using pooled data include Harris (1993), Auerbach and Hassett (1993) and Cummins and Hubbard (1995). Other pooled data sources are Labor Department Surveys, utilized by Bond (1981), and Commerce Department Surveys, utilized by Ondrich and Wasylenko (1993). The time-series estimates that use BEA data tend to find an elasticity of investment with respect to the after-tax return in the vicinity of 1. This is true even through the most recent study of Swenson (1994), who investigates the effect of the Tax Reform Act of 1986. Cross-sectional results are more varied. Hines and Rice (1994) find an elasticity of the demand for capital with respect to the tax rate of about -3 while Grubert and Mutti (1991) find an elasticity of only -0.11. Cummins and Hubbard (1995), using an unbalanced panel of foreign subsidiaries of US firms, find an elasticity of investment with respect to the after-tax cost of capital of between -1 and -2. Hines (1996c) finds a large impact of taxes on FDI coming from tax-credit as opposed to exemption countries. While his elasticity is not quite comparable to those mentioned, his finding that a 1 percent reduction in tax results in a 9-11 percent increase in the share of investment coming from tax-credit countries suggests a large tax impact.

The overall conclusion of this literature is that taxes play a statistically significant role in determining the location of foreign direct investment, but the magnitude of the impact of taxes remains uncertain. While time-series studies seem to produce similar elasticities of about 1, the rather large range of elasticity estimates that result from cross-sectional estimates indicates some uncertainty about the magnitude of the effect that taxes have on foreign investment. Additional panel studies that control for unobserved heterogeneity across firms, such as that of Cummins and Hubbard, may provide additional confidence concerning the range of estimates. One possible reason for the large effect found by Hines is that, by studying investment in a single country and using state dummies, he has effectively controlled for some unobserved heterogeneity that cross-country regressions lack.

One aspect that a firm needs to consider as it evaluates an investment project is how that project will be financed. In general, a project can be financed from debt or equity; the way in which a multinational finances a project will have different tax consequences. For instance, as discussed earlier, those profits of a CFC of a US multinational (or the CFC equivalent of a non-US multinational) that are financed by equity (and not subject to Subpart F in the US or equivalent rules in other countries) are not taxable by the home country until repatriated as dividends. If the CFC is instead financed by debt issued by the parent, the interest paid by the CFC is taxable foreign source income for the parent. The interest payments are (usually) deductible in the country in which the CFC is located. As mentioned previously, withholding taxes (often reduced by treaty) are also usually owed to the host country for interest (as well as dividend and royalty) payments.

If interest paid by a CFC is deductible and interest received by the parent is taxable foreign source income, a multinational that has a CFC located in a high-tax (including withholding taxes) country would do better to finance the CFC's investment by debt since it will save money by deducting the interest in the high-tax country and paying tax at home. Countries tend to restrict the use of debt to some extent by using 'thin-capitalization' rules that specify certain limits in terms of a debt-to-asset ratio.

The financing decision of the multinational is a bit more complex for the case of a subsidiary located in a low-tax country because of the Hartman (1985) argument. Traditionally, the argument is that an excess credit multinational might prefer to finance an investment project by equity since it could use deferral to avoid paying the high home country tax for a while. As explained above, however, the implication of Hartman (1985) is that deferral has no value because the present value of the deferred dividend will equal that of the repatriated dividend. Since after-tax returns are equated in equilibrium, there is no advantage to deferral in this view.

One of the first studies to examine the dividend decisions of multinationals is Kopits (1972), who uses aggregate country-level data. Mutti (1981) is able to take advantage of tax return data for subsidiaries and finds that higher US taxes reduce dividend payments. Hines and Hubbard's (1990) paper is the first in a series of modern studies on the dividend repatriation decision. They are able to take advantage of a data set constructed using three separate US tax forms filed by multinationals in 1984: the basic corporate Form 1120, the foreign tax credit Form 1118, and the controlled foreign corporation Form 5471. This data set details information on the parent company (including whether the parent is in excess or deficit of credit) and the repatriations of the parent CFCs. They not only find that higher taxes on dividends reduce dividend payments, but also that the excess credit position of the parent matters in the repatriation decision; excess credit firms tend to have a higher dividend pay-out ratio. This is inconsistent with the Hartman (1985) hypothesis. Two studies, the first by Altshuler and Newlon (1993) and the second by Altshuler, Newlon, and Randolph (1995), extend the Hines and Hubbard study. The first of these studies uses 1986 tax return data and specifies somewhat more completely the tax price of dividend repatriations. The second study uses a panel of tax data for the years 1980, 1982, 1984 and 1986 to investigate the effect of transitory versus permanent tax changes. Transitory changes are found to influence dividend repatriations, while permanent changes do not. This is consistent with Hartman's view of dividend repatriation.

One other study of dividend behavior focuses on a slightly different issue. Hines (1996a) compares dividend payout rates of foreign and domestic subsidiaries. He finds that foreign subsidiaries tend to have a much higher dividend payout rate than domestic subsidiaries; the additional personal tax that is owed on these dividends implies that the cost of capital from foreign investment may be higher than previously thought.

As noted above, a multinational with subsidiaries in high-tax locations will normally do better (from a tax perspective) by financing an investment project by debt so that it can deduct the interest payments in the high-tax location.

Grubert (1995) confirms this pattern. Hines (1994a) develops a model in which the opposite (a positive correlation between greater use of debt finance and lower tax locations) may result over a certain range. This is confirmed in his empirical work in which he finds a quadratic relationship between tax rates and debt levels across countries.

Although most studies concentrate on the effect of taxes on one form of finance, taxes may cause substitution among different sources of finance. For instance, the 1986 Tax Reform Act (TRA86) restricted the deductibility of interest expenses. Interest expenses deemed to be 'foreign' are only allowed to be deducted against foreign, not US, income. The consequence of this is that foreign interest expense will benefit a firm in a deficit of credit position, but not one in an excess credit position. The deficit of credit firm will reduce its taxable income (and maximum credit) by the amount of interest expense; since it has not reached the limit of its foreign tax credit this means that it will reduce its US tax liability. An excess credit firm reduces its taxable income, but also its foreign tax credit by the amount of interest expense; hence, this type of firm does not benefit from foreign interest expense. Two studies (Collins and Shackelford, 1992, and Altshuler and Mintz, 1995) find that firms tended to substitute debt-like instruments for debt after TRA86.

Grubert (1995) and Grubert (forthcoming) are the first studies to jointly estimate separate equations for dividend, interest, and royalty payments. Grubert (forthcoming) finds that taxes have a large effect on the composition of repatriations. That is, differential tax treatment of interest, dividends, and royalties is found to influence the form in which income is repatriated. Similarly, Altshuler and Grubert (1996) examine the complex incentives created when repatriation can flow through several entities. Rather than repatriating through different forms of income, however, they examine the flows between a multinational's CFCs and find that tax incentives have significant effects.

Finally, with respect to repatriation decisions, the role of exchange rate gains and losses should be mentioned. As the world moved from an era of fixed to flexible exchange rates, issues of how and when transactions would be translated into the home currency became relevant. One of the first discussions of the issues involved is Musgrave (1975). As she describes, the taxpayer was given much latitude in the translation of profits into the home currency. This can create problems for the taxing authority because the taxpayer will naturally attempt to time the translation so as to minimize taxes. Wahl (1989) notes that TRA86 in the United States tightened up on translation rules so that most hedging transactions are taxed on accrual, leaving the taxpayer little latitude to time the transactions. However, some transactions are still taxed on realization, which may lead to some loss in revenue through judicious timing of the translation.

Although most empirical studies tend to confirm that multinationals are sensitive to tax considerations in their financial decisions, Hines (1996b), after a thorough survey of the literature, suggests that a more complete analysis would consider the fact that taxes influence financial and investment decisions simultaneously. This is one avenue for further study. In addition, nontax considerations may also play a major role in financial and investment decisions. As we have noted, the local public finance literature suggests that consideration of the expenditure side of the budget is important. This suggests that such factors as road and transportation networks, communications facilities, the quality of the local workforce (and hence investment in schools), and other public infrastructure investments may be important. Other regulatory issues, such as bankruptcy or bank secrecy laws, may also be a reason that firms willingly pay taxes when deciding where to invest. Finally, a country's economic and political stability may also be an important consideration.

We next turn to issues in intra-multinational transfer pricing. Multinational corporations, usually organized as a set of separate entities, typically involve a parent corporation and a set of subsidiaries. The parent is typically the major stockholder in its subsidiaries, often controlling 100 percent of a subsidiary's stock. Various transactions may occur between the parent and subsidiary companies within the multinational, such as the sale by a subsidiary of an input that is used in the parent's production process or sale of a trademark by the parent to a subsidiary. The prices attached to these transactions that occur between corporations within a multinational are referred to as 'transfer prices'. While transfer pricing occurs (implicitly or explicitly) with any intrafirm transfer, the feature that has made transfer pricing so important and controversial is its possible use to avoid taxes. For instance, suppose that the parent is located in a high-tax country while the subsidiary is located in a low-tax country. Assuming that the multinational is trying to minimize its total tax payments, the multinational will try to price transfers so that most of its profits appear in the low-tax country. For example, if the subsidiary is providing the parent with an input, there is an incentive to charge a very high price for the input. Since this will result in high revenue in the low-tax country and high costs in the high-tax country, the effect will be to transfer profits from the high-tax to the low-tax country. The multinational's taxes will be lower and its after-tax profits higher than would otherwise be the case.

Transfers between entities that make up a multinational firm can be bi-directional. We first consider the transfer pricing decisions of a home country multinational that invests abroad (outbound investment), and then the transfer pricing decision of a foreign multinational that owns a corporation in a home country (inbound investment). For each category, we discuss the general nature of the problem and the empirical literature. Finally, we discuss some solutions that governments have implemented to try to reduce tax avoidance and tax evasion by means of transfer pricing.

Transfer pricing can be used to reduce taxes for either the source/territorial or the resident/worldwide tax system. The simplest cases can be illustrated for a multinational that has foreign profits generated in a single foreign country as well as profits generated at home. Abuses under the territorial system are perhaps the most obvious: taxes can be reduced by transferring profits out of the high-tax country and into the low-tax country.

A purported advantage of the worldwide system is that this incentive disappears for a multinational that invests in a single foreign country with a tax rate lower than the home country. In this case, income derived from the foreign investment will be taxed at the home country tax rate and the incentive to shift income is eliminated.

However, several complications of the tax systems of countries that purport to use the worldwide system of taxation allow multinationals to use transfer pricing to reduce taxes. First, consider a multinational in a low-tax country that invests in a single high-tax country. By definition, this firm would be in an excess credit position. The multinational will not receive a credit in its home country for some of the taxes paid in the high-tax country unless it is able to shift some income back to its low-tax home. The multinational can use transfer prices to shift profits to the home country. Second, since multinationals typically have investments in a variety of foreign countries, the way in which the credit is computed is important. As mentioned above, some countries aggregate income over all foreign countries in determining the limit. In addition, the use of 'mixer' companies in countries that use a per-country limitation can also result in income averaging. For these countries, a multinational with a large proportion of income coming from investments in high-tax countries and a small proportion of income coming from investments in low-tax foreign countries will not obtain full credit for foreign taxes paid. This firm would then have an incentive to use transfer prices to shift income from high-tax to low-tax foreign countries and thereby obtain credit for all foreign taxes paid. Third, the use of deferral effectively converts a worldwide tax system into a territorial system, at least until profits are repatriated. Although Subpart F provisions in the United States have limited deferral, the transfer pricing problems associated with territorial tax systems become relevant when a worldwide system incorporates deferral.

The evidence on the use of transfer pricing is consistent with tax-minimizing behavior, although the magnitude of abusive transfer pricing appears to be moderate. Outbound investment by US multinationals has been investigated by Harris, et al. (1993), who use Compustat data to investigate whether taxes paid to the US are influenced by the location of the multinational's profits overseas. Since the US taxes multinationals based on a worldwide system and computes the foreign tax credit by aggregating on a worldwide basis, the multinational can get credit for income tax paid in a country with a tax rate higher than the US rate by judicious use of transfer pricing. It simply needs to shift income from a high tax to a low tax location so as to avoid hitting the credit limit. Harris, et al. find that a multinational that has a subsidiary in a low (high) tax country has a lower (higher) than average ratio of US tax to US assets. This is consistent with the use of transfer pricing to minimize worldwide taxes, although they find that the aggregate effect on US tax revenues is moderate. Hines and Rice (1994) investigate transfer pricing of outbound investment by concentrating on the use of 'tax havens' (a set of very low-tax foreign countries) by US multinationals. They find that reported profit rates are sensitive to local tax rates, although they note that this may not be bad for US revenue since the US is now a relatively low-tax country. A US multinational whose foreign source income comes primarily from a high tax country will not be subject to additional US tax. If however, the multinational is able to shift income so that its foreign source income appears to come primarily from a low tax country, the US will gain tax revenue equal to the difference between taxes paid and what would be paid in the US

We next consider transfer prices used by foreign corporations operating in the home country (that is, inbound investment) to transfer profits out and so avoid home country taxes. This has become an important topic, particularly in the United States, because the aggregate rate of return for foreign-controlled companies in the US is observed to be much lower than the rate of return of domestically controlled companies. A concern expressed by the US Congress is that foreign-controlled US corporations are not paying their fair share of US taxes. The suggested culprit is transfer pricing.

There are several reasons other than transfer pricing that might explain low rates of return of foreign-controlled companies operating in a home country. First, foreign companies may at first experience a lower than average rate of return because of the revaluation of the assets of new acquisitions or because of the start-up costs of a new business. Second, a low average rate of return in any one year may not be indicative of a long-run trend. That is, although foreign companies may have difficulty in adjusting to the nuances of a foreign market at first, one would expect this to change over time as the firms mature. Finally, unexpected changes in exchange rates can have a large effect on profits. An unexpected fall in the dollar, for instance, would increase the cost of components imported into the US and therefore temporarily decrease the profits of a foreign-controlled company in the US. This effect also would be expected to diminish over time.

Inbound investment in the US is investigated by Grubert, Goodspeed and Swenson (1993) using both a 1987 cross-section and a 1980-87 panel data set. They use data from the tax returns of US corporations to investigate the difference in taxes paid by foreign-controlled as opposed to US-controlled corporations. The aggregate data suggests a much lower ratio of taxable income to assets for foreign-controlled corporations. However, the authors find that the revaluation of assets after merger or acquisition (captured by an age effect), exchange rate changes and a maturation effect account for about half of the difference. The remaining difference could be due to transfer pricing, and the authors present some evidence that indicates that foreign-controlled companies tend to be more concentrated at zero taxable income than domestic companies. They also remain in the zero-profit state longer than domestic companies. This suggests that transfer pricing may be used to some extent to reduce taxes, although less than feared when the transfer pricing issue first arose in the US Congress.

Grubert (1997) updates the study of Grubert, Goodspeed and Swenson by repeating the previous analysis (with some modifications) for a 1993 cross-section and a 1987-1993 panel. He finds that for some specifications purely cross-sectional variables can explain almost 50 percent of the difference in rates of return, rather than the 25 percent explained in the previous study. This appears to be partly due to the fact that US companies are receiving more income from foreign dividends. The panel estimation corroborates the earlier finding of a maturation effect. Overall, Grubert is able to explain somewhat more than the earlier 50 percent (up to 75 percent) of the difference between foreign-controlled and US-controlled corporate returns in the US.

Since transfer pricing can be used to evade taxes, governments have naturally developed a set of rules to try to minimize this potential source of tax evasion. The problem is to find an 'objective' way of valuing tangible and intangible assets transferred across national boundaries by multinational corporations. The widely accepted international standard is that such transfers be assigned the prices that would have been charged if the transactions had occurred between independent entities. Such prices are referred to as 'arm's length' prices. The basic notion is that a transaction between a parent and its subsidiary should be priced as if it had occurred between two unrelated parties in a competitive market.

However, arm's length transfer prices are not always easy to calculate because comparable transactions by unrelated parties may not exist. This issue is pervasive for intangible assets because the value of most intangible asset arises from market power generated by the intangible. For example, how should McDonald's price the right to use its golden arches? McDonald's does not sell use of its golden arches to unrelated parties. The value of the golden arches arises from the rents that the use of this trademark generates. There are no comparable arm's length prices and alternative methods for pricing this type of transfer must be used.

A general framework and some specific standards for transfer pricing are suggested in OECD (1979). Revisions have recently been proposed in OECD (1995). Specific rules that are acceptable to a country's taxing authority generally vary from country to country but, in general, the prices charged in comparable arm's length transactions are preferred. (See Ault, 1997, for a discussion of practices in several countries, and Molina Gómez-Arnáu, 1997, for the case of Spain.) When exactly comparable transactions do not exist, the government often provides some guidance in the form of regulations or case law (usually based on OECD, 1979) on the range of transfer prices that will be deemed acceptable. Such guidance may include a cost-plus calculation, reference to some industry average such as a rate of return on assets or a margin on sales, or attempts to adjust 'inexact' comparables to obtain transfer prices. Profit-based methods (for example, 'comparable profits') as opposed to transactions methods tend to be the most controversial. Some countries do not allow comparable profits methods.

The methodology used to determine the proper transfer price has become increasingly sophisticated. Frisch (1989) and Witte and Chipty (1990) suggest the use of the capital asset pricing model to determine a proper return for a project. Appropriate transfer prices are then calculated as the prices necessary for the project to have that rate of return. Horst (1993) suggests using regression analysis to determine an appropriate rate of return.

The US Internal Revenue Service (IRS) has adopted an open approach on the methods used to obtain transfer prices. Multinational companies may now propose a method for determining transfer prices. The IRS examines the proposed method and determines whether or not the methodology is acceptable. If the methodology is acceptable, the IRS enters into an 'advanced pricing agreement' (APA) with the multinational. The agreement allows the multinational to use the mutually agreed upon methodology to set transfer prices for the firm for a period of 3 to 5 years. The APA may involve the other countries impacted by the agreed transfer price. APAs are also possible in some other countries (for example, Germany and The Netherlands).

One of the more subtle elements of corporate international taxation is that the tax system can be used to create subsidies. Although the thrust of the General Agreement on Tariffs and Trade (GATT) is to prohibit discrimination between domestic and foreign produced goods, corporate tax systems have been used to subsidize exports and investment. We consider below two specific US tax provisions (foreign sales corporations and sales source rules) that provide subsidies for goods exported from the US. We then consider the general concept of tax holidays, and its relation to tax sparing in tax treaties.

The US Congress created Domestic International Sales Corporations (DISCs) in 1971. DISCs were essentially conduits through which export transactions could be recorded. Exports carried out through DISCs received favorable tax treatment. This subsidy was found to be in violation of GATT's prohibition of export subsidies in 1976. The reaction of the US was to replace DISCs by Foreign Sales Corporations (FSCs), which perform much the same function, but are able to pass muster under GATT rules. As long as title is passed overseas, a portion of FSC income is exempt from US tax; hence, a subsidy is created for a product to be produced domestically and exported rather than manufactured and sold abroad.

A second type of export incentive in the US tax code is that produced by the sales source rules (Section 863(b) of the US Internal Revenue Code). These rules allow a multinational to reclassify part of its export income as foreign source. If a multinational is in an excess credit position, the US tax rate times foreign source income is the binding constraint on the foreign tax credit. Hence, each dollar that an excess credit firm is able to reclassify as foreign rather than domestic source will result in extra foreign tax credit equal to the US tax rate. For example, if a multinational is in an excess credit position and faces a US tax rate of 35 percent, each dollar that it is able to reclassify as foreign rather than domestic source will result in savings of $0.35. The rules thus provide an incentive for US excess credit multinationals to export rather than produce abroad.

While the US Treasury issues periodic reports on FSCs, little academic literature has investigated the export incentives hidden in corporate tax codes. An early exception is Horst and Pugel (1977). One recent study is Rousslang and Tokarick (1994), who use a general equilibrium model to examine the consequences of the tax-based export incentives. They find that the tax provisions increase the volume of trade but that domestic welfare is worsened because the terms of trade are worsened for the US.

Apart from export incentives, a second set of tax subsidies arise because of developing countries' efforts to attract multinational investment. Many developing countries give multinationals 'tax holidays'. During periods of tax holiday, multinationals may pay no taxes or, at a minimum, lower taxes than would otherwise be due. Such tax breaks only provide incentives for multinationals to invest in the developing country if the multinational's home country taxes on a source basis. For countries that tax on a worldwide basis, tax holidays provide no incentive to locate in the developing country since the income of the multinational will be taxed at the home country rate. Recognizing this, some countries (for example, Germany and Japan) that tax on a worldwide basis allow their multinationals credit for such tax holidays; that is, they allow credit for taxes that have not actually been paid. This is often referred to as 'tax sparing'. Tax sparing provisions are often written into tax treaties between a developed and a developing country.

Although most countries grant tax sparing in treaties with many developing countries, the US does not. However, the US has had a set of rules (contained in Section 936 of the US Internal Revenue Code) that provide tax subsidies for corporations that locate in US Possessions (the primary beneficiary being Puerto Rico). In part, Section 936 allows tax sparing, and since Puerto Rico offers tax holidays, US multinationals received tax credits for taxes that were not actually paid to Puerto Rico. The 936 rules were tightened in 1993, however, through a limitation on the allowable tax credit. Further, 1996 legislation began a phase out of Section 936. It is scheduled to be eliminated completely by 2005. While the US Treasury provides periodic reports on the tax treatment of Possessions' corporations, the academic literature on the effect of Section 936 is sparse. One older study is that of Bond (1981). Grubert and Slemrod (1994) provide a more recent study of the effect of Section 936 in Puerto Rico. Grubert and Slemrod's findings suggest that firms with high levels of intangible assets (for example, drug companies) located in Puerto Rico because it was relatively easy, through transfer pricing, to shift profits to Puerto Rico. The profits thus shifted gained the tax advantage provided by Section 936.

4. Issues in International Indirect Taxation

The destination and origin principles for indirect taxation are analogous to the source and resident principles for direct taxation. The difference between the destination and origin principles is that the destination principle imposes tax where consumption takes place whereas the origin principle imposes tax where production takes place. As with source taxation, one might argue that the origin principle distorts the location of production. As with resident taxation, one might argue that the destination principle causes distortions in relative savings decisions across countries.

Despite the analogy of the destination and origin principles for indirect taxation and the source and resident principles for direct taxation, and our previous discussion of the efficiency differences of the source and resident principles for direct taxation, much has been made of the fact that the destination and origin principles of indirect taxation are, under certain conditions, equivalent. This is noted in Cnossen and Shoup (1987) and demonstrated formally in Lockwood, de Meza and Myles (1994a). The equivalence comes from the fact that balanced trade implies that aggregate production and aggregate consumption are the same. Consequently, a destination based tax (on aggregate consumption) and an origin-based tax (on aggregate production) are equivalent.

However, this result requires some very strong assumptions, and there are several models, outlined in Keen and Smith (1996), in which the equivalence result fails to hold. One such model is an overlapping generations model of Bovenberg (1994) in which the two principles can have different intergenerational effects. A second situation in which equivalence fails is when countries do not tax all commodities at a uniform rate. See Sinn (1990) and Feldstein and Krugman (1990).

Assuming that the equivalence result does not hold brings us back to our discussion concerning efficiency for direct taxation and the trade-off between production efficiency and exchange efficiency. Again appeal might be made to the Diamond and Mirrlees (1971) result that the optimal commodity tax system is characterized by production efficiency, which would suggest a preference for the destination principle. However, the Diamond-Mirrlees framework is one of perfect competition and 100 percent taxation of pure profits. Some interesting new work relaxes some of these assumptions and indicates some scope for origin taxation in an optimal tax system. For instance, Keen and Lahiri (1996) consider a model of Cournot duopolists. As noted in Keen and Smith (1996), part of the difference in this type of setting is that, unlike the Diamond-Mirrlees framework, it is recognized that countries have their own distinct revenue constraints. Again, the relevance of the fiscal federalism literature, which studies the relationship between jurisdictions with distinct revenue constraints, is evident. A somewhat different tact would be to investigate models of illegal activity. For instance, there may be an incentive under destination taxes to bypass legal rules and smuggle goods from low-tax/low-enforcement countries to countries with high and well enforced consumption taxes.

Much of the recent interest in these issues has arisen because of the elimination of controls on the movement of both capital and labor in the European Union. (But see also Grubert and Newlon, 1995 for an examination of recent proposals in the US to replace the income tax with a consumption tax.) European countries typically raise a substantial portion of revenue through value-added taxes (VATs). As these countries eliminate controls on the movement of both capital and labor, there is increasing concern about the possibility of cross-border shopping that could result from VAT systems that have different tax rates applied to the same products. A good review of some of the early concerns can be found in Cnossen and Shoup (1987) and Lee, Pearson and Smith (1988); a more recent treatment is that of Keen and Smith (1996). The issues here are whether consumers would engage in cross-border shopping to avoid high taxes, whether competition would force these taxes to some common rate, and the welfare impacts of these possibilities. These issues are directly related to the tax competition literature mentioned earlier, and some papers mentioned there (for example, Mintz and Tulkens, 1986; Kanbur and Keen, 1993) explicitly address tax competition for indirect rather than direct taxes.

One practical set of issues for the European Union's concerns how countries can best make 'border adjustments', that is, the rebate of VAT on export and its imposition on import. The required tax adjustments have been made at the border and, hence, the term border adjustments. Cnossen (1983) has proposed that a 'clearinghouse' be set up to handle border adjustments. Under the clearinghouse proposal, a country would, in the aggregate, either be net owers or receivers of VAT revenue depending on their trade balance and VAT rates.

The function of the clearinghouse would be to determine the net position of each country rather than have countries give or receive VAT on a transaction by transaction basis. The European Commission has considered this proposal, but has not been able to come to agreement. Instead, they moved in 1993 to a transitional system. This system has eliminated border adjustments for consumer purchases for personal use (so that personal consumption purchases are now taxed on the origin principle), although border adjustments are still made for transactions between firms.

Keen and Smith (1996) point out a number of problems with the transitional system, and propose an alternative, which they call a Viable Integrated VAT (VIVAT). They compare the VIVAT to the transitional system as well as other systems (including a clearinghouse mechanism), and suggest that the VIVAT is superior. VIVAT, as described by them, is a combination of harmonized VAT rates and different retail sales tax rates. Their proposal combines the origin and destination principles, and offers the advantage of national autonomy in setting taxes (emphasized in the fiscal federalism literature) with the self-policing advantages often ascribed to VAT.

5. Some Suggestions for Future Research

To date, work on the efficiency effects of various methods of international taxation have assumed a first-best world. The complexity and many distortions present in the international arena suggest that work that considers a world with distortions other than those caused by the international tax regime would be useful.

The administration of international taxes has received relatively little attention. Careful examination of the administrative provisions of tax treaties might provide a useful base for thinking about administrative issues. Application of the arm's length standard often involves very high transaction costs. Tax agencies experiences with Advanced Pricing Agreements might provide some guidance for alternative systems. It would be important to estimate and compare both the efficiency and transactions costs of the arm's length standard and other proposed systems.

To date most work on international taxation has considered only efficiency effects. Interesting new insights might be obtained by examining equity and public choice considerations. In this context examinations of tax sparing provision might be interesting. Comparisons of the US that does not have tax sparing provisions (except with Possessions) with European countries and Japan that have tax sparing provisions with many developing countries could be revealing.

Increases in the flow of financial services and the opening of telecommunication markets raise important new issues regarding the way in which international tax and regulatory regimes interact. While research that introduces regulations as well as taxation would be difficult, such work could provide important new insights.

Trade blocks have become increasingly important and, yet, we have no work that tells us the implication of such blocks for international taxation. Close examination of the development of the tax systems of the European Union as the Union becomes more closely integrated would be valuable. Work that considers both the implications of changes for the Union, and for other countries and trading blocks would be informative.

To date the literatures on foreign investment and international taxation have been largely distinct. Integration of insights from the two literatures would enhance our understanding of the way in which multinational corporations operate.

Models used to discern the effects of international taxes have generally assumed perfect information and abstracted from risk. Such assumptions do not well characterize the international arena. Relaxation of these assumptions would be fruitful.

Bibliography on International Taxation (6080)

Aaron, Henry J. (ed.) (1981), *The Value-Added Tax: Lessons from Europe*, Washington, Brookings Institution.

ABA (1984), *Unitary Tax: International Taxation - Up for Grabs? (Program Material)*, Chicago, American Bar Association.

Aliber, R.Z. and Click, R.W. (eds) (1993), *Readings in International Business: A Decision Approach*, Cambridge, MA, MIT Press.

Allegra, F.M. (1994), 'Section 482: Mapping the Contours of the Abuse of Discretion Standard of Judicial Review', **13** *Virginia Tax Review*, 423 ff.

Altshuler, Rosanne and Cummins, J. (1997), 'Tax Policy and the Dynamic Demand for Domestic and Foreign Capital by Multinational Corporations', Unpublished paper.

Altshuler, Rosanne and Fulghieri, Paolo (1994), 'Dynamic Effects of Foreign Tax Credits on Multinational Corporations', **47** *National Tax Journal*, 349-361.

Altshuler, Rosanne and Grubert, Harry (1996), 'Balance Sheets, Multinational Financial Policy, and the Cost of Capital at Home and Abroad', Unpublished paper.

Altshuler, Rosanne and Mintz, Jack M. (1995), 'U.S. Interest-Allocation Rules: Effects and Policy', **2** *International Tax and Public Finance*, 7-35.

Altshuler, Rosanne and Newlon, T. Scott (1993), 'The Effects of U.S. Tax Policy on the Income Repatriation Patterns of U.S. Multinational Corporations', in Giovannini, A., Hubbard, R.G. and Slemrod, J. (eds), *Studies in International Taxation*, Chicago, University of Chicago Press.

Altshuler, Rosanne, Newlon, T. Scott and Randolph, W.C. (1995), 'Do Repatriation Taxes

Matter? Evidence From the Tax Returns of U.S. Multinationals', in Feldstein, M., J.R.H., Jr and Hubbard, R.G. (eds), *The Effects of Taxation on Multinational Corporations*, Chicago: University of Chicago Press.

Alworth, J.S. (1987), 'Taxation and the Cost of Capital: A Comparison of Six EC Countries', in Cnossen, S. (ed.), *Tax Coordination In The European Community*, London: Kluwer Law and Taxation, 253-283.

Alworth, J.S. (1988), *The Finance, Investment, and Taxation Decisions of Multinational Firms*, Oxford, Basil Blackwell.

Ambardar, M. (1995), 'Comment: The Taxation of Deferred Compensation Under I.R.C. 864(c)(6) and Income Tax Treaties: A Rose is Not Always Arose', **19** *Fordham International Law Journal*, 736 ff.

Andel, N. (1987), 'Determination of Company Profits', in Cnossen, S. (ed.), *Tax Coordination In The European Community*, London, Kluwer Law and Taxation, 287-304.

Auerbach, Alan J. (1983), 'Taxes, Firm Financial Policy, and the Cost of Capital', **21** *Journal of Economic Literature*, 905-940.

Auerbach, Alan J. and Hassett, K. (1993), 'Taxation and Foreign Direct Investment in the United States: A Reconsideration of the Evidence', in Giovannini, A., Hubbard, R.G. and Slemrod, J. (eds), *Studies in International Taxation*, Chicago: University of Chicago Press.

Ault, Hugh (1992), 'Colloquium on Corporate Integration: Corporate Integration, Tax Treaties and the Division of the International Tax Base: Principles and Practices', **47** *New York University Tax Law Review*, 565 ff.

Ault, Hugh (1997), *Comparative Income Taxation: A Structural Analysis*, The Hague, Kluwer Law International.

Ault, Hugh and Bradford, David F. (1990), 'Taxing International Income: An Analysis of the U.S. System and its Economic Premises', in Razin and Slemrod (eds), *Taxation in the Global Economy*, Chicago, University of Chicago Press, 11-54.

Avi-Yonah, R.S. (1995), 'The Rise and Fall of Arm's Length: A Study in the Evolution of U.S. International Taxation', **15** *Virginia Tax Review*, 89 ff.

Avi-Yonah, R.S. (1996), 'The Structure of International Taxation: A Proposal for Simplification', **74** *Texas Law Review*, 1301 ff.

Avramovich, M. (1995), 'Development of the Democratic Institutions and the Rule of Law in the Former Soviet Union: Note: Intercompany Transfer Pricing Regulations Under Internal Revenue Code Section 482: The Noose Tightens on Multinational Corporations', **28** *John Marshall Law Review*, 915 ff.

Azrieli, A. (1993), 'Improving Arbitration Under the U.S.-Israel Free Trade Agreement: A Framework for a Middle-East Free Trade Zone', **67** *St. John's Law Review*, 187 ff.

Barone, S.L. and Zerrenner, K. (1995), 'Note: Over the Edge: State Taxation of Multinational Corporations in the Wake of Barclays', **10** *St. John's Journal of Legal Commentary*, 343 ff.

Bartik, Timothy J. (1985), 'Business Location Decisions in the United States: Estimates of the effects of Unionization, Taxes, and Other Characteristics of States', **3** *Journal of Business and Economic Statistics*, 14-22.

Bernard, Jean Thomas and Weiner, Robert J. (1990), 'Multinational Corporations, Transfer Prices, and Taxes: Evidence from the U.S. Petroleum Industry', in Razin and Slemrod (eds), *Taxation in the Global Economy*, Chicago, University of Chicago Press.

Betten, Rijkele (1986), 'OECD Report: Trends in International Taxation: Taxation Issues Relating to International Hiring out of Labor', **40(7)** *Bulletin for International Fiscal Documentation*, 330-334.

Bhattacharya, Sudipto (1979), 'Imperfect Information, Dividend Policy, and the Bird in the Hand Fallacy', **10** *Bell Journal of Economics*, 259-270.

Biehl, Dieter (1982), 'Towards a General Theory of Taxing International Transactions: A Taxonomy of International Taxation Principles', **37(2)** *Public Finance*, 189-205.

Bird, Richard M. (1987), 'Corporate Personal Tax Integration', in Cnossen, S. (ed.), *Tax Coordination in the European Community*, London, Kluwer Law and Taxation, 227-251.

Bird, Richard M. (1994), 'Colloquium on NAFTA and Tradition: Commentary: A View From the North', **49** *Tax Law Review*, 745 ff.

Bird, Richard M. and Mintz, Jack M. (eds) (1992), *Taxation to 2000 and Beyond*, Toronto, Canadian Tax Foundation.

Blatt, W.S. (1986), 'A Review of Decisions of the United States Court of Appeals for the Federal Circuit: Area Summary: The Federal Circuit's 1985 Tax Cases: The Exercise of Equity', **35** *American University Law Review*, 1097 ff.

Block, W. and Walker, M. (1984), 'Taxation: International Evidence', in Block, W. and Walker, M. (eds), *Taxation: An International Perspective: Proceedings of An International Conference*, Vancouver, Fraser Institute, 3-19.

Blum, C. (1986), 'Rollover: An Alternative Treatment of Capital Gains', **41** *Tax Law Review*, 385 ff.

Blum, C. (1988), 'How the United States Should Tax Foreign Shareholders', **7** *Virginia Tax Review*, 583-696.

Blumenthal, Marsha and Slemrod, Joel B. (1995), 'The Compliance Cost of Taxing Foreign-Source Income: Its Magnitude, Determinants, and Policy Implications', **2** *International Tax and Public Finance*, 37-53.

Bond, Eric W. (1981), 'Tax Holidays and Industry Behavior', **63** *Review of Economics and Statistics*, 88-95.

Bond, Eric W. and Samuelson, Larry (1989), 'Strategic Behaviour and the Rules for International Taxation of Capital', **99(398)** *Economic Journal*, 1099-1111.

Boskin, Michael J. and Gale, W.G. (1987), 'New Results on the Effects of Tax Policy on the International Location of Investment', in Feldstein, M. (ed.), *The Effects of Taxation on Capital Accumulation*, Chicago, University of Chicago Press.

Bovenberg, L. (1994), 'Destination- and Origin-Based Taxation Under International Capital Mobility', **1** *International Tax and Public Finance*, 247-273.

Bovenberg, L., Anderson, K., Aramake, K. and Chand, S. (1990), 'Tax Incentives and International Capital Flows: The Case of the United States and Japan', in Razin and Slemrod (eds), *Taxation in the Global Economy*, Chicago, University of Chicago Press, 283-330.

Bradford, David F. (1981), 'The Incidence and Allocation Effects of a Tax on Corporate Capital', **15** *Journal of Public Economics*, 1-22.

Brean, D.J.S. (1992), 'Here or There? The Source and Residence Principles of International Taxation', in Bird, R.M. and Mintz, J.M. (eds), *Taxation to 2000 and Beyond.Canadian Tax Paper*, Toronto, Canadian Tax Foundation, 303-333.

Brown, F.B. (1993), 'Federal Income Taxation of U.S. Branches of Foreign Corporations: Separate Entity or Separate Rules?', *New York University Tax Law Review*.

Burgess, Robin and Stern, Nicholas (1993), 'Taxation and Development', **31** *Journal of Economic Literature*, 762-830.

Cameron, R. and Bovykin, V.I.E. (1992), 'International Banking 1870-1914', **26** *George Washington Journal of International Law and Economics*, 221 ff.

Campolongo, Alberto (1978), 'Tassazione Internazionale Per Lo Sviluppo (International Taxation for Development (With English summary)', **31(1-2)** *Economia Internazionale*, 3-17.

Canzoneri, Matthew B. and Rogers (1990), 'Is the European Community an Optimal Currency Area? Optimal Taxation versus the Cost of Multiple Currencies', **80** *American Economic Review*, 419-433.

Caves, Richard E. (1982), *Multinational Enterprise and Economic Analysis*, Cambridge, Cambridge University Press.

Clark, R.G. (1993), 'Comment: Transfer Pricing, Section 482, and International Tax Conflict: Getting Harmonized Income Allocation Measures from Multinational Cacophony', **42** *American University Law Review*, 1155 ff.

Cnossen, Sijbren (1983), 'Harmonization of Indirect Taxes in the EC', *British Tax Review*.

Cnossen, Sijbren (1987a), 'Tax Coordination in the European Community: Introduction', in Cnossen, S. (ed.), *Tax Coordination in the European Community*, London, Kluwer Law and Taxation, 1-15.

Cnossen, Sijbren (1987b), 'Tax Structure Developments', in Cnossen, S. (ed.), *Tax Coordination in the European Community*, London, Kluwer Law and Taxation, 19-55.

Cnossen, Sijbren and Shoup, Carl S. (1987), 'Coordination of Value-Added Taxes', in Cnossen, S. (ed.), *Tax Coordination in the European Community*, London, Kluwer Law and Taxation, 59-84.

Collins, Julie H. and Shackelford, D.A. (1992), 'Foreign Tax Credit Limitations and Preferred Stock Issuances', **30(S)** *Journal of Accounting Research*, 103-124.

Collins, Julie H. and Shackelford, D.A. (1995), 'Corporate Domicile and Average Effective Tax Rates: The Cases of Canada, Japan, the United Kingdom, and the United States', **2** *International Tax and Public Finance*, 55-83.

Connolly, C.F. (1995), 'Comment: The New Transfer Pricing and Penalty Regulations: Increased Burdens, and the Search for a Safe Harbor', **16** *University of Pennsylvania Journal of International Business*, 339 ff.

Corrado, M.G. (1988), 'Comment: The Supreme Court's Impact on Swiss Banking Secrecy: Societe Nationale Industrielle Aerospatiale v. United States District Court', **37** *American University Law Review*, 827 ff.

Coughlin, C.C., Terza, J.V. and Arromdee, V. (1991), 'State Characteristics and the Location of Foreign Direct Investment within the United States', **68** *Review of Economics and Statistics*, 675-683.

Coven, G.E. (1993), 'Corporate Tax Policy for the Twenty-First Century: Integration and Redeeming Social Value', **50** *Washington and Lee Law Review*, 495 ff.

Cummins, J. and Hassett, K. (1997), 'The Giant Sucking Sound:Structural Estimates of Factor Substitution from Firm-Level Panel Data on Multinational Corporations', Unpublished paper.

Cummins, J. and Hubbard, R. Glenn (1995), 'The Tax Sensitivity of Foreign Direct Investment: Evidence From Firm-Level Panel Data', in Feldstein, M., J.R.H., Jr and Hubbard, R.G. (eds), *The Effects of Taxation on Multinational Corporations*, Chicago, University of Chicago Press.

Cummins, J., Harris, T.S. and Hassett, K. (1995), 'Accounting Standards Information Flow, and Firm Investment Behavior', in Feldstein, M., J.R.H., Jr and Hubbard, R.G. (eds), *The Effects of Taxation on Multinational Corporations*, Chicago: University of Chicago Press.

Daly, Michael and Weiner, Joann (1993), 'Corporate Tax Harmonization and Competition in Federal Countries: Some Lessons for the European Community?', **441** *National Tax Journal*, 461 ff.

Davlin, J.A. (1994), 'Note: The Uncertainty of Foreign Blocked Income: Trying to Reconcile the 1994 482 Regulations With Procter & Gamble', **5** *Duke Journal of Comparative and International Law*, 117 ff.

Denys, L.A. (1987), 'The Proposed Belgian Tax Reform: Aspects of International Taxation', **41(8-9)** *Bulletin for International Fiscal Documentation*, 383-390.

Devereux, Michael and Freeman, Harold (1995), 'The Impact of Tax on Foreign Direct Investment: Empirical Evidence and the Implications for Tax Integration Schemes', **2** *International Tax and Public Finance*, 85-106.

Devereux, Michael and Pearson (1991), *Capital Export Neutrality, Capital Import Neutrality, and European Tax Harmonization: An Empirical Assessment*, Cambridge, National Bureau of Economic Research Summer Institute.

Diamond, Peter and Mirrlees, J.A. (1971), 'Optimal Taxation and Public Production I: Production Efficiency', **61** *American Economic Review*, 8-27.

Dixit, A. (1985), 'Tax Policy in Open Economies', in Auerbach, Alan and Feldstein, Martin (eds), *Handbook in Public Economics*, North-Holland, Amsterdam, 313-374.

Doernberg, Richard L. (1985), 'A Workable Flat Rate Consumption Tax. Iowa University', **70** *Iowa Law Review*, 425 ff.

Douvier, Pierre Jean (1993), 'Major Measures Concerning International Taxation: The Finance Act 1993 and Transfer of Assets Abroad', **47(4)** *Bulletin for International Fiscal Documentation*, 214-219.

Dutton, John (1982), 'The Optimal Taxation of International Investment Income: A Comment', **96** *Quarterly Journal of Economics*, 373-380.

Easson, Alex J. (1991), 'A New International Tax Order Responding to the Challenge: International', **45(10)** *Bulletin for International Fiscal Documentation*, 465-472.

Easson, Alex J. and Jinyan, L. (1986), 'Taxation of Foreign Business and Investment in the People's Republic of China', **7** *Journal of International Law and Business*, 666 ff.

Elitzur, R. Ramy and Mintz, Jack M. (1995), 'Transfer Pricing Rules and Corporate Tax Competition', **60** *Journal of Public Economics*, 401-422.

Fargeix, Andr and Perloff, Jeffrey M. (1989), 'The Effects of Tariffs in Markets with Vertical Restraints', **26** *Journal of International Economics*, 99-117.

Feldstein, Martin (1994), 'Taxes, Leverage and the National Return on Outbound Foreign Direct Investment', Cambridge, National Bureau of Economic Research, Working Paper, No. 4689.

Feldstein, Martin (1995), 'The Effects of Outbound Foreign Direct Investment on the Domestic Capital Stock', in Feldstein, M., J.R.H., Jr and Hubbard, R.G. (eds), *The Effects of Taxation on Multinational Corporations*, Chicago: University of Chicago Press.

Feldstein, Martin (1997), 'Tax Policy and International Capital Flows', Cambridge, National Bureau of Economic Research, Working Paper, No. 4851.

Feldstein, Martin and Hartman, D. (1979), 'The Optimal Taxation of Foreign Source Investment Income', **93** *Quarterly Journal of Economics*, 613-630.

Feldstein, Martin and Krugman, Paul R. (1990), 'International Trade Effects of Value-Added Tax', in Razin and Slemrod (eds), *Taxation in the Global Economy*, Chicago: University of Chicago Press.

Finnerty, J.J.I. (1993), 'Note: The "Mother Court" and the Foreign Plaintiff: Does Rule 10b-5 Reach Far Enough', **62** *Fordham Law Review*.

Fischel, William A. (1975), 'Fiscal and Environmental Considerations in the Location of Firms in Suburban Communities', in Mills, Edwin S. and Oates, Wallace E. (eds), *Fiscal Zoning and Land Use Controls*, Lexington, MA, Lexington Books.

Fischer Zernin, Justus (1987), 'GATT versus Tax Treaties? The Basic Conflicts between International Taxation Methods and the Rules and Concepts of GATT', **21(3)** *Journal of World Trade Law*, 39-62.

Franson, M. D. (1984), 'Comment: The Repeal of the Thirty Percent Withholding Tax on Portfolio Interest Paid to Foreign Investors', **6** *Journal of International Law and Business*, 930 ff.

Freed, A. (1996), 'Progress versus Protectionism: The Double Taxation of Computer Software in Korea', **47** *Hastings Law Journal*, 473 ff.

Freiman, B.M. (1991), 'Comment: The Japanese Consumption Tax: Value-Added Model or Administrative Nightmare?', **40** *American University Law Review*, 1265 ff.

Frenkel, Jacob A., Razin, Assaf and Sadka, Efraim (1990), 'Basic Concepts of International Taxation', Cambridge, National Bureau of Economic Research, Working Paper, No. 3540.

Frenkel, Jacob A., Razin, Assaf and Sadka, Efraim (1991), *International Taxation in an Integrated World*, Cambridge, MA, MIT Press.

Frisch, Daniel (1983), 'Issues in the Taxation of Foreign Source Income', in Feldstein (ed.), *Simulation Methods in Tax Policy Analysis*, Chicago, University of Chicago Press.

Frisch, Daniel (1989), 'The BALRM Approach to Transfer Pricing', **42** *National Tax Journal*, 261-271.

Frisch, Daniel and Hartman, D. (1983), 'Taxation and the Location of U.S. Investment Abroad', Cambridge, NBER, Working Paper, No. 1241.

Froot, K.A. and Hines, J. (1995), 'Interest Allocation Rules, Financing Patterns, and the Operations of U.S. Multinationals', in Feldstein, M., J.R.H., Jr and Hubbard, R.G. (eds), *The Effects of Taxation on Multinational Corporations*, Chicago, University of Chicago Press.

Galston, N.M. and Smit, H. (1984), *Sale of Goods*, New York, Matthew Bender.

Gammie, M. (1994), 'Colloquium on NAFTA and Tradition: The Taxation of Inward Direct Investment in North America Following the Free Trade Agreement', **49** *New York University Tax Law Review*, 615 ff.

Gann, P.B. (1982), 'The Concept of an Independent Treaty Foreign Tax Credit', **38** *New York University Tax Law Review*, 1 ff.

Garbarino, C. and Colucci, P.A. (1992), 'La Tassazione del Reddito Transnazionale', **April** *American Journal of International Law*.

Gazur, W.M. (1994), 'The Forgotten Link: "Control" in Section 482', **15** *Journal of International Law and Business*, 1 ff.

Gazur, W.M. and Goff, N.M. (1991), 'Assessing the Limited Liability Company', **41** *Case Western Reserve Law Review*, 387 ff.

Gentry, William M. (1995), 'Comment', in Feldstein, M., J.R.H., Jr and Hubbard, R.G. (eds), *The Effects of Taxation on Multinational Corporations*, Chicago, University of Chicago

Press.

Gersovitz (1987), 'The Effects of Domestic Taxes on Foreign Private Investment', in Newberry and Stern (eds), *The Theory of Taxation for Developing Countries: World Bank*.

Giovannini, Alberto (1989), 'National Tax Systems vs. The European Capital Market', **9** *Economic Policy*,

Giovannini, Alberto (1991), *International Capital Mobility and Tax Avoidance*, New York, Columbia University Press.

Giovannini, Alberto and Hines, J. (1990), 'Capital Flight and Tax Competition: Are There Viable Solutions to both Problems?', CEPR Discussion Papers.

Giovannini, Alberto, Glenn, H.R. and Slemrod, Joel (eds) (1993), *Studies in International Taxation*, Chicago, National Bureau of Economic Research.

Glautier, M.W.E. and Bassinger, F.W. (1987), *A Reference Guide to International Taxation: Profiting From Your International Operations*, Lexington, MA, Lexington Books.

Gliksberg, D. (1994), 'The Effect of the Statist-Political Approach to International Jurisdiction of the Income Tax Regime - The Israeli Case', **15** *Michigan Journal of International Law*, 460 ff.

Goodspeed, Timothy J. (1989), 'A Re-Examination of the Use of Ability to Pay Taxes by Local Governments', **38** *Journal of Public Economics*, 319-342.

Goodspeed, Timothy J. (1995), 'Local Income Taxation: An Externality, Pigouvian Solution, and Public Policies', **25** *Regional Science and Urban Economics*, 279-296.

Goodspeed, Timothy J. (1997), 'Transfer Pricing', in Warner, Malcolm (ed.), *International Encyclopedia of Business and Management. Volume 5*, London, Routledge Limited.

Goodspeed, Timothy J. and Frisch, Daniel (1989), 'U.S. Tax Policy and the Overseas Activities of U.S. Multinational Corporations: A Quantitative Assessment', Mimeo.

Gordon, Roger H. (1983), 'An Optimal Taxation Approach to Fiscal Federalism', **567** *Quarterly Journal of Economics*, 586 ff.

Gordon, R.H. (1986), 'Taxation of Investment and Savings in a World Economy', **76** *American Economic Review*, 1086-1102.

Gordon, Roger H. (1990), 'Canada-U.S. Free Trade and Pressures for Tax Harmonization', NBER Working Paper, No. 3327.

Gordon, R.H. (1992), 'Can Capital Income Taxes Survive in Open Economies?', **47** *Journal of Finance*, 1159-1180.

Gordon, R.H. and Bovenberg, A. Lans (1993), 'Why is Capital so Immobile Internationally?', Cambridge, National Bureau of Economic Research, Working Paper, No. 4796.

Gordon, R.H. and Jun, J. (1993), 'Taxes and the Form of Ownership of Foreign Corporate Equity', in Giovannini, A., Hubbard, R.G. and Slemrod, J. (eds), *Studies in International Taxation*, Chicago, University of Chicago Press.

Gordon, R.H. and Mackie-Mason, Jeffrey K. (1995), 'Why is There Corporate Taxation in a Small Open Economy? The Role of Transfer Pricing and Income Shifting', in Feldstein, M., J.R.H., Jr and Hubbard, R.G. (eds), *The Effects of Taxation on Multinational Corporations*, Chicago, University of Chicago Press.

Gramwell, A., Merrill, P. and Dubert, C. (1996), *Taxation of U.S. Corporations Doing Business Aborad: U.S. Rules and Competitiveness Issues*, Morristown, New Jersey, Financial Executives Research Foundation, Inc.

Green, R.A. (1993), 'The Future of Source-Based Taxation of the Income of Multinational

Enterprises', **80** *Cornell Law Review*,

Grubert, Harry (1995), 'Royalties, Dividends, and R&D', Paper presented at the Proceedings of the Eighty-Seventh Annual Conference on Taxation, Columbus, OH.

Grubert, Harry (1997), 'Taxes and the Division of Foreign Operating Income Among Royalties, Interest, Dividends, and Retained Earnings', *Journal of Public Economics*, forthcoming.

Grubert, Harry and Mutti, John (1991), 'Taxes, Tariffs and Transfer Pricing in Multinational Corporation Decision Making', **33** *Review of Economics and Statistics*, 285-293.

Grubert, Harry and Newlon, T. Scott (1995), 'The International Implications of Consumption Tax Proposals', **48** *National Tax Journal*, 619-647.

Grubert, Harry and Slemrod, Joel (1994), 'The Effects of Taxes on Investment and Income Shifting to Puerto Rico', Cambridge, NBER Working Paper, No. 4869.

Grubert, Harry, Goodspeed, Timothy J. and Swenson, D. (1993), 'Explaining the Low Taxable Income of Foreign-Controlled Companies in the United States', in Giovannini, A., Hubbard, R.G. and Slemrod, J. (eds), *Studies in International Taxation*, Chicago: University of Chicago Press.

Grubert, Harry and Newlon, T. Scott (1997), *Taxing Consumption in a Global Economy*, Washington, DC, AEI Press.

Grundy, M. (1984), *The World of International Tax Planning*, New York, Cambridge University Press.

Hall, Bronwyn H. (1993), 'R&D; Tax Policy During The 1980s: Success or Failure?', in Poterba, J.M. (ed.), *Tax Policy and the Economy Vol. 7*, Cambridge, MA, MIT Press.

Hamilton, Bruce W. (1976), 'Capitalization of Interjurisdictional Differences in Local Tax Prices', **66** *American Economic Review*, 743-753.

Hanna, C.H. (1995), 'The Virtual Reality of Eliminating Tax Deferral', **12** *American Journal of Tax Policyv*, 449 ff.

Harris, C.M. (1994), 'The European Community's Parent-Subsidiary Directive', **9** *Florida International Law Journal*, 111 ff.

Harris, D.G. (1993), 'The Impact of U.S. Tax Law Revision on Multinational Corporations' Capital Location and Income-Shifting Decisions', **31(S)** *Journal of Accounting Research*, 111-140.

Harris, D.G., Morck, Randall, Slemrod, Joel and Yeung, B. (1993), 'Income Shifting in U.S. Multinational Corporations', in Giovannini, A., Hubbard, R.G. and Slemrod, J. (eds), *Studies in International Taxation*, Chicago, University of Chicago Press.

Hartman, D. (1980), 'The Effects of Taxing Foreign Investment Income', **13** *Journal of Public Economics*, 213-230.

Hartman, D. (1981), 'Domestic Tax Policy and Foreign Investment: Some Evidence', Cambridge, NBER Working Paper, No. 784.

Hartman, D. (1984), 'Tax Policy and Foreign Direct Investment in the United States', **37** *National Tax Journal*, 475-487.

Hartman, D. (1985), 'Tax Policy and Foreign Direct Investment', **26** *Journal of Public Economics*, 107-121.

Hartman, P.J. (1984), 'Constitutional Limitations on State Taxation of Corporate Income From Multinational Corporations', **37** *Vanderbilt Law Review*.

Higinbotham, Harlow N., Asper, D.W., Stoffregen, P.A. and Wexler, R.P. (1987), 'Effective Application of the Section 482 Transfer Pricing Regulations', **42** *Tax Law Review*, 295 ff.

Hines, James R., Jr (1988), 'Taxation and U.S. Multinational Investment', in Summers, Lawrence H. (ed.), *Tax Policy and the Economy, Volume 2*, Cambridge, MIT Press.

Hines, James R., Jr (1991), 'The Flight Paths of Migratory Corporations', **6** *Journal of Accounting Auditing, and Finance*, 447-479.

Hines, James R., Jr (1993), 'On the Sensitivity of R&D; to Delicate Tax Changes: The Behavior of U.S. Multinationals in the 1980s', in Giovannini, A., Hubbard, R.G., Slemrod, J. (eds), *Studies in International Taxation*, Chicago, University of Chicago Press.

Hines, James R., Jr (1994a), 'Credit and Deferral as International Investment Incentives', **55** *Journal of Public Economics*, 323-347.

Hines, James R., Jr (1994b), 'No Place Like Home: Tax Incentives and the Location of R&D, by American Multinationals', in Poterba, J.M. (ed.), *Tax Policy and the Economy Vol. 7*, Cambridge, MA, MIT Press.

Hines, James R., Jr (1995a), 'Taxes, Technology Transfer, and the R&D; activities of Multinational Firms', in Feldstein, M., J.R.H., Jr and Hubbard, R.G. (eds), *The Effects of Taxation on Multinational Corporations*, Chicago, University of Chicago Press.

Hines, James R., Jr (1995b), 'Forbidden Payment: Foreign Bribery and American Business After 1977', Cambridge, NBER Working Paper, No. 5266.

Hines, James R., Jr (1996a), 'Dividends and Profits: Some Unsubtle Foreign Influences', **51** *Journal of Finance*.

Hines, James R., Jr (1996b), 'Tax Policy and the Activities of Multinational Corporations', Mimeo.

Hines, James R., Jr (1996c), 'Altered States: Taxes and the Location of Foreign Direct Investment In America', **86** *American Economic Review*, 1076-1094.

Hines, James R., Jr and Hubbard, R. Glenn (1990), 'Coming Home to America: Dividend Repatriations by U.S. Multinationals', in Razin and Slemrod (eds), *Taxation in the Global Economy*, Chicago, University of Chicago Press.

Hines, James R., Jr and Rice, Edward M. (1994), 'Fiscal Paradise: Foreign Tax Havens and American Business', **109** *Quarterly Journal of Economics*, 149-182.

Hodder, James E. and Senbet, Lemma W. (1990), 'International Capital Structure Equilibrium', **45(5)** *Journal of Finance*, 1495-1516.

Hornberger, W.H. (1994), 'U.S. Taxation of U.S. Persons Doing Business or Investing in Mexico: An Overview', **26** *St. Mary's Law Journal*, 107 ff.

Horst, Thomas (1977), 'American Taxation of Multinational Firms', **67** *American Economic Review*, 376-389.

Horst, Thomas (1980), 'A Note on the Optimal Taxation of International Investment Income', **94** *Quarterly Journal of Economics*, 793-798.

Horst, Thomas (1982), 'Reply', **96** *Quarterly Journal of Economics*, 381 ff.

Horst, Thomas (1993), 'The Comparable Profits Method', **14** *Tax Notes International*, 1443-1458.

Horst, Thomas and Pugel, Thomas (1977), 'The Impact of DISC on the Prices and Profitability of U.S. Exports', **7** *Journal of Public Economics*, 72-87.

Hreha, K.S. (1990), 'The Current State of Graduate Education in International Taxation (Report of the 1987-1988 Joint International Accounting Section--American Taxation Association Research Committee on International Taxation)', in Jones, S.M. (ed.), *Advances in Taxation*, Greenwich, JAI Press, 249-259.

Hubbard, R. Glenn (1993), 'Comment', in Giovannini, A., Hubbard, R.G.and Slemrod, J. (eds), *Studies in International Taxation*, Chicago, University of Chicago Press, 231-234.

Hudson, D.M. (1984), 'International and Interstate Approaches to Taxing Business Income', **6** *Journal of International Law and Business*, 562 ff.

Hufbauer, Gary (1992), *U.S. Taxation of International Income: Blueprint for Reform*, Washington, DC, Institute for International Economics.

Hufbauer, Gary, Elliot, K. and Maldonado, E. (1988), *Tax Treaties and American Interests. A Report to the National Foreign Trade Council*, Washington, DC.

Huizinga, Harry (1994), 'International Interest Withholding Taxation: Prospects for a Common European Policy', **1(3)** *International Tax and Public Finance*, 277-291.

Huston, J., Miyatake, T. and Griffith, W. (1985), *Japanese International Taxation*, New York, Matthew Bender.

Isenbergh, Joseph (1990a), *International Taxation: U.S. Taxation of Foreign Taxpayers and Foreign Income*, Boston, Little Brown.

Isenbergh, Joseph (1990b), 'The End of Income Taxation', **45** *Tax Law Review*, 283 ff.

Jacob, Friedhelm (1984), 'Unitary Approaches in International Taxation', **38(3)** *Bulletin for International Fiscal Documentation*, 99-120.

Jacobson, H.K. (1983), 'Resources, Regimes, World Order. By Antony J. Dolman, Book Review', **77** *American Journal of International Law*, 688 ff.

Janeba, Eckhard (1996), 'Foreign Direct Investment under Oligopoly: Profit Shifting or Profit Capturing?', **60** *Journal of Public Economics*, 423-445.

Jenkins, G.P. and B.D.W. (1975), 'Taxation of Income of Multinational Corporations: The Case of the United States Petroleum Industry', **57** *Review of Economics and Statistics*, 1-11.

Jensen, Michael C. and Meckling, William H. (1976), 'Theory of the Firm: Managerial Behavior, Agency Costs, and Ownership Structures', **3** *Journal of Financial Economics*, 305-360.

Jones, S.M. (1990), *Advances in Taxation. Volume 3*, Greenwich, JAI Press.

Kalinka, S. (1993), 'Acts 1990, No. 1009: The Repeal of Provisions for Separation From Bed and Board Increases the Federal Income Tax Burden of Separated Spouses in Louisiana', **53** *Louisiana Law Review*, 597 ff.

Kanbur, Ravi and Keen, Michael (1993), 'Jeux Sans Frontièrs: Tax Competition and Tax Coordination When Countries Differ in Size', **83** *American Economic Review*, 877-892.

Kaplan, Richard L. (1983), 'Creeping Xenophobia and the Taxation of Foreign-Owned Real Estate', **71** *Georgetown Law Journal*.

Kay, John A. and Keen, Michael (1987), 'Alcohol and Tobacco Taxes: Criteria For Harmonisation', in Cnossen, S. (ed.), *Tax Coordination in the European Community*, London, Kluwer Law and Taxation, 85-111.

Keely, M.G. (1995), 'Comment: Barclays Bank PLC v. The Franchise Tax Board: Has the Supreme Court Emasculated the One Voice Doctrine?', **8** *DePaul Business Law Journal*, 133 ff.

Keen, Michael (1990), *Corporate Tax, Foreign Direct Investment and the Single Market*, University of Essex.

Keen, Michael (1991), 'Corporate Tax, Foreign Direct Investment and the Single Market', in Winters, L. and A.V. (ed.), *The Impact of 1992 on European Trade and Industry*, Cambridge, Cambridge University Press.

Keen, Michael (1992), 'Harmonization of Taxes on Capital Income', in Newman, Peter,

Milgate, Murray and Eatwell, John (eds), *The New Palgrave Dictionary of Money and Finance*, London, Macmillan.

Keen, Michael and Lahiri, S. (1996), 'The Comparison Between Destination and Origin Taxation Under Imperfect Competition', Unpublished paper.

Keen, Michael and Smith, Steven D. (1996), 'The Future of Value Added Taxion the European Union', *Economic Policy*, 375-420.

Kemsley, D. (1995), *The Effect of Taxes on the Choice Between Exports and Foreign Production*, New York, Columbia Business School.

King, Mervyn A. (1974), 'Dividend Behavior and the Theory of the Firm', **41** *Economica*, 25-34.

Kingson, C.I. (1992), 'U.S. International Taxation, by Joel D. Kuntz and Robert J. Peroni, Book Review', **26** *George Washington Journal of International Law and Economics*, 213 ff.

Klassen, K., et al. (1993), 'Geographic Income Shifting by Multinational Corporations in Response to Tax Rate Changes', **31** *Journal of Accounting Research*, 141-173.

Klein, William A. and Zolt, Eric M. (1995), 'LLCs, LLPs and the Evolving Corporate Form: A Symposium Sponsored by the University of Colorado Law Review: Business Form, Limited Liability, and Tax Regimes: Lurching Toward a Coherent Outcome?', **66** *University of Colorado Law Review*, 1001 ff.

Kole, D.V. (1986), 'Tax Efficient Forex Management, Book Review', **8** *Journal of International Law and Business*.

Kole, D.V. (1988), 'Perspective: The Status of United States International Taxation: Another Fine Mess We've Gotten Ourselves Into', **9** *Journal of International Law and Business*, 49 ff.

Kopits, G.F. (1972), 'Dividend Remittance Behavior Within the International Firm: A Cross-Country Analysis', **54** *Review of Economics and Statistics*, 339-342.

Kopits, G.F. (1976), 'Intra-Firm Royalties Crossing Frontiers and Transfer-Pricing Behaviour', **86** *Economic Journal*, 791-805.

Kozusko, D.D. and J.A.S. (eds) (1991), *International Estate Planning Principles and Strategies*, American Bar Association.

Kurlander, G. (1983), 'The Economic Recovery Tax Act of 1981: The Foreign Earned Income Exclusion: Redefining the Exception for Amounts Paid by the United States Under IRC @ 911', **70** *Cornell Law Review*.

Kwall, J.L. (1985), 'Subchapter G of the Internal Revenue Code: Crusade Without a Cause?', **5** *Virginia Tax Review*, 223 ff.

LaFrance, M. (1995), 'The Separate Tax Status of Loan-Out Corporations', **48** *Vanderbilt Law Review*.

Laity, E.T. (1996), 'Defining the Passive Income of Controlled Foreign Corporations', **20** *North Carolina Journal of International Law and Commercial Regulation*, 293 ff.

Lanciano, G.C. (1992), 'Comment: Procter & Gamble Co. v. Commissioner: Should Foreign Law Control U.S. Tax Liability of U.S. Shareholders?', **17** *Delaware Journal of Corporate Law*, 515 ff.

Lee, Catherine, Pearson, Mark and Smith, Stephen (1988), *Fiscal Harmonization: An Analysis of the European Commision's Proposals*, London, Institute for Fiscal Studies.

Leechor, Chad and J.M. (1993), 'On the Taxation of Multinational Corporate Investment When the Deferral Method is Used by the Capital-Exporting Country', **51** *Journal of Public Economics*, 75-96.

Levey, M.M. and Vonk, W.J.K. (eds) (1990), 'Foreign Investment in the United States: Law,Taxation, Finance', **84** *American Journal of International Law*,

Lipsey, R.E. (1995), 'Outward Direct Investment and the U.S. Economy', in Feldstein, M., J.R.H., Jr and Hubbard, R.G. (eds), *The Effects of Taxation on Multinational Corporations*, Chicago, University of Chicago Press.

Livingston, Michael (1993), 'Risky Business: Economics, Culture and the Taxation of High-Risk Activities', **48** *New York University Tax Law Review*, 163-232.

Lockwood, B., de Meza, D. and Myles, G. (1994a), 'When are Origin and Destination Regimes Equivalent', **1** *International Tax and Public Finance*, 5-24.

Lockwood, B., de Meza, D. and Myles, G. (1994b), 'The Equivalence between Destination and Non-reciprocal Restricted Origin Tax Regimes', **96** *Scandinavian Journal of Economics*, 696 ff.

Lord, C.J. (1986), 'Stapled Stock and I.R.C. Section 269B: Ill-Conceived Change in the Rules of International Tax Jurisdiction', **73** *Cornell Law Review*,

Loss, Louis (1989), 'The Evolving Antarctic Legal Regime: Michigan Yearbook of International Legal Studies: Volume 9, Book Review', **83** *American Journal of International Law*, 696 ff.

Lowell, C.H., Burge, M. and Briger, P. (1994), *Understanding Transfer Pricing*, Boston, Waren, Gorham & Lamont.

Lyon, A.B.R. (1994), 'Review of: Studies in International Taxation', **32** *Journal of Economic Literature*, 702-703.

Lyon, A.B.R. and G.S. (1995), 'The Alternative Minimum Tax and the Behavior of Multinational Corporations', in Feldstein, M., J.R.H., Jr., Hubbard, R.G. (eds), *The Effects of Taxation on Multinational Corporations*, Chicago: University of Chicago Press.

Lyons, C.M. (1995), 'The Constitutionality of the Worldwide Combined Reporting Method of Taxation of Multinational Corporations: Barclays Bank v. Franchise Tax Board', **37** *Boston College Law Review*, 183 ff.

MacKenzie, G.W. (1993), 'ICSID Arbitration as a Strategy for Levelling the Playing Field Between International Non-Governmental Organizations and Host', *Syracuse Journal of International Law and Commerce*.

Malinvaud, E. (1989), 'Comments', in Giovannini, A. (ed.), *National Tax System vs. The European Market: Economic Policy 9*.

Marx, R.S. (1995), 'Transforming International Politics: An American Role for the Post Cold War', **64** *University of Cincinnati Law Review*, 119 ff.

Mason, Z.D. (1994), 'Implications of the Income Tax Treaty Between the United States and Mexico', **25** *St. Mary's Law Journal*, 1213 ff.

McDaniel, P.R. (1984), 'In Memoriam: Stanley S. Surrey: Celebrating Stanley's Gifts', **98** *Harvard Law Review*.

McDaniel, P.R. (1987), 'Personal Income Taxes: The Treatment of Tax Expenditures', in Cnossen, S. (ed.), *Tax Coordination In The European Community*, London, Kluwer Law and Taxation, 319-333.

McDaniel, P.R. (1994), 'Colloquium on NAFTA and Tradition: Formulary Taxation in the North American Free Trade Zone', **49** *Tax Law Review*, 691 ff.

McDaniel, P.R. and Ault, H.J. (1989), *Introduction To United States International Taxation*, Norwell, Kluwer Law and Taxation.

McDonald, J. (1987), 'Comment: Anti-Deferred: A Proposal for the Reform of International Tax Law', **16** *Journal of International Law and Business*, 248 ff.

McIntyre, M.J. (1994), 'Colloquium on NAFTA and Tradition: Commentary: The Design of Tax Rules for the North American Free Trade Alliance', *New York University Tax Law Review*.

McIntyre, R.S. (1989), 'Tax Americana', **200** *New Republic*, 18-20.

McLure, Charles (1980), 'The State Corporate Income Tax: Lambs in Wolves' Clothing?', in Aaron, H. (ed.), *The Economics of Taxation*, Washington, Brookings Institution.

McLure, Charles (1981), 'The Elusive Incidence of the Corporate Income Tax: The State Case', **395** *Public Finance Quarterly*, 413 ff.

McLure, Charles E., Jr (1994), 'Review of: U.S. Taxation of International Income: Blueprint For Reform', **32** *Journal of Economic Literature*, 148-150.

Mick, J. (1992), 'A Proposal for the Indexation of Debt for Inflation (Comment)', **140** *University of Pennsylvania Law Review*.

Mintz, Jack M. and Tulkens, Henry (1984), 'Strategic Use of Tax Rates and Credits in a Model of International Corporate Income Tax Competition', CORE Discussion Paper, No. 9073.

Mintz, Jack M. and Tulkens, Henry (1986), 'Commodity Tax Competition Between Member States of a Federation: Equilibrium and Efficiency', **29** *Journal of Public Economics*, 133-172.

Misey, R.J. (1992), 'Simplifying International Jurisdiction for United States Transfer Taxes: Retain Citizenship and Replace Domicile with the Green Cardtest', *Marquette Law Review*,

Molina Gómez-Arnáu, Pilar (1997), 'Spanish Rules on Transfer Pricing', **23** *International Tax Journal*, 42-61.

Mundstock, G. (1993), 'Section 902 is too Generous', *New York University Tax Law Review*.

Murfin, A. (1987), 'Price Discrimination and Tax Differences in the European Motor Industry', in Cnossen, S. (ed.), *Tax Coordination In The European Community*, London, Kluwer Law and Taxation, 171-194.

Musgrave, Peggy B. (1969), *United States Taxation of Foreign Investment Income: Issues and Arguments*, Cambridge, MA, International Tax Program, Harvard Law School.

Musgrave, Peggy B. (1975), 'Exchange Rate Aspects in the Taxation of Foreign Income', **27** *National Tax Journal*, 405-413.

Musgrave, Peggy B. (1987), 'Interjurisdictional Coordination of Taxes on Capital Income', in Cnossen, S. (ed.), *Tax Coordination In The European Community*, London, Kluwer Law And Taxation, 197-225.

Muten, L. (1983), 'Some Topical Issues Concerning International Double Taxation', in Cnossen, S. (ed.), *Comparative Tax Studies: Essays in Honor of Richard Goode*, Amsterdam, North-Holland.

Mutti, John (1981), 'Tax Incentives and Repatriation Decisions of U.S. Multinational Corporations', **31** *National Tax Journal*, 241-248.

Mutti, John (1993), 'Comment', in Giovannini, A., Hubbard, R.G.and Slemrod, J. (eds), *Studies in International Taxation*, Chicago, University of Chicago Press.

Mutti, John and Grubert, Harry (1985), 'The Taxation of Capital Income in an Open Economy: The Importance of Resident-Nonresident Tax Treatment', **28** *Journal of Public Economics*.

Newlon, T. Scott (1987), 'Tax Policy and the Multinational Firm's Financial Policy and Investment Decisions', Unpublished Ph.D. Dissertation, Princeton University, Princeton.

Nutter, S.E. (1994), 'Corporate Foreign Tax Credit, 1990: An Industry Focus', **13** *Statistics of Income Bulletin*, 78-106.

Oates, Wallace E. (1972), *Fiscal Federalism*, Princeton, Harcourt, Brace and Jovanovich.

Oates, Wallace E. (1994), 'Federalism and Government Finance', in Quigley, J.M. and Smolensky, E. (eds), *Modern Public Finance*, Cambridge, Harvard University Press.

Oates, Wallace E. and Schwab, Robert M. (1988), 'Economic Competition Among Jurisdictions: Efficiency Enhancing or Distortion Inducing?', **35** *Journal of Public Economics*, 333-354.

OECD (1995), *Transfer Pricing Guidelines for Multinational Enterprises and Tax Administrations*, Paris, OECD.

Office of Management and Budget (1996), *Budget of the United States Government, Fiscal Yesr 1997, Analytical Perspectives, Chapter 5, Tax Expenditures*, Washington,Office of Management and Budget.

Ohlenforst, C.M., Dorrill, J.W. and Christmann, K.A. (1994), 'Taxation', **47** *SMU Law Review*.

Ohlenforst, C.M., Dorrill, J.W. and Goodin, K.L. (1995), 'Taxation', **48** *SMU Law Review*.

Ondrich, J. and Wasylenko, M. (1993), *Foreign Direct Investment in the United States: Issues, Magnitudes, and Location Choice of New Manufacturing Plants*, Kalamazoo, MI, W.E. Upjohn Institute.

Orland, L. (1991), 'Exchange, Commentary: Teaching Antitrust after Chicago and Perestroika', **66** *New York University Law Review*.

Osgood, R.K. (1983), 'Symposium: The Economic Recovery Tax Act of 1981: The Ages and Themes of Income Taxation: Savings and Investment', **70** *Cornell Law Review*.

Owens, Jeffrey (1991), 'International Taxation and International Investment Flows between OECD and Non OECD Countries', **45(5)** *Bulletin for International Fiscal Documentation*, 219-220.

Papke, L.E. (1991), 'Interstate Business Tax Differentials and New Firm Location', **45** *Journal of Public Economics*, 47-68.

Pires, M. (1989), *International Juridical Double Taxation of Income*, Norwell, Kluwer Law and Taxation.

Plasschaert, Sylvain R.F. (1981), 'The Design of Schedular and Global Systems of Income Taxation, the International Dimension', **35(8-9)** *Bulletin for International Fiscal Documentation*, 409-416.

Pollack, S.D. (1994), 'Tax Complexity, Reform, and the Illusions of Tax Simplification', **2** *George Mason Law Review*, 319 ff.

Pomp, R.D. (1994a), 'Issues in the Design of Formulary Apportionment in the Context of NAFTA', *New York University Tax Law Review*.

Pomp, R.D. (1994b), 'The Foreign Tax Credit Limitation: An Analysis of the President's Tax Proposals', *International Lawyer*.

Postlewaite, P.F., Collins, M.P. and Macdonald, J.R. (1983), 'Book Review: International Individual Taxation', **77** *American Journal of International Law*, 708 ff.

Pratt, K.T. (1995), 'Federal Tax Sources Recommended for Law School Libraries', **87** *Law Library Journal*, 387 ff.

Razin, Assaf and Sadka, Efraim (1989), 'Optimal Incentives to Domestic Investment in the Presence of Capital Flight', International Monetary Fund, Research and Fiscal Affairs Department, No. 89/79.

Razin, Assaf and Sadka, Efraim (1990), 'Capital Market Integration: Issues of International

Taxation', in Frech, H.E. (ed.), *Regulating Doctors' Fees: Competition, Benefits, and Controls under Medicare*, Washington, DC, American Enterprise Institute.

Razin, Assaf and Sadka, Efraim (1991a), 'International Fiscal Policy Coordination and Competition: An Exposition', Cambridge, National Bureau of Economic Research, No. 3779.

Razin, Assaf and Sadka, Efraim (1991b), 'Vanishing Tax on Capital Income in the Open Economy', Cambridge, National Bureau of Economic Research, No. 3796.

Razin, Assaf and Sadka, Efraim (1991c), 'International Tax Competition and the Gains from Tax Harmonization', **37** *Economic Letters*, 69-76.

Razin, Assaf and Yuen, C.W. (1992), 'Convergence in Growth Rates: The Role of Capital Mobility and International Taxation', Cambridge, National Bureau of Economic Research, No. 4214.

Razin, Assaf and Yuen, C.W. (1993), 'Convergence in Growth Rates: A Quantitative Assessment of the Role of Capital Mobility and International Taxation', Cambridge: National Bureau of Economic Research, No. 4336.

Redmiles, L. (1992), 'International Boycott Participation', **12** *Statistics of Income Bulletin*, 88-89.

Redmiles, L. (1994), 'Individual Foreign-Earned Income and Foreign Tax Credit, 1991', **14** *Statistics of Income Bulletin*, 113-122.

Robin, J. (1988), 'United They Stand, Divided They Fall: Public Choice Theory and the Tax Code', **75** *Cornell Law Review*.

Robin, J. (1989), 'The Grand Illusion: A Neutral System For The Taxation of International Transactions', **75** *Virginia Law Review*.

Robin, J. (1994), 'Adding Insult to Injury: The "Enhancement" of § 163(j) and the Tax Treatment of Foreign Investors in the United States', *New York University Tax Law Review*.

Rose, M. (1987), 'Optimal Tax Perspective on Tax Coordination', in Cnossen, S. (ed.), *Tax Coordination in the European Community*, London, Kluwer Law and Taxation, 113-138.

Rosenbloom, D.H. (1994), 'Sovereignty and the Regulation of International Business in the Tax Area', **20** *Canada-United States Law Journal*, 267 ff.

Rothman, D.J. and Marx, R.S. (1984), *The World of International Tax Planning by Milton Grundy (Review)*.

Rousslang, Donald J. and Tokarick, S.P. (1994), 'The Trade and Welfare Consequences of U.S. Export-Enhancing Tax Provisions', **41(4)** *IMF Staff Papers*, 675-683.

Rubinfeld, D. (1987), 'The Economics of the Local Public Sector', in Auerbach, A.J. and Feldstein, M. (eds), *Handbook of Public Economics*, vol. 2, Amsterdam, North Holland, 571-646.

Rudnick, R.S. (1989), 'Who Should Pay the Corporate Tax in a Flat Tax World?', **39** *Case Western Reserve Law Review*, 965 ff.

Sabransky, R. (1995), 'Notes: Note, Barclays Bank PLC v. Franchise Tax Board: California's Taxation of Foreign-based Multinational Corporations', **31** *California Western Law Review*, 317 ff.

Samuels, L.B. and Brown, Patricia A. (1990), 'Observations on the Taxation of Global Securities Trading', *New York University Tax Law Review*

Sanford, C. (ed.) (1993), *Key Issues inTax Reform*, Bath, Fiscal Publications.

Sawyer, Adrian J. (1995), 'International Taxation: A Complete Approach At Last? New

Zealand', **49(10)** *Bulletin for International Fiscal Documentation*, 472-481.

Schenk, D.H. (1994), 'Colloquium on NAFTA and Tradition: Foreword', **49** *New York University Tax Law Review*, 525 ff.

Schjelderup, Guttorm (1991), *Optimal Taxation, Capital Mobility and Tax Evasion*, Norwegian School of Economics and Business Administration.

Scholes, Myron S. and Wolfson, Mark A. (1992), *Taxes and Business Strategy: A Planning Approach*, Englewood Cliffs (NJ), Prentice-Hall.

Schwarz, J.C. (1992), 'Note: Trawling for Taxpayers: Section 6038A and Transfer Pricing Regulations', **42** *Case Western Reserve Law Review*, 933 ff.

Shaffer, G.C. (1988), 'An Alternative to Unilateral Immigration Controls: Toward a Coordinated U.S.-Mexico Binational Approach', **40** *Stanford Law Review*.

Shaviro, Daniel N. (1992), 'An Economic and Political Look at Federalism in Taxation', **90** *Michigan Law Review*.

Shuldiner, R. (1992), 'A General Approach to the Taxation of Financial Instruments', *Texas Law Review* in Frech, H. E. (ed.), *Regulating Doctors' Fees: Competition, Benefits, and Controls under Medicare*, Washington, DC, American Enterprise Institute.

Sinn, Hans-Werner (1984), 'Die Bedeutung des Accelerated Cost Recovery System fur den Internationalen Kapitalverkehr (The Importance of the Accelerated Cost Recovery System for International Capital Transfers)', **37** *Kyklos*, 542-576.

Sinn, Hans-Werner (1990), 'Tax Harmonization and Tax Competition in Europe', **34** *European Economic Review*.

Sinn, Hans-Werner (1993), 'Taxation and the Birth of Foreign Subsidiaries', in Herberg, H. and Long, N.V. (eds), *Trade Welfare, and Economic Policies: Essays in Honor of Murray C Kemp*, Ann Arbor: University of Michigan Press, 325-352.

Sinn, Stefan (1990), 'Capital Market Integration: Issues of International Taxation: Comment', in Siebert, H. (ed.), *Reforming Capital Income Taxation*, Westview Press, 166-169.

Siverson, S.E. (1994), 'Where a Tax Disadvantage Looms Large: Interest Expense and the American Corporate Return to South Africa', *Pace International Law Review*,

Slemrod, Joel B. (1988), 'Effect of Taxation with International Capital Mobility', in Aaron, Henry J., Galper, Harveu and Pechman, Joseph A. (eds), *Uneasy Compromise: Problems of a Hybrid Income-Consumption Tax*, Washington, Brookings Institution.

Slemrod, Joel B. (1990a), 'Optimal Taxation and the Optimal Tax System', **4** *Journal of Economic Perspectives*, 157-178.

Slemrod, Joel B. (1990b), 'Tax Effects on Foreign Direct Investment in the United States: Evidence From a Cross-Country Comparison', in Slemrod, J. and Razin, A. (eds), *Taxation in the Global Economy*, Chicago, University of Chicago Press.

Slemrod, Joel B. (1992), 'Here or There? The Source and Residence Principles of International Taxation: Comment', in Bird, R.M. and Mintz, J.M. (eds), *Taxation to 2000 and Beyond. Canadian Tax Paper*, Toronto, Canadian Tax Foundation, 333-337.

Slemrod, Joel B. (1995), 'Free Trade Taxation and Protectionist Taxation', **2(3)** *International Tax and Public Finance*, 471-489.

Smith, E.J. (1993), 'The U.S.-Mexico Tax Treaty', **8** *Florida International Law Journal*, 97 ff.

Smith, Robert S. (1987), 'Motor Vehicle Tax Harmonization', in Cnossen, S. (ed.), *Tax Coordination in the European Community*, London, Kluwer Law and Taxation, 141-170.

Sorensen, Peter Birch (1988), 'Optimal Taxation of Capital and Labor in a Small Open Economy', Paper presented at the International Conference On 'Tax Reform for Tax Neutrality', University of Bielefeld, Germany, May 30 - June 2, 1988.

Sorensen, Peter Birch (1992), 'Coordination of Capital Income Taxes in the Economic and Monetary Union: What Needs to be Done?', Mimeo.

Sowle, L.A. (1989), 'International Debt for Equity Swaps: Does Revenue Ruling 87-124 Make Sense? (Comment)', **83** *Northwestern University Law Review*.

Steines, J.P. (1994), 'Colloquium on NAFTA and Tradition: Commentary: Income Tax Implications of Free Trade', **49** *New York University Tax Law Review*, 675 ff.

Stevens, G.V.G. and Lipsey, R.E. (1992), 'Interactions Between Domestic and Foreign Investment', **11** *Journal of International Money and Finance*, 40-62.

Stockmann, Frank (1995), 'Should the Exemption Method Have Priority over the Credit Method in International Tax Law?', **49(6)** *Bulletin for International Fiscal Documentation*, 285-288.

Sullivan, Mark (1984), 'In Memoriam: Stanley S. Surrey: Appendix', **97** *Harvard Law Review*.

Surrey, Stanley S. (1958), 'The United States Taxation of Foreign Income', **1** *Journal of Law and Economics*, 72-96.

Swenson, D. (1994), 'The Impact of U.S. Tax Reform on Foreign Direct Investment in the United States', **54** *Journal of Public Economics*, 243-266.

Tanzi, V. and Minassian, T.T. (1987), 'The European Monetary System and Fiscal Policies', in Cnossen, S. (ed.), *Tax Coordination in the European Community*, London, Kluwer Law and Taxation.

Tanzi, Vito (1995), *Taxation in an Integrating World*, Washington, Brookings Institution.

Tatarowicz, P.M. and Mims-Velarde, R.F. (1986), 'Symposium on State and Local Taxation: An Analytical Approach to State Tax Discrimination Under the Commerce Clause', **39** *Vanderbilt Law Review*.

Tiebout, Charles M. (1956), 'A Pure Theory of Local Expenditures', **56** *Journal of Political Economy*, 416-424.

Tillinghast, D.R. (1996), 'Tax Treaty Issues', **50** *University of Miami Law Review*,

Trachtman, J.P. (1991), 'Recent Initiatives in International Financial Regulation and Goals of Competitiveness, Effectiveness, Consistency and Cooperation', **12** *Journal of International Law and Business*, 241 ff.

U.S. Congress, Joint Commitee on Taxation (1987), *General Explanation of the Tax Reform Act of 1986*, Washington, Government Printing Office.

U.S. Congress, Joint Commitee on Taxation (1991), *Factors Affecting the International Competitiveness of the United States*, Washington, Government Printing Office.

Ulph, D.T. (1987), 'Tax Harmonisation and Labour Mobility', in Cnossen, S. (ed.), *Tax Coordination in the European Community*, London, Kluwer Law and Taxation, 305-317.

Utz, S.G. (1994), 'Taxation Panel: Tax Harmonization and Coordination in Europe and America', **9** *Connecticut Journal of International Law*, 767 ff.

Vagts, D.F. (1981), 'Comment: Are There No International Lawyers Anymore?', **75** *American Journal of International Law*, 134 ff.

Vann, Richard J. and Parsons, Ross W. (1986), 'The Foreign Tax Credit and Reform of International Taxation', **3(2)** *Australian Tax Forum*, 131-221.

Vernon, R. (1977), *Storm Over the Multinationals: The Real Issues*, Cambridge, Harvard

University Press.

Wahl, J. (1989), 'Tax Treatment of Foreign Exchange Gains and Losses and the Tax Reform Act of 1986', **42(1)** *National Tax Journal*, 59-68.

Waterland, L.J. (1985), 'Note: Container Corporation of America v. Franchise Tax Board: The Supreme Court Encourages Apportionment Taxation', **26** *William & Mary Law Review*, 683 ff.

Weinberg, K. S. (1994), 'Arbitration Procedures in the United States-German Income Tax', **12** *Boston University International Law Journal*, 180 ff.

Weiner, Joann (1996a), 'Using the Experience of the U.S. States to Evaluate Issues in Implementing Formula Apportionment at the International Level', **Dec. 23** *Tax Notes International*, 2113-2144.

Weiner, Joann (1996b), 'Estimates of How the Unitary Tax Affects Business Investment', Working Paper, Jan. 3, 1996.

Wheeler, J.E. (1988), 'An Academic Look at Transfer Pricing in a Global Economy', **87** *Tax Notes*, 96 ff.

Whitman, D.S. (1995), 'Recent Developments: Barclays Bank v. Franchise Tax Board of California: Worldwide Combined Reporting Survives For State Taxation of Multinational Enterprises', **3** *Tulane Journal of International and Comparative Law*, 265 ff.

Wildasin, David E. (1986), *Urban Public Finance*, New York, Harwood Academic Press.

Willard, Kristen L. (1994), *Essays On International Taxation*, Princeton, Princeton University Press.

Wilson, G.P. (1993), 'The Role of Taxes in Location and Sourcing Decisions', in Giovannini, A., Hubbard, R.G. and Slemrod, J. (eds), *Studies in International Taxation*, Chicago, University of Chicago Press.

Wong Pakshong, Michael (1980), 'The Future Position of Singapore in International Taxation', **34(4)** *Bulletin for International Fiscal Documentation*, 146-149.

Workman, D.J. (1982), 'Comment: The Use of Offshore Tax Havens for the Purpose of Criminally Evading Income Taxes', **73** *Journal of Criminal Law and Criminology*, 675 ff.

Young, Garry (1994), 'International Competitiveness, International Taxation and Domestic Investment', **0(148)** *National Institute Economic Review*, 44-48.

Young, K.H. (1988), 'The Effects of Taxes and Rates of Return on Foreign Direct Investment Into the United States', **41** *National Tax Journal*, 109-121.

Zodrow, George R. (1991), 'On the "Traditional" and "New" Views of Dividend Taxation', **44** *National Tax Journal*, 497-509.

Zodrow, George R. and Mieszkowski, Peter (1986), 'Pigou, Tiebout, Property Taxation, and the Underprovision of Public Goods', **19** *Journal of Urban Economics*, 356-370.

Zucker, D. (1983), 'Note: MCA, Inc. v. United States: Judicial Recognition of the Separate Interests Theory', **5** *Journal of International Law and Business*, 680 ff.

6110
Optimal Techniques of Redistribution

Christopher Curran
Associate Professor, Emory University Department of Economics

Abstract

Legal scholars have often argued that a legal system in providing a 'level playing field' for consumers and producers should be designed to help in society's efforts to achieve an optimal distribution of income. This chapter reviews research by law and economics scholars that challenges this premise. Using neoclassical welfare economics most of these scholars conclude that there exists a taxation scheme that achieves a desired income distribution and is preferred by all members of society to any plan for redistributing income using the legal system. An implication of this research is that economic efficiency and not fairness is the appropriate criteria for evaluating any legal rule.
JEL classification: K0, H2
Keywords: Income Redistribution, Taxation

1. Introduction

In this chapter we examine the issue of whether income redistribution goals are more efficiently achieved by using the tax system or by incorporating these goals into the design and implementation of a legal system. As stated, this question takes as given that some amount of income redistribution is desirable and ignores the extensive literature on (1) the desirability of income redistribution and (2) the effectiveness of income redistribution in combating poverty. While the problem that remains - that of developing the most cost effective method of achieving the desired income distribution - has a strong production flavor, the answer has important implications both for the study and practice of law. If the arguments of Kaplow and Shavell (1994) and others are correct, then law and economics scholars should adopt their suggestion that 'it is appropriate for economic analysis of legal rules to focus on efficiency and to ignore the distribution of income in offering normative judgments' (Kaplow and Shavell, 1994, p. 677). If their analysis is flawed or if, as some authors suggest, traditional neoclassical economics models contain serious deficiencies, then the arguments of Calabresi (1991), Kronman (1980), Kennedy (1982) and Arlen (1992) that the courts should consider income distribution when evaluating legal rules have merit.

2. Two Lines of Research

It is not unusual for legal scholars to assume that courts ought to be concerned with the proper distribution of income. Indeed, given that allowing the courts to consider issues of income distribution in judging cases will increase the demand for the services of lawyers and the legal system, it would be surprising if legal scholars were unanimous in concluding that courts ought to ignore the implications of legal policies on the income distribution (see, for example, Polinsky and Shavell, 1991). Moreover, Friedman's (1981) and Lott's (1987) papers imply that a court should consider a party's wealth when that consideration leads to optimal deterrence. Rather than reviewing all of this literature, this chapter focuses on articles directly addressing the issue of whether it is more efficient to use the legal system or taxation to redistribute income. Heavy reliance on neoclassical economic theory and (usually) mathematical models characterizes the articles contributing to this discussion.

3. Related Literature

While Shavell (1981) is the first law and economics scholar to address the issue of the most efficient way to redistribute income, his arguments draw directly from the optimal taxation literature of the 1970s. (See Auerbach, 1985, and Stiglitz, 1985, for thorough reviews of the optimal taxation literature and Drèze and Stern, 1985, for a review of the cost-benefit literature.) Shavell acknowledges his particular intellectual debt to two articles in this literature. In the first, Mirrlees (1971) demonstrates that commodities whose demand are independent of income should not be taxed (with a fixed per unit tax) when there is an optimal income taxation system in place. In the second, Hylland and Zeckhauser (1979, p. 266) demonstrate that 'in the optimal arrangement, distributional objectives are achieved through the tax system alone'. Moreover, Hylland and Zeckhauser conclude that, in the presence of the optimal income tax, government programs should be adopted based purely on efficiency criteria. Shavell's 1981 paper reaches a conclusion that echoes that of Hylland and Zeckhauser. In particular, Shavell (1981, p. 414) argues that 'despite imperfect ability to redistribute income through taxation, everyone would strictly prefer that legal rules be chosen only on the basis of their efficiency'.

4. Legal Scholarship

The conclusions of Shavell (1981) are contrary to those made by earlier legal scholars. Scholars such as Ackerman (1973), Kennedy (1976), Michelman (1978), and Kronman (1980) argue that an important role of legal institutions is to redistribute income. Indeed, Kronman (1980, p. 510) argues that the choice between using the legal system and using taxation to redistribute income depends on 'contextual considerations that are likely to vary from one situation to the next'. Kronman suggests that all of the alleged problems with using courts to redistribute income are equally likely to be problems with taxation. For instance, critics of using the courts to redistribute income claim that there is no reason to believe that judges can correctly assess the distributional consequences of any particular decision. Kronman counters that difficulty in applying egalitarian rules in individual cases does not mean that we cannot use egalitarian principles when designing the legal system. To the claim that the legal system should 'remain neutral between the aims and activities of its citizens' (Kronman, 1980, p. 502), Kronman responds that taxation is no more neutral than are the courts and the relative neutrality of the two methods of redistributing income is an empirical issue. Kronman responds in a similar manner to claims that regulation is more injurious to its intended beneficiaries and is more expensive to administer than is taxation by asserting that these are empirical issues than cannot be resolved through the use of theory alone, a conclusion not supported by Shavell (1981).

5. Shavell Forgotten

Not only does Shavell's research offer conclusions contrary to earlier research, it appears to have been ignored by legal scholars during the ten years following its publication. Calabresi (1991), Donohue (1989), Ellis (1982) and Kennedy (1982) all discuss the role of the legal system in achieving the proper distribution of income without mentioning Shavell's 1981 seminal article. Abraham and Jeffries (1989), who argue that information about a defendant's wealth should not be considered in determining punitive awards, do not reference Shavell. In their defense, the connection of Shavell's conclusion to the issue that Abraham and Jeffries discuss is not obvious. Abraham and Jeffries argue that the consideration of a defendant's wealth is not germane to the issue of punitive damages and invites jury speculation about issues about which they have no information. They argue that traditional arguments that the legal system needs punitive damages in order to deter individuals from inflicting harm for personal satisfaction and to neutralize the effects of underenforcement are incorrect. While Abraham and Jeffries do not point out the connection, their arguments echo those of both Hylland and Zeckhauser (1979) and Shavell (1981) that distributional goals are best achieved through the tax system while government programs - including legal regulation - should ignore distributional goals in favor of efficiency criteria. Thus, by Hylland and Zeckhauser's and Shavell's logic one would consider the defendant's wealth only in cases wealth is correlated with deterrence, a conclusion that matches Abraham and Jeffries' result.

6. Shavell Remembered

Arlen (1992) appears to be the first author to acknowledge Shavell's 1981 article. While the model that Shavell develops assumes that people are risk neutral, he points out that his results are independent of this assumption. Arlen argues, incorrectly it turns out, that Shavell's conclusions do not hold when individuals are risk averse. The most recent contributions to this literature are in direct response to what Kaplow and Shavell (1994) and Miceli and Segerson (1995) perceive as a general misunderstanding of Shavell's 1981 article by legal scholars, including Arlen (1992). In what follows, we discuss Shavell (1981) and Kaplow and Shavell (1994) together because of the similarities in the two articles. We then review Miceli and Segerson (1995). Since the model in Miceli and Segerson (1995) corrects and places Arlen's results in the context of the Shavell model, we include Arlen (1992) in this discussion.

7. Shavell's Analysis

The arguments in Shavell (1981) and Kaplow and Shavell (1994) are essentially identical. These authors argue that all efforts to redistribute income - be these efforts through the legal system or through the tax system - distort work efforts (see Hausman, 1981, for an empirical justification of this point). Redistributing income through the legal system creates additional inefficiencies in the activities affected by the legal rules. Thus, we should be able to construct a new tax schedule that we can combine with efficient legal rules that will have the same distortions of work effort but none of the inefficiencies that arise when we use the legal system to redistribute income.

8. Achieving a Desired Income Distribution

Since this result is key, we consider it here in some detail. Shavell (1981) and Kaplow and Shavell (1994) assume that individuals are risk neutral maximizers of expected utility, which is equal to their income net of taxes, expected liability costs, expected damages, and the costs of work effort and care taking. The tax schedule is a function of income while the expected liability and damages are functions of the level of care taken by the individual. In order to simplify the analysis, these authors assume that (1) an individual's income is a linear function of his work effort and (2) in the aggregate the government returns all taxes collected. Following existing literature, they define the efficient level of care as that care level that minimizes sum of the total costs of care and the expected accident costs. As Shavell (1981, p. 416) and Kaplow and Shavell (1994, p. 678) note, the level of care that is efficient is independent of an individual's income. These authors show that we can replace *any* regime having an inefficient legal rule and a tax schedule with a regime with an efficient legal rule and a properly modified tax schedule that raises the same level of taxes. More importantly, they also show that all members of society prefer the regime with the efficient legal rule.

9. Modification of the Tax Schedule

The modification to the tax schedule under the inefficient legal rule offers some insight into what drives these results. The modified tax schedule is equal to the tax schedule in the inefficient regime plus the total accident costs in the inefficient regime minus the total accident costs in the efficient regime (see Kaplow and Shavell, 1994, p. 678). Substitution of the new tax schedule into the expected utility function yields the results that the expected utility is the same in the efficient regime (with the modified tax schedule) as it is in the inefficient regime. Moreover, this new tax schedule yields a greater level of revenue. Remember that the modified tax schedule is equal to the old tax schedule plus the efficiency savings that come from switching to the efficient legal rule. Thus, if we rebate these savings uniformly to the population in the form of a lump sum (negative) tax, no-one's incentive to work is affected and everyone is better off by the amount of the rebate in taxes.

10. Other Reasons for Using the Tax System to Achieve Distributional Goals

Kaplow and Shavell (1994, pp. 674-676) offer several other, more traditional reasons for favoring the use of the tax system over the legal system to redistribute income. First, the tax system can allocate the impact of income redistribution on all of the rich and all of the poor. By contrast, using the legal system to redistribute income yields haphazard results. The legal system can only affect those individuals involved in a lawsuit. Moreover, in many cases consumer response is bound to mute or completely negate efforts to use the courts to redistribute income. For instance, individuals bound by contracts will adjust prices to take account of efforts by the courts to redistribute income. Similarly, corporations may well be able to pass on to consumers the income redistribution efforts by the courts. Second, Kaplow and Shavell (1994, p. 675) argue that claims that the legal system should be involved in income redistribution efforts because the political system is unable to achieve the ideal amount of income redistribution do not stand close examination. In particular, the legal system operates under the influence of the politicians and there is no reason to believe that efforts by the courts to redistribute income in ways not intended by the politicians will escape their scrutiny. Thus, Kaplow and Shavell (1994, p. 677) conclude that their analysis 'suggests that it is appropriate for economic analysis of legal rules to focus on efficiency and to ignore the distribution of income in offering normative judgments'.

11. A General Model

Miceli and Segerson (1995) offer the most complete analysis of the issue of role of income distribution in setting efficient levels of care. These authors analyze the role of risk aversion in the Shavell (1981) and Kaplow and Shavell (1994) model. In doing so, they correct and reconcile Arlen's (1992) results with the other models. Miceli and Segerson argue that of the three potential optimal choice criteria - Pareto efficiency, the Pareto criterion, and aggregate welfare - Pareto efficiency is the proper one to use. They define Pareto efficiency by the following choice problem:

Max U_i subject to U_v U_v^o (1) where U_i is the utility level of the injurer, U_v is the utility level of victim, and U_v^o is some arbitrarily fixed level of utility for the victim. The Pareto criterion has the same definition as (1), except that U_v^o is set equal to the victim's original utility level, $U(W_v^o)$. Finally, aggregate welfare is the solution to the following choice problem:

Max $U_i + U_v$(2) is where some weight placed on the victim's utility. Miceli and Segerson (1995, p. 194) illustrate the three concepts with the utility possibilities frontier (UPF) shown in Figure 1. The UPF contains all of the Pareto optimal points. As illustrated in Figure 1, the Pareto criterion and the aggregate welfare each pick points that are subsets of the Pareto optimal points. The authors prefer to use Pareto optimality as their choice criterion for two reasons. First, unlike the other concepts, Pareto optimality does not involve interpersonal comparisons of utility. Second, we can specify any income distribution by varying U_v^o.

Figure 1 The utility possibility curve (UPC) for injurer and victim

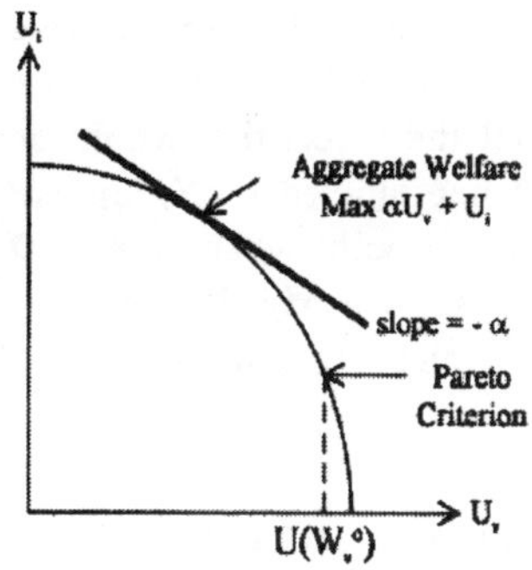

12. Definition of Terms

Miceli and Segerson (1995, p. 197) define $P(X)$ to be the probability of an accident (where $P' >$ and $P'' < 0$); X, the injurer's care level; m, the damages that the victim suffers if there is an accident; W_i and W_v, the injurer's and victim's preaccident wealth levels, respectively; D, the damages paid by the injurer in case of an accident; and T, a (positive or negative) transfer from the injurer to the victim that occurs independent of whether an accident occurs. As Miceli and Segerson (1995, p. 197) note, the addition of the variable T allows them to 'decouple distribution and cost minimization issues'. They then split the analysis into two distinct parts. In the first they derive the first-best care levels while in the second they analyze the ability of various liability rules to give individuals the incentives necessary to take these first-best care levels.

13. Efficient Care Standards

Miceli and Segerson (1995) show that in the presence of fully working insurance markets, the first-best care standards are independent of both injurer's and victim's wealth levels as long as the policymaker is free to choose the care standard and the amount of the transfer, T. Only in the case where the policymaker can only set the care standard is the care standard a function of the injurer's wealth. For instance, Arlen (1992) implicitly assumes in her analysis that the amount of the transfer, T, and the amount of damages, D, are preset such that $T = D = 0$. Figure 2 illustrates the case when the policymaker can only set the care standard. The solid curve labeled UPF_1 is the utility possibilities frontier that faces the policymaker who is free to set the care standard and the amount of the transfer. Since the policymaker's choice set is restricted, the utility possibilities frontier available to the policy maker who can only set the care standard must lie inside the unrestricted UPF at all points except the point where T and D by coincidence equal the levels that would occur in the unrestricted case. In Figure 2 the dashed line labeled UPF_2 represents the restricted UPF, while point A represents the one point where T and D equal the values they would have in the unrestricted case. Clearly, there exist solutions on UPF_1 where both the victim and the injurer can achieve higher utility levels than they can on the restricted UPF_2.

Figure 2 Restricted and unrestricted utility possibility curves

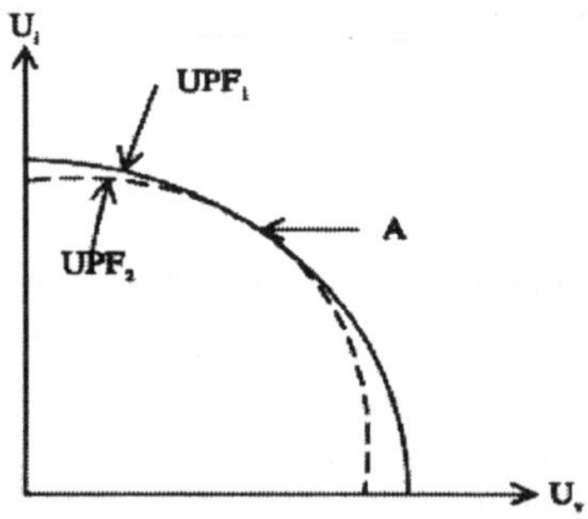

14. Efficiency of the Legal Rules

By choosing appropriate liability rules society attempts to induce injurers to take the efficient level of care. The potential success of society in achieving this goal while concurrently attempting to reach an ideal distribution of income depends on the number of policy tools available to the policy makers. Miceli and Segerson (1995, pp. 200-202) analyze the efficiency of strict liability and negligence under various assumptions about the choice variables available to the policy makers. As they note, the efficient care level solves Max U_i subject to U_v U_v^o and X maximized $U_i(3)$ given the liability rule. Miceli and Segerson demonstrate that, when policymakers can set the care standard X, the damage award D, and the transfer from the injurer to the victim T, both strict liability and negligence rules are efficient. The reason for this result is that the policy makers have three tools - X, D, and T - with which to achieve three goals - income distribution, cost minimization and efficient incentives for the injurer. Thus, the policy makers can set *X* to minimize total social cost, *D* to give the injurer the proper incentives, and *T* to redistribute income, resulting in society attaining a point somewhere on UPF_1, as shown in Figure 2. In contrast, if one or two of the three control instruments are not available to the policymakers, then society can achieve the three goals only by coincidence.

15. An Existence Theorem

The results presented by Shavell (1981), Miceli and Segerson (1995) and Kaplow and Shavell (1994) comprise an existence theorem - if society decides to redistribute income, there exists a tax schedule for redistributing income that everyone prefers to any other way of redistributing income, including the use of legal rules or institutions. As Kaplow and Shavell (1994, p. 675) note, the importance of this result to legal scholars is that it demonstrates that it is appropriate to evaluate legal rules only on the basis of efficiency criteria.

Bibliography on Optimal Techniques of Redistribution (6110)

Abraham, Kenneth S. and Jeffries, John C. Jr (1989), 'Punitive Damages and the Rule of Law: The Role of Defendant's Wealth', **28** *Journal of Legal Studies*, 415-425.

Ackerman, Bruce (1973), 'Regulating Slum Housing Markets on Behalf of the Poor: Of Housing Codes, Housing Subsidies and Income Redistribution Policy', **80** *Yale Law Journal*, 1093-1197.

Arlen, Jennifer H. (1992), 'Should Defendants' Wealth Matter?', **21** *Journal of Legal Studies*, 413-429.

Hylland, Aanund and Zeckhauser, Richard (1979), 'Distributional Objectives Should Affect Taxes but Not Program Choice or Design', **81** *Scandinavian Journal of Economics*, 264-284.

Kaplow, Louis and Shavell, Steven (1994), 'Why the Legal System is Less Efficient than the Income Tax in Redistributing Income', **23** *Journal of Legal Studies*, 667-681.

Miceli, Thomas J. and Segerson, Kathleen (1995), 'Defining Efficient Care: The Role of Income Distribution', **24** *Journal of Legal Studies*, 189-208.

Shavell, Steven (1981), 'A Note on Efficiency vs. Distributional Equity in Legal Rulemaking: Should Distributional Equity Matter Given Optimal Income Taxation?', **71** *American Economic Review*, 414-418.

Other References

Auerbach, Alan J. (1985), 'The Theory of Excess Burden and Optimal Taxation', in Auerbach, Alan J. and Feldstein, Martin (eds), *Handbook of Public Economics*, Amsterdam, Elsevier Science Publishers B.V. (North Holland), 61-127.

Calabresi, Guido (1991), 'The Pointlessness of Pareto: Carrying Coase Further', **100** *Yale Law Journal*, 1211-1237.

Donohue, John J. III (1989), 'Diverting the Coasean River: Incentive Schemes to Reduce Unemployment Spells', **99** *Yale Law Journal*, 549-609.

Drèze, Jean and Stern, Nicholas (1985), 'The Theory of Cost-Benefit Analysis', in Auerbach, Alan J. and Feldstein, Martin (eds), *Handbook of Public Economics*, Amsterdam, Elsevier Science Publishers B.V. (North Holland), 909-989.

Ellis, Dorsey D., Jr (1982), 'Fairness and Efficiency in the Law of Punitive Damages', **56** *Southern California Law Review*, 1-78.

Friedman, David D. (1981), 'Reflections on Optimal Punishment, or: Should the Rich Pay Higher Fines', **3** *Research in Law and Economics*, 185-205.

Hausman, Jerry A. (1981), 'Labor Supply', in Aaron, Henry J. and Pechman, Joseph A. (eds) *How Taxes Affect Economic Behavior*, Washington, DC, Brookings Institution, 27-72.

Kennedy, Duncan (1976), 'Form and Substance in Private Law Adjudication', **89** *Harvard Law Journal*, 1685-1778.

Kennedy, Duncan (1982), 'Distributive and Paternalist Motives in Contract and Tort Law, with Special Reference to Compulsory terms and Unequal Bargaining Power', **41** *Maryland Law Review*, 563-658.

Kronman, Anthony T. (1980), 'Contract Law and Distributive Justice', **89** *Yale Law Journal*, 472-511.

Lott, John R., Jr. (1987), 'Should the Wealthy Be Able to "Buy Justice?"', **95** *Journal of Political Economy*, 1307-1316.

Michelman, Frank I. (1978), 'Norms and Normativity in the Economic Theory of the Law', **62** *Minnesota Law Review*, 1015-1048.

Mirrlees, J.A. (1971), 'An Exploration in the Theory of Optimum Income Taxation', **38** *Review of Economic Studies*, 175-208.

Polinsky, A. Mitchell and Shavell, Steven (1991), 'A Note on Optimal Fines When Wealth Varies Among Individuals', **81** *American Economic Review*, 618-621.

Shavell, Steven (1982), 'On Liability and Insurance', **13** *Bell Journal of Economics*, 120-132.

Stiglitz, Joseph E. (1985), 'Pareto Efficient and Optimal Taxation and the New New Welfare Economics', in Auerbach, Alan J. and Feldstein, Martin (ed.) *Handbook of Public Economics*, Amsterdam, Elsevier Science Publishers B.V. (North Holland), 991-1042.

6120
PENSIONS

Koen Algoed and Frans Spinnewyn
University of Leuven

Abstract

This chapter discusses the different pension systems. Pension systems are a means of transferring purchasing power from the working phase to the retirement phase of the life cycle. Formal pension systems are organised in two ways. In the funded or the capital-reserve system, the agents save to accumulate a fund which finances an annuity to the survivors. In the pay-as-you-go system, the payment of the pensions to the retired population are financed by the contributions of the working population. It is shown that capital-reserve systems and pay-as-you-go systems, two variants of providing retirement income, may yield the same outcome or may yield allocations differing only in their second order effects. Capital-reserve systems are superior to pay-as-you-go systems in the definition of the future rights of the retired population. Pay-as-you-go systems are better suited to redistribute the burden of major shocks among the working generations and the retired generations.

Reforms fixing the individual rights of the retired population conditional on the state of the economy and the record of individual contributions are desirable. Alternatively, adapting the tax status of funded pension plans to the state of the economy in a well-defined way could improve the risk-sharing properties of the capital-reserve system.
JEL classification: H55
Keywords: Overlapping Generations, Pay-as-you-go, Capital Reserve, Aaron's Rule, Social Risk

1. Saving for Retirement

Old-age pension plans are a means of transferring purchasing power from the working phase to the retirement phase of the life cycle. The wages earned while working constitute a claim on the output of the economy. By refraining from consuming part of this claim, output can be devoted to investment or consumption of collective goods.. The contributions to a pension fund are an example. Through the pension fund, these financial means are lent to firms for the acquisition of capital assets or to the government for providing collective goods. In this way, the retired population derives a claim on the output of the economy, either by sharing in the income appropriated by the capital owners or by sharing in the taxes levied by the government to service the debt. This income finances consumption after retirement.

Alternatively, working children can share their claim on the output of the economy with their retired parents. In this way, the parents are given the opportunity to satisfy their consumption needs after retirement. In the extended family, the children care for their parents in the hope of being cared for by their children in old age. On a broader scale, in a formal pension plan part of the wages earned by the working population are transferred to the retired population. In this way, the retired generation obtains a claim on the output of the economy even when they are no longer involved in the production process.

Like private saving, old-age pension plans therefore smooth consumption over the life cycle. However, the transfer of purchasing power in a pension plan is conditional on the survival after retirement. Formal pension plans covering large populations redistribute income from the short-lived to the long-lived. In addition to the transfer of purchasing power, formal pension plans offer insurance against longevity. Old-age pensions insure against the risk that the retiree will outlive the amount saved for the provision of retirement income (Bodie, 1990a). In this way, those who have contributed for a pension but die before or live only for a short while after retirement contribute to and increase the retirement income of those who are blessed with a long life. The rate of return for the survivors in a pension plan exceeds the rate of return on saving, the difference being equal to the mortality rate. The reason is that the rights of those who die are transferred to the survivors. Restricting transfers to the survivors is motivated by the fact that only the survivors still have consumption needs. In contrast, the wealth accumulated through saving is bequeathed to the heirs. Due to the stochastic nature of the length of life, the bequest at the time of death has a random component. Using the techniques of insurance, formal pension plans can control for this random component. The exchanges between the young and the old generation are therefore better defined in the formal pension plans than in the extended family.

2. The Capital-Reserve System and the Pay-As-You-Go-System

Formal pension plans are organised in two ways. In the funded or the capital-reserve system, the agents save to accumulate a fund which finances an annuity to the survivors. At each point of time, the accumulated fund of a cohort of agents together with the contributions which are still due from the surviving members of the cohort before retirement, will meet the future pension rights of the survivors in the cohort. In the pay-as-you-go system, the payment of the pensions to the retired population are financed by the contributions of the working population. When the former exceed the latter, the accounts are balanced either by a subsidy of the government financed by taxes or by running down reserves. A pay-as-you-go system can therefore be viewed as a plan of transfer payments from the working population to the retired population. The contributions made while working, provide the agent with a right to receive a pension while retired.

From this description, it is concluded that the distinguishing feature between the capital-reserve system and the pay-as-you-go system is the redistribution of income between generations which takes place in the latter but not in the former (Verbon, 1989; Marchand and Pestieau, 1991). However, this conclusion needs the following qualifications.

First, workers, capital owners and the taxing authorities have competing claims on the output. Depending on the organisation of the pension plan and the definition of the pension rights, the income of the retired population will depend on the solution of this basic conflict. If the pensions are linked to the income of the working population, as in the pay-as-you-go system, the old-age pensioners gain from an increase in the wage bill. But the interests diverge when both parties bargain over the share of the wage bill accruing to the old-age pensioners. If the pensions are linked to the income of the capital owners, as in the capital-reserve system, then the working generation increases its share at the expense of the retired generation.

Second, the transfers between generations in the formal pension plans are complemented by voluntary transfers or bequests. Abstracting from uncertainties, differences in transfer payments between young and old in the pension plans will be offset by changes in the bequests. This neutrality theorem of Barro (1974) is a variant of Ricardian equivalence of government fiscal actions and is based on the life cycle model of savings (Modigliani and Brumberg, 1954). In this model, a consumption profile has the discounted sum of lifetime after-tax income as one of its arguments. Two after-tax income profiles with the same present value result in the same consumption profile. Two pension plans leading to two different profiles of after-tax income but with the same present value do not change consumption. If consumption does not change, investment and the capital formation are not affected by the choice of the pension plan. Barro's neutrality result has been criticised by the fact that it may require negative bequests at the individual level in order to establish the neutrality of public actions. This will be the case when at the collective level the burden to the future generations of servicing the public debt is low.

3. Equivalence of Pension Systems Under Certainty

In the comparison of formal pension plans, consider an environment without uncertainty apart from the risk of longevity. In the capital-reserve system, the contributions to a pension plan grow with the interest rate which is linked to the marginal productivity of capital. Samuelson (1958) and Aaron (1966) have shown that the contributions to the pay-as-you-go system also earn a return which is composed of the growth rate of the population (Samuelson's 'biological' rate of interest) and the growth rate of wages.

Equivalence on the Golden Rule Path

Assume that in the capital-reserve system, the age profile of contributions and benefits of any two succeeding generations are obtained from each other by a parallel vertical shift reflecting the growth rate of wages. It then follows that in the steady state the two systems are equivalent if the interest rate is equal to the sum of population and wage growth rates. This can be established as follows. In the capital-reserve system, the capital which has been accumulated during the working life is equal to the discounted future liability of the pension fund at the date of retirement. Consider a pay-as-you-go system in which contributions and benefits of each individual are equal to those of the capital-reserve system. Compare in the pay-as-you-go system the own contributions of the retiring generation when they started working and the current contributions of the youngest generation. The contributions of the youngest generation have increased at a rate equal to the sum of the growth rate of the population and the growth rate of wages for a period equal to the length of the working life. By assumption, this sum is equal to the rate of interest. It follows that the current contribution of the youngest generation in the pay-as-you-go system is equal to the capitalized value of the contributions of the retiring generation as young workers in the capital-reserve system. By shortening the period for which they were contributing each time by one year, the same holds for each of the older working generations. Similarly, for each of the retired generations, the total transfer payments in the pay-as-you-go system are equal to the present value of the future transfer payments of the pension funds when the current retiring generation will be of the same age. In the pay-as-you-go-system, the older retired generations are less numerous and have a lower pension reflecting the lower wage earned in their working life. By assumption, the sum of these effects is matched by the effect of discounting the future liability of the pension fund in the capital-reserve system. Since at the retirement date, the capitalised contributions are equal to the present value of the liabilities in the capital-reserve system, it follows that the pay-as-you-go system which mimics the capital-reserve system breaks even.

If the interest rate is equal to the growth rate, the economy is at the golden rule. At the golden rule the consumption per head is maximised. The consumption per head is obtained as the difference between the production per head and the investment per head needed to keep the capital-labour ratio constant. The labour force is measured in efficiency units. Consumption per head is then a function of the capital-labour ratio. There is over-accumulation if the capital-labour ratio in the steady state is larger than the ratio in the golden rule. The golden rule is Pareto superior to any steady state with over-accumulation. This is established as follows. Let the capital stock fall by delaying investment until the capital-labour ratio has fallen to the one in the golden rule. Without investment, the consumption of the generations living in the transition can be increased. In the new steady state satisfying the golden rule, the consumption is larger than in the steady state with over-accumulation. The government debt is adjusted to obtain equality between private financial wealth and the sum of the government debt and the value of the capital stock.

There is under-accumulation if the capital-labour ratio in the steady state is smaller than the ratio in the golden rule. In this case, one cannot increase the capital-labour ratio without decreasing the consumption of the generations living in the transition. The steady state with under-accumulation is therefore Pareto efficient.

Equivalence off the Golden Rule Path

Restricting the analysis to Pareto-efficient situations, we conclude that the rate of return on saving in the capital-reserve system is at least as large as the one in the pay-as-you-go system. By and large, the interest rate has always exceeded the growth rate of the economy. From Aaron (1966) to Feldstein (1976), economists as well as politicians have concluded that for that reason the capital-reserve system is more efficient than the pay-as-you-go system. In this comparison, it is implicitly assumed that government debt is the same in the two systems. In an economy with lump-sum taxation, the equivalence of the two systems is re-established when in the pay-as-you-go system the government debt is reduced by an appropriate amount (Bewley, 1981; Myles, 1995). The argument is based on the life-cycle model stating that the consumption profile is unaffected by a change in the after-tax income profile which does not change its present value. When compared to the capital-reserve system, the pay-as-you-go system has higher taxes before retirement but lower taxes after retirement. If the interest rate exceeds the growth rate of the economy, the two systems yield the same consumption profile for an average tax rate which is larger in the capital-reserve system than in the pay-as-you-go system. The tax rate is increased in the capital-reserve system by increasing the taxes needed to service a larger government debt.

The same conclusion is obtained when it is assumed that the pay-as-you-go system mimics the capital-reserve system. If the interest rate exceeds the growth rate of the economy, it follows from the previous discussion that per retiring agent the contributions of the working generations in the pay-as-you-go system fall short of his or her accumulated savings in the capital-reserve system. The transfer payments to the retired generations in the pay-as-you-go system exceed the present value of the future liability to a retiring agent in the capital-reserve system. From the equality of the accumulated savings and the present value of future liabilities at the retirement date in the capital-reserve system, it follows that the pay-as-you-go system runs a deficit. When the government subsidy needed to restore the balance is equal to the tax saving from a lower government debt, the two systems are equivalent.

The conversion of a pay-as-you-go system to a capital-reserve system shows that, *ceteris paribus*, the government debt must be larger in the latter than in the former (Townley, 1981; Breyer, 1989; Verbon, 1989). In the transition period, the retired generations receive pension payments equivalent to those they would have received for the fraction of their working life that they contributed under the old system. No generation is therefore sacrificed. The gap needed to compensate these generations is closed by an increase in government debt which is taken up by the pension funds. But then, after the transition period, no generation will benefit from the higher rate of return of the capital-reserve system. The government subsidy which was needed under the pay-as-you-go system is replaced by an increase in the average tax rate to service the larger debt.

Although a consensus on the issue of the performance of pension systems has not been reached, we conclude that investment needed to raise the capital stock in a state of under-accumulation can be achieved only by reducing aggregate consumption at the outset. Consider an environment without uncertainty and without distortionary taxation. For a given rate of interest, the utility-maximising consumption profile is chosen within the intertemporal budget of each generation. An increase in the capital stock requires a higher investment rate and, therefore, an adjustment in the consumption profile. An adjustment of an optimal consumption profile is possible only by decreasing the lifetime utility. It then follows that increasing the capital stock is impossible unless at least one generation is made worse off.

From this conclusion it does not follow that the different definition of the rights of pensioners in the capital-reserve system and in the pay-as-you-go system is unimportant. The definition of the rights in each of the systems and in their variants determines the risk borne by the retirees and the risk sharing between the agents in the economy. In addition, the allocation of pension rights provide different incentives to contribute to a pension system affecting both the level of contributions and the choice of the retirement age. Finally, market imperfections in the form of asymmetric information on survival risks, transaction costs, myopia and free riding must be taken into account.

4. Pension as Retirement Income Insurance

Through contributions during the working years, pension plans are designed to protect an economic agent against economic insecurity in retirement. In addition to the longevity risk, the following major sources of retirement income risk can be distinguished (Bodie, 1990a; Disney, 1996).

First, the replacement rate inadequacy reflects the risk that the retiree is unable to maintain the same standard of living after retiring as during the pre-retirement years. Consumption is smoothed by linking the pension to some measure of final earnings and the years of service. Occupational pensions of the 'defined benefit' form and pensions of civil servants belong to this type. In contrast, personal pensions of the 'defined contribution' form depend on the total contributions and investment earnings of the accumulation in the account of the employee.

Capital market uncertainty reflects the risk that the retirement income will be inadequate because of poor performance of the capital market. Inflation risk affects the purchasing power of retirement savings. Pay-as-you-go systems are insulated from these two previous sources of risk, since the pension benefits are related to the contributions of the wage earners. Wage income fluctuates less than rental incomes and wages are adjusted to inflation.

Finally, by the time the retirement age is reached, the individual risks that either the social insurance provisions in the pay-as-you-go system or the tax status of the pensions in the capital-reserve system have been changed.

In defining the rights of the retiree in an optimal pension plan, the reduction of economic insecurity in one direction will imply greater economic insecurity in another direction. The reason is that aggregate production varies from year to year so that the uncertainty on the production side must somehow be reflected on the consumption side. If none of the pension plans dominates the others, agents may participate in pension plans of different types and, in addition, accumulate private wealth for retirement. In particular, human capital and housing property are a hedge against inflation risk (Feldstein, 1983; Summers, 1983). The choice between the various pension instruments and private saving can be described using the theory of portfolio selection (Augier, Chaveau and Loupias, 1995). The retirement income in the capital-reserve system depends on the stochastic rate of return of investments in physical capital and the tax status of pension plans. For the retirement income in the pay-as-you-go system, the stochastic rate of return depends on the wage growth, on the population growth and on changing social security provisions. The choice of the mix depends on the expected return and the systematic risk of each alternative. A pension plan with a greater exposure to economic insecurity will compensate the participant with a larger rate of return.

5. Optimal Risk Sharing

The final appraisal of the efficiency of a mix of pension instruments should depend on its potential to eliminate idiosyncratic risks at the individual level (Borch, 1962; Fisher, 1983; Townsend, 1994). Optimal risk sharing is achieved when changing consumption levels of individuals living at the same time can be explained by changes in their aggregate endowment. Other peculiarities, in particular whether an individual is retired or not, should have no further explaining power. As a result, the individual consumption levels should move together with the aggregate endowment. Otherwise, a reallocation of endowments is welfare improving. Consider an individual or a small group of individuals with a high income when the income of others is low in a bad state and with a low income when the income of others is high in a good state. Then this group should give to the others in the bad state in return for a gift in the good state. When chosen appropriately, such a reallocation which gives to everybody an income which is lower in the bad state than in the good state is welfare improving for risk averse agents. Everybody's income as a donor exceeds his or her income as a beneficiary in the reallocation of the endowments. The marginal cost of giving is therefore less than the marginal gain of receiving.

From the perspective of optimal risk sharing, the income received by the old age pensioners and the income of the working population should move together. For this reason, Musgrave (1981) proposed a pension plan which determines old-age pensions as a fixed proportion of labour income per worker. Assume that workers transfer a fixed proportion of their income to old-age pensioners, that the ratio of old-age pensioners to workers is constant over time and that the share of labour income in total income is fixed. This definition of pension rights in a pay-as-you-go system is well suited to achieve optimal risk sharing when the growth rate of income is uncertain.

Note that in a capital-reserve system, capital market risk and inflation risk could be eliminated by the government issuing bonds with a risk-free real rate of return. But from the perspective of optimal risk sharing, insulating the retired population from economic insecurity by shifting aggregate risk completely to the working population is inappropriate. Instead, Merton (1983a) proposed the issuing of bonds with a rate of return linked to the growth rate of per capita consumption. If wages and consumption are perfectly correlated, the proposals of Musgrave and Merton are equivalent.

By the equality of the accumulated savings and the present value of future liabilities within each cohort at the time of retirement, the capital-reserve system excludes intergenerational transfers. In contrast, intergenerational transfers required by optimal risk sharing can take place in a pay-as-you-go system operating under a softer budget constraint. It is not guaranteed that the opportunities of a softer budget constraint will be used to improve intergenerational risk sharing. The government may yield to the demands of pressure groups which oppose the welfare improving adjustments. But the risk of government failure in the process of intergenerational risk sharing does not imply that the Pareto inefficient status quo without intergenerational transfers is the best choice.

The previous argument in favour of the pay-as-you-go system takes the tax status of pension plans as given. However, the tax status of pension plans has redistributive consequences. By choosing an appropriate tax status and by adjusting taxation to the state of the economy, a capital-reserve system may improve intergenerational risk sharing as well.

6. Limits to Insurance

Moral Hazard

The link between the benefits of the retiree and the contributions in the working period affects the willingness to contribute in a pension scheme. The high fertility rates in the informal pension schemes is an example. A mandatory pay-as-you-go system which offers a basic (flat rate) pension financed by a payroll tax implies a distortionary tax affecting the choice of the labour input. With distortionary taxes, the pay-as-you-go system and the capital-reserve system may no longer be equivalent (Breyer, 1989; Homberg, 1990; Breyer and Straub, 1993). This conclusion depends on the level of government debt in each of the systems and on the distortionary effects of taxes needed to service the debt. In addition, if one wants to guarantee a minimum income to the retired belonging to the lower income classes for redistributive purposes, then these transfer payments have to be financed by distortionary taxes. Finally, the rights of the pensioners can be defined proportionally to the contributions and to the years of service in the pay-as-you-go system as well as in the capital-reserve system.

Linking retirement income to the years of service raises problems in the case of early retirement. The optimal retirement date will vary both with the disutility of working and with the worker's productivity at an older age. Since the latter depends on a variety of random factors, from an insurance point of view it is desirable to adjust the retirement date accordingly without changing retirement income. But since the factors determining the retirement date cannot be measured in an objective way, early retirement demanded by the worker or induced by the employer will result in abuses. In the second best, the retirement income should therefore depend on the years of service (Diamond and Mirrlees, 1986).

Adverse Selection

Like any insurance contract, pension plans face the problem of adverse selection arising from the asymmetric information about the survival probability. Individuals who privately know that their survival probability is below average may prefer to save in assets instead of life insurance. For them, the rate of return on life insurance is lower since the terms of life insurance policies are based on the average survival probability of the particular group to which the insurance policy is sold. Since the individuals with a lower survival probability do not buy life insurance, the cost to the others increases. The unattractive annuity rates prevent the full development of a market for annuities. Adverse selection can be circumvented by compulsory schemes, in which good and bad risks are pooled (Eckstein, Eichenbaum and Peled, 1985). Employer pension plans and publicly organized pension plans are examples.

7. The Arguments for Publicly Organised Pension Plans

The arguments for state intervention in the provision of retirement income are income redistribution, market failures, paternalism and efficiency (Diamond, 1977). Pay-as-you-go systems, unlike capital-reserve systems, usually need the authority of a government. In comparing the relative performance of each system, the need for government intervention on the grounds of these arguments have already been dealt with. We add some comments.

In the absence of mandatory social insurance, the lower income classes may not have an incentive to save for retirement income. Welfare assistance cares for people without income. People with a low income during their working life have therefore little to lose when they do not save for retirement income. Unless they accept a dramatic cut in their consumption as workers, they will be unable to increase their retirement income by retirement savings above the lost welfare benefit. This free-rider problem is resolved by a mandatory scheme. A redistributive public pension plan will reduce the cost to the low incomes and their willingness to participate in the labour market.

In addition, people may be myopic and not save enough for retirement. Information on how much to save and where to invest the savings is costly to obtain. People may therefore accept the coercion of a mandated plan which provides the necessary discipline and offers a reasonable and trustworthy solution to an intricate problem. Adverse selection already requires pooling and does not leave much choice in tailoring a retirement policy to individual preferences. Many do not know or are unsure about their true preferences. The operating expenses of a public scheme are much lower than those of the life insurance industry with large selling costs. All these are additional arguments in favour of government intervention in the provision of retirement income.

8. The Demographic Problem

Demographic ageing threatens the financial viability of pay-as-you-go systems. The creation of social security schemes operating on a pay-as-you-go basis in most European countries after the Second World War forced young generations to make transfers to aged generations with the promise of being refunded when their own retirement would come. This operation was easy in an environment of demographic and economic growth. The transfer from the young to the aged population is painful in the current setting with demographic ageing (Marchand and Pestiau, 1991).

In order to bring the problem of demographic ageing in the right perspective, it is important to distinguish between the higher lifetime expectancy and the fall in fertility rates. Starting from the capital-reserve system, an increase in the survival probability after retirement requires higher contributions to provide adequate income after retirement for the same retirement age. The same carries over to the pay-as-you-go system. Without changing the contribution rate of the working generations, either the replacement rate must be reduced or the average retirement date has to be increased. The main causes of the falling activity rates of the aged are early retirement and the rise of unemployment among the aged. Changing early retirement incentives by penalising the retired who voluntarily quit the labour force or the firm which induces involuntary unemployment may be needed. But consumption smoothing and risk sharing requires adjustments in all the available instruments to achieve the equilibrium between contributions and liabilities in any pension system.

As explained above, a fall in population growth will increase the deficit of the pay-as-you-go system which adjusts its contribution and replacement rates to those of a capital-reserve system operating in the same environment. Without corrective measures, this will increase the public debt in the pay-as-you-go-system. The fall in the labour force is due to the declining birth rate which run at high levels from 1946 to the mid 1960s. The fertility rate fell partly because of an increased female participation in the labour force. Since demographic changes are gradual and to some extent predictable many years in advance, it possible to plan ahead by smoothing the contribution rates and by building up reserves in the pay-as-you-go system (Hagemann and Nicoletti, 1989; Marchand and Pestieau, 1991). Transfer payments between countries experiencing differently paced demographic shocks or early repayment of the public debt in countries with large public debt are examples. But note that such measures can be taken in combination with alternative measures affecting the activity rates of the aged and the young in the population and the migration rates. In addition, a fall in the labour force will lower the costs of education of children unless fewer children are provided with more human capital.

From the equality of the accumulated contributions and future liabilities of each retiring cohort, it is often claimed that a capital-reserve system offers better protection against demographic changes. But irrespective of the pension system, the dissaving of a large retiring generation exceeds the saving of the smaller succeeding generation. In the transition, the desired consumption claims may be satisfied only if the output is adjusted by changing the capital-labour ratio after an adjustment of the government debt. Otherwise, the income distribution problem between generations may cause inflation eroding the purchasing power of retirement income.

9. Concluding Remarks

The basic conflict between the working generations and the retired generations in the division of output cannot be resolved in an easy way. The mode of financing retirement income will affect the outcome of this basic conflict. But, in evaluating the relative merits of each system, compensating effects should be taken into account. As has been shown, two variants of providing retirement income may yield the same outcome or may yield allocations differing only in their second order effects. Any reform of an existing pension scheme should therefore be modest in the setting of its goals. It should not disappoint people by promises which it cannot deliver because of unforeseen compensating effects. As a consequence, any reform should be gradual as well. Although the outcome may not differ very much in the long run after agents have adjusted their behaviour, the outcome may imply dramatic changes for the generations living in the transition to the new equilibrium as they are unable to adjust their behaviour.

Capital-reserve systems are superior to pay-as-you-go systems in the definition of the future rights of the retired population. Although income security after retirement is desired by each individual, it is not optimal from the risk-sharing point of view to insulate one group of the population from the collective risks which have to be borne by the society as a whole and which have to be shared between generations. Pay-as-you-go systems are well suited to redistribute the burden of major shocks among the working generations and the retried generations. But reforms fixing the individual rights of the retired population conditional on the state of the economy and the record of individual contributions are desirable. Alternatively, adapting the tax status of funded pension plans to the state of the economy in a well-defined way could improve the risk-sharing properties of the capital-reserve system.

Bibliography on Pensions (6120)

Aaron, Henry J. (1966), 'The Social Insurance Paradox', **32** *Canadian Journal of Economics and Political Science*, 371-374.

Augier, L., Chaveau, T. and Loupias, C (1995), 'Epargne Privée et Retraite par Répartition dans un Modèle de Croissance Optimale, en Avenir Incertain et avec Générations d'Agents', **46** *Revue Economique*, 195-215.

Barr, N. (1992), 'Economic Theory and the Welfare State: a Survey and Interpretation', **30** *Journal of Economic Literature*, 675-740.

Barro, Robert J. (1974), 'Are Government Bonds Net Wealth?', **82** *Journal of Political Economy*, 1095-1117.

Bernheim, B. Douglas and Levin, Lawrence (1989), 'Social Security and Personal Saving: An Analysis of Expectations', **79** *American Economic Review. Papers and Proceedings*, 97-102.

Bewley, T (1981), *The Relation between Social Security, Saving and Investment in a Life-cycle Model*, North Western, Department of Economics, Discussion Paper, No. 492.

Bodie, Zvi (1990a), 'Pensions as Retirement Income Insurance', **28** *Journal of Economic Literature*, 28-49.

Bodie, Zvi (1990b), 'Inflation Insurance', **57** *Journal of Risk and Insurance*, 634-645.

Bodie, Zvi, Shoven, John B. and Wise, David A. (eds) (1987), *Issues in Pension Economics*, Chicago, University of Chicago Press, 376 p.

Borch, K. (1962), 'Equilibrium in a Reinsurance Market', **30** *Econometrica*, 424-444.

Breyer, Friedrich (1989), 'On the Intergenerational Pareto-efficiency of Pay-as-you-go Financed Pension Systems', **145** *Journal of Institutional and Theoretical Economics*, 643-658.

Breyer, F. and Straub, M. (1993), 'Welfare Effects of Unfunded Pension Systems when labor supply is endogenous', **50** *Journal of Public Economics*, 77-93.

Browning, Edgar K. (1973), 'Social Insurance and Intergenerational Transfers', **16** *Journal of Law and Economics*, 215-237.

Chapman, Bruce (1987), 'Pensions, Sex Discrimination, and the Value of Life after Death', **7** *International Review of Law and Economics*, 193-214.

Diamond, Peter A. (1965), 'National Debt in a Neoclassical Growth Model', **55** *American Economic Review*, 1126-1150.

Diamond, Peter A. (1977), 'A Framework for Social Security Analysis', **8** *Journal of Public Economics*, 275-298.

Diamond, Peter A. and Hausman, J.A. (1984), 'Individual Retirement and Savings Behavior', **23** *Journal of Public Economics*, 81-114.

Diamond, Peter A. and Mirrlees, J.A. (1978), 'A Model of Social Insurance with Variable Retirement', **10** *Journal of Public Economics*, 295-336.

Diamond, Peter A. and Mirrlees, J.A. (1985), 'Insurance Aspects of Pensions', in Wise, D.A. (ed.), *Pensions, Labor, and Individual Choice*, Chicago, IL, University of Chicago Press, 317-356.

Diamond, Peter A. and Mirrlees, J.A. (1986), 'Payroll-Tax Financed Social Insurance with Variable Retirement', **88** *Scandinavian Journal of Economics*, 25-50.

Diamond, Peter A., Helms, L.J. and Mirrlees, J.A. (1980), 'Optimal Taxation in a Stochastic Economy: a Cobb-Douglas Example', **14** *Journal of Public Economics*, 1-29.

Disney (1996), 'Pensions as Insurance', **21** *Geneva Papers on Risk and Insurance*, 258-270.

Dnes, Anthony W. (1981), 'Structural Change and British Employment Trends', **8(1)** *Journal of Industrial Affairs*, 40-48.

Eckstein, Z., Eichenbaum, M. and Peled, D. (1985a), 'Uncertain Lifetimes and the Welfare Enhancing Properties of Annuity Markets and Social Security'', **26** *Journal of Public Economics*, 303-326.

Eckstein, Z., Eichenbaum, M. and Peled, D. (1985b), 'The Distribution of Wealth and Welfare in the Presence of Incomplete Annuity Markets', **100** *Journal of Public Economics*, 789-806.

Fabel, Oliver (1994), *The Economics of Pensions and Variable Retirement Schemes*, New York, John Wiley and Sons, 221 p.

Feldstein, Martin S. (1974), 'Social Security, Induced Retirement, and Aggregate Capital Accumulation', **82** *Journal of Political Economy*, 905-926.

Feldstein, Martin S. (1976), 'Social Security and the Distribution of Wealth', **71** *Journal of the American Statistical Association*, 800-807.

Feldstein, Martin S. (1978), 'Do Private Pensions Increase National Savings', **10** *Journal of Public Economics*, 277-293.

Feldstein, Martin S. (1983), 'Social Security and Private Savings: Reply', **90** *Journal of Political Economy*, 630-642.

Fisher, S. (1983), 'Welfare Aspects of Government Issue of Indexed Bonds', in Dornbusch, R. and Simonson, M.H. (eds), *Inflation, Debt and Indexation*, Cambridge, MA, MIT Press.

Gordon, R.H. and Varian, H.R. (1988), 'Intergenerational Risk Sharing', **37** *Journal of Public Economics*, 185-202.

Green, Jerry R. (1988), 'Demographics, Market Failure, and Social Security', in Wachter, M.S. (ed.), *Social Security and Private Pensions*, Lexington, MA, Lexington Books, 3-16.

Gunderson, Morley and Pesando, James (1988), 'The Case for Allowing Mandatory Retirement', **14** *Canadian Public Policy*, 32-39.

Gustman, Alan L. and Steinmier, Thomas L. (1991), 'The Effects of Pensions and Retirement Policies on Retirement in Higher Education', **81** *American Economic Review. Papers and Proceedings*, 111-115.

Hagemann, R.P. and Nicoletti G. (1989), 'Aging Populations: Economic Effects and Implications for Public Finance', **12** *OECD Economic Studies*, 59-110.

Hansson, Ingemar and Stuart, Charles (1989), 'Social Security as Trade Among Living Generations', **79** *American Economic Review*, 1182-1195.

Homberg, S. (1990), 'The Efficiency of Unfunded Pension Schemes', **146** *Journal of Institutional and Theoretical Economics*, 640-647.

Honig, Marjorie and Reimers, Cordelia (1989), 'Is It Worth Eliminating the Retirement Test?', **79** *American Economic Review. Papers and Proceedings*, 103-107.

Huerta De Soto, Jesús (1989), 'Los Planes de Pensiones Privados y sus Fondos Financieros (Private Pensions and their Financial Funding)', in Martinez Lafuente, Antonio (ed.), *Estudios Sobre Planes y Fondos de Pensiones*, Ariel, Barcelona, 169-187.

Huerta De Soto, Jesús (1994a), *Planes de Pensiones Privados* (Private Pension Plans), Madrid, San Martín, 294 p.

Huerta De Soto, Jesús (1994b), 'The Crisis of Social Security: An Economic Analysis from the Austrian Perspective', **5** *Journal des Economistes et des Etudes Humaines*, 127-155.

Hurd, Michael D. (1990), 'Research on the Elderly: Economic Status, Retirement, and Consumption and Saving', **28** *Journal of Economic Literature*, 565-637.

Ippolito, Richard A. (1985), 'The Economic Function of Underfunded Pension Plans', **28** *Journal of Law and Economics*, 611-651.

Ippolito, Richard A. (1987), 'Pension Security: Has ERISA had any Effect?', **11(2)** *Regulation*, 15-22.

Ippolito, Richard A. (1988), 'A Study of the Regulatory Effect of the Employee Retirement Income Security Act', **31** *Journal of Law and Economics*, 85-125.

Ippolito, Richard A. (1989), *The Economics of Pension Insurance*, Homewood, Irwin for the University of Pennsylvania, Wharton School, Pension Research Council, 270 p.

Keating, Daniel (1991), 'Pension Insurance, Bankruptcy, and Moral Hazard', **67** *Wisconsin Law Review*, 65-108.

Krashinsky, Michael (1988), 'The Case for Eliminating Mandatory Retirement: Why Economics and Human Rights Need Not Conflict', **14** *Canadian Public Policy*, 40-51.

Marchand, M. and Pestieau P. (1991), 'Public Pensions: Choices for the Future', **35** *European Economic Review*, 441-453.

Merton, R.C. (1983a), 'On Consumption-indexed Public Pension Plans', in Bodie, Z. and Shoven, J.B. (eds), *Financial Aspects of the United States Pension System*, Chicago, IL, University of Chicago Press.

Merton, R.C. (1983b), 'On the Role of Social Security as a Means for Efficient Risk-sharing in an Economy where Human Capital is Not Tradeable', in Bodie, Z.

and Shoven, J.B. (eds), *Financial Aspects of the United States Pension System*, Chicago, IL, University of Chicago Press.

Modigliani, Franco and Brumberg (1954), 'Utility Analysis and the Consumption Function: An Interpretation of Cross-section Data', in Kurihana, K.K. (ed.), *Post-Keynesian Economics*, New Brunswick, NJ, Rutgers University Press.

Musgrave, Richard A. (1981), 'A Reappraisal of Social Security Financing', in Skidmore, F. (ed.), *Social Security Financing*, Cambridge, MA, MIT Press.

Myles, Gareth D. (1995), *Public Economics*, Cambridge, Cambridge University Press, 546 p.

Peters, W. (1988), 'A Pension Insurance Model in an Overlapping Generations Model', **144** *Journal of Institutional and Theoretical Economics*, 813-830.

Rea, Samuel A., Jr and James E. (1977), *Pesando, Public and Private Pensions In Canada: An Economic Analysis*, Toronto, University of Toronto Press.

Ricardo-Campbell, Rita and Lazear, Adward P. (eds) (1988), *Issues in Contemporary Retirement*, Stanford, Hoover Institute Press, Stanford University, 427 p.

Rothschild, Michael and Stiglitz, Joseph E. (1976), 'Equilibrium in Competitive Insurance Markets: An Essay on the Economics of Imperfect Information', **90** *Quarterly Journal of Economics*, 629-649.

Samuelson, Paul A. (1958), 'An Exact Consumption-Loan Model of Interest With or Without the Social Contrivance of Money', **66** *Journal of Political Economy*, 467-482.

Samuelson, Paul A. (1975), 'Optimum Social Security in a Life-cycle Growth Model', **16** *International Economic Review*, 531-538.

Schmahl, Winfried (ed.) (1989), *Redefining the Process of Retirement: An International Perspective*, London, Springer, 179 p.

Schulenburg, J. Matthias Graf Von Der (1990), 'Demographischer Wandel, intergenerationale Gerechtigkeit und Stabilität des Generationenvertrages (Demographic Change, Intergenerational Justice and Stability of the Contact Between Generations)', in Gahlen, B., Hesse, H. And Ramser, H.J. (eds), *Theorie und Politik der Sozialversicherung, Schriftenreihe des Wirtschaftswissenschaftlichen Seminars Ottobeuren Bd. 19*, Tübingen, Mohr/Siebeck, 269-300.

Schulenburg, J. Matthias Graf Von Der and Breyer, F. (1989), 'Umlagefinanzierte Rentenversicherung bei abnehmender Bevölkerung unter den Bedingungen eines demokratischen Wahlmechanismus (Pension Insurance Financed by Contributions in Times of Decreasing Population Under the Conditions of a Democratic Election Mechanism)', in Boettcher, Erik, Herder-Dorneich, Philipp and Schenk, Karl-Ernst (eds), *Jahrbuch für Neue Politische Ökonomie*, Tübingen, Mohr, 126-139.

Smith, Sharon P. (1991), 'Ending Mandatory Retirement in the Arts and Sciences', **81** *American Economic Review. Papers and Proceedings*, 106-110.

Solow, R.M. (1956), 'A Contribution to the Theory of Economic Growth', **70** *Quarterly Journal of Economics*, 65-94.

Strauss, Peter J., Wolf, Robert G. and Shilling, Dana (1990), *Aging and the Law*, Chicago, Commerce Clearing House, 892 p.

Summers, Lawrence H. (1983), 'Observations on the Indexation of Old-age Pensions', in Bodie, Z. and Shoven, J.B. (eds), *Financial Aspects of the United States Pension System*, Chicago, IL, University of Chicago Press.

Townley, P.G.C. (1981), 'Public Choice and the Social Insurance Paradox: A Note', **14** *Canadian Journal of Economics*, 712-717.

Townley, P.G.C. and Boadway, Robin W. (1988), 'Social Security and the Failure of Annuity Markets', **35** *Journal of Public Economics*, 75-96.

Townsend, Robert M. (1994), 'Risk and Insurance in Village India', **3** *Econometrica*, 539-591.

Verbon, Harrie A.A. (1985), 'On the Independence of Financing Methods and Redistributive Aspects of Public Pensions', **40** *Public Finance*, 280-289.

Verbon, Harrie A.A. (1987), 'On the Independence of Financing Methods and Redistributive Aspects of Public Pensions: Reply', **42** *Public Finance*, 454-456.

Verbon, Harrie A.A. (1988a), *The Evolution of Public Pension Scemes*, Berlin, Springer, 287 p.

Verbon, Harrie A.A. (1988b), 'Explaining Pay-as-you-go Financed Public Pensions', **28** *Economics Letters*, 181-187.

Verbon, Harrie A.A. and Van Winden, Frans A.A.M. (1986), 'Public Pensions and Political Decision Making', in Graf Von Der Schulenburg, J.-Matthias (ed.), *Essays in Social Security Economics*, Berlin, Springer, 32-53.

Verbon, Harrie A.A. (1989), 'Conversion Policies for Public Pension Plans in a small open Economy', in Gustafsson, B.A. and Klevmarken, N.A. (ed.), *The Political Economy of Social Security*, Amsterdam, North-Holland.

Viscusi, W. Kip (1979), *Welfare for the Elderly: An Economic Analysis and Policy Prescription*, New York, Wiley, 251 p.

Wachter, Susan M. (ed.) (1988), *Social Security and Private Pensions: Providing for Retirement in the Twenty-First Century*, Lexington, MA, Lexington Books, 232 p.

Wilson, C. (1977), 'A Model of Insurance Markets with Incomplete Information', **16** *Journal of Economic Theory*, 167-207.

Woodford, M. (1989), *Equilibrium Models of Endogenous Fluctuations: an Introduction*, University of Chicago Discussion Paper.

Yaari, M.E. (1964), 'On the Consumer's Lifetime Allocation Process', **5** *International Economic Review*, 304-317.

Yaari, M.E. (1965), 'Uncertain Lifetime, Life Insurance, and the Theory of the Consumer', **32** *Review of Economic Studies*, 137-150.

6200
TAKINGS

Thomas J. Miceli and Kathleen Segerson
Department of Economics
University of Connecticut

Abstract

This chapter provides an overview of the law and economics literature on government takings of private property under eminent domain. The first part of the chapter addresses questions pertaining to physical acquisitions of property, including the meaning of the public use and just compensation requirements, and the impact of takings for development decisions of landowners. The second part of the chapter turns to the question of whether or when a land use regulation ever becomes so burdensome to the landowner as to require compensation under the takings clause. Regulations that cross this threshold are referred to as regulatory takings. The chapter first discusses the economic justification for government (public) control of externalities, and then considers factors that affect the compensation question, including the intent of the regulation, the impact of the regulation on the landowner, incentives for efficient land use, fairness considerations, and whether capitalization nullifies the need for compensation.
JEL Classification: K11, K32, Q24
Keywords: Eminent Domain, Compensation, Regulatory Takings, Police Power, Land Use

1. Introduction

This chapter provides an overview of the law and economics literature on government 'takings' through acquisition or regulation of private property. Unlike private individuals who must bargain with owners when they wish to acquire property, the government can acquire private property for public use without the owner's consent provided that it pays just compensation. In the United States, this authority is granted by the 'takings clause' of the Fifth Amendment of the Constitution, which states: 'nor shall private property be taken for public use, without just compensation'. In addition, nearly all state constitutions contain takings clauses (Fischel, 1995b, p. 180). The law and economics literature has addressed a number of issues relating to the government's taking power, including the economic justification for the government's power of eminent domain, the meaning of the public use and 'just' compensation requirements, and the implications of eminent domain for the land development decisions of property owners. In the first part of this chapter, we provide an overview of these issues and the related literature.

In contrast to physical acquisitions or intrusions for which compensation is nearly always paid, government regulation of private property generally does not require compensation. Instead, it is viewed as a legitimate exercise of the government's police power. There is a long-standing question, however, about whether or when a regulation ever becomes so burdensome to a property owner as to require compensation under the takings clause. Regulations that cross this threshold are referred to as 'regulatory takings'. In the second part of this chapter, we review the law and economics literature on regulatory takings. We begin by discussing economic justifications for government regulation, and then turn to factors that affect the compensation question, including the nature of the government action and the impact of the regulation on landowners. We argue that various 'rules' for determining whether or not compensation should be paid, which appear at first to be different, are in fact consistent under certain conditions. We conclude by proposing compensation rules that balance the incentives of regulators against the incentives of landowners.

A. The Economics of Eminent Domain

The Fifth Amendment to the US Constitution guarantees, in part, that the government shall not take private property for public use without paying 'just compensation'. This seemingly straightforward protection of private property from arbitrary government seizure has generated a large literature attempting to interpret and justify its various components.

2. The Justification for Eminent Domain

Eminent domain gives the government the power to acquire property from private individuals through non-consensual transfers. Thus, a private individual's property is protected by a liability rule, rather than a property rule, *vis-à-vis* the government (Calabresi and Melamed, 1972). A common justification for this power is that it prevents individuals from refusing to sell their property to the government at a 'reasonable' price. This argument is faulty, however, because the subjective value an individual attaches to his or her property is worthy of protection in economic exchange - indeed, an important reason for protecting property by a property rule is to allow individuals to refuse transactions that do not make them better off (Posner, 1992, Ch. 3; Munch, 1976).

Since subjective value is important, and property rules protect subjective value, there must be another justification for eminent domain. The answer is that, when the government is assembling a large amount of land to build a public project like a highway, individual owners whose land is necessary for the project acquire monopoly power in their dealing with the government. That is, they can hold out for prices in excess of their true (subjective) valuation of the land given that it would be costly, once the project is begun, for the government to seek alternative locations (Cohen, 1991). Although the government theoretically could solve this problem by acquiring all the necessary land prior to construction, it would be difficult to conceal the project as the pattern of acquisitions was revealed. Moreover, because the project is publicly funded, it usually is public knowledge well in advance due to the need to appropriate funds. Private developers assembling a large number of properties clearly face the same problem. One argument for why they do not have eminent domain power is that it would be easier for them to acquire the property while disguising their ultimate intent, for example, through the use of 'dummy' buyers.

The real justification for eminent domain, then, is the need to prevent hold-outs, which is a form of transactions cost. This justification is therefore a special case of the argument that property rules are desirable when transactions costs are low and liability rules are desirable when transaction costs are high (Calabresi and Melamed, 1972; Krier and Schwab, 1995; Kaplow and Shavell, 1996).

3. The Public Use Requirement

The government's eminent domain power is restricted by the public use requirement included in the Fifth Amendment (Merrill, 1986a; Paul 1987b; Rubenfeld, 1993; LaCroix and Rose, 1995). One interpretation of this requirement is that the government can only use its taking power to acquire property for the provision of public goods (Ulen, 1992). While this seems to be a natural interpretation of 'public use', the economic theory of public goods does not imply that acquiring the inputs for public goods creates a hold-out problem (Cornes and Sandler, 1986, Ch. 5; Cohen, 1991). While coerced contributions to the *funding* of public goods is necessitated by the free-rider problem, coerced *acquisition* of the resources used to produce them is not.

Another interpretation of the public use requirement is that it is synonymous with the hold-out problem. This view, however, implies that private individuals faced with the hold-out problem also ought to have eminent domain power. Fischel (1995b, pp. 71-73) in fact suggests that private interests (for example, railroads) have often been granted the taking power by legislatures, and courts have been deferential (though not universally so) to this practice. Bouckaert and

De Geest (1995) provide a transactions cost justification for private takings.

Epstein (1985, Ch. 12) argues that the presence of a hold-out problem should be a necessary, but not sufficient condition for the public use limitation to be satisfied. In addition, some provision should be made to prevent private interests from acquiring all of the surplus from a forced sale. The basis for this additional requirement is that forced acquisitions with compensation set at market value prevent the owner of the acquired property from realizing both his subjective value, and a share of the gains from the sale (the value of the property in its proposed use minus the owner's subjective value). To prevent this, Epstein proposes as the second prong of a two-pronged public use test something like the above public goods requirement in order to ensure that the gains from a forced sale accrue widely to the public rather than to a private interest endowed with taking power.

Epstein does not, however, use this second prong to argue that private interests should never have taking power. Private interests can legitimately have taking power under Epstein's public use test if, in addition to facing the hold-out problem, they make some effort to pay a share of the surplus from the taking to the victim of the taking. An example is the Mill Acts, which granted private individuals the right to erect dams for purposes of operating mills provided that they paid flooded upstream owners compensation equal to 150 percent of their market value. Note that this sharing of the surplus, while serving the interest of fairness, also helps to counteract the tendency to overtake under market value compensation (see the next section).

4. Just Compensation

The Fifth Amendment allows the government to take private property for public use if it pays just compensation. Courts generally define just compensation to be 'fair market value'. However, this amount almost certainly undercompensates landowners, possibly by a large amount, since owners do not generally view land and wealth as perfect substitutes, whereas market value compensates them as if they did. Fair market value is not only unfair to landowners, it also potentially leads to an excessive transfer of private property to public use because the government does not have to pay the true opportunity cost of the resources it acquires. (We pursue this point in more detail in the discussion of fiscal illusion below.) Thus, while the hold-out problem precludes the efficient assembly of property through market exchange, eminent domain with market value compensation potentially leads to too much assembly (Munch, 1976; Fischel, 1995a).

Of course, the takings clause does not *define* just compensation to be fair market value, so it is not a necessary feature of eminent domain that it result in undercompensation. However, the problem with setting compensation equal to the owner's true valuation is that this amount is unobservable, and owners would clearly have an incentive to overstate it (Knetsch and Borcherding, 1979). Thus, taking measurement costs into account, fair market value may be the best proxy for just compensation.

A related issue, suggested by Epstein (1985, Ch. 18), is that money raised to finance compensation is a 'taking' from taxpayers for which they receive 'in-kind' compensation in the form of benefits from the public project. Based on this insight, Fischel (1995b, p. 211) suggested that market value compensation may be the best way to balance 'the undercompensation of the market-based rule against the greater loss incurred by higher taxes and [foregone] public works that full, consensual compensation would require'.

5. Eminent Domain and Land Use Incentives

The feature of eminent domain that has drawn the most attention from economists, especially recently, is its impact on land use incentives. In particular, how does the possible threat of condemnation affect a landowner's incentive to invest in developing his land? The first formal analysis of this question was by Blume, Rubinfeld and Shapiro (1984). The principal result that they derived (or at least the one that has received the most attention) was that full compensation for takings results in inefficient investment decisions by landowners while no compensation results in efficient incentives. Intuitively, compensation that is positively related to the value of the property, and hence the level of investment in that property, creates a moral hazard problem by providing the landowner insurance against the possibility of a taking. When a taking occurs, a social cost is incurred because an irreversible investment is lost. An efficient investment decision must therefore reflect the likelihood that this cost will be incurred (that is, the probability that a taking will occur). However, as is true of unlimited expectation damages for promisees in contract cases (Cooter, 1985), if the landowner is guaranteed full compensation, he will not incur any private loss if a taking occurs. Hence, he will ignore the possibility of a taking when making his investment decision and overinvest.

Blume, Rubinfeld and Shapiro (1984) show that this overinvestment incentive can be eliminated by making the compensation lump-sum, that is, independent of the amount of investment in the property. Since lump-sum compensation is the same regardless of how much the landowner invests, increases in the level of investment lead to increased losses if a taking occurs. Thus, under lump-sum compensation the landowner is not fully insured and hence considers the possibility of a taking when making his investment decision. He thus chooses an efficient level of investment. Note that a special case of lump sum compensation is no compensation. Thus, Blume, Rubinfeld and Shapiro (1984) conclude that a rule of never paying compensation will lead to efficient landowner investment decisions. Kaplow (1986, 1992) has also endorsed the no compensation result for government takings, and more broadly for many forms of legal change that have distributional and allocative implications.

Although no compensation is consistent with efficient land use incentives, several arguments have been made against it. The first and most common objection is that a rule of no compensation allows the government to acquire resources at no cost. This is not a problem if the government is unswervingly devoted to acquiring resources only when it is efficient to do so. Fischel and Shapiro (1988, 1989) refer to such a government as 'Pigouvian'. However, modern public choice theory suggests that this is unlikely to be the case (Mueller, 1989). A more realistic view treats the government like any other economic agent who responds to economic incentives. If compensation is zero in this case,

> The resources under the control of the central authority will be perceived to be costless. The opportunity costs will be ignored, and land use regulation without compensation will lead to overproduction of environmental amenities .... (Johnson, 1977, p. 65)

Such a government is said to have 'fiscal illusion' (Blume, Rubinfeld and Shapiro (1984). In the current setting, this implies that the government will make its taking decision by comparing the benefit of the public good to the amount of compensation it must pay to the owners of the land that it takes. If it is not required to pay any compensation, it will tend to take property too often since it will view the taking as having positive benefits but no costs. Thus, a rule of zero compensation creates a moral hazard problem for the government. Full compensation can solve this problem and at the same time protect the rights of politically under-represented groups (Paul, 1987a; Epstein, 1985, 1995, Ch. 7; Burrows, 1991; Farber, 1992; Fischel, 1995b; and Yandle, 1995).

As noted above, full compensation for takings results in inefficient investment because it allows landowners to ignore the social costs that result if a taking occurs. At the same time, full compensation is necessary to prevent overregulation by the government. In the presence of this trade-off, Fischel and Shapiro (1989) examined a compensation rule under which the level of compensation would be proportional to the value of the property, and they showed that the optimal (second-best) solution requires partial compensation. In contrast, Hermalin (1995) showed that the first-best outcome is attainable under a pair of compensation rules. Under the first, the government pays the landowner compensation equal to the social value of the taking. Note that this rule has the same effect as a property rule in that the owner receives compensation in excess of his value of the land (assuming that the taking is efficient), implying that the transfer is essentially consensual. The efficiency of this rule is thus consistent with the efficiency of property rules as discussed by Fischel and Shapiro (1988, p. 275).

Under Hermalin's second rule, the landowner has the option to buy back the land for a price equal to its social value. As noted above, actual compensation rules tie payment to the fair market value of the land to the owner rather than its value in public use, and owner's do not ordinarily have a buy-back option. Thus both of Hermalin's are purely normative in that they do not explain the actual practice of courts.

Breach of contract remedies suggest yet another solution to the trade-off between moral hazard and fiscal illusion, namely, limit compensation to the full value of the land to the owner, evaluated not at the actual level of investment but rather at the efficient level of investment (Cooter, 1985; Rose-Ackerman, 1992). Note first that this rule will induce efficient behavior by the government because it requires full compensation. In addition, in equilibrium it will induce all landowners to choose an efficient level of investment because compensation is still lump-sum.

Even when the government does not have fiscal illusion, there is an argument for paying compensation for takings if the likelihood of a taking depends on the value of the property (Miceli, 1991; Trefzger and Colwell, 1996). The model in Blume, Rubinfeld and Shapiro (1984) assumed that landowners view the probability of a taking as independent of their investment decision. However, in reality, the government may be less likely to take land that is more valuable in private use. For example, by taking undeveloped rather than developed land, it can reduce the social cost of the taking. If landowners anticipate that by increasing their investment in land they can reduce the chance that their land will be taken, they will adjust their investment decisions accordingly. To avoid this problem, Miceli (1991) shows that, even in the absence of fiscal illusion, compensation must be equal to the full value of the land at the optimal level of investment, net of any compensation tax. The intuition for this result is as follows. When the landowner expects zero compensation (or, generally, undercompensation), he will *overinvest* in order to reduce the probability of a taking. On the other hand, if he expects overcompensation he will *underinvest* in order to increase the probability of a taking. Only full compensation at the efficient level of investment eliminates these incentives to over- or underinvest.

The question is whether landowners in fact view the probability of a taking as being a function of their level of investment. This is unlikely in the context of physical acquisitions of land, which rarely occur. Indeed, the probability of a physical taking is probably near zero for most landowners. However, government regulations preventing certain land uses such as zoning and environmental restrictions are widespread and generally apply to all plots in a given area. In that case, the probability of a land use restriction that reduces their property values is not necessarily small, and it may be possible for landowners to affect its magnitude by their land use decisions (Miceli and Segerson, 1996, Chs 7 and 8). Thus, this issue is likely to arise in the context of regulatory takings discussed below.

The preceding discussion has shown that a compensation rule that pays landowners the full value of their land at the efficient level of investment results in both efficient investment in land and efficient takings decisions when the government has fiscal illusion. One problem with this rule is that it requires courts to be able to calculate the efficient level of investment, a task that may prove difficult in practice. However, this problem has not prevented courts from adopting rules in other areas of the law that require similar calculations. For example, negligence rules require calculation of due standards of care in accident settings (Landes and Posner, 1987, Ch. 4; Cooter and Ulen, 1988, Ch. 8; *U.S. v. Carroll Towing*, 159 F.2d 169 (1947)). Moreover, existing community standards for 'normal' land use can often provide a good proxy for efficient development levels (Fischel, 1985, Ch. 8).

Two additional arguments against the no compensation result have been made in the literature. The first was by Michelman (1967) in perhaps the most influential article on takings to date. Michelman used a utilitarian standard for deciding, first, when a government should enact a taking, and second, when it should pay compensation. The standard is based on three factors: efficiency gains, demoralization costs, and settlement costs. Efficiency gains simply represent the social benefits minus the costs of a public project. A *necessary* condition for enactment of the project under Michelman's standard is that the project generates efficiency gains.

In addition to efficiency gains, Michelman introduced two types of costs. The first is the demoralization costs associated with non-payment of compensation. Demoralization costs represent the total of (1) the dollar value necessary to offset disutilities which accrue to losers and their sympathizers specifically from the realization that no compensation is offered, and (2) the present capitalized dollar value of lost future production (reflecting either impaired incentives or social unrest) caused by demoralization of uncompensated losers, their sympathizers, and other observers disturbed by the thought that they themselves may be subjected to similar treatment on some other occasion (Michelman, 1967, p. 1214).

The second type of cost is the settlement (or transaction) costs associated with payment of compensation. Settlement costs represent 'the dollar value of time, effort, and resources which would be required to reach compensation settlements adequate to avoid demoralization costs' (Michelman, 1967, p. 1214). Michelman's standard for compensation is that it should be paid if settlement costs are less than demoralization costs, and not paid if the reverse is true. Further, the public project should be enacted if and only if the efficiency gain exceeds the lower of the settlement and demoralization costs. Note that this standard is intermediate between the Pareto and Kaldor-Hicks criteria for efficiency. It is more permissive than Pareto since a project should be enacted without compensation if the efficiency gains exceed the demoralization costs and the demoralization costs are less than the settlement costs. However, it is less permissive than Kaldor-Hicks since even if there are efficiency gains, the project should not be enacted if those gains are less than the lower of the settlement and demoralization costs (Fischel and Shapiro, 1988, p. 280).

The final argument against the no compensation result is based on the idea that compensation acts as a form of public insurance for risk-averse landowners against the possibility of government expropriation of their property (Blume and Rubinfeld, 1984, 1987; Rose-Ackerman, 1992). The need for public rather than private insurance is that moral hazard and adverse selection problems, and the infrequency of takings, prevent formation of a private insurance market for takings risk. Because of the administrative costs and incentive effects of compensation, however, it should only be paid when landowners are very risk-averse and losses are large.

B. Regulation and Takings

Thus far we have focused on physical acquisitions of private property, which have been universally accepted by courts as compensable government takings. There has been much more controversy, however, both in the courts and in the academic literature, over government regulations that reduce private property values and the extent to which these should be compensable (Knetsch, 1983; Epstein, 1985; Paul, 1987a; Fischel, 1995b; and Yandle, 1995). Courts have generally granted the government broad powers to regulate private property in the interest of protecting public welfare. However, some government regulations can become so restrictive as to cause a substantial reduction in the value of private property. When this happens, courts have occasionally found the regulation to be a taking and ordered payment of compensation. The problem is to determine where to set the threshold that separates non-compensable regulations (police power actions) from compensable ones (regulatory takings). We begin our discussion of this question by considering the rationale for the existence of the government's regulatory power. We then provide an overview of the issues that have arisen in trying to define a threshold for compensable regulatory actions.

6. Justifications for Government Regulation

One of the principal uses of the government's regulatory power is in the context of externalities, or incompatible uses of property (Cornes and Sandler, 1986, Chs 3 and 4). There are, however, private (common law) remedies available for dealing with such incompatibilities. Thus, prior to addressing the question of whether the government should pay compensation for a regulation, we first need to answer the question of why government (public) intervention is economically justified at all.

Trespass and nuisance are the principal common law remedies available to property owners faced with violations of their property rights. Trespass ordinarily allows owners to exclude, or enjoin, future intrusions regardless of the benefits to the intruder, whereas under nuisance law the court generally enjoins the intrusion or awards damages only after determining that the victim's harm is substantial and the nuisance-creating activity is unreasonable (Keeton, et al., 1984, pp. 622-623). According to Merrill (1985), this distinction can be explained in terms of transactions costs. Specifically, when transactions costs between the intruder and the victim are low, trespass is the efficient remedy because it forces the parties to resolve the incompatibility through a voluntary transaction - a solution that guarantees a mutually beneficial outcome. When transactions costs are high, however, nuisance law is the appropriate remedy because the parties may be unable to resolve the dispute through bargaining. In that case, the court conducts a sort of cost-benefit analysis before determining if the victim is entitled to relief. In a sense, the court coerces an efficient exchange (a 'private taking') or prohibits an inefficient one when bargaining is expected to fail. The case of *Boomer v. Atlantic Cement* (309 N.Y.S.2d 312 (1970)) illustrates this common law (private) approach to externalities.

The preceding theory implies that private remedies initiated by the victim of an externality are available for both low and high transaction costs cases. The question then is where direct government regulation of externalities fits into this scheme. One answer is that if the external cost is dispersed across a large number of victims, then no one victim may have an incentive to seek a private remedy, even when the aggregate cost outweighs the benefit of the injurer's activity. In that case, the government acts as an 'agent' of the victims by regulating the injurer's activity directly. The government thereby overcomes a collective action problem among victims (Landes and Posner, 1987, Ch. 2).

While many regulations are designed to address externality problems, government intervention can be justified on other grounds as well, such as protection of individual rights. For example, laws designed to protect the rights of disabled people, to guarantee free speech, or to ensure equal access or opportunity, can result in requirements that impose costs on property owners and reduce the value of private property. Alternatively, government regulation (such as public utility regulation) can arise in response to other market failures, including imperfect competition and imperfect information. Regulatory takings issues have arisen in these contexts as well.

The preceding discussion identifies situations in which government regulation of private property may be justified, but it does not address the question of whether the landowner should be compensated for the resulting private loss. Although from an economic perspective the distinction between physical invasions and value-reducing regulations is not a meaningful one (Rose-Ackerman, 1992, p. 29), courts have routinely denied compensation for the latter (with some notable exceptions). In the following sections, we review the key issues relating to the question of when compensation should be paid for regulations that reduce the value of private property without physically acquiring it.

7. The Nature of the Government Action

As noted, courts have historically granted governments wide powers to regulate without paying compensation, provided that the regulation somehow protects the public interest. This justification for non-payment of compensation thus focuses on the nature of the government action.

7.1 Regulation of 'Harmful' or 'Noxious' Uses

An early case that established the nature of the government action as relevant for the compensation question is *Mugler v. Kansas* (123 U.S. 623 (1887)). The case concerned a law passed by the State of Kansas prohibiting the operation of breweries because they were public nuisances. The plaintiff argued that operation of his brewery predated the law, and further, that it did not constitute a nuisance. The Court nevertheless upheld the law based on the state's right to regulate, without compensation, land uses that are injurious to public welfare. Specifically, the Court held that there is no taking if a regulation is aimed at preventing uses that are 'injurious to the health, morals, or safety of the community' (*Mugler v. Kansas*, 1887, 668-669). This argument has become known as the 'noxious use' doctrine and remains an important basis for government regulations under the police power.

Concern with the nature of the government's action was re-affirmed in *Penn Central Transportation Co. v. City of New York* (438 U.S. 104 (1978)). Echoing the noxious use doctrine from *Mugler*, the court noted that 'in instances in which a state tribunal reasonably concluded that "the health, safety, morals, or general welfare" would be promoted by prohibiting particular contemplated uses of land, this court has upheld land-use regulations that destroyed or adversely affected recognized real property interests' (*Penn Central v. City of New York*, 1978, p. 125). Thus, according to the Court, if the public benefit of the regulation is sufficiently large, it may not constitute a taking even when the landowner suffers a significant loss.

Finally, in *Lucas v. South Carolina Coastal Council* (112 S. Ct. 2886 (1992)), the Court introduced a provision that would allow the government to avoid paying compensation if it could show that the activity a landowner planned to pursue would be prohibited under the state's common law of nuisance. Thus, the Court recognized that government actions consistent with nuisance law are non-compensable. This provision of the *Lucas* decision is known as the 'nuisance exception'.

The academic literature has also looked to the nature of the government action to determine if a regulation should be compensable. Much of the literature is based on property rights principles. Property rights approaches to the takings question typically begin by implicitly defining a distribution of property rights that the law protects. If a government action deprives a property owner of a right protected by this distribution, compensation is due, whereas if it deprives him of an unprotected right, no compensation is due.

The 'harm-benefit' rule exemplifies this approach (Fischel, 1985, pp. 154-155). According to this rule, compensation is not due for regulations that prevent a landowner from imposing an external cost on society (for example, pollution), but compensation is due for regulations that compel the landowner to provide an external benefit (for example, open space). The underlying basis for this distinction is that landowners do not have the right to impose costs, but they do have the right to withhold conferral of benefits.

Joseph Sax has offered two theories of takings that fall within this property rights approach. His first theory (Sax, 1964) argues that the government owes compensation when it acquires property rights for use as an enterprise - for example, when it provides a public good; but it does not owe compensation when it merely arbitrates private disputes - for example, when it regulates an externality. (Rose, 1983, advances a similar argument.) According to this view, regulatory takings for the most part fall within the category of non-compensable actions since, as noted above, they generally are aimed at preventing an external cost or correcting a market failure or inequity.

Sax's second theory (Sax, 1971) suggests that the government does not owe compensation for any action that involves the internalization of spillover effects (negative externalities). Bromley adopts a similar view, arguing that compensation for regulations that prevent externalities would represent 'indemnification for an inability to continue to impose unwanted costs on others' (Bromley, 1993, p. 677). Like the harm-benefit rule, this view is based on the idea that the law does not protect an individual's property right when that right infringes on other individuals' rights. Note that a similar delineation of property rights underlies the noxious use doctrine (Mercuro, 1992a, p. 3) and the *Lucas* nuisance exception. The nuisance exception is also a fundamental feature of Richard Epstein's view of takings law (Epstein, 1985, Ch. 9, 1992; Epstein, et. al., 1992), which holds that landowners should generally receive compensation for regulations except when the offending land use would have been prohibited by the state's common law of nuisance.

Property rights approaches to the compensation question are not necessarily consistent with economic theory, especially those based on the harm-benefit approach. For example, it is well known that there does not exist a meaningful economic distinction between a harm imposed and a benefit conferred, given that a harm is equivalent to a foregone benefit, and a benefit is equivalent to an avoided harm (Coase, 1960; Fischel, 1985, p. 158). What is lacking is a 'benchmark of neutral conduct' for defining the threshold between harms and benefits (Michelman, 1967, p. 1197). The basis for harm-benefit rules can be made consistent with economic logic, however, by appealing to administrative, or transaction, costs as a way of identifying such a neutral point.

7.2 Standards of 'Normal' Behavior

Fischel employs a transaction costs approach in proposing a rule based on a 'normal behavior' (Fischel, 1985, Ch. 8, 1995b; Ellickson, 1973, 1977). This rule resembles the harm-benefit rule in that it says that no compensation is due for regulations that prevent 'subnormal' land uses, but compensation is due for regulations that compel 'super-normal' land uses. The rule differs from the harm-benefit rule in that 'normal' behavior is defined according to local community standards based on what a landowner could reasonably expect to do with his land without government restriction. A reasonableness standard for land use thus replaces the arbitrary distinction between a harm and a benefit.

The importance of transactions costs to this rule is that, by using normal behavior as the 'zero compensation' point, the transactions costs of compelling normal behavior are minimized. In particular, since most people will engage in normal behavior without state intervention, only a few transactions will be needed to fine those who engage in subnormal behavior and to compensate those who undertake supernormal behavior. Wittman (1984) uses a similar transactions cost approach to distinguish compensable from non-compensable regulations. He argues that administrative costs are minimized if compensation is paid only when the government acts inefficiently since 'we would expect the government to act efficiently more often than not' (Wittman, 1984, p. 74).

In addition to minimizing transaction costs associated with paying compensation, Fischel's normal behavior standard avoids what he views as a major problem with a rule that conditions compensation solely on the loss in value to the owner (the diminution of value rule) - namely, the possibility of paying compensation for regulations that restrict truly inappropriate land uses while imposing substantial losses on the landowner, for example, prohibiting pulp mills in residential neighborhoods. Fischel recognizes, however, the need to balance the costs of regulations against their benefits. He therefore argues that forcing 'super-normal' behavior on landowners need not require compensation if the benefits of the regulation exceed the cost to the private landowner and the transaction costs are excessive (Fischel, 1985, p. 165). Since the presumption is that requiring landowners to conform with social norms would generate benefits in excess of its costs, Fischel's rule is essentially one of paying compensation for inefficient regulations and not paying compensation for efficient ones.

To the extent that noxious uses and nuisances represent subnormal (inefficient) uses, non-compensation for regulation of these types of activities is consistent with Fischel's and Wittman's rules for minimizing transactions costs. Moreover, all of these rules are essentially versions of the harm-benefit approach to defining compensable regulations in that they rely on a distinction between 'good' and 'bad' behavior by the landowner, which in turn defines a threshold for determining compensation. Thus, while these various theories appear at first to be quite different, they are in fact consistent with each other when the thresholds are defined on the basis of economic principles. In addition, they are consistent with the threshold-based rules proposed by Miceli and Segerson (1994, 1996) (see Section 9 below).

7.3 The 'Essential Nexus' Requirement

While the foregoing suggests that the nature of the government action can justify uncompensated regulations, courts have required that those actions must bear at least some relationship to the regulated land use. In particular, the doctrine of 'unconstitutional conditions' holds that 'the government may not require a person to give up a constitutional right ... in exchange for a discretionary benefit conferred by the government where the property right sought has little or no reasonable relationship to the benefit' (*Dolan v. City of Tigard*, 114 S.Ct. 2309, 2317 (1994)). This condition arises in takings cases when the government requires a landowner to dedicate some property to public use without just compensation in exchange for a permit to develop.

In *Nollan v. California Coastal Comm'n* (438 U.S. 825 (1987)), the Court held that in order for a permit condition to be valid, there must exist an 'essential nexus' between the condition (that is, the required dedication of property) and the proposed development for which the permit is sought. The case concerned a state requirement that the Nollans allow public access to their beach in return for a permit to replace an existing beachfront bungalow with a three bedroom house. The State's interest in imposing the condition of beach access was purportedly to counteract the fact that the larger house proposed by the Nollans would diminish the view of the ocean from the roadway. However, the

Court held that the essential nexus requirement was *not* met in this case because access to the beach did not serve to enhance the view of the ocean from the road; that is, it did not counteract the impact of the proposed development.

The Court re-examined this issue in *Dolan v. City of Tigard* (1994). While the Court reaffirmed the essential nexus requirement, it also found that mere *existence* of a nexus was not enough to validate the permit condition. In addition, 'the degree of the exactions demanded [must] bear the required relationship to the impact of the petitioner's proposed development' (*Dolan v. City of Tigard*, 1994, p. 2318). The Court adopted a 'rough proportionality' test to assess this relationship. When the court applied this test to the facts of *Dolan*, it concluded that the government's conditions did not bear the required 'reasonable relationship' to the impact of the proposed development.

Miceli and Segerson (1996, Chapter 4) argue that the essential nexus requirement represents a generalized condition for determining whether or not a government regulation is efficient in cases where landowners have the ability to mitigate the external costs of their proposed development. The regulatory decision is assumed to have two separate components: first, the government decides whether or not to attach conditions to the permit if it is granted, and second, it decides whether or not to grant the permit given those conditions. In this context, the efficiency of the regulatory decision includes efficiency of both the decision of whether or not to grant the permit, and the efficiency of any conditions attached to the permit. The essential nexus and rough proportionality tests in combination can be viewed as an attempt to ensure the efficiency of the permit conditions.

In contrast to Miceli and Segerson (1996), Innes (1995, 1997) argues that the essential nexus and proportionality requirements should not be applied in takings cases. He argues instead that the focus should be on providing equal protection to owners of similarly situated land (the equal protection requirement). This argument, however, is based on consideration of the incentives of landowners rather than the efficiency of the regulatory decision (see Section 8.3 below).

8. The Impact of the Regulation on the Landowner

In addition to the nature of the government action, the other major factor used to evaluate regulatory takings cases is the impact of the regulation on the landowner. This criterion is best exemplified by Holmes's diminution of value test.

8.1 The Diminution of Value Test

The impact of the regulation on the landowner was first advanced as a test for compensation in *Pennsylvania Coal Co. v. Mahon* (260 U.S. 393 (1922)), which is one of the most influential takings cases in US history. This case challenged a Pennsylvania statute, the Kohler Act, which prohibited coal companies from any mining that threatened the safety of surface owners due to cave-ins. The majority opinion, written by Justice Oliver Wendell Holmes, found the regulation to be a taking requiring compensation because it went 'too far' in reducing the landowner's rights. Specifically, Holmes's ruling provided that the government can regulate private property without compensation unless the regulation goes too far in diminishing the value of the property to the owner. This rule is thus referred to as the 'diminution of value' test. Holmes did not articulate a general test for establishing when a regulation had gone too far, however, leaving it instead to be determined on a case by case basis.

Holmes's ruling in *Pennsylvania Coal* marked a watershed in takings law because, prior to this case, takings were usually limited to physical acquisitions of property by the government; most efforts to obtain compensation for 'mere regulations' failed, due in large part to the noxious use doctrine (Friedman, 1986). The diminution of value test broke with this tradition by introducing the loss in value to the owner into the equation. It thus 'put the police power on a continuum with the power of eminent domain' (Mercuro, 1992a, p. 4).

Holmes did not argue for a general rule of compensation because he recognized that the government 'could hardly go on if to some extent values incident to property could not be diminished without paying for every such change in the law' (*Pennsylvania Coal v. Mahon*, 1922, p. 413). At the same time, however, he acknowledged that a rule of no compensation for regulations would, given 'the natural tendency of human nature', result in overregulation until 'at last private property disappear[ed]'. Thus, Holmes recognized the fundamental trade-off between the costs of compensation (a stifled government) and the benefits of compensation (protection of private property and a limitation of government excess): 'The general rule at least is that while property may be regulated to a certain extent, if regulation goes too far it will be recognized as a taking' (*Pennsylvania Coal v. Mahon*, 1922, p. 415).

Most takings cases since *Pennsylvania Coal* have generally applied some form of Holmes's diminution of value test. An example is the previously cited case of *Lucas v. South Carolina Coastal Council* (1992), which concerned a developer (Lucas) who had purchased two beachfront lots in South Carolina with the intent of developing them for residential use. Although development was permitted at the time Lucas purchased the lots, the State subsequently passed a law, the Beachfront Management Act, that prohibited development. Lucas acknowledged the state's right to impose such a law, but he argued that it reduced the value of his property so much that it constituted a taking for which compensation was due. The South Carolina Supreme Court ruled in favor of the State, based on the broad regulatory powers that have been granted to state and local governments. However, the US Supreme Court reversed the decision and found that compensation was due.

Environmental groups had feared such a decision in the belief that the need to pay compensation would greatly reduce the ability of governments to protect the environment against the unrestrained actions of private property owners. However, the decision in *Lucas* awarded compensation on narrow grounds. In particular, the Court found that compensation was due because 'when the owner of real property has been called upon to sacrifice *all* economically beneficial uses in the name of the common good, that is to leave his property economically idle, he has suffered a taking' (*Lucas v. S. Carolina Coastal Council*, 1992, p. 2895).

Thus, the Court found that the regulation had clearly crossed the threshold set by the diminution of value test and that a taking had therefore occurred. However, the opinion offered no guidance as to the exact location of the threshold.

While the diminution of value test has been widely applied, it has been criticized on efficiency grounds. As noted above, for example, if only the loss in property value is considered when deciding whether to compensate, then the resulting outcome may be inefficient since the benefit of the regulation will not be balanced against the cost (the loss in private property value) (Fischel, 1985, pp. 156-157). Similarly, if compensation is not required when the reduction in property value is small, then a government that considers only actual cost outlays rather than social costs, that is, a government with fiscal illusion, will view such regulations as costless and thus overregulate. If some balancing between these two effects is to take place, as proposed in the original Holmes ruling, then a standard for deciding when a regulation has gone 'too far' must be available. We will propose such a standard below.

8.2 Investment-Backed Expectations

In *Penn Central Transportation Co. v. City of New York* (1978), the US Supreme Court faced the question of whether the City of New York could prevent the owners of Grand Central Terminal from erecting an office tower over the terminal by declaring it an historical landmark. The Court held that it could without being obliged to pay compensation. In reaching its decision, the Court identified several factors to be weighed in determining whether a regulation constitutes a taking, including the nature of the government action and the economic impact of the regulation on the claimant. The former reflects the noxious use doctrine from *Mugler* and the latter the diminution of value rule from *Pennsylvania Coal*. While Holmes did not offer any criterion for determining when a regulation goes too far under the diminution of value rule, the *Penn Central* court did. Specifically, the Court said that a regulation 'may so frustrate distinct investment-backed expectations as to amount to a taking' (*Penn Central v. City of New York*, 1978, p. 127), whereas it is not a taking if it does 'not interfere with interests that [are] sufficiently bound up with reasonable expectations of the claimant to constitute "property" for 5th amendment purposes' (*Penn Central v. City of New York*, 1978, pp. 124-125). Thus, a relevant factor for determining whether a regulation requires compensation is whether the regulation interferes with distinct investment-backed expectations by the claimant.

Justice Brennan's majority opinion in the *Penn Central* case relied heavily on Michelman's (1967) view that, in order for a landowner to put his land to productive use, he must have a reasonable expectation of being allowed to retain the fruits of his investment (Mandelker, 1987, pp. 10-13). Nevertheless, Michelman asserts that compensation is *not* due in every case of investment-backed expectations (Michelman, 1967, p. 1213). For example, compensation would not be due if demoralization costs are low and settlement costs are high (see the discussion of Michelman above).

Miceli and Segerson (1996, Ch. 7) also argue that a rule of paying compensation if and only if the landowner's expectations are investment-backed will be inefficient. In particular, they show that it can lead to overinvestment. However, they also show that efficient land use decisions will be made under a 'good faith' rule based on 'reasonable' (efficient) land use decisions. In particular, in the event of a regulation, such a rule would require compensation for landowners who acted in good faith, either by investing when it was efficient to do so or not investing when investment was inefficient, and it would not require compensation for those who did not act in good faith (Mandelker, 1987).

8.3 Singling Out and Equal Protection

An additional factor identified in the *Penn Central* case for determining when a taking occurs was proposed by Justice Rehnquist in a dissenting opinion. This factor concerns whether the government action applies to a broad class of landowners or whether it 'singles out' individuals. Rehnquist noted that 'Even where the government prohibits a noninjurious use, the court has ruled that a taking does not take place if the prohibition applies over a broad cross section of land and thereby "secure[s] an average reciprocity of advantage"' (*Penn Central v. City of New York* (1978, p. 147), Rehnquist dissent, quoting from *Pennsylvania Coal v. Mahon* (1922, p. 415)). In contrast, regulations that single-out landowners are more likely to be judged a taking according to this criterion. In *Agins v. Tiburon* (447 U.S. 255 (1980)), the Court similarly held that a landowner subject to a zoning ordinance 'will share with other owners the benefits and burdens of the city's exercise of its police power. In assessing the fairness of the zoning ordinances, these benefits must be considered along with any diminution in market value that the appellants might suffer' (*Agins v. Tiburon*, 1980, p. 262). Even Epstein (1995, pp. 134-137), who argues generally in favor of compensation, recognizes that regulations that spread benefits and costs over the same population offer in-kind compensation.

The singling out criterion also forms the basis for Michelman's (1967) proposed fairness standard for compensation:

> A decision not to compensate is not unfair as long as the disappointed claimant ought to be able to appreciate how such decisions might fit into a consistent practice which holds forth a lesser long run risk to people like him than would any consistent practice which is naturally suggested by the opposite decision. (p. 1223)

Such a rule can be defended by a 'veil of ignorance' argument that legitimizes rules that people would have approved prior to learning of their actual position in society (Rawls, 1971, pp. 136-142; Posner, 1980). This rule prevents landowners from being singled out to bear costs for society as a whole, as when a single landowner is compelled to give up his property without compensation to provide a public good (Rose-Ackerman, 1992). At the same time, it allows uncompensated regulations that potentially apply equally to all landowners, such as broadly-based zoning laws. Such a rule therefore depends on the extent to which a regulation applies to few versus many landowners.

Singling out can also occur when compensation is not paid for restrictions that are placed on undeveloped land if comparable developed land is exempted from the restriction, that is, when there is not 'equal protection' for developed and undeveloped land. In addition to the fairness implications of an equal protection requirement, it can also have efficiency effects. Specifically, because it is often efficient for the government to take undeveloped land before developed land, uncompensated takings can provide an incentive for landowners to develop 'too early' in an effort to reduce the likelihood that their land will be taken (Innes, 1995, 1997). For example, a developer might begin construction in an effort to beat an anticipated downzoning (Dana, 1995). This is consistent with the result discussed above that zero compensation will not be efficient if landowners can influence the probability of a taking (Miceli, 1991; Miceli and Segerson, 1996, Chs 7 and 8).

Compensating owners of undeveloped land that is taken, or affording equal protection to both developed and undeveloped land, can offset the incentive for premature development (Innes, 1995; Miceli and Segerson, 1996, Ch. 8). Thus, such a rule can achieve both equity and efficiency objectives. However, Miceli and Segerson (1996, Ch. 8) show that, while equal protection is sufficient for efficient incentives, it is not necessary. Other rules are capable of simultaneously satisfying efficiency and equity goals as well.

In some cases, a developer will begin investing in a project only to find that a change in the zoning regulations prevents its completion. While recognizing that local governments need to have some freedom to revise their zoning laws in response to changing circumstances, landowners also need some protection of their sunk investments when a zoning change occurs (Mandelker, 1993, pp. 234-244; Kaplow, 1986). The courts have provided a basis for such protection in the form of 'vested rights'. A vested right allows the landowner to proceed with the project despite the zoning change under certain conditions.

In order for a landowner to acquire a vested right, he generally must have made a 'substantial' investment in the property in reliance on a valid building permit. In this sense, his expectations must be 'investment-backed' (see the related discussion above). How much investment is necessary to be deemed substantial is not clear. Generally courts engage in a balancing test that weighs the costs and benefits of the zoning change. For example, in addition to making substantial investments, the landowner must have acted in 'good faith' by not rushing the development process in an effort to beat an impending zoning change. More generally, the good faith test asks 'whether a landowner's conduct was consistent with how a reasonable property owner would have acted in the same circumstances' (Mandelker, 1993, p. 239). Miceli and Segerson (1996, Chs 7 and 8) show that, if good faith or 'reasonableness' are judged on efficiency grounds, then a good faith rule can induce efficient land use decisions by awarding a vested right if development was efficient but not awarding one if development was not efficient.

Note, however, that the threat to withhold a vested right if the landowner developed prematurely is only effective if the development is *reversible* - that is, only if the development process can be halted and the resulting external cost avoided or eliminated if the landowner developed inefficiently. This will not always be possible, as when a landowner harvests timber prematurely, or destroys wildlife in order to avoid the imposition of regulations aimed at preserving the habitat of an endangered species (a practice known as 'shoot, shovel, and shut up') (Epstein, 1995, p. 294). In such cases, it may be necessary to promise compensation for the threatened regulation in order to offset the incentive for preemptive development or destruction of wildlife and habitat. The magnitude of compensation cannot be too large, however, for then landowners may have an incentive to *delay* development inefficiently. One way to ensure efficient incentives is to condition the payment of compensation on efficiency of the landowner's decision - that is, on whether his decision either to develop or to postpone development was efficient (Miceli and Segerson, 1996, Ch. 8)

8.4 The Role of Capitalization

As noted above, an important factor in evaluating the fairness of a regulation is the extent to which it interferes with the landowner's reasonable expectations.

One issue that arises in this context is whether the threat of a regulation was known to the landowner when he first purchased the land. A frequent argument made against paying compensation for regulations is that when landowners purchased land subject to the threat of a regulation, they paid a price that discounted (or 'capitalized') the possibility of that regulation. Consequently, they have already received 'implicit' compensation (Posner, 1980). Although this argument owes much to Michelman (1967), courts understood it as far back as 1823 when, in the case of *Callender v. Marsh* (1 Pick. 417, 430 (1823)), the court said: 'Those who purchase house lots ... are supposed to calculate the chance of [regulations]..., and as their purchase is always voluntary, they may indemnify themselves in the price of the lot which they buy.'

If the purchase price discounted (or capitalized) the threat of regulation, then the case for compensation is weakened because the landowner 'got exactly what [he] meant to buy'. Michelman concludes that compensation in this case would be analogous to refunding the price of a losing lottery ticket (Michelman, 1967, p. 1238; Rose-Ackerman, 1992). This is a persuasive argument that has found its way into fairly recent judicial decisions defending rulings against compensation (*HFH Ltd. v. Superior Court*, 542 P.2d 237 (1975)).

Several authors have suggested, however, that the capitalization argument against compensation is flawed (Epstein, 1985, pp. 151-158; Fischel, 1985, pp. 184-186; Fischel and Shapiro, 1988; Miceli and Segerson, 1996, Ch. 6). The reason is that, even if the purchaser had full knowledge of the threat of a regulation when he bought the land (and therefore paid a discounted price), the threat had to arise at some previous point in time, and the owner at that point suffered a capital loss. The only way that the original landowner is fully protected against this capital loss is if any subsequent owner who is regulated expects to receive full compensation, that is, compensation equal to the difference between the value of the property with and without the regulation. Compensation based on other measures, such as the purchase price of the land or reliance expenditures, will not eliminate landowner losses (or gains) even when capitalization occurs (Miceli and Segerson, 1996, Ch. 6).

9. Government Incentives versus Land Use Incentives

The above discussion of land use incentives in the presence of a takings threat identified a moral hazard problem associated with compensation. Specifically, paying compensation for the full value of the confiscated land will generally lead to overinvestment by landowners. While this result was first demonstrated in the case of physical takings (Blume, Rubinfeld and Shapiro 1984), the basic logic applies to regulatory takings as well (Miceli and Segerson, 1996, Ch. 3). Specifically, with full compensation landowners will act as if they are fully insured against the risk of a regulation and hence will overinvest. To remedy this problem, compensation must be lump sum, or independent of the amount that was invested in the land. Since a special case of lump sum compensation is zero compensation, an implication of the Blume, Rubinfeld and Shapiro (1984) model is that zero compensation will lead to efficient land use decisions in the case of regulatory takings as well.

If regulatory agencies have fiscal illusion, however, then a rule of no compensation potentially leads to excessive regulation (Epstein, 1985, Ch. 17; Johnson, 1977). This threat is especially severe for groups who are underrepresented in the political process or owners of immobile assets who cannot escape uncompensated regulations (Farber, 1992; Fischel, 1995a;Yandle, 1995). Hence, there is a potential trade-off between two effects: the moral hazard problem - which argues against compensation - and regulatory fiscal illusion - which argues for compensation.

Miceli and Segerson (1994) explicitly examine the trade-off between moral hazard and fiscal illusion in the context of regulatory takings by considering a compensation rule that conditions the amount of compensation on whether or not the regulator acted in an efficient manner. They show that a rule under which compensation must be paid if and only if the government made an inefficient regulatory decision (the '*ex post*' rule) will lead to efficient incentives not only for the regulator but also for the landowner. Under this rule, compensation is full when it is inefficient to impose the regulation ex post, but zero when it is efficient to impose the regulation *ex post*. This definition of the threshold for compensation induces the regulator to act efficiently because by doing so he can 'avoid' paying compensation. Moreover, since compensation is zero for efficient regulations, landowners will make the correct land use decisions as well.

In light of this conclusion, Miceli and Segerson (1996, Ch. 5) argue that, under appropriate definitions of 'noxious use' and 'nuisance', the *ex post* rule is consistent with both the noxious use doctrine and the nuisance exception. In addition, it is consistent with Fischel's (1985, Ch. 8) rule of paying compensation for inefficient regulations and not paying compensation for efficient ones (see the discussion above). Finally, it defines a threshold for determining when a regulation goes too far under the diminution of value test.

While compensation under the *ex post* rule hinges on the nature of the government action, Miceli and Segerson (1994, 1996, Ch. 4) show that efficient incentives for both regulators and landowners can also be achieved under an alternative rule that determines compensation on the basis of the efficiency of the landowner's decision (the '*ex ante*' rule). Under this rule, compensation is paid if and only if the landowner made an efficient land use decision at the time the that the original investment was made. Note that both the *ex post* and *ex ante* rules induce efficiency by both parties for the same reason that negligence rules work in bilateral care accident cases (Landes and Posner, 1987, Ch. 4;

Cooter and Ulen, 1988, Ch. 8). Specifically, they specify a threshold for one of the parties such that, by acting efficiently, that party can 'avoid liability'. As a result, the other party bears 'full liability' in equilibrium and therefore also acts efficiently. Since Miceli and Segerson (1994, 1996, Ch. 4) identify two alternative rules that are efficient, factors other than efficiency can be used to choose between them. Two such factors are fairness and transactions costs. Fairness generally argues for payment of compensation in equilibrium (the *ex ante* rule), whereas transactions cost considerations argue against compensation (the *ex post* rule). Note that these options mirror Michelman's (1967) comparison of demoralization and settlement costs for determining compensation.

As noted above, Hermalin (1995) also proposed rules that solve the moral hazard and fiscal illusion problems in the context of full takings. However, in contrast to Hermalin's proposals, the rules proposed by Miceli and Segerson permit attainment of the first-best outcome even when compensation is tied to the value of the land to the landowner, and the landowner does not have a buy-back option. Thus, while both the Miceli-Segerson rules and those of Hermalin induce efficient behavior by both landowners and regulators, the former are more closely linked to actual takings law and hence have greater positive significance.

Fischel and Shapiro (1989) also proposed a resolution to the trade-off between moral hazard and fiscal illusion in the context of a constitutional choice (veil of ignorance) model. They concluded that partial compensation for regulations optimally balances the costs of these two problems. However, a partial compensation rule only achieves a second-best solution. In addition, it fails to explain actual decisions of courts, which typically award either zero or full compensation. Note, however, that to the extent that compensation is based on fair market value, which is often less than the subjective value of the property (see Section 4 above), courts might in fact be awarding partial compensation for takings that are found to be compensable. Under this form of partial compensation, the rules proposed by Miceli and Segerson (1994, 1996) would yield second-best outcomes as well.

Acknowledgements

We acknowledge the very helpful comments of two reviewers.

Bibliography on Takings (6200)

Adelstein, Richard P. (1974), 'Just Compensation and the Assassin's Bequest: A Utilitarian Approach', **122** *University of Pennsylvania Law Review*, 1012-1032.

Baxter, W. and Altree, L. (1972), 'Legal Aspects of Airport Noise', **15** *Journal of Law and*

Economics, 1-113.

Been, Vicki (1991), ''Exit' as a Constraint of Land Use Exactions: Rethinking the Unconstitutional Conditions Doctrine', **91** *Columbia Law Review*, 473-545.

Benson, Bruce L. (1992), 'The Development of Criminal Law and Its Enforcement: Public Interest or Political Transfers', **3** *Journal des Economistes et des Etudes Humaines*, 79-108.

Benson, Bruce L. (1994), 'Emerging From the Hobbesian Jungle: Might Takes and Makes Rights', **5** *Constitutional Political Economy*, 129-158. Translated into Spanish and republished (1995) Las Instituciones y Los Derechos de Propiedad al Emerger de la Jungla Hobbesiana: La Fuerza Quita los Reprinted Derechos y los Crea Libertas, 12, 35-75.

Berger, L. (1991), 'Inclusionary Zoning as Takings: The Legacy of the Mount Laurel Cases', **70** *Nebraska Law Review*, 186-228.

Blume, L. and Rubinfeld, D. (1984), 'Compensation for Takings: An Economic Analysis', **72** *California Law Review*, 569-624.

Blume, L. and Rubinfeld, Daniel L. (1987), 'Compensation for Takings: An Economic Analysis', **10** *Research in Law and Economics*, 53-104.

Blume, L., Rubinfeld, Daniel L. and Shapiro, P. (1984), 'The Taking of Land: When Should Compensation Be Paid?', **99** *Quarterly Journal of Economics*, 71-92.

Bouckaert, Boudewijn and De Geest, Gerrit (1995), 'Private Takings, Private Taxes, Private Compulsory Services: The Economic Doctrine of Quasi Contracts', **15** *International Review of Law and Economics*, 463-487.

Bromley, Daniel W. (1993), 'Regulatory Takings: Coherent Concept or Logical Contradiction', **17** *Vermont Law Review*, 647-682.

Buchanan, James M. (1972), 'Politics, Property, and the Law: An Alternative Interpretation of Miller et al. v. Schoene', **15** *Journal of Law and Economics*, 439-452.

Burrows, Paul (1989), 'Getting a Stranglehold with the Eminant Domain Clause', **9** *International Review of Law and Economics*, 129-147.

Burrows, Paul (1991), 'Compensation for Compulsory Acquisition', **67** *Land Economics*, 49-63.

Cohen, Lloyd R. (1991), 'Holdouts and Free Riders', **20** *Journal of Legal Studies*, 351-362.

Connors, C. (1990), 'Back to the Future: The 'Nuisance Exception' to the Just Compensation Clause', **19** *Capital University Law Review*, 139-185.

Disheroon, F. (1993), 'After Lucas: No More Wetland Takings?', **13** *Vermont Law Review*, 683-693.

Dudley, B. and MacDonald, J. (1995), 'Lucas v. South Carolina Coastal Council, Takings, and the Search for the Common Good', **33** *American Business Law Journal*, 153-178.

Durham, James Geoffrey (1985), 'Efficient Just Compensation as a Limit on Eminent Domain', **69** *Minnesota Law Review*, 1277-1313.

Echeverria, J. and Dennis, S. (1993), 'The Takings Issue and the Due Process Clause: A Way Out of a Doctrinal Confusion', **17** *Vermont Law Review*, 695-721.

Epstein, Richard A. (1985), *Takings: Private Property and the Power of Eminent Domain*, Cambridge, Harvard University Press, 362 p.

Epstein, Richard A. (1987), 'Takings: Descent and Resurrection', *Supreme Court Review*, 1-45.

Epstein, Richard A. (1992), 'Ruminations on Lucas v. South Carolina Coastal Council: An Introduction to Amicus Curiae Brief', **25** *Loyola of Los Angeles Law Review*,

1225-1232.

Epstein, Richard A., W., Mellor III. C., Bolick, J. Emord and Bullock, S. (1992), 'David Lucas v. South Carolina Coastal Council: Brief for the Institute for Justice as Amicus Curiae in Support of Petitioner', **25** *Loyola of Los Angeles Law Review*, 1233-1258.

Farber, Daniel A. (1992), 'Economic Analysis and Just Compensation', **12** *International Review of Law and Economics*, 125-138.

Fischel, William A. (1987), 'The Economics of Land Use Exactions: A Property Rights Analysis', **50** *Law and Contemporary Problems*, 101-113. Reprinted in Stein, Jay M. (ed.) (1996), *Classic Readings in Real Estate and Development*, Washington, DC, ULI - the Urban Land Institute.

Fischel, William A. (1988), 'Introduction: Utilitarian Balancing and Formalism in Takings', **88** *Columbia Law Review*, 1581-1599.

Fischel, William A. (1991), 'Exploring the Kozinski Paradox: Why Is More Efficient Regulation a Taking of Property?', **67** *Chicago-Kent Law Review*, 865-912.

Fischel, Wiliam A. (1992), 'Exploring the Kozinsky Paradox: Why is More Efficient Regulation a Taking of Property?', **67** *Chicago-Kent Law Review*, 865-912.

Fischel, William A. (1995a), 'The Offer/Ask Disparity and Just Compensation for Takings: A Constitutional Choice Perspective', **15** *International Review of Law and Economics*, 187-203.

Fischel, William A. (1995b), *Regulatory Takings: Law, Economics, and Politics*, Cambridge, MA, Harvard University Press.

Fischel, William A. (1996), 'The Political Economy of Just Compensation: Lessons from the Military Draft for the Takings Issue', *Harvard Journal of Law and Public Policy*.

Fischel, William A. and Shapiro, Perry (1988), 'Takings, Insurance and Michelman: Comments on Economic Interpretations of "Just Compensation" Law', **17** *Journal of Legal Studies*, 269-293. Reprinted in Ellickson, Robert, Rose, Carol and Ackerman, Bruce (eds), *Perspectives on Property Law*, 2dn edn, 514-530, Boston, Little Brown, 1995.

Fischel, William A. and Shapiro, Perry (1989), 'A Constitutional Choice Model of Compensation for Takings', **9** *International Review of Law and Economics*, 115-128.

Fisher, W. III. (1988), 'The Significance of Public Perceptions of the Takings Doctrine', **88** *Columbia Law Review*, 1774-1794.

Fisher, W. III. (1993), 'The Trouble with Lucas', **45** *Stanford Law Review*, 1393-1410.

Francis, L (1984), 'Eminent Domain Compensation in Western States', **1984** *Utah Law Review*, 429-484.

Frech, H. Edward III (1982), 'The California Coastal Commissions: Economic Impacts', in Johnson, Bruce (ed.), *Resolving the Housing Crisis: Government Policy, Decontrol and the Public Interest*, Ballinger, 259-274.

Frech, H. Edward III and Lafferty, Ronald N. (1976), 'The Economic Impact of the California Coastal Commission: Land Use and Land Values', in Johnson, Bruce M. (ed.), *The California Coastal Plan: A Critique*, Institute for Contemporary Studies, 69-91.

Frech, H. Edward III and Lafferty, Ronald N. (1978), 'Community Environment and the Market Value of Single-Family Homes: The Effect of Dispersion of Land Uses', **21** *Journal of Law and Economics*, 381-396.

Freyer, T. (1981), 'Reassessing the Impact of Eminent Domain in Early American Economic Development', **57** *Wisconsin Law Review*, 1263-1286.

Friedman, L. (1986), 'A Search for Seizure: Pennsylvania Coal Co. v. Mahon in Context',

4 *Law and History Review*, 1-22.

Gecker, Frances F. (1987), 'Comment: The Recovery of Opportunity Costs as Just Compensation: A Takings Analysis of Adequate Protection', **81** *Northwestern University Law Review*, 953-1025.

Ghosh, Shubha (1997), 'Takings, the Exit Option and Just Compensation', **17** *International Review of Law and Economics*, 157-176.

Goldberg, Victor P., Merrill, Tom and Unumb, Daniel (1987), 'Bargaining in the Shadow of Eminent Domain: Valuing and Apportioning Condemnation Awards Between Landlord and Tenant', **34** *UCLA Law Review*, 1083-1187.

Hermalin, Benjamin E. (1995), 'An Economic Analysis of Takings', **11** *Journal of Law, Economics and Organization*, 64-86.

Hippler, T. (1987), 'Reexamining 100 Years of Supreme Court Regulatory Taking Doctrine: The Principles of 'Noxious Use', 'Average reciprocity of Advantage', 'and 'Bundle of Rights' for Mugler to Keystone Bituminous Coal', **14** *Boston College Environmental Affairs Law Review*, 653-727.

Innes, R. (1994), *Takings, Compensation and Equal Protection for Owners of Developed and Undeveloped Land*, Mimeo, University of Arizona.

Innes, R. (1995), 'An Essay on Takings: Concepts and Issues', **4** *Choices*.

Innes, R. (1997), 'Takings, Compensation and Equal Protection for Owners of Developed and Undeveloped Land', *Journal of Law and Economics*, forthcoming.

Johnson, M. Bruce (1977), 'Planning without Prices: A Discussion of Land Use Regulation Without Compensation', in Siegan, Bernard H. (ed.), *Planning Without Prices*, Lexington, MA, Lexington Books, 63-111.

Kaplow, Louis (1986), 'An Economic Analysis of Legal Transitions', **99** *Harvard Law Review*, 509-617.

Kaplow, Louis (1987), 'Optimal Transition Policy: Replacing Horizontal Equity with an Ex Ante Incentives Perspective', Dissertation accepted by Harvard University Department of Economics.

Kaplow, Louis (1992), 'Government Relief for Risk Associated with Government Action', **94** *Scandinavian Journal of Economics*, 525-541.

Kmiec, D. (1981), 'Regulatory Takings: The Court Runs Out of Gas in San Diego', **57** *Indiana Law Journal*, 45-81.

Kmiec, D. (1988), 'The Original Understanding of the Taking Clause is Neither Weak Nor Obtuse', **88** *Columbia Law Review*, 1630-1666.

Knetsch, Jack L. (1983), *Property Rights and Compensation: Compulsory Acquisitions and Other Losses*, Toronto, Butterworths.

Knetsch, Jack L. (1990), 'Environmental Policy Implications of Disparities between Willingness to Pay and Compensation Demanded Measures of Values', **18** *Journal of Environmental Economics and Management*, 227-237.

Knetsch, Jack L. and Borcherding, T. (1979), 'Expropriation of Private Property and the Basis for Compensation', **29** *University of Toronto Law Journal*, 237-252.

La Croix, Summer and Rose, L. (1995), 'Public Use, Just Compensation, and Land Reform in Hawaii', **17** *Research in Law and Economics*, 17 ff.

Levmore, Saul (1990), 'Just Compensation and Just Politics', **22** *Connecticut Law Review*, 285-322.

Levmore, Saul (1991), 'Takings, Torts, and Special Interests', **77** *Virginia Law Review*, 1333-1368.

Levmore, Saul and Stuntz, William J. (1990), 'Remedies and Incentives in Private and Public Law: A Comparative Essay', **66** *Wisconsin Law Review*, 483-499.

Lodise, John P. (1988), 'Retroactive Compensation and the Illusion of Economic Efficiency: An Analysis of the First English Decision', **35** *UCLA Law Review*, 1267-1290.

Lunney, G. (1992), 'A Critical Reexamination of the Takings Jurisprudence', **90** *Michigan Law Review*, 1892-1965.

MacKaay, Ejan (1987), 'Le Paradoxe des Droits Acquis (The Paradox of Acquired Rights)', in, *De 'l'Ancienne' à la 'Nouvelle' Economie. Essais à l'Occasion de la Dixième Université d'Eté de la Nouvelle Economie*, Aix-en-Provence, Librairie de l'Université, 205-219.

Mandelker, D. (1987), 'Investment-Backed Expectations: Is There a Taking?', **31** *Journal of Urban and Contemporary Problems*, 3-43.

Manheim, K. (1989), 'Tenant Eviction and the Takings Clause', **65** *Wisconsin Law Review*, 925-1019.

McKenzie, Richard B. (1986), 'Eminent Domain: A New Industrial Policy Tool', **142** *Journal of Institutional and Theoretical Economics*, 27-38.

Medema, S. (1992a), 'Making Choices and Making Law: An Institutional Perspective on the Taking Issue', in Mercuro, Nicholas, *Taking Property and Just Compensation: Legal and Economic Perspectives of the Takings Issue*, Boston, Kluwer Academic Publishers.

Medema, Steven G. (1992b), 'Probing the Legal-Economic Nexus: Takings, 1978-1988', **26** *Journal of Economic Issues*, 525-534.

Medema, Steven G. (1992c), *Legal Economic Perspectives on the Taking Issue*, Boston, Kluwer Academic Publishers.

Mercuro, Nicholas (ed.) (1992a), *Taking Property and Just Compensation: Legal and Economics Perspectives of the Takings Issue*, Boston, Kluwer Academic Publishers.

Mercuro, Nicholas (1992b), 'The Takings Issue: A Continuing Dilemma in Law and Economics', in Mercuro, Nicholas (ed.), *Taking Property and Just Compensation: Law and Economics Perspectives of the Takings Issue*, Boston, Kluwer Academic Publishers, 1-23.

Mercuro, Nicholas and Ryan, Thimothy P. (1980), 'Property Rights and Welfare Economics: Miller et al. v. Schoene Revisited: Reply', **56** *Land Economics*, 202-212.

Mercuro, Nicholas and Ryan, Thimothy P. (1981), 'Property Rights and Welfare Economics: Miller et al. v. Schoene Revisited: Reply', **57** *Land Economics*, 657-659.

Merrill, T. (1986a), 'The Economics of Public Use', **72** *Cornell Law Review*, 61-116.

Merrill, T. (1986b), 'Rent Seeking and the Compensation Principle', **80** *Northwestern Law Review*, 1561-1589.

Miceli, Thomas J. (1991), 'Compensation for the Taking of Land Under Eminent Domain', **147** *Journal of Institutional and Theoretical Economics*, 354-363.

Miceli, Thomas J. and Segerson, Kathleen (1994), 'Regulatory Takings: When Should Compensation be Paid?', **23** *Journal of Legal Studies*, 749-776.

Miceli, Thomas J. and Segerson, Kathleen (1995), 'Government Regulation and Compensation for Takings: Implications for Agriculture', **77** *American Journal of Agricultural Economics*, 1177-1182.

Miceli, Thomas J. and Segerson, Kathleen (1996), *Compensation for Regulatory Takings: An Economic Analysis with Applications*, Greenwich, CT, JAI Press.

Michelman, Frank I. (1967), 'Property, Utility and Fairness: Comments on the Ethical

Foundations of 'Just Compensation' Law', **80** *Harvard Law Review*, 1165-1258. Reprinted in Ackerman, Bruce A. (ed.) (1975), *Economic Foundations of Property Law*, Boston, Little Brown, 100 ff.

Michelman, Frank I. (1988), 'Takings', **88** *Columbia Law Review*, 1600-1629.

Munch, Patricia (1976), 'An Economic Analysis of Eminent Domain', **84** *Journal of Political Economy*, 473-497.

Paul, E. (1987a), *Property Rights and Eminent Domain*, New Brunswick, NJ, Transaction Press.

Paul, Ellen Frankel (1987b), 'Public Use: A Vanishing Limitation on Governmental Takings', in Dorn, James A. and Manne, Henry G. (eds), *Economic Liberties and the Judiciary*, Fairfax, George Mason University Press, 357-373.

Peterson, Andrew A. (1989), 'The Takings Clause: In Search of Underlying Principles', **77** *California Law Review*, 1299-1363.

Poirier, M. (1993), 'Takings and Natural Hazards Policy: Public Choice on the Beachfront', **46** *Rutgers Law Review*, 243-347.

Rose, Carol M. (1984), 'Mahon Reconstructed: Why the Takings Issue is Still a Muddle', **57** *Southern California Law Review*, 561-599.

Rose-Ackerman, Susan (1988), 'Against Ad Hocery: A Comment on Michelman', **88** *Columbia Law Review*, 1697-1711.

Rose-Ackerman, Susan (1992), 'Regulatory Takings: Policy Analysis and Democratic Principles', in Mercuro, Nicholas (ed.), *Taking Property and Just Compensation: Law and Economics Perspectives of the Takings Issue*, Boston, Kluwer Academic Publishers, 25-44.

Ross, Thomas W. (1994), 'Raising an Army: A Positive Theory of Military Recruitment', **37** *Journal of Law and Economics*, 109-131.

Rowley, Charles K. (1992), 'The Supreme Court and Takings Judgments: Constitutional Political Economy versus Public Choice', in Mercuro, Nicholas (ed.), *Taking Property and Just Compensation: Law and Economics Perspectives of the Takings Issue*, Boston, Kluwer Academic Publishers, 79-124.

Rubenfeld, J. (1993), 'Usings', **102** *Yale Law Journal*, 1077-1163.

Runge, C. (1993), 'Economic Implications of Wider Compensation for 'Takings' or, What if Agricultural Policies Ruled the World?', **17** *Vermont Law Review*, 723-739.

Samuels, Warren J. (1974), 'Commentary: An Economic Perspective on the Compensation Problem', **21** *Wayne Law Review*, 113-134. Reprinted in Samuels, Warren J. and Schmid, A. Allen (eds) (1981), *Law and Economics: An Institutional Perspective*, Boston, Nijhoff, 1981, 188-209.

Samuels, Warren J. and Mercuro, Nicholas (1979), 'The Role and Resolution of the Compensation Principle in Society: Part One - The Role', **1** *Research in Law and Economics*, 157-194.

Samuels, Warren J. and Mercuro, Nicholas (1980), 'The Role and Resolution of the Compensation Principle in Society: Part Two - The Resolution', **2** *Research in Law and Economics*, 103-128.

Sax, Joseph L. (1964), 'Takings and the Police Power', **74** *Yale Law Journal*, 36-76.

Sax, Joseph L. (1971), 'Takings, Private Property and Public Rights', **81** *Yale Law Journal*, 149-186. Reprinted in Ackerman, Bruce A. (ed.) (1975), *Economic Foundations of Property Law*, Boston, Little Brown, 146-158.

Schill, M. (1989), 'Intergovernmental Takings and Just Compensation: A Question of

Federalism', **137** *University of Pennsylvania Law Review*, 829-901.

Siegan, Bernard H. (1972), *Land Use Without Zoning*, Lexington, MA, Lexington Books.

Stake, Jeffrey E. (1995), 'Loss Aversion and Involuntary Transfers of Title', in Malloy, Robbin P. and Braun, Christopher K. (eds), *Law and Economics: New and Critical Perspectives*, New York, Lang, 331-360.

Stein, G (1995), 'Regulatory Takings and Ripeness in Federal Courts', **48** *Vanderbilt Law Review*, 1-99.

Stoebuck, W. (1969), 'The Property Right of Access versus the Power of Eminent Domain', **47** *Texas Law Review*, 733-765.

Stoebuck, W. (1972), 'A General Theory of Eminent Domain', **47** *Washington Law Review*, 553-608.

Swank, W. (1976), 'Note. Inverse Condemnation: The Case for Diminution in Property Values as Compensable Damage', **28** *Stanford Law Review*, 779-804.

Symposium (1988), 'Symposium on Takings', **88** *Columbia Law Review*, 1581-1794.

Thompson, B. (1990), 'Judicial Takings', **76** *Virginia Law Review*, 1449-1544.

Tideman, N. (1988), 'Takings, Moral Evolution, and Justice', **88** *Columbia Law Review*, 1714-1730.

Tiefer, C. (1996), 'Controlling Federal Agencies by Claims on Their Appropriations? the Takings Bill and the Power of the Purse', **13** *Yale Journal on Regulation*, 501-534.

Treanor, W. (1985), 'The Origins and Original Significance of the Just Compensation Clause of the Fifth Amendment', **94** *Yale Law Journal*, 694-716.

Trefzger, J. and Colwell, P. (1996), 'Investor Efficiency in the Face of Takings', **12** *Journal of Real Estate Finance and Economics*, 23-35.

Ulen, Thomas S. (1992), 'The Public Use of Private Property: A Dual Constraint Theory of Efficient Government Takings', in Mercuro, Nicholas (ed.), *Taking Property and Just Compensation: Law and Economics Perspectives of the Takings Issue*, Boston, Kluwer Academic Publishers, 163-198.

Werin, Lars (1978), 'Expropriation - en Studie i Lagstiftningsmotiv och Ersättningsrättsliga Grundprinciper (Expropriation - A Study in Legislative Motives and Compensatory Basic Principles)', *Svensk Juristtidning*, 81-120.

Wittman, Donald A. (1995), *The Myth of Democratic Failure: Why Political Institutions are Efficient*, Chicago, University of Chicago Press.

Wittman, Donald A. and Grofman, Bernard (eds) (1989), *The Federalist Papers: The New Institutionalism and the Old*, Edison, NJ, Agathon Press.

Yandle, Bruce (1995), *Land Rights: The 1990's Property Rights Rebellion*, Lanham, MD, Rowman and Littlefield.

Other References

Calabresi, Guido and Melamed, A. Douglas (1972), 'Property Rules, Liability Rules, and Inalienability: One View of the Cathedral', **85** *Harvard Law Review*, 1089-1128.

Coase, Ronald H. (1960), 'The Problem of Social Cost', **3** *Journal of Law and Economics*, 1-44.

Cooter, Robert D. (1985), 'Unity in Tort, Contract, and Property: The Model of Precaution', **73** *California Law Review*, 1-51.

Cooter Robert D. and Ulen, Tom (1988), *Law and Economics*, New York, Harper Collins.

Cornes, R. and Sandler, Todd (1986), *The Theory of Externalities, Public Goods, and Club Goods*, Cambridge, Cambridge Univ. Press.

Dana, D. (1995), 'Natural Preservation and the Race to Develop', **143** *University of Pennsylvania Law Review*, 655-708.

Ellickson, Robert (1973), 'Alternatives to Zoning: Covenants, Nuisance Rules, and Fines as Land Use Controls', **40** *University of Chicago Law Review*, 681-782.

Ellickson, Robert (1977), 'Suburban Growth Controls: An Economic and Legal Analysis', **86** *Yale Law Journal*, 385-511.

Epstein, Richard (1995), *Simple Rules for a Complex World*, Cambridge, Harvard University Press.

Fischel, William (1985), *The Economics of Zoning Laws*, Baltimore, Johns Hopkins University Press.

Kaplow, Louis and Shavell, Steven (1996), 'Property Rules versus Liability Rules: An Economic Analysis', **109** *Harvard Law Review*, 715-790.

Keeton, W.P., Dobbs, D., Keeton, R. and Owen, D. (1984), *Prosser and Keeton on the Law of Torts*, 5th edn, St. Paul, West.

Krier, James and Schwab, Stuart (1995), 'Property Rules and Liability Rules: The Cathedral in Another Light', **70** *New York University Law Review*, 440-483.

Landes, William, and Posner, Richard A. (1987), *The Economic Structure of Tort Law*, Cambridge, Harvard University Press.

Mandelker, D. (1993), *Land Use Law*, 3rd edn, Charlottesville, Michie.

Merrill, T. (1985), 'Trespass, Nuisance, and the Costs of Determining Property Rights', **14** *Journal of Legal Studies*, 13-48.

Mueller, Dennis C. (1989), *Public Choice II*, Cambridge, Cambridge University Press.

Posner, Richard A. (1980), 'The Ethical and Political Basis of the Efficiency Norm in Common Law Adjudication', **8** *Hofstra Law Review*, 487-507.

Posner, Richard A. (1992), *Economic Analysis of Law*, 4th edn, Boston, Little Brown.

Rawls, John (1971), *A Theory of Justice*, Cambridge, Harvard University Press.

Rose, Carol (1983), 'Planning and Dealing: Piecemeal Land Controls as a Problem of Local Legitimacy', **71** *California Law Review*, 837-912.

Wittman, Donald (1984), 'Liability for Harm or Restitution for Benefit?', **13** *Journal of Legal Studies*, 57-80.

List of Cases

Agins v. City of Tiburon (1980), 447 U.S. 255.
Boomer v. Atlantic Cement (1970), 309 N.Y.S.2d 312.
Callender v. Marsh (1823), 1 Pick. 417.
Dolan v. City of Tigard (1994), 114 S.Ct. 2309.
HFH Ltd. v. Superior Court (1975), 542 P.2d 237.
Lucas v. South Carolina Coastal Council (1992), 112 S.Ct. 2886.
Mugler v. Kansas (1887), 123 U.S. 623.
Nollan v. California Coastal Comm'n (1987), 438 U.S. 825.
Penn Central Transportation Co. v. City of New York (1978) 438 U.S. 104.
Pennsylvania Coal Co. v. Mahon (1922), 260 U.S. 393.
U.S. v. Carroll Towing (1947), 159 F.2d 169.

6300
ADMINISTRATIVE LAW

Bibliography Collected by the Editors

Arruñada, Benito (1994), 'Competencia y Privatización en el Mercado Educativo (Competition and Privatization in the Education Market)', **59** *Boletín del Círculo de Empresarios*, 265-275.

Arruñada, Benito (1995), 'Diseño Organizativo y Gestión de Personal en la Sanidad Pública (Organization and Management of Human Resources in the Public Healthcare System)', in A.E.S. (ed.), *Cambios en la Regulación Sanitaria*, Barcalona, SG Editores, 64-119.

Audretsch, David B., Sleuwaegen, L. and Yamawaki, H. (1989), *The Convergence of International and Domestic Markets*, Amsterdam, North-Holland, 317 p.

Auster, Richard D. and Silver, Morris (1979), *The State as a Firm: Economic Forces in Political Development*, Den Haag, Martinus Nijhoff, 178 p.

Backhaus, Jürgen G. (1977), *Public Enterprise: Forms and Functions*, Haag & Herchen, 1977 (1st edn), 441 p., 1980 (2nd edn), 535 p.

Backhaus, Jürgen G. (1991), 'Law: Cooperation between Lawyers, Economists and Common Denominator', **45(10)** *Wirtschaftswoche*, 149-150.

Bandin Tomislav (1988), 'Politicko Jedinstvo kao Faktor Ostvarivanja Dogovorene Ekonomske i Razvojne Politike (Political Unity as a Factor of Implementation of Agreed Economic and Development Policy)', **1** *Ekonomist*, 29-31.

Bardach, Eugene and Kagan, Robert A. (1982), *Going By The Book: The Problem of Regulatory Unreasonableness*, Philadelphia, Temple University Press, 375 p.

Bawn, Kathleen (1997), 'Choosing Strategies to Control the Bureaucracy: Statutory Constraints, Oversight, and the Committee System', **13** *Journal of Law, Economics, and Organization*, 101-126.

Berge, J.B.J.M. Ten (1991), 'Rechtseconomie en Staatsrecht/Bestuursrecht (Law and Economics and Constitutional/Administrative Law)', in Hondius, E.H., Schippers, J.J. and Siegers, J.J. (eds), *Rechtseconomie en Recht*, Zwolle, Tjeenk Willink, 149-162.

Bishop, William (1990), 'A Theory of Administrative Law', **19** *Journal of Legal Studies*, 489-530.

Boardman, Anthony E. and Vining, Aidan R. (1989), 'Ownership and Performance in Competitive Environments: A Comparison of the Performance of Private, Mixed, and State-owned Enterprises', **32** *Journal of Law and Economics*, 1-33.

Borjas, George J. (1982), 'The Politics of Employment Discrimination in the Federal Bureaucracy', **25** *Journal of Law and Economics*, 271-299.

Breyer, Stephen G. (1993), *Breaking the Vicious Circle: Toward Effective Risk Regulation*, Cambridge, Harvard University Press, 127 p.

Buxbaum, Hertig and Hirsch, Hopt (eds), *European Economic and Business Law, Legal and Economic Analyses on Integration and Harmonization*, Berlin, 401 p.

Calabresi, Guido (1970), *The Costs of Accidents: A Legal and Economic Analysis*, New Haven, Yale University Press, 340 p.

Clarckson, Kenneth W. and Martin, Donald L. (eds) (1979), *The Economics of Nonproprietary Institutions (Supplement 1 to Research in Law and Economics)*, Greenwood, JAI Press, 330 p.

Clarckson, Kenneth W. and Tollison, Robert D. (1979), 'Toward a Theory of Government Advertising', **1** *Research in Law and Economics*, 131-143.

Cooter, Robert D. and Topakian, G. (1980), 'Political Economy of a Public Corporation: The Pricing Objectives of BART', **13** *Journal of Public Economics*.

Cragg, Michael (1997), 'Performance Incentives in the Public Sector: Evidence From the Job Training Partnership Act', **13** *Journal of Law, Economics, and Organization*, 147-168.

Cranor, Carl F. (1993), *Regulating Toxic Substances: A Philosophy of Science and the Law*, New York, Oxford Press, 252 p.

De Kraan, D.J. (1982a), 'Deregulering: Een Begripsbepaling (Deregulation: A Definition)', **9** *Beleid en Maatschappij*, 177-181.

De Kraan, D.J. (1982b), 'Deregulering (Deregulation)', **62** *Economisch-Statistische Berichten*, 692-696.

Desouza, Patrick J. (1985), 'Regulating Fraud in Military Procurement: A Legal Process Model', **95** *Yale Law Journal*, 390-413.

Diver, Colin S. (1983), 'The Optimal Precision of Administrative Rules', **93** *Yale Law Journal*, 65-109.

Doel, J. v.d. and Van Velthoven, Ben C.J. (1990), *Democratie en Welvaartstheorie* (3rd edn) *(Democracy and Welfare Economics)*, Alphen a.d. Rijn, Samsom H.D. Tjeenk Willink, 232 p.

Doel, J. v.d. and Van Velthoven, Ben C.J. (1993), *Democracy and Welfare Economics: An Introduction Into New Political Economy*, 2nd edn, Cambridge, Cambridge University Press, 212 p.

Farber, Daniel A. and Frickey, Philip P. (1988), 'Integrating Public Choice and Public Law: A Reply to DeBow and Lee', **66** *Texas Law Review*, 1013-1019.

Ferris, James M. and Graddy, Elizabeth (1994), 'Organizational Choices for Public Service Supply', **10** *Journal of Law, Economics, and Organization*, 126-141.

Finkelstein, M.O. (1973), 'Regression Models in Administrative Proceedings', **86** *Harvard Law Review*, 1442-1475.

Fiorina, M. (1982), 'Legislative Choice of Regulatory Forms: Legal Process or Administrative Proces?', **39** *Public Choice*, 33 ff.

Frech, H.Edward III and Lafferty, Ronald N. (1984), 'The Effect of the California Coastal Commission on Housing Prices', **16** *Journal of Urban Economics*, 105-123.

Friedman, David D. (1993), 'The Political Economy of the Decline of American Public Education: Comments', **36** *Journal of Law and Economics*, 371-378.

Gantner, Manfred (1988), 'Öffentliche (De-)Regulierung im Zusammenhang mit der österreichischen Post- und Telegraphenverwaltung (Public Deregulation of Postal Serevices)', **8** *Finanzwissenschaftliche Diskussionsreihe*.

Gantner, Manfred (ed.) (1991), *Handbuch des öffentlichen Haushaltswesens* (The Handbook of Public Budgeting), Vienna, Manz, 416 p.

Gantner, Manfred (ed.) (1994), *Budgetausgliederung - Fluch(t) oder Segen?* (Budgetary Disembodyment - Vice or Virtue?), Vienna, Manz, 232 p.

Garcia Villarejo, Salinas, Avelino and Sánchez, Javier (1993), *Manual de Hacienda Pública general y de España* (Public Treasury Manual), Madrid, Tecnos.

Geelhoed, L.A. (1993), 'Deregulering, Herregulering en Zelfregulering (Deregulation, Re-regulation and Selfregulation)', in Eijlander, Ph. (ed.), *Government and Selfregulation*, Deventer, W.E.J. Tjeenk Willink, 33-51.

Gimeno Ullastres, Juan A., *La Situación de las Facultades de Derecho y Económicas: Análisis y Propuestas* (Analysis and Proposals for Law and Economics Schools), Secretaría de Estado de Universidades e Investigación, Ministerio de Educación y Ciencia, 67 p.

Gimeno Ullastres, Juan A. and Ruiz Huerta, Jesús, 'Los Costes de los Servicios Universitarios (The Cost of Universities)', in X (ed.), *La Financiación de la Enseñanza Superior*, Madrid, Consejo de Universidades, 181-209.

Ginsburg, Douglas H. and Demuth, Christopher C. (1986), 'White House Review of Agency Rulemaking', **99** *Harvard Law Review*, 1075 ff.

Greene, Kenneth V. and Moulton, George D. (1986), 'Municipal Employee Residency Requirement Statutes: An Economic Analysis', **9** *Research in Law and Economics*, 185-204.

Greenstein, Shane (1993), 'Procedural Rules and Procurement Regulations: Complexity Creates Tradeoffs', **9** *Journal of Law, Economics, and Organization*, 159-180.

Grossekettler, Heinz (1984), 'Verwaltungsstrukturpolitik (Public Administration Structure Policy)', in Ewers, H.-J. and Schuster (ed.), *Probleme der Ordnungs- und Strukturpolitik*, Göttingen, Vandenhoeck & Ruprecht, 16-51.

Hackney, James R., Jr (1988), 'A Proposal for State Funding of Municipal Tort Liability', **98** *Yale Law Journal*, 389-407.

Harmathy, Attila (1980), 'Allami Támogatások Jogi Kérdéseiröl (Legal Questions on State Subsidies)', **1** *Allam- és Jogtudomány*, 33-61.

Harmathy, Attila (1983), *Szerzödések, Allamigazgatás, Gazdaságirányitás* (Contract, Administration, Business Governing), Budapest, Akadémiai Kiadó, 210 p.

Hill, Jeffrey S. and Brazier, James E. (1991), 'Constraining Administrative Decisions: A Critical Examination of the Structure and Process Hypothesis', **7** *Journal of Law, Economics, and Organization*, 373-400.

Hondius, E.H., Schippers, Joop J. and Siegers, Jacques J. (1991), *Rechtseconomie en Recht. Kennismaking met een Vakgebied in Opkomst* (Law and Economics: Introduction to a Growing Field of Science), Zwolle, Tjeenk Willink, 201 p.

Howard, Philip K. (1994), *The Death of Common Sense: How Law is Suffocating America*, New York, Random House, 202 p.

Howse, Robert, Prichard, J. Robert S. and Trebilcock, Michael J. (1990), 'Smaller or Smarter Government?', **40** *University of Toronto Law Journal*, 498-541.

Johnson, Ronald N. and Libecap, Gary D. (1989), 'Bureaucratic Rules, Supervisor Behavior, and the Effect on Salaries in the Federal Government', **5** *Journal of Law, Economics, and Organization*, 53-82.

Kramer, Larry and Sykes, Alan O. (1987), 'Municipal Liability under Section 1983: A Legal and Economic Analysis', *Supreme Court Review*, 249-301.

Künneke, R.W. (1986), 'Privatisation of Municipal Utilities', **18(5)** *Openbare Uitgaven*, 218-228.

Labus Miroljub (1990), 'Devalvacija i Administrativna Kontrola Cena (Devaluation and Administrative Control of Prices)', **1** *Ekonomska misao*, 1-24.

Lane, J.-E. (ed.) (1985), *State and Market; The Politics of the Public and the Private*, London, Sage, 304 p.

Mackaay, Ejan (1992), 'The Public's Right to Information', in Korthals Altes, Willem F., Dommering, Egbert J., Hugenholtz, P. Bernt and Kabel, Jan J.C. (eds), *Information Law Towards the 21st Century*, Deventer, Kluwer, 167-175.

Marshall, Robert C., Meurer, Michael J. and Richard, Jean Francois (1994), 'Multiple Litigants with a Public Good Remedy', **16** *Research in Law and Economics*, 151-173.

Martin, Dolores Tremewan and Wagner, Richard E. (1978), 'The Institutional Framework for Municipal Incorporation: An Economic Analysis of Local Agency Formation Commissions in California', **21** *Journal of Law and Economics*, 409-425.

Mashaw, Jerry L. (1985), 'Prodelegation: Why Administrators Should Make Political Decisions', **1** *Journal of Law, Economics, and Organization*, 81-100.

Mashaw, Jerry L. (1990), 'Explaining Administrative Process: Normative, Positive, and Critical Stories of Legal Devopment', **6(S)** *Journal of Law, Economics, and Organization*, 267-298.

McCubbins, Mathew D., Noll, Roger G. and Weingast, Barry R. (1987), 'Administrative Procedures as Instruments of Political Control', **3** *Journal of Law, Economics, and Organization*, 243-277.

McCubbins, Mathew D., Noll, Roger G. and Weingast, Barry R. (1990), 'Positive and Normative Models of Procedural Rights: An Integrative Approach to Administrative Procedures', **6(S)** *Journal of Law, Economics, and Organization*, 307-332.

McGarity, Thomas O. (1991), *Reinventing Rationality: The Role of Regulatory Analysis in the Federal Bureaucracy*, New York, Cambridge University Press, 384 p.

Miller, Geoffrey P., Litt, David, Macey, Jonathan R. and Rubin, Edward L. (1990), 'Politics, Bureaucracies, and Financial Markets: Bank Entry Into Commercial Paper Underwriting in the United States and Japan,', **139** *University of Pennsylvania Law Review*, 20 ff.

Morgan, Thomas D. (1978), 'Toward a Revised Strategy for Ratemaking', **21** *University of Illinois Law Forum*.

Morgan, Thomas D. (1979), 'Procedural Impediments to Optimal Rate Making', in Sichel, Werner (ed.), *Public Utility Rate Making in an Energy-Conscious Environment*, Boulder, Westview Press.

Neelen, G.H.J.M. (1990), 'Efficiency Differences Between Organizations Within the Public Sector: The Dutch Social Housing Sector', **2** *Tinbergen Institute Research Bulletin*, 33-41.

Ommeren, F.J. Van (1990), 'Bestuurscompensatie, Draagkracht en Rechtseconomie (Administrative Compensation, Financial Capacity and Economic Analysis of Law)', **39(10)** *Ars Aequi*, 682-691.

Owen, Bruce M. and Willig, Robert D. (1983), 'Economic and Postal Pricing Policy', in Fleishman, J. (ed.), *The Future of the Postal Service*, New York, Praeger Publishing Company.

Pastor, Santos (1988), 'Elementos para un Análisis Económico de la Justicia: el Gasto Público en Justicia en España' (Public Expenditure in the Courts: Reflections on Method and Scope), **110** *Hacienda Pública Española*.

Pastor, Santos (1990), 'A Propósito de la Eficacia del Gasto Público. Notas Sobre una Asignatura Pendiente del Sector Público Español (The Efficiency of Public Expenditure)', **680** *Información Comercial Española*, 151-157.

Pastor, Santos (1991), 'Las Políticas de no Intervención Estatal en Economía: una Revisión (The State in a Market Economy: A Review)', **113** *Hacienda Pública Española*, 147-159.

Pastor, Santos (1993), 'Composición, Estructura y Características de la Litigiosidad Contencioso-Administrativa: Un Análisis Muestral (Litigation in Contentious-Administrative Courts. An Empirical Analysis)', **111** *Boletín de Información del Consejo General del Poder Judicial*, 205-288.

Peeters, Bruno (1989), De Continuïteit van het Overheidsondernemen: een Begrippenanalyse en een Kritiek op de Uitvoeringsimmuniteit (The Continuity Principle of Governmental Activities: A Concept Analysis and a Critique on the Execution Immunity), Antwerpen, Maklu, 559 p.

Peltzman, Sam (1993), 'The Political Economy of the Decline of American Public Education', **36** *Journal of Law and Economics*, 331-370.

Petrovic Milenko (1995), 'Funkcije drzave u Savremenoj Trzisnoj Privredi (State Functions in a Contemporary Market Economy)', **3-4** *Ekonomska misao*, 207-224.

Philipson, Tomas and Posner, Richard A. (1994), 'Public Spending on AIDS Education: An Economic Analysis', **37** *Journal of Law and Economics*, 17-38.

Preite, Disiano (1987), 'Sovrapprezzo, aste Competitive e Mercato Mobiliare' (Overpricing, Competitive Auctions and Security Market)', *Giurisprudenza commerciale*, 882-924.

Puy Fraga, Pedro (1992), 'La Economía Política del Servicio Militar (Political Economy of Recruiting)', *Revista de Derecho Financiero y Hacienda Pública*, 471-500. 1ª edición, Boletín de Información del Ministerio de Defensa, nº 227, 1992, páxs 9-29. 2ªre ed., Monografías del Ceseden: Cuatro aspectos de la defensa nacional, Ministerio de Defensa, Madrid, 1993, páxs. 137-165.

Puy Fraga, Pedro (1993), 'O Procedemento Administrativo como Factor na Toma de Decisións Públicas (Comentarios desde a economía política á Lei 30/1992 do 26 de Novembro, de réxime xurídico das administracións públicas e do procedemento administrativo común) (The Role of Administrative Procedure in Public Decision Making)', **5** *Revista Galega de Administracion Publica*, 163-181.

Puy Fraga, Pedro (1994), 'Indices de Voluntariedad para el Servicio Militar: Una Visión desde la Economía Política (Voluntary Indexes from a Political Economy Approach to the Mandatory Military Service)', in Segado, F. Fernández (ed.), *El Servicio Militar: Aspectos Jurídicos y Socioeconómicos*, Madrid, Editorial Dikynson, 275-295. Reedición e traducción do artig.: 'Indices de voluntariedade e custos do servicio militar: Unha visión desde a economía política', Revista Galega da Economía, vol. 2, nº 1, 1993, páxs. 231-243.

Rogerson, William P. (1989), 'Profit Regulation of Defense Contractors and Prizes for Innovation', **97** *Journal of Political Economy*, 1284-1305.

Rose-Ackerman, Susan (1986), 'Reforming Public Bureaucracy through Economic Incentives?', **2** *Journal of Law, Economics, and Organization*, 131 ff.

Rose-Ackerman, Susan (1988), 'Progressive Law and Economics - and the New Administrative Law', **98** *Yale Law Journal*, 341-368.

Rose-Ackerman, Susan (1990a), 'Deregulation and Reregulation: Rhetoric and Reality', **6** *Journal of Law and Politics*, 287-309.

Rose-Ackerman, Susan (1990b), 'Defending the State: A Skeptical Look at "Regulatory Reform" in the Eighties' , **61** *University of Colorado Law Review*, 517-535.

Rose-Ackerman, Susan (1994a), 'Consensus Versus Incentives: A Skeptical Look at Regulatory Negotiation', **43** *Duke Law Journal*, 1206-1220.

Rose-Ackerman, Susan (1994b), 'American Administration Law under Siege: Is Germany a Model?', **107** *Harvard Law Review*, 1279-1302.

Ryssdal, Stray A.C. (1993), *Antitrust Enforcement - An Inquiry into Policy Analysis of Competition Law*, Working Paper, Centre for Research in Economics & Business Administration, Bergen, No. 89.

Sagoff, Mark (1988), *The Economy of the Earth: Philosophy, Law, and the Environment*, New York, Cambridge University Press, 271 p.

Salinas, Javier, *Presupuestos y Financiación de la Unión Europea* (Coordination of Budget Policy Through Legislation), Valladolid, Editorial Lex Nova.

Salinas, Javier, 'Racionalidad Económica y Derecho Presupuestario (Economic Rationality and Budget Law)', **132** *Hacienda Pública Española*, 21-51.

Salinas, Javier (1991), *Economía Política del Federalismo Fiscal Español* (Political Economy of the Spanish Fiscal Federalism), Madrid, Instituto de Estudios Fiscales.

Salinas, Javier (1993), Economía Política Constitucional de los Presupuestos Públicos (Constitutional Political Economy of the Budget), Madrid, Tecnos.

Salinas, Javier (1995), 'Economía Constitucional de la Descentralización del Sector Público en España (Constitutional Economy of Descentralization of the Spanish Public Sector)', in Capítulo del libro, *La Financiación de las Comunidades Autonomas, Análisis y Orientación desde la Teoría del Federalismo Fiscal*, Valladolid, Consejeria de Economía, Junta de Castilla y León, 29-54.

Salinas, Javier (1996a), 'Economía Constitucional de la Política Fiscal Española y la Convergencia Europea (Constitutional Economy of Spanish Tax Policy and European

Covergence)', in X (ed.), *Proceedings, XVIII Jornadas de la Dirección General del Servicio Juridico del Estado sobre la Constitución Española y el Ordenamiento Comunitario Europeo*, Madrid, Ministerio de Justicia.

Salinas, Javier (1996b), *Elementos Institucionales de la Organización Territorial del Sector Público en Castilla y León* (Institutional Elements of the Public Sector's Territorial Organization in Castilla and Leon), Valladolid, Consejería de Economía, Junta de Castilla y León.

Salvador Coderch, Pablo, Lloveras Y., Ferrer, M.R.Y., Seuba Y. and Torreblanca, J.C (1995), 'Del Servicio Público al Servicio a la Comunidad (From Public Service to Service for the Community)', **136** *Revista de Administración Pública*, 69 ff.

Samuels, Warren J. (1993), 'The Growth of Government', **7** *Critical Review*, 445-460.

Sanjiao Otero, Francisco Javier (1994), 'Economía de las Instituciones: Análisis de la Política Museística en 'Galicia (Economics of Institutions: Policy on Museums in Galicia)', **3** *Dereito, Revista Xurídica da Universidade de Santiago de Compostela*, 127-158.

Sanjiao Otero, Francisco Javier (1995), 'Análise Económico das Medidas Públicas para o Fomento do Teatro Privado Galego (Economic Analysis of Public Policy to Promote Private Galician Theatre)', in Leiceaga, Fernández, Rodríguez, M. Jordán, Iglesias, E. López and Deza, X. Vence (eds), *Estudos en homenaxe ó profesor Xose Manuel Beiras Torrado*, Universidade de Santiago de Compostela, 439-460.

Schenk, Karl-Ernst (1976), 'Demokratie oder Bürokratie? Dezentralisierung - Selbstverwaltung - Entbürokratisierung (Democracy or Bureaucracy? Decentralization, Self-Administration, De-Bureaucratisation)', in Geißler, H. (ed.), *Verwaltete Bürgergesellschaft in Fesseln. Bürokratisierung und ihre Folgen für den Staat, Wirtschaft und Gesellschaft*, Frankfurt (M), Berlin Wien.

Schenk, Karl-Ernst, Schmidtchen, Dieter and Streit, Manfred E. (eds) (1996), *Vom Hoheitsstaat zum Konsensualstaat, Neue Formen der Kooperation zwischen Staat und Privaten Jahrbuch für Neue Politische Ökonomie 15* (From Sovereignity to Consensus, New Forms of Cooperation Between State and Citizens), Tübingen, Mohr.

Schwartz, Bernard (1985), 'Cost-Benefit Analysis in Administrative Law: Does it Make Priceless Procedural Right Worthless?', **37** *Administrative Law Review*, 1-14.

Schwarzer, Stephan (1985), ''Wirtschaftsrecht und Okonomische Effizienz (Commercial Law and Economic Efficiency)', *Wirtschaftspolitische Blätter*, 26-31.

Siekmann, Hans (1996), 'Corporate Governance und Offentlich-Rechtliche Unternehmen (Corporate Governance and Public Enterprises)', in Schenk, Karl-Ernst, Schmidtchen, Dieter Streit, Manfred E. (eds), *Vom Hoheitsstaat zum Konsensualstaat, Neue Formen der Kooperation zwischen Staat und Privaten Jahrbuch für Neue Politische Ökonomie 15*, Tübingen, Mohr.

Spence, David B. (1997), 'Modeling Away the Delegation Problem', **7** *Journal of Public Administration Research and Theory*, 199-219.

Spiller, Pablo T. and Ferejohn, John A. (1992), 'The Economics and Politics of Administrative Law and Procedures: An Introduction', **8** *Journal of Law, Economics, and Organization*, 1-17.

Sunstein, Cass R. (1983), 'Is Cost-Benefit Analysis a Panacea for Administrative Law?', **29** *Law School Record*, 19-21.

Sunstein, Cass R. (1990a), *After the Rights Revolution: Reconceiving the Regulatory State*, Cambridge, Harvard University Press, 284 p.

Sunstein, Cass R. (1990b), 'Political Economy, Administrative Law: A Comment', **6(S)** *Journal of Law, Economics, and Organization*, 299-306.

Sunstein, Cass R. (1991), 'Administrative Substance', **1991** *Duke Law Journal*, 607-646.

Sunstein, Cass R. (1993), 'Against Interest Group Theory: A Comment (on the Political Economy of the Decline of American Public Education)', **36** *Journal of Law and Economics*, 379-383.

Sunstein, Cass R. (1996), 'Legislative Forward: Congress, Constitutional Moments, and the Cost-Benefit State', **48** *Stanford Law Review*, 247-309.

Sunstein, Cass R. (1997), *Free Markets and Social Justice*, New York, Oxford Press, 407 p.

Supper, Meinhard (1988), 'Das Niederösterreichische Landesrecht und die ökonomische Analyse des Rechts (The Law of the Province of Lower Austria and Economic Analysis of Law)', in Funk, Bernd-Christian (Project Management) (ed.), *Deregulierung und Entbürokratisierung am Beispiel*, Vienna, Austrian Economic Publishers Company, 43-48.

Turnbull, Shann (1995), 'Best Practice in the Governance of GBEs', in Gutrie, James (ed.), *The Australian Public Sector: Pathways to Change in the 1990s*, Sydney, IIR Pty. Limited, 99-109.

Vickrey, William (1980), 'The City as a Firm in Feldstein', in M.S. and Inman, R.S. (eds), *The Economics of Public Services*, London, Macmillan, 334-343.

Wilson, James Q. (1989), *Bureaucracy: What Government Agencies Do and Why they Do It*, New York, Basic Books.

Wolff, Birgitta (1996), 'Public-Private Partnerships', in Schenk, Karl-Ernst, Schmidtchen, Dieter and Streit, Manfred E. (eds), *Vom Hoheitsstaat zum Konsensualstaat, Neue Formen der Kooperation zwischen Staat und Privaten Jahrbuch für Neue Politische Ökonomie 15*, Tübingen, Mohr.

Zalm, G. (1982), 'Deregulation', **67** *Economisch-Statistische Berichten*, 692-696.